Lecture Notes in Computer Science 4783

Commenced Publication in 1973
Founding and Former Series Editors:
Gerhard Goos, Juris Hartmanis, and Jan van Leeuwen

T0223147

Jan Holub   Jan Žďárek (Eds.)

Implementation and Application of Automata

12th International Conference, CIAA 2007
Prague, Czech Republic, July 16-18, 2007
Revised Selected Papers

 Springer

Volume Editors

Jan Holub
Czech Technical University in Prague
Faculty of Electrical Engineering
Department of Computer Science and Engineering
Karlovo náměstí 13, Praha 2, CZ–121 35, Czech Republic
E-mail: holub@fel.cvut.cz

Jan Žďárek
Czech Technical University in Prague
Faculty of Electrical Engineering
Department of Computer Science and Engineering
Karlovo náměstí 13, Praha 2, CZ–121 35, Czech Republic
E-mail: zdarekj@fel.cvut.cz

Library of Congress Control Number: 2007937688

CR Subject Classification (1998): F.1.1-3, F.4.2-3, F.2

LNCS Sublibrary: SL 1 – Theoretical Computer Science and General Issues

ISSN   0302-9743
ISBN-10   3-540-76335-X Springer Berlin Heidelberg New York
ISBN-13   978-3-540-76335-2 Springer Berlin Heidelberg New York

Springer is a part of Springer Science+Business Media

springer.com

© Springer-Verlag Berlin Heidelberg 2007
Printed in Germany

Typesetting: Camera-ready by author, data conversion by Scientific Publishing Services, Chennai, India
Printed on acid-free paper   SPIN: 12182312   06/3180   5 4 3 2 1 0

Preface

The 12th International Conference on Implementation and Application of Automata CIAA 2007 was held at the Czech Technical University in Prague, Czech Republic on July 16–18, 2007.

These proceedings contain the papers that were presented at CIAA 2007, as well as the abstracts of the poster papers that were displayed during the conference. The proceedings also include the abstracts and extended abstracts of four invited lectures presented by Gheorghe Păun, Michael Riley, Moshe Vardi, and Bruce W. Watson.

The 23 regular papers and 7 poster papers were selected from 79 submitted papers covering various topics in the theory, implementation, and application of automata and related structures. Each submitted paper was reviewed by at least three Program Committee members, with the assistance of referees. The authors of the papers presented here come from the following countries: Canada, Czech Republic, Denmark, Finland, France, Germany, Greece, Israel, Italy, Poland, Romania, Russia, South Africa, Spain, Sweden, UK, and USA.

We wish to thank all those who made this meeting possible: the authors for submitting papers, the Program Committee members and external referees (listed on pages VII and VIII) for their excellent work, and last but not least our four invited speakers. Finally, we wish to express our sincere appreciation to the sponsors and local organizers.

July 2007

Jan Holub
Jan Žďárek

Organization

Program Committee

Marie-Pierre Béal	Université de Marne-la-Vallée, France
Cristian S. Calude	University of Auckland, New Zealand
Jean-Marc Champarnaud	Université de Rouen, France
Erzsébet Csuhaj-Varjú	Hungarian Academy of Sciences, Hungary
Jürgen Dassow	University of Magdeburg, Germany
Jacques Farré	ESSI, France
Jozef Gruska	Masaryk University, Czech Republic
Tero Harju	University of Turku, Finland
Jan Holub, *Co-chair*	Czech Technical University in Prague, Czech Republic
Markus Holzer	Technische Universität München, Germany
Juraj Hromkovič	ETH Zurich, Switzerland
Oscar H. Ibarra	University of California, Santa Barbara, USA
Masami Ito	Kyoto Sangyo University, Japan
Kazuo Iwama	Kyoto University, Japan
Juhani Karhumäki	University of Turku, Finland
Werner Kuich	Vienna University of Technology, Austria
Denis Maurel	Université François-Rabelais de Tours, France
Giancarlo Mauri	Università degli Studi di Milano–Bicocca, Italy
Bořivoj Melichar, *Co-chair*	Czech Technical University in Prague, Czech Republic
Mehryar Mohri	New York University, USA
Gheorghe Păun	Romanian Academy, Romania
Giovanni Pighizzini	Università degli Studi di Milano, Italy
Jean-Éric Pin	LIAFA, France
Bala Ravikumar	Sonoma State University, USA
Wojciech Rytter	Warsaw University, Poland
Kai Salomaa	Queen's University, Canada
Pierluigi San Pietro	Politecnico di Milano, Italy
Bow-Yaw Wang	Academia Sinica, Taiwan
Bruce Watson	University of Pretoria, South Africa; Sagantec, USA
Hsu-Chun Yen	National Taiwan University, Taiwan
Sheng Yu	University of Western Ontario, Canada

Steering Committee

Jean-Marc Champarnaud   Université de Rouen, France
Oscar H. Ibarra   University of California, Santa Barbara, USA
Denis Maurel   Université François-Rabelais de Tours, France
Derick Wood   Hong Kong University of Science and
                          Technology, Hong Kong
Sheng Yu, *Chair*   University of Western Ontario, Canada

External Referees

Cyril Allauzen   Paul Gastin   Cyril Nicaud
Bruno Apolloni   Cagdas Gerede   Hidenosuke Nishio
Béatrice Bouchou   Massimiliano Goldwurm   Alexander Okhotin
Sakthi Balan   Hermann Gruber   Beatrice Palano
Miroslav Balík   Franck Guingne   Andrei Paun
Pawel Baturo   Vesa Halava   Klaus Reinhardt
Franziska Biegler   Mika Hirvensalo   Dominique Revuz
Paola Bonizzoni   Florian Horn   Jacques Sakarovitch
Daniel Brown   Pao-Ann Hsiung   Nicolae Santean
Gregory Budzban   Lucian Ilie   Sylvain Schmitz
Elena Calude   Costas Iliopoulos   Sebastian Seibert
Pascal Caron   Christos Kapoutsis   Patrick Solé
Christian Choffrut   Ernest Ketcha Ngassam   Paola Spoletini
Loek Cleophas   Derrick Kourie   Lynn Stauffer
Julien Clément   Gregory Kucherov   Ralf Stiebe
Jean-Michel Couvreur   Martin Kutrib   Tinus Strauss
Eugen Czeizler   Slawomir Lasota   Sophie Tison
Zhe Dang   Alberto Leporati   Nicholas Tran
Gianluca Della Vedova   Martin Leucker   Kumar Neeraj Verma
Michael Domaratzki   Andreas Malcher   Halava Vesa
Claudio Ferretti   Carlo Mereghetti   Farn Wang
Markus Forsberg   Manal Mohamed   Claudio Zandron
Dominik Freydenberger   Mark-Jan Nederhof
Anna Frid   Florent Nicart

Organizing Committee

Miroslav Balík, *Co-chair*
Jan Holub, *Co-chair*
Ladislav Vagner
Michal Voráček
Jan Žďárek

URL: http://www.stringology.org/

Conference Sponsors

 Czech Technical University in Prague

 IBM Czech Republic

 Sun Microsystems Czech

Table of Contents

III   Poster Abstracts

Spiking Neural P Systems
Used as Acceptors and Transducers
(Extended Abstract of an Invited Talk)

Gheorghe Păun

Institute of Mathematics of the Romanian Academy
PO Box 1-764, 014700 Bucureşti, Romania
george.paun@imar.ro, gpaun@us.es

Keywords: membrane computing, spiking neural P system, Turing computability, string processing.

The study of spiking neural P systems is a branch of membrane computing (comprehensive information about this area of natural computing can be found in [24], [9], or at the web page [31]) initiated in [18]. The goal is to build a model of the way the neurons cooperate in (large) neural nets, communicating by means of spikes, electrical impulses of identical shapes. "Computing by spiking" is a vivid research area in neural computing, which promises to lead to a neural computing "of the third generation" – see [12], [22], etc.

Very briefly, the resulting models, called *spiking neural P systems* (in short, SN P systems), consists of a set of *neurons* (cells, consisting of only one membrane) placed in the nodes of a directed graph and sending signals (*spikes*, denoted in what follows by the symbol a) along *synapses* (arcs of the graph). Thus, the architecture is that of a tissue-like P system, with only one kind of objects present in the cells. The objects evolve by means of *spiking rules*, which are of the form $E/a^c \to a; d$, where E is a regular expression over $\{a\}$ and c, d are natural numbers, $c \geq 1, d \geq 0$. The meaning is that a neuron containing k spikes such that $a^k \in L(E), k \geq c$, can consume c spikes and produce one spike, after a delay of d steps. This spike is sent to all neurons to which a synapse exists outgoing from the neuron where the rule was applied. There also are *forgetting rules*, of the form $a^s \to \lambda$, with the meaning that $s \geq 1$ spikes are removed, provided that the neuron contains exactly s spikes. We say that the rules "cover" the neuron, all spikes are taken into consideration when using a rule.

The system works in a synchronized manner, i.e., in each time unit, each neuron which can use a rule should do it, but the work of the system is sequential in each neuron: only (at most) one rule is used in each neuron. If there are several rules which can be applied in a neuron, then one of them is chosen in a non-deterministic way.

There are various ways of using such a device. For instance, we can consider one of the neurons as the *input neuron* and one of them as the *output neuron*. Spikes can be introduced in the former one, at various steps, while the spikes

Jan Holub and Jan Žd'árek (Eds.): CIAA 2007, LNCS 4783, pp. 1–4, 2007.

of the output neuron are sent to the environment. The moments of time when a spike is emitted by the output neuron are marked with 1, the other moments are marked with 0. The binary sequence obtained in this way is called the *spike train* of the system – it might be infinite if the computation does not stop. A binary sequence is similarly associated with the spikes entering the system.

If we do not consider an input neuron, then the system is used in the *generative* mode: we start from an initial configuration and all spike trains produced by the system by means of computations constitute the set of binary strings/sequences generated by the system; various sets of numbers can be associated with the spike trains, such as the distance in time between the first two spikes, between all consecutive spikes, the total number of spikes (in the case of halting computations), and so on. If we only consider an input neuron, then an SN P system can be used in the *accepting* mode: we introduce a string of symbols 0 and 1 (as a sequence of steps, with 1 associated with time units when spikes enters the system), or a number represented by such a string (e.g., as the number of steps elapsed between the first two spikes entering the system), and the input is accepted/recognized if and only if the computation stops. When both an input and an output neuron are considered, the system can be used as a *transducer*, both for strings and infinite sequences, as well as for computing numerical functions.

Two main types of results were obtained in the generative and the accepting modes: computational completeness in the case when no bound was imposed on the number of spikes present in the system, and a characterization of semilinear sets of numbers in the case when a bound was imposed (hence for finite SN P systems). In the transducing mode, a large class of (Boolean) functions can be computed, but strong restrictions exist in the case of morphisms – details can be found in [28] and [29].

Also strings/languages on arbitrary alphabets can be handled, for instance, using extended rules, i.e., rules of the form $E/a^c \rightarrow a^p; d$: when the rule is used, p spikes are produced and sent (after d steps) to all neighboring neurons. Then, with a step when the system sends out i spikes, we associate a symbol b_i, and thus we get a language over an alphabet with as many symbols as the number of spikes simultaneously produced. This case was investigated in [7].

The proofs of all computational completeness results known up to now in this area are based on simulating register machines. Starting the proofs from small universal register machines, as those produced in [20], one can find small universal SN P systems. This idea was explored in [23].

In the initial definition of SN P systems several ingredients are used (delay, forgetting rules), some of them of a general form (general synapse graph, general regular expressions). As shown in [15], rather restrictive normal forms can be found, in the sense that some ingredients can be removed or simplified without losing the computational completeness. For instance, the forgetting rules or the delay can be removed, both the indegree and the outdegree of the synapse graph can be bounded by 2, while the regular expressions from firing rules can be of very restricted forms.

There were investigated many other types of SN P systems: with several output neurons ([16], [17]), with a non-synchronous use of rules ([2]), with an exhaustive use of rules (whenever enabled, a rule is used as much as possible for the number of spikes present in the neuron, [19]), with packages of spikes sent along specified synapse links ([1]), etc. We refer the reader to the bibliography of this note, with many papers being available at [31].

This area of research is fast developing and there are many research topics and open problems formulated in the literature (see, e.g., [25]). We recall here only some general ideas: bring more ingredients from neural computing, especially related to learning/training/efficiency; incorporate other facts from neurobiology, such as the role played by astrocytes, the way the axon not only transmits impulses, but also amplifies them; consider not only "positive" spikes, but also inhibitory impulses; define a notion of *memory* in this framework, which can be read without being destroyed; provide ways for generating an exponential working space (by splitting neurons? by enlarging the number of synapses?), in such a way to trade space for time and provide polynomial solutions to computationally hard problems; define systems with a dynamical synaptic structure; compare the SN P systems as generator/acceptor/transducers of infinite sequences with other devices handling such sequences; investigate further the systems with exhaustive and other parallel ways of using the rules, as well as systems working in a non-synchronized way; find classes of (accepting) SN P systems for which there is a difference between deterministic and non-deterministic systems; find classes which characterize levels of computability different from those corresponding to finite automata (semilinear sets of numbers or regular languages) or to Turing machines (recursively enumerable sets of numbers or languages).

For the reader convenience, the bibliography provided below mentions many of the papers circulated at this moment in the literature of spiking neural P systems.

References

1. Alhazov, A., Freund, R., Oswald, M., Slavkovik, M.: Extended variants of spiking neural P systems generating strings and vectors of non-negative integers. In [14], pp. 123–134
2. Cavaliere, M., Egecioglu, E., Ibarra, O.H., Ionescu, M., Păun, Gh., Woodworth, S.: Asynchronous spiking neural P systems; decidability and undecidability (submitted, 2006)
3. Chen, H., Freund, R., Ionescu, M., Păun, Gh., Pérez-Jiménez, M.J.: On string languages generated by spiking neural P systems. In [13], vol. I, pp. 169–194
4. Chen, H., Ionescu, M., Ishdorj, T.-O.: On the efficiency of spiking neural P systems. In [13], vol. I, pp. 195–206. In: Proc. 8th Intern. Conf. on Electronics, Information, and Communication, Ulanbator, Mongolia, pp. 49–52 (June 2006)
5. Chen, H., Ionescu, M., Păun, A., Păun, Gh., Popa, B.: On trace languages generated by spiking neural P systems. In [13], Proc. DCFS 2006, Las Cruces, NM, vol. I, pp. 207–224 (June 2006)
6. Chen, H., Ishdorj, T.-O., Păun, Gh.: Computing along the axon. In [13], vol. I, pp. 225–240

7. Chen, H., Ishdorj, T.-O., Păun, Gh., Pérez-Jiménez, M.J.: Spiking neural P systems with extended rules. In [13], vol. I, pp. 241–265
8. Chen, H., Ishdorj, T.-O., Păun, Gh., Pérez-Jiménez, M.J.: Handling languages with spiking neural P systems with extended rules. Romanian J. Information Sci. and Technology 9(3), 151–162 (2006)
9. Ciobanu, G., Păun, Gh., Pérez-Jiménez, M.J. (eds.): Applications of Membrane Computing. Springer, Berlin (2006)
10. Freund, R., Oswald, M.: Spiking neural P systems with inhibitory axons. In: Proc. AROB Conf., Japan (2007)
11. García-Arnau, M., Peréz, D., Rodriguez-Patón, A., Sosík, P.: Spiking neural P systems. Stronger normal forms (submitted, 2007)
12. Gerstner, W., Kistler, W.: Spiking Neuron Models. Single Neurons, Populations, Plasticity. Cambridge Univ. Press, Cambridge (2002)
13. Gutiérrez-Naranjo, M.A., et al. (eds.): Proceedings of Fourth Brainstorming Week on Membrane Computing, Fenix Editora, Sevilla (February 2006)
14. Hoogeboom, H.J., Păun, Gh., Rozenberg, G., Salomaa, A. (eds.): WMC 2006. LNCS, vol. 4361. Springer, Heidelberg (2006)
15. Ibarra, O.H., Păun, A., Păun, Gh., Rodríguez-Patón, A., Sosík, P., Woodworth, S.: Normal forms for spiking neural P systems. In [13], Vol. II, 105–136. Theoretical Computer Sci. 372(2-3), 196–217 (2007)
16. Ibarra, O.H., Woodworth, S.: Characterizations of some restricted spiking neural P systems. In [14], pp. 424–442
17. Ibarra, O.H., Woodworth, S., Yu, F., Păun, A.: On spiking neural P systems and partially blind counter machines. In: UC 2006. Proceedings of Fifth Unconventional Computation Conference, York, UK (September 2006)
18. Ionescu, M., Păun, Gh., Yokomori, T.: Spiking neural P systems. Fundamenta Informaticae 71(2-3), 279–308 (2006)
19. Ionescu, M., Păun, Gh., Yokomori, T.: Spiking neural P systems with exhaustive use of rules. Intern. J. Unconventional Computing (to appear)
20. Korec, I.: Small universal register machines. Theoretical Computer Science 168, 267–301 (1996)
21. Leporati, A., Zandron, C., Ferretti, C., Mauri, G.: On the computational power of spiking neural P systems (submitted, 2007)
22. Maass, W., Bishop, C. (eds.): Pulsed Neural Networks. MIT Press, Cambridge (1999)
23. Păun, A., Păun, Gh.: Small universal spiking neural P systems. In [13], BioSystems II, 213–234 (in press)
24. Păun, Gh.: Membrane Computing. An Introduction. Springer, Berlin (2002)
25. Păun, Gh.: Twenty six research topics about spiking neural P systems. Available at [31], (2006)
26. Păun, Gh.: Spiking neural P systems. Power and efficiency. In: Proc. IWINAC, Mar Menor, Spain (2007)
27. Păun, Gh., Pérez-Jiménez, M.J., Rozenberg, G.: Spike trains in spiking neural P systems. Intern. J. Found. Computer Sci. 17(4), 975–1002 (2006)
28. Păun, Gh., Pérez-Jiménez, M.J., Rozenberg, G.: Infinite spike trains in spiking neural P systems (submitted, 2005)
29. Păun, Gh., Pérez-Jiménez, M.J., Rozenberg, G.: Computing morphisms by spiking neural P systems. Intern. J. Found. Computer Sci. (to appear)
30. Ramírez-Martínez, D., Gutiérrez-Naranjo, M.A.: A software tool for dealing with spiking neural P systems (submitted, 2007)
31. The P Systems Web Page: http://psystems.disco.unimib.it

Linear-Time Model Checking: Automata Theory in Practice

(Extended Abstract of an Invited Talk)

Moshe Y. Vardi*

Rice University, Department of Computer Science, Houston, TX 77251-1892, U.S.A.
vardi@cs.rice.edu
http://www.cs.rice.edu/~vardi

Abstract. In automata-theoretic model checking we compose the design under verification with a Büchi automaton that accepts traces violating the specification. We then use graph algorithms to search for a counterexample trace. The basic theory of this approach was worked out in the 1980s, and the basic algorithms were developed during the 1990s. Both explicit and symbolic implementations, such as SPIN and and SMV, are widely used. It turns out, however, that there are still many gaps in our understanding of the algorithmic issues involved in automata-theoretic model checking. This paper covers the fundamentals of automata-theoretic model checking. The conference talk also reviews the reduction of the theory to practice and outlines areas that require further research.

Keywords: Büchi automata, model checking, linear-temporal logic.

1 Introduction

Formal verification is a process in which mathematical techniques are used to guarantee the correctness of a design with respect to some specified behavior. Automated formal-verification tools, such as COSPAN [15], SPIN [16] and SMV [7,20], based on *model-checking technology* [8,22], have enjoyed a substantial and growing use over the last few years, showing an ability to discover subtle flaws that result from extremely improbable events [9]. While until recently these tools were viewed as of academic interest only, they are now routinely used in industrial applications, resulting in decreased time to market and increased product integrity [10,11,18]. It is fair to say that automated verification is one of the most successful applications of automated reasoning in computer science.

As model-checking technology matured, the demand for specification language of increased expressiveness increased interest in linear-time formalisms [2]. The automata-theoretic approach offers a uniform algorithmic framework for model checking linear-time properties [17,23,26]. It turns out, however, that

---

* Supported in part by NSF grants CCR-9988322, CCR-0124077, CCR-0311326, and ANI-0216467, by BSF grant 9800096, and by a grant from the Intel Corporation.

Jan Holub and Jan Žd'árek (Eds.): CIAA 2007, LNCS 4783, pp. 5–10, 2007.

there are still many gaps in our understanding of the algorithmic issues involved in automata-theoretic model checking [25]. This paper covers the fundamental theory of automata-theoretic model checking. The conference talk also reviews the reduction of the theory to practice and outlines areas that require further research.

2   Basic Theory

The first step in formal verification is to come up with a *formal specification* of the design, consisting of a description of the desired behavior. One of the more widely used specification languages for designs is *temporal logic* [21]. In *linear* temporal logics, time is treated as if each moment in time has a unique possible future. Thus, linear temporal formulas are interpreted over linear sequences, and we regard them as describing the behavior of a single computation of a system. (An alternative approach is to use *branching* time. For a discussion of linear vs. branching time, see [24].)

In the linear temporal logic LTL, formulas are constructed from a set *Prop* of atomic propositions using the usual Boolean connectives as well as the unary temporal connectives X ("next"), F ("eventually"), G ("always"), and the binary temporal connective U ("until"). For example, the LTL formula $G(request \rightarrow F\ grant)$, which refers to the atomic propositions *request* and *grant*, is true in a computation precisely when every state in the computation in which *request* holds is followed by some state in the future in which *grant* holds. The LTL formula $G(request \rightarrow (request\ U\ grant))$ is true in a computation precisely if, whenever *request* holds in a state of the computation, it holds until a state in which *grant* holds is reached. In LTL model checking we assume that the specification is given in terms of properties expressed by LTL formulas.

LTL is interpreted over *computations*, which can be viewed as infinite sequences of truth assignments to the atomic propositions; i.e., a computation is a function $\pi : I\!N \rightarrow 2^{Prop}$ that assigns truth values to the elements of *Prop* at each time instant (natural number). For a computation π and a point $i \in I\!N$, the notation $\pi, i \models \varphi$ indicates that a formula φ holds at the point i of the computation π. In particular, $\pi, i \models X\varphi$ if $\pi, i+1 \models \varphi$, and $\pi, i \models \varphi U \psi$ if for some $j \geq i$, we have $\pi, j \models \psi$ and for all k, $i \leq k < j$, we have $\pi, k \models \varphi$. The connectives F and G can be defined in terms of the connective U: $F\varphi$ is defined as $\mathbf{true}\ U\varphi$, and $G\varphi$ is defined as $\neg F \neg \varphi$. We say that π *satisfies* a formula φ, denoted $\pi \models \varphi$, iff $\pi, 0 \models \varphi$. We denote by models(φ) the set of computations satisfying φ.

Designs can be described using a variety of formalisms. Regardless of the formalism used, a *finite-state design* can be abstractly viewed as a *labeled transition system*, i.e., as a structure of the form $M = (W, W_0, R, V)$, where W is the finite set of states that the system can be in, $W_0 \subseteq W$ is the set of initial states of the system, $R \subseteq W^2$ is a transition relation that indicates the allowable state transitions of the system, and $V : W \rightarrow 2^{Prop}$ assigns truth values to the atomic propositions in each state of the system. (A labeled transition system is essentially a Kripke structure.) A *path* in M that *starts at* u is a possible infinite behavior of the system starting at u, i.e., it is an infinite sequence $u_0, u_1, \ldots$ of states in W such that $u_0 = u$, and $(u_i, u_{i+1}) \in R$ for all $i \geq 0$. The sequence $V(u_0), V(u_1), \ldots$ is a *computation* of M that *starts at* u. It is the sequence of truth assignments visited by the path, and can be viewed as a function from $I\!N$ to 2^{Prop}. The *language* of M, denoted $L(M)$, consists of all computations of M that start at a state in W_0. Note that $L(M)$ can be viewed as a language of infinite words over the alphabet 2^{Prop}. The language $L(M)$ can be viewed as an abstract description of the system M, describing all possible "traces". We say that M *satisfies* an LTL formula φ if all computations in $L(M)$ satisfy φ, that is, if $L(M) \subseteq \text{models}(\varphi)$. When M satisfies φ we also say that M is a model of φ, which explains why the technique is known as *model checking* [9].

One of the major approaches to automated verification is the *automata-theoretic approach*, which underlies model checkers that can handle linear-time specifications (for a precursor, see [19]). The key idea underlying the automata-theoretic approach is that, given an LTL formula φ, it is possible to construct a finite-state automaton A_φ on infinite words that accepts precisely all computations that satisfy φ. The type of finite automata on infinite words we consider is the one defined by Büchi [4]. A *Büchi automaton* is a tuple $A = (\Sigma, S, S_0, \rho, F)$, where Σ is a finite alphabet, S is a finite set of states, $S_0 \subseteq S$ is a set of initial states, $\rho : S \times \Sigma \to 2^S$ is a nondeterministic transition function, and $F \subseteq S$ is a set of accepting states. A *run* of A over an infinite word $w = a_1 a_2 \cdots$, is a sequence $s_0 s_1 \cdots$, where $s_0 \in S_0$ and $s_i \in \rho(s_{i-1}, a_i)$ for all $i \geq 1$. A run $s_0, s_1, \ldots$ is *accepting* if there is some accepting state that repeats infinitely often, i.e., for some $s \in F$ there are infinitely many i's such that $s_i = s$. The infinite word w is *accepted* by A if there is an accepting run of A over w. The *language* of infinite words accepted by A is denoted $L(A)$. The following fact establishes the correspondence between LTL and Büchi automata [27] (for a tutorial introduction to this correspondence, see [23]):

Theorem 1. *Given an LTL formula φ, one can build a Büchi automaton $A_\varphi = (\Sigma, S, S_0, \rho, F)$, where $\Sigma = 2^{Prop}$ and $|S| \leq 2^{O(|\varphi|)}$, such that $L(A_\varphi) = \text{models}(\varphi)$.*

This correspondence reduces the verification problem to an automata-theoretic problem as follows [26]. Suppose that we are given a system M and an LTL formula φ. We check whether $L(M) \subseteq \text{models}(\varphi)$ as follows: (1) construct the automaton $A_{\neg\varphi}$ that corresponds to the *negation* of the formula φ (this automaton is called the *complementary* automaton), (2) take the *cross product* of the system M and the automaton $A_{\neg\varphi}$ to obtain an automaton $A_{M,\varphi}$, such that $L(A_{M,\varphi}) = L(M) \cap L(A_{\neg\varphi})$, and (3) check whether the language $L(A_{M,\varphi})$ is empty, i.e., $A_{M,\varphi}$ accepts *no* input.

Theorem 2. *Let M be a labeled transition system and φ be an LTL formula. Then M satisfies φ iff $L(A_{M,\varphi}) = \emptyset$.*

If $L(A_{M,\varphi})$ is empty, then the design is correct. Otherwise, the design is incorrect and the word accepted by $L(A_{M,\varphi})$ is an incorrect computation.

The *emptiness* problem for an automaton is to decide, given an automaton A, whether $L(A) = \emptyset$, i.e., if the automaton accepts no word. Algorithms for emptiness are based on testing *fair reachability* in graphs: an automaton is *nonempty* if starting from some initial state we can reach an accepting state from where there is a cycle back to itself [6]. An algorithm for nonemptiness is the following: (i) decompose the transition graph of the automaton into *maximal strongly connected components* (MSCCs) (linear cost depth-first search [12]); (ii) verify that one of the MSCCs intersects with F (linear cost). More sophisticated Büchi nonemptiness algorithms have been studied, e.g., [13,14]. When the automaton is nonempty, nonemptiness algorithms return a witness in the shape of a "lasso": an initial finite prefix followed by a finite cycle. (If the accepting states are "sink" states, then the finite cycle following the initial prefix can be ignored.) Thus, once the automaton $A_{\neg \varphi}$ is constructed, the verification task is reduced to automata-theoretic problems, namely, intersecting automata and testing emptiness of automata, which have highly efficient solutions [23]. Furthermore, using data structures that enable compact representation of very large state spaces makes it possible to verify designs of significant complexity [3,5].

The linear-time framework is not limited to using LTL as a specification language. ForSpec and PSL are recent extensions of LTL, designed to address the need of the semiconductor industry [1,2]. There are also those who prefer to use automata on infinite words as a specification formalism [27]; in fact, this is the approach of COSPAN [15,17]. In this approach, we are given a design represented as a finite transition system M and a property represented by a Büchi (or a related variant) automaton P. The design is correct if all computations in $L(M)$ are accepted by P, i.e., $L(M) \subseteq L(P)$. This approach is called the *language-containment* approach. To verify M with respect to P, we: (1) construct the automaton P^c that *complements* P, (2) take the product of the system M and the automaton P^c to obtain an automaton $A_{M,P}$, and (3) check that the automaton $A_{M,P}$ is nonempty. As before, the design is correct iff $A_{M,P}$ is empty. Thus, the verification task is again reduced to automata-theoretic problems, namely complementing and intersecting automata and testing emptiness of automata.

References

1. Albin, K., et al.: Property Specification Language Reference Manual. Technical Report Version 1.1, Accellera (2004)
2. Armoni, R., Fix, L., Flaisher, A., Gerth, R., Ginsburg, B., Kanza, T., Landver, A., Mador-Haim, S., Singerman, E., Tiemeyer, A., Vardi, M.Y., Zbar, Y.: The ForSpec temporal logic: A new temporal property-specification logic. In: Katoen, J.-P., Stevens, P. (eds.) ETAPS 2002 and TACAS 2002. LNCS, vol. 2280, pp. 211–296. Springer, Heidelberg (2002)
3. Biere, A., Cimatti, A., Clarke, E.M., Zhu, Y.: Symbolic model checking without BDDs. In: Cleaveland, W.R. (ed.) ETAPS 1999 and TACAS 1999. LNCS, vol. 1579, Springer, Heidelberg (1999)
4. Büchi, J.R.: On a decision method in restricted second order arithmetic. In: Proc. Int. Congress on Logic, Method, and Philosophy of Science. 1960, pp. 1–12. Stanford University Press (1962)

5. Burch, J.R., Clarke, E.M., McMillan, K.L., Dill, D.L., Hwang, L.J.: Symbolic model checking: 10^{20} states and beyond. Information and Computation 98(2), 142–170 (1992)
6. Choueka, Y.: Theories of automata on ω-tapes: A simplified approach. Journal of Computer and Systems Science 8, 117–141 (1974)
7. Cimatti, A., Clarke, E.M., Giunchiglia, E., Giunchiglia, F., Pistore, M., Roveri, M., Sebastiani, R., Tacchella, A.: Nusmv 2: An opensource tool for symbolic model checking. In: Brinksma, E., Larsen, K.G. (eds.) CAV 2002. LNCS, vol. 2404, pp. 359–364. Springer, Heidelberg (2002)
8. Clarke, E.M., Emerson, E.A., Sistla, A.P.: Automatic verification of finite-state concurrent systems using temporal logic specifications. ACM Transactions on Programming Languages and Systems 8(2), 244–263 (1986)
9. Clarke, E.M., Grumberg, O., Peled, D.: Model Checking. MIT Press, Cambridge (1999)
10. Clarke, E.M., Kurshan, R.P.: Computer aided verification. IEEE Spectrum 33, 61–67 (1986)
11. Clarke, E.M., Wing, J.M.: Formal methods: State of the art and future directions. ACM Computing Surveys 28, 626–643 (1996)
12. Cormen, T.H., Leiserson, C.E., Rivest, R.L.: Introduction to Algorithms. MIT Press and McGraw-Hill (1990)
13. Courcoubetis, C., Vardi, M.Y., Wolper, P., Yannakakis, M.: Memory efficient algorithms for the verification of temporal properties. Formal Methods in System Design 1, 275–288 (1992)
14. Emerson, E.A., Lei, C.-L.: Efficient model checking in fragments of the propositional μ-calculus. In: Proc. 1st IEEE Symp. on Logic in Computer Science, pp. 267–278. IEEE Computer Society Press, Los Alamitos (1986)
15. Hardin, R.H., Har'el, Z., Kurshan, R.P.: COSPAN. In: Alur, R., Henzinger, T.A. (eds.) CAV 1996. LNCS, vol. 1102, pp. 423–427. Springer, Heidelberg (1996)
16. Holzmann, G.J.: The model checker SPIN. IEEE Transactions on Software Engineering 23(5), 279–295 (1997)
17. Kurshan, R.P.: Computer Aided Verification of Coordinating Processes. Princeton Univ. Press, Princeton, NJ (1994)
18. Kurshan, R.P.: Formal verification in a commercial setting. In: Proc. 34st Design Automation Conf., vol. 34, pp. 258–262 (1997)
19. Lichtenstein, O., Pnueli, A.: Checking that finite state concurrent programs satisfy their linear specification. In: Proc. 12th ACM Symp. on Principles of Programming Languages, pp. 97–107. ACM Press, New York (1985)
20. McMillan, K.L.: Symbolic Model Checking. Kluwer Academic Publishers, Dordrecht (1993)
21. Pnueli, A.: The temporal logic of programs. In: Proc. 18th IEEE Symp. on Foundations of Computer Science, pp. 46–57. IEEE Computer Society Press, Los Alamitos (1977)
22. Queille, J.P., Sifakis, J.: Specification and verification of concurrent systems in Cesar. In: Dezani-Ciancaglini, M., Montanari, U. (eds.) International Symposium on Programming. LNCS, vol. 137, pp. 337–351. Springer, Heidelberg (1982)
23. Vardi, M.Y.: An automata-theoretic approach to linear temporal logic. In: Moller, F., Birtwistle, G. (eds.) Logics for Concurrency. LNCS, vol. 1043, pp. 238–266. Springer, Heidelberg (1996)
24. Vardi, M.Y.: Branching vs. linear time: Final showdown. In: Margaria, T., Yi, W. (eds.) ETAPS 2001 and TACAS 2001. LNCS, vol. 2031, pp. 1–22. Springer, Heidelberg (2001)

25. Vardi, M.Y.: Automata-theoretic model checking revisited. In: Cook, B., Podelski, A. (eds.) VMCAI 2007. LNCS, vol. 4349, pp. 137–150. Springer, Heidelberg (2007)
26. Vardi, M.Y., Wolper, P.: An automata-theoretic approach to automatic program verification. In: Proc. 1st IEEE Symp. on Logic in Computer Science, pp. 332–344. IEEE Computer Society Press, Los Alamitos (1986)
27. Vardi, M.Y., Wolper, P.: Reasoning about infinite computations. Information and Computation 115(1), 1–37 (1994)

OpenFst: A General and Efficient Weighted Finite-State Transducer Library
(Extended Abstract of an Invited Talk)

Cyril Allauzen[1], Michael Riley[2,*], Johan Schalkwyk[2], Wojciech Skut[2], and Mehryar Mohri[1]

[1] Courant Institute of Mathematical Sciences
251 Mercer ST, New York, NY 10012, USA
{allauzen,mohri}@cs.nyu.edu
[2] Google, Inc.
111 Eighth AV, New York, NY 10011, USA
{riley,johans,wojciech}@google.com

Abstract. We describe *OpenFst*, an open-source library for *weighted finite-state transducers* (WFSTs). OpenFst consists of a C++ template library with efficient WFST representations and over twenty-five operations for constructing, combining, optimizing, and searching them. At the shell-command level, there are corresponding transducer file representations and programs that operate on them. OpenFst is designed to be both very efficient in time and space and to scale to very large problems.

This library has key applications speech, image, and natural language processing, pattern and string matching, and machine learning.

We give an overview of the library, examples of its use, details of its design that allow customizing the labels, states, and weights and the lazy evaluation of many of its operations.

Further information and a download of the OpenFst library can be obtained from http://www.openfst.org.

Keywords: weighted automata, finite-state transducers, rational power series.

1 Introduction

A *weighted finite-state transducer* (WFST) is a finite automaton for which each transition has an input label, an output label, and a weight. Figure 1 depicts a weighted finite state transducer:

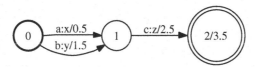

Fig. 1. An example weighted finite-state transducer

---

* Corresponding author.

Jan Holub and Jan Žd'árek (Eds.): CIAA 2007, LNCS 4783, pp. 11–23, 2007.
© Springer-Verlag Berlin Heidelberg 2007

The initial state is labeled 0. The final state is 2 with final weight of 3.5. Any state with non-infinite final weight is a final state. There is a transition from state 0 to 1 with input label a, output label x, and weight 0.5. This machine transduces, for instance, the string ac to xz with weight 6.5 (the sum of the arc and final weights).

Weighted finite-state transducers have been used in speech recognition and synthesis, machine translation, optical character recognition, pattern matching, string processing, machine learning, information extraction and retrieval among others. Having a comprehensive software library of weighted transducer representations and core algorithms is key for using weighted transducers in these applications and for the development of new algorithms and applications.

To our knowledge, the first such software library was the AT&T FSM Library developed by Mohri, Pereira, and Riley for their work on transducer algorithms and applications [1]. It is available from AT&T for non-commercial use as executable binary programs. Since then, there have been various other weighted transducer library efforts [2,3,4,5]. Our motivation for OpenFst was to create a library as comprehensive and efficient as the AT&T FSM Library, but that was an open-source project. We also sought to make this library as flexible and customizable as possible given the wide range of applications WFSTs have enjoyed in recent years. It is a C++ template library, allowing it to be both very customizable and efficient.

This paper is an overview of this new library. Section 2 introduces some definitions and notation. Section 3 describes the representation and construction of transducers in this library. Section 4 briefly outlines the available algorithms. Section 5 provides examples of the library's use and discusses some new, simplified implementations of several algorithms. Section 6 gives more detail about the transducer representation and discusses the lazy evaluation of algorithms.

The OpenFst library is available for download from `http://www.openfst.org` and is released under the Apache license. Detailed documentation is also available at this site.

2   Definitions and Notation

The OpenFst Library closely parallels its mathematical foundations in the theory of rational power series [6,7,8]. The library user can define the alphabets and weights that label transitions. The weights may represent any set so long as they form a *semiring*.

A semiring $(\mathbb{K}, \oplus, \otimes, \bar{0}, \bar{1})$ is specified by a set of values $\mathbb{K}$, two binary operations $\oplus$ and $\otimes$, and two designated values $\bar{0}$ and $\bar{1}$. The operation $\oplus$ is associative, commutative, and has $\bar{0}$ as identity. The operation $\otimes$ is associative, has identity $\bar{1}$, distributes with respect to $\oplus$, and has $\bar{0}$ as annihilator: for all $a \in \mathbb{K}, a \otimes \bar{0} = \bar{0} \otimes a = \bar{0}$. If $\otimes$ is also commutative, we say that the semiring is *commutative*.

Table 1 lists some common semirings. All but the last are defined over subsets of the real numbers (extended with positive and negative infinity). In addition

Table 1. Semiring examples. $\oplus_{\log}$ is defined by: $x \oplus_{\log} y = -\log(e^{-x} + e^{-y})$

Semiring	Set	$\oplus$	$\otimes$	$\bar{0}$	$\bar{1}$
Boolean	$\{0,1\}$	$\vee$	$\wedge$	0	1
Probability	$\mathbb{R}_+$	$+$	$\times$	0	1
Log	$\mathbb{R} \cup \{-\infty, +\infty\}$	$\oplus_{\log}$	$+$	$+\infty$	0
Tropical	$\mathbb{R} \cup \{-\infty, +\infty\}$	min	$+$	$+\infty$	0
String	$\Sigma^* \cup \{\infty\}$	lcp	$\cdot$	∞	ε

to the familiar Boolean semiring, and the probability semiring used to combine probabilities, two semirings often used in applications are the *log semiring* which is isomorphic to the probability semiring via the negative-log mapping, and the *tropical semiring* which is similar to the *log semiring* except the $\oplus$ operation is min. The *left (right) string semiring*, which is defined over strings, has longest common prefix (suffix) and concatenation as its operations, and has the (extended element) *infinite string* and the empty string for its identity elements. It only distributes on the left (right).

A *weighted finite-state transducer* $T = (\mathcal{A}, \mathcal{B}, Q, I, F, E, \lambda, \rho)$ over a semiring $\mathbb{K}$ is specified by a finite input alphabet $\mathcal{A}$, a finite output alphabet $\mathcal{B}$, a finite set of states Q, a set of initial states $I \subseteq Q$, a set of final states $F \subseteq Q$, a finite set of transitions $E \subseteq Q \times (\mathcal{A} \cup \{\varepsilon\}) \times (\mathcal{B} \cup \{\varepsilon\}) \times \mathbb{K} \times Q$, an initial state weight assignment $\lambda : I \rightarrow \mathbb{K}$, and a final state weight assignment $\rho : F \rightarrow \mathbb{K}$. $E[q]$ denotes the set of transitions leaving state $q \in Q$.

Given a transition $e \in E$, $p[e]$ denotes its origin or previous state, $n[e]$ its destination or next state, $i[e]$ its input label, $o[e]$ its output label, and $w[e]$ its weight. A *path* $\pi = e_1 \cdots e_k$ is a sequence of consecutive transitions: $n[e_{i-1}] = p[e_i]$, $i = 2, \ldots, k$. The functions n, p, and w on transitions can be extended to paths by setting: $n[\pi] = n[e_k]$ and $p[\pi] = p[e_1]$ and by defining the weight of a path as the $\otimes$-product of the weights of its constituent transitions: $w[\pi] = w[e_1] \otimes \cdots \otimes w[e_k]$. More generally, w is extended to any finite set of paths R by setting $w[R] = \bigoplus_{\pi \in R} w[\pi]$; if the semiring is closed, this is defined even for infinite R. We denote by $P(q, q')$ the set of paths from q to q' and by $P(q, x, y, q')$ the set of paths from q to q' with input label $x \in \mathcal{A}^*$ and output label $y \in \mathcal{B}^*$. These definitions can be extended to subsets $R, R' \subseteq Q$ by $P(R, R') = \cup_{q \in R, \, q' \in R'} P(q, q')$, $P(R, x, y, R') = \cup_{q \in R, \, q' \in R'} P(q, x, y, q')$.

A transducer T is *regulated* if the weight associated by T to any pair of input-output string (x, y) given by:

$$[\![T]\!](x, y) = \bigoplus_{\pi \in P(I, x, y, F)} \lambda[p[\pi]] \otimes w[\pi] \otimes \rho[n[\pi]] \tag{1}$$

is well-defined and in $\mathbb{K}$. If $P(I, x, y, F) = \emptyset$, then $T(x, y) = \bar{0}$. A weighted transducer without ε-cycles is regulated.

3 Transducer Representation and Construction

In the OpenFst Library, a transducer can be constructed from either the C++ level using class constructors and mutators or from a shell-level program using a textual file representation. We describe the former here.

This C++ code creates the transducer in Figure 1:

```
// A vector FST is a general mutable FST
VectorFst<StdArc> fst;

// Add state 0 to the initially empty FST and make it the initial state
fst.AddState();  // 1st state will be state 0 (returned by AddState)
fst.SetStart(0);  // arg is state ID

// Add two arcs exiting state 0
// Arc constructor args: ilabel, olabel, weight, dest state ID
fst.AddArc(0, StdArc(1, 1, 0.5, 1));  // 1st arg is src state ID
fst.AddArc(0, StdArc(2, 2, 1.5, 1));

// Add state 1 and its arc
fst.AddState();
fst.AddArc(1, StdArc(3, 3, 2.5, 2));

// Add state 2 and set its final weight
fst.AddState();
fst.SetFinal(2, 3.5);  // 1st arg is state ID, 2nd arg weight
```

The steps consist of first constructing an empty VectorFst, which is a general-purpose transducer that uses an adjacency list representation (stored in STL vectors). Next, its mutator member functions are used to add states and transitions ('arcs') and to set the intial state[1] and final weights. States are identified by integer labels. The result can be saved to a file with fst.Write('out.fst').

The VectorFst, like all transducer representations and algorithms in this library, is templated on the transition type. This permits customization of the labels, state IDs and weights in a transducer. StdArc defines the library-standard transition representation:

```
struct StdArc {
    typedef int Label;
    typedef TropicalWeight Weight;
    typedef int StateId;

    Label ilabel;         // Transition input label
    Label olabel;         // Transition output label
    Weight weight;        // Transition weight
    StateId nextstate;    // Transition destination state
};
```

---

[1] Only one initial state is permitted and it has weight $\bar{1}$.

This uses 32-bit integer labels and state IDs and the class `TropicalWeight` for its weight.

A Weight class holds the set element and provides the semiring operations. `TropicalWeight` uses a single-precision float to hold the set element, has member functions that define the identity elements $\bar{0}$ and $\bar{1}$ and has associated functions `Plus` and `Times` that implement $\oplus$ and $\otimes$, respectively:

```
class TropicalWeight {
public:
  TropicalWeight(float f) : value_(f) {}
  static TropicalWeight Zero() { return TropicalWeight(Infinity); }
  static TropicalWeight One() { return TropicalWeight(0.0); }
private:
  float value_;
};
TropicalWeight Plus(TropicalWeight w1, TropicalWeight w2) {
    return w1.value_ < w2.value_ ? w1 : w2;
};
```

The class `LogWeight` is also defined in this library. Users may define their own weight classes and transition types. So long as the weights form a semiring, either a library algorithm will work correctly, or in the case where additional requirements are placed on the weights (such as commutivity), an error will be signalled if the condition is not met.

One simple customization is to use smaller or larger precision labels, state IDs or weights for a more compact or higher capacity representation, respectively. A less trivial extension is to use the `ProductWeight` template, also provided by the library:

```
template <typename W1, typename W2>
class ProductWeight {
public:
  ProductWeight(W1 w1, W2 w2) : value1_(w1), value2_(w2) {}
  static ProductWeight Zero() {
    return ProductWeight(W1::Zero(), W2::Zero());
  }
  static ProductWeight One() {
    return ProductWeight(W1::One(), W2::One());
  }
private:
  W1 value1_;
  W2 value2_;
};
```

For instance, the product semiring of the tropical semiring with itself can be created with

```
ProductWeight<TropicalWeight, TropicalWeight>.
```

Defined over $(\mathbb{R} \cup \{-\infty, +\infty\}) \times (\mathbb{R} \cup \{-\infty, +\infty\})$, this weight class could be used, for example, in speech recognition applications to store both the acoustic and language model scores in recognizer output hypothesis set ('lattice').

Another example of a semiring defined on pairs is the *expectation semiring*. Let $\mathbb{K}$ denote $(\mathbb{R} \cup \{+\infty, -\infty\}) \times (\mathbb{R} \cup \{+\infty, -\infty\})$. For pairs (x_1, y_1) and (x_2, y_2) in $\mathbb{K}$, define the following:

$$(x_1, y_1) \oplus (x_2, y_2) = (x_1 + x_2, y_1 + y_2)$$
$$(x_1, y_1) \otimes (x_2, y_2) = (x_1 x_2, x_1 y_2 + x_2 y_1)$$

The system $(\mathbb{K}, \oplus, \otimes, (0,0), (1,0))$ defines a commutative semiring. [9] show how to use this semiring to compute the relative entropy between probabilistic automata. This algorithm is trivially implemented in this library by adding the expectation semiring and using the intersection and shortest-distance library algorithms.

4   Transducer Algorithms

4.1   Algorithm Implementation Types

The algorithms in the library fall into three implementation types. The *destructive* algorithms modify in place. e.g., "Invert(&fst)". The *constructive* algorithms copy their result into a provided mutable transducer, e.g., "Reverse(fst, &inverted_fst)". Both have a complexity that is a function of the number of states and transitions in the result. The *lazy* (or *delayed*) algorithms are separate transducer C++ classes, e.g., "InvertFst<StdArc> inverted_fst(fst)". They do no computation on construction and their complexity is a function of the number of states and transitions *visited*. This is useful in applications where the whole result may not be visited, e.g., with Dijsktra's algorithm (with positive weights) or in a pruned search. In Section 6, the implementation of lazy algorithms is described.

4.2   Available Algorithms

The library provides over twenty-five transducer operations. We briefly describe some of them below.

Table 2 shows the library operations for the sum, product, and Kleene closure of weighted transducers. Both destructive implementations, using the Thompson construction, and lazy implementations are provided.

Table 3 shows the elementary unary operations for reversing the strings in an automaton, inverting a transduction, and projecting a transduction onto its domain or range. Invert and Project have both destrucive and lazy implementations, while Reverse has a constructive implementation. In Section 6, we outline the implementation of both forms of Invert.

Table 2. The rational operations

OPERATION	DEFINITION
Union	$[\![T_1 \oplus T_2]\!](x,y) = [\![T_1]\!](x,y) \oplus [\![T_2]\!](x,y)$
Concat	$[\![T_1 \otimes T_2]\!](x,y) = \displaystyle\bigoplus_{x=x_1x_2,y=y_1y_2} [\![T_1]\!](x_1,y_1) \otimes [\![T_2]\!](x_2,y_2)$
Closure	$[\![T^*]\!](x,y) = \displaystyle\bigoplus_{n=0}^{\infty} [\![T]\!]^n(x,y)$

Table 3. Elementary unary operations

OPERATION	DEFINITION AND NOTATION	LAZY
Reverse	$[\![\widetilde{T}]\!](x,y) = [\![T]\!](\tilde{x},\tilde{y})$	No
Invert	$[\![T^{-1}]\!](x,y) = [\![T]\!](y,x)$	Yes
Project	$[\![A]\!](x) = \displaystyle\bigoplus_{y} [\![T]\!](x,y)$	Yes

Table 4 shows several binary operations based on the composition algorithm: the composition of transducers, the intersection of acceptors, and the difference of an acceptor and an unweighted, deterministic acceptor [6,7]. Composition is a fundamental operation used to apply or cascade transductions (see Section 5). All have lazy implementations.

Table 4. Fundamental binary operations

OPERATION	DEFINITION AND NOTATION	CONDITION
Compose	$[\![T_1 \circ T_2]\!](x,y) = \displaystyle\bigoplus_{z} [\![T_1]\!](x,z) \otimes [\![T_2]\!](z,y)$	$\mathbb{K}$ commutative
Intersect	$[\![A_1 \cap A_2]\!](x) = [\![A_1]\!](x) \otimes [\![A_2]\!](x)$	$\mathbb{K}$ commutative
Difference	$[\![A_1 - A_2]\!](x) = [\![A_1 \cap \overline{A_2}]\!](x)$	A_2 unweighted & deterministic

Table 5 shows operations that optimize transducers: trimming, epsilon-removal, and weighted determinization and minimization. Several of these algorithms have specific semiring conditions for their use. Not all weighted transducers can be determinized [10,11,12].

Table 5. Optimization operations

OPERATION	DESCRIPTION	LAZY
Connect	Removes non-accessible/non-coaccessible states	No
RmEpsilon	Removes ε-transitions	Yes
Determinize	Creates equivalent deterministic transducr	Yes
Minimize	Creates equivalent minimal deterministic transducer	No

Table 6 shows operations for sorting a transducer's transitions or states, for pushing their weights and labels toward the initial or final states, for placing all input ε's after the non-ε's and for synchronizing the ε delay [13,12].

Table 6. Normalization operations

OPERATION	DESCRIPTION	LAZY
TopSort	Topologically sorts an acyclic transducer	No
ArcSort	Sorts state's arcs given an order relation	Yes
Push	Creates equivalent pushed/stochastic machine	No
EpsNormalize	Places input ε's after non-ε's on paths	No
Synchronize	Produces monotone ε delay	Yes

Table 7 shows operations that search for shortest paths or distances in a weighted automaton or prune away states and transitions on paths that have weights that exceed a threshold [13].

Table 7. Search operations

OPERATION	DESCRIPTION
ShortestPath	Finds n-shortest paths
ShortestDistance	Finds single-source shortest-distances
Prune	Prunes states and transitions by path weight

Usage information, graphical examples, and complexities of all library operations are provided in the documentation available at http://www.openfst.org.

5   Examples

In this section, we give examples of the use of the library algorithms. First, we give a simple example of transducer application:

```
// Reads in an input FST.
StdFst *input = StdFst::Read("input.fst");

// Reads in the transduction model.
StdFst *model = StdFst::Read("model.fst");

// The FSTs must be sorted along the dimensions they will be joined.
// In fact, only one needs to be so sorted.
// This could have instead been done for "model.fst" when it was created.
ArcSort(input, StdOLabelCompare());
ArcSort(model, StdILabelCompare());

// Container for composition result.
StdVectorFst result;

// Create the composed FST
Compose(*input, *model, &result);

// Just keeps the output labels
Project(&result, PROJECT_OUTPUT);
```

An input automaton and a transducer to which the input will be applied are first read from files. Then these automata are sorted as required by the composition algorithm. Next, they are composed and the result is projected onto the output labels.

Next we give an example of using different semirings to compute the shortest distance from the initial state to each state q [13]:

```
// Tropical semiring
Fst<StdArc> *input = Fst<StdArc>::Read("input.fst");
vector<StdArc::Weight> distance;
ShortestDistance(*input, &distance);

// Log semiring
Fst<LogArc> *input = Fst::Read("input.fst");
vector<LogArc::Weight> distance;
ShortestDistance(*input, &distance);

// Right string semiring
typedef StringArc<TropicalWeight, STRING_RIGHT> SR;
Fst<SR> *input = Fst::Read("input.fst");
vector<SR::Weight> distance;
ShortestDistance(*input, &distance);

// Left string semiring
typedef StringArc<TropicalWeight, STRING_LEFT> SL;
Fst<SL> *input = Fst::Read("input.fst");
vector<SL::Weight> distance;
ShortestDistance(*input, &distance);
ERROR: ShortestDistance: Weights need to be right distributive
```

With the tropical semiring, the minimum path weight to q is computed. With the log semiring, the (log) sum of path weights to q is computed. With the right string semiring, the longest common suffix among paths to q is computed. With the left string semiring, an error is signalled, since the semiring is only left-distributive.

We have represented a transition as:

$$e \in Q \times (\mathcal{A} \cup \{\varepsilon\}) \times (\mathcal{B} \cup \{\varepsilon\}) \times \mathbb{K} \times Q.$$

This treats the input and output labels symmetrically, is space-efficient since there is a single output-label per transition, and is the natural representation for the composition algorithm whose efficiency is critical in many applications. However, an alternative representation of a transition is:

$$e \in Q \times (\mathcal{A} \cup \{\varepsilon\}) \times \mathcal{B}^* \times \mathbb{K} \times Q.$$

or equivalently,

$$e \in Q \times (\mathcal{A} \cup \{\varepsilon\}) \times \mathbb{K}' \times Q, \qquad \mathbb{K}' = \mathcal{B}^* \times \mathbb{K}.$$

This treats string and $\mathbb{K}$ outputs uniformly and is the natural representation for weighted transducer determinization, minimization, label pushing, and epsilon normalization [10,11,13,12]. Implementing these algorithms in the original transition representation is awkward and complex.

We can use the alternative transition representation in this library, combining each transitions output label and weight into a new product weight, with:

```
typedef ProductWeight⟨StringWeight,TropicalWeight⟩CompositeWeight;
```

The following shows how this composite weight is used to implement weighted determinization:

```
Fst<StdArc> *input = Fst::Read("input.fst");
// Converts into alternative transition representation
MapFst<StdArc, CompositeArc> composite(*input, ToCompositeMapper);
WeightedDeterminizeFst<CompositeArc> det(composite);
// Ensures only one output label per transition (functional input)
FactorWeightFst<CompositeArc> factor(det);
// Converts back from alternative transition representation
MapFst<CompositeArc> result(factor, FromCompositeMapper);
```

First, the input is converted to the alternate representation using an operation that maps a conversion function (object) across all transitions. Next, generic weighted (acceptor) determiniztaion is applied, and then the result is converted back to the original transition representation. Performance is not sacrificed given efficient lazy computation and string semiring implementations. Weighted transducer minimization, label pushing and epsilon normalization are easily implemented in a similar way using this change of transition representation and the generic (acceptor) weighted minimization, weight pushing, and ε-removal algorithms.

6   Transducer Class Design and Lazy Evaluation

In this section, the details of the transducer representations used and the implementation of lazy evaluation are described. In this library there are many transducer represenations. Some are mutable containers like VectorFst, others are immutable containers like ConstFst, while others implement the lazy evaluation of operations like InvertFst. They all share the abstract base Fst class:

```
template <class Arc>
class Fst {
public:
  virtual StateId Start() const = 0;          // Initial state
  virtual Weight Final(StateId) const = 0;    // State's final weight
  static Fst<Arc> *Read(const string filename);
}
```

Two companion classes, StateIterator and ArcIterator, are defined that each have methods Next, Done, and Value. These classes provide the minimum information needed to specify a transducer. This includes its initial state, final weights, and operations to step through the states of the transducer and the transitions of a state. Any class that derives from Fst and correctly implements these methods can be used with any algorithm that accepts this base type as its argument.

The destructive algorithms mutate their input. They use as arguments another abstract class, MutableFst, that derives from Fst. This class adds methods SetStart, SetFinal. AddState, and AddArc and has a companion class MutableArcIterator that adds method SetValue to ArcIterator.

The following shows the implementation of destructive Invert using these classes. The states and transitions are traversed and the input and output swapped in place:

```
template <class Arc> void Invert(MutableFst<Arc> *fst) {
  for (StateIterator< MutableFst<Arc> > siter(*fst);
    !siter.Done();
    siter.Next()) {
      StateId s = siter.Value();
      for (MutableArcIterator< MutableFst<Arc> > aiter(fst, s);
        !aiter.Done();
        aiter.Next()) {
          Arc arc = aiter.Value();
          Label l = arc.ilabel;
          arc.ilabel = arc.olabel;
          arc.olabel = l;
          aiter.SetValue(arc);
      }
  }
}
```

The following shows the implementation of lazy InvertFst:

```
template <class Arc> class InvertFst : public Fst<Arc> {
public:
  virtual StateId Start() const { return fst_->Start(); }
  ...
private:
  const Fst<Arc> *fst_;
}

template <class F> Arc ArcIterator<F>::Value() const {
  Arc arc = arcs_[i_];
  Label l = arc.ilabel;
  arc.ilabel = arc.olabel;
  arc.olabel = l;
  return arc;
}
```

This is a new class that derives from `Fst`. It forwards most of its methods to the input transducer. However, its companion `ArcIterator` swaps the input and output labels when a transition is requested. Note the input transducer is not modified and no computation is performed until requested. While the lazy inversion operation is trivial, more complex operations like composition and determinization are naturally implemented in this way as well.

7 Conclusion

This paper has presented an overview of a new comprehensive and flexible weighted finite-state transducer library whose source code is freely available. We encourage readers to visit `http://www.openfst.org` to download the library. There is an easy-to-use shell-level interface that we did not describe here, but that is documented on the web site and is a good place to start. It is our hope that others will find this library useful in the years to come.

Acknowledgments

The research of Cyril Allauzen and Mehryar Mohri was partially supported by the New York State Office of Science Technology and Academic Research (NYS-TAR). This project was also sponsored in part by the Department of the Army Award Number W81XWH-04-1-0307. The U.S. Army Medical Research Acquisition Activity, 820 Chandler Street, Fort Detrick MD 21702-5014 is the awarding and administering acquisition office. The content of this material does not necessarily reflect the position or the policy of the Government and no official endorsement should be inferred.

References

1. Mohri, M., Pereira, F., Riley, M.: The design principles of a weighted finite-state transducer library. Theoretical Computer Science 231, 17–32 (2000)
2. Adant, A.: WFST: a finite-state template library in C++ (2000), http://membres.lycos.fr/adant/tfe
3. Hetherington, L.: The MIT finite-state transducer toolkit for speech and language processing. In: Proceedings of the ICSLP, Jeju, South Korea (2004)
4. Kanthak, S., Ney, H.: FSA: An efficient and flexible C++ toolkit for finite state automata using on-demand computation. In: Proceedings of 42nd Meeting of the ACL, pp. 510–517 (2004)
5. Lombardy, S., Régis-Gianas, Y., Sakarovitch, J.: Introducing VAUCANSON. Theoretical Computer Science 328, 77–96 (2004)
6. Salomaa, A., Soittola, M.: Automata-Theoretic Aspects of Formal Power Series. Springer, New York (1978)
7. Kuich, W., Salomaa, A.: Semirings, Automata, Languages. Number 5 in EATCS Monographs on Theoretical Computer Science. Springer, Germany (1986)
8. Berstel, J., Reutenauer, C.: Rational Series and Their Languages. Springer, New York (1988)

9. Cortes, C., Mohri, M., Rastogi, A., Riley, M.: On the computation of the relative entropy of probabilistic automata. International Journal of Foundations of Computer Science (2007)

10. Mohri, M.: Finite-state transducers in language and speech processing. Computational Linguistics 23 (1997)

11. Mohri, M.: Minimization algorithms for sequential transducers. Theoretical Computer Science 234, 177–201 (2000)

12. Mohri, M.: Generic epsilon-removal and input epsilon-normalization algorithms for weighted transducers. International Journal of Foundations of Computer Science 13, 29–143 (2002)

13. Mohri, M.: Semiring frameworks and algorithms for shortest-distance problems. Journal of Automata, Languages and Combinatorics 7, 321–350 (2002)

Automata Applications in Chip-Design Software
(Extended Abstract of an Invited Talk)

Bruce W. Watson

FASTAR, University of Pretoria, South Africa
Sagantec Corp., Fremont, USA
bw@bruce-watson.com
www.fastar.org

Abstract. In this paper, I present several new automata applications in software for *electronic design automation* (EDA) — chip design. EDA software has typically been implemented by and for microelectronic engineers, and the associated algorithmics remains underdeveloped. In several cases, overly complex algorithms have been used whereas automata could have been applied after abstracting from the problem details.

Keywords: EDA, integrated circuit layout, pattern matching, design rule checking, chip design.

The term *EDA* refers to software supporting the entire chip-design flow, consisting roughly of the following sequence:

1. Specification: the desired chip functionality is formally defined.
2. Functional simulation: the specification and a block-form of the chip is simulated to match the specification against end-user expectations.
3. Synthesis: specified components are compiled into circuit elements and library building blocks.
4. Library-block selection: specific library building blocks are selected and instantiated.
5. Floor-planning: the building blocks are placed on the intended *die* (chip) area.
6. Routing: building blocks are interconnected as required.
7. Electrical characterization: the electrical behaviour is simulated, detecting undesirable interactions.
8. Timing analysis: the resultant electrical behaviour, along with the layout, is used to determine the timing of signals and detect race conditions.
9. Lithography simulation: the printability of the circuit element and their interaction with nearby circuit elements is simulated.
10. Physical-layout fixing: problems detected in lithography simulation are fixed, and the physical layout is *biased* to compensate for the fact that the lithography-light wavelength (193 nanometers) is considerably bigger than the circuit feature sizes (65 nanometers).
11. Mask-data preparation: the physical layout is put in a format suitable for manufacturing the *masks*.

Jan Holub and Jan Žd'árek (Eds.): CIAA 2007, LNCS 4783, pp. 24–26, 2007.

In many of the first phases, automata are used implicitly or explicitly in modeling circuit behaviour — and those areas are well explored. (For comprehensive overviews of these phases, see [1,2].) The outputs of each successive phase in the chip-design flow increase dramatically: for a medium-sized microprocessor, a specification measures under a megabyte, while the physical-layout data and mask-data would measure in the hundreds of gigabytes. The most performance constrained phases are presently from lithography simulation onwards — largely due to the massive data sizes.

In physical-layout form, the chip design consists of several layers (upwards of 11 layers, each of which will be physically manufactured on the wafer, yielding the chip). Each layer consists of *polygons* (with edges aligned to the x and y axes, or at 45 degrees). The polygons on different layers together form the wires, and (where they overlap electrically) the transistors, capacitors and resistors of the circuit. A modern chip of 300 million transistors will easily consist of a billion or more polygons when counting the interconnecting wires, etc. Such complexity presents formidable challenges:

- As mentioned above, the data-sizes for a physical design can reach several hundred gigabytes.
- With Moore's law[1], the file size of a physical design doubles every 18 months. Necessarily, the hardware used to *run* EDA software is at least one generation behind, giving a factor of two in required- versus available-capacity (virtual memory, running time, etc.).
- Hardware for running EDA software is increasingly parallel (e.g. server farms and multi-core CPU's).

Our algorithmic and implementation efforts show that these challenges can be met by applying automata of various types. Some further advantages of using automata include: simple computational model, well-explored theoretical foundations, and the potential to implement them in specialized-hardware.

We are applying automata in several specific physical design problem areas, yielding the above-mentioned advantages over current solutions:

- Design-rule (DR) checking: DR's are factory ('fab')-specified physical layout rules that restrict allowable layouts to make them lithographically/manufacturing viable. Designers who violate such rules risk chips which are not electrically correct or fail other standards such as timing. Checking DR's can be expressed as an automata-based pattern matching problem.
- Pattern-based layout modification: problems in the physical layout (perhaps a DR violation, or a lithographically weak polygon configuration) often occur repetitively (and identically) in uniformly structured chips such as FPGAs and memory devices. Once a fix is determined (by moving, replacing, reshaping, or deleting some polygons), it is usually applied everywhere the problematic configuration occurs. This can be done by a form of transducer.

---

[1] Moore's law states that the complexity (transistor count, density, etc.) of chips doubles roughly every 18 months.

- Repetition detection: sometimes layouts are manually designed or edited (by a 'layouter' who literally hand-places polygons), and repetitive structures are coincidental and ad-hoc. In such cases, designers would prefer to detect such repetitions and *factor* them, making the design more maintainable. Similar to their use in strings, such repetitions can be detected using various two-dimensional index-oriented automata.
- Optical proximity correction (OPC) and Phase-shift masking (PSM): these advanced lithography-aware design techniques are used to change the physical-layout polygon shapes ('bias' them) so that the actual printed polygons more closely resemble the original ones. (As mentioned above, such techniques are necessary because the lithography light's wavelength is so much longer than the chip feature sizes.) OPC and PSM can also be implemented using two-dimensional transductions.

These automata applications will be presented in further detail, along with performance data indicating the trade-off between the traditionally used EDA algorithms and automata-based solutions.

Note: Several of the solutions presented in this paper are the subject of ongoing patent filings.

References

1. Jansen, D. (ed.): The Electronic Design Automation Handbook. Kluwer Academic Publishers, Boston (2003)
2. McFarland, G.: Microprocessor Design. McGraw-Hill, New York (2006)

Synchronizing Automata
Preserving a Chain of Partial Orders[*]

Mikhail V. Volkov

Department of Mathematics and Mechanics,
Ural State University, 620083 Ekaterinburg, Russia
`Mikhail.Volkov@usu.ru`

Abstract. We present a new class of automata which strictly contains the class of aperiodic automata and shares with the latter certain synchronization properties. In particular, every strongly connected automaton in this new class is synchronizing and has a reset word of length $\left\lfloor \frac{n(n+1)}{6} \right\rfloor$ where n is the number of states of the automaton.

Keywords: deterministic finite automaton, synchronizing automaton, Černý conjecture, congruence on an automaton, weakly monotonic automaton, strongly connected automaton.

Background and Motivation

Let $\mathscr{A} = \langle Q, \Sigma, \delta \rangle$ be a *deterministic finite automaton* (DFA), where Q is the state set, Σ stands for the input alphabet, and $\delta : Q \times \Sigma \to Q$ is the transition function defining an action of the letters in Σ on Q. The action extends in a unique way to an action $Q \times \Sigma^* \to Q$ of the free monoid Σ^* over Σ; the latter action is still denoted by δ. The DFA $\mathscr{A}$ is called *synchronizing* if there exists a word $w \in \Sigma^*$ whose action resets $\mathscr{A}$, that is to leave the automaton in one particular state no matter which state in Q it starts at: $\delta(q, w) = \delta(p, w)$ for all $q, p \in Q$. Any such word w is said to be a *reset word* for the DFA.

It is rather natural to ask how short a reset word for a given synchronizing automaton may be. The question is not easy: given a DFA $\mathscr{A}$ and a positive integer ℓ, the problem whether or not $\mathscr{A}$ has a reset word of length at most ℓ is known to be NP-complete (see [4] or [7] or [12]). On the other hand, there are some upper bounds on the minimum length of reset words for synchronizing automata with a given number of states. The best such bound known so far is due to Pin [10] (it is based on a combinatorial theorem conjectured by Pin and then proved by Frankl [5]): for each synchronizing automaton with n states, there exists a reset word of length at most $\frac{n^3-n}{6}$. In 1964 Černý [3] constructed for each $n > 1$ a synchronizing automaton with n states which shortest reset word has length $(n-1)^2$. Soon after that he conjectured that those automata represent the worst possible case, that is, every synchronizing automaton with n states can be reset

---

[*] Supported by the Russian Foundation for Basic Research, grant 05-01-00540.

Jan Holub and Jan Žd'árek (Eds.): CIAA 2007, LNCS 4783, pp. 27–37, 2007.
© Springer-Verlag Berlin Heidelberg 2007

by a word of length $(n-1)^2$. By now this simply looking conjecture is arguably the most longstanding open problem in the combinatorial theory of finite automata. The reader is referred to the survey [8] for an interesting overview of the area and its relations to multiple-valued logic and symbolic dynamics; applications of synchronizing automata to robotics are discussed in [4,6]. (A more recent survey [13] contains a detailed account of algorithmic and complexity issues in the field but unfortunately omits some important references.)

While the Černý conjecture remains open in general, some progress has been achieved for various restricted classes of synchronizing automata. In particular, some attention has been paid to the synchronization issues within the class **Ap** of *aperiodic automata*. Recall that a DFA is called *aperiodic* (or *counter-free*) if its transition monoid has only singleton subgroups. Aperiodic automata play a distinguished role in many aspects of formal language theory and its connections to logic, see the classic monograph [9]. Thus, studying synchronization of aperiodic automata appears to be well justified, especially if one takes into account that the problem of finding short reset words is known to remain difficult when restricted to **Ap**. Indeed, inspecting the reductions from 3-SAT used in [4] or [7] or [12], one can observe that in each case the construction results in an aperiodic automaton, and therefore, the question of whether or not a given aperiodic automaton admits a reset word which length does not exceed a given positive integer, is NP-complete.

Recently Trahtman [14] has proved that every synchronizing aperiodic automaton with n states admits a reset word of length at most $\frac{n(n-1)}{2}$. Thus, the Černý conjecture holds true for synchronizing aperiodic automata. However, the problem of establishing a precise bound for the minimum length of reset words for synchronizing aperiodic automata with n states still remains open, and moreover, we do not even have a reasonably justified conjecture for this case. Indeed, in all concrete examples of synchronizing aperiodic automata the minimum length of reset words is bounded by a linear function of the number of states, namely, by $n + \lfloor \frac{n}{2} \rfloor - 2$. (A series of examples reaching this bound for $n \geq 7$ appeared in [1].) This phenomenon creates a feeling, first, that the upper bound $\frac{n(n-1)}{2}$ is rather rough, and second, that some arguments from [14] may apply to a larger class of automata.

In Section 1 we define such a new class of automata which we call *weakly monotonic*. Their definition resembles the one of generalized monotonic automata introduced and motivated in [2] and is in fact obtained by a slight relaxation of the latter notion. But, while generalized monotonic automata form a proper subclass of the class **Ap** of aperiodic automata [2], the class of weakly monotonic automata can be shown to strictly contain **Ap**, see Propositions 1 and 2.

In Section 2 we discuss synchronization properties of weakly monotonic automata. Here we restrict ourselves to the case when the underlying digraph of the automaton in question is strongly connected (for brevity, we refer to such automata as to *strongly connected*). The restriction is rather natural since it is known (and easy to verify, see the discussion following Proposition 3) that the

Černý conjecture readily reduces to this case. We prove, and this is the main result of the paper, that every strongly connected weakly monotonic automaton is synchronizing and has a reset word of length $\left\lfloor \frac{n(n+1)}{6} \right\rfloor$ where n is the number of states of the automaton. This upper bound is new even for the aperiodic case.

1 Weakly Monotonic Automata

Let X be a set and $\rho \subseteq X \times X$ a binary relation on X. We denote by $\mathrm{Eq}(\rho)$ the *equivalence closure* of ρ, that is, the least equivalence relation containing ρ. It is well known and easy to see that a pair $(x, y) \in X \times X$ belongs to $\mathrm{Eq}(\rho)$ if and only if there exist elements $x_0, x_1, \dots, x_k \in X$ such that $x = x_0$, $x_k = y$, and for each $i = 1, \dots, k$ either $x_{i-1} = x_i$ or $(x_{i-1}, x_i) \in \rho$ or $(x_i, x_{i-1}) \in \rho$.

A binary relation ρ on the state set Q of a DFA $\mathscr{A} = \langle Q, \Sigma, \delta \rangle$ is said to be *stable* if $(p, q) \in \rho$ implies $\big(\delta(p, a), \delta(q, a)\big) \in \rho$ for all states $p, q \in Q$ and all letters $a \in \Sigma$. From the above description of the equivalence closure it easily follows that $\mathrm{Eq}(\rho)$ is stable whenever ρ is.

Recall that a stable equivalence π on the state set of a DFA is called a *congruence*. Given a congruence π of $\mathscr{A} = \langle Q, \Sigma, \delta \rangle$ and a state $q \in Q$, we denote by $[q]_\pi$ the π-class containing q. The *quotient* $\mathscr{A}/\pi$ is the DFA $\langle Q/\pi, \Sigma, \delta_\pi \rangle$ where $Q/\pi = \big\{ [q]_\pi \mid q \in Q \big\}$ and the transition function δ_π is defined by the rule $\delta_\pi([q]_\pi, a) = [\delta(q, a)]_\pi$ for all $q \in Q$ and $a \in \Sigma$. Observe that every stable relation $\rho \subseteq Q \times Q$ containing π induces a stable relation on Q/π, namely, the relation $\rho/\pi = \big\{ ([p]_\pi, [q]_\pi) \mid (p, q) \in \rho \big\}$.

We call a DFA $\mathscr{A} = \langle Q, \Sigma, \delta \rangle$ *weakly monotonic of level* ℓ if it has a strictly increasing chain of stable binary relations

$$\rho_0 \subset \rho_1 \subset \cdots \subset \rho_\ell \tag{1}$$

satisfying the following conditions:

WM1) ρ_0 is the equality relation $\{(q, q) \mid q \in Q\}$;
WM2) for each $i = 1, \dots, \ell$, the congruence $\pi_{i-1} = \mathrm{Eq}(\rho_{i-1})$ is contained in ρ_i and the relation ρ_i/π_{i-1} is a (partial) order on Q/π_{i-1};
WM3) π_ℓ is the universal relation $Q \times Q$.

Slightly abusing terminology, we refer to any chain of the form (1) satisfying WM1–WM3 as to a *chain of partial orders preserved by* $\mathscr{A}$. (It should be clear that in fact the ρ_i's with $i > 1$ are preorders on Q but not orders as they cannot be antisymmetric.)

First of all, since the definition of a weakly monotonic automaton is rather involved, we illustrate it by a transparent example. Consider the DFA in the left part of Fig. 1; we denote it by $\mathscr{E}$. We want to show that $\mathscr{E}$ is weakly monotonic of level 2. Let ρ_0 be the equality relation. Then so is $\pi_0 = \mathrm{Eq}(\rho_0)$, of course. We define $\rho_1 = \pi_0 \cup \{(1, 2), (3, 4)\}$. Then it is easy to check that ρ_1 is a stable partial order and the congruence $\pi_1 = \mathrm{Eq}(\rho_1)$ is the partition of $\{1, 2, 3, 4\}$ into 2 classes $Q_1 = \{1, 2\}$ and $Q_2 = \{3, 4\}$ (the partition is shown in Fig. 1 by the dashed line). The quotient $\mathscr{E}/\pi_1$ is shown in Fig. 1 on the right. Next, we define $\rho_2 = \pi_1 \cup Q_1 \times Q_2$. Then we immediately see that ρ_2/π_1 is a stable order with respect to the quotient $\mathscr{E}/\pi_1$ and $\pi_2 = \mathrm{Eq}(\rho_2)$ is the universal relation.

We mention in passing that one can show that $\mathscr{E}$ is in fact weakly monotonic of level 1. (For this, one should check that the partial order $\pi_0 \cup \{(1,2), (1,3),$ $(1,4), (2,4), (3,4)\}$ also is stable with respect to $\mathscr{E}$.)

Now we give two mass examples of weakly monotonic automata. The first of them constitutes our main motivation for considering this class.

Proposition 1. *Every aperiodic automaton is weakly monotonic.*

Proof. Let $\mathscr{A} = \langle Q, \Sigma, \delta \rangle$ be an aperiodic automaton. We induct on $|Q|$ and, since the claim is trivial for $|Q| = 1$, we assume $|Q| > 1$. We have to construct a strictly increasing chain of stable relations satisfying the conditions WM1–WM3. In [14] it is shown that every non-trivial aperiodic automaton admits a non-trivial stable partial order. Let ρ_1 be such an order with respect to $\mathscr{A}$ and $\pi_1 = \mathrm{Eq}(\rho_1)$. The quotient automaton $\mathscr{A}/\pi_1$ is aperiodic again because its transition monoid is a quotient of the transition monoid of $\mathscr{A}$. Thus, $\mathscr{A}/\pi_1$ preserves a chain of partial orders by the induction assumption. Lifting this chain back to Q, we obtain, for some ℓ, a chain of stable relations $\rho_0' \subset \rho_1' \subset \cdots \subset \rho_\ell'$ satisfying WM2 and WM3 and such that $\rho_0' = \pi_1$. Now it is easy to see that the chain $\rho_0 \subset \rho_1 \subset \rho_1' \subset \cdots \subset \rho_\ell'$, in which ρ_0 is the equality relation on Q, satisfies WM1–WM3. □

The second group of examples shows, in particular, that the converse of Proposition 1 is not true. Recall that a state s of a DFA $\mathscr{A} = \langle Q, \Sigma, \delta \rangle$ is called a *sink* if $\delta(s, a) = s$ for all $a \in \Sigma$.

Proposition 2. *Every DFA with a unique sink is weakly monotonic.*

Proof. Let $\mathscr{A} = \langle Q, \Sigma, \delta \rangle$ be a DFA with a unique sink $s \in Q$. We define a partial order ρ_1 on the set Q by letting the sink s be less than each state in $Q \setminus \{s\}$ and leaving all states in $Q \setminus \{s\}$ incomparable. It is easy to see that ρ_1 is preserved by all the transformations $\delta(\sqcup, a)$ where $a \in \Sigma$ and that $\mathrm{Eq}(\rho_1) = Q \times Q$. Thus, the chain $\rho_0 \subset \rho_1$, in which ρ_0 is the equality on Q, satisfies WM1–WM3, and $\mathscr{A}$ is weakly monotonic of level 1. □

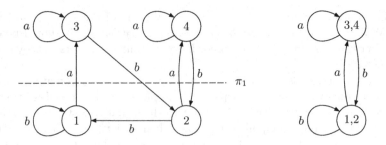

Fig. 1. An example of a weakly monotonic automaton

Of course, a DFA $\mathscr{A}$ with a unique sink need not be aperiodic. For instance, some of the input letters of $\mathscr{A}$ can act as a cyclic permutation of the non-sink states thus inducing a non-singleton cyclic subgroup in the transition monoid of $\mathscr{A}$.

2   Strongly Connected Weakly Monotonic Automata

First, we explain why one may concentrate on strongly connected automata when studying synchronization issues such as the minimum length of reset words for automata with a given number of states.

Proposition 3. *Let* **C** *be any class of automata closed under taking subautomata and quotients, and let* $\mathbf{C}_n$ *stand for the class of all automata with* n *states in* **C**. *Further, let* $f : \mathbb{Z}^+ \to \mathbb{N}$ *be any function such that*

$$f(n) \geq f(n - m + 1) + f(m) \ \text{whenever} \ n \geq m \geq 1. \tag{2}$$

If each synchronizing automaton in $\mathbf{C}_n$ *which either is strongly connected or possesses a unique sink has a reset word of length* $f(n)$, *then the same holds true for all synchronizing automata in* $\mathbf{C}_n$.

Proof. Let $\mathscr{A} = \langle Q, \Sigma, \delta \rangle$ be a synchronizing automaton in $\mathbf{C}_n$. Consider the set S of all states to which the automaton $\mathscr{A}$ can be synchronized and let $m = |S|$. If $q \in S$, then there exists a reset word $w \in \Sigma^*$ such that $Q.w = \{q\}$. Then wa also is a reset word and $Q.wa = \{\delta(q, a)\}$ whence $\delta(q, a) \in S$. This means that, restricting the transition function δ to $S \times \Sigma$, we get a subautomaton $\mathscr{S}$ with the state set S. Obviously, $\mathscr{S}$ is synchronizing and strongly connected and, since the class **C** is closed under taking subautomata, we have $\mathscr{S} \in \mathbf{C}$. Hence, $\mathscr{S}$ has a reset word v of length $f(m)$.

Now consider the partition π of Q into $n - m + 1$ classes one of which is S and all others are singletons. It is easy to see that π is a congruence of the automaton $\mathscr{A}$. Clearly, the quotient $\mathscr{A}/\pi$ is synchronizing and has S as a unique sink. Since the class **C** is closed under taking quotients, we have $\mathscr{A}/\pi \in \mathbf{C}$. Hence, $\mathscr{A}/\pi$ has a reset word u of length $f(n - m + 1)$.

Since $Q.u \subseteq S$ and $S.v$ is a singleton, we conclude that also $Q.uv \subseteq S.v$ is a singleton. Thus, uv is reset word for $\mathscr{A}$, and the length of this word does not exceed $f(n - m + 1) + f(m) \leq f(n)$ according to (2). □

It is easy to check that the function $f(n) = (n - 1)^2$ satisfies (2). Thus, applying Proposition 3 to the class of all automata, we see that it suffices to prove the Černý conjecture for strongly connected automata and for automata with a unique sink. It is known (see, e.g., [11]) that every synchronizing automaton with a unique sink has a reset word of length $\frac{n(n-1)}{2} \leq (n - 1)^2$, whence only the strongly connected case remains open.

Similarly, applying Proposition 3 to the class **Ap** of all aperiodic automata and to the function $f(n) = \frac{n(n-1)}{2}$, we see that Trahtman's upper bound [14] for the length of reset words for synchronizing aperiodic automata follows from its restriction to strongly connected automata.

In view of Proposition 2, weak monotonicity does not impose any extra restriction on automata with a unique sink. In contrast, we will prove that strongly connected weakly monotonic automata are rather specific from the synchronization viewpoint.

Theorem 1. *Every strongly connected weakly monotonic automaton $\mathscr{A} = \langle Q, \Sigma, \delta \rangle$ is synchronizing and has a reset word of length $\lfloor \frac{n(n+1)}{6} \rfloor$ where $n = |Q|$.*

Proof. We induct on n and observe that the case $n = 1$ is obvious. Thus, we assume that $n > 1$.

By the definition of weakly monotonic automata there exist a non-trivial stable partial order relation ρ_1 on Q. For $S \subseteq Q$, we denote by $\min(S)$ and $\max(S)$ the sets of the minimal and the maximal elements of S with respect to the order ρ_1.

For $S \subseteq Q$ and $w \in \Sigma^*$, we denote the set $\{\delta(q, w) \mid q \in S\}$ by $S.w$. It is convenient to isolate the following observation.

Lemma 1. *For every word $v \in \Sigma^*$, one has $\min(S.v) \subseteq \min(S).v$.*

Proof. In order to improve readability, we write $\leq$ instead of ρ_1. Take any state $p' \in \min(S.v)$ and consider its arbitrary preimage $p \in S$. There exists $q \in \min(S)$ such that $q \leq p$. Since the order $\leq$ is stable, we then have $q' = \delta(q, v) \leq \delta(p, v) = p'$. The state q' belongs to the set $S.v$, and therefore, $q' = p'$ because p' has been chosen to be a minimal element in this set. Thus, we have found a preimage for p' in $\min_K(S)$ whence $\min_K(S.v) \subseteq \min_K(S).v$. $\qquad\square$

We say that a subset $T \subseteq Q$ is *linked* if for every pair $(q, p) \in T \times T$ there exist states $q_0, q_1, \ldots, q_k \in T$ such that $q = q_0$, $q_k = p$, and for each $i = 1, \ldots, k$ either $(q_{i-1}, q_i) \in \rho_1$ or $(q_i, q_{i-1}) \in \rho_1$. (This simply means that the Hasse diagram of the poset $\langle T, \rho_1 \rangle$ is connected as a graph.) Let $\pi_1 = \mathrm{Eq}(\rho_1)$. It is clear that each π_1-class is a linked set and that any linked set is contained in a single π_1-class. Further, since the order ρ_1 is stable, we immediately get the following observation:

Lemma 2. *If $T \subseteq Q$ is linked, then for every word $v \in \Sigma^*$ the set $T.v$ is linked.*

We will often use the following property of linked sets:

Lemma 3. *If T is linked and $|T| > 1$, then $\min(T) \cap \max(T) = \varnothing$.*

Proof. Again, we write $\leq$ instead of ρ_1. Take any state $q \in \min(T)$, and let p be any state in $T \setminus \{q\}$. Since T is linked, there is a sequence of states $q_0, q_1, \ldots, q_k \in T$ such that $q = q_0$, $q_k = p$, and for each $i = 1, \ldots, k$ either $q_{i-1} \leq q_i$ or $q_i \leq q_{i-1}$. If we choose $q_0, q_1, \ldots, q_k$ to be such a sequence of minimum length, then no adjacent states can be equal, in particular, $q_0 \neq q_1$. Therefore either $q_0 \lneq q_1$ or $q_1 \lneq q_0$. As the latter inequality would contradict the fact that $q_0 = q \in \min(T)$, we conclude that $q = q_0 \lneq q_1$ whence q is not a maximal element of T. Thus, no minimal element of T can be in the same time a maximal element. $\qquad\square$

The core of our argument is contained in the following

Lemma 4. *Let $T \subseteq Q$ be a linked set, $\ell = |\min(T)\backslash\max(T)|$ and $k = |\max(Q)|$. Then there exists a word $w \in \Sigma^*$ of length at most $b(\ell, k) = \ell(n - k + 1) - \frac{\ell(\ell+1)}{2}$ such that $|T.w| = 1$.*

Proof. We induct on ℓ. If $\ell = 0$, then $b(\ell, k) = 0$. Besides that, from the definition of the number ℓ it follows that in T each minimal element is in the same time a maximal element. By Lemma 3 this is only possible if T is a singleton. Then the empty word can play the role of w.

Let $\ell > 0$. By Lemma 3 we then have $\ell = |\min(T)|$. Since the DFA $\mathscr{A}$ is strongly connected, there is a directed path from $\min(T)$ to $\max(Q)$ in its underlying digraph. Choose such a path of minimum length. This path cannot visit any state twice, only its first state can belong to $\min(T)$ and only its last state can lie in $\max(Q)$. Therefore the number of the edges in the path cannot exceed $|Q \setminus (\min(T) \cup \max(Q))| + 1$. From Lemma 3 it follows that $\min(T) \cap \max(Q) = \varnothing$ whence the cardinality of the set $Q \setminus (\min(T) \cup \max(Q))$ is equal to $n - \ell - k$ (in particular, $n - \ell - k \geq 0$). Thus, if u is the word that labels a path of minimum length from $\min(T)$ to $\max(Q)$, then the length of u does not exceed $n - \ell - k + 1$.

Observe that

$$b(\ell - 1, k) + (n - \ell - k + 1) = (\ell - 1)(n - k + 1) - \frac{(\ell - 1)\ell}{2} + (n - \ell - k + 1) =$$

$$\ell(n - k + 1) - \frac{\ell(\ell + 1)}{2} = b(\ell, k). \quad (3)$$

Since $n - \ell - k \geq 0$, this implies that $b(\ell, k) > b(\ell - 1, k)$ whenever $\ell > 0$.

Now consider the set $T.u$. It is linked by Lemma 2. By Lemma 1 $\min(T.u) \subseteq \min(T).u$. Let $q \in \min(T)$ be the state at which the path labelled u starts. If $q' = \delta(q, u) \notin \min(T.u)$, then

$$|\min(T.u)| < |\min(T).u| \leq |\min(T)| = \ell,$$

and the induction assumption applies to the set $T.u$. We have observed that the number $b(\ell, k)$ increases with ℓ, and therefore, we may assume that there is a word $v \in \Sigma^*$ of length at most $b(\ell - 1, k)$ such that $|(T.u).v| = 1$. Then we can let $w = uv$: we have $T.w = (T.u).v$ whence $|T.w| = 1$ and (3) ensures that the length of w does not exceed $b(\ell, k)$.

It remains to consider the case when $q' = \delta(q, u) \in \min(T.u)$. Recall that by the choice of our path $q' \in \max(Q)$. Thus, the state q' which is minimal in $T.u$ is also maximal in Q whence it is of course maximal in $T.u$ as well. By Lemma 3 this implies that $|T.u| = 1$, and we can let $w = u$. The fact that the length of u (which does not exceed $n - \ell - k + 1$) is less than or equal to $b(\ell, k)$ follows from the equality (3) if one takes into account that $b(\ell - 1, k) \geq 0$. $\square$

We will also use the following arithmetical observation which elementary proof is omitted due to the space constraints:

Lemma 5. *If $0 \le \ell \le k$, then $b(\ell, k) \le \lfloor \frac{n(n+1)}{6} \rfloor$.*

Now we can return to the proof of Theorem 1. Since π_1 is not the equality relation on Q, the number m of π_1-classes is strictly less than n. We subdivide the proof in 3 cases depending on m.

Case 1: $m = 1$. In this case the whole set Q forms a π_1-class, and therefore, it is linked. Let $\ell = |\min(Q)|$, $k = \max(Q)$. If $\ell \le k$, then, applying Lemma 4 for $T = Q$, we get a reset word of length at most $b(\ell, k)$, and by Lemma 5 we obtain the desired upper bound. If $\ell > k$, we may apply the dual of Lemma 4 in which we interchange the roles of minimal and maximal elements. This gives a reset word of length at most $b(k, \ell)$, and again a reference to Lemma 5 concludes the proof.

Thus, for the rest of the proof we may assume that $m > 1$. The quotient automaton $\mathscr{A}/\pi_1$ is weakly monotonic and strongly connected. Applying the induction hypothesis, we obtain that $\mathscr{A}/\pi_1$ possesses a reset word u of length at most $\lfloor \frac{m(m+1)}{6} \rfloor$. This means that in the automaton $\mathscr{A}$ we have $Q.u \subseteq T$ where T is a π_1-class.

Case 2: $m > \frac{n}{2}$. It is easy to calculate that in this case the congruence π_1 has at least $2m - n$ singleton classes and at most $n - m$ non-singleton classes. Since the automaton $\mathscr{A}/\pi_1$ is strongly connected, there is a path from the class T to a singleton class, and the length of the shortest path with this property does not exceed the number of non-singleton classes. Let v be the word of length at most $n - m$ labelling such a path. Since $|T.v| = 1$, we have $|Q.uv| = 1$, that is, uv is a reset word for $\mathscr{A}$ of length at most $\lfloor \frac{m(m+1)}{6} \rfloor + (n - m)$. It is not hard to check that for all n and m satisfying $n > m > \frac{n}{2}$ the latter sum does not exceed $\lfloor \frac{n(n+1)}{6} \rfloor$. Indeed, consider the difference

$$\frac{n(n+1)}{6} - \frac{m(m+1)}{6} - (n - m) = \frac{1}{6}(n - m)(n + m - 5). \qquad (4)$$

Clearly, $n = 3$ and $m = 2$ are the only admissible values of n and m such that (4) is equal to 0, and for all other n and m satisfying $n > m > \frac{n}{2}$ the difference (4) is positive. Thus, if $(n, m) \ne (3, 2)$, then

$$\left\lfloor \frac{m(m+1)}{6} \right\rfloor + (n - m) \le \frac{m(m+1)}{6} + (n - m) < \frac{n(n+1)}{6}.$$

Since the left-hand side of this inequality is an integer, we conclude that

$$\left\lfloor \frac{m(m+1)}{6} \right\rfloor + (n - m) \le \left\lfloor \frac{n(n+1)}{6} \right\rfloor,$$

and the latter inequality also holds for the exceptional pair $(n, m) = (3, 2)$.

Case 3: $2 \le m \le \frac{n}{2}$. This is the most complicated case which proof involves a combination of the ideas from the two previous cases with some extra twists.

Denote the π_1-classes by $T_1, \ldots, T_m$. For each $i = 1, \ldots, m$ we consider $\ell_i = |\min(T_i)|$ and $k_i = |\max(T_i)|$. Let ℓ be the least number in the set $\{\ell_1, \ldots, \ell_m, k_1, \ldots, k_m\}$.

We partition the set of the π_1-classes into 4 subsets:

$$M_{00} = \{T_i \mid \ell_i = \ell, \ k_i = \ell\}, \qquad M_{01} = \{T_i \mid \ell_i = \ell, \ k_i > \ell\},$$
$$M_{10} = \{T_i \mid \ell_i > \ell, \ k_i = \ell\}, \qquad M_{11} = \{T_i \mid \ell_i > \ell, \ k_i > \ell\}.$$

Some of these subsets may be empty but at least one of the subsets M_{00}, M_{01} and M_{10} has to be non-empty by the choice of the number ℓ. Let m_{st} denote the cardinality of the set M_{st}, $s, t \in \{0, 1\}$. Using, if necessary, the up-down symmetry, we can always assume that $m_{01} \geq m_{10}$. Observe that this assumption implies that $M_{00} \cup M_{01} \neq \varnothing$. Indeed, if $M_{00} \cup M_{01} = \varnothing$, then $m_{00} = m_{01} = 0$ and from the assumed inequality $m_{01} \geq m_{10}$ it would also follow that $m_{10} = 0$. Then all the three subsets M_{00}, M_{01} and M_{10} would be empty, a contradiction.

Each π_1-class $T_i \in M_{00} \cup M_{01}$ has exactly ℓ minimal elements. Since every π_1-class is a linked set, we may apply Lemma 4 to each such π_1-class. Thus, letting $k = |\max(Q)|$, we obtain that for every $T_i \in M_{00} \cup M_{01}$ there exists a word $w_i \in \Sigma^*$ of length at most $b(\ell, k) = \ell(n - k + 1) - \frac{\ell(\ell+1)}{2}$ such that $|T_i.w_i| = 1$.

Since the congruence π_1 is the equivalence closure of the order ρ_1, any two ρ_1-comparable states always belong to the same π_1-class. In particular, the set $\max(Q)$ of all maximal elements of Q is a disjoint union of the sets of all maximal elements of the π_1-classes, and the cardinality k of $\max(Q)$ is equal to the sum $k_1 + \cdots + k_m$. Recall that $k_i = \ell$ if $T_i \in M_{00} \cup M_{10}$ and $k_i \geq \ell + 1$ if $T_i \in M_{01} \cup M_{11}$. Therefore $k \geq \ell m + m_{01} + m_{11}$. As $b(\ell, k)$ is a decreasing function of k, we can conclude that $b(\ell, \ell m + m_{01} + m_{11}) \geq b(\ell, k)$.

Recall that there is a word u of length at most $\lfloor \frac{m(m+1)}{6} \rfloor$ such that $Q.u \subseteq T$ where T is a certain π_1-class. Since the automaton $\mathscr{A}/\pi_1$ is strongly connected, there is a path from T to a class $T_i \in M_{00} \cup M_{01}$, and the length of the shortest path with this property does not exceed $m_{10} + m_{11}$. Let v be a word that labels such a shortest path. Then $Q.uv = (Q.u).v \subseteq T.v \subseteq T_i$ whence the product uvw_i is a reset word for the automaton $\mathscr{A}$. Its length does not exceed

$$\left\lfloor \frac{m(m+1)}{6} \right\rfloor + (m_{10} + m_{11}) + b(\ell, \ell m + m_{01} + m_{11}), \qquad (5)$$

and it remains to verify that this sum does not exceed $\lfloor \frac{n(n+1)}{6} \rfloor$.

To start with, consider the sum of the second and the third summands:

$$(m_{10} + m_{11}) + b(\ell, \ell m + m_{01} + m_{11}) =$$
$$(m_{10} + m_{11}) + \ell(n - \ell m - m_{01} - m_{11} + 1) - \frac{\ell(\ell+1)}{2} =$$
$$(m_{10} + m_{11}) + b(\ell, \ell m) - \ell(m_{01} + m_{11}).$$

Since $\ell \geq 1$ and $m_{01} \geq m_{10}$, we see that it does not exceed $b(\ell, \ell m)$. Now considering $b(\ell, \ell m) = \ell(n - \ell m + 1) - \frac{\ell(\ell+1)}{2}$ as a quadratic polynomial of ℓ, one sees that its maximum value is $\frac{(2n+1)^2}{8(2m+1)}$. Thus,

$$b(\ell, \ell m) < \frac{(2n+1)^2}{8(2m+1)} \leq \frac{(2n+1)^2}{40}. \tag{6}$$

Here the first inequality is strict because $b(\ell, \ell m)$ is an integer while $\frac{(2n+1)^2}{8(2m+1)}$ is not, and the second inequality follows from the fact that $m \geq 2$ in the case under consideration.

On the other hand, we have

$$\left\lfloor \frac{m(m+1)}{6} \right\rfloor \leq \frac{m(m+1)}{6} \leq \frac{n(n+2)}{24}. \tag{7}$$

Here the first inequality is clear and the second follows from another condition of the case, namely, $m \leq \frac{n}{2}$. From (6) and (7) we conclude that the sum (5) is strictly less than the sum

$$\frac{n(n+2)}{24} + \frac{(2n+1)^2}{40}$$

which can be easily seen to be strictly less than $\frac{n(n+1)}{6}$ for all $n \geq 2$. Since the sum (5) is an integer, it does not exceed $\lfloor \frac{n(n+1)}{6} \rfloor$, as required.   □

As an immediate consequence of Proposition 1 and Theorem 1 we get

Corollary 1. *Every strongly connected aperiodic automaton is synchronizing and has a reset word of length* $\lfloor \frac{n(n+1)}{6} \rfloor$ *where n is the number of states of the automaton.*

The fact that strongly connected aperiodic automata are synchronizing is known [14] but our upper bound for the minimum length of reset words is considerably better than the bound $\frac{n(n-1)}{2}$ established in [14]. However, we strongly believe that our bound can be further improved.

Acknowledgement

The paper has been completed during the author's stay at the University of Turku under the Finnish Mathematical Society International Visitors Program 2006–2007 "Algorithmic and Discrete Mathematics".

References

1. Ananichev, D.S.: The mortality threshold for partially monotonic automata. In: De Felice, C., Restivo, A. (eds.) DLT 2005. LNCS, vol. 3572, pp. 112–121. Springer, Heidelberg (2005)
2. Ananichev, D.S., Volkov, M.V.: Synchronizing generalized monotonic automata. Theoret. Comput. Sci. 330, 3–13 (2005)

3. Černý, J.: Poznámka k homogénnym eksperimentom s konečnými automatami. Mat.-Fyz. Cas. Slovensk. Akad. Vied. 14, 208–216 (1964) (in Slovak)
4. Eppstein, D.: Reset sequences for monotonic automata. SIAM J. Comput. 19, 500–510 (1990)
5. Frankl, P.: An extremal problem for two families of sets. Eur. J. Comb. 3, 125–127 (1982)
6. Goldberg, K.: Orienting polygonal parts without sensors. Algorithmica 10, 201–225 (1993)
7. Goralčik, P., Koubek, V.: Rank problems for composite transformations. Algebra and Computation 5, 309–316 (1995)
8. Mateescu, A., Salomaa, A.: Many-valued truth functions, Černý's conjecture and road coloring. EATCS Bull. 68, 134–150 (1999)
9. McNaughton, R., Papert, S.A.: Counter-free automata. MIT Press, Cambridge (1971)
10. Pin, J.-E.: On two combinatorial problems arising from automata theory. Ann. Discrete Math. 17, 535–548 (1983)
11. Rystsov, I.: Reset words for commutative and solvable automata. Theoret. Comput. Sci. 172, 273–279 (1997)
12. Salomaa, A.: Composition sequences for functions over a finite domain. Theoret. Comput. Sci. 292, 263–281 (2003)
13. Sandberg, S.: Homing and synchronizing sequences. In: Broy, M., Jonsson, B., Katoen, J.-P., Leucker, M., Pretschner, A. (eds.) Model-Based Testing of Reactive Systems. LNCS, vol. 3472, pp. 5–33. Springer, Heidelberg (2005)
14. Trahtman, A.N.: The Černý conjecture for aperiodic automata. Discrete Math. Theoret. Comp. Sci. 9(2), 3–10 (2007)

Reducing Acyclic Cover Transducers

Jean-Marc Champarnaud[1], Franck Guingne[2], and Jacques Farré[2]

[1] Laboratoire LITIS, Université de Rouen, France
jean-marc.champarnaud@univ-rouen.fr
[2] Laboratoire I3S, Université de Nice – Sophia Antipolis and CNRS, France
guingne@i3s.unice.fr, Jacques.Farre@unice.fr

Abstract. Finite languages and finite subsequential functions can be represented by possibly cyclic finite machines, respectively called cover automata and cover transducers. In general, reduced cover machines have much fewer states than the corresponding minimal machines, yielding a compact representation for lexicons or dictionaries. We present here a new algorithm for reducing the number of states of an acyclic transducer.

Keywords: finite state transducer, state reduction, subsequential transducer, cover transducer for a finite subsequential function.

1   Introduction

A cover transducer for a finite subsequential function can be defined as follows: given two alphabets Σ and Ω, and a function $\alpha : \Sigma^* \to \Omega^*$ of order l (the maximal length of a word in the domain of α), a cover transducer for α is any subsequential transducer that realizes the function α when its input is restricted to $\Sigma^{\leq l}$, the subset of Σ^* of words with a length not greater than l. This definition is similar to the one introduced by Câmpeanu, Paun and Yu [1,2] for a cover automaton for a finite language.

The main interest in reduced cover machines is that they generally have much fewer states than the corresponding minimal machines. Such size reductions would be of a great interest in natural language processing applications, providing compact representations for lexicons or dictionaries, or in bioinformatics, for sets of genetic sequences.

Concerning automata, cover minimization via state merging is based on a (unique) state relation involving right languages. This relation is underlied by a similarity relation on $\Sigma^{\leq l}$ [3,4,5], which allows to define the notion of a minimal cover automaton for a finite language. Several algorithms exist for computing a minimal cover automaton [6,1,2,7]. Concerning cover transducers, the situation is more complex: it seems quite difficult to give a straightforward characterization of a minimal cover transducer for a finite subsequential function, since it is possible to define several relations that involve state right functions and that allow to perform cover reduction via state merging [8]. Unfortunately, the more powerful these relations are, the less transitive they become.

This paper addresses the acyclic case, where the input is a transducer that realizes the function. Former algorithms [8] were based on the notion of k-function

Jan Holub and Jan Žd'árek (Eds.): CIAA 2007, LNCS 4783, pp. 38–50, 2007.

of a state, for $0 \leq k \leq l$, that is the restriction to $\Sigma^{\leq k}$ of the right function. The notion of prefix k-function is introduced, and a new algorithm is described, based on the computation of prefix k-functions. Moreover, a new technique involving linearly dependent prefix k-functions is discussed. These results improve the algorithm of reduction via a minimization of the underlying cover automaton described in [8].

This short introduction is completed by Section 3, which is devoted to an illustrated overview of the problem of cover transducer reduction. In order to fix notation this overview is preceded by some preliminaries (Section 2). Our new approach, which is an algorithm based on the identification of the prefix k-functions and a technique involving linearly dependent prefix k-functions, is developed in the last section.

2   Preliminaries

Finite subsequential functions are realized by subsequential transducers [9,10,11]. Given a mapping f from a set A to a set B, the domain of f will be denoted by $\mathrm{dom}(f)$.

A *subsequential transducer* is a tuple $\mathcal{S} = (\Sigma, \Omega, Q, q_-, F, \mathtt{i}, \mathtt{t}, \cdot, \star)$ where:

- Σ (resp. Ω) is the *input* (resp. *output*) *alphabet*,
- Q is the finite set of *states* and $q_- \in Q$ is the *initial state*,
- $\mathtt{i} \in \Omega^*$ is the *initialization value* and $\mathtt{t} : Q \rightarrow \Omega^*$ is the *termination function*,
- $F = \mathrm{dom}(\mathtt{t})$ is the set of *final states*,
- the *transition function*, denoted by $\cdot$, maps $(q, a) \in Q \times \Sigma$ to $q \cdot a \in Q$,
- the *output function*, denoted by $\star$, maps $(q, a) \in Q \times \Sigma$ to $q \star a \in \Omega^*$.

The transition and output functions have the same $Q \times \Sigma$ domain that can be extended to $Q \times \Sigma^*$. A *path* is a finite sequence $((q_i, a_i, b_i, q_{i+1}))_{i=0,\ldots,n-1}$ of tuples in $Q \times \Sigma \times \Omega^* \times Q$ with $q_i \cdot a_i = q_{i+1}$ and $q_i \star a_i = b_i$. A *successful* path is a final path starting in $q_0 = q_-$ and ending in $q_n \in F$. The word $a_0 \cdots a_{n-1} \in \Sigma^*$ (resp. $\mathtt{i}b_0 \cdots b_{n-1}\mathtt{t}(q_n) \in \Omega^*$) is the *input* (resp. *output*) label of the path. A transducer is said to be *trim* if each state $q \in Q$ lies on a successful path.

A subsequential transducer $\mathcal{S}$ realizes a *subsequential* function $S : \Sigma^* \rightarrow \Omega^*$ such that for all x in $\mathrm{dom}(S)$, $S(x) = \mathtt{i}(q_- \star x)\mathtt{t}(q_- \cdot x)$. The subsequential transducer $\mathcal{S}_p$ is deduced from $\mathcal{S}$ by letting p be the new initial state and ε be the initialization value. The function S_p realized by $\mathcal{S}_p$ is called the *right function* of p; it is such that for all x in $\mathrm{dom}(S_p)$, $S_p(x) = (p \star x)\mathtt{t}(p \cdot x)$. Two subsequential transducers $\mathcal{S}$ and $\mathcal{S}'$ are said to be *equivalent* if they realize the same function.

The *order* l of a function $\alpha : \Sigma^* \rightarrow \Omega^*$ is the maximal length of a word in $\mathrm{dom}(\alpha)$. In the sequel, we deal with transducers realizing a function with a finite order l. Given a state p, the restriction to $\Sigma^{\leq k}$ of the function S_p, called the *k-function* of p, is denoted by S_p^k. The *height* of a state q, denoted by $\mathrm{height}(q)$, is equal to l minus the length of a shortest path from the initial state q_- to q.

Definition 1. *Let α be a function of order l. A subsequential transducer S is a cover transducer for α if and only if for all $x \in \Sigma^{\le l}$, $S(x) = \alpha(x)$.*

Let Σ^* be a free monoid and $z, y \in \Sigma^*$. The word z is said to be a *prefix* of y ($z \preceq y$) if there exists a word t of Σ^* such that $y = zt$. The word t is denoted by $z^{-1}y$. Let $E \subset \Sigma^*$. We denote by $\bigwedge_{u \in E} u$ the *longest common prefix* (lcp for short) of the words in E. By convention the lcp of the empty set is denoted by 0 and for all u in E, $\bigwedge\{u, 0\} = u$. By convention too, the notation $(\bigwedge_{u \in E} u)^{-1}E$ applies when E is empty, with: $0^{-1}\emptyset = \emptyset$.

Definition 2. *Let S be an acyclic cover transducer for a function α of order l. Let p be a state of S. We define the following longest common prefixes:*
- $\nu_S(p, k) = \bigwedge_{x \in \Sigma^{\le k}} S_p(x)$, *with* $0 \le k \le \text{height}(p)$,
- $\mu_S(p) = \nu_S(p, \text{height}(p)) = \bigwedge_{x \in \Sigma^{\le \text{height}(p)}} S_p(x)$.

Definition 3. *Let $S = (\Sigma, \Omega, Q, q_-, F, i_S, t_S, \cdot, \star_S)$ be an acyclic subsequential transducer. The prefix transducer of S is the transducer $\mathcal{P} = (\Sigma, \Omega, Q, q_-, F, i, t, \cdot, \star)$ such that:*
- $i = i_S \mu_S(q_-)$ *and* $\forall p \in \text{dom}(t)$, $t(p) = \mu_S(p)^{-1} t_S(p)$,
- $p \star a = \mu_S(p)^{-1}(p \star_S a)\mu_S(p \cdot a)$, $\forall p \in Q$, $\forall a \in \Sigma$.

Let X be an ordered set (the order is denoted by $\le$). A relation $\sim$ over X is *semi-transitive* if and only if for all x, y, z in X such that $x \le y \le z$, the following implications hold: $x \sim y$ and $y \sim z \Rightarrow x \sim z$, and $x \sim y$ and $x \sim z \Rightarrow y \sim z$. A reflexive, symmetric and semi-transitive relation is a *similarity relation*.

3   An Overview

We give here an informal illustration of both the topic of cover transducer reduction and our new results. Precise definitions will be given in next sections.

Given two alphabets Σ and Ω and a positive integer l, we deal with functions f from $\Sigma^{\le l}$ to Ω^*, called finite subsequential functions. Throughout this section we will consider the function[1] $\alpha : \{a, b\}^3 \to \{a, b\}^*$ of order $l = 3$, and defined by Table 1.

A finite subsequential function f is straightforwardly realized by a prefix-tree subsequential transducer S. Figure 1 shows the transducer S_α that realizes the function α. The implicit label of the transition from state u to state ua is $a|\varepsilon$. Every final state u has an output label equal to $\alpha(u)$. Notice that there exists a sink state in S_α (for clarity it has not been drawn).

We now address the problem of turning S into an equivalent transducer, with a size as small as possible. We first illustrate two possible solutions: the algorithm for minimizing a sequential transducer [12,13,14] and the algorithm based on the minimization of the underlying cover automaton [8].

The minimization algorithm allows us to compute the minimal subsequential transducer $\mathcal{M}$ of the function α (actually this algorithm does not require the

---

[1] This function is derived from the example in [12].

Table 1. The function α ...

dom(α)	α
a	$abba$
ab	$abbaba$
ba	$babba$
aaa	$abbababba$
abb	$abbababa$
bab	$babbaba$
bba	$bbabba$

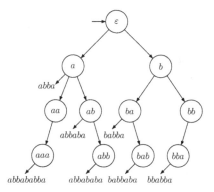

Fig. 1. ... and its prefix-tree transducer S_α

subsequential function to be a finite one). First the lcps of the (outputs of the) right functions in S are computed. For example, the right function of the state ab is the set $S_{ab} = \{(\varepsilon, abbaba), (b, abbababa)\}$ and the associated lcp is $\mu_S(ab) =$ lcp($abbaba, abbababa$) = $abbaba$. Then the prefix transducer $\mathcal{P}$ of S is computed according to Definition 3.

Finally the minimization of $\mathcal{P}$ amounts to the minimization of its underlying automaton. The key here is that checking whether two right functions are equal amounts to checking whether the associated weighted graphs coincide in $\mathcal{P}$. Figure 2 shows the partition of the set of states of $\mathcal{P}_\alpha$ according to right functions (states with the same box shape being in the same subset). Notice that the label $u \star a$ of the transition from state u to state ua stands for $a|u \star a$. This convention also holds for the trees of Figures 4, 6 and 10. Figure 3 shows the minimal transducer $\mathcal{M}_\alpha$.

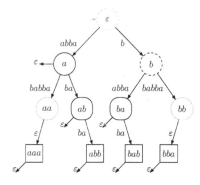

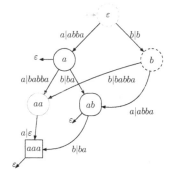

Fig. 2. Partitioning $\mathcal{P}_\alpha$ according to right functions

Fig. 3. Minimal transducer $\mathcal{M}_\alpha$

Another solution comes from the notion of cover transducer, which is likely to bring new space savings. The transducers S_α and $\mathcal{P}_\alpha$ are both cover transducers for α. Our aim is to compute a smaller cover transducer for α from $\mathcal{S}_\alpha$ (or $\mathcal{P}_\alpha$). The reduction techniques proposed in [8] are based on the notion of k-function. For example, the k-functions of state b in $\mathcal{P}_\alpha$ are: $P_b^0 = \emptyset$, $P_b^1 = \{(a, abba)\}$ and $P_b^2 = \{(a, abba), (ab, abbaba), (ba, babba)\}$.

A basic reduction consists in merging two states p and q (such that height$(p) \geq$ height(q)) having identical k-functions for $k =$ height(q). However, the drawback is that checking whether two k-functions are equal is not equivalent to checking whether the associated weighted graphs coincide in either $\mathcal{S}$ or $\mathcal{P}$. For example the states ε and b are such that $P_\varepsilon^2 = P_b^2 = \{(a, abba), (ab, abbaba), (ba, babba)\}$ but their weighted graphs in $\mathcal{P}$ do not coincide. Figure 4 shows the partition of the set of states of $\mathcal{P}_\alpha$ according to the weighted graphs of the k-functions. Figure 5 shows the corresponding reduced cover transducer $\mathcal{R}_\alpha^1$, obtained by minimization of the underlying cover automaton [8].

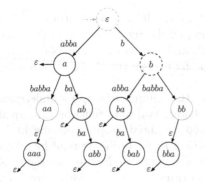

Fig. 4. Approximate k-function partitioning of $\mathcal{P}_\alpha$

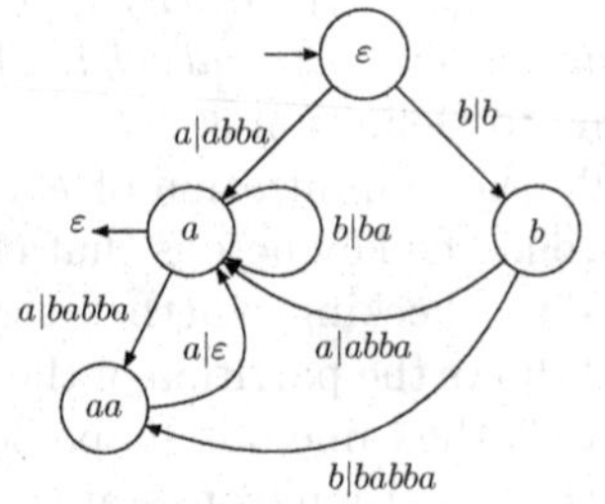

Fig. 5. Reduced cover transducer $\mathcal{R}_\alpha^1$

We now introduce two techniques (that will be developed in the next section) to avoid the above-mentioned drawback. They are both based on the notion of a prefix k-function. Let p be a state in $\mathcal{P}$ and $\nu_P(p, k)$ be the lcp of the k-function of p. We call *prefix k-function* of p the set $\nu_P(p, k)^{-1} P_p^k$. Now if p and q have identical prefix h-functions with $h =$ height(q), we get: $\nu_P(p, h)^{-1} P_p^h = P_q$, where P_q is the right function of q, since $\nu_P(q, h) = \varepsilon$ and $P_p^h = P_q$.

There are two cases. The first case is when $\nu_P(p, h) = \varepsilon$. Checking the equality of two k-functions is then equivalent to checking the equality of the associated prefix k-functions. The advantage is that it can be achieved by checking the coincidence of the weighted graphs of the prefix k-functions. Figure 6 shows the exact partition of the set of states of $\mathcal{P}_\alpha$ according to their k-functions. Figure 7 shows the corresponding reduced cover transducer $\mathcal{R}_\alpha^2$.

The second case, when $\nu_P(p, h) \neq \varepsilon$, leads to a more sophisticated reduction. Indeed, since the set $\nu_P(p, h)^{-1} P_p^h$ cannot be computed on the graph of $\mathcal{P}$, the only way to merge p and q is to compute the set $\nu_P(p, h) P_q$. Merging q into p

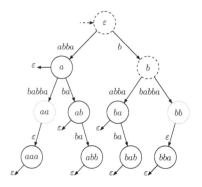

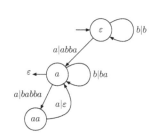

Fig. 6. Exact k-function partitioning of $\mathcal{P}_\alpha$ via prefix k-functions

Fig. 7. Reduced cover transducer $\mathcal{R}_\alpha^2$

is then possible if $\nu_{\mathcal{P}}(p,h)$ is a suffix of the label w of any transition (r,a,w,q) in $\mathcal{P}$ since such a transition is replaced by $(r,a,w\,\nu_{\mathcal{P}}(p,h)^{-1},p)$.

For example, in Figure 8 and Figure 9, the states b and aa can be merged since $\nu_{\mathcal{P}}(b,1) = abba$, $P_b^1 = abba\ P_{aa}^1$ and $abba$ is a suffix of the label $babba$ of the transition from a to aa in $\mathcal{P}$.

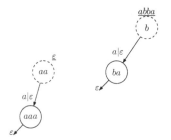

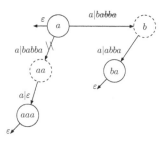

Fig. 8. Prefix 1-functions of states b and aa

Fig. 9. Merging b and aa in $\mathcal{P}_\alpha$ w.r.t. prefix 1-functions

The same reasoning holds for the states b and bb, ε and bb and finally ε and aa. Thus the classes $\{aa, bb\}$ and $\{\varepsilon, b\}$ can be merged. The resulting two-states cover transducer $\mathcal{R}_\alpha^3$ is shown in Figure 11.

4   Towards an Efficient Reduction Algorithm

Let α be a finite subsequential function. We assume here that the input is the (acyclic) prefix-tree $\mathcal{S}$ of α. We consider the reduction of $\mathcal{S}$ via the weighted graph of its prefix version $\mathcal{P}$. In the following we assume that p and q are two states of $\mathcal{S}$ (and hence of $\mathcal{P}$) such that $\text{height}(p) \geq \text{height}(q) = h$.

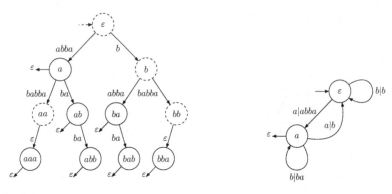

Fig. 10. Partitioning $\mathcal{P}_\alpha$ according to prefix k-functions   **Fig. 11.** Reduced cover transducer $\mathcal{R}_\alpha^3$

Minimization involves comparisons between state right functions while cover reduction involves comparisons between state k-functions. In fact, the reduction algorithm described in [8] only performs a partial identification of the set of k-functions.

For $0 \leq k \leq \text{height}(p)$, the *prefix k-function* of a state p is defined as $\nu_P(p, k)^{-1} P_p^k$. In this section, we first show how to compute prefix k-functions and to check the equality of two prefix k-functions. Then we describe a reduction algorithm where a full identification of the set of k-functions is achieved through the associated prefix k-functions. Finally we present a more sophisticated reduction where the merging of two states can be considered even though they do not have identical k-functions.

4.1   Computation and Identification of Prefix k-Functions

Definition 4. *For $0 \leq k < l$, two states p and q are said to be k-comparable ($p \cong_k q$) if and only if their prefix k-functions are identical: $p \cong_k q \Longleftrightarrow \nu_P(p, k)^{-1} P_p^k = \nu_P(q, k)^{-1} P_q^k$.*

Let us set $Q_k = \{p \in Q \mid \text{height}(p) \geq k\}$. The equivalence relation $\cong_k$ on Q_k, for $0 \leq k < l$, can be computed according to the following lemma.

Lemma 5. *The following two properties hold:*
1) For $k = 0$, $p \cong_0 q \Longleftrightarrow (p \in F \Leftrightarrow q \in F)$.
2) For $1 \leq k < l$, two states p and q are k-comparable iff the following four conditions are satisfied:
    (a) $p \cong_{k-1} q$,
    (b) $\forall a \in \Sigma$, $p \cdot a \cong_{k-1} q \cdot a$,
    (c) $\nu_P(p, k)^{-1} \mathbf{t}[p] = \nu_P(q, k)^{-1} \mathbf{t}[q]$,
    (d) $\forall a \in \Sigma$, $\nu_P(p, k)^{-1}(p \star a) = \nu_P(q, k)^{-1}(q \star a)$.

We now describe Algorithm 1, which computes the partition of Q_k w.r.t. $\cong_k$, for $0 \leq k < l$, according to Lemma 5. We will use the following notation: given a relation R over X, any partition of X w.r.t. R can be denoted by $\widehat{X}_R$ or simply $\widehat{X}$ when there is no ambiguity. The function Partition(X,t) returns a partition $\widehat{X}$ w.r.t. the key t. The initializations at Line 4 come from Lemma 5 (case 1). Let us assume that the set of prefixes $(\nu_P(p, k-1))_{p \in Q_{k-1}}$ has been computed, as well as the partition C_{k-1} w.r.t. $\cong_{k-1}$. For all p in Q_k, the following elements are computed: the prefix $\nu_P(p, k)$ (Line 10), the weight $\nu_P(p, k)^{-1}t[p]$ (Line 14), and for all a in Σ, the weight $\nu_P(p, k)^{-1}(p \star a)$ (Lines 15–17). These elements are used to identify the prefix k-function P_p^k. The partition C_k w.r.t. $\cong_k$ is deduced from C_{k-1} according to Lemma 5 (case 2): condition (a) is checked at Line 9 and conditions (b,c,d) are checked at Line 19.

Let $t_{max} = \max_{p \in Q}\{\text{length}(t[p])\}$ be the length of a longest word labeling a final state. Let $k_{max} = (|\Sigma| + 1)t_{max} + |\Sigma| + s$, where s is the size of an integer.

Algorithm 1. Computation and identification of prefix k-functions

---

1: Input: $\mathcal{P} = (\Sigma, \Omega, Q, q_-, F, \mathbf{i}, \mathbf{t}, \cdot, \star)$, the prefix of the prefix-tree transducer of α.
2: Output: the partition C_k of Q_k w.r.t. $\cong_k$, $\forall 0 \leq k < l$.
3: Comments: $N[p, k]$ is the rank of the class of p in C_k $(0 \leq N[p, k] \leq |C_k| - 1)$.
4: Initializations: $\nu_P(p, 0) = \mathbf{t}[p]$, $\forall p \in Q$; $C_0 = \{Q \setminus F, F\}$.
5: **for all** $k \in 1 .. l - 1$ **do**
6:      Computation of the relation $\cong_k$
7:      **for all** $C \in C_{k-1}$ **do**
8:          $C^+ = \{p \in C \mid \text{height}(p) \geq k\}$
9:          **for all** $p \in C^+$ **do**
10:             $\nu_P(p, k) = \bigwedge_{a \in \Sigma}(\mathbf{t}[p], (p \star a)\nu_P(p \cdot a, k - 1))$
11:             Computation of the key keya of p
12:             IF $\nu_P(p, k) = 0$ THEN $A[p] = 0$; $\forall a \in \Sigma$, $B[p, a] = 0$
13:             ELSE
14:                 $A[p] = \nu_P(p, k)^{-1}\mathbf{t}[p]$
15:                 **for all** $a \in \Sigma$ **do**
16:                     $B[p, a] = \nu_P(p, k)^{-1}(p \star a)$
17:                 **end for**
18:             FI
19:             keya$[p] = ((N[p \cdot a, k - 1])_{a \in \Sigma}, A[p], (B[p, a])_{a \in \Sigma})$
20:         **end for**
21:         $\widehat{C^+} = \text{Partition}(C^+, \text{keya})$
22:         Insert the blocks of $\widehat{C^+}$ into the set C_k.
23:     **end for**
24: **end for**

Proposition 6. *Let $n = |Q|$. Algorithm 1 computes the partition of Q_k w.r.t. $\cong_k$, for $0 \leq k < l$, in $O(k_{max}nl)$ overall time, where $O(l)$ is between $O(\log(n))$ and $O(n)$.*

Proof. Correctness is from Lemma 5. Complexity depends on the function Partition that can be implemented via a bucket sort algorithm [15,16]. □

The computation of the partition C_k of Q_k w.r.t. $\cong_k$, for $0 \leq k < l$, is illustrated by Example 7. For each state, the associated integer in the table is the rank of its class.

Example 7.

	ε	b	aa	bb	a	ab	ba	aaa	abb	bab	bba
$\cong_0$	0	0	0	0	1	1	1	1	1	1	1
$\cong_1$	0	0	0	0	1	1	1				
$\cong_2$	0	0			1						

4.2 Reduction Based on the Equality of h-Functions

Definition 8. *Two states p and q (with $\mathrm{height}(p) \geq \mathrm{height}(q) = h$) are said to be ε-mergeable ($p \sim_\varepsilon q$) if and only if their h-functions are identical: $p \sim_\varepsilon q \Longleftrightarrow P_p^h = P_q$.*

Proposition 9. *The relation $\sim_\varepsilon$ is a similarity relation.*

We will show now how to compute the relation $\sim_\varepsilon$ from the set of prefix k-functions.

Definition 10. *Two states p and q (such that $\mathrm{height}(p) \geq \mathrm{height}(q) = h$) are said to be comparable ($p \cong q$) if and only if their prefix h-functions are identical:*

$$p \cong q \Longleftrightarrow p \cong_h q \Longleftrightarrow \nu_\mathcal{P}^{-1}(p,h)P_p^h = \nu_\mathcal{P}^{-1}(q,h)P_q$$

Lemma 11. *Two states p and q (with $\mathrm{height}(p) \geq \mathrm{height}(q) = h$) are ε-mergeable ($p \sim_\varepsilon q$) if and only if they are comparable and if $\nu_\mathcal{P}(p,h)$ and $\nu_\mathcal{P}(q,h)$ are identical.*

Since $\mathcal{P}$ is the prefix version of a prefix-tree transducer, the following equalities hold: $\nu_\mathcal{P}(q,h) = \mu_\mathcal{P}(q) = 0$ or ε. Given a state p, the word $\nu_\mathcal{P}(p,k)$, for $0 \leq k \leq \mathrm{height}(p)$, only depends on the height k. We say that $\nu_\mathcal{P}(p,k)$ is the k-gap of p. Lemma 11 deals with the case where the h-gap of p is equal to 0 or to ε. The main point in this case is that a complete identification of the h-functions is possible through prefix h-functions. The case where the h-gap of p is neither 0 nor ε is studied in the next section.

Algorithm 2 computes a minimal partition of Q w.r.t. $\sim_\varepsilon$ according to Lemma 12 and Lemma 13. Let us fix some notation. For all $X \subseteq Q$, set $X^+ = \{p \in X \mid \mathrm{height}(p) \geq k\}$ and $X^- = X \setminus X^+$. The partition produced by Algorithm 2 is denoted by $D_{\sim_\varepsilon}$ and the content of this partition at the end of step k by D_k. We make use of two functions: $\mathrm{Pref}(s)$ that respectively returns 0, 1, or 2 depending on whether $s = 0$, $s = \varepsilon$, or $s \succ \varepsilon$ and $\mathrm{Partition}(X,t)$ that returns a partition $\widehat{X}$ w.r.t. the key t.

Let us run Algorithm 2 in order to list the cases where a new block is inserted into D_k. Let D be a block of D_{k-1}, with $D^+ = \{p \in D \mid \mathrm{height}(p) \geq k-1\}$. If $D^+ = \emptyset$, D is definitively a block of $D_{\sim_\varepsilon}$. Hence D is inserted into D_k (case 1). Otherwise, partitioning D w.r.t. $\cong_k$ only involves the set D^+. The handling of D^- will be explained later.

Algorithm 2. Reduction based on the equality of k-functions

1: Input: $\mathcal{P} = (\Sigma, \Omega, Q, q_{\text{-}}, F, \mathbf{i}, \mathbf{t}, \cdot, \star)$, the prefix of the prefix-tree transducer of α.
2: Output: a minimal partition $D_{\sim_\varepsilon}$ of Q w.r.t. $\sim_\varepsilon$.
3: Initializations: $\nu_\mathcal{P}(p, 0) = \mathbf{t}[\mathbf{p}], \forall p \in Q$.
4: Initializations: $D_0 = \{Q \setminus F, F_1, F_2\}$, with $F_1 = \{p \in F \mid \nu_\mathcal{P}(p, 0) = \varepsilon\}$ and
    $F_2 = F \setminus F_1$.
5: **for all** $k \in 1 .. l - 1$ **do**
6:     Computation of the partition D_k
7:     **for all** $D \in D_{k-1}$ **do**
8:         IF $D^+ = \emptyset$ THEN Insert D into the partition D_k
9:         ELSE
10:        **for all** $p \in D^+$ **do**
11:            Computation of a partition of D^+ w.r.t. $\cong_k$
12:            $\overline{\nu_\mathcal{P}(p, k) = \bigwedge_{a \in \Sigma}(\mathbf{t}[\mathbf{p}], (\mathbf{p} \star \mathbf{a})\nu_\mathcal{P}(\mathbf{p} \cdot \mathbf{a}, \mathbf{k} - 1))}$
13:            $\text{keyb}[p] = \text{Pref}(\nu_\mathcal{P}(p, k))$
14:            Compute keya[p] according to Lines 11–19 of the Algorithm 1
15:        **end for**
16:        $\widehat{D^+} = \text{Partition}(D^+, \text{keya})$
17:        $linked = \text{false}$
18:        **for all** $C \in \widehat{D^+}$ **do**
19:            Computation of a partition of C w.r.t. $\sim_\varepsilon$
20:            IF $\exists p \in C \mid \text{height}(p) = k$
21:            THEN $\widehat{C} = \text{Partition}(C, \text{keyb})$
22:                $\widehat{C} = \{E_1, E_2\}$, with $E_2 = \{p \mid \nu_\mathcal{P}(p, k) \succ \varepsilon\}$
23:                IF $\neg linked$ THEN $E_1 = E_1 \cup D^-$; $linked = \text{true}$ FI
24:                Insert E_1 into the partition D_k
25:            ELSE IF $\neg linked$ THEN $C = C \cup D^-$; $linked = \text{true}$ FI
26:                Insert C into the partition D_k
27:            FI
28:        **end for**
29:        FI
30:    **end for**
31: **end for**

Let C be a block of $\widehat{D^+}_{\cong_k}$. Notice that $C^- = \{p \in C \mid \text{height}(p) = k\}$. If there exists no state p with height k in C, the block C is generally inserted into D_k (case 2). Otherwise, C is partitioned into two blocs, E_1 and E_2, with $E_2 = \{p \mid \nu_\mathcal{P}(p, k) \succ \varepsilon\}$. The block E_2 is systematically inserted into D_k (case 3). The block E_1 is generally inserted into D_k (case 4).

Let X be the first block C (case 2) or block E_1 (case 4) to appear. Instead of inserting C or E_1 we then insert $C \cup D^-$ (case 5) or $E_1 \cup D^-$ (case 6).

The correctness of Algorithm 2 is proved by checking that inserted blocks satisfy the following conditions. Let $X \subseteq Q$. We set $P_1(X) \Leftrightarrow (p, q \in X^+ \Rightarrow p \cong_k q)$, $P_2(X) \Leftrightarrow (p \in X, q \in X^- \Rightarrow p \sim_\varepsilon q)$ and $P(X) \Leftrightarrow P_1(X) \wedge P_2(X)$. Given a partition $\widehat{X}$ of X w.r.t. a relation R, we set: $P(\widehat{X}) \Longleftrightarrow \forall Y \in \widehat{X}, P(Y) = \text{true}$.

Lemma 12. *The condition $P(D_k)$ is an invariant of the main loop of Algorithm 2.*

We now address the problem of minimality of $D_{\sim_\varepsilon}$. Two classes X and X' in $D_{\sim_\varepsilon}$ are said to be *dissimilar* if and only if there exist $p \in X$ and $p' \in X'$ such that $p \not\sim_\varepsilon p'$. A partition of Q w.r.t. $\sim_\varepsilon$ is a *minimal partition* if and only if its classes are pairwise dissimilar.

Lemma 13. *The partition of Q w.r.t. $\sim_\varepsilon$ produced by Algorithm 2 is a minimal one.*

Proposition 14. *Algorithm 2 computes a minimal partition of Q w.r.t. $\sim_\varepsilon$ in $O(k_{max}nl)$ time.*

4.3   Reduction Based on the Equality of Prefix h-Functions

We have seen that two comparable states p and q are such that: $P_p^h = \nu_P(p,h)P_q$. We consider here the case where $\nu_P(p,h) \succeq \varepsilon$. Since the set $\nu_P(p,h)^{-1}P_p$ makes no sense on the graph of $\mathcal{P}$, the only way to merge p and q is to compute the set $\nu_P(p,h)P_q$, which requires that the h-gap of p to be a suffix of the label of any in-coming transition of q in $\mathcal{P}$.

Definition 15. *Two states p and q are said to be mergeable ($p \sim q$) if and only if the following two conditions are satisfied:*
   (i) p and q are comparable: $P_p^h = \nu_P(p,h)P_q$,
   (ii) for all transition (r,a,w,q) in $\mathcal{P}$, $\nu_P(p,h)$ is a suffix of w.

We first examine our current example.

	ε	b	aa	bb	a	ab	ba	aaa	abb	bab	bba
$\cong_0$	0	0	0	0	1	1	1	1	1	1	1
$\nu_P(p,0)$	0	0	0	0	ε	ε	ε	ε	ε	ε	ε
$\sim_\varepsilon$	0	0	0	0	1	1	1	1	1	1	1
$\sim$	0	0	0	0	1	1	1	1	1	1	1
$\cong_1$	0	0	0	0	1	1	1				
$\nu_P(p,1)$	abba	abba	ε	ε	ε	ε	ε				
$\sim_\varepsilon$	2	2	0	0	1	1	1	1	1	1	1
$\sim$	0	0	0	0	1	1	1	1	1	1	1
$\cong_2$	0	0			1						
$\nu_P(p,2)$	ε	ε			ε						
$\sim_\varepsilon$	2	2	0	0	1	1	1	1	1	1	1
$\sim$	0	0	0	0	1	1	1	1	1	1	1

Example 16. (label at left of $\cong_1$ / $\nu_P(p,1)$ rows)

We consider the initial class $C = Q \setminus F = \{\varepsilon, b, aa, bb\}$. Partitioning w.r.t. $\cong_1$ lets it unchanged while partitioning w.r.t. $\sim_\varepsilon$ breaks it into two blocks: $\{aa, bb\}$ where 1-gaps are equal to ε, and $\{\varepsilon, b\}$ where 1-gaps are different from ε. On the opposite, partitioning w.r.t. $\sim$ does not break this class: the 1-gap of ε is $abba$

which is a suffix of the label $babba$ of the unique transition coming into aa and thus $\varepsilon \sim aa$ holds; similarly, we have: $\varepsilon \sim bb$, $b \sim aa$ and $b \sim bb$.

The behavior of the relation $\sim$ on our current example is a best-case one, where two classes w.r.t. $\sim_\varepsilon$ can be merged. The general behavior is much more complex since it can be checked that the relation $\sim$ is neither transitive nor semi-transitive, which leads to a first brute-force algorithm based on the computation of a partition of Q w.r.t. $\sim$ as a partition into cliques.

However, since the relation $\sim_\varepsilon$ is smaller than the relation $\sim$, an alternative is to first compute a minimal partition w.r.t. $\sim_\varepsilon$ (and simultaneously the set of couples (p, q) such that $p \sim q$ and $p \not\sim_\varepsilon q$) and then reduce this partition according to specific properties of $\sim$, such as the following ones.

Lemma 17. *Let* $D, D' \in D_{\sim_\varepsilon}$. *Let* $p, q \in D, p' \in D'$ *and* $height(p) \geq height(q) \geq height(p')$. *Then we have:* $(p \sim_\varepsilon q, q \sim p') \Rightarrow p \sim p'$.

Lemma 18. *Let* $D, D' \in D_{\sim_\varepsilon}$. *Let* h *be the minimal height of a state in* D *and* H' *be the maximal height of a state in* D'. *We suppose that for all* p *with height* h *in* D *and for all* q *with height* H' *in* D' *we have:* $p \sim q$. *Then the classes* D *and* D' *can be merged.*

Lemma 19. *Let* $D, D_1, \ldots, D_m \in D_{\sim_\varepsilon}$. *Assume that there is a partition* $(d_1, \ldots, d_m)$ *of* D *such that for all* $i = 1 .. m$ *the condition* $(p \in D_i, q \in d_i) \Rightarrow p \sim q$ *holds. Then it is possible to reduce the size of* $D_{\sim_\varepsilon}$ *by merging* d_i *into* D_i, *for* $i = 1 .. m$.

5   Conclusion

We have shown how to improve a previous algorithm for reducing cover trans-ducers, using the $\sim_\varepsilon$ relation. One of our future objectives is to design heuristical techniques to compute a partitioning as small as possible with respect to the re-lation $\sim$. This implies to develop the experimental study started in [8]. Other issues are to extend this study to possibly cyclic cover transducers and also to consider minimality according to the finite subsequential function itself.

References

1. Păun, A., Sântean, N., Yu, S.: An $O(n^2)$ algorithm for constructing minimal cover automata for finite languages. In: Yu, S., Păun, A. (eds.) CIAA 2000. LNCS, vol. 2088, pp. 243–251. Springer, Heidelberg (2001)
2. Câmpeanu, C., Păun, A., Yu, S.: An efficient algorithm for constructing minimal cover automata for finite languages. Int. J. Found. Comput. Sci. 13, 83–97 (2002)
3. Kaneps, J., Freivalds, R.: Running time to recognize nonregular languages by 2-way probabilistic automata. In: Leach Albert, J., Monien, B., Rodríguez-Artalejo, M. (eds.) Automata, Languages and Programming. LNCS, vol. 510, pp. 174–185. Springer, Heidelberg (1991)
4. Dwork, C., Stockmeyer, L.: A time complexity gap for two-way probabilistic finite-state automata. SIAMJC 19, 1011–1023 (1990)

5. Champarnaud, J.M., Guingne, F., Hansel, G.: Similarity relations and cover automata. RAIRO Theoret. Informatics Appl. 39, 115–123 (2005)
6. Câmpeanu, C., Sântean, N., Yu, S.: Minimal cover-automata for finite languages. Theor. Comput. Sci. 267, 3–16 (2001)
7. Körner, H.: A time and space efficient algorithm for minimizing cover automata for finite languages. Int. J. Found. Comput. Sci. 14, 1071–1086 (2003)
8. Champarnaud, J.M., Guingne, F., Hansel, G.: Cover transducers for functions with finite domain. Int. J. Found. Comput. Sci. 16, 851–865 (2005)
9. Schützenberger, M.P.: Sur une variante des fonctions séquentielles. Theor. Comput. Sci. 4, 47–57 (1977)
10. Choffrut, C.: Contribution à l'étude de quelques familles remarquables de fonctions rationnelles. Thèse d'État, Université Paris 7, Mathématiques (1978)
11. Berstel, J.: Transductions and Context-Free Languages. vol. 38 of Leitfäden der angewandten Mathematik und Mechanik LAMM. Teubner (1979)
12. Choffrut, C.: Minimizing subsequential transducers: a survey. Theor. Comput. Sci. 292, 131–143 (2003)
13. Béal, M.P., Carton, O.: Computing the prefix of an automaton. RAIRO Theoret. Informatics Appl. 34, 503–514 (2000)
14. Mohri, M.: Minimization algorithms for sequential transducers. Theor. Comput. Sci. 234, 177–201 (2000)
15. Aho, A.V., Hopcroft, J.E., Ullman, J.D.: Data Structures and Algorithms. Addison-Wesley, Reading (1983)
16. Paige, R., Tarjan, R.E.: Three partition refinement algorithms. SIAM J. Comput. 16, 973–989 (1987)

On-the-Fly Stuttering in the Construction of Deterministic ω-Automata

Joachim Klein and Christel Baier*

Institute of Theoretical Computer Science, Dresden University of Technology
01062 Dresden, Germany
j.klein@ltl2dstar.de, baier@tcs.inf.tu-dresden.de

Abstract. We propose to use the knowledge that an ω-regular property is stutter insensitive to construct potentially smaller deterministic ω-automata for such a property, e.g. using Safra's determinization construction. This knowledge allows us to skip states that are redundant under stuttering, which can reduce the size of the generated automaton. In order to use this technique even for automata that are not completely insensitive to stuttering, we introduce the notion of partial stutter insensitiveness and apply our construction only on the subset of symbols for which stuttering is allowed. We evaluate the benefits of this heuristic in practice using multiple sets of benchmark formulas.

Keywords: stuttering, LTL, determinization, Rabin, deterministic, ω-automaton.

1 Introduction

Automata on infinite words, ω-automata [1,2], play a vital role in the automata theoretic approach [3,4] to formal verification. In this context, ω-regular properties specifying desired behavior, often formalized in Linear Temporal Logic (LTL) [5], are translated into nondeterministic Büchi automata (NBA), which can then be used to verify, using graph algorithms, that the property is not violated by a given system design. In some situations, e.g. the quantitative analysis of Markov decision processes [6,7,8], deterministic instead of nondeterministic automata are needed. The determinization construction from NBA to deterministic Rabin automata (DRA) can lead to a worst-case $2^{\mathcal{O}(n \log n)}$ blow-up in automata size, making the whole translation from LTL formula to DRA double exponential.

Despite this complexity, in practice and using several minimization heuristics [9], we were able to generate automata of usable size for many benchmark formulas using Safra's determinization algorithm [10]. The automata generated by our tool *ltl2dstar* are used in practice for example by *LiQuor* [11], an explicit state model checker for Markov decision processes, providing quantitative and qualitative analysis of ω-regular properties.

---

* Both authors are supported by the EU project CREDO.

Jan Holub and Jan Žd'árek (Eds.): CIAA 2007, LNCS 4783, pp. 51–61, 2007.
© Springer-Verlag Berlin Heidelberg 2007

One desirable characteristic for ω-regular properties is *insensitiveness to stutter*, i.e. that the property can not distinguish between traces that differ only by *stuttering*, the finite repetition of similar states. Stutter insensitive specifications provide an abstraction from the implementation choices [12] and are a prerequisite for the application of powerful optimizations like partial order reduction in model checking [13,14,15].

We propose to use knowledge about the stutter insensitiveness of a formula and the corresponding automaton during the determinization construction by modifying the transition function to skip states that are redundant under stuttering, with the goal of generating smaller DRA in practice. Our construction can be applied on-the-fly, i.e. without building the whole original deterministic automaton first. This has the benefit that the intermediate, skipped states do not have to be fully expanded. We can apply this construction as well for automata that are only partially stutter insensitive, by determining the set of symbols for which stuttering is allowed. Our technique is independent of the underlying determinization construction and can also be used e.g. in the construction of the union automaton for two DRA. It can also easily be adapted for deterministic Streett or parity automata.

After defining our basic notations, LTL and the automata used in Section 2, we explain our construction in Section 3. We have incorporated this proposed heuristic in our tool *ltl2dstar* (http://www.ltl2dstar.de/) and report on experimental evaluation using benchmark formulas in Section 4.

2   Notations, LTL and Automata

For a (non-empty) set S, let S^* denote the set of finite sequences $s = s_0, s_1, \ldots, s_n$ over S and let S^ω denote the set of infinite sequences $s = s_0, s_1, \ldots$ over S, with $s_i \in S$. Let $s|_i$ be the suffix $s_i, s_{i+1}, \ldots$ of a sequence s starting at index i. If S is an alphabet Σ, the sequences are called *words over* Σ. For two words $\alpha \in \Sigma^*$ and $\beta \in (\Sigma^* \cup \Sigma^\omega)$, the concatenation of α and β is denoted by $\alpha \cdot \beta$. For a letter $a \in \Sigma$, the word a^i consists of the i-times repetition of the letter a, a^0 being the empty word ε. A language $\mathcal{L}$ over Σ is a subset of Σ^ω: $\mathcal{L} \subseteq \Sigma^\omega$. The complement language, denoted by $\overline{\mathcal{L}}$, is defined as the words from Σ^ω that are not in $\mathcal{L}$, $\overline{\mathcal{L}} = \Sigma^\omega \setminus \mathcal{L}$. For a set S, 2^S denotes the power set of S (the set of all subsets of S).

Linear Temporal Logic (LTL). The set of LTL formulas over a set of atomic propositions AP is defined by the grammar

$$\varphi ::= \textbf{true} \mid p \mid \neg\varphi \mid \varphi \vee \varphi \mid \textbf{X}\,\varphi \mid \varphi\,\textbf{U}\,\varphi,$$

with $p \in$ AP. The temporal operators X and U are called "Next" and "Until", respectively.

Let $\alpha = \alpha_0, \alpha_1, \ldots$ be an infinite word over $\Sigma = 2^{\text{AP}}$ and let φ be an LTL formula over AP. Satisfaction of φ by α, $\alpha \models \varphi$, is defined as follows:

$$\alpha \models \text{true} \qquad\qquad \alpha \models p \in \text{AP iff } p \in \alpha_0$$
$$\alpha \models \neg\varphi \text{ iff } \alpha \not\models \varphi \qquad \alpha \models \varphi_1 \lor \varphi_2 \text{ iff } \alpha \models \varphi_1 \text{ or } \alpha \models \varphi_2$$
$$\alpha \models \mathsf{X}\,\varphi_1 \text{ iff } \alpha|_1 \models \varphi_1$$
$$\alpha \models \varphi_1 \mathsf{U}\varphi_2 \text{ iff } \exists k \geq 0 : \alpha|_k \models \varphi_2 \text{ and } \forall 0 \leq i < k : \alpha|_i \models \varphi_1$$

The language of an LTL formula φ is $\mathcal{L}(\varphi) = \{\alpha \in \Sigma^\omega : \alpha \models \psi\}$. From the basic operators defined above, we derive the usual propositional operators, e.g. conjunction ($\wedge$) and implication ($\rightarrow$), as well as the temporal operators "Finally" ($\mathsf{F}\varphi \equiv \text{true}\,\mathsf{U}\varphi$) and "Globally" ($\mathsf{G}\varphi \equiv \neg\,\mathsf{F}\neg\varphi$).

Automata. A nondeterministic ω-automaton over an alphabet Σ is defined as $\mathcal{A} = (Q, \Sigma, \delta, q_0, \Omega)$ with a finite set Q of states, initial state $q_0 \in Q$ and transition function $\delta : Q \times \Sigma \rightarrow 2^Q$. For deterministic ω-automata, the transition function associates exactly one successor state ($|\delta(q, a)| = 1$) per transition and can thus be considered as $\delta : Q \times \Sigma \rightarrow Q$, which can be naturally extended to take a finite word from Σ^* as input by applying δ successively on each letter. Ω is the acceptance condition, depending of the type of the automaton.

A run of an ω-automaton $\mathcal{A}$ over a word $\alpha \in \Sigma^\omega$ is an infinite sequence of states $\pi = \pi_0, \pi_1, \ldots$ with $\pi_0 = q_0$ and $\pi_{i+1} \in \delta(\pi_i, \alpha_i)$. Let $\inf(\pi) \subseteq Q$ be the set of states of $\mathcal{A}$ that are visited infinitely often in the run π. In a *Büchi automaton* the acceptance condition Ω is a set of states $F \subseteq Q$, and a run π is called accepting iff F is visited infinitely often: $\inf(\pi) \cap F \neq \emptyset$. In a *Rabin automaton*, the acceptance condition Ω consists of k acceptance pairs of subsets of the states: $\Omega = \{(L_1, U_1), \ldots, (L_k, U_k)\}$, where $L_i \subseteq Q$ and $U_i \subseteq Q$. A run π of the automaton is called accepting, iff there exists an i such that L_i is visited infinitely often and U_i is visited only finitely often: $\exists i \in \{1, \ldots, k\} : \inf(\pi) \cap L_i \neq \emptyset \wedge \inf(\pi) \cap U_i = \emptyset$. The language $\mathcal{L}(\mathcal{A})$ of a (non-)deterministic automaton is the set of words $\alpha \in \Sigma^\omega$ for which there exists an accepting run in $\mathcal{A}$. We abbreviate nondeterministic Büchi automaton as NBA and deterministic Rabin automaton as DRA.

In this paper, we will additionally use an alternative, equivalent encoding of Rabin acceptance: For every state of a Rabin automaton, we can encode its *acceptance signature* as a k-tuple $\vec{r} = (\vec{r}[1], \ldots, \vec{r}[k]) \in Acc^k$, where $Acc = \{white, green, red\}$. Let $\text{acc} : Q \rightarrow Acc^k$ calculate the acceptance signature for a given state q: $\text{acc}(q) = \vec{r} = (\vec{r}[1], \ldots, \vec{r}[k])$, with $\vec{r}[i] = red$ iff $q \in U_i$, $\vec{r}[i] = green$ iff $q \in L_i \wedge q \notin U_i$ and $\vec{r}[i] = white$ else. We naturally extend this function to a subset of the states, $\text{acc} : 2^Q \rightarrow 2^{Acc^k}$, $\text{acc}(Q') = \{\text{acc}(q) : q \in Q'\}$ to get the set of acceptance signatures for the states. We then specify a total order $white < green < red$ on the three different values of Acc and define the operator $\max : 2^{Acc^k} \rightarrow Acc^k$,

$$\max\{\vec{r_1}, \ldots, \vec{r_n}\} = \vec{r_{max}} \text{ with } \vec{r_{max}}[i] = \max\{\vec{r_j}[i] : 1 \leq j \leq n\}, 1 \leq i \leq k,$$

i.e. separately calculating the maximum for each of the k elements for a set of acceptance signatures, according to the order on Acc.

With these tools, we can reformulate Rabin acceptance as follows: Let $R_{inf} = \text{acc}(\inf(\pi))$ be the set of acceptance signatures of the states that occur infinitely often in a run π, then $\overrightarrow{r_{inf}} = \max(R_{inf})$ represents the element-wise maximum of these acceptance signatures. Then π is accepting iff there exists at least one $1 \leq i \leq k$ such that $\overrightarrow{r_{inf}}[i] = green$.

3   Stuttering the Determinization Construction

3.1   Stuttering

In the literature (e.g. [12,16,17,18]), stuttering is usually considered in the context where all the different letters from the alphabet Σ are allowed to be stuttered. For our purposes, we refine this notion and more generally consider the effect on the language of allowing stuttering for only a subset $S \subseteq \Sigma$ of the letters (partial stuttering). The usual definitions of stuttering are then obtained by using $S = \Sigma$.

Let Σ^ω be the set of infinite words over Σ and let $S \subseteq \Sigma$ be a subset of Σ. Let $\alpha = \alpha_0, \alpha_1, \ldots$ be an infinite word from Σ^ω. A letter α_i is called *redundant* iff $\alpha_i = \alpha_{i+1}$ and there exists a $j > i$ such that $\alpha_i \neq \alpha_j$.

Let $\natural_S : \Sigma^\omega \to \Sigma^\omega$ be an operator that removes all the redundant occurrences of all symbols $\sigma \in S$ from α. Two words $\alpha, \beta \in \Sigma^\omega$ are called *S-stutter equivalent* iff $\natural_S(\alpha) = \natural_S(\beta)$. We denote by $[\alpha]_{\cong S} = \{\beta \in \Sigma^\omega : \natural_S(\alpha) = \natural_S(\beta)\}$ the equivalence class of S-stutter equivalent words of α.

A language $\mathcal{L}$ over Σ is called *closed under S-stuttering* iff for every $\alpha \in \mathcal{L}$, all the S-stutter equivalent words are in $\mathcal{L}$ as well, $[\alpha]_{\cong S} \subseteq \mathcal{L}$. Note that if a language $\mathcal{L}$ is closed under S-stuttering then $\mathcal{L}$ is also closed under S'-stuttering for any subset $S' \subseteq S$ and that if $\mathcal{L}$ is closed under S_1- and S_2-stuttering then $\mathcal{L}$ is closed under $S_1 \cup S_2$-stuttering.

An LTL formula φ is called *S-stutter invariant* iff the language $\mathcal{L}(\varphi)$ is closed under S-stuttering. An automaton $\mathcal{A}$ is called *S-stutter insensitive* iff the language $\mathcal{L}(\mathcal{A})$ is closed under S-stuttering.

3.2   Checking for Closure Under Stuttering

Unfortunately, checking whether the language of a given LTL formula or NBA is closed under Σ-stuttering is PSPACE-complete [18], assuming a fixed (nontrivial) alphabet Σ. However, for any formula φ from the subset of formulas LTL\X that do not contain the Next operator X, it can be shown that φ is Σ-stutter invariant [12,17] and can thus be easily identified by a simple syntactic check.

For the other formulas that do contain the X operator, we would like to determine the maximal set $S \subseteq \Sigma = 2^{\text{AP}}$ for which such a formula φ with atomic propositions AP is S-stutter invariant.

In a prototypical implementation in our tool, we accomplish this by successively checking for all the symbols $\sigma \in \Sigma$ whether φ is $\{\sigma\}$-stutter invariant, i.e. $\mathcal{L}(\varphi)$ is closed under stuttering of σ. Checking for $\{\sigma\}$-stutter invariance of a formula φ is PSPACE-complete as well, again assuming a fixed alphabet Σ:

Membership in PSPACE can be shown by allowing only stuttering of σ in the algorithm for Σ-stutter invariance checking from [18]. PSPACE-hardness follows from the fact that Σ-stutter invariance checking can be reduced to checking $\{\sigma\}$-stutter invariance for all the $\sigma \in \Sigma$.

Our implementation checks $\{\sigma\}$-stutter invariance by calculating the *stutter-closure* under stuttering of the symbol σ, denoted by $cl_{\cong\sigma}(\mathcal{A})$, for the nondeterministic Büchi automaton $\mathcal{A}$ obtained from φ, similar to what is proposed in [19]. By construction, $\mathcal{L}(cl_{\cong\sigma}(\mathcal{A})) = \bigcup_{\alpha\in\mathcal{L}(\mathcal{A})} [\alpha]_{\cong\sigma}$. Then, $\mathcal{A}$ is $\{\sigma\}$-stuttering insensitive iff $\mathcal{L}(cl_{\cong\sigma}(\mathcal{A})) = \mathcal{L}(\mathcal{A})$ which is equivalent to $\mathcal{L}(cl_{\cong\sigma}(\mathcal{A}))\cap\overline{\mathcal{L}(\mathcal{A})} = \emptyset$. This condition can be checked using a standard emptiness check on the product automaton $cl_{\cong\sigma}(\mathcal{A}) \times \overline{\mathcal{A}}$. Rather than obtaining $\overline{\mathcal{A}}$ by complementing $\mathcal{A}$, we simply generate the NBA for the negated formula $\neg\varphi$.

Clearly, this approach to checking stutter invariance is computationally hard, but our experiments in Section 4 suggest that – at least for our benchmark formulas – determining S can be performed in a reasonable amount of time. Alternative approaches like [18] or [20] should be evaluated for their performance in practice.

3.3 The Stuttered Deterministic Rabin Automaton

Given a DRA $\mathcal{A} = (T, \Sigma, \delta, t_0, \Omega)$ with $\Omega = \{(L_1, U_1), \ldots, (L_k, U_k)\}$ which is S-stutter insensitive, we will provide a construction for a DRA $\mathcal{B} = (Q, \Sigma, \delta_{\cong S}, q_0, \Omega^{\mathcal{B}})$, which we call the stuttered DRA and which accepts the same language as automaton $\mathcal{A}$.

A state from the set of states $Q = T \times Acc^k$ of $\mathcal{B}$ consists of a state from $\mathcal{A}$ augmented with an acceptance signature, $(t, \overrightarrow{r}) \in Q$. The acceptance condition $\Omega^{\mathcal{B}} = \{(L_1^{\mathcal{B}}, U_1^{\mathcal{B}}), \ldots, (L_k^{\mathcal{B}}, U_k^{\mathcal{B}})\}$ of $\mathcal{B}$ is determined as follows: For every state $(t, \overrightarrow{r}) \in Q$ and every $1 \leq i \leq k$, the state $(t, \overrightarrow{r}) \in L_i^{\mathcal{B}}$ iff $\overrightarrow{r}[i] = green$ and $(t, \overrightarrow{r}) \in U_i^{\mathcal{B}}$ iff $\overrightarrow{r}[i] = red$, i.e. the acceptance condition is chosen to correspond to the acceptance signature $\overrightarrow{r}$. The initial state $q_0 = (t_0, \overrightarrow{r_0})$ with $\overrightarrow{r_0} = acc(t_0)$ is a copy of the initial state from $\mathcal{A}$ with its acceptance signature.

To determine $\delta_{\cong S}(q, a)$ for a state $q = (t, \overrightarrow{r})$ we consider the sequence of states $t_i = \delta(t, a^i)$, with $i = 1, \ldots$ (i.e. the infinite run on the word a^ω in $\mathcal{A}$ starting at t). As all $t_i \in T$ and T is finite, there will eventually be a cycle of states that are visited infinitely often. Thus we can partition the sequence into a prefix segment and a cycle segment as follows:

$$t \xrightarrow{a} \underbrace{t_1 \xrightarrow{a} \cdots \xrightarrow{a} t_{prefix}}_{\text{prefix}} \xrightarrow{a} \underbrace{t_{cycle} \xrightarrow{a} \cdots \xrightarrow{a} t_{cycle+i} \xrightarrow{a} \cdots \xrightarrow{a} t_{cycle+c} = t_{cycle}}_{\text{cycle}}$$

Note that the prefix may be empty, i.e. $t_{cycle} = t_1$. We now choose one of the cycle states from $\{t_{cycle}, \ldots, t_{cycle+c}\}$ in such a way that, whenever we have to chose from the same cycle, always the same state is chosen. This can be accomplished e.g. by defining an order on T and always choosing the smallest state w.r.t. this order. Let $t_{cycle+i}$ be that chosen state and let $stutter_{t,a} = cycle + c + i$. It is now easy to see that $\delta(t, a^{stutter_{t,a}}) = t_{stutter_{t,a}} = t_{cycle+c+i} = t_{cycle+i}$, i.e. we go from t to the chosen state with a number of stutter$_{t,a}$ consecutive a-transitions visiting every state on the prefix and cycle and then continuing to the chosen state:

$$\underbrace{t \xrightarrow{a} \overbrace{t_1 \xrightarrow{a} \cdots \xrightarrow{a} t_{prefix}}^{\text{all states in prefix}} \xrightarrow{a} \overbrace{t_{cycle} \xrightarrow{a} \cdots \xrightarrow{a} t_{cycle+c}}^{\text{all states on cycle}} \xrightarrow{a} \overbrace{\cdots \xrightarrow{a} t_{cycle+c+i}}^{\text{go to chosen state again}}}_{\text{stutter}_{t,a} \text{ transitions}}$$

We now define $\delta_{\cong S}((t, \overrightarrow{r}), a) = (t', \overrightarrow{r}')$ with $t' = t_{\text{stutter}_{t,a}}$ and $\overrightarrow{r}' = \max(\text{acc}(\{t_1, \ldots, t_{cycle+c}\}))$. If the automaton $\mathcal{A}$ is not S-stutter insensitive for symbol a, $a \notin S$, then we set stutter$_{t,a} = 1$, i.e. we go to the state $(t_1, \text{acc}(t_1))$ just as in the original, unstuttered automaton $\mathcal{A}$.

With this construction, we skip ahead stutter$_{t,a} - 1$ states and modify the acceptance signature of the resulting state to reflect the acceptance signatures of the skipped states.

Structure of $\mathcal{B}$. For a given state q in $\mathcal{B}$ and an $a \in S$, this construction leads to the following structure, with q_{cycle} having an a-self loop:

$$\underbrace{(t, \overrightarrow{r})}_{q=(t,\overrightarrow{r})} \xrightarrow{a} \underbrace{(t', \max(\text{acc}\{t_1, \ldots, t_{cycle+c}\}))}_{q_{prefix}=(t',\overrightarrow{r_p})} \xrightarrow{a} \underbrace{(t', \max(\text{acc}\{t_{cycle}, \ldots, t_{cycle+c}\}))}_{q_{cycle}=(t',\overrightarrow{r_c})}$$

When $\overrightarrow{r_p} = \overrightarrow{r_c}$, both q_{prefix} and q_{cycle} collapse to a single state. In the special case that $\max\{\overrightarrow{r}, \overrightarrow{r_p}, \overrightarrow{r_c}\} = \max\{\overrightarrow{r}, \overrightarrow{r_c}\}$ and $a \in S$, we can stutter skip q_{prefix} and set $\delta_{\cong S}(q, a) = q_{cycle}$, i.e. behave as if reading two a's instead of one, which is safe as $\mathcal{B}$ is S-stutter insensitive, too.

Please note that the intermediate q_{prefix} states can not be avoided in general: Consider for example the LTL formula $\varphi = \mathsf{GF}a \wedge \mathsf{GF}\neg a$, with $AP = \{a\}$, $\Sigma = 2^{AP}$. Assume there is a DRA recognizing $\mathcal{L}(\varphi)$ with no q_{prefix} states, i.e. with every state q having a self loop for symbol $a \in \Sigma$ if there is an incoming edge to q with symbol a. As $\mathcal{L}(\varphi)$ is non-empty, there exists a state q, reachable from q_0 via the prefix $\alpha \cdot a$, with $\alpha \in \Sigma^*$ and $a \in \Sigma$, such that the acceptance signature of q has at least one *green* element. But by assumption, q has an a-self loop and the word $\alpha \cdot a^\omega$ would be accepted, contradicting the fact that it is not in $\mathcal{L}(\varphi)$.

Proposition 1. *$\mathcal{A}$ and $\mathcal{B}$ accept the same language, $\mathcal{L}(\mathcal{A}) = \mathcal{L}(\mathcal{B})$.*

Proof. We first show how we can relate runs in $\mathcal{B}$ with runs in $\mathcal{A}$. Given an infinite word $\beta = \beta_0, \beta_1, \ldots$ and the corresponding run $\pi_\mathcal{B}(\beta)$ in automaton $\mathcal{B}$, we can construct a word α and corresponding run $\pi_\mathcal{A}(\alpha)$ in the original automaton $\mathcal{A}$. Let $\pi_\mathcal{B}(\beta) = q_0, q_1, \ldots$, with $q_i = (t_{q_i}, \overrightarrow{r_{q_i}})$, be the run in $\mathcal{B}$ for β. We know for each transition $(t_{q_i}, \overrightarrow{r_{q_i}}) \xrightarrow{\beta_i} (t_{q_{i+1}}, \overrightarrow{r_{q_{i+1}}})$ the number $st_i = \text{stutter}_{t_{q_i}, \beta_i}$ used in the construction of $\delta_{\cong S}$ to determine the number of states to skip for this transition. By constructing $\alpha = \beta_0^{st_0} \cdot \beta_1^{st_1} \cdots$, i.e. stuttering the symbols β_i the appropriate number of times st_i, we get the corresponding run in $\mathcal{A}$, $\pi_\mathcal{A}(\alpha)$.

By construction, α and β are S-stutter-equivalent, $\alpha \in [\beta]_{\cong S}$, because we only stutter symbols in S as our construction guarantees that $st_i = 1$ for all $\beta_i \notin S$.

The two runs $\pi_{\mathcal{A}}(\alpha)$ and $\pi_{\mathcal{B}}(\beta)$ then run in parallel, for every transition with β_i in $\pi_{\mathcal{B}}(\beta)$ there are st_i transitions with β_i in $\pi_{\mathcal{A}}(\alpha)$:

$$\pi_{\mathcal{B}}(\beta) : \overset{\beta_{i-1}}{\leadsto} q_i = (t_{q_i}, \overrightarrow{r_{q_i}}) \xrightarrow{\hspace{1.5cm}\beta_i\hspace{1.5cm}} q_{i+1} = (t_{q_{i+1}}, \overrightarrow{r_{q_{i+1}}}) \overset{\beta_{i+1}}{\leadsto}$$

$$\pi_{\mathcal{A}}(\alpha) : \overset{\beta_{i-1}}{\leadsto} t_{q_i} \xrightarrow{\beta i} t_{q_i,1} \xrightarrow{\beta i} \cdots \xrightarrow{\beta i} t_{q_i,st_i} \overset{\beta_{i+1}}{\leadsto}$$

By construction, $t_{q_{i+1}} = t_{q_i,st_i}$ and $\overrightarrow{r_{q_{i+1}}} = \max(\mathrm{acc}(\{t_{q_i,1}, \ldots, t_{q_i,st_i}\}))$.

Lemma 2. $\pi_{\mathcal{B}}(\beta)$ *and* $\pi_{\mathcal{A}}(\alpha)$ *are both accepting or both rejecting.*

We show $\max(\mathrm{acc}(\inf(\pi_{\mathcal{A}}(\alpha)))) = \max(\mathrm{acc}(\inf(\pi_{\mathcal{B}}(\beta))))$, which is an even stronger claim. To determine the sets $\inf(\pi_{\mathcal{A}}(\alpha))$ and $\inf(\pi_{\mathcal{B}}(\beta))$ of infinitely visited states, we determine the index j for β such that, from that point on, all transitions that occur in $\pi_{\mathcal{B}}(\beta)|_j$ appear infinitely often. As the set of possible transitions $Q \times \Sigma$ is finite and the run is infinite, such a j is guaranteed to exist. Let $j' = \Sigma_{i=0}^{i<j} st_i$ be the corresponding index for α such that $\pi_{\mathcal{A}}(\alpha)|_{j'}$ is synchronized with $\pi_{\mathcal{B}}(\beta)|_j$. In general, $\inf(\pi) = \inf(\pi|_j)$ for any j as we consider only the infinitely repeating behavior, which allows us to start as "late" in the run as we want. It is easy to see that the set of infinitely visited states in the run are exactly the states that occur as the destination states of the infinitely occurring transitions. Because the two runs are synchronized, for every transition visited infinitely often in $\pi_{\mathcal{B}}(\beta)|_j$ with destination state $q_{i+1} = (t_{q_{i+1}}, \overrightarrow{r_{q_{i+1}}})$, the corresponding transitions with destination states $t_{q_i,1}, \ldots, t_{q_i,st_i}$ in $\pi_{\mathcal{A}}(\alpha)|_{j'}$ are visited infinitely often, too. As every infinitely occurring transition in $\pi_{\mathcal{A}}(\alpha)|_{j'}$ can be related to at least one infinitely occurring transition in $\pi_{\mathcal{B}}(\beta)|_j$, this approach covers all the transitions and thus also all infinitely visited states in $\pi_{\mathcal{A}}(\alpha)|_{j'}$.

Because $\max(\mathrm{acc}(q_{i+1})) = \max(\overrightarrow{r_{q_{i+1}}}) = \max(\mathrm{acc}(\{t_{q_i,1}, \ldots, t_{q_i,st_i}\}))$ for all the transitions in $\pi_{\mathcal{B}}(\beta)|_j$, it follows that $\max(\mathrm{acc}(\inf(\pi_{\mathcal{A}}(\alpha)|_{j'}))) = \max(\mathrm{acc}(\inf(\pi_{\mathcal{B}}(\beta)|_j)))$.

We will now use the above to show language equivalence of $\mathcal{A}$ and $\mathcal{B}$:

$\mathcal{L}(\mathcal{A}) \subseteq \mathcal{L}(\mathcal{B})$: Let $\beta \in \mathcal{L}(\mathcal{A})$ and let $\pi_{\mathcal{B}}(\beta)$ be the run for β in the modified automaton $\mathcal{B}$. As shown above, we can construct a word α by only stuttering $a \in S$. By Lemma 2, the run $\pi_{\mathcal{A}}(\alpha)$ in $\mathcal{A}$ is accepting iff $\pi_{\mathcal{B}}(\beta)$ is accepting. Because α is S-stutter equivalent to β and $\mathcal{A}$ is S-stutter insensitive, it follows that $\alpha \in \mathcal{L}(\mathcal{A})$ and that $\pi_{\mathcal{A}}(\alpha)$ is accepting, hence $\pi_{\mathcal{B}}(\beta)$ is accepting, too, and $\beta \in \mathcal{L}(\mathcal{B})$.

$\mathcal{L}(\mathcal{A}) \supseteq \mathcal{L}(\mathcal{B})$: Let $\beta \in \mathcal{L}(\mathcal{B})$ and let $\pi_{\mathcal{B}}(\beta)$ be the accepting run for β in $\mathcal{B}$. As shown above, we can construct α and the corresponding accepting run $\pi_{\mathcal{A}}(\alpha)$ in the original automaton $\mathcal{A}$. It follows that $\alpha \in \mathcal{L}(\mathcal{A})$. Because α and β are S-stutter equivalent and $\mathcal{A}$ is S-stutter insensitive, it follows that $\beta \in \mathcal{L}(\mathcal{A})$. $\square$

Number of states. Our construction merges states along path fragments in the DRA $\mathcal{A}$. This can lead to $\mathcal{B}$ having more reachable states than $\mathcal{A}$ if the states, transitions and acceptance signatures in $\mathcal{A}$ are arranged in a compact, interleaved way that is destroyed by merging the stuttered transitions. Therefore our technique should be considered as an additional heuristic in the toolbox to generate smaller automata. In practice, only in three of the cases evaluated in Section 4 were the stuttered automata $\mathcal{B}$ larger than the corresponding standard automaton $\mathcal{A}$.

If $\mathcal{A}$ has n reachable states and k acceptance pairs, the number of reachable states n' in $\mathcal{B}$ is bound by $n' \leq n \cdot |Acc^k| = n \cdot 3^k$. Ignoring the special case of skipping q_{prefix} which can only lead to fewer states, n' is bound as well by the number of reachable transitions in $\mathcal{A}$, $n' \leq n \cdot |\Sigma|$, as $\delta_{\cong S}(q, a)$ for $q = (t, \overrightarrow{r})$ is uniquely determined by t and a.

4   Implementation and Experimental Results

In our tool *ltl2dstar*, we have implemented the construction of stuttered DRA for Safra's construction and for the union construction, which generates two DRA for each of the subformulas in a formula $\varphi = \varphi_1 \vee \varphi_2$ and then builds the DRA for φ by building the union automaton from the two subformula automata. Each of the subformula automata can be constructed again with stuttering, with potentially differing sets of stutter insensitive symbols for φ_1 and φ_2.

As we are interested in generating small automata in practice, we performed an evaluation of our heuristic. We used the standard tool *ltl2ba* from [21] as the external generator for the nondeterministic Büchi automata from LTL formulas.

Example formula. We consider the formula $\varphi = \mathsf{GF}a \rightarrow \mathsf{GF}b \equiv \mathsf{FG}\neg a \vee \mathsf{GF}b$, representing a strong fairness condition ("infinitely often a implies infinitely often b"). The NBA generated by *ltl2ba* has 5 states, from which our implementation of Safra's algorithm, with the heuristics presented in [9] disabled, generates a DRA with 61 states. With our minimization heuristics enabled, the generated DRA has 12 states, which is mostly thanks to the use of the union construction. With the stuttered construction, our tool generates a DRA with only 4 states, by building the union of the two now stuttered DRA for the subformulas, each having the minimal size of two states per automaton (Fig. 1 shows the DRA for the subformula $\mathsf{GF}b$).

Benchmark. We have evaluated the effect of our stuttering construction on the benchmark formulas we used in [9]. We distinguish between the formulas without and with the X operator, i.e. those where we can stutter all symbols from Σ and those where we may be only allowed to stutter a subset of Σ. The sets of benchmark formulas consist of 39 formulas from [22] and [23] (25 without X), 1000 randomly generated formulas (415 without X) and 55 pattern formulas [24], which can be regarded as typical formula types used in practice (30 without X)[1].

---

[1] The tests were carried out with an Intel Pentium M 1.5 GHz, 512 MB RAM, running Linux. The same machine was used for the benchmarks in [9].

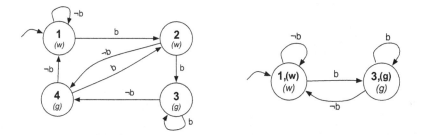

Fig. 1. DRA for LTL formula `GFb` as generated by *ltl2dstar*, left without stuttering, right with our stuttering technique. **Bold**: State, *Italics*: Acceptance signature.

We compared the automata sizes without and with our stuttered transition function. The other heuristics described in [9] (on-the-fly improvements of Safra's algorithm, union construction, bisimulation, etc.) were enabled. The results of our experiments are shown in Table 1, once for generating DRA and once for generating deterministic Rabin or Streett automata (DSA). Depending on the formula, using the dual Streett acceptance instead of Rabin acceptance can lead to exponentially smaller automata, and vice versa. If the user can handle both acceptance types, we compute a DRA and a DSA and return the smaller. For further details we refer to [9].

In addition to listing the sum of the number of states of the automata, the time needed for computing the automata is detailed. For the formulas with the

Table 1. Combined number of states of the automata and time spent during the construction. For the formulas with **X**, how much time of the construction was spent calculating the set of stutter insensitive symbols S and the average fraction of the alphabet Σ that is stutter insensitive.

Formula set (without X)	DRA states Normal	Stuttered	Time Norm.	Stutt.	DRA/DSA states Normal	Stuttered	Time Norm.	Stutt.
[22,23]	278	168 (-39.6%)	0.3s	0.3s	215	140 (-34.9%)	0.5s	0.5s
Patterns	311	189 (-39.2%)	0.3s	0.3s	126	121 (-4.0%)	0.3s	0.3s
Random	1820	1499 (-17.6%)	3.9s	4.0s	1621	1405 (-13.3%)	4.6s	4.8s

Formula set (with X)	DRA states Normal	Stuttered	Time Normal	Stuttered	Calc. S	Average $|S|/|\Sigma|$
[22,23]	107	79 (-26.2%)	0.3s	6.8s	6.5s	75.9%
Patterns	103318	17731 (-82.8%)	207.5s	99.4s	15.5s	92.7%
Random	3441	3081 (-10.5%)	5.6s	10.6s	3.8s	49.6%

Formula set (with X)	DRA/DSA states Normal	Stuttered	Time Normal	Stuttered	Calc. S	Average $|S|/|\Sigma|$
[22,23]	53	51 (-3.8%)	0.3s	6.9s	6.5s	75.9%
Patterns	6273	2731 (-56.5%)	55.3s	78.8s	15.4s	92.7%
Random	2882	2750 (-4.6%)	6.5s	12.1s	3.9s	49.6%

X operator, we list how much of that time was spent calculating the set S of stutter insensitive symbols and the average of how many symbols of Σ for each formula are stutter insensitive.

The results show that significant reductions are obtainable using our proposed heuristic, even for the formulas containing the X operator. While determining the exact set S for theses formulas takes a significant amount of time, it allows reductions especially for the practically relevant pattern formulas, with large subsets of Σ being stutter insensitive. As explained in Section 3.3, in three cases the stuttered automata were slightly larger (170 states instead of 157, 14 instead of 11 and 9 instead of 8). It should be noted that all the reductions in the size of the automata are in addition to those achieved by the other heuristics and bisimulation quotienting.

5 Conclusion

We have shown that, in practice, stuttering the determinization construction is a useful tool to obtain smaller deterministic ω-automata, even for properties that are only partially insensitive to stuttering.

The problem of efficiently determining in practice the exact set $S \subseteq \Sigma$ for which an NBA or LTL formula is S-stutter insensitive provides opportunities for further research. It would be especially interesting to find heuristics for syntactically determining or approximating S.

Acknowledgments

We would like to thank Carsten Fritz for his input and the anonymous reviewers for helpful comments.

References

1. Thomas, W.: Languages, automata, and logic. Handbook of formal languages 3, 389–455 (1997)
2. Grädel, E., Thomas, W., Wilke, T. (eds.): Automata, Logics, and Infinite Games. LNCS, vol. 2500. Springer, Heidelberg (2002)
3. Vardi, M.Y., Wolper, P.: An automata-theoretic approach to automatic program verification. In: LICS, pp. 332–344. IEEE Computer Society Press, Los Alamitos (1986)
4. Vardi, M.Y.: An automata-theoretic approach to linear temporal logic. In: Moller, F., Birtwistle, G. (eds.) Logics for Concurrency. LNCS, vol. 1043, pp. 238–266. Springer, Heidelberg (1996)
5. Pnueli, A.: The temporal logic of programs. In: FOCS, pp. 46–57. IEEE Computer Society Press, Los Alamitos (1977)
6. de Alfaro, L.: Formal Verification of Probabilistic Systems. PhD thesis, Stanford University, Department of Computer Science (1997)
7. Baier, C., Kwiatkowska, M.: Model checking for a probabilistic branching time logic with fairness. Distributed Computing 11, 125–155 (1998)

8. Vardi, M.: Probabilistic linear-time model checking: An overview of the automata-theoretic approach. In: Katoen, J.-P. (ed.) AMAST-ARTS 1999, ARTS 1999, and AMAST-WS 1999. LNCS, vol. 1601, pp. 265–276. Springer, Heidelberg (1999)
9. Klein, J., Baier, C.: Experiments with deterministic ω-automata for formulas of linear temporal logic. Theoretical Computer Science 363, 182–195 (2006)
10. Safra, S.: Complexity of Automata on Infinite Objects. PhD thesis, The Weizmann Institute of Science, Rehovot, Israel (1989)
11. Ciesinski, F., Baier, C.: LiQuor: A tool for qualitative and quantitative linear time analysis of reactive systems. In: QEST, pp. 131–132. IEEE Computer Society Press, Los Alamitos (2006)
12. Lamport, L.: What Good is Temporal Logic? In: IFIP Congress, pp. 657–668 (1983)
13. Holzmann, G.J., Peled, D.: An improvement in formal verification. In: FORTE, pp. 197–211. Chapman & Hall, Sydney, Australia (1994)
14. Valmari, A.: A stubborn attack on state explosion. Formal Methods in System Design 1, 297–322 (1992)
15. Baier, C., D'Argenio, P.R., Größer, M.: Partial order reduction for probabilistic branching time. Electr. Notes Theor. Comput. Sci. 153, 97–116 (2006)
16. Etessami, K.: Stutter-invariant languages, omega-automata, and temporal logic. In: Halbwachs, N., Peled, D.A. (eds.) CAV 1999. LNCS, vol. 1633, pp. 236–248. Springer, Heidelberg (1999)
17. Peled, D., Wilke, T.: Stutter-invariant temporal properties are expressible without the next-time operator. Inf. Process. Lett. 63, 243–246 (1997)
18. Peled, D., Wilke, T., Wolper, P.: An Algorithmic Approach for Checking Closure Properties of Temporal Logic Specifications and omega-Regular Languages. Theor. Comput. Sci. 195, 183–203 (1998)
19. Holzmann, G., Kupferman, O.: Not checking for closure under stuttering. In: Proceedings of the 2nd International Workshop on the SPIN Verification System, DIMCAS, pp. 163–169 (1996)
20. Etessami, K.: A note on a question of Peled and Wilke regarding stutter-invariant LTL. Inf. Process. Lett. 75, 261–263 (2000)
21. Gastin, P., Oddoux, D.: Fast LTL to Büchi automata translation. In: Berry, G., Comon, H., Finkel, A. (eds.) CAV 2001. LNCS, vol. 2102, pp. 53–65. Springer, Heidelberg (2001)
22. Etessami, K., Holzmann, G.J.: Optimizing Büchi automata. In: Palamidessi, C. (ed.) CONCUR 2000. LNCS, vol. 1877, pp. 153–167. Springer, Heidelberg (2000)
23. Somenzi, F., Bloem, R.: Efficient Büchi automata from LTL formulae. In: Emerson, E.A., Sistla, A.P. (eds.) CAV 2000. LNCS, vol. 1855, pp. 248–263. Springer, Heidelberg (2000)
24. Dwyer, M.B., Avrunin, G.S., Corbett, J.C.: Patterns in property specifications for finite-state verification. In: ICSE, pp. 411–420 (1999)

Average Value and Variance of Pattern Statistics in Rational Models*

Massimiliano Goldwurm and Roberto Radicioni

Università degli Studi di Milano
Dipartimento di Scienze dell'Informazione
Via Comelico 39, 20135 Milano, Italy
{goldwurm,radicioni}@dsi.unimi.it

Abstract. We study the pattern statistics representing the number of occurrences of a given string in a word of length n generated at random by rational stochastic models, defined by means of weighted finite automata. We get asymptotic estimations for the mean value and the variance of these statistics under the hypothesis that the matrix of all transition weights is primitive. Our results extend previous evaluations obtained by assuming ergodic stationary Markovian sources and they yield a general framework to determine analogous estimations under several stochastic models. In particular they show the role of the stationarity hypothesis in such models.

Keywords: bioinformatics, Markov chains, pattern statistics, rational formal series.

1 Introduction

The classical problem of evaluating the number of occurrences of a given string (usually called pattern) in a random text has been mainly studied assuming the text generated by a Markovian source [1,2,3]. Here we assume more general stochastic models, called rational, which were first considered in [4] and studied in details in [5]. The rational models are defined by means of weighted finite automata and are able to generate a random string of given length in a regular language under uniform distribution. In this work we determine asymptotic expressions of average value and variance of the number of occurrences of a pattern in a string of length n generated at random in such models. We compare our results with analogous evaluations obtained in [1,2,4]. Our approach yields a general framework where the previous evaluations appear as special cases. We also relax the stationarity hypothesis assumed in [1,2] and show how such a condition affects the evaluations of mean value and variance of our statistics.

---

* This work has been supported by the Project MIUR PRIN 2005-2007 "Automata and Formal Languages: mathematical and applicative aspects".

Jan Holub and Jan Žd'árek (Eds.): CIAA 2007, LNCS 4783, pp. 62–72, 2007.

2 Preliminary Notions

Given a set X and an integer $m > 0$, we denote by X^m and $X^{m \times m}$, respectively, the set of all vectors and the set of all square matrices of size m with coefficients in X. Any $x \in X^m$ is considered as a column vector, while x' is its transposed (row) vector. Denoting by $\mathbb{R}_+$ the set of nonnegative real numbers, we recall that a matrix $M \in \mathbb{R}_+^{m \times m}$ is called primitive if $M^n > 0$ for some integer $n > 0$, meaning that all entries of M^n are greater than 0. By the Perron–Frobenius theorem [6, Sect.1], it is well-known that every primitive matrix $M \in \mathbb{R}_+^{m \times m}$ admits a real positive eigenvalue λ, called the Perron–Frobenius eigenvalue of M, which is a simple root of the characteristic polynomial of M, such that $|\nu| < \lambda$ for every eigenvalue $\nu \neq \lambda$.

The properties of nonnegative matrices are widely used to study the behaviour of Markov chains [7,8,6]. We recall that a real vector $\pi' = (\pi_1, \pi_2, \dots, \pi_m)$ is stochastic if $0 \leq \pi_i \leq 1$ for every i and $\sum_{i=1}^{n} \pi_i = 1$. A matrix $P \in \mathbb{R}^{m \times m}$ is stochastic if all its rows are stochastic vectors. It is easy to see that any stochastic matrix P has eigenvalue 1, with a corresponding right eigenvector $\underline{1}' = (1, 1, \dots, 1)$, while $|\gamma| \leq 1$ for any other eigenvalue γ of P.

A stochastic vector π and a stochastic matrix P of same size m allows us to define a Markov chain over the set of states $Q = \{1, 2, \dots, m\}$, i.e. a sequence of random variables $\{X_n\}_{n \in N}$ taking on values in Q, such that $\Pr(X_0 = i) = \pi_i$ and

$$\Pr(X_{n+1}{=}j \mid X_n{=}i, X_{n-1}{=}i_{n-1}, \dots, X_0{=}i_0) = \Pr(X_{n+1} = j \mid X_n = i) = P_{ij}$$

for every integer $n > 0$, and any tuple of states $j, i, i_0 \dots, i_{n-1} \in Q$. The arrays π and P are called, respectively, the initial vector and the transition matrix of the Markov chain. Note that $\Pr(X_n = j) = (\pi' P^n)_j$, for each $j \in Q$ and every $n \in \mathbb{N}$. Moreover, if P is primitive, by the Perron–Frobenius theorem one can prove that

$$P^n = \underline{1} v' + \mathrm{O}(\varepsilon^n) , \qquad (1)$$

where $0 \leq \varepsilon < 1$ and v' is the left eigenvector of P corresponding to the eigenvalue 1 such that $v'\underline{1} = 1$. Observe that $\underline{1} v'$ is a stable matrix, i.e. all its rows equal v'; moreover, v' is a stochastic vector, called the stationary vector of the chain, and it is the unique stochastic vector such that $v'P = v'$. If further $\pi = v$ then the Markov chain is called stationary, since $\pi' P^n = \pi'$ for every $n \in \mathbb{N}$, and hence $\Pr(X_n = j) = \pi_j$ for any state j.

Now, let us fix our notation on words and formal series [9]. Given a finite alphabet A, for every $x \in A^*$, $|x|$ is the length of x and $|x|_a$ is the number of occurrences of a symbol $a \in A$ in x. We also denote by A^n the set $\{x \in A^* \mid |x| = n\}$ for every $n \in \mathbb{N}$. A formal series over A with coefficients in $\mathbb{R}_+$ is a function $r : A^* \longrightarrow \mathbb{R}_+$, usually represented in the form $r = \sum_{x \in A^*} r(x) \cdot x$, where $r(x)$ denotes the value of r at $x \in A^*$. We denote by $\mathbb{R}_+\langle\!\langle A \rangle\!\rangle$ the family of all formal series over A with coefficients in $\mathbb{R}_+$. This set forms a semiring with respect to the traditional operations of sum and Cauchy product. As an example of formal series in $\mathbb{R}_+\langle\langle A\rangle\rangle$, we recall the notion of *probability measure* on A^*, defined as a map $f : A^* \longrightarrow [0,1]$, such that $f(\epsilon) = 1$ and $\sum_{a\in A} f(xa) = f(x)$, for every $x \in A^*$ [10].

A formal series $r \in \mathbb{R}_+\langle\langle A\rangle\rangle$ is called rational if it admits a linear representation, that is a triple $\langle\xi, \mu, \eta\rangle$ where, for some integer $m > 0$, ξ and η are (column) vectors in $\mathbb{R}_+^m$ and $\mu : A^* \longrightarrow \mathbb{R}_+^{m\times m}$ is a monoid morphism, such that $r(x) = \xi'\mu(x)\eta$ holds for each $x \in A^*$. We say that m is the *size* of the representation. Such a triple $\langle\xi, \mu, \eta\rangle$ can be interpreted as a weighted nondeterministic automaton, where the set of states is given by $\{1, 2, \ldots, m\}$ and the transitions, the initial and the final states are assigned weights in $\mathbb{R}_+$ by μ, ξ and η, respectively. To avoid redundancy it is convenient to assume that $\langle\xi, \mu, \eta\rangle$ is trim, i.e. for every index i there are two indexes p, q and two words $x, y \in A^*$ such that $\xi_p\mu(x)_{pi} \neq 0$ and $\mu(y)_{iq}\eta_q \neq 0$. The total transition matrix M of $\langle\xi, \mu, \eta\rangle$ is defined by $M = \sum_{a\in A} \mu(a)$. We say that $\langle\xi, \mu, \eta\rangle$ is primitive if such a matrix M is primitive.

Several properties of the formal series in $\mathbb{R}_+\langle\langle A\rangle\rangle$ can be studied by considering their commutative image. To define it formally, consider the canonical morphism $\Phi : A^* \longrightarrow \mathcal{M}(A)$, where $\mathcal{M}(A)$ is the free totally commutative monoid over A. Such a monoid morphism extends to a semiring morphism from $\mathbb{R}_+\langle\langle A\rangle\rangle$ to the traditional ring $\mathbb{R}[[A]]$ of formal series with real coefficients and commutative variables in A. We recall that, if $r \in \mathbb{R}_+\langle\langle A\rangle\rangle$ is rational, then also $\Phi(r)$ is rational in $\mathbb{R}[[A]]$, i.e. $\Phi(r) = pq^{-1}$ for two polynomials $p, q \in \mathbb{R}[A]$.

3   Stochastic Models on Words

Several stochastic models have been proposed in the literature to study probability measures on free monoids [11,10]. Here, we intuitively consider a stochastic (probabilistic) model over a finite alphabet A as a device to define a probability function on the set A^n for every integer $n > 0$, equipped with an effective procedure to generate on input n a word in A^n with the prescribed probability.

In this section we discuss three types of probabilistic models introduced in [5] and called, respectively, Markovian, sequential and rational models. Here, we recall their main properties and differences. These models include the classical Markovian sequences of any order and the rational probability measure studied in [10]. They can be seen as special cases of more general probabilistic devices studied in [11].

The simplest probabilistic model on words is the well-known Bernoullian model. A *Bernoullian* model $\mathcal{B}$ over A is defined by a function $p : A \to [0,1]$ such that $\sum_{a\in A} p(a) = 1$. A word $x \in A^+$ is generated in this model by choosing each letter of x under the distribution defined by p independently of one another. Thus, the probability of $x = x_1 x_2 \cdots x_n$, where $x_i \in A$ for each i, is given by $\Pr_{\mathcal{B}}(x) = p(x_1)p(x_2) \cdots p(x_n)$, which clearly defines a probability function over A^n for every integer $n > 0$.

3.1   Markovian Models

A *Markovian* model over A is defined as a pair $\mathcal{M} = (\pi, \mu)$ where, for some integer $k > 0$, $\pi \in [0,1]^k$ is a stochastic vector and μ is a function $\mu : A \rightarrow [0,1]^{k \times k}$ such that, for every $a \in A$, each row of $\mu(a)$ has at most one non-null entry and the matrix $M = \sum_{a \in A} \mu(a)$ is stochastic.

The probability of a word $x = x_1 x_2 \cdots x_n$, where $x_i \in A$ for each $i = 1, 2, \ldots, n$, is given by

$$\mathrm{Pr}_{\mathcal{M}}(x) = \pi' \mu(x_1) \mu(x_2) \cdots \mu(x_n) \underline{1}.$$

Thus, $\mathrm{Pr}_{\mathcal{M}}$ is a rational formal series in $\mathbb{R}_+ \langle\!\langle A \rangle\!\rangle$ with linear representation $\langle \pi, \mu, \underline{1} \rangle$. Also, since both π and M are stochastic arrays, $\mathrm{Pr}_{\mathcal{M}}$ defines a probability function over A^n for each positive integer n. This model implicitly defines a Markov chain taking on values in the set of states $\{1, 2, \ldots, k\}$, that has initial vector π and transition matrix M; we may call it the *underlying* Markov chain of $\mathcal{M}$.

Note that every Bernoullian model is a Markovian model. Moreover, the pair $\mathcal{M} = (\pi, \mu)$ defines a deterministic finite state automaton where transitions are weighted by probabilities: the set of states is $Q = \{1, 2, \ldots, k\}$, the transition function $\delta_{\mathcal{M}} : Q \times A \longrightarrow Q \cup \{\bot\}$ is defined so that for every $i \in Q$ and every $a \in A$, $\delta_{\mathcal{M}}(i, a) = j$ if $\mu(a)_{ij} \neq 0$, and the same value $\mu(a)_{ij}$ is the weight of the transition, while $\delta_{\mathcal{M}}(i, a) = \bot$ if $\mu(a)_{ij} = 0$ for all j. Clearly, $\delta_{\mathcal{M}}$ can be extended to all words in A^*. Thus, the sum of weights of all transitions outgoing from any state equals 1 and, since the automaton is deterministic, for every word $x \in A^*$ and every $i \in Q$ there exists at most one path labeled by x starting from i. These properties lead to prove the following lemma, which gives an asymptotic property of the probabilities defined in Markovian models.

Lemma 1. *[5] Let $\mathcal{M} = (\pi, \mu)$ be a Markovian model of size k over the alphabet A and let $x \in A^+$. Then, there exists $0 \leq \beta \leq 1$ such that $\mathrm{Pr}_{\mathcal{M}}(x^n) = \Theta(\beta^n)$, as n tends to $+\infty$* [1].

This lemma plays a role similar to classical pumping lemma in formal languages in the sense that it can be used to show that a given probabilistic model on A is not Markovian simply by showing that, for a word $x \in A^+$, the probability of x^n is not of the order $\Theta(\beta^n)$ for any constant $\beta \geq 0$.

Observe that the Markovian models can generate the traditional Markov sequences of order m over A (for any $m \in \mathbb{N}$), where the probability of the next symbol occurrence only depends on the previous m symbols. To define these sources in our context we say that a Markovian model $\mathcal{M}$ over A is of *order* m if for every word $w \in A^m$ either there exists j such that $\delta_{\mathcal{M}}(i, w) = j$ for every $i \in Q$ or $\delta_{\mathcal{M}}(i, w) = \bot$ for every $i \in Q$, and m is the smallest integer with such a property.

---

[1] This means that for some positive constants c_1, c_2, the relation $c_1 \beta^n \leq \mathrm{Pr}_{\mathcal{M}}(x^n) \leq c_2 \beta^n$ holds for any n large enough.

A relevant case occurs when $m = 1$. In this case, the set of states Q can be reduced to A and $\mathrm{Pr}_{\mathcal{M}}$ is called Markov probability measure in [10]. Also observe that there exist Markovian models that are not of order m, for any $m \in \mathbb{N}$. For instance, if $\mathcal{M}$ is defined by the following (weighted) finite automaton, then $\delta_{\mathcal{M}}(1, x) \neq \delta_{\mathcal{M}}(2, x)$ for every $x \in \{a, b\}^*$.

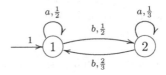

Hence our notion of Markovian model properly includes the traditional sources of Markovian sequences.

3.2   Sequential Models

A natural proper extension of the previous model can be obtained by allowing nondeterminism in the corresponding finite state device. In this way the model corresponds to a stochastic sequential machine, as defined in [11], with a unary input alphabet. Moreover, it is characterized by the rational probability measures, i.e. the probability measures on A^* that are rational formal series in $\mathbb{R}_+\langle\!\langle A \rangle\!\rangle$ [10].

Formally, we define a *sequential* stochastic model over A as a pair $\mathcal{Q} = (\pi, \mu)$ where $\pi \in [0, 1]^k$ is a stochastic vector and μ is a function $\mu : A \to [0, 1]^{k \times k}$ such that $M = \sum_{a \in A} \mu(a)$ is a stochastic matrix. Clearly, any Markovian model is also a sequential model. In particular, as in the Markovian models, μ defines a monoid morphism from A^* to $[0, 1]^{k \times k}$, and the probability of a word $x = x_1 x_2 \cdots x_n \in A^*$ is given by

$$\mathrm{Pr}_{\mathcal{Q}}(x) = \pi' \mu(x)\underline{1} = \pi' \mu(x_1)\mu(x_2) \cdots \mu(x_n)\underline{1}$$

Also in this case, $\mathrm{Pr}_{\mathcal{Q}}$ is a rational formal series, taking on values in $[0, 1]$, that admits the linear representation $\langle \pi, \mu, \underline{1} \rangle$ and defines a probability function over A^n, for every positive integer n. Furthermore, it is easy to see that $\mathrm{Pr}_{\mathcal{Q}}$ is a rational probability measure on A^*. Actually, that is a characterization of the sequential models, in the sense that, as proved in [10], for every rational probability measure f on A^* there exists a sequential model $\mathcal{Q}$ such that $f = \mathrm{Pr}_{\mathcal{Q}}$.

Analogously, one can define the underlying Markov chain on the set of states $Q = \{1, 2, \ldots, k\}$ with initial vector π and transition matrix M. We say that the sequential model is primitive if M is a primitive matrix; if further π is the stationary vector then the model is said to be stationary too. Moreover, the pair $\mathcal{Q} = (\pi, \mu)$ can be interpreted as a finite state automaton equipped with probabilities associated with transitions; the main difference, with respect to the Markovian models, is that now the automaton is nondeterministic. For any $a \in A$, every non-null entry $\mu(a)_{ij}$ is the weight of the transition from i to j

labeled by a and, for every word x, $\mathrm{Pr}_Q(x)$ is the sum of the weights of all paths labeled by x in the corresponding transition diagram.

However, in spite of these similarities, the sequential models seem to be much more general than Markovian models. In particular, their probability functions do not satisfy Lemma 1. In fact, it is easy to find a sequential model Q such that $\mathrm{Pr}_Q(a^n) = \Theta(n\varepsilon^n)$ for some $a \in A$ and $0 < \varepsilon < 1$.

Further properties of sequential models concern the commutative image of the probability functions. Since Pr_Q is rational, also its commutative image $\Phi(\mathrm{Pr}_Q)$ is rational in $\mathbb{R}[\![A]\!]$; such a series is given by $\Phi(\mathrm{Pr}_Q) = \pi'(I - \sum_{a \in A} \mu(a)a)^{-1}\underline{1}$ and it represents the generating function of the probabilities of occurrences of symbols in A. In other words, setting $A = \{a_1, a_2, \ldots, a_s\}$, we have

$$\Phi(\mathrm{Pr}_Q) \;=\; \sum_{i \in \mathbb{N}^s} \; \sum_{|x|_{a_1}=i_1,\ldots,|x|_{a_s}=i_s} \mathrm{Pr}_Q(x)\, a_1^{i_1} \cdots a_s^{i_s}\,.$$

3.3   Rational Models

Consider a rational formal series $r \in \mathbb{R}_+\langle\!\langle A \rangle\!\rangle$ and, for every positive integer n, assume $r(w) \neq 0$ for some $w \in A^n$. Then r defines a probability function over A^n, given by

$$\mathrm{Pr}_r(x) = \frac{r(x)}{\sum_{w \in A^n} r(w)} \qquad \text{for every } x \in A^n\,. \tag{2}$$

Observe that if r is the characteristic series χ_L of a regular language $L \subseteq A^*$, then Pr_r represents the uniform probability function over $L \cap A^n$, for each n.

Since r is rational it admits a linear representation (ξ, μ, η) and hence

$$\mathrm{Pr}_r(x) = \frac{\xi'\mu(x)\eta}{\xi'M^n\eta} \qquad \text{for every } x \in A^n, \tag{3}$$

where $M = \sum_{a \in A} \mu(a)$. Thus any linear representation (ξ, μ, η) defines a rational model; we say that the model is primitive if M is a primitive matrix. Also observe that Pr_r is a sort of Hadamard division of two rational formal series. Well-known algorithms for the generation of random words in regular languages can be easily modified in order to compute, for an input $n \in \mathbb{N}$, a word x with probability $\mathrm{Pr}_r(x)$ [12,13].

It is clear that every sequential model over A is a rational model over the same alphabet. However, $\Phi(\mathrm{Pr}_r)$ is not always a rational series. As shown in [5], such a function may even be non-holonomic (and hence transcendental). This occurs for rather simple r as, for instance, the characteristic series of the language $(b+ab)^*$. The key property here is that the Hadamard division of two rational series is not necessarily rational. This proves that the rational models are a proper extension of the sequential models.

Thus, we can summarize the discussion presented in this section by the following statement.

Proposition 2. *The chain of inclusions*

$$\text{Markovian models} \subset \text{Sequential models} \subset \text{Rational models}$$

is strict. Moreover, the Markovian models strictly include the Bernoullian models and can generate the Markovian sequences of order m, for every integer $m \geq 1$.

4   Average Number of Pattern Occurrences

In this section we evaluate the average number of occurrences of a pattern $w \in A^*$ in a string $x \in A^*$ of length n, generated at random in a rational model, assuming that the corresponding series admits a primitive linear representation.

Let (ξ, μ, η) be a linear representation of size m over the alphabet A as defined in Section 2. We assume the matrix $M = \sum_{a \in A} \mu(a)$ is primitive. Let λ be its Perron-Frobenius eigenvalue and denote by v and u, respectively, the left and right (strictly positive) eigenvector of M corresponding to λ such that $v'u = 1$. We know (see for instance [6]) that for every $n \in \mathbb{N}$

$$M^n = \lambda^n(uv' + C(n)) \tag{4}$$

where $C(n)$ is a real matrix such that $C(n) = O(\varepsilon^n)$, for some $0 < \varepsilon < 1$. Thus, we can define the matrix $C = \sum_{n=0}^{+\infty} C(n)$, which turns out to be an analogous of the fundamental matrix in Markov chains [8, Sect. 4.3]. In fact, the following identities are easy to prove:

$$C = \left(I - \left(\frac{M}{\lambda} - uv'\right)\right)^{-1} - uv' , \quad v'C = Cu = 0 ,$$

$$CM = MC = \lambda(C - I + uv') , \quad \sum_{n=0}^{+\infty} nC(n) = \frac{CMC}{\lambda} = C^2 - C .$$

Now, let $w \in A^*$ be a pattern of length $m \geq 1$ and let $x \in A^*$ be a word of length $n \geq m$, generated at random in the rational model defined by the linear representation (ξ, μ, η). We can consider the random variable O_n representing the number of occurrences of w in x, i.e. $O_n = |x|_w$. Clearly, O_n takes on values in $\{0, 1, \ldots, n - m + 1\}$ and for each i in that set we have

$$\Pr(O_n = i) = \sum_{y \in A^n, |y|_w = i} \frac{\xi'\mu(y)\eta}{\xi'M^n\eta}$$

Setting $x = x_1 \cdots x_n$ with $x_i \in A$ for each i, we can consider O_n as a sum of random variables of the form

$$O_n = I_m + I_{m+1} + \cdots + I_n \tag{5}$$

where, for every $j = m, m+1, \ldots, n$

$$I_j = \begin{cases} 1 \text{ if } x_1 x_2 \cdots x_j \in A^* w \\ 0 \text{ otherwise} \end{cases}$$

Note that each I_j is a Bernoullian random variable such that

$$\Pr(I_j = 1) = \frac{\xi' M^{j-m} \mu(w) M^{n-j} \eta}{\xi' M^n \eta}$$

Proposition 3. *Let O_n be the number of occurrences of a nonempty pattern $w \in A^m$ in a string of length $n \geq m$ generated at random in a rational model defined by a primitive linear representation (ξ, μ, η) of size m. Then, its average value is given by*

$$E(O_n) = \beta(n - m + 1) + a + b + O(\varepsilon^n) , \qquad (|\varepsilon| < 1)$$

where β, a and b are real constants defined by

$$\beta = \frac{v' \mu(w) u}{\lambda^m}, \quad a = \frac{\xi' C \mu(w) u}{\lambda^m \xi' u}, \quad b = \frac{v' \mu(w) C \eta}{\lambda^m v' \eta}$$

with λ, v, u and C defined as above.

Proof. From (4) it is easy to derive the equations

$$\xi' M^n \eta = \lambda^n (\xi' u v' \eta + O(\varepsilon^n)) \tag{6}$$

and

$$\sum_{j=m}^{n} \xi' M^{j-m} \mu(w) M^{n-j} \eta =$$

$$\lambda^{n-m} \left\{ \xi' \left[(n - m + 1) u v' \mu(w) u v' + C \mu(w) u v' + u v' \mu(w) C \right] \eta + O(\varepsilon^n) \right\} \tag{7}$$

Thus, the result follows by replacing the right hand sides of (6) and (7) into the expression

$$E(O_n) = \sum_{j=m}^{n} \frac{\xi' M^{j-m} \mu(w) M^{n-j} \eta}{\xi' M^n \eta}$$

As a comment to the previous result we now make the following remarks:

1. If $m = 1$ the pattern w is reduced to an element of A and we get the average number of symbol occurrences in a primitive rational model obtained in [4].
2. If (ξ, μ, η) is a sequential model then M is a stochastic matrix. Therefore, $\lambda = 1$, $\eta = u = \underline{1}$ and v is the stationary distribution of the underlying Markov chain, here defined by the initial vector ξ and the transition matrix M. As a consequence, we also have $C\eta = 0$, and hence

$$E(O_n) = v' \mu(w) \underline{1} (n - m + 1) + \xi' C \mu(w) \underline{1} + O(\varepsilon^n). \tag{8}$$

In this case the leading constant $\beta = v' \mu(w) \underline{1}$ is the probability of generating w in the stationary sequential model (v, μ) (i.e. a sort of stationary probability of w).

3. If (ξ, μ, η) is a stationary sequential model (i.e. $\xi = v$), then $\xi'C = 0$ and we get

$$E(O_n) = v'\mu(w)\underline{1}\,(n - m + 1)\,, \tag{9}$$

which is the equation obtained in [1] (see also [2] Eq. (7.2.25)) in a stationary (primitive) Markovian model of order 1. Thus, our proposition extends the same equality to all stationary (primitive) sequential models.

4. Note that Equation (9) is not true if the sequential model is not stationary (i.e. $\xi \neq v$); in this case constant $\xi'C\mu(w)\underline{1}$ of Equation (8) is not null in general. This means that the stationarity hypothesis is necessary to get (9), even in the Markovian models of order 1.

5   Analysis of the Variance

In this section we study the variance of O_n under the same assumptions of the previous section. Our goal is to determine an asymptotic expression of the form $Var(O_n) = \gamma n + O(1)$ where γ is a real constant depending on the pattern w and the linear representation (ξ, μ, η).

It turns out that γ is also related to the autocorrelation set of w, a classical notion we here define following the approach proposed in [2]. Assume $w = w_1 \cdots w_m$, where $w_i \in A$ for each i. For every $1 \leq i \leq j \leq m$ let $w_i^j \in A^+$ be given by $w_i^j = w_i \cdots w_j$. Then, we define the set of indices S and the matrix $P(w)$ given by

$$S = \{k \in \{1, 2, \ldots, m - 1\} \mid w_1^k = w_{m-k+1}^m\}\,, \quad P(w) = \sum_{k \in S} \lambda^k \mu(w_{k+1}^m)$$

Clearly, if $m = 1$ then $S = \emptyset$ and $P(w) = 0$.

Proposition 4. *Under the assumptions of Proposition 3 we have*

$$Var(O_n) = \gamma n + c + O(\varepsilon^n)\,, \qquad (|\varepsilon| < 1)$$

where γ and c are real constants, the first one being given by

$$\gamma = \beta - (2m - 1)\beta^2 + 2\frac{v'\mu(w)\,[C\mu(w) + P(w)]\,u}{\lambda^{2m}} \tag{10}$$

Proof. By Equation (5) and Proposition 3 we have

$$E(O_n^2) = \sum_{j=m}^{n} E(I_j^2) + 2\sum_{i=m}^{n-1}\sum_{j=i+1}^{n} E(I_i I_j) =$$
$$= (n - m - 1)\beta + a + b +$$
$$+ 2\sum_{i=m}^{n-m}\sum_{j=i+m}^{n} E(I_i I_j) + 2\sum_{i=m}^{n-1}\sum_{j=i+1}^{\min\{i+m-1,n\}} E(I_i I_j) \tag{11}$$

Observe that $E(I_iI_j)$ is easy to evaluate when $i + m \leq j$ since in this case there is no overlap in the occurrences of w at positions i and j. Hence, for every $i = m, \ldots, n - m$ and every $j = i + m, \ldots, n$, we have

$$E(I_iI_j) = \Pr(I_i = 1, I_j = 1) = \frac{\xi' M^{i-m}\mu(w)M^{j-m-i}\mu(w)M^{n-j}\eta}{\xi' M^n \eta}$$

Thus, replacing (4) in the previous equation, by some computation one obtains

$$2 \sum_{i=m}^{n-m} \sum_{j=i+m}^{n} E(I_iI_j) =$$

$$= n^2\beta^2 + n\left(2\beta(a+b) - \beta^2(4m-3) + 2\frac{v'\mu(w)C\mu(w)u}{\lambda^{2m}}\right) + O(1) \quad (12)$$

Now consider the last sum in the right hand side of (11); this term exists only if $m > 1$ and in this case (being $m \notin S$) it can be proved that

$$2 \sum_{i=m}^{n-1} \sum_{j=i+1}^{\min\{i+m-1,n\}} E(I_iI_j) = 2 \sum_{i=m}^{n-m+1} \sum_{k \in S} E(I_iI_{i+m-k}) + O(1)$$

Again applying (4) we get

$$2 \sum_{i=m}^{n-m+1} \sum_{k \in S} E(I_iI_{i+m-k}) = 2n\frac{v'\mu(w)P(w)u}{\lambda^{2m}} + O(1) \quad (13)$$

Thus, replacing (12) and (13) in (11) and recalling that $Var(O_n) = E(O_n^2) - E(O_n)^2$, the result follows.

Now, let us discuss the previous result in some special cases.

1. In the case $m = 1$ we get the same evaluation of the variance obtained in [4], with $\gamma = \beta - \beta^2 + 2(v'\mu(w)C\mu(w)u)/\lambda^2$.
2. If (ξ, μ, η) is a sequential model (and hence $\beta = v'\mu(w)\underline{1}$) we get

$$\gamma = \beta - (2m-1)\beta^2 + 2v'\mu(w)\left[C\mu(w) + \sum_{k \in S}\mu(w_{k+1}^m)\right]\underline{1}$$

which generalizes and extends the evaluation of the leading term of the variance obtained in [1] in stationary (primitive) Markovian models of order 1(see also [2, Th. 7.2.8]).
3. If (ξ, μ, η) is just a Markovian model of order 1, Equation (10) is equivalent to Equation (7.2.27) in [2]. Note that the leading term γ does not depend on the initial distribution ξ and is the same as in the stationary case.

4. Also the constant c can be computed explicitly as a function of w and (ξ, μ, η). In particular, in the sequential model, reasoning as in Proposition 4 one gets

$$c = (3m^2 - 4m + 1)\beta^2 - 2(2m - 1)v'\mu(w)C\mu(w)\underline{1} - 2v'\mu(w)CMC\mu(w)\underline{1} +$$

$$-(m - 1)\beta - 2(m - 1)v'\mu(w)P(w)\underline{1} + 2v'\mu(w) \sum_{\ell=2}^{m-1} \sum_{k \in S, k \geq \ell} \mu(w_{k+1}^m)\underline{1} +$$

$$+a - a^2 - 2\beta\xi'CMC\mu(w)\underline{1} + 2\xi'C\mu(w)C\mu(w)\underline{1} + 2\xi'C\mu(w)P(w)\underline{1} .$$

Note that, as for the average value, the constant term of the variance depends on the initial distribution ξ. If the sequential model is stationary, the above expression of c further simplifies and the equation reduces to the first two rows, all terms of the third one being null. Hence, the terms in the third row represent the contribution given to the variance by the non-stationary hypothesis.

References

1. Régnier, M., Szpankowski, W.: On pattern frequency occurrences in a Markovian sequence. Algorithmica 22, 631–649 (1998)
2. Jacket, P., Szpankowski, W.: Analytic approach to pattern matching. In: Lothaire, M. (ed.) Applied Combinatorics on Words. Encyclopedia of Mathematics and its Applications, vol. 105, Cambridge University Press, Cambridge (2005)
3. Nicodème, P., Salvy, B., Flajolet, P.: Motif statistics. Theoret. Comput. Sci. 287, 593–617 (2002) Algorithms (Prague, 1999)
4. Bertoni, A., Choffrut, C., Goldwurm, M., Lonati, V.: On the number of occurrences of a symbol in words of regular languages. Theoret. Comput. Sci. 302, 431–456 (2003)
5. Goldwurm, M., Radicioni, R.: Probabilistic models for pattern statistics. Theor. Inform. Appl. 40, 207–225 (2006)
6. Seneta, E.: Non-negative matrices and Markov chains. Springer Series in Statistics. Springer, New York (2006)
7. Gantmacher, F.R.: The theory of matrices. Translated by K.A. Hirsch, vol. 2. Chelsea Publishing Co., New York (1959)
8. Iosifescu, M.: Finite Markov processes and their applications. Wiley Series in Probability and Mathematical Statistics. John Wiley & Sons Ltd., Chichester (1980)
9. Berstel, J., Reutenauer, C.: Rational series and their languages. EATCS Monographs on Theoretical Computer Science, vol. 12. Springer, Berlin (1988)
10. Hansel, G., Perrin, D.: Rational probability measures. Theoret. Comput. Sci. 65, 171–188 (1989)
11. Paz, A.: Introduction to probabilistic automata. Academic Press, New York (1971)
12. Flajolet, P., Zimmerman, P., Van Cutsem, B.: A calculus for the random generation of labelled combinatorial structures. Theoret. Comput. Sci. 132, 1–35 (1994)
13. Denise, A.: Génération aléatoire uniforme de mots de langages rationnels. Theoret. Comput. Sci. 159, 43–63 (1996) Selected papers from the "GASCOM '94" (Talence, 1994) and the "Polyominoes and Tilings" (Toulouse, 1994) Workshops.

Weighted Automata and Weighted Logics with Discounting

Manfred Droste[1] and George Rahonis[2]

[1] Institute of Computer Science, Leipzig University
D-04009 Leipzig, Germany
droste@informatik.uni-leipzig.de
[2] Department of Mathematics, Aristotle University of Thessaloniki
54124 Thessaloniki, Greece
grahonis@math.auth.gr

Abstract. We introduce a weighted logic with discounting and we establish Büchi's and Elgot's theorem for weighted automata over finite words and arbitrary commutative semirings. Then we investigate Büchi and Muller automata with discounting over the max-plus and the min-plus semiring. We show their expressive equivalence with weighted MSO-sentences with discounting. In this case our logic has a purely syntactic definition. For the finite case, we obtain a purely syntactically defined weighted logic if the underlying semiring is additively locally finite.

Keywords: weighted automata, weighted Büchi and Muller automata, formal power series, weighted MSO logic, discounting.

1 Introduction

In automata theory, Büchi's and Elgot's fundamental theorems [3,4,14] established the coincidence of regular languages of finite or infinite words with languages definable in monadic second-order logic. At the same time, Schützenberger [34] characterized the behaviors of finite automata enriched with weights for the transitions as rational formal power series. Both of these results have led to various extensions and also to practical applications, e.g. in verification of finite state programs [1,26,29], in digital image compression [5,18,19] and in speech-to-text processing [21,31]. For surveys and monographs on weighted automata see [2,23,25,33]. Recently, in [9] a logic with weights was developed for finite words and shown to be expressively equivalent to weighted automata.

It is the goal of this paper to provide a weighted logic for infinite words which is again expressively equivalent to weighted automata, thereby combining Büchi's and Schützenberger's approaches to achieve a quantitative model for non-terminating behavior. Whereas in the results of [9] for finite words the weights can be taken in an arbitrary semiring, it is clear that for weighted automata on infinite words questions of summability and convergence arise. Therefore we assume that the weights are taken in the real numbers, and we ensure convergence of infinite sums by discounting: in a path, later transitions get less

Jan Holub and Jan Žďárek (Eds.): CIAA 2007, LNCS 4783, pp. 73–84, 2007.

weight. This method of discounting is classical in mathematical economics for systems with non-terminating behavior, also in Markov decision processes and game theory [16,35]. Recently, for a theory of systems engineering, it was investigated in [8]. For weighted automata, it was introduced in [10], and the discounting behaviors of weighted Büchi automata were characterized as the ω-rational formal power series; this was further investigated in [15,24]. As semirings, here we consider the max-plus and the min-plus semiring which are fundamental in max-plus algebra [7,17] and algebraic optimization problems [38].

As our main contributions, we will:

(1) extend the weighted logic of [9] to weighted automata with discounting for finite words and arbitrary commutative semirings as investigated in [10,15,24]; our present form of discounting is slightly more general;

(2) provide for the max-plus and min-plus semirings of real numbers a weighted logic with discounting which is expressively equivalent to the weighted Büchi automata on infinite words of [10]; we will also show equivalence to weighted Muller automata;

(3) show that for a large class of semirings, a purely syntactically defined fragment of the weighted logics suffices to achieve the equivalences of (1) and (2).

In our approach, it was not clear how to define a discounted semantics of weighted formulas. Somewhat surprisingly, we can almost completely take over the *undiscounted* semantics as given in [9], changing only the semantics of the universal quantifier. For the general result of [9], the weighted formula employed require certain semantically described restrictions; clearly, a purely syntactic definition would be desirable. In (3), we present a new, purely syntactic definition of a class of weighted formulas and show that they are expressively equivalent to the weighted automata with discounting of (1) and (2). For these formulas, the equivalent automata can be constructed effectively. Our arguments combine the methods of [9,10,11], suitably adjusted to the discounted setting.

We note that a different approach of weighted automata acting on infinite words has been considered before in connection with digital image processing by Culik and Karhumäki [6]. Another approach requires the semirings to be *complete*, i.e., to have (built-in) infinitary sum and product operations. This was investigated deeply e.g. in [13,23,15]. Recently, in [11] we presented weighted Büchi and Muller automata and a weighted logics for complete semirings and showed their expressive equivalence. The present paper shows the robustness of the weighted logics approach also for infinite words in case of discounting. For weighted logics and automata on trees, pictures, traces and texts we refer the reader to [12,27,28,30]. Due to space limitations, almost all proofs are left out here; they are contained in the full version of the paper.

2   Weighted Automata with Discounting

Let A be a finite alphabet. The set of all finite (resp. infinite) words over A is denoted as usually by A^* (resp. A^ω). We let ε denote the empty word. The length of a finite word w is denoted by $|w|$. If w is finite (resp. infinite) for any $0 \le i \le |w|$ (resp. $i \ge 0$) we shall denote by $w_{\le i}$ the finite prefix of w with length i. Obviously $w_{\le 0} = \varepsilon$.

A *semiring* $(K, +, \cdot, 0, 1)$ (denoted simply also by K) is called *commutative* if $a \cdot b = b \cdot a$ for all $a, b \in K$. The following structures constitute important examples of commutative semirings: the semiring $(\mathbb{N}, +, \cdot, 0, 1)$ of *natural numbers*; the *arctic semiring* or *max-plus semiring* $\mathbb{R}_{\max} = (\mathbb{R}_+ \cup \{-\infty\}, \max, +, -\infty, 0)$ where $\mathbb{R}_+ = \{r \in \mathbb{R} \mid r \ge 0\}$ and $-\infty + x = -\infty$ for each $x \in \mathbb{R}_+$; the *tropical* or *min-plus semiring* $\mathbb{R}_{\min} = (\mathbb{R}_+ \cup \{\infty\}, \min, +, \infty, 0)$; each bounded distributive lattice with the operations supremum and infimum, in particular the *fuzzy semiring* $([0, 1], \sup, \inf, 0, 1)$ and the *Boolean semiring* $\mathbf{B} = (\{0, 1\}, \vee, \wedge, 0, 1)$.

The semiring K is called *additively locally finite* if each finitely generated submonoid of $(K, +, 0)$ is finite. Important examples of such semirings include: all idempotent semirings, in particular the arctic and the tropical semirings and all bounded distributive lattices; all fields of characteristic p, for any prime p; all products $K_1 \times \cdots \times K_n$ (with operations defined pointwise) of additively locally finite semirings K_i $(1 \le i \le n)$; the semiring of polynomials $(K[X], +, \cdot, 0, 1)$ over a variable X and an additively locally finite semiring K.

A homomorphism $f : K \to K$ is an *endomorphism* of K. The set $End(K)$ of all endomorphisms of K is a monoid with operation the usual composition mapping $\circ$ and unit element the identity mapping id on K. If no confusion arises, we shall simply denote the operation $\cdot$ of K and the composition operation $\circ$ of $End(K)$ by concatenation.

Example 1. Let $K = \mathbb{R}_{\max}$, the max-plus semiring. Choose any $p \in \mathbb{R}_+$ and put $p \cdot (-\infty) = -\infty$. Then the mapping $\overline{p} : \mathbb{R}_{\max} \to \mathbb{R}_{\max}$ given by $x \longmapsto p \cdot x$ is an endomorphism of $\mathbb{R}_{\max}$ which can be considered as a discounting of $\mathbb{R}_{\max}$. Conversely, every endomorphism of $\mathbb{R}_{\max}$ is of this form (cf. [10]). The same result can be proved for $\mathbb{R}_{\min}$ where $p \cdot \infty = \infty$.

A Φ-*discounting over A and K* is a family $\Phi = (\Phi_a)_{a \in A}$ of endomorphisms of K, i.e. $\Phi_a \in End(K)$ for all $a \in A$. Then Φ induces a monoid morphism $\Phi : A^* \to End(K)$ determined by $\Phi(w) = \Phi_{a_0} \circ \Phi_{a_1} \circ \cdots \circ \Phi_{a_{n-1}}$ for any $w = a_0 a_1 \cdots a_{n-1} \in A^+, (a_i \in A$ for $0 \le i \le n - 1)$, and $\Phi(\varepsilon) = id$. We shall use the notation $\Phi_w = \Phi(w)$ for any $w \in A^*$. In particular, due to Example 1, for $K = \mathbb{R}_{\max}$ (or $\mathbb{R}_{\min}$), a Φ'-discounting over A and $\mathbb{R}_{\max}$ will be of the form $\Phi' = (\overline{p_a})_{a \in A}$ where $0 \le p_a < 1$ for all $a \in A$. For any finite word $w = a_0 a_1 \cdots a_{n-1} \in A^+$ $(a_i \in A$ for $0 \le i \le n - 1)$ we put $p_w = \prod_{a \in A} p_a^{|w|_a}$ where $|w|_a$ denotes the number of a's in w. Then $\Phi'_w(x) = p_w \cdot x$ for each $x \in \mathbb{R}_{\max}$. Note that if $m_{\Phi'} = \max\{p_a \mid a \in A\}$ then $0 \le m_{\Phi'} < 1$ and $p_w \le m_{\Phi'}^{|w|}$ for each $w \in A^*$.

A *finitary* (resp. *infinitary*) *formal power series* or *series* for short is a mapping $S : A^* \to K$ (resp. $S : A^\omega \to \mathbb{R}_{\max}$). The class of all finitary (resp. infinitary) series over A and K (resp. $\mathbb{R}_{\max}$) is denoted by $K\langle\langle A^* \rangle\rangle$ (resp. $\mathbb{R}_{\max}\langle\langle A^\omega \rangle\rangle)$. We refer the reader to [13,23] for notions and results on finitary series, and to [11,15] for infinitary ones.

For the rest of the paper we fix a finite alphabet A, *a semiring* K *and a* Φ-*discounting (resp.* Φ'-*discounting) over* A *and* K *(resp.* $\mathbb{R}_{\max}$*).*

Definition 2. *A weighted automaton over* A *and* K *is a quadruple* $\mathcal{A} = (Q, in, wt, out)$, *where* Q *is the finite state set,* $in : Q \to K$ *is the initial distribution,* $wt : Q \times A \times Q \to K$ *is a mapping assigning weights to the transitions of the automaton, and* $out : Q \to K$ *is the final distribution.*

Now we define the Φ-behavior of $\mathcal{A}$ as follows. Given a word $w = a_0 a_1 \cdots a_{n-1} \in A^*$, a *path of* $\mathcal{A}$ *over* w is a finite sequence of transitions $P_w := (t_i)_{0 \le i \le n-1}$ so that $t_i = (q_i, a_i, q_{i+1})$ for all $0 \le i \le n-1$. We define the *running weight* $rwt(P_w)$ of P_w by $rwt(P_w) = \prod_{0 \le i \le n-1} \Phi_{w \le i}(wt(t_i))$. Then the Φ-*weight* (or simply *weight*) of P_w is the value $weight(P_w) := in(q_0) \cdot rwt(P_w) \cdot \Phi_w(out(q_n))$. The Φ-*behavior* (or simply *behavior*) of $\mathcal{A}$ is the formal power series $\|\mathcal{A}\| : A^* \to K$ whose coefficients are given by $(\|\mathcal{A}\|, w) = \sum_{P_w} weight(P_w)$ for any $w \in A^*$.

A series $S : A^* \to K$ is said to be Φ-*recognizable* if there is a weighted automaton $\mathcal{A}$ over A and K so that $S = \|\mathcal{A}\|$. We shall denote by $K^{\Phi-rec} \langle\langle A^* \rangle\rangle$ the class of all Φ-recognizable series over A and K. A power series $S : A^* \to K$ is called a *recognizable step function* if $S = \sum_{1 \le j \le n} k_j 1_{L_j}$ where $k_j \in K$ and $L_j \subseteq A^*$ $(1 \le j \le n$ and $n \in \mathbb{N})$ are recognizable languages.

For intuition, note that if $K = \mathbb{R}_{\max}$ and $\Phi_a = \overline{p_a}$ for some $p_a \in (0, 1)$ $(a \in A)$, say, as in Example 1, then in the computation of $rwt(P_w)$ later transitions get less weight, hence $\|\mathcal{A}\|$ models a discounted behavior of $\mathcal{A}$. If Φ is the *trivial* discounting, i.e. Φ_a is the identity on K for each $a \in A$, then the Φ-behavior coincides with the usual behavior of weighted automata.

By standard arguments (cf. [13]) we can show that:

(a) the class of Φ-recognizable series (resp. recognizable step functions) is closed under sum and scalar products; furthermore, if K is commutative, then it is closed under Hadamard products;

(b) given two finite alphabets A, B and a strict alphabetic homomorphism $h : A^* \to B^*$, i.e. such that $h(A) \subseteq B$, then $h : K \langle\langle A^* \rangle\rangle \to K \langle\langle B^* \rangle\rangle$ and $h^{-1} : K \langle\langle B^* \rangle\rangle \to K \langle\langle A^* \rangle\rangle$ preserve Φ-recognizability;

(c) if $L \subseteq A^*$ is a recognizable language then its characteristic series $1_L \in K \langle\langle A^* \rangle\rangle$ is Φ-recogizable. The next result is new and its proof is non-trivial.

Proposition 3. *Let* K *be additively locally finite. Let* A, B *be two finite alphabets and* $h : A^* \to B^*$ *be a strict alphabetic homomorphism. If* $S \in K \langle\langle A^* \rangle\rangle$ *is a recognizable step function then* $h(S) \in K \langle\langle B^* \rangle\rangle$ *is also a recognizable step function.*

Next, we turn to weighted automata over infinite words. More precisely, we present two automata models acting on infinite words. Weighted Büchi automata with discounting were introduced and investigated in [10]. Here we define this model in a slightly more general form. On the other hand, weighted Muller automata were studied in [11] in connection to weighted MSO logics over infinite words. Our Muller automaton model here is equipped with a discounting Φ' so that convergence problems will not be encountered. The max-plus semiring $\mathbb{R}_{\max}$ and the min-plus semiring $\mathbb{R}_{\min}$ will be our underlying semirings. But now we intend to compute over infinite words, hence we will use sup and inf instead of max and min, respectively. The problem of summing up infinitely many factors will be faced by using a discounting parameter.

Definition 4. *(a) A weighted Muller automaton (WMA for short) over A and $\mathbb{R}_{\max}$ is a quadruple $\mathcal{A} = (Q, in, wt, \mathcal{F})$, where Q is the finite state set, $in : Q \rightarrow \mathbb{R}_{\max}$ is the initial distribution, $wt : Q \times A \times Q \rightarrow \mathbb{R}_{\max}$ is a mapping assigning weights to the transitions of the automaton, and $\mathcal{F} \subseteq \mathcal{P}(Q)$ is the family of final state sets.*

(b) A WMA $\mathcal{A}$ is a weighted Büchi automaton (WBA for short) if there is a set $F \subseteq Q$ such that $\mathcal{F} = \{S \subseteq Q \mid S \cap F \neq \emptyset\}$.

Given an infinite word $w = a_0 a_1 \cdots \in A^\omega$, a *path* P_w of $\mathcal{A}$ over w is an infinite sequence of transitions $P_w := (t_i)_{i \geq 0}$, so that $t_i = (q_i, a_i, q_{i+1})$ for all $i \geq 0$. The Φ'-*weight of* P_w (or simply *weight*) is the value $weight(P_w) := in(q_0) + \sum_{i \geq 0} p_{w_{\leq i}} \cdot wt(t_i)$. Observe that this infinite sum converges; its value is bounded by $M \cdot \sum_{i \geq 0} m_{\Phi'}^i = M \cdot 1/(1 - m_{\Phi'})$, where $M = max\{wt(t) \mid t \in Q \times A \times Q\}$. We denote by $In^Q(P_w)$ the set of states that appear infinitely many times in P_w, i.e., $In^Q(P_w) = \{q \in Q \mid \exists^\omega i : t_i = (q, a_i, q_{i+1})\}$. The path P_w is called *successful* if the set of states that appear infinitely often along P_w constitute a final state set, i.e., $In^Q(P_w) \in \mathcal{F}$. The Φ'-*behavior* (or simply *behavior*) of $\mathcal{A}$ is the infinitary power series $\|\mathcal{A}\| : A^\omega \rightarrow \mathbb{R}_{\max}$ with coefficients specified for $w \in A^\omega$ by $(\|\mathcal{A}\|, w) = \sup_{P_w}(weight(P_w))$ where the supremum is taken over all successful paths P_w of $\mathcal{A}$ over w. Again, this supremum exists in $\mathbb{R}_{\max}$ since the values $weight(P_w)$ are uniformly bounded.

A series $S : A^\omega \rightarrow \mathbb{R}_{\max}$ is called Φ'-*Muller recognizable* (resp. Φ'-*Büchi recognizable* or Φ'-ω-*recognizable*) if there is a WMA (resp. WBA) $\mathcal{A}$, such that $S = \|\mathcal{A}\|$. The class of all Φ'-Muller recognizable (resp. Φ'-ω-recognizable series) over A and $\mathbb{R}_{\max}$ is denoted by $\mathbb{R}_{\max}^{\Phi'-M-rec} \langle\langle A^\omega \rangle\rangle$ (resp. $\mathbb{R}_{\max}^{\Phi'-\omega-rec} \langle\langle A^\omega \rangle\rangle$). We will call an infinitary series $S : A^\omega \rightarrow \mathbb{R}_{\max}$ *Muller recognizable step function* (or ω-*recognizable step function*) if $S = \max_{1 \leq j \leq n} (k_j + 1_{L_j})$ where $k_j \in \mathbb{R}_{\max}$ and $L_j \subseteq A^\omega$ ($1 \leq j \leq n$ and $n \in \mathbb{N}$) are ω-recognizable languages.

Droste and Kuske [10] considered WBA over $\mathbb{R}_{\max}$ where $p_a = p$ ($0 \leq p < 1$) for any $a \in A$. Our first main result (in the next theorem) can be proved using similar arguments as in Theorem 25 in [11].

Theorem 5. $\mathbb{R}_{\max}^{\Phi'-\omega-rec} \langle\langle A^\omega \rangle\rangle = \mathbb{R}_{\max}^{\Phi'-M-rec} \langle\langle A^\omega \rangle\rangle$.

The next proposition refers to closure properties of Φ'-ω-recognizable series and ω-recognizable step functions.

Proposition 6. *(a) The class* $\mathbb{R}_{\max}^{\Phi'-\omega-rec}\langle\langle A^\omega\rangle\rangle$ *(resp. of ω-recognizable step functions) is closed under max, scalar sum and sum.*
(b) Let A, B be two alphabets, $h : A^\omega \to B^\omega$ be a strict alphabetic homomorphism and $S \in \mathbb{R}_{\max}\langle\langle A^\omega\rangle\rangle$ be a Φ'-ω-recognizable series (resp. ω-recognizable step function). Then $h(S) \in \mathbb{R}_{\max}\langle\langle B^\omega\rangle\rangle$ is Φ'-recognizable (resp. ω-recognizable step function). Furthermore, $h^{-1} : \mathbb{R}_{\max}\langle\langle B^\omega\rangle\rangle \to \mathbb{R}_{\max}\langle\langle A^\omega\rangle\rangle$ preserves Φ'-ω-recognizability.
(c) Let $L \subseteq A^\omega$ be an ω-recognizable language. Then its characteristic series $1_L \in \mathbb{R}_{\max}\langle\langle A^\omega\rangle\rangle$ is Φ'-ω-recognizable.

3   Weighted MSO Logic with Discounting

In this section, we introduce our weighted monadic second order logic with discounting (weighted MSO logic with discounting, for short) and we interpret the semantics of MSO-formulas in this logic as formal power series. Let $\mathcal{V}$ be a finite set of first and second order variables. A word $w \in A^*$ (resp. $w \in A^\omega$) is represented by the relational structure $(dom(w), \leq, (R_a)_{a \in A})$ where $dom(w) = \{0, \ldots, |w| - 1\}$ (resp. $dom(w) = \omega = \{0, 1, 2, \ldots\}$), $\leq$ is the natural order and $R_a = \{i \mid w(i) = a\}$ for $a \in A$. A $(w, \mathcal{V})$-*assignment* σ is a mapping associating first order variables from $\mathcal{V}$ to elements of $dom(w)$, and second order variables from $\mathcal{V}$ to subsets of $dom(w)$. If x is a first order variable and $i \in dom(w)$, then $\sigma[x \to i]$ denotes the $(w, \mathcal{V} \cup \{x\})$-assignment which associates i to x and acts as σ on $\mathcal{V} \setminus \{x\}$. For a second order variable X and $I \subseteq dom(w)$, the notation $\sigma[X \to I]$ has a similar meaning.

In order to encode pairs (w, σ) for all $w \in A^*$ (resp. $w \in A^\omega$) and any $(w, \mathcal{V})$-assignment σ, we use an extended alphabet $A_\mathcal{V} = A \times \{0, 1\}^\mathcal{V}$. Each pair (w, σ) is a word in $A_\mathcal{V}^*$ (resp. in $A_\mathcal{V}^\omega$) where w is the projection over A and σ is the projection over $\{0, 1\}^\mathcal{V}$. Then σ is a valid $(w, \mathcal{V})$-assignment if for each first order variable $x \in \mathcal{V}$ the x-row contains exactly one 1. In this case, we identify σ with the $(w, \mathcal{V})$-assignment so that for each first order variable $x \in \mathcal{V}$, $\sigma(x)$ is the position of the 1 on the x-row, and for each second order variable $X \in \mathcal{V}$, $\sigma(X)$ is the set of positions labelled with 1 along the X-row.

It is well-known that the set $N_\mathcal{V} = \{(w, \sigma) \in A_\mathcal{V}^* \mid \sigma$ is a valid $(w, \mathcal{V})$-assignment$\}$ (resp. $N_\mathcal{V}^\omega = \{(w, \sigma) \in A_\mathcal{V}^\omega \mid \sigma$ is a valid $(w, \mathcal{V})$-assignment$\}$) is recognizable (resp. ω-recognizable).

Let φ be an MSO-formula [20,32,36,37]. Then Büchi's and Elgot's theorem [3,14] states that for $Free(\varphi) \subseteq \mathcal{V}$ the language $\mathcal{L}_\mathcal{V}(\varphi) = \{(w, \sigma) \in N_\mathcal{V} \mid (w, \sigma) \models \varphi\}$ defined by φ over $A_\mathcal{V}$ is recognizable. Conversely, each recognizable language $L \subseteq A^*$ is definable by an MSO-sentence φ, i.e., $L = \mathcal{L}(\varphi)$.

The fundamental Büchi's theorem [4] for infinite words proves that the language $\mathcal{L}_\mathcal{V}^\omega(\varphi) = \{(w, \sigma) \in N_\mathcal{V}^\omega \mid (w, \sigma) \models \varphi\}$ defined by φ over $A_\mathcal{V}$ is ω-recognizable. Conversely, each ω-recognizable language $L \subseteq A^\omega$ is definable by an MSO-sentence φ, i.e., $L = \mathcal{L}^\omega(\varphi)$.

We simply write $\mathcal{L}(\varphi) = \mathcal{L}_{Free(\varphi)}(\varphi)$ (resp. $\mathcal{L}^\omega(\varphi) = \mathcal{L}_{Free(\varphi)}^\omega(\varphi)$).

Now we turn to weighted MSO logic with discounting.

Definition 7. *The syntax of formulas of the weighted MSO logic with Φ-discounting over K is given by*

$$\varphi := k \mid P_a(x) \mid \neg P_a(x) \mid Last(x) \mid \neg Last(x) \mid S(x, y) \mid \neg S(x, y)$$
$$\mid x \in X \mid \neg(x \in X) \mid \varphi \vee \psi \mid \varphi \wedge \psi \mid \exists x . \varphi \mid \exists X . \varphi \mid \forall x . \varphi$$

where $k \in K$, $a \in A$. We shall denote by $MSO(K, A)$ the set of all such weighted MSO-formulas φ.

Definition 8. *Let $\varphi \in MSO(K, A)$ and V be a finite set of variables with $Free(\varphi) \subseteq V$. The Φ-semantics of φ is a formal power series $\|\varphi\|_V \in K \langle\langle A_V^* \rangle\rangle$. Consider an element $(w, \sigma) \in A_V^*$. If σ is not a valid assignment, then we put $\|\varphi\|_V (w, \sigma) = 0$. Otherwise, we inductively define $(\|\varphi\|_V, (w, \sigma)) \in K$ as follows:*

- $(\|k\|_V, (w, \sigma)) = k$
- $(\|P_a(x)\|_V, (w, \sigma)) = \begin{cases} 1 \text{ if } w(\sigma(x)) = a \\ 0 \text{ otherwise} \end{cases}$
- $(\|Last(x)\|_V, (w, \sigma)) = \begin{cases} 1 \text{ if } \sigma(x) = |w| - 1 \\ 0 \text{ otherwise} \end{cases}$
- $(\|S(x, y)\|_V, (w, \sigma)) = \begin{cases} 1 \text{ if } \sigma(x) + 1 = \sigma(y) \\ 0 \text{ otherwise} \end{cases}$
- $(\|x \in X\|_V, (w, \sigma)) = \begin{cases} 1 \text{ if } \sigma(x) \in \sigma(X) \\ 0 \text{ otherwise} \end{cases}$
- $(\|\neg\varphi\|_V, (w, \sigma)) = \begin{cases} 1 \text{ if } (\|\varphi\|_V, (w, \sigma)) = 0 \\ 0 \text{ if } (\|\varphi\|_V, (w, \sigma)) = 1 \end{cases}$, $\begin{array}{l} \text{provided that } \varphi \text{ is of} \\ \text{the form } P_a(x), \; Last(x), \\ S(x, y) \; or \; (x \in X) \end{array}$
- $(\|\varphi \vee \psi\|_V, (w, \sigma)) = (\|\varphi\|_V, (w, \sigma)) + (\|\psi\|_V, (w, \sigma))$
- $(\|\varphi \wedge \psi\|_V, (w, \sigma)) = (\|\varphi\|_V, (w, \sigma)) \cdot (\|\psi\|_V, (w, \sigma))$
- $(\|\exists x . \varphi\|_V, (w, \sigma)) = \displaystyle\sum_{i \in dom(w)} \left(\|\varphi\|_{V \cup \{x\}}, (w, \sigma[x \to i]) \right)$
- $(\|\exists X . \varphi\|_V, (w, \sigma)) = \displaystyle\sum_{I \subseteq dom(w)} \left(\|\varphi\|_{V \cup \{X\}}, (w, \sigma[X \to I]) \right)$
- $(\|\forall x . \varphi\|_V, (w, \sigma)) = \displaystyle\prod_{i \in dom(w)} \Phi_{w \leq i} \left(\left(\|\varphi\|_{V \cup \{x\}}, (w, \sigma[x \to i]) \right) \right)$

where the product is taken in the natural order.

We simply write $\|\varphi\|$ for $\|\varphi\|_{Free(\varphi)}$. If φ is a sentence, i.e, it has no free variables, then $\|\varphi\| \in K \langle\langle A^* \rangle\rangle$. We note that if Φ is the trivial discounting, then the Φ-semantics coincides (apart from the slight changes in the syntax) with the semantics of weighted formulas as defined in [9]. The reader should find in [9,11] examples of possible interpretations of weighted MSO formulas. In the following, we give an example employing discounting.

Example 9. Consider the alphabet $A = \{a, b, c\}$, the max-plus semiring $\mathbb{R}_{max}$ and the discounting $\Phi = \{\overline{p_a}, \overline{p_b}, \overline{p_c}\}$ with $p_a = p_b = 1$ and $p_c = 0$. Let $\varphi \in MSO(\mathbb{R}_{max}, A)$ given by $\varphi = \forall x . (\neg P_a(x) \vee (P_a(x) \wedge \exists y . (S(x, y) \wedge P_b(y) \wedge 1)))$. Then, for any word $w \in A^*$ the MSO-formula φ counts in w the occurrences of the subword ab before the first appearance of c.

Now, we turn to weighted MSO logics over infinite words. Let Φ' be a discounting over $\mathbb{R}_{\max}$. The syntax of formulas of the weighted MSO logic with Φ'-discounting over $\mathbb{R}_{\max}$ is almost the same as in the finite case (cf. Definition 7). The only difference is that we exclude $Last(x)$ and we add the atomic formula $x \leq y$ and its negation. We shall denote by $MSO(\mathbb{R}_{\max}, A)$ the set of all weighted MSO-formulas over $\mathbb{R}_{\max}$. Let $\varphi \in MSO(\mathbb{R}_{\max}, A)$ and $\mathcal{V}$ be a finite set of variables with $Free(\varphi) \subseteq \mathcal{V}$. We define the Φ'-semantics of φ as a formal power series $\|\varphi\|_{\mathcal{V}} \in \mathbb{R}_{\max} \langle\langle A_{\mathcal{V}}^{\omega} \rangle\rangle$ as follows. For any $(w, \sigma) \in A_{\mathcal{V}}^{\omega}$, if σ is not a valid assignment, then we put $(\|\varphi\|_{\mathcal{V}}, (w, \sigma)) = -\infty$. Otherwise, we define $(\|\varphi\|_{\mathcal{V}}, (w, \sigma))$ as in Definition 8, where $K = \mathbb{R}_{\max}$ and the semiring operations are taking suprema and addition in the reals; also we put

$$- (\|x \leq y\|_{\mathcal{V}}, (w, \sigma)) = \begin{cases} 0 & \text{if } \sigma(x) \leq \sigma(y) \\ -\infty & \text{otherwise} \end{cases}.$$

Observe that the definitions of semantics are valid for each formula $\varphi \in MSO(K, A)$ (resp. $\varphi \in MSO(\mathbb{R}_{\max}, A)$) and each finite set $\mathcal{V}$ of variables containing $Free(\varphi)$. In fact, the Φ-semantics (resp. Φ'-semantics) $\|\varphi\|_{\mathcal{V}}$ depends only on $Free(\varphi)$. More precisely,

Proposition 10. *Let $\varphi \in MSO(K, A)$ (resp. $\varphi \in MSO(\mathbb{R}_{\max}, A)$) and $\mathcal{V}$ be a finite set of variables such that $Free(\varphi) \subseteq \mathcal{V}$. Then $(\|\varphi\|_{\mathcal{V}}, (w, \sigma)) = (\|\varphi\|, (w, \sigma|_{Free(\varphi)}))$ for each $(w, \sigma) \in A_{\mathcal{V}}^{*}$ (resp. $(w, \sigma) \in A_{\mathcal{V}}^{\omega}$) where σ is a valid $(w, \mathcal{V})$-assignment. Furthermore, $\|\varphi\|$ is Φ-recognizable (resp. a recognizable step function, Φ'-ω-recognizable, an ω-recognizable step function) iff $\|\varphi\|_{\mathcal{V}}$ is Φ-recognizable (resp. a recognizable step function, Φ'-ω-recognizable, an ω-recognizable step function).*

Let now $Z \subseteq MSO(K, A)$ (resp. $Z \subseteq MSO(\mathbb{R}_{\max}, A)$). A series $S \in K \langle\langle A^{*} \rangle\rangle$ (resp. $S \in \mathbb{R}_{\max} \langle\langle A^{\omega} \rangle\rangle$) is called Φ-Z-definable (resp. Φ'-Z-definable) if there is a sentence $\varphi \in Z$ such that $S = \|\varphi\|$. The main results of this section compare Φ-Z-definable (resp. Φ'-Z-definable) with Φ-recognizable (resp. Φ'-ω-recognizable) series for suitable fragments Z in the context of our weighted MSO logic with discounting. First, we show that $K^{\Phi-rec} \langle\langle A^{*} \rangle\rangle$ is not in general closed under universal quantifications.

Example 11. Let $K = (\mathbb{N}, +, \cdot, 0, 1)$. It is easy to see that the series $T = \|\exists x \,.\, 1\|$ is recognizable. Let $S = \|\forall y \,.\, \exists x \,.\, 1\|$. Then $(S, w) = |w|^{|w|}$. But if $\mathcal{A}$ is a weighted automaton, there is a constant $C \in \mathbb{N}$ such that for all $w \in A^{*}$ we have $(\|\mathcal{A}\|, w) \leq C^{|w|}$. Hence S is not recognizable. Note that T takes on infinitely many values. In contrast, over the max-plus semiring $K = \mathbb{R}_{\max}$, T takes on only two values, and the series S would be recognizable.

The previous example states that unrestricted universal quantification is too strong to preserve Φ-recognizability, and thus motivates the following definitions.

Definition 12. *(cf. [9]) (a) A formula $\varphi \in MSO(K, A)$ will be called restricted if whenever φ contains a universal first order quantification $\forall x \,.\, \psi$, then $\|\psi\|$ is a recognizable step function.*

(b) A formula $\varphi \in MSO(K, A)$ will be called almost existential *if whenever φ contains a universal first order quantification $\forall x \cdot \psi$, then ψ does not contain any universal quantifier.*

We let $RMSO(K, A)$ comprise all restricted formulas of $MSO(K, A)$. Furthermore, let $REMSO(K, A)$ contain all *restricted existential* MSO-formulas φ, i.e., φ is of the form $\exists X_1, \ldots, X_n \cdot \psi$ with $\psi \in RMSO(K, A)$ containing no set quantification. We shall denote by $AEMSO(K, A)$ the set of all almost existential formulas of $MSO(K, A)$. We let $K^{\Phi-rmso} \langle\langle A^* \rangle\rangle$ (resp. $K^{\Phi-remso} \langle\langle A^* \rangle\rangle$, $K^{\Phi-aemso} \langle\langle A^* \rangle\rangle$) contain all series $S \in K \langle\langle A^* \rangle\rangle$ which are Φ-definable by some sentence in $RMSO(K, A)$ (resp. in $REMSO(K, A)$, $AEMSO(K, A)$). For the case $K = \mathbb{R}_{\max}$ the corresponding classes of infinitary series $\mathbb{R}_{\max}^{\Phi'-rmso} \langle\langle A^\omega \rangle\rangle$ (resp. $\mathbb{R}_{\max}^{\Phi'-remso} \langle\langle A^\omega \rangle\rangle$, $\mathbb{R}_{\max}^{\Phi'-aemso} \langle\langle A^\omega \rangle\rangle$) are defined analogously.

Next, we state our second main result.

Theorem 13. *Let A be a finite alphabet, K any commutative semiring and Φ any discounting over A and K. Then*

(a) $K^{\Phi-rec} \langle\langle A^* \rangle\rangle = K^{\Phi-rmso} \langle\langle A^* \rangle\rangle = K^{\Phi-remso} \langle\langle A^* \rangle\rangle$.

(b) If K is additively locally finite, then $K^{\Phi-rec} \langle\langle A^* \rangle\rangle = K^{\Phi-aemso} \langle\langle A^* \rangle\rangle$.

In our proof of the inclusion $K^{\Phi-rmso} \langle\langle A^* \rangle\rangle \subseteq K^{\Phi-rec} \langle\langle A^* \rangle\rangle$ resp. $K^{\Phi-aemso} \langle\langle A^* \rangle\rangle \subseteq K^{\Phi-rec} \langle\langle A^* \rangle\rangle$, we proceed by induction on the structure of a restricted or almost existential formula φ and we exploit closure properties of Φ-recognizable series. A crucial point is dealing with the universal quantifier; here we analyze a corresponding result of [9] (for restricted formula) resp. we employ Proposition 3 (for almost existential formula). For the converse inclusion $K^{\Phi-rec} \langle\langle A^* \rangle\rangle \subseteq K^{\Phi-aemso} \langle\langle A^* \rangle\rangle$ (and also for $K^{\Phi-rec} \langle\langle A^* \rangle\rangle \subseteq K^{\Phi-remso} \langle\langle A^* \rangle\rangle$), given a weighted automaton $\mathcal{A}$ we give an explicit $AEMSO(K, A)$-formula φ with $\|\mathcal{A}\| = \|\varphi\|$. Observe that Theorem 13, part (a) generalizes the main result of [9] which we obtain by letting Φ be the trivial discounting.

The last theorem contains our third main result. For its proof we use similar arguments as for the finitary case.

Theorem 14. *Let A be a finite alphabet and Φ' any discounting over A and $\mathbb{R}_{\max}$. Then*

$$\mathbb{R}_{\max}^{\Phi'-\omega-rec} \langle\langle A^\omega \rangle\rangle = \mathbb{R}_{\max}^{\Phi'-rmso} \langle\langle A^\omega \rangle\rangle = \mathbb{R}_{\max}^{\Phi'-remso} \langle\langle A^\omega \rangle\rangle = \mathbb{R}_{\max}^{\Phi'-aemso} \langle\langle A^\omega \rangle\rangle.$$

Corollary 15 (Büchi's Theorem). *An infinitary language is ω-recognizable iff it is definable by a EMSO-sentence.*

Finally, we turn to constructibility and decision problems.

Corollary 16. *Let K be a computable, additively locally finite, commutative semiring, or let $K = \mathbb{R}_{\max}$ or $K = \mathbb{R}_{\min}$. Let Φ be a discounting over A and K. Given an $AEMSO(K, A)$-formula φ whose atomic entries from K are effectively given, we can effectively compute a weighted automaton, resp. a weighted Muller automaton $\mathcal{A}$, such that $\|\varphi\| = \|\mathcal{A}\|$.*

Proof. We proceed by induction on the structure of φ. During the first steps we will be dealing with formulas ψ such that $\|\psi\|$ is a recognizable (resp. ω-recognizable) step function, say $\|\psi\| = \sum\limits_{i=1,\ldots,n} k_i \cdot 1_{L_i}$. Then we always try to compute all values k_i and automata (resp. Muller automata) for the languages L_i $(i = 1, \ldots, n)$. For atomic formulas and their negations, this is clear. If ψ, ψ' are of this form, by the constructions given in the full proofs of our corresponding results, we obtain the required values and automata for $\psi \vee \psi'$, $\psi \wedge \psi'$, $\exists x \cdot \psi$ and $\exists X \cdot \psi$. When we deal with $\forall x \cdot \psi$, our constructions produce a weighted automaton (resp. weighted Muller automaton) for $\|\forall x \cdot \psi\|$. Now assume that ψ, ψ' are subformulas of φ and we have constructed weighted automata (resp. weighted Muller automata) $\mathcal{A}$, $\mathcal{A}'$ with $\|\psi\| = \|\mathcal{A}\|$ and $\|\psi'\| = \|\mathcal{A}'\|$. Then we also obtain weighted automata (resp. weighted Muller automata) for $\psi \vee \psi'$, $\psi \wedge \psi'$, $\exists x \cdot \psi$ and $\exists X \cdot \psi$ effectively by our constructions.

Unfortunately, for such semirings K as in Corollary 16, the equality $\|\varphi\| = \|\varphi'\|$ on A^*, i.e. finite words, for two $AEMSO(K, A)$-sentences φ, φ' is in general undecidable. Consider $K = \mathbb{R}_{\max}$, and suppose there was a decision procedure for this equality. By Theorem 13, part (a) we would obtain a decision procedure for weighted automata $\mathcal{A}$, $\mathcal{A}'$ of whether $\|\mathcal{A}\| = \|\mathcal{A}'\|$ (as series over A^*). But this is impossible by a result of Krob [22]. Here the interesting open problem arises whether due to the discounting we might achieve better decidability results for the semirings $\mathbb{R}_{\max}$ or $\mathbb{R}_{\min}$ over infinite words.

4   Conclusion

We introduced a weighted logics with discounting over finite words, and we proved its expressive equivalence to discounted behaviors of weighted automata. We gave a logic with a purely syntactic definition whenever the underlying semiring is additively locally finite. Then we investigated Büchi and Muller automata with discounting over the max-plus and min-plus semiring and we characterized their behaviors as definable series in a discounting weighted logic over infinite words. This logic also possesses a syntactic definition. In this way, we obtained an extension of classical and recent results of the theory of formal languages and formal power series, and this provides an automata (and thus algorithmic) and logical theoretic way to describe the discounting concept which is widely used in game theory and mathematical economics.

References

1. Arnold, A.: Finite Transition Systems. International Series in Computer Science. Prentice Hall, Englewood Cliffs (1994)
2. Berstel, J., Reutenauer, C.: Rational Series and Their Languages. In: EATCS Monographs in Theoretical Computer Science, vol. 12, Springer, Heidelberg (1988)
3. Büchi, J.R.: Weak second-order arithmetic and finite automata. Z. Math. Logik Grundlager Math. 6, 66–92 (1960)

4. Büchi, J.R.: On a decision method in restricted second order arithmetic. In: Proc. 1960 Int. Congr. for Logic, Methodology and Philosophy of Science, pp. 1–11 (1962)
5. Culik II, K., Kari, J.: Image compression using weighted finite automata. Computer and Graphics 17, 305–313 (1993)
6. Culik, K., Karhumäki, J.: Finite automata computing real functions. SIAM J. Comput. 23(4), 789–814 (1994)
7. Cuninghame-Green, R.A.: Minimax algebra and applications. Adv. in Imaging Electron Phy. 90, 1–121 (1995)
8. de Alfaro, L., Henzinger, T.A., Majumda, R.: Discounting the future in systems theory. In: Baeten, J.C.M., Lenstra, J.K., Parrow, J., Woeginger, G.J. (eds.) ICALP 2003. LNCS, vol. 2719, pp. 1022–1037. Springer, Heidelberg (2003)
9. Droste, M., Gastin, P.: Weighted automata and weighted logics. Theoret. Comput. Sci. 380, 69–86 (2007) extended abstract In: Caires, L., Italiano, G.F., Monteiro, L., Palamidessi, C., Yung, M. (eds.) ICALP 2005. LNCS, vol. 3580, pp. 513–525. Springer, Heidelberg (2005)
10. Droste, M., Kuske, D.: Skew and infinitary formal power series. Theoret. Comput. Sci. 366, 189–227 (2006). extended abstract In: Baeten, J.C.M., Lenstra, J.K., Parrow, J., Woeginger, G.J. (eds.) ICALP 2003. LNCS, vol. 2719, pp. 426–438. Springer, Heidelberg (2003)
11. Droste, M., Rahonis, G.: Weighted automata and weighted logics on infinite words. In: Ibarra, O.H., Dang, Z. (eds.) DLT 2006. LNCS, vol. 4036, pp. 49–58. Springer, Heidelberg (2006)
12. Droste, M., Vogler, H.: Weighted tree automata and weighted logics. Theoret. Comput. Sci. 366, 228–247 (2006)
13. Eilenberg, S.: Automata, Languages and Machines, vol. A. Academic Press, London (1974)
14. Elgot, C.: Decision problems of finite automata design and related arithmetics. Trans. Amer. Math. Soc. 98, 21–52 (1961)
15. Ésik, Z., Kuich, W.: A semiring-semimodule generalization of ω-regular languages I and II. Special issue on "Weighted automata". In: Droste, M., Vogler, H. (eds.) J. of Automata Languages and Combinatorics 10, 203–242, 243–264 (2005)
16. Filar, J., Vrieze, K.: Competitive Marcov Decision Processes. Springer, Heidelberg (1997)
17. Gaubert, S., Plus, M.: Methods and applications of (max, +) linear algebra, Techical Report 3088, INRIA, Rocquencourt (January 1997)
18. Jiang, Z., Litow, B., de Vel, O.: Similarity enrichment in image compression through weighted finite automata. In: Du, D.-Z., Eades, P., Sharma, A.K., Lin, X., Estivill-Castro, V. (eds.) COCOON 2000. LNCS, vol. 1858, pp. 447–456. Springer, Heidelberg (2000)
19. Katritzke, F.: Refinements of data compression using weighted finite automata, PhD thesis, Universität Siegen, Germany (2001)
20. Khoussainov, B., Nerode, A.: Automata Theory and its Applications, Birkhäuser Boston (2001)
21. Knight, K., Graehl, J.: Machine transliteration. Comput. Linguist. 24(4), 599–612 (1998)
22. Krob, D.: The equality problem for rational series with multiplicities in the tropical semiring is undecidable. Intern. J. of Information and Computation 4, 405–425 (1994)
23. Kuich, W.: Semirings and formal power series: Their relevance to formal languages and automata theory. In: Rozenberg, G., Salomaa, A. (eds.) Handbook of Formal Languages, vol. 1, pp. 609–677. Springer, Heidelberg (1997)

24. Kuich, W.: On skew formal power series. In: Bozapalidis, S., Kalampakas, A., Rahonis, G. (eds.) Proceedings of the Conference on Algebraic Informatics, Thessaloniki, pp. 7–30 (2005)
25. Kuich, W., Salomaa, A.: Semirings, Automata, Languages. EATCS Monographs in Theoretical Computer Science, vol. 5. Springer, Heidelberg (1986)
26. Kurshan, R.P.: Computer-Aided Verification of Coordinating Processes. Princeton Series in Computer Science. Princeton University Press, Princeton (1994)
27. Mathissen, C.: Definable transductions and weighted logics for texts. In: Proceedings of DLT 2007. 11th International Conference on Developments in Language Theory (DLT) 2007. LNCS, vol. 4588, pp. 324–336 (2007)
28. Mäurer, I.: Weighted picture automata and weighted logics. In: Durand, B., Thomas, W. (eds.) STACS 2006. LNCS, vol. 3884, pp. 313–324. Springer, Heidelberg (2006)
29. McMillan, K.: Symbolic Model Checking. Kluwer Academic Publishers, Dordrecht (1993)
30. Meinecke, I.: Weighted logics for traces. In: Grigoriev, D., Harrison, J., Hirsch, E.A. (eds.) CSR 2006. LNCS, vol. 3967, pp. 235–246. Springer, Heidelberg (2006)
31. Mohri, M., Pereira, F., Riley, M.: The design principles of a weighted finite-state transducer library. Theoret. Comput. Sci. 231, 17–32 (2000)
32. Perrin, D., Pin, J.E.: Infinite Words. Elsevier, Amsterdam (2004)
33. Salomaa, A., Soittola, M.: Automata-Theoretic Aspects of Formal Power Series. Texts and Monographs in Computer Science. Springer, Heidelberg (1978)
34. Schützenberger, M.: On the definition of a family of automata. Inf. Control 4, 245–270 (1961)
35. Shapley, L.S.: Stochastic games. Roc. National Acad. of Sciences 39, 1095–1100 (1953)
36. Thomas, W.: Automata on infinite objects. In: Leeuwen, J.v. (ed.) Handbook of Theoretical Computer Science, vol. B, pp. 135–191. Elsevier Science Publishers, Amsterdam (1990)
37. Thomas, W.: Languages, automata and logic. In: Rozenberg, G., Salomaa, A. (eds.) Handbook of Formal Languages, vol. 3, pp. 389–485. Springer, Heidelberg (1997)
38. Zimmermann, U.: Combinatorial Optimization in Ordered Algebraic Structures, Annals of Discrete Mathematics, North-Holland, Amsterdam, vol. 10 (1981)

Regulated Nondeterminism
in Pushdown Automata

Martin Kutrib[1], Andreas Malcher[2], and Larissa Werlein[1]

[1] Institut für Informatik, Universität Giessen,
Arndtstr. 2, 35392 Giessen, Germany
kutrib@informatik.uni-giessen.de
[2] Institut für Informatik,
Johann Wolfgang Goethe-Universität Frankfurt,
60054 Frankfurt am Main, Germany
a.malcher@em.uni-frankfurt.de

Abstract. A generalization of pushdown automata towards regulated nondeterminism is studied. The nondeterminism is governed in such a way that the decision, whether or not a nondeterministic rule is applied, depends on the whole content of the stack. More precisely, the content of the stack is considered as a word over the stack alphabet, and the pushdown automaton is allowed to act nondeterministically, if this word belongs to some given set R of control words. Otherwise its behavior is deterministic. The computational capacity of such R-PDAs depends on the complexity of R. It turns out that non-context-free languages are accepted even if R is a linear, deterministic context-free language. On the other hand, regular control sets R do not increase the computational capacity of nondeterministic pushdown automata. This raises the natural question for the relations between the structure and complexity of regular sets R on one hand and the computational capacity of the corresponding R-PDA on the other hand. Clearly, if R is empty, the deterministic context-free languages are characterized. For $R = \{a, b\}^*$ one obtains all context-free languages. Furthermore, if R is finite, then the regular closure of the deterministic context-free languages is described. We investigate these questions, and discuss closure properties of the language classes in question under AFL operations.

Keywords: regulated nondeterminism, limited nondeterminism, pushdown automata, closure properties.

1 Introduction

In order to explore the power of nondeterminism in bounded-resource computations, in [5,13] the study of nondeterminism as a measurable resource has been initiated. The well-known proper inclusion between the deterministic and nondeterministic real-time multitape Turing machine languages is refined by showing an infinite hierarchy between the deterministic real-time Turing machine languages and the languages acceptable by real-time Turing machines whose number of nondeterministic steps is logarithmically bounded. In [15] this result is

Jan Holub and Jan Žd'árek (Eds.): CIAA 2007, LNCS 4783, pp. 85–96, 2007.

further generalized to arbitrary dimensions, and extended to time complexities in the range between real time and linear time. Extensive investigations are also made on limited nondeterminism in the context of finite automata [7,8,14]. A good survey of limited nondeterminism reflecting the state-of-the-art at its time is [6]. The quantitative study of nondeterminism in context-free languages originates from [22], and is continued in [20,21]. The so-called branching as measure of nondeterminism, introduced for finite automata [7], is studied in [11] in connection with pushdown automata, where infinite hierarchies in between the deterministic context-free and context-free languages depending on the amount of nondeterminism or on the amount of ambiguity are shown. In [9] lower bounds for the minimum amount of nondeterminism to accept certain context-free languages are established. Pushdown automata with limited nondeterminism were investigated in [16] from the viewpoint of context-dependent nondeterminism. One important result obtained there is an automata characterization of the regular closure of deterministic context-free languages (DCFL). This is an interesting language class, since it properly extends DCFL but still has a linear-time membership problem [2]. Thus, the limitation of nondeterminism increases the generative capacity but preserves the computational complexity of the model.

Another cornerstone concept in formal language theory is regulated rewriting. Roughly speaking, that is, given some grammar, to impose restrictions on how to use the productions. The restrictions are usually realized by some control device. Extensive investigations of this concept in many areas of formal language theory have been done. There are too many fundamental approaches to mention them in an introduction. Valuable sources for results and references are [3] and [4].

The concept of regulated rewriting has been adapted to automata in [17,18]. Basically, the idea is to limit the computations in such a way that the sequence of transition steps has to form some words of a given control language. Even for very simple context-free control languages the power of one-turn regulated pushdown automata suffices to characterize the recursively enumerable languages.

The main goal of this paper is to investigate pushdown automata with regulated nondeterminism. Again, we want to achieve that regulation increases the generative capacity and avoids additional complexity. The use of transition rules is controlled in a weak sense. We provide two independent transition functions, where one is deterministic and the other one is nondeterministic. The regulation concerns the application of the nondeterministic function. Moreover, the control device is not directly defined by the words formed by sequences of transition steps. Rather the content of the stack is used. More precisely, the content of the stack is considered as a word over the stack alphabet, and the pushdown automaton is allowed to act nondeterministically, if this word belongs to some given set R of control words. Otherwise, the deterministic transition function is applied. This mechanism extends the context dependent nondeterminism of [16]. Context-dependence means that nondeterministic transition steps may appear only within certain contexts, i.e., in configurations that meet particular conditions. When these conditions concern the stack content only, there is a bridge to the approach considered here. For example, it is known that automata, which have to empty their stack up to the initial symbol in order to behave nondeterministically, are characterized by the regular closure of DCFL. In our terms, these are pushdown automata with regulated nondeterminism whose control language contains the empty word only.

The paper is organized as follows. In the following section we recall briefly some basic notions and definitions. In Section 3 we introduce pushdown automata with regulated nondeterminism and present some examples in order to provide a flavor of the concept. Clearly, the computational capacity of R-PDAs depends on the complexity of R. It turns out that non-context-free languages are accepted even if R is a linear, deterministic context-free language. However, we show that regular control sets R do not increase the computational capacity of nondeterministic pushdown automata. This raises the natural question for the relations between the structure and complexity of regular sets R on one hand, and the computational capacity of the corresponding R-PDA on the other hand. Clearly, if R is empty, the deterministic context-free languages are characterized. For $R = \{a, b\}^*$ one obtains all context-free languages since, in general, the number of necessary stack symbols can be reduced to two [10]. Furthermore, we deal with finite and infinite languages and show that the regular closure of the deterministic context-free languages is characterized by finite control sets. In Section 4 a hierarchy of four classes is established, where the main results are the non-acceptance of witness languages. Finally, in Section 5 the closure properties of the families in question under AFL operations (union, concatenation, Kleene star, homomorphism, inverse homomorphism, intersection with regular languages) are discussed and summarized in Table 1.

2 Preliminaries

Let Σ^* denote the set of all words over the finite alphabet Σ. The empty word is denoted by λ. For convenience, we use Σ_λ for $\Sigma \cup \{\lambda\}$. The reversal of a word w is denoted by w^R, and for the length of w we write $|w|$. Set inclusion is denoted by $\subseteq$, and strict set inclusion by $\subset$.

A *pushdown automaton* is a system $\mathcal{M} = \langle Q, \Sigma, \Gamma, \delta, q_0, Z_0, F \rangle$, where Q is a finite set of states, Σ is the finite input alphabet, Γ is a finite set of stack symbols, δ is a mapping from $Q \times \Sigma_\lambda \times \Gamma$ to finite subsets of $Q \times \Gamma^*$ called the transition function, $q_0 \in Q$ is the initial state, $Z_0 \in \Gamma$ is a distinguished stack symbol, called the bottom-of-stack symbol, which initially appears on the pushdown store, and $F \subseteq Q$ is the set of accepting states.

A *configuration* of a pushdown automaton is a triple (q, w, γ), where q is the current state, w the unread part of the input, and γ the current content of the stack, the leftmost symbol of γ being the top symbol. If p, q are in Q, a is in Σ_λ, w is in Σ^*, γ and β are in Γ^*, and Z is in Γ, then we write $(q, aw, Z\gamma) \vdash_{\mathcal{M}} (p, w, \beta\gamma)$, if the pair (p, β) is in $\delta(q, a, Z)$. In order to simplify matters, we require that during any computation the bottom-of-stack symbol appears only at the bottom of the stack. Formally, we require that if (p, β) is in $\delta(q, a, Z)$, then either β does not contain Z_0 or $\beta = \beta' Z_0$, where β' does not contain Z_0, and $Z = Z_0$. As usual, the reflexive transitive closure of $\vdash_{\mathcal{M}}$ is denoted by $\vdash^*_{\mathcal{M}}$. The subscript $\mathcal{M}$ will be dropped whenever the meaning remains clear.

The *language accepted* by $\mathcal{M}$ is

$$T(\mathcal{M}) = \{w \in \Sigma^* \mid (q_0, w, Z_0) \vdash^* (q, \lambda, \gamma), \text{ for some } q \in F \text{ and } \gamma \in \Gamma^*\}.$$

A pushdown automaton is *deterministic*, if there is at most one choice of action for any possible configuration. In particular, there must never be a choice of using an input symbol or of using λ input. Formally, a pushdown automaton $\mathcal{M} = \langle Q, \Sigma, \Gamma, \delta, q_0, Z_0, F \rangle$ is *deterministic* if (i) $\delta(q, a, Z)$ contains at most one element, for all a in Σ_λ, q in Q, and Z in Γ, and (ii) for all q in Q and Z in Γ: if $\delta(q, \lambda, Z)$ is not empty, then $\delta(q, a, Z)$ is empty for all a in Σ.

In general, we denote the *family of languages accepted* by devices of type X by $\mathscr{L}(X)$.

3 Pushdown Automata with Regulated Nondeterminism

In this section, we introduce the concept of regulated nondeterminism for pushdown automata. In contrast to the general model of nondeterministic pushdown automata, where nondeterministic steps may be performed at any time and in any situation, we regulate the use of nondeterministic steps. In detail, we provide some control language R such that nondeterministic steps are only allowed when the current content of the stack forms a word belonging to R. Recall that the bottom-of-stack symbol appears at the bottom of the stack only. A formal definition is as follows.

Let $\mathcal{M} = \langle Q, \Sigma, \Gamma, \delta, q_0, Z_0, F \rangle$ be a PDA and $R \subseteq (\Gamma \setminus Z_0)^*$ be some control language. Then $\mathcal{M}$ is called an *R-PDA* if

(i) for all $q \in Q$, $a \in \Sigma_\lambda$, and $Z \in \Gamma$, δ can be decomposed as

$$\delta(q, a, Z) = \delta_d(q, a, Z) \cup \delta_n(q, a, Z),$$

where $\langle Q, \Sigma, \Gamma, \delta_d, q_0, Z_0, F \rangle$ is a DPDA and $\langle Q, \Sigma, \Gamma, \delta_n, q_0, Z_0, F \rangle$ is a PDA,
(ii) for all $q, q' \in Q$, $a \in \Sigma_\lambda$, $w \in \Sigma^*$, $Z \in \Gamma$, and $\gamma \in \Gamma^*$,
   (a) $(q, aw, Z\gamma) \vdash (q', w, \gamma'\gamma)$, if $(q', \gamma') \in \delta_n(q, a, Z)$ and $Z\gamma = \gamma''Z_0$ with $\gamma'' \in R$,
   (b) $(q, aw, Z\gamma) \vdash (q', w, \gamma'\gamma)$, if $\delta_d(q, a, Z) = (q', \gamma')$ and $Z\gamma = \gamma''Z_0$ with $\gamma'' \notin R$.

Before we continue with the systematic study of the properties of R-PDAs, let us discuss some examples. The first question is whether regulating the nondeterminism gains additional power for PDAs due to additional control mechanisms, or weaker devices due to restrictions on the nondeterminism. Clearly, there is no definite answer, since it may depend on the choice of the control language.

Example 1. Let $R = \{b^n a^n \mid n \geq 1\}$ be a bounded, linear, deterministic context-free language. Then we construct an R-PDA $\mathcal{M}$ accepting the non-context-free language $\{a^n b^n c^n \mid n \geq 2\}$ as follows.

First, all as read are pushed on the stack. When the first b is read, an a is popped from the stack. The following bs are pushed on the stack. When the first c appears in the input, there are two possibilities. Either the stack contains some word of R, which implies that the number of already consumed as matches the number of already consumed bs, or the deterministic transition function has to be applied. Thus, $\mathcal{M}$ can check whether the number of as and bs is equal, and continues with comparing the number of cs from the input with the number of bs on the stack. If all bs are popped and the last c from the input is matched against the topmost a on the stack, then the input is accepted, and rejected otherwise.   □

The example reveals that the regulation of nondeterminism may result in an increase of the computational capacity going beyond the computational capacity of PDAs. Let us continue with some more or less immediate observations.

Trivially, if $R = \emptyset$, then no nondeterminism is allowed at all. Therefore, the $\emptyset$-PDAs characterize the deterministic context-free languages (DCFL). At the other extreme, we have the set $R = (\Gamma \setminus Z_0)^*$. In this case, R-PDAs are allowed to perform nondeterministic steps at any time. Thus, $(\Gamma \setminus Z_0)^*$-PDAs characterize the context-free languages (CFL). The following lemma shows that an important property of R-PDAs is the structure of the set R and not the number of symbols which may always be decreased to two.

Lemma 2. *The family $\mathscr{L}(\{a, b\}^*\text{-PDA})$ is equal to the context-free languages.*

Proof. In [10] it is shown that any PDA can be converted to an equivalent PDA with a binary stack alphabet. Thus, any PDA can be converted to an equivalent $\{a, b\}^*$-PDA.   □

To some extent, the next lemma builds a bridge between regulated nondeterminism and context-dependent nondeterminism. It has been shown in latter terms in [16].

Lemma 3. *The family $\mathscr{L}(\{\lambda\}\text{-PDA})$ is equal to the regular closure of the deterministic context-free languages, i.e., the least language class containing DCFL and being closed under the regular operations union, concatenation, and Kleene star.*

Since two stack symbols are sufficient, we have to consider the class of R-PDAs with unary stack alphabet (up to the bottom-of-stack symbol). A pushdown automaton with unary stack alphabet is called *one-counter*, and a context-free language is a one-counter language, if it is accepted by a one-counter PDA. But $\{a\}^*$-PDAs are strictly more powerful than nondeterministic one-counter PDAs.

Lemma 4. *The family of one-counter languages is a proper subfamily of the family $\mathscr{L}(\{a\}^*\text{-PDA})$.*

Proof. Clearly, every one-counter language is accepted by an $\{a\}^*$-PDA. For the strictness of the inclusion consider the context-free language $L = \{a^n b w c w^R b a^n \mid n \geq 1, w \in \{a, b\}^*\}$, which trivially belongs to $\mathscr{L}(\{a\}^*\text{-PDA})$. But L is not a one-counter language according to the discussion in [1].   □

We have seen that the computational capacity of R-PDAs may be increased to accept non-context-free languages. So, the question arises how complex R must be in order to obtain such a power. By the witness language $L = \{b^n a^n \mid n \geq 1\}$ we know a rough upper bound since L is bounded, linear, and deterministic context-free. We next show that this upper bound is in some sense tight, i.e., R-PDAs accept context-free languages as long as R is regular. Furthermore, the next theorem shows that an R-PDA can check the property (ii) in its definition itself, if R is regular.

Theorem 5. *Let R be a regular set and $\mathcal{M} = \langle Q, \Sigma, \Gamma, \delta, q_0, Z_0, F \rangle$ an R-PDA. Then an equivalent PDA $\mathcal{M}'$ can effectively be constructed.*

Proof. The idea of the construction is to consider the stack of $\mathcal{M}'$ to have two components. The first component simulates the stack of $\mathcal{M}$. In the second component, the history of a computation of a DFA $\mathcal{A}$ is stored, which is used to check whether or not the current content of the stack belongs to R. The details are omitted due to space constraints. □

In order to investigate the range between the deterministic and nondeterministic context-free languages with respect to the complexity and structure of the control set R, in the sequel we are mainly interested in regular sets. As a first step we study the power of finite sets, and start to explore the role played by the empty word. Besides, for constructions it is sometimes useful to know whether an R-PDA may perform nondeterministic steps with empty stack. It is obvious that this is possible, if R contains λ. Our next construction shows that this is always possible as long as R is not empty.

Theorem 6. *Let $R \neq \{\lambda\}$ be not empty. Then the families $\mathscr{L}((R \cup \{\lambda\})$-PDA) and $\mathscr{L}((R \setminus \{\lambda\})$-PDA) are equal.*

Proof. The inclusion $\mathscr{L}((R \setminus \{\lambda\})$-PDA$) \subseteq \mathscr{L}((R \cup \{\lambda\})$-PDA$)$ is obvious. For the converse inclusion, we consider an $(R \cup \{\lambda\})$-PDA $\mathcal{M} = \langle Q, \Sigma, \Gamma, \delta, q_0, Z_0, F \rangle$. Let $w = a_1 a_2 \cdots a_n \in R$ be a shortest and non-empty word in R. We construct an equivalent $(R \setminus \{\lambda\})$-PDA $\mathcal{M}'$. The idea is to simulate $\mathcal{M}$ directly, unless the stack is empty. If the stack is empty and, therefore, $\mathcal{M}$ may perform a nondeterministic step, then $\mathcal{M}'$ stores the next input symbol in its state and pushes w on the stack. Now, $\mathcal{M}'$ can guess and simulate the step that $\mathcal{M}$ had performed with empty stack. The result of the guess is remembered by states of $\mathcal{M}'$. Next, $\mathcal{M}'$ empties its stack via λ-transitions and, finally, performs the previously guessed step of $\mathcal{M}$. □

By the previous theorem, we may assume without loss of generality that R includes the empty word. We now turn to prove that a finite control set R is as powerful as a control set consisting of the empty word only. Nevertheless, in [16] it is shown that the family $\mathscr{L}(\{\lambda\}$-PDA) characterizes the regular closure of the deterministic context-free languages, which clearly is a proper superset of the deterministic context-free languages.

Theorem 7. *Let R be finite and not empty. Then the families $\mathscr{L}(R\text{-}PDA)$ and $\mathscr{L}(\{\lambda\}\text{-}PDA)$ are equal.*

Proof. Due to Theorem 6 we may assume that R includes the empty word, and obtain $\mathscr{L}(\{\lambda\}\text{-}PDA) \subseteq \mathscr{L}(R\text{-}PDA)$.

To show the converse inclusion, let R be finite and non-empty, and $\mathcal{M}$ be an R-PDA. Due to the construction given in Theorem 5, we may assume without loss of generality that the second component of the state indicates whether $\mathcal{M}$ may perform a nondeterministic transition, i.e., whether the current content of the stack is a word of R. An equivalent $\{\lambda\}$-PDA $\mathcal{M}'$ works as follows. If the stack of $\mathcal{M}'$ contains no word from R, then $\mathcal{M}'$ works the same way as $\mathcal{M}$. If $\mathcal{M}'$ recognizes a word $w \in R$ in its stack, then w is stored in the state and the stack is emptied via λ-transitions. Then, if the stack is empty, $\mathcal{M}'$ may guess the nondeterministic step of $\mathcal{M}$ and the successor stack content is pushed again on the stack. The details of the construction are omitted due to space constraints.

□

4 Hierarchy

In this section, we consider a hierarchy of four classes defined by control sets R. Since $\emptyset \subset \{\lambda\} \subset \{a\}^* \subset \{a,b\}^*$, we know that we have inclusions between the language classes accepted by the corresponding R-PDAs. Our main results concern the non-acceptance of witness languages, from which the strictness of the inclusions follows.

In the following, we need the known closure of deterministic context-free languages under the prefix operation. Let $w = a_1 a_2 \cdots a_n \in \Sigma^n$ be some word. The *set of prefixes* of w is defined to be $\{\lambda, a_1, a_1 a_2, \ldots, a_1 \cdots a_n\}$. For a language $L \subseteq \Sigma^*$ and a natural number $i \geq 1$ let

$$P_i(L) = \{w \in L \mid \text{exactly } i \text{ prefixes of } w \text{ belong to } L\}.$$

Lemma 8. *Let $i \geq 1$ be a constant. If $L \in DCFL$, then $P_i(L) \in DCFL$.*

Proof. The state set of a deterministic pushdown automaton M accepting L is extended by a finite counter. The counter is increased every time an accepting state appears, i.e., a prefix belongs to L. Now, M can easily be modified such that it accepts if and only if the input and exactly i prefixes belong to L.   □

Lemma 9. *The language $L = \{a^n bwba^n b \mid n \geq 1, w \in \{a,b\}^*\}$ does not belong to the family $\mathscr{L}(\{\lambda\}\text{-}PDA)$.*

Proof. In contrast to the assertion assume some $\{\lambda\}$-PDA accepts L. In [16] it is shown that the family $\mathscr{L}(\{\lambda\}\text{-}PDA)$ is characterized by the regular closure of DCFL. Thus, L has a representation as regular expression $\mathcal{E}$ with atoms from DCFL. In the following, we want to show that L can be represented as an expression inductively built from finite unions of deterministic context-free languages and concatenations with singletons from right or left. To this end, consider the following languages $L_{\ell,r}, L_{\ell,b}$ for constants $\ell, r \geq 0$ and a procedure decompose.

$$L_{\ell,r} = \{a^{n-\ell}bwba^{n-r} \mid n \geq 1, w \in \{a,b\}^*\},$$
$$L_{\ell,b} = \{a^{n-\ell}bwba^{n}b \mid n \geq 1, w \in \{a,b\}^*\}.$$

The procedure decompose is defined for languages K of the form $L_{\ell,r}$ or $L_{\ell,b}$. Clearly, for $\ell = 0$ also language L itself is of the form $L_{\ell,b}$.

If $K \in$ DCFL, then decompose(K) returns K, i.e., a deterministic context free language is not further decomposed.

Assume K has a representation $K = L_1^*$, for some language L_1, then $L_1 \subseteq K$. Moreover, K either contains two words $a^{n_1-\ell}bw_1ba^{n_1-r}$ and $a^{n_2-\ell}bw_2ba^{n_2-r}$, or two words $a^{n_1-\ell}bw_1ba^{n_1}b$ and $a^{n_2-\ell}bw_2ba^{n_2}b$ with different numbers n_1 and n_2. But this implies $L_1^* \not\subseteq K$, since in the first case $a^{n_1-\ell}bw_1ba^{n_1-r}a^{n_2-\ell}bw_2ba^{n_2-r}$, and in the second case $a^{n_1-\ell}bw_1ba^{n_1}ba^{n_2-\ell}bw_2ba^{n_2}b$ belongs to L_1^*, but does not belong to K. Therefore, K cannot have a representation $K = L_1^*$ and decompose is undefined in this case.

Next, we consider the possible representation $K = L_1L_2$. Without loss of generality we assume $L_1 \neq \{\lambda\}$ and $L_2 \neq \{\lambda\}$. Since K is infinite, at least one of the languages L_1 or L_2 has to be infinite. If L_1 contains two different words a^i and a^j, then we obtain a contradiction, since $a^iv \in K$ implies $a^jv \notin K$. If L_1 contains some word a^ibv, then all words $x \in L_2$ must have the property $a^ibvx \in K$. Due to the necessary number of as in the suffixes, all words in L_2 must have the same number of as in their suffixes. That is, they all are either a^k or a^kb, or of the form vba^k or vba^kb, depending on whether K is of the form $L_{\ell,r}$ or $L_{\ell,b}$. In the first case, L_2 is a singleton. In the second case, we obtain a contradiction since, for example, there are words in K which end with ba^{k+1} or $ba^{k+1}b$. But these words cannot belong to L_1L_2. Therefore, if $K = L_1L_2$, then either $L_1 = \{a^i\}$, $i \geq 1$, or dependent on K, L_2 is one of the singletons $\{a^k\}$ or $\{a^kb\}$, $k \geq 1$. In either case, we continue the inductive consideration with the quotient of the languages. That is, for $K = L_{\ell,r}$ resp. $K = L_{\ell,b}$, if $L_1 = \{a^i\}$, we set $\ell' = \ell+i$, $r' = r$ resp. $r' = b$, otherwise we set $\ell' = \ell$, $r' = r+k$ resp. $r' = k$, and apply decompose to $K' = L_{\ell',r'}$.

If K is represented as union $K = L_1 \cup L_2$, we continue with decompose(L_1) and decompose(L_2).

It can be observed that decompose$(\mathcal{E})$ returns the desired representation of L, which is an expression built inductively from finite unions of deterministic context-free languages and concatenations with singletons from right or left.

On the other hand, sub-expressions having the form $(L_1 \cup \cdots \cup L_n)L_0$ and $L_0(L_1 \cup \cdots \cup L_n)$ are equivalent to $L_1L_0 \cup \cdots \cup L_nL_0$ and $L_0L_1 \cup \cdots \cup L_0L_n$, respectively. Since deterministic context-free languages are closed under concatenation with singletons from right as well as from left, the sub-expressions have an equivalent representation of the form $L_1' \cup \cdots \cup L_n'$, where the L_i' are deterministic context-free languages. Continuing inductively, we finally end up with a representation $L = \bigcup_{i=1}^m L_i''$, where all L_i'' are deterministic context free.

Since the deterministic context-free languages are closed under intersection with regular languages, the languages $L_i''' = L_i'' \cap a^*bba^*ba^*ba^*b$ are also deterministic context free, for $1 \leq i \leq m$. Due to Lemma 8, so are the languages $P_3(L_i''')$. Since $P_3(L \cap a^*bba^*ba^*ba^*b) = \{a^nbba^nba^nba^nb \mid n \geq 1\}$ is infinite, and $P_3(L \cap a^*bba^*ba^*ba^*b) = P_3(L_1''') \cup \cdots \cup P_3(L_m''')$, at least for one $1 \leq i \leq m$ language $P_3(L_i''')$ is an infinite subset of $\{a^nbba^nba^nba^nb \mid n \geq 1\}$. But any infinite subset of $\{a^nbba^nba^nba^nb \mid n \geq 1\}$ is not even context free. The contradiction completes the proof. $\square$

Lemma 10. *The language $L = \{a^mb^ncww^Rcb^na^m \mid m,n \geq 1, w \in \{a,b\}^*\}$ does not belong to the family $\mathscr{L}(\{a\}^*\text{-PDA})$.*

Proof. Contrarily assume some $\{a\}^*$-PDA $\mathcal{M} = \langle Q, \Sigma, \{a, Z_0\}, \delta, q_0, Z_0, F \rangle$ accepts L. We consider accepting computations and, in particular, configurations with so-called unary stacks, that is, the stacks contain as only (apart from the bottom-of-stack symbol). Suppose there is a pair (m, n) such that for any word $a^mb^ncww^Rcb^na^m$, $w \in \{a,b\}^*$, there is an accepting computation where no unary stack appears while processing the input infix cww^Rc. In this case, one can construct a $\{\lambda\}$-PDA $\mathcal{M}'$ accepting the language $\{ww^R \mid w \in \{a,b\}^*\}$ as follows. During a first phase, on input ww^R automaton $\mathcal{M}'$ simulates the behavior of $\mathcal{M}$ on the prefix a^mb^nc in its finite control with empty stack. Next, $\mathcal{M}$ is simulated directly on ww^R. The latter is possible since during this phase no unary stack appears in the computation of $\mathcal{M}$, thus, the computation is deterministic. Finally, $\mathcal{M}'$ simulates the behavior of $\mathcal{M}$ on the suffix cb^na^m with the help of its finite control and the current stack content. Since it is shown in [16] that the language $\{ww^R \mid w \in \{a,b\}^*\}$ is not accepted by any $\{\lambda\}$-PDA, we obtain a contradiction. Therefore, for any pair (m, n) there is a word $a^mb^ncww^Rcb^na^m$, $w \in \{a,b\}^*$, such that in any accepting computation there appears a unary stack while processing the input infix cww^Rc.

Now we consider accepting computations of inputs $a^mb^ncww^Rcb^na^m$ in more detail. We may choose m and n arbitrarily large. Moreover, we always find w such that in any accepting computation there appears a unary stack while processing the input infix cww^Rc. With respect to the accepting computations, the input $a^mb^ncww^Rcb^na^m$ admits a factorization uvx as follows. First, let the last unary stack that appears while processing the prefix a^mb^n be reached after processing u, which clearly is of the form a^*b^*. The height of this last stack is denoted by k. Secondly, let v be the infix of the form $a^*b^*c\{a,b\}^*$ such that the unary stack of height k reappears for the first time after processing uv. Finally, x denotes the remaining suffix. So, we are concerned with computations

$$(q_0, uvx, Z_0) \vdash^* (q_1, vx, a^k Z_0) \vdash^* (q_2, x, a^k Z_0) \vdash^* (q_f, \lambda, \gamma Z_0),$$

where $q_1, q_2 \in Q$, $q_f \in F$, and $\gamma \in \Gamma^*$.

Next we consider the number k. Disregarding λ-transitions while $\mathcal{M}$ processes u, we obtain $k \leq p|u| \leq p(m + n)$, for some constant $p \geq 1$. On the other hand, there are $\sum_{i=1}^{m+n-1}(m + n - i) = \frac{(m+n)^2 - m - n}{2}$ different pairs

(m', n') such that $m' + n' \leq m + n$. Therefore, for m and n large enough, we have $|Q|k \leq |Q|p(m+n) < \frac{(m+n)^2 - m - n}{2}$. We conclude that there are at least two different pairs (m_1, n_1) and (m_2, n_2) with the same number k such that for both pairs the accepting computation is in the same state, say q_2, after processing the corresponding prefixes uv, respectively. The same is true when $\mathcal{M}$ performs λ-transitions in order to increase the unary stack height. In this case the computation loops, and the pairs can be chosen such that it loops on both pairs. In particular, we have two inputs $a^{m_1} b^{n_1} c w_1 w_1^R c b^{n_1} a^{m_1} = u_1 v_1 x_1$ and $a^{m_2} b^{n_2} c w_2 w_2^R c b^{n_2} a^{m_2} = u_2 v_2 x_2$. Let

$$(q_0, u_1 v_1 x_1, Z_0) \vdash^* (q_1, v_1 x_1, a^k Z_0) \vdash^* (q_2, x_1, a^k Z_0) \vdash^* (q_f, \lambda, \gamma Z_0)$$

as above be an accepting computation. Then

$$(q_0, u_2 v_2 x_1, Z_0) \vdash^* (q_1', v_2 x_1, a^k Z_0) \vdash^* (q_2, x_1, a^k Z_0) \vdash^* (q_f, \lambda, \gamma Z_0)$$

is an accepting computation, either. Since the accepted input $u_2 v_2 x_1$ has the prefix $a^{m_2} b^{n_2} c$ and the suffix $c b^{n_1} a^{m_1}$, a contradiction follows.   □

Theorem 11.

$$\mathscr{L}(\emptyset\text{-}PDA) \subset \mathscr{L}(\{\lambda\}\text{-}PDA) \subset \mathscr{L}(\{a\}^*\text{-}PDA) \subset \mathscr{L}(\{a,b\}^*\text{-}PDA)$$

Proof. We know that $\mathscr{L}(\emptyset\text{-}PDA) = \text{DCFL}$ and $\mathscr{L}(\{\lambda\}\text{-}PDA)$ is equivalent to the regular closure of DCFL. Since DCFL is not closed under any of the regular operations, we conclude that the first inclusion is strict. The properness of the second inclusion is shown by the language $L = \{a^n bwba^n b \mid n \geq 1, w \in \{a, b\}^*\}$. It is easy to see that L is a one-counter language. Therefore, L belongs to $\mathscr{L}(\{a\}^*\text{-}PDA)$ by Lemma 4. On the other hand, $L \notin \mathscr{L}(\{\lambda\}\text{-}PDA)$ due to Lemma 9.

Finally, the language $L' = \{a^m b^n cww^R cb^n a^m \mid m, n \geq 1, w \in \{a, b\}^*\}$ is context free. Since any context-free language can be accepted by some PDA with binary stack alphabet [10], we derive $L' \in \mathscr{L}(\{a, b\}^*\text{-}PDA)$. But L' does not belong to $\mathscr{L}(\{a\}^*\text{-}PDA)$ due to Lemma 10.   □

5   Closure Properties

Now we turn to closure properties of pushdown automata languages with regulated nondeterminism. We consider the AFL operations (union, concatenation, Kleene star, homomorphism, inverse homomorphism, intersection with regular languages) and summarize the properties in Table 1.

Theorem 12. *Let R be a non-empty regular set. Then, $\mathscr{L}(R\text{-}PDA)$ is closed under union, intersection with regular sets, and inverse homomorphism, but is not closed under complementation. If $\mathscr{L}(R\text{-}PDA) \neq CFL$, then it is not closed* *under homomorphism. For $R = \{\lambda\}$, the family is closed under concatenation and Kleene star.*

Proof. Let $\mathcal{M}_1$ and $\mathcal{M}_2$ be two R-PDAs. The R-PDA $\mathcal{M}$ that accepts $T(\mathcal{M}_1) \cup T(\mathcal{M}_2)$ is easily constructed. It decides nondeterministically in its first step whether to simulate $\mathcal{M}_1$ or $\mathcal{M}_2$. The nondeterministic choice is possible, since due to Theorem 6 we may assume $\lambda \in R$.

The proofs of closure under intersection with regular sets and inverse homomorphism are straightforward adaptions of the proofs for pushdown automata given in [12], since the corresponding constructions neither affect the stack behavior nor the deterministic and nondeterministic behavior of the PDA.

It is shown in [16] that there is a language $L \in \mathcal{L}(\{\lambda\}\text{-PDA})$ whose complement is the non-context-free language $\{a^n b^n c^n \mid n \geq 0\}$. Since $\lambda \in R$, we obtain $\mathcal{L}(\{\lambda\}\text{-PDA}) \subseteq \mathcal{L}(R\text{-PDA})$ and, thus, non-closure under complementation.

Since DCFL $\subseteq \mathcal{L}(R\text{-PDA})$ and every context-free language can be represented as the homomorphic image of a deterministic context-free language (cf. [19]), we obtain that $\mathcal{L}(R\text{-PDA})$ is not closed under homomorphism unless $\mathcal{L}(R\text{-PDA}) = \text{CFL}$.

For $R = \{\lambda\}$, the closure under concatenation and Kleene star follows from the characterization of $\mathcal{L}(\{\lambda\}\text{-PDA})$ by the regular closure of DCFL [16]. Obviously, the regular closure is closed under regular operations. $\square$

Table 1. Closure properties of pushdown automata languages with regulated nondeterminism, where R is a non-empty regular set such that $\mathcal{L}(R\text{-PDA}) \neq \text{CFL}$

Language Class	$\cup$	$\bullet$	$*$	h	h^{-1}	$\cap_{reg}$	$\sim$
$\mathcal{L}(1\text{-counter})$	+	+	+	+	+	+	−
$\mathcal{L}(\emptyset\text{-PDA})$	−	−	−	−	+	+	+
$\mathcal{L}(\{\lambda\}\text{-PDA})$	+	+	+	−	+	+	−
$\mathcal{L}(R\text{-PDA})$	+	?	?	−	+	+	−
CFL	+	+	+	+	+	+	−

For $\{\lambda\}$-PDAs and $\{a, b\}^*$-PDAs it is known that empty stack and accepting states are equivalent acceptance modes. It is not clear whether this is also true for R-PDAs with infinite regular sets R such that $\mathcal{L}(R\text{-PDA}) \neq \text{CFL}$. Thus, it is not clear whether such language classes are closed under concatenation and Kleene star, since the standard construction requires acceptance by empty stack.

Acknowledgments

We would like to thank Jürgen Dassow for his suggestion to consider this generalization of context-dependent nondeterminism.

References

1. Autebert, J.M., Berstel, J., Boasson, L.: Context-free languages and pushdown automata. In: Handbook of Formal Languages, vol. 1, pp. 111–174. Springer, Berlin (1997)
2. Bertsch, E., Nederhof, M.J.: Regular closure of deterministic languages. SIAM J. Comput. 29, 81–102 (1999)
3. Dassow, J., Păun, G.: Regulated Rewriting in Formal Language Theory. Springer, Berlin (1989)
4. Dassow, J., Păun, G., Salomaa, A.: Grammars with controlled derivations. In: Handbook of Formal Languages, vol. 2, pp. 101–154. Springer, Berlin (1997)
5. Fischer, P.C., Kintala, C.M.R.: Real-time computations with restricted nondeterminism. Math. Systems Theory 12, 219–231 (1979)
6. Goldsmith, J., Levy, M.A., Mundhenk, M.: Limited nondeterminism. SIGACT News 27, 20–29 (1996)
7. Goldstine, J., Kintala, C.M.R., Wotschke, D.: On measuring nondeterminism in regular languages. Inform. and Comput. 86, 179–194 (1990)
8. Goldstine, J., Leung, H., Wotschke, D.: On the relation between ambiguity and nondeterminism in finite automata. Inform. and Comput. 100, 261–270 (1992)
9. Goldstine, J., Leung, H., Wotschke, D.: Measuring nondeterminism in pushdown automata. J. Comput. System Sci. 71, 440–466 (2005)
10. Goldstine, J., Price, J.K., Wotschke, D.: On reducing the number of stack symbols in a PDA. Math. Systems Theory 26, 313–326 (1993)
11. Herzog, C.: Pushdown automata with bounded nondeterminism and bounded ambiguity. Theoret. Comput. Sci. 181, 141–157 (1997)
12. Hopcroft, J.E., Ullman, J.D.: Introduction to Automata Theory, Languages, and Computation. Addison-Wesley Publishing Co., Reading, Mass. (1979)
13. Kintala, C.M.R.: Computations with a restricted number of nondeterministic steps. PhD thesis, Pennsylvania State University (1977)
14. Kintala, C.M.R., Wotschke, D.: Amounts of nondeterminism in finite automata. Acta Inform. 13, 199–204 (1980)
15. Kutrib, M.: Refining nondeterminsim below linear time. J. Autom. Lang. Comb. 7, 533–547 (2002)
16. Kutrib, M., Malcher, A.: Context-dependent nondeterminism for pushdown automata. Theoret. Comput. Sci. 376, 101–111 (2007)
17. Meduna, A., Kolář, D.: Regulated pushdown automata. Acta Cybernet. 14, 653–664 (2000)
18. Meduna, A., Kolář, D.: One-turn regulated pushdown automata and their reduction. Fund. Inform. 51, 399–405 (2002)
19. Salomaa, A.: Formal Languages. Academic Press, New York (1973)
20. Salomaa, K., Yu, S.: Limited nondeterminism for pushdown automata. Bull. EATCS 50, 186–193 (1993)
21. Salomaa, K., Yu, S.: Measures of nondeterminism for pushdown automata. J. Comput. System Sci. 49, 362–374 (1994)
22. Vermeir, D., Savitch, W.J.: On the amount of nondeterminism in pushdown automata. Fund. Inform. 4, 401–418 (1981)

Deterministic Caterpillar Expressions*

Kai Salomaa[1], Sheng Yu[2], and Jinfeng Zan[1]

[1] School of Computing, Queen's University, Kingston, Ontario K7L 3N6, Canada
{ksalomaa,zan}@cs.queensu.ca
[2] Department of Computer Science, University of Western Ontario, London, Ontario
N6A 5B7, Canada
syu@csd.uwo.ca

Abstract. Caterpillar expressions have been introduced by Brüggemann-Klein and Wood for applications in markup languages. A caterpillar expression can be implemented as a tree walking automaton operating on unranked trees. Here we give a formal definition of determinism of caterpillar expressions that is based on the language of instruction sequences defined by the expression. We show that determinism of caterpillar expressions can be decided in polynomial time.

Keywords: regular expressions, tree walking automata, determinism, decidability.

1 Introduction

Tree-walking automata have been used for the specification of context in structured documents and for tree pattern matching, for references see e.g. [21,22]. Differing from the classical tree automata, these applications typically use unranked trees where the number of children of a given node is finite but unbounded. In the unranked case, for example, when considering down moves of a tree walking automaton the finite transition function cannot directly specify an arbitrary child node where the automaton moves to.

Brüggemann-Klein and Wood [7,8] introduced caterpillar expressions as a convenient tool to specify style sheets for XML documents. For possible applications of caterpillar expressions see also [13,20,23]. A caterpillar expression is, roughly speaking, a regular expression built from atomic instructions and such expressions provide an intuitive and simple formalism for specifying the operation of tree walking automata on unranked trees. Each atomic instruction specifies the direction of the next move or a test on the current node label. The sequences of legal instructions define the computations of a tree walking automaton on an unranked input tree.

Concerning tree walking automata in general, it is easy to see that any tree language recognized by a tree walking automaton is regular, and consequently the same holds for tree languages defined by caterpillars. It has been a long-standing open question whether tree walking automata recognize all regular tree

* Work supported in part by the Natural Sciences and Engineering Research Council of Canada grants OGP0147224 (Salomaa) and OGP0041630 (Yu).

languages. A negative answer was conjectured by Engelfriet et al. [11,12] and finally Bojańczyk and Colcombet [3] have established this result. Neven and Schwentick [23] and Okhotin et al. [24] have investigated restricted classes of tree walking automata and obtained negative recognizability results for these classes.

Given a caterpillar expression a crucial question is whether the computation it defines is deterministic. Recently Bojańczyk and Colcombet [2] have shown that nondeterministic tree walking automata cannot, in general, be simulated by the deterministic variant.

In their original paper Brüggemann-Klein and Wood discussed the notion of determinism only informally and presented examples of deterministic caterpillars. Here we will give a formal definition of determinism of caterpillar expressions in terms of the set of instruction sequences defined by the expression. We show that determinism of caterpillar expressions can be decided in polynomial time. The general algorithm is based on ideas that have been used to test code properties of regular languages [1,17]. We develop a more direct algorithm to test determinism of caterpillar expressions where the corresponding instruction language has fixed polynomial density. Also, we show that general caterpillar expressions have the same expressive power as nondeterministic tree walking automata.

2 Preliminaries

We assume that the reader is familiar with the basic notions associated with regular expressions and finite automata [18,28].

The set of words over an alphabet Ω is Ω^* and the empty word is λ. The length of a word $u \in \Omega^*$ is $|u|$. If u is nonempty, the first symbol of u is denoted $\text{first}(u)$. The prefix-relation for words over alphabet Ω is denoted $\leq_p$, that is, for $u, v \in \Omega^*$, $u \leq_p v$ if and only if $v = uu'$ for some $u' \in \Omega^*$. Similarly the "strict prefix" relation is denoted by $<_p$. We denote $u \simeq_p v$ if $u \leq_p v$ or $v \leq_p u$. The longest common prefix of words u and v is denoted as $\text{lcp}(u, v)$. The left-quotient of v by u, $u \setminus v$, is equal to w where $uw = v$ if $u \leq_p v$, and $u \setminus v$ is undefined otherwise.

A nondeterministic finite automaton (NFA) is a tuple $A = (\Omega, Q, q_0, F, \delta)$ where Ω is the input alphabet, Q is the finite set of states, $q_0 \in Q$ is the start state, $F \subseteq Q$ is the set of accepting states and $\delta \subseteq Q \times \Omega \times Q$ is the set of transitions. The language recognized by A is denoted $L(A) \subseteq \Omega^*$.

The NFA A is said to be *reduced* if for any state $q \in Q$ there is a path from q_0 to q and a path from q to some accepting state. The NFA A is a deterministic finite automaton (DFA) if for any $q \in Q$ and $b \in \Omega$ there exists at most one $q' \in Q$ such that $(q, b, q') \in \delta$. The nondeterministic and deterministic finite automata recognize exactly the regular languages.

The density function of a language $L \subseteq \Omega^*$ is defined as $\varrho_L(n) = |L \cap \Omega^n|$, $n \in \mathbb{N}$. Here $\mathbb{N}$ denotes the set of positive integers. We recall the following characterization of polynomial density regular languages from [27,28], similar results can be found also e.g. in [10].

Proposition 1. *A regular language R over Ω has density in $O(n^k)$, $k \geq 0$, iff R can be denoted by a finite union of regular expressions of the form*

$$w_0 u_1^* w_1 u_2^* \cdots u_{m+1}^* w_{m+1}, \quad m \leq k \tag{1}$$

where $w_i, u_j \in \Omega^*$, $i = 0, \ldots, m+1$, $j = 1, \ldots, m+1$.

We call finite unions of regular expressions as in (1), *k-bounded regular expressions over Ω.*

Below we still recall a few notions associated with trees and tree automata. General references for tree automata are [9,14] and aspects specific to unranked trees are discussed e.g. in [5].

In the following Σ denotes always a finite alphabet that is used to label the nodes of the trees. A *tree domain* D is a subset of $\mathbb{N}^*$ such that if $u \in D$ then every prefix of u is in D and there exists $m_u \geq 0$ such that for $j \in \mathbb{N}$, $u \cdot j \in D$ iff $j \leq m_u$. A Σ-labeled tree is a mapping $t : D \to \Sigma$ where $D = \mathrm{dom}(t)$ is a tree domain. If Σ is a ranked alphabet, each symbol $\sigma \in \Sigma$ has a fixed rank denoted $\mathrm{rank}(\sigma) \in \mathbb{N} \cup \{0\}$, and the rank determines the number of children of all nodes labeled by σ. In the general case, when referring to unranked trees, the label $t(u)$ of a node u does not specify the number of children of u, m_u (and there is no apriori upper bound for m_u). The set of Σ-labeled trees is denoted T_Σ.

3   Caterpillars and Determinism

Caterpillar expressions have been introduced in [7]. Here we present a somewhat streamlined definition that includes only what will be needed below for discussing determinism.

Definition 2. *Let Σ be a set of node labels for the input trees. The set of atomic caterpillar instructions is*

$$\Delta = \Sigma \cup \{isFirst, isLast, isLeaf, isRoot, Up, Left, Right, First, Last\}. \tag{2}$$

A caterpillar expression is a regular expression over Δ.

An atomic instruction $a \in \Sigma$ tests whether the label of the current node is a. The instructions *isFirst*, *isLast*, *isLeaf* and *isRoot* test whether the current node is the first (leftmost) sibling of its parent, the last sibling, a leaf node or the root node, respectively. The above are the *test instructions.*

The *move instructions Up, Left, Right, First* and *Last*, respectively, make the caterpillar to move from the current node to its parent, the next sibling to the left, the next sibling to the right, the leftmost child of the current node, or the rightmost child of the current node, respectively.

Let α be a caterpillar expression. By the *instruction language of α*, $L(\alpha)$, we mean the set of all sequences of instructions over Δ that are denoted by the expression α (when α is viewed as an ordinary regular expression). Below we define the configurations and the computation relation associated with expression α. Intuitively, the computations can be viewed as a tree walking automaton that, on an input tree t, implements all possible sequences of instructions $w \in L(\alpha)$.

Formally, a *t-configuration* of α is a pair (u, w) where $t \in T_\Sigma$ is the input tree, $u \in \mathrm{dom}(t)$ is the current node and and $w \in \Delta^*$ is the remaining sequence of instructions. The single step computation relation between t-configurations is defined by setting $(u, w) \vdash (u', w')$ if $w = cw'$, $c \in \Delta$, $w' \in \Delta^*$, $u, u' \in \mathrm{dom}(t)$, and the following holds:

(i) If c is a test instruction, c returns true at node $u \in \mathrm{dom}(t)$ and $u' = u$.

(ii) If c is one of the move instructions *Up*, *Left*, *Right*, *First* or *Last* then, respectively, $u = u'j$, $j \in \mathbb{N}$ (u' is the parent of u), $u = v(j+1)$, $u' = vj$, $v \in \mathbb{N}^*$, $j \in \mathbb{N}$ (u' is the sibling of u immediately to the left), $u = vj$, $u' = v(j+1)$, $v \in \mathbb{N}^*$, $j \in \mathbb{N}$ (u' is the sibling of u immediately to the right), $u' = u1$ (u' is the leftmost child of u), or $u' = uj$, $j \in \mathbb{N}$ and $u(j+1) \notin \mathrm{dom}(t)$ (u' is the rightmost child of u).

Let α be a caterpillar expression. The tree language defined by α is

$$T(\alpha) = \{\, t \in T_\Sigma \mid (\exists w \in L(\alpha))\ (\lambda, w) \vdash^* (u, \lambda) \text{ for some } u \in \mathrm{dom}(t) \,\}.$$

Thus $t \in T(\alpha)$ if and only if some sequence of instructions denoted by α can be executed to completion where the computation begins at the root of t and ends at an arbitrary node of t. The definition could alternatively require that the caterpillar has to return to the root of t at the end of the computation.

Example 3. Let $a, b \in \Sigma$. Define α as the expression

$$(First \cdot Right^*)^* \cdot isFirst \cdot (isLeaf \cdot a \cdot Right)(isLeaf \cdot b \cdot Right)(isLeaf \cdot a \cdot isLast).$$

The caterpillar α defines the set of trees that contain a node with precisely three children that are all leaves and labeled, respectively, by a, b, a.

The behavior of a caterpillar expression is described using a tree walking automaton and, conversely, we show that caterpillar expressions can simulate arbitrary tree walking automata. We state the result below comparing the expressive power of caterpillar expressions and tree walking automata only for tree languages over a ranked alphabet. Most of the work on tree walking automata, e.g., [2,12,23], uses trees over ranked alphabets.

Theorem 4. *Let Σ be a ranked alphabet. Caterpillar expressions define the same sets of Σ-labeled trees as the nondeterministic tree walking automata.*

Proof. We need to show only how to simulate a tree walking automaton A by a caterpillar expression. We denote the set of states of A as Q and m is the maximum rank of elements of Σ. The transitions of A are defined as a set of tuples (q, σ, j, q'), where $q \in Q$ is the current state, $\sigma \in \Sigma$ is the current node label, $j \in \{0, 1, \ldots, \mathrm{rank}(\sigma)\}$ is the direction of the next move and $q' \in Q$ is the state after the move. Here "0" is an up move and "i", $1 \leq i \leq \text{rank}(\sigma)$, denotes a move to the ith child.

Denote $\Omega = Q \times \Sigma \times \{0, 1, \ldots, m\} \times Q$. The set of *semi-computations* of A is the regular language $L_{sc} \subseteq \Omega^*$ that consists of all words $\omega_1 \cdots \omega_k$, where $\omega_i \in \Omega$ is a tuple that represents a transition of A, $i = 1, \ldots, k$, and $\pi_1(\omega_1)$ is the start state of A, $\pi_4(\omega_k)$ is an accepting state of A and $\pi_4(\omega_i) = \pi_1(\omega_{i+1})$, $i = 1, \ldots, k-1$. Here π_j is the projection to the jth component.

Any accepting computation of A corresponds to a word of L_{sc} but, conversely, words of L_{sc} need not represent an accepting computation since the definition of L_{sc} requires only that the computation is locally correct and does not verify that the number of up moves does not exceed the number of down moves. However, the language L_{sc} will give the following correspondence with instruction languages defined by caterpillar expressions.

Let Δ be as in (2) and define a mapping $f : \Omega^* \to \Delta^*$ by setting

$$f(q, \sigma, j, q') = \begin{cases} \sigma \cdot First \cdot (Right)^{j-1} & \text{if } 1 \leq j \leq \text{rank}(\sigma), \\ \sigma \cdot Up & \text{if } j = 0. \end{cases} \tag{3}$$

Now the language $f(L_{sc})$ is regular and hence it is denoted by some caterpillar expression α_{sc}. The instruction sequences of $L(\alpha_{sc})$ correspond to semi-computations of A where we have deleted the state information, and any $u \in L(\alpha_{sc})$ can be completed to a semi-computation according to the correspondence (3). As observed above, a semi-computation need not represent a correct computation of A due to the possibility of trying to make an up move at the root of the tree. In this situation also the execution of the corresponding sequence of caterpillar instructions obtained via the function f gets blocked. This means that $w \in L_{sc}$ encodes a valid computation on $t \in T_\Sigma$ iff the sequence of caterpillar instructions $f(w)$ can be successfully executed on t. Hence $T(\alpha_{sc})$ is exactly the tree language recognized by A. □

The result of Theorem 4 can be straightforwardly extended for unranked trees assuming we extend the operation of tree walking automata to unranked trees in some reasonable way, e.g., the down moves could be made only to the first or last child and then the automaton could make moves to the closest sibling node. The proof of Theorem 4 didn't use several of the caterpillar instructions. For example, the test *isLeaf* is not needed because on ranked trees this property can be decided by looking at the node label. Similarly, (deterministic) tree walking automata on unranked trees would need a mechanism to detect whether the node is a leaf. For unranked trees the details of the simulation would depend on the precise definition of the tree walking automaton model.

Next we turn to the notion of determinism. By definition, a caterpillar expression can be simulated by a tree walking automaton [8,12,24] and, intuitively, we say that a caterpillar is deterministic if the computation performing the simulation is deterministic. This operational definition was used by Brüggemann-Klein and Wood [7,8] to deal with the notion of determinism.

In order to, for example, algorithmically decide determinism of given caterpillar expressions, it is necessary to have a more direct definition of determinism in terms of the sequences of instructions denoted by an expression.

Let Δ be the set of atomic instructions given in Definition 2. Let $t \in T_\Sigma$ be arbitrary. We say that instruction $c \in \Delta$ is *successfully executed* at node $u \in \text{dom}(t)$ if there exist $w \in \Delta^*$ and $u' \in \text{dom}(t)$ such that $(u, cw) \vdash (u', w)$. (Without loss of generality we could choose w to be λ.)

Definition 5. *Let $c, c' \in \Delta$. We say that instructions c and c' are* mutually exclusive *if either*

(i) *$c, c' \in \Sigma$ and $c \neq c'$, that is, c and c' are tests on distinct symbols of Σ, or,*
(ii) *$\{c, c'\}$ is one of the sets $\{First, isLeaf\}$, $\{Last, isLeaf\}$, $\{Up, isRoot\}$, $\{Left, isFirst\}$, or $\{Right, isLast\}$.*

The following lemma can be verified by a straightforward case analysis.

Lemma 6. *For any $c, c' \in \Delta$, $c \neq c'$, the following two conditions are equivalent.*

(i) *There exists $t \in T_\Sigma$ and $u \in \text{dom}(t)$ such that c and c' can be successfully executed at node u.*
(ii) *The instructions c and c' are not mutually exclusive.*

In order for a caterpillar expression α to define a deterministic computation, we require that in computations controlled by α on any input tree there cannot be a situation where the computation could successfully execute two different instructions as the next step. Formally, we define the notion of determinism associated with caterpillar expressions as follows.

Definition 7. *Let α be a caterpillar expression over Δ. We say that α is* deterministic *if the following implication holds. If wc_1w_1 and wc_2w_2 are in $L(\alpha)$ where $w, w_1, w_2 \in \Delta^*$, $c_1, c_2 \in \Delta$, $c_1 \neq c_2$, then c_1 and c_2 are mutually exclusive.*

The definition says that for any instruction sequences w and w' defined by α that are not prefixes of one another, the pair of instructions following the longest common prefix of w and w' has to be mutually exclusive. Note that if $w, w' \in L(\alpha)$ where w is a proper prefix of w', this corresponds to a situation where the corresponding tree walking automaton has reached an accepting state after simulating the instructions of w and the tree walking automaton can execute further moves. According to our definition this does not constitute an instance of nondeterminism. By Lemma 6, Definition 7 coincides with the operational definition of determinism discussed earlier.

Note that the condition of Definition 7, strictly speaking, depends only on the instruction language of α. In the following, when there is no confusion, we say that a language $L \subseteq \Delta^*$ is deterministic if L satisfies the condition of Definition 7. Also, we note that it might seem that determinism of caterpillar expressions is related to unambiguity of regular expressions [4,6]. However, it is not difficult to verify that deterministic expressions need not be unambiguous or vice versa.

The caterpillar of Example 3 is obviously nondeterministic. The subexpression $(First \cdot Right^*)^*$ involves choices between instructions $First$ and $Right$, and these allow the caterpillar to move from the root to an arbitrary node.

Example 8. [7] Consider the caterpillar expression

$$\alpha_{\mathrm{trav}} = First^* \cdot isLeaf \cdot (Right \cdot First^* \cdot isLeaf)^* \cdot isLast \cdot$$
$$\left(Up \cdot (Right \cdot First^* \cdot isLeaf)^* \cdot isLast \right)^* \cdot isRoot$$

Here the subexpression $First^* \cdot isLeaf$ finds the leftmost leaf of the tree. Next the subexpression $(Right \cdot First^* \cdot isLeaf)^* \cdot isLast$ finds the leftmost leaf of the current subtree that is the last child of its parent. The process is then iterated by going one step up in the subexpression $(Up \cdots isLast)^*$ and in this way it can be verified that the expression α_{trav} defines a computation that traverses an arbitrary input tree in depth-first left-to-right order.

Furthermore, it is easy to verify that α_{trav} is deterministic. In the notations of Definition 7 possible pairs of instructions c_1, c_2 that may occur in the instruction sequences are $\{First, isLeaf\}$, $\{Right, isLast\}$ and $\{Up, isRoot\}$ and these are all mutually exclusive.

In Theorem 4 we have seen that general caterpillar expressions can simulate nondeterministic tree walking automata. The morphism f used in the proof of Theorem 4, roughly speaking, erases the state information from encodings of (semi-)computations and the instruction language ($\subseteq \Delta^*$) corresponding to a deterministic tree walking automaton need not be deterministic in the sense of Definition 7. On the other hand, the deterministic caterpillar expression considered in Example 8 can traverse an arbitrary input tree which indicates that it may not be very easy to show that some particular tree language (recognized by a deterministic tree walking automaton) cannot be defined by any deterministic caterpillar expression.

Problem 9. Do the deterministic tree walking automata define a strictly larger family of tree languages than the tree languages defined by deterministic caterpillar expressions?

4   Deciding Determinism

First we develop a reasonably efficient algorithm to decide determinism of k-bounded caterpillar expressions, that is, expressions where the instruction language has polynomial density. This algorithm is based only on structural properties of the caterpillar expressions. Afterwards we consider an algorithm to test determinism of general expressions.

Let Δ be as in (2). In the following $k \in \mathbb{N}$ is fixed and we consider caterpillar expressions that are sums of expressions of the form

$$x_0 y_1^* x_1 y_2^* x_2 \cdots y_{m+1}^* x_{m+1}, \quad x_i, y_j \in \Delta^*, y_j \neq \lambda, \tag{4}$$

$i = 0, \ldots, m + 1$, $j = 1, \ldots, m + 1$, $m \le k$. Note that above the assumption $y_j \ne \lambda$ can be made without loss of generality. If α is as above, by the length of α we mean $|\alpha| = |x_0| + \sum_{i=1}^{m+1} |x_i y_i|$.

We say that an expression (4) is *normalized* if

$$\text{for each } 1 \le i \le m + 1, \quad \text{lcp}(x_i, y_i) = \lambda, \text{ and } x_j \ne \lambda, \text{ for each } 1 \le j \le m. \quad (5)$$

The proof of the following lemma can be found in the full version of the paper [25].

Lemma 10. *Consider an arbitrary expression α of length n as in (4) and let k be the constant bounding m. The expression α can be written as the sum of $O(n^k)$ normalized expressions each having length $O(k \cdot n)$.*

Let α be as in (4). We say that α is *well-behaved* if $x_i \ne \lambda$ implies that $\text{first}(y_i)$ and $\text{first}(x_i)$ are mutually exclusive, $1 \le i \le m + 1$.

Note that always $y_i \ne \lambda$. If α is normalized, then x_i can be the empty word only when $i = m + 1$. When considering prefixes of $L(\alpha)$, where α is normalized, after the last symbol of y_i the next symbol can be one of $\text{first}(y_i)$ and $\text{first}(x_i)$ and these are known to be distinct. Hence the following lemma is immediate.

Lemma 11. *If α as in (4) is normalized and deterministic, then α is well-behaved.*

Due to Lemmas 10 and 11, in order to test determinism of k-bounded expressions it is sufficient to consider sums of well-behaved normalized expressions. Consider two well-behaved normalized k-bounded caterpillar expressions over Δ,

$$\alpha = x_0 y_1^* x_1 \cdots y_{m+1}^* x_{m+1}, \quad \beta = u_0 v_1^* u_1 \cdots v_{q+1}^* u_{q+1}, \quad m, q \le k. \quad (6)$$

We describe an algorithm `TestNormalizedExpr` to test whether or not $\alpha + \beta$ is deterministic where α and β are as in (6). By Lemma 11 it is sufficient to determine whether there exist $w_\alpha \in L(\alpha)$ and $w_\beta \in L(\beta)$ such that

$$w_\alpha \text{ and } w_\beta \text{ violate the condition of determinism.} \quad (7)$$

Intuitively, the algorithm works as follows. We are dealing with longest common prefixes of z_α and z_β where z_α is a prefix of $L(\alpha)$ and z_β is a prefix of $L(\beta)$, and the algorithm tries to find a situation where the longest common prefix can be extended by two symbols that are not mutually exclusive. In case z_α is a prefix of z_β the algorithm can expand z_α by appending a word y_r or x_r, $1 \le r \le m+1$, where the algorithm keeps track of the current index r. (If z_β is a prefix of z_α, we have a symmetric situation.) Since α is normalized, y_r and x_r are nonempty and $\text{first}(y_r) \ne \text{first}(x_r)$. This means that only one of the expanded words can be in the prefix relation with z_β and only this option will need to be pursued further. Only in the case where $z_\alpha = z_\beta$ there can be two distinct ways to expand the words where the algorithm doesn't get the answer "right away", and the number of this type of instances is bounded by $2k$.

We introduce the following notation:

(i) $Y(i_1, \ldots, i_r) = x_0 y_1^{i_1} x_1 y_2^{i_2} \cdots x_{r-1} y_r^{i_r}$, $1 \le r \le m+1$, $i_b \ge 0$, $b = 1, \ldots, r$.

(ii) $V(j_1, \ldots, j_s) = u_0 v_1^{j_1} u_1 v_2^{j_2} \cdots u_{s-1} v_s^{j_s}$, $1 \le s \le q+1$, $j_b \ge 0$, $b = 1, \ldots, s$.

A word $Y(i_1, \ldots, i_r)$ (respectively, $V(j_1, \ldots, j_s)$) is a prefix of a word in $L(\alpha)$ (respectively, in $L(\beta)$). Note that if $r < m+1$ then $Y(i_1, \ldots, i_r, 0) = Y(i_1, \ldots, i_r)x_{i_r}$ and the words $V(j_1, \ldots, j_s)$ satisfy a similar property.

We say that the *index* of a pair of words $(Y(i_1, \ldots, i_r), V(j_1, \ldots, j_s))$ is (r, s). Note that since α is normalized, always when $r \ne r'$ we have $Y(i_1, \ldots, i_r) \ne Y(i'_1, \ldots, i'_{r'})$ independently of the parameters $i_1, \ldots, i_r$ and $i'_1, \ldots, i'_{r'}$. The V-words have the analogous property since β is normalized and this means that the index of a pair of words is uniquely defined.

The algorithm uses a method Compare(w_1, w_2) that for given $w_1, w_2 \in \Delta^*$ finds their longest common prefix and looks at the following symbols of w_1 and w_2. Only in the case where w_1 is a prefix of w_2 or vice versa, Compare(w_1, w_2) does not directly give an answer, and the algorithm has to continue comparing possible continuations of w_1 and w_2.

The algorithm begins by comparing $Y(0) = x_0$ and $V(0) = u_0$. For the general case, we consider a method call

$$\text{Compare}(Y(i_1, \ldots, i_r), V(j_1, \ldots j_s)), \quad r, s \ge 1. \tag{8}$$

of the recursive algorithm. The essential idea will be that the algorithm employs a counter that keeps track of the number of recursive calls (8) that have taken place since the index was changed. Consider a method call (8) where the index of the of the argument words is (r, s). If this is followed by a sequence of compare method calls where the index of each pair of argument words remains (r, s), this means that we are consecutively appending copies of y_r to $Y(i_1, \ldots, i_r)$ and copies of v_s to $V(j_1, \ldots, j_s)$, and the resulting words $Y(i_1, \ldots, i_r+b)$, $V(j_1, \ldots, j_s+c)$ always remain in the prefix relation. Recall that when the argument words are not in the prefix relation, the next compare method call gives a definitive answer. Thus, if we have a sequence of $|y_r| + |v_s|$ method calls where the index remains (r, s), the computation must be in a cycle. (A more detailed description of the choices after a recursive call (8) and of why we can bound the counter by $|y_r| + |v_s|$ is included in the the full version of the paper [25].)

One call of the compare method (8) uses linear time as a function of the argument word lengths. The length of the arguments of (8) can be longer than the input length $n = |\alpha| + |\beta|$. We have observed that in the arguments of (8) we can always restrict $i_r, j_s \le |y_r| + |v_s|$ and hence $|Y(i_1, \ldots, i_r)|, |V(j_1, \ldots, j_s)| \in O(n^2)$. Strictly speaking, according to the above description, one branch of the computation makes $O(n)$ calls to the compare method, but by keeping track of the current positions in prefixes of $L(\alpha)$ and $L(\beta)$ the total time of one branch of the computation can also be bounded by $O(n^2)$.

The computation may branch into two cases when in a recursive call (8) we have $Y(i_1, \ldots, i_r) = V(j_1, \ldots, j_s)$. With a fixed index (r, s) this branching needs to be done only once. Putting all the above together we have seen that the algorithm operates in time $2^{2k} \cdot O(n^2)$.

Combining Lemma 10 with the algorithm `TestNormalizedExpr` we get the following:

Proposition 12. *Let Δ be as in (2) and k is fixed. Given a k-bounded caterpillar expression α over Δ (i.e., α is a sum of arbitrarily many expressions as in (4)) we can decide in polynomial time whether or not α is deterministic.*

Note that the time bound of `TestNormalizedExpr` to decide determinism of a sum of normalized expressions is of the form $f(k)O(n^2)$. In the time bound the function f depends exponentially on k but, since the branching occurs only when the current prefixes coincide, in fact, on most inputs the running time should be essentially better. Arbitrary k-bounded expressions need to be written as sums of normalized expressions (according to Lemma 10) and the worst-case behaviour of the algorithm of Proposition 12 would not be better than the behaviour of the general algorithm we will discuss below. The algorithm of Proposition 12 may be useful in cases where the input expressions are in a normalized form.

To conclude this section we show that determinism can be decided in polynomial time also for general caterpillar expressions. Given a caterpillar expression α it would not be difficult to verify whether or not α satisfies the condition of Definition 7 assuming we can construct the minimal DFA for the instruction language of α. However, this approach would result in an exponential time algorithm due to the exponential worst-case blow-up of converting a regular expression to a DFA.

Here we give an algorithm to test determinism that is based on the state-pair graph associated with a reduced NFA recognizing the instruction language of α. The construction relies on ideas that have been used to test code properties of regular languages [1,17].

Definition 13. *Let $A = (\Omega, Q, q_0, F, \delta)$ be an NFA. The state-pair graph of A is defined as a directed graph $G_A = (V, E)$ where the set of nodes is $V = Q \times Q$ and the set of Ω-labeled edges is*

$$E = \{((p, q), b, (p', q')) \mid (p, b, p') \in \delta, (q, b, q') \in \delta, \ b \in \Omega\}.$$

Lemma 14. *Assume $A = (\Delta, Q, q_0, F, \delta)$ is a reduced NFA with input alphabet Δ as in (2). The language $L(A)$ is not deterministic if and only if there exist $p, q \in Q$ such that*

(i) *The state-pair graph G_A has a path from (q_0, q_0) to (p, q).*
(ii) *There exist $c_1, c_2 \in \Delta$, $c_1 \neq c_2$, such that $(p, c_1, p') \in \delta$ and $(q, c_2, q') \in \delta$ for some $p', q' \in Q$, and c_1, c_2 are not mutually exclusive.*

Proof. First assume that $L(A)$ is not deterministic in the sense of Definition 7. Thus, there exist $w, w_1, w_2 \in \Delta^*$, $c_1, c_2 \in \Delta$, $c_1 \neq c_2$, where c_1 and c_2 are not mutually exclusive, such that $w c_i w_i \in L(A)$, $i = 1, 2$. Let C_i be an accepting computation of A on the word $w c_i w_i$, and let p_i be the state of C_i after reading the prefix w. This means that in the graph G_A the node (p_1, p_2) is reachable from (q_0, q_0) and a transition on c_i is defined in state p_i. Thus, the conditions (i) and (ii) hold.

Conversely, assume that $p, q, p', q' \in Q$ and $c_1, c_2 \in \Delta$ are as in (i) and (ii). Since G_A has a path from (q_0, q_0) to (p, q) there exists $w \in \Delta^*$ such that both p and q are reachable from q_0 on word w. Since A is reduced, there exists $w_{p'}$ (respectively, $w_{q'}$) that reaches an accepting state from p' (respectively, q'). Thus $wc_1 w_{p'}, wc_2 w_{q'} \in L(A)$ and $L(A)$ is not deterministic.   □

In the second part of the proof, note that we require that (p, q) is reachable from (q_0, q_0) in the graph G_A whereas the accepting states can be reached from p' and q' along computations of A not necessarily along the same word.

Lemma 15. *Given a caterpillar expression α of size n over an alphabet Δ as in (2) we can construct in time $O(n^2 \log^4 n)$ the state-pair graph G_A of an NFA A that recognizes the instruction language $L(\alpha)$ of α.*

Proof. For α having size n we can construct an NFA (without ε-transitions) with $O(n \cdot (\log n)^2)$ transitions and the transformation can be done in time $O(n \log n + m)$ where m is the size of the output [16,19,26]. The NFA can be reduced and the corresponding state-pair graph can be constructed in square time in the size of the NFA.   □

Note that if Δ is considered to be fixed, the upper bound for the regular expression-to-NFA conversion can be improved [15,26]. Combining the results of Lemma 14 and 15 with any graph reachability algorithm we have:

Theorem 16. *Given an alphabet Δ as in (2) and a caterpillar expression α over Δ we can decide in polynomial time whether or not α is deterministic.*

References

1. Berstel, J., Perrin, D.: Theory of Codes. Academic Press, Inc., London (1985)
2. Bojańczyk, M., Colcombet, T.: Tree walking automata cannot be determinized. Theoret. Comput. Sci. 350, 164–173 (2006)
3. Bojańczyk, M., Colcombet, T.: Tree-walking automata do not recognize all regular languages. In: Proceedings of STOC 2005, pp. 234–243. ACM Press, New York (2005)
4. Book, R.V., Even, S., Greibach, S., Ott, G.: Ambiguity in graphs and expressions. IEEE Trans. on Computers 20, 149–153 (1971)
5. Brüggemann-Klein, A., Murata, M., Wood, D.: Regular tree and regular hedge languages over unranked alphabets. Technical Report HKUST-TCSC-2001-0, The Hongkong University of Science and Technology (2001)
6. Brüggemann-Klein, A., Wood, D.: One-unambiguous regular languages. Inform. Computation 142, 182–206 (1998)
7. Brüggemann-Klein, A., Wood, D.: Caterpillars: A context-specification technique. Mark-up Languages: Theory & Practice 2, 81–106 (2000)
8. Brüggemann-Klein, A., Wood, D.: Caterpillars, context, tree automata and tree pattern matching. In: Rozenberg, G., Thomas, W. (eds.) DLT 1999, pp. 270–285. World Scientific, Singapore (2000)

9. Comon, H., Gilleron, R., Jacquemard, F., Lugiez, D., Tison, S., Tommasi, M.: Tree Automata Techniques and Applications (1997), http://www.grappa.univ-lille3.fr/tata
10. Eilenberg, S.: Automata, Languages, and Machines, vol. A. Academic Press, New York (1974)
11. Engelfriet, J., Hoogeboom, H.J.: Tree-walking pebble automata. In: Karhumäki, J., Maurer, H., Păun, Gh., Rozenberg, G. (eds.) Jewels are forever, pp. 72–83. Springer, Heidelberg (1999)
12. Engelfriet, J., Hoogeboom, H.J., van Best, J.P.: Trips on trees. Acta Cybern. 14, 51–64 (1999)
13. Fernau, H.: Learning XML grammars. In: Perner, P. (ed.) MLDM 2001. LNCS (LNAI), vol. 2123, pp. 73–87. Springer, Heidelberg (2001)
14. Gécseg, F., Steinby, M.: Tree languages. In: Rozenberg, G., Salomaa, A. (eds.) Handbook of Formal Languages, vol. 3, pp. 1–68. Springer, Heidelberg (1997)
15. Geffert, V.: Translation of binary regular expressions into nondeterministic ε-free automata with $O(n \log n)$ transitions. J. Comput. System Sci. 66, 451–472 (2003)
16. Hagenah, C., Muscholl, A.: Computing ε-free NFA from regular expressions in $O(n \log^2(n))$ time. R.A.I.R.O. Theoret. Inform. Appl. 34, 257–277 (2000)
17. Han, Y.-S., Salomaa, K., Wood, D.: Intercode regular languages. Fund. Informaticae 76, 113–128 (2007)
18. Hopcroft, J.E., Ullman, J.D.: Introduction to Automata Theory, Languages, and Computation. Addison-Wesley, Reading (1979)
19. Hromkovič, J., Seibert, S., Wilke, T.: Translating regular expressions into small ε-free nondeterministic automata. J. Comput. System Sci. 62, 565–588 (2001)
20. Kilpeläinen, P., Wood, D.: SGML and XML document grammars and exceptions. Inform. Computation 163, 230–251 (2001)
21. Milo, T., Suciu, D., Vianu, V.: Typechecking for XML transformers. J. Comput. System Sci. 66, 66–97 (2002)
22. Murata, M., Lee, D., Mani, M.: Taxonomy of XML schema languages using formal language theory. ACM Trans. Internet Technology 5 (2005)
23. Neven, F., Schwentick, T.: On the power of tree walking automata. Inform. Computation 183, 86–103 (2003)
24. Okhotin, A., Salomaa, K., Domaratzki, M.: One-visit caterpillar tree automata. Fund. Informaticae 52, 361–375 (2002)
25. Salomaa, K., Yu, S., Zan, J.: Deterministic caterpillar expressions. School of Computing, Queen's University, Tech. Report No. 2007–533 (2007)
26. Schnitger, G.: Regular expressions and NFA without ε-transitions. In: Durand, B., Thomas, W. (eds.) STACS 2006. LNCS, vol. 3884, pp. 432–443. Springer, Heidelberg (2006)
27. Szilard, A., Yu, S., Zhang, K., Shallit, J.: Characterizing regular languages with polynomial densities. In: Havel, I.M., Koubek, V. (eds.) Mathematical Foundations of Computer Science 1992. LNCS, vol. 629, pp. 494–503. Springer, Heidelberg (1992)
28. Yu, S.: Regular languages. In: Rogenberg, G., Salomaa, A. (eds.) Handbook of Formal Languages, vol. 1, pp. 41–110. Springer, Heidelberg (1997)

Backward and Forward Bisimulation Minimisation of Tree Automata

Johanna Högberg[1], Andreas Maletti[2], and Jonathan May[3]

[1] Dept. of Computing Science, Umeå University, S–90187 Umeå, Sweden
johanna@cs.umu.se
[2] Faculty of Computer Science, Technische Universität Dresden,
D–01062 Dresden, Germany
maletti@tcs.inf.tu-dresden.de
[3] Information Sciences Institute, University of Southern California, Marina Del Rey,
CA 90292
jonmay@isi.edu

Abstract. We improve an existing bisimulation minimisation algorithm for tree automata by introducing backward and forward bisimulations and developing minimisation algorithms for them. Minimisation via forward bisimulation is also effective for deterministic automata and faster than the previous algorithm. Minimisation via backward bisimulation generalises the previous algorithm and is thus more effective but just as fast. We demonstrate implementations of these algorithms on a typical task in natural language processing.

Keywords: bisimulation, tree automata, minimisation, natural language processing.

1 Introduction

Automata minimisation has a long and studied history. For deterministic finite (string) automata (dfa) efficient algorithms exist. The well-known algorithm by Hopcroft [1] runs in time $O(n \log n)$ where n is the number of states of the input automaton. The situation is worse for non-deterministic finite automata (nfa). The minimisation problem for nfa is PSPACE-complete [2] and cannot even be efficiently approximated within the factor $o(n)$ unless P = PSPACE [3]. The problem must thus be restricted to allow algorithms of practical value, and one possibility is to settle for a partial minimisation. This was done in [4] for *non-deterministic tree automata* (nta), which are a generalisation of nfa that recognise tree languages and are used in applications such as model checking [5] and natural language processing [6].

The minimisation algorithm in [4] was inspired by a partitioning algorithm due to Paige and Tarjan [7], and relies heavily on *bisimulation*; a concept introduced by R. Milner as a formal tool for investigating transition systems. Intuitively, two states are bisimilar if they can simulate each other, or equivalently, the observable behaviour of the two states must coincide. Depending on the capacity of the

Jan Holub and Jan Žd'árek (Eds.): CIAA 2007, LNCS 4783, pp. 109–121, 2007.

observer, we obtain different types of bisimulation. In all cases we assume that the observer has the capacity to observe the final reaction to a given input (i.e., the given tree is either accepted or rejected), so the presence of bisimilar states in an automaton indicates redundancy. Identifying bisimilar states allows us to reduce the size of the input automaton, but we are not guaranteed to obtain the smallest possible automaton. In this work we extend the approach of [4] in two ways: (i) we relax the constraints for state equivalence, and (ii) we introduce a new bisimulation relation that (with effect) can be applied to deterministic (bottom-up) tree automata (dta) [8]. Note that [4] is ineffective on dta. Thus we are able to find smaller automata than previously possible.

The two ways correspond, respectively, to two types of bisimulation: *backward* and *forward* bisimulation [9]. In a forward bisimulation on an automaton M, bisimilar states are restricted to have identical futures (i.e., the observer can inspect what will happen next). The future of a state q is the set of *contexts* (i.e., trees in which there is a unique leaf labelled by the special symbol $\square$) that would be recognised by M, if the (bottom-up) computation starts with the state q at the unique $\square$-labelled node in the context. By contrast, backward bisimulation uses a local condition on the transitions to enforce that the past of any two bisimilar states is equal (i.e., the observer can observe what already happened). The past of a state q is the language that would be recognised by the automaton if q were its only final state.

Both types of bisimulation yield efficient minimisation procedures, which can be applied to arbitrary nta. Further, forward bisimulation minimisation is useful on dta. It computes the unique minimal dta recognising the same language as the input dta (see Theorem 29). More importantly, it is shown in Theorem 27 that the asymptotic time-complexity of our minimisation algorithm is $O(rm \log n)$, where r is the maximal rank of the symbols in the input alphabet, m is the size of the transition table, and n is the number of states. Thus our algorithm supersedes the currently best minimisation algorithm [8] for dta, whose complexity is $O(rmn)$. Backward bisimulation, though slightly harder to compute, has great practical value as well. Our backward bisimulation is weaker than the bisimulation of [4]. Consequently, the nta obtained by our backward bisimulation minimisation algorithm will have at most as many states as the automata obtained by the minimisation algorithm of [4]. In addition, the asymptotic time-complexity of our algorithm (see Theorem 15), which is $O(r^2 m \log n)$, is the same as the one for the minimisation algorithm of [4]. In [4] the run time $O(rm' \log n)$ is reported with $m' = rm$.

Finally, there are advantages that support having two types of bisimulation. First, forward and backward bisimulation minimisation only yield nta that are minimal with respect to the respective type of bisimulation. Thus applying forward and backward bisimulation minimisation in an alternating fashion commonly yields even smaller nta (see Sect. 5). Second, in certain domains only one type of bisimulation minimisation is effective. For example, backward bisimulation minimisation is ineffective on dta because no two states of a dta have the same past.

Including this Introduction, the paper has 6 sections. In Sect. 2, we define basic notions and notations. We then proceed with backward minimisation and the algorithm based on it. In Sect. 4, we consider forward bisimulation. Finally, in Sect. 5 we demonstrate our algorithms on a typical task in natural language processing and conclude in Sect. 6.

2   Preliminaries

We write $\mathbb{N}$ to denote the set of natural numbers including zero. The set $\{k, k+1, \ldots, n\}$ is abbreviated to $[k, n]$, and the cardinality of a set S is denoted by $|S|$. We abbreviate $Q \times Q$ as Q^2, and the inclusion $q_i \in D_i$ for all $i \in [1, k]$ as $q_1 \cdots q_k \in D_1 \cdots D_k$.

Let $\mathcal{R}$ and $\mathcal{P}$ be equivalence relations on S. We say that $\mathcal{R}$ is *coarser* than $\mathcal{P}$ (or equivalently: $\mathcal{P}$ is a *refinement* of $\mathcal{R}$), if $\mathcal{P} \subseteq \mathcal{R}$. The *equivalence class* (or *block*) of an element s in S with respect to $\mathcal{R}$ is the set $[s]_{\mathcal{R}} = \{s' \mid (s, s') \in \mathcal{R}\}$. Whenever $\mathcal{R}$ is obvious from the context, we simply write $[s]$ instead of $[s]_{\mathcal{R}}$. It should be clear that $[s]$ and $[s']$ are equal if s and s' are in relation $\mathcal{R}$, and disjoint otherwise, so $\mathcal{R}$ induces a partition $(S/\mathcal{R}) = \{[s] \mid s \in S\}$ of S.

A *ranked alphabet* is a finite set of symbols $\Sigma = \bigcup_{k \in \mathbb{N}} \Sigma_{(k)}$ which is partitioned into pairwise disjoint subsets $\Sigma_{(k)}$. The set T_Σ of *trees* over Σ is the smallest language over Σ such that $f\, t_1 \cdots t_k$ is in T_Σ for every f in $\Sigma_{(k)}$ and all $t_1, \ldots, t_k$ in T_Σ. To improve readability we write $f[t_1, \ldots, t_k]$ instead of $f\, t_1 \cdots t_k$ unless k is zero. Any subset of T_Σ is called a *tree language*.

A *non-deterministic tree automaton* (for short: nta) is a tuple $M = (Q, \Sigma, \delta, F)$, where Q is a finite set of *states*, Σ is a ranked alphabet, and δ is a finite set of *transitions* of the form $f(q_1, \ldots, q_k) \to q_{k+1}$ for some symbol f in $\Sigma_{(k)}$ and $q_1, \ldots, q_{k+1} \in Q$. Finally, $F \subseteq Q$ is a set of *accepting* states. To indicate that a transition $f(q_1, \ldots, q_k) \to q_{k+1}$ is in δ, we write $f(q_1, \ldots, q_k) \xrightarrow{\delta} q_{k+1}$. In the obvious way, δ extends to trees yielding a mapping $\delta \colon T_\Sigma \to \mathfrak{P}(Q)$; i.e., $\delta(t) = \{q \mid f(q_1, \ldots, q_k) \xrightarrow{\delta} q$ and $q_i \in \delta(t_i)$ for all $i \in [1, k]\}$ for $t = f[t_1, \ldots, t_k]$ in T_Σ. For every $q \in Q$ we denote $\{t \in T_\Sigma \mid q \in \delta(t)\}$ by $\mathcal{L}(M)_q$. The tree language *recognised* by M is $\mathcal{L}(M) = \bigcup_{q \in F} \mathcal{L}(M)_q$. Finally, we say that a state q in Q is *useless* if $\mathcal{L}(M)_q = \emptyset$.

3   Backward Bisimulation

Foundation. We first introduce the notion of *backward bisimulation* for a nta M. This type of bisimulation requires bisimilar states to recognise the same tree language. Next, we show how to collapse a block of bisimilar states into just a single state to obtain a potentially smaller nta M'. The construction is such that M' recognises exactly $\mathcal{L}(M)$. Finally, we show that there exists a coarsest backward bisimulation on M, which leads to the smallest collapsed nta.

Definition 1 (cf. [9, Definition 4.1]). *Let $M = (Q, \Sigma, \delta, F)$ be a nta, and let $\mathcal{R}$ be an equivalence relation on Q. We say that $\mathcal{R}$ is a* backward bisimulation *on M if for every $(p, q) \in \mathcal{R}$, symbol f of $\Sigma_{(k)}$, and sequence $D_1, \dots, D_k \in (Q/\mathcal{R})$*

$$\bigvee_{p_1 \cdots p_k \in D_1 \cdots D_k} f(p_1, \dots, p_k) \xrightarrow{\delta} p \quad \Longleftrightarrow \quad \bigvee_{q_1 \cdots q_k \in D_1 \cdots D_k} f(q_1, \dots, q_k) \xrightarrow{\delta} q \ .$$

Example 2. Suppose we want to recognise the tree language $L = \{f[a, b], f[a, a]\}$ over the ranked alphabet $\Sigma = \Sigma_{(2)} \cup \Sigma_{(0)}$ with $\Sigma_{(2)} = \{f\}$ and $\Sigma_{(0)} = \{a, b\}$. We first construct nta N_1 and N_2 that recognise only $f[a, b]$ and $f[a, a]$, respectively. Then we construct N by disjoint union of N_1 and N_2. In this manner we could obtain the nta $N = ([1, 6], \Sigma, \delta, \{3, 6\})$ with

$$a() \xrightarrow{\delta} 1 \quad b() \xrightarrow{\delta} 2 \quad f(1, 2) \xrightarrow{\delta} 3 \quad a() \xrightarrow{\delta} 4 \quad a() \xrightarrow{\delta} 5 \quad f(4, 5) \xrightarrow{\delta} 6 \ .$$

Let $\mathcal{P} = \{1, 4, 5\}^2 \cup \{2\}^2 \cup \{3\}^2 \cup \{6\}^2$. We claim that $\mathcal{P}$ is a backward bisimulation on N. In fact, we only need to check the transitions leading to 1, 4, or 5 in order to justify the claim. Trivially, the condition of Definition 1 is met for such transitions because (i) $a() \to q$ is in δ and (ii) $b() \to q$ is not in δ for every state $q \in \{1, 4, 5\}$. $\quad\square$

Next we describe how a nta $M = (Q, \Sigma, \delta, F)$ may be collapsed with respect to an equivalence relation $\mathcal{R}$ on Q. In particular, we will invoke this construction for some $\mathcal{R}$ that is a backward (in the current section) or forward (in Sect. 4) bisimulation on M.

Definition 3 (cf. [9, Definition 3.3]). *Let $M = (Q, \Sigma, \delta, F)$ be a nta, and let $\mathcal{R}$ be an equivalence relation on Q. The* aggregated nta *(with respect to M and $\mathcal{R}$), denoted by $(M/\mathcal{R})$, is the nta $((Q/\mathcal{R}), \Sigma, \delta', F')$ given by $F' = \{[q] \mid q \in F\}$ and*

$$\delta' = \{f([q_1], \dots, [q_k]) \to [q] \mid f(q_1, \dots, q_k) \xrightarrow{\delta} q\} \ .$$

The nta $(M/\mathcal{R})$ has as many states as there are equivalence classes with respect to $\mathcal{R}$. Thus $(M/\mathcal{R})$ cannot have more states than M.

Example 4. Let N be the nta and $\mathcal{P}$ the backward bisimulation of Example 2. According to Definition 3, the aggregated nta $(N/\mathcal{P})$, which should recognise the language $\{f[a, b], f[a, a]\}$, is $(Q', \Sigma, \delta', F')$ where $Q' = \{[1], [2], [3], [6]\}$ and $F' = \{[3], [6]\}$ and

$$a() \xrightarrow{\delta'} [1] \quad b() \xrightarrow{\delta'} [2] \quad f([1], [2]) \xrightarrow{\delta'} [3] \quad f([1], [1]) \xrightarrow{\delta'} [6] \ . \quad\square$$

For the rest of this section, we let $M = (Q, \Sigma, \delta, F)$ be an arbitrary but fixed nta and $\mathcal{R}$ be a backward bisimulation on M. Next we prepare Corollary 6, which follows from Lemma 5. This corollary shows that M and $(M/\mathcal{R})$ recognise the same tree language. The linking property is that the states q and $[q]$ (in their respective nta) recognise the same tree language. In fact, this also proves that bisimilar states in M recognise the same tree language.

Lemma 5 (cf. [9, Theorem 4.2]). *For any state q of M, $\mathcal{L}((M/\mathcal{R}))_{[q]} = \mathcal{L}(M)_q$.* □

Corollary 6 (cf. [9, Theorem 4.2]). *$\mathcal{L}((M/\mathcal{R})) = \mathcal{L}(M)$.* □

Clearly, among all backward bisimulations on M the coarsest one yields the smallest aggregated nta. Further, this nta admits only the trivial backward bisimulation.

Theorem 7. *There exists a coarsest backward bisimulation $\mathcal{P}$ on M, and the identity is the only backward bisimulation on $(M/\mathcal{P})$.*

Minimisation algorithm. We now present a minimisation algorithm for nta that draws on the ideas presented. Algorithm 1 searches for the coarsest backward bisimulation $\mathcal{R}$ on M by producing increasingly refined equivalence relations $\mathcal{R}_0, \mathcal{R}_1, \mathcal{R}_2, \ldots$. The first of these is the coarsest possible candidate solution. The relation $\mathcal{R}_{i+1}$ is derived from $\mathcal{R}_i$ by removing pairs of states that prevent $\mathcal{R}_i$ from being a backward bisimulation. The algorithm also produces an auxiliary sequence of relations $\mathcal{P}_0, \mathcal{P}_1, \mathcal{P}_2, \ldots$ that are used to find these offending pairs. When $\mathcal{P}_i$ eventually coincides with $\mathcal{R}_i$, the relation $\mathcal{R}_i$ is the coarsest backward bisimulation on M.

Before we discuss the algorithm, its correctness, and its time complexity, we extend our notation.

Definition 8. *For every $q \in Q$ and $k \in \mathbb{N}$ let $obs_q^k : \Sigma_{(k)} \times \mathfrak{P}(()Q)^k -> \mathbb{N}$ be the mapping given by*

$$obs_q^k(f, D_1 ... D_k) = |q_1 .. q_k \in D_1 ... D_k | f(q_1, ..., q_k) -> q| \ ,$$

for every $f \in \Sigma_{(k)} and D_1 ... D_k \in \mathfrak{P}(()Q)^k$.

Intuitively, $obs_q^k(f, D_1 \cdots D_k)$, the *observation*, is the number of f-transitions that lead from blocks $D_1, \ldots, D_k$ to q, and thus a local observation of the properties of q (cf. Definition 1). As we will shortly see, we discard (q, q') from our maintained set of bisimilar states should obs_q^k and $obs_{q'}^k$ disagree in the sense that one is positive whereas the other is zero.

Definition 9. *Let B be a subset of Q, $i \in \mathbb{N}$, and $L, L' \subseteq \mathfrak{P}(Q)^*$ be languages.*

- *Let $r = \max\{k \mid \Sigma_{(k)} \neq \emptyset\}$.*
- *The notation L_i will abbreviate $(Q/\mathcal{P}_i)^0 \cup \cdots \cup (Q/\mathcal{P}_i)^r$.*
- *We use $L(B)$ to abbreviate $\{D_1 \cdots D_k \in L \mid D_i = B \text{ for some } i \in [1, k]\}$.*
- *We write $cut(B)$ for the subset $(Q^2 \setminus B^2) \setminus (Q \setminus B)^2$ of $Q \times Q$.*
- *We write $split(L)$ for the set of all (q, q') in $Q \times Q$ for which there exist $f \in \Sigma_{(k)}$ and a word $w \in L$ of length k such that exactly one of $obs_q^k(f, w)$ and $obs_{q'}^k(f, w)$ is zero.*

```
[input:    a nta M = (Q, Σ, δ, F);
[initially:
    P₀    := Q × Q;
    R₀    := P₀ \ split(L₀);
    i     := 0;
[while Rᵢ ≠ Pᵢ:
    choose Sᵢ ∈ (Q/Pᵢ) and Bᵢ ∈ (Q/Rᵢ) such that
            Bᵢ ⊂ Sᵢ and |Bᵢ| ≤ |Sᵢ|/2;
    Pᵢ₊₁  := Pᵢ \ cut(Bᵢ);
    Rᵢ₊₁  := (Rᵢ \ split(Lᵢ₊₁(Bᵢ))) \ splitn(Lᵢ(Sᵢ), Lᵢ₊₁(Bᵢ));
    i     := i + 1;
[return:   the nta (M/Rᵢ);
```

Alg. 1. A minimisation algorithm for non-deterministic tree automata

– *Finally, we write* $\mathrm{splitn}(L, L')$ *for the set of all* (q, q') *in* $Q \times Q$ *such that there exist a symbol* f *in* $\Sigma_{(k)}$ *and a word* $D_1 \cdots D_k \in L$ *of length* k *such that*

$$\mathrm{obs}_p^k(f, D_1 \cdots D_k) = \sum_{\substack{C_1 \cdots C_k \in L', \\ \forall i \in [1,k]: \, C_i \subseteq D_i}} \mathrm{obs}_p^k(f, C_1 \cdots C_k)$$

holds for either $p = q$ *or* $p = q'$ *but not both.*   □

Let us briefly discuss how the sets $L_0, L_1, L_2, \ldots$ that are generated by Alg. 1 relate to each other. The set L_0 contains a single word of length k, for each $k \in [0, r]$, namely Q^k. Every word w of length k in the set L_{i+1} is in either in L_i, or of the form $D_1 \cdots D_k$, where $D_j \in \{B_i, S_i \setminus B_i\}$ for some $j \in [1, k]$ and $D_l \in (Q/P_{i+1})$ for every $l \in [1, k]$.

Example 10. We trace the execution of the minimisation algorithm on the automaton N of Example 2. Let us start with the initialisation. State 2 can be separated from $[1, 6]$ since only obs_2^0 is non-zero for the symbol b and the empty word $\epsilon \in L_0$. Similarly, states 3 and 6 differ from 1, 4, and 5, as obs_3^2 and obs_6^2 are both non-zero for the symbol f and word QQ. Thus $P_0 = Q \times Q$ and $R_0 = \{1, 4, 5\}^2 \cup \{2\}^2 \cup \{3, 6\}^2$.

In the first iteration, we let $S_0 = Q$ and $B_0 = \{2\}$. The algorithm can now use the symbol f and word $w = (Q \setminus \{2\})\{2\}$ in $L_1(B_1)$ to distinguish between state 3 and state 6, as $\mathrm{obs}_3^2(f, w) > 0$ whereas $\mathrm{obs}_6^2(f, w) = 0$. The next pair of relations is then:

$$P_1 = \{2\}^2 \cup (Q \setminus \{2\})^2 \text{ and } R_1 = \{1, 4, 5\}^2 \cup \{2\}^2 \cup \{3\}^2 \cup \{6\}^2 .$$

As the states in $\{1, 4, 5\}$ do not appear at the left-hand side of any transition, this block will not be further divided. Two more iterations are needed before P_3 equals R_3.   □

Next we establish that the algorithm really computes the coarsest backward bisimulation on M. We use the notations introduced in the algorithm.

Lemma 11. *The relation $\mathcal{R}_i$ is a refinement of $\mathcal{P}_i$, for all $i \in \{0, 1, 2, \dots\}$.* □

Lemma 11 assures that $\mathcal{R}_i$ is a proper refinement of $\mathcal{P}_i$, for all $i \in \{0, \dots, t-1\}$ where t is the value of i at termination. Up to the termination point t, we can always find blocks $B_i \in (Q/\mathcal{R}_i)$ and $S_i \in (Q/\mathcal{P}_i)$ such that B_i is contained in S_i, and the size of B_i is at most half of that of S_i. This means that checking the termination criterion can be combined with the choice of S_i and B_i, because we can only fail to choose these blocks if $\mathcal{R}$ and $\mathcal{P}$ are equal. Lemma 11 also guarantees that the algorithm terminates in less than n iterations.

Theorem 12. *$\mathcal{R}_t$ is the coarsest backward bisimulation on M.* □

Let us now analyse the running time of the minimisation algorithm on M. We use n and m to denote the size of the sets Q and δ, respectively. In the complexity calculations, we write δ_L, where $L \subseteq \mathfrak{P}(Q)^*$, for the subset of δ that contains entries of the form $f(q_1, \dots, q_k) \to q$, where $f \in \Sigma_{(k)}$, $q \in Q$, and $q_1 \cdots q_k$ is in $B_1 \cdots B_k$ for some $B_1 \cdots B_k \in L$. Our computation model is the random access machine [10], which supports indirect addressing, and thus allows the use of pointers. This means that we can represent each block in a partition $(Q/\mathcal{R})$ as a record of two-way pointers to its elements, and that we can link each state to its occurrences in the transition table. Given a state q and a block B, we can then determine $[q]_\mathcal{R}$ in constant time, and δ_L, where $L \subseteq \mathfrak{P}(Q)^*$, in time proportional to the number of entries.

To avoid pairwise comparison between states, we hash each state q in Q using $(\mathrm{obs}_q^k)_{k \in [0,r]}$ as key, and then inspect which states end up at the same positions in the hash table. Since a random access machine has unlimited memory, we can always implement a collision free hash h; i.e., by interpreting the binary representation of $(\mathrm{obs}_q^k)_{k \in [0,r]}$ as a memory address, and the time required to hash a state q is then proportional to the size of the representation of $(\mathrm{obs}_q^k)_{k \in [0,r]}$.

The overall time complexity of the algorithm is

$$O\left(\mathrm{INIT} + \sum_{i \in [0, t-1]} (\mathrm{SELECT}_i + \mathrm{CUT}_i + \mathrm{SPLIT}_i + \mathrm{SPLITN}_i) + \mathrm{AGGREGATE}\right),$$

where INIT, SELECT_i, CUT_i, SPLIT_i, SPLITN_i, and $\mathrm{AGGREGATE}$ are the complexity of: the initialisation phase; the choice of S_i and B_i; the computation of $\mathcal{P}_i \setminus \mathrm{cut}(B_i)$; the computation of $\mathcal{R}_i \setminus \mathrm{split}(L_{i+1}(B_i))$; the subtraction of $\mathrm{splitn}(L_i(S_i), L_{i+1}(B_i))$; and the construction of the aggregated automaton $(M/\mathcal{R}_t)$; respectively.

Lemma 13. INIT *and* $\mathrm{AGGREGATE}$ *are in* $O(rm + n)$, *whereas, for every i in* $[0, t-1]$, SELECT_i *is in* $O(1)$, CUT_i *is in* $O(|B_i|)$, *and* SPLIT_i *and* SPLITN_i *are in* $O\left(r \, |\delta_{L_{i+1}(B_i)}|\right)$. □

Lemma 14. *For each $q \in Q$ we have* $|\{B_i \mid i \in [0, t-1] \text{ and } q \in B_i\}| \le \log n$. □

Theorem 15. *The backward minimisation algorithm is in* $O(r^2 m \log n)$. $\square$

Proof. By Lemma 13 the time complexity of the algorithm can be written as

$$O\left((rm+n) + \sum_{i\in[0,t-1]} (1 + |B_i| + r\,|\delta_{L_{i+1}(B_i)}| + r\,|\delta_{L_{i+1}(B_i)}|) + (rm+n)\right) .$$

Omitting the smaller terms and simplifying, we obtain $O\left(r\sum_{i\in[0,t-1]} |\delta_{L_{i+1}(B_i)}|\right)$. According to Lemma 14, no state occurs in more than $\log n$ distinct B-blocks, so no transition in δ will contribute by more than $r \log n$ to the total sum. As there are m transitions, the overall time complexity of the algorithm is $O(r^2 m \log n)$. $\square$

We next compare the presented backward bisimulation to the bisimulation of [4].

Definition 16 (cf. [4, Sect. 5]). *Let* $\mathcal{P}$ *be an equivalence relation on* Q. *We say that* $\mathcal{P}$ *is an AKH-bisimulation on* M, *if for every* $(p,q) \in \mathcal{P}$ *we have (i)* $p \in F$ *if and only if* $q \in F$; *and (ii) for every symbol* f *in* $\Sigma_{(k)}$, *index* $i \in [1,n]$, *and sequence* $D_1, \ldots, D_n$ *of blocks in* $(Q/\mathcal{P})$

$$\bigvee_{\substack{p_1 \cdots p_n \in D_1 \cdots D_n, \\ p_i = p}} f(p_1, \ldots, p_k) \xrightarrow{\delta} p_n \iff \bigvee_{\substack{q_1 \cdots q_n \in D_1 \cdots D_n, \\ q_i = q}} f(q_1, \ldots, q_k) \xrightarrow{\delta} q_n$$

where $n = k+1$. $\square$

Lemma 17. *Every AKH-bisimulation on* M *is a backward bisimulation on* M.
    $\square$

The coarsest backward bisimulation $\mathcal{R}$ on M is coarser than the coarsest AKH-bisimulation $\mathcal{P}$ on M. Hence $(M/\mathcal{R})$ has at most as many states as $(M/\mathcal{P})$. Since our algorithm for minimisation via backward bisimulation is computationally as efficient as the algorithm of [4] (see Theorem 15 and [4, Sect. 3]), it supersedes the minimisation algorithm of [4].

4   Forward Bisimulation

Foundation. In this section we consider a computationally simpler notion of bisimulation. Minimisation via forward bisimulation coincides with classical minimisation on deterministic nta. In addition, the two minimisation procedures greatly increase their potential when they are used together in an alternating fashion (see Sect. 5).

Definition 18. *Let* $M = (Q, \Sigma, \delta, F)$ *be a nta, and let* $\mathcal{R}$ *be an equivalence relation on* Q. *We say that* $\mathcal{R}$ *is a forward bisimulation on* M *if for every* (p,q) *in* $\mathcal{R}$ *we have (i)* $p \in F$ *if and only if* $q \in F$; *and (ii) for every symbol* f *in* $\Sigma_{(k)}$, *index* $i \in [1,k]$, *sequence of states* $q_1, \ldots, q_k$ *in* Q, *and block* D *in* $(Q/\mathcal{R})$

$$\bigvee_{r\in D} f(q_1, \ldots, q_{i-1}, p, q_{i+1}, \ldots, q_k) \xrightarrow{\delta} r \iff \bigvee_{r\in D} f(q_1, \ldots, q_{i-1}, q, q_{i+1}, \ldots, q_k) \xrightarrow{\delta} r .$$

    $\square$

Note that Condition (ii) in Definition 18 is automatically fulfilled for all nullary symbols. Let us continue Example 4 (the aggregated nta is defined in Definition 3).

Example 19. Recall the aggregated nta from Example 4. An isomorphic nta N is given by $([1, 4], \Sigma, \delta, \{3, 4\})$ with

$$a() \xrightarrow{\delta} 1 \qquad b() \xrightarrow{\delta} 2 \qquad f(1, 2) \xrightarrow{\delta} 3 \qquad f(1, 1) \xrightarrow{\delta} 4 \ .$$

We have seen in Example 10 that N admits only the trivial backward bisimulation. Let us consider $\mathcal{P} = \{1\}^2 \cup \{2\}^2 \cup \{3, 4\}^2$. We claim that $\mathcal{P}$ is a forward bisimulation on N. Condition (i) of Definition 18 is met, and since $(1, 2) \notin \mathcal{P}$ and the states 3 and 4 only appear on the right hand side of $\xrightarrow{\delta}$, also Condition (ii) holds. Thus $\mathcal{P}$ is a forward bisimulation.

The aggregated nta $(N/\mathcal{P})$ is $(Q', \Sigma, \delta', F')$ with $Q' = \{[1], [2], [3]\}$ and $F' = \{[3]\}$ and

$$a() \xrightarrow{\delta'} [1] \qquad b() \xrightarrow{\delta'} [2] \qquad f([1], [2]) \xrightarrow{\delta'} [3] \qquad f([1], [1]) \xrightarrow{\delta'} [3] \ . \qquad \square$$

For the rest of this section, we let $M = (Q, \Sigma, \delta, F)$ be an arbitrary but fixed nta and $\mathcal{R}$ be a forward bisimulation on M. In the forward case, a collapsed state of $(M/\mathcal{R})$ functions like the combination of its constituents in M (cf. Sect. 3). In particular, bisimilar states need not recognise the same tree language. However, $(M/\mathcal{R})$ and M do recognise the same tree language.

Lemma 20 (cf. [9, Theorem 3.1]). $\mathcal{L}((M/\mathcal{R}))_{[q]} = \bigcup_{p \in [q]} \mathcal{L}(M)_p$ *for every* $q \in Q$. $\qquad \square$

Theorem 21 (cf. [9, Corollary 3.4]). $\mathcal{L}((M/\mathcal{R})) = \mathcal{L}(M)$. $\qquad \square$

The coarsest of all forward bisimulations on M yields the smallest aggregated nta. This nta cannot be reduced further by collapsing it with respect to some forward bisimulation.

Theorem 22. *There exists a coarsest forward bisimulation $\mathcal{P}$ on M, and the identity is the only forward bisimulation on $(M/\mathcal{P})$.* $\qquad \square$

Minimisation algorithm. We now modify the algorithm of Sect. 3 so as to minimise with respect to forward bisimulation. As in Sect. 3 this requires us to extend our notation. We denote by C_Q^k the of set of *contexts* over Q: the set of k-tuples over $Q \cup \{\square\}$ that contain the special symbol $\square$ exactly once. We denote by $c[\![q]\!]$, where $c \in C_Q^k$ and $q \in Q$, the tuple that is obtained by replacing the unique occurrence of $\square$ in c by q.

Definition 23. *For each state q in Q and $k \in \mathbb{N}$, the map $\mathrm{obsf}_q^k \colon \Sigma_{(k)} \times C_Q^k \times \mathfrak{P}(Q) \to \mathbb{N}$ is defined by $\mathrm{obsf}_q^k(f, c, D) = |\{q' \in D \mid f(c[\![q]\!]) \xrightarrow{\delta} q'\}|$ for every symbol $f \in \Sigma_{(k)}$, context $c \in C_Q^k$, and set $D \subseteq Q$ of states.* $\qquad \square$

Like obs_q^k, obsf_q^k is a local observation of the properties of q. The difference here, is that $\text{obsf}_q^k(f, c, D)$ is the number of f-transitions that match the sequence $c[\![q]\!]$ and lead to a state of D. In contrast, obs_q^k looked from the other side of the rule.

Definition 24. *Let D and D' be subsets of Q.*

- *We write* $\text{splitf}(D)$ *for the set of all pairs* (q, q') *in* $Q \times Q$, *for which there exist* $f \in \Sigma_{(k)}$ *and* $c \in C_Q^k$ *such that exactly one of* $\text{obsf}_q^k(f, c, D)$ *and* $\text{obsf}_{q'}^k(f, c, D)$ *is non-zero.*
- *Similarly, we write* $\text{splitfn}(D, D')$ *for the set of all pairs* (q, q') *in* $Q \times Q$, *for which there exist* $f \in \Sigma_{(k)}$ *and* $c \in C_Q^k$ *such that* $\text{obsf}_p^k(f, c, D) = \text{obsf}_p^k(f, c, D')$ *holds for either* $p = q$ *or* $p = q'$ *but not both.* □

We can now construct a minimisation algorithm based on forward bisimulation by replacing the initialisation of $\mathcal{R}_0$ in Alg. 1 with $\mathcal{R}_0 = ((Q \backslash F)^2 \cup F^2) \backslash \text{splitf}(Q)$ and the computation of $\mathcal{R}_{i+1}$ with $\mathcal{R}_{i+1} = (\mathcal{R}_i \backslash \text{splitf}(B_i)) \backslash \text{splitfn}(S_i, B_i)$.

Example 25. We show the execution of the minimisation algorithm on the nta N from Example 19. In the initialisation of $\mathcal{R}_0$, states 3 and 4 are separated because they are accepting. State 1 is distinguished as only obsf_1^2 is non-zero on the symbol f, context $(\Box, 2) \in C_{[1,4]}^2$, and block Q in $\mathcal{P}_0$. We thus have the relations $\mathcal{P}_0 = Q \times Q$ and $\mathcal{R}_0 = \{1\}^2 \cup \{2\}^2 \cup \{3, 4\}^2$. As neither 3 nor 4 appear on a left-hand side of any transition, they will not be separated, so the algorithm terminates with $(M/\mathcal{R}_0)$ in the second iteration, when $\mathcal{P}_0$ has been refined to $\mathcal{R}_0$. □

Note that also the modified algorithm is correct and terminates in less than n iterations where n is the cardinality of Q.

Theorem 26. $\mathcal{R}_t$ *is the coarsest forward bisimulation on* M. □

The time complexity of the backward bisimulation algorithm is computed using the same assumptions and notations as in Sect. 3. Although the computations are quite similar, they differ in that when the backward algorithm would examine every transition in δ of the form $f(q_1 \cdots q_k) \to q$, where $q_j \in B_i$ for some $j \in [1, k]$, the forward algorithm considers only those transitions that are of the form $f(q_1 \cdots q_k) \to q$, where $q \in B_i$. Since the latter set is on average a factor r smaller, we are able to obtain a proportional speed-up of the algorithm.

Theorem 27. *The forward minimisation algorithm is in* $O(rm \log n)$. □

Next, we show that forward bisimulation minimisation coincides with classical minimisation and yields the minimal deterministic nta.

Definition 28. *We say that M is* deterministic *(respectively,* complete*), if for every symbol f in $\Sigma_{(k)}$, and sequence $(q_1, \ldots, q_k) \in Q^k$ of states there exists at most (respectively, at least) one state q in Q such that $f(q_1, \ldots, q_k) \to q$ is in δ.* □

Clearly, the automaton $(M/\mathcal{R})$ is deterministic and complete whenever M is so. Moreover, there exists a unique minimal complete and deterministic nta N that recognises the language $\mathcal{L}(M)$. The next theorem shows that N is isomorphic to $(M/\mathcal{R})$ if $\mathcal{R}$ is the coarsest forward bisimulation on M.

Theorem 29. *Let M be a deterministic and complete nta without useless states. Then $(M/\mathcal{R}_t)$ is a minimal deterministic and complete nta recognising $\mathcal{L}(M)$.*

5   Implementation

In this section, we present some experimental results that we obtained by applying a prototype implementation of Alg. 1 to the problem of *language modelling* in the natural language processing domain [11]. A language model is a formalism for determining whether a given sentence is in a particular language. Language models are particularly useful in many applications of natural language and speech processing such as translation, transliteration, speech recognition, character recognition, etc., where transformation system output must be verified to be an appropriate sentence in the domain language. Recent research in natural language processing has focused on using tree-based models to capture syntactic dependencies in applications such as machine translation [12,13]. Thus, the problem is elevated to determining whether a given syntactic tree is in a language. Language models are naturally representable as finite-state acceptors. For efficiency and data sparsity reasons, whole sentences are not typically stored, but rather a sliding window of partial sentences is verified. In the string domain this is known as *n-gram* language modelling. We instead model *n-subtrees*, fixed-size pieces of a syntactic tree.

Table 1. Reduction of states and rules using backward, forward, and AKH bisimulation

TREES	ORIGINAL		BACKWARD		FORWARD		AKH	
	states	rules	states	rules	states	rules	states	rules
58	353	353	252	252	286	341	353	353
161	953	953	576	576	749	905	953	953
231	1373	1373	781	781	1075	1299	1373	1373
287	1726	1726	947	947	1358	1637	1726	1726

Table 2. Reduction of states and rules when combining backward and forward bisimulation

TREES	ORIGINAL		BW AFTER FW		FW AFTER BW	
	states	rules	states	rules	states	rules
58	353	353	185	240	180	235
161	953	953	378	534	356	512
231	1373	1373	494	718	468	691
287	1726	1726	595	874	563	842

We prepared a data set by collecting 3-subtrees, i.e. all subtrees of height 3, from sentences taken from the Penn Treebank corpus of syntactically bracketed English news text [14]. An initial nta was constructed by representing each 3-subtree in a single path. We then wrote an implementation of the forward and backward variants of Alg. 1 in Perl and applied them to data sets of various sizes of 3-subtrees. To illustrate that the two algorithms perform different minimisations, we then ran the forward algorithm on the result from the backward algorithm, and vice-versa. As Table 2 shows, the combination of both algorithms reduces the automata nicely, to less than half the size (in the sum of rules and states) of the original.

Table 1 includes the state and rule count of the same automata after minimisation with respect to AKH-bisimulation. As these figures testify, the conditions placed on an AKH-bisimulation are much more restrictive than those met by a backward bisimulation. In fact, Definition 16 is obtained from Definition 1 if the two-way implication in Definition 1 is required to hold for *every* position in a transition rule (i.e. not just the last), while insisting that the sets of accepting and rejecting states are respected.

6 Conclusion

We have introduced a general algorithm for bisimulation minimisation of tree automata and discussed its operation under forward and backward bisimulation. The algorithm has attractive runtime properties and is useful for applications that desire a compact representation of large non-deterministic tree automata. We plan to include a refined implementation of this algorithm in a future version of the tree automata toolkit described in [15].

Acknowledgements. The authors acknowledge the support and advice of Frank Drewes and Kevin Knight. We thank Lisa Kaati for providing data and information relevant to the details of [4]. We would also like to thank the referees for extensive and useful comments. This work was partially supported by NSF grant IIS-0428020.

References

1. Hopcroft, J.E.: An $n \log n$ algorithm for minimizing states in a finite automation. In: Kohavi, Z. (ed.) Theory of Machines and Computations, Academic Press, London (1971)
2. Meyer, A.R., Stockmeyer, L.J.: The equivalence problem for regular expressions with squaring requires exponential space. In: Proc. 13th Annual Symp. Foundations of Computer Science, pp. 125–129. IEEE Computer Society Press, Los Alamitos (1972)
3. Gramlich, G., Schnitger, G.: Minimizing NFAs and regular expressions. In: Diekert, V., Durand, B. (eds.) STACS 2005. LNCS, vol. 3404, pp. 399–411. Springer, Heidelberg (2005)

4. Abdulla, P.A., Högberg, J., Kaati, L.: Bisimulation minimization of tree automata. In: IJFCS (2007)
5. Abdulla, P.A., Jonsson, B., Mahata, P., d'Orso, J.: Regular tree model checking. In: Brinksma, E., Larsen, K.G. (eds.) CAV 2002. LNCS, vol. 2404, pp. 555–568. Springer, Heidelberg (2002)
6. Knight, K., Graehl, J.: An overview of probabilistic tree transducers for natural language processing. In: Gelbukh, A. (ed.) CICLing 2005. LNCS, vol. 3406, pp. 1–24. Springer, Heidelberg (2005)
7. Paige, R., Tarjan, R.: Three partition refinement algorithms. SIAM Journal on Computing 16, 973–989 (1987)
8. Comon, H., Dauchet, M., Gilleron, R., Jacquemard, F., Lugiez, D., Tison, S., Tommasi, M.: Tree automata: Techniques and applications (1997), Available on http://www.grappa.univ-lille3.fr/tata
9. Buchholz, P.: Bisimulation relations for weighted automata (unpublished, 2007)
10. Papadimitriou, C.H.: Computational Complexity. Addison-Wesley, Reading (1994)
11. Jelinek, F.: Continuous speech recognition by statistical methods. Proc. IEEE 64, 532–557 (1976)
12. Galley, M., Hopkins, M., Knight, K., Marcu, D.: What's in a translation rule? In: Proc. 2004 Human Language Technology Conf. of the North American Chapter of the Association for Computational Linguistics, pp. 273–280 (2004)
13. Yamada, K., Knight, K.: A syntax-based statistical translation model. In: Proc. 39th Meeting of the Association for Computational Linguistics, pp. 523–530. Morgan Kaufmann, San Francisco (2001)
14. Marcus, M.P., Marcinkiewicz, M.A., Santorini, B.: Building a large annotated corpus of english: The Penn treebank. Computational Linguistics 19, 313–330 (1993)
15. May, J., Knight, K.: Tiburon: A weighted tree automata toolkit. In: Ibarra, O.H., Yen, H.-C. (eds.) CIAA 2006. LNCS, vol. 4094, pp. 102–113. Springer, Heidelberg (2006)

An Implementation of Deterministic Tree Automata Minimization

Rafael C. Carrasco[1], Jan Daciuk[2], and Mikel L. Forcada[3]

[1] Dep. de Lenguajes y Sistemas Informáticos, Universidad de Alicante, E-03071
Alicante, Spain
carrasco@dlsi.ua.es
[2] Knowledge Engineering Department, Gdańsk University of Technology,
Ul. G. Narutowicza 11/12, 80-952 Gdańsk, Poland
jandac@eti.pg.gda.pl
[3] Dep. de Llenguatges i Sistemes informàtics, Universitat d'Alacant, E-03071
Alacant, Spain
mlf@dlsi.ua.es

Abstract. A frontier-to-root deterministic finite-state tree automaton
(DTA) can be used as a compact data structure to store collections of
unranked ordered trees. DTAs are usually sparser than string automata,
as most transitions are undefined and therefore, special care must be
taken in order to minimize them efficiently. However, it is difficult to
find simple and detailed descriptions of the minimization procedure in
the published literature. Here, we fully describe a simple implementation
of the standard minimization algorithm that needs a time in $\mathcal{O}(|A|^2)$,
with $|A|$ being the size of the DTA.

Keywords: sminimal deterministic tree automata, minimization of
automata.

1 Introduction

A data structure that stores unranked ordered tree data efficiently is a minimal
frontier-to-root deterministic tree automaton (DTA) where each subtree which is
common to several trees in the collection is assigned a single state. Furthermore,
the number of such states is minimized by assigning a single state to groups
of subtrees that may appear interchangeably in the collection. The general procedure to obtain a minimal DTA is well known [1,2,3]. However, it is difficult
to find detailed descriptions of the minimization algorithm. Here, we describe a
simple and efficient implementation of the algorithm to minimize DTAs.

Given an *alphabet*, that is, a finite set of symbols $\Sigma = \{\sigma_1, \ldots, \sigma_{|\Sigma|}\}$, we define
T_Σ as the set of unranked ordered trees with labels in Σ: every symbol $\sigma \in \Sigma$
belongs to T_Σ and every $\sigma(t_1 \cdots t_m)$ with $\sigma \in \Sigma$, $m > 0$ and $t_1, \ldots, t_m \in T_\Sigma$ is
also a tree in T_Σ. The trees so defined are ordered and unranked, that is, the
order of descendents $t_1, \ldots, t_m$ is relevant but symbols in Σ are not assigned a
fixed *valence* m. Any subset of T_Σ will be called a *tree language*. In particular,

Jan Holub and Jan Žd'árek (Eds.): CIAA 2007, LNCS 4783, pp. 122–129, 2007.

the language of subtrees sub(t) of $t = \sigma(t_1,\ldots,t_m)$ is the union of $\{t\}$ and $\bigcup_{k=1}^{m}$ sub(t_k).

A *finite-state frontier-to-root tree automaton* is defined as $A = (Q, \Sigma, \Delta, F)$, where $Q = \{q_1,\ldots,q_{|Q|}\}$ is a finite set of *states*, $\Sigma = \{\sigma_1,\ldots,\sigma_{|\Sigma|}\}$ is the *alphabet*, $F \subseteq Q$ is the subset of *accepting states*, and $\Delta = \{\tau_1,\ldots,\tau_{|\Delta|}\} \subseteq \bigcup_{m=0}^{\infty} \Sigma \times Q^{m+1}$ is a finite set of *transitions*.

A tree automaton A is a *deterministic finite-state frontier-to-root automaton*, or deterministic tree automaton (DTA) for short, if for every argument $(\sigma, i_1,\ldots,i_m)$ there is at most one possible output, that is, for all $\sigma \in \Sigma$, for all $m \geq 0$ and for all $(i_1,\ldots,i_m) \in Q^m$, there is at most one $j \in Q$ such that $(\sigma, i_1,\ldots,i_m,j) \in \Delta$. In a DTA, the transition output for argument $(\sigma, i_1,\ldots,i_m)$ is

$$\delta_m(\sigma, i_1,\ldots,i_m) = \begin{cases} j & \text{if } (\sigma, i_1,\ldots,i_m,j) \in \Delta \\ \perp & \text{if no such } j \text{ exists} \end{cases} \tag{1}$$

where the symbol $\perp$ will be interpreted as a special *absorption state* such that $\perp \in Q - F$ but cannot appear in Δ. With this convention, Δ remains finite but the output for all possible transition arguments is a state in Q. The *size* of the DTA is defined as the size of its transition function (which, in contrast with string automata, cannot be directly obtained from its number of transitions, that is,

$$|A| = \sum_{n=1}^{|\Delta|} |\tau_n|, \tag{2}$$

with $|(\sigma, i_1,\ldots,i_m,j)| = m+1$.

The output $A(t)$ when DTA A operates on $t \in T_\Sigma$ is the state in Q recursively computed as

$$A(t) = \begin{cases} \delta_0(\sigma) & \text{if } t = \sigma \in \Sigma \\ \delta_m(\sigma, A(t_1),\ldots,A(t_m)) & \text{if } t = \sigma(t_1 \cdots t_m) \in T_\Sigma - \Sigma \end{cases} \tag{3}$$

The tree *language $L_A(q)$ accepted* at state $q \in Q$ is the subset of T_Σ with output q

$$L_A(q) = \{t \in T_\Sigma : A(t) = q\} \tag{4}$$

and the tree language $L(A)$ accepted by A is the subset of trees in T_Σ accepted at the states in F

$$L(A) = \bigcup_{q \in F} L_A(q) = \{t \in T_\Sigma : A(t) \in F\}. \tag{5}$$

In a DTA A, a state q is *inaccessible* if $L_A(q) = \emptyset$, that is, if there is no tree t in T_Σ such that $A(t) = q$. Therefore, inaccessible states and the transitions using them are useless and can be safely removed from Q and Δ respectively without affecting $L(A)$. It is worth to note that in DTAs the absorption state $\perp$ is always accessible because Δ is a finite subset of $\bigcup_{m=0}^{\infty} \Sigma \times Q^{m+1}$ and there is an infinite number of arguments leading to $\perp$. A DTA with no inaccessible state is said to be *reduced*.

An accessible state $q \in Q$ is said to be *coaccessible* in A if there is at least one tree $t \in L(A)$ containing a subtree s such that $q = A(s)$. States which are not coaccessible (and accessible) are *useless*. In particular, as no transition in Δ contains $\perp$, the absorption state is useless. As will be shown later, the identification of inaccessible and useless states can be done in time $\mathcal{O}(|A|)$.

2   Minimal Deterministic Tree Automata

The standard procedure to minimize [1,2,3] a deterministic tree automaton A removes its inaccessible states and then merges all its equivalent states.

On the one hand, the subset $I \subseteq Q$ of inaccessible states can be easily identified by means of an iterative procedure: start with $n \leftarrow 0$ and $I_0 \leftarrow Q$ and while there is a transition $(\sigma, i_1, \ldots, i_m, j) \in \Delta$ such that $j \in I_n$ and $(i_1, \ldots, i_m) \in (Q - I_n)^m$, make $I_{n+1} \leftarrow I_n - \{j\}$ and $n \leftarrow n + 1$. A detailed implementation of this procedure, which runs in time $\mathcal{O}(|A|)$, is shown in Figure 1.

Algorithm findInaccessible
Input: A DTA $A = (Q, \Sigma, \Delta, F)$
Output: The subset of inaccessible states in A.
Method:

1. For all q in Q create an empty list R_q.
2. For all $\tau_n = (\sigma, i_1, \ldots, i_m, j)$ in Δ do
   - $B_n \leftarrow m$ (* Store num. of inaccessible positions in argument of τ_n *).
   - For $k = 1, \ldots, m$ append n to R_{i_k} (* Store all occurrences in $i_1, \ldots, i_m$ *).
3. $K \leftarrow \{\delta_0(\sigma) : \sigma \in \Sigma\}$; $I \leftarrow Q - K$
4. While $K \neq \emptyset$ and $I \neq \emptyset$ remove a state q from K and for all n in R_q do
   - $B_n \leftarrow B_n - 1$
   - If $B_n = 0$ and output$(\tau_n) \in I$ then move output(τ_n) from I to K.
5. Return $I - \{\perp\}$.

Fig. 1. Algorithm for the identification of inaccessible states in a DTA

On the other hand, equivalent states can be found, as shown in figure 2, by creating a partition $P_0 = (Q)$ and iteratively refining this partition until it becomes a congruence. A *congruence* $\simeq$ on A is an equivalence relation such that $p \simeq q$ implies:

1. $p \in F$ if and only if $q \in F$.
2. If $m > 0$, $k \leq m$ and $(\sigma, r_1, \ldots, r_m) \in \Sigma \times Q^m$ then

$$\delta_m(\sigma, r_1, \ldots, r_{k-1}, p, r_{k+1}, \ldots, r_m) \simeq \delta_m(\sigma, r_1, \ldots, r_{k-1}, q, r_{k+1}, \ldots, r_m) \quad (6)$$

In other words, the equivalence relation is closed under context and, thus, equivalent states are interchangeable as the output of automaton A on any tree or subtree without any effect on $L(A)$.

As the standard algorithms [4,5,6] for the minimization of deterministic finite-state automata do, the minimization of DTAs partitions the set of states Q into equivalence classes by iterative refinement. In the following, P_n will denote the partition at iteration n, $\Phi_n[p]$ will denote the class in P_n that contains p and we will write $p \sim_n q$ if and only if $\Phi_n[p] = \Phi_n[q]$. We will say that P_n is *inconsistent* if there exist $m > 0$, $k \leq m$ and $(\sigma, r_1, \ldots, r_m) \in \Sigma \times Q^m$ such that

$$\delta_m(\sigma, r_1, \ldots, r_{k-1}, p, r_{k+1}, \ldots, r_m) \not\sim_n \delta_m(\sigma, r_1, \ldots, r_{k-1}, q, r_{k+1}, \ldots, r_m) \quad (7)$$

Then, the standard algorithm refines the partition until it becomes consistent, as shown in Figure 2.

Algorithm minimizeDTA
Input: a reduced DTA $A = (Q, \Sigma, \Delta, F)$ with $F \neq \emptyset$.
Output: a minimal DTA $A^{\min} = (Q^{\min}, \Sigma, \Delta^{\min}, F^{\min})$ equivalent to A.
Method:

1. Create the initial partition $P_0 \leftarrow (Q)$, $P_1 \leftarrow (F, Q - F)$ and set $n \leftarrow 1$.
2. While $P_n \neq P_{n-1}$ create P_{n+1} by refining P_n so that $p \sim_{n+1} q$ if and only if for all $m > 0$, for all $k \leq m$ and for all $(\sigma, r_1, \ldots, r_m) \in \Sigma \times Q^m$

$$\delta_m(\sigma, r_1, \ldots, r_{k-1}, p, r_{k+1}, \ldots, r_m) \sim_n \delta_m(\sigma, r_1, \ldots, r_{k-1}, q, r_{k+1}, \ldots, r_m)$$

3. Output $(Q^{\min}, \Sigma, \Delta^{\min}, F^{\min})$ with
   - $Q^{\min} = \{\Phi_n[q] : q \in Q\}$;
   - $F^{\min} = \{\Phi_n[q] : q \in F\}$;
   - $\Delta^{\min} = \{(\sigma, \Phi_n[i_1], \ldots, \Phi_n[i_m], \Phi_n[j]) : (\sigma, i_1, \ldots, i_m, j) \in \Delta \wedge j \not\sim_n \perp\}$.

Fig. 2. Standard algorithm for DTA minimization. Function $\Phi_n(q)$ returns the identifier of the class in P_n that contains q.

However, the efficient implementation of this procedure requires a fast method to search for arguments $(\sigma, r_1, \ldots, r_m) \in \Sigma \times Q^m$ where replacing r_k with p and q leads to non-equivalent outputs and a correct treatment of undefined transitions. The implementation of the algorithm shown in Figure 4 meets these requirements and realizes it as follows.

- Initialization: All useless states in the automaton are replaced by a single one (the absorption state $\perp$) and then, the partition P is initialized with classes where all states have identical signature, the *signature* of a state being a set defined as

$$\text{sig}(q) = \begin{cases} \{(\sigma, m, k) : \exists(\sigma, i_1, \ldots, i_m, j) \in \Delta : i_k = q\} \cup \{(\#, 1, 1)\} & \text{if } q \in F \\ \{(\sigma, m, k) : \exists(\sigma, i_1, \ldots, i_m, j) \in \Delta : i_k = q\} & \text{otherwise} \end{cases}$$

where # is a symbol not in Σ used to distinguish accepting and non-accepting states. Useless states can be identified in time $\mathcal{O}(|A|)$ by means of the procedure shown in Figure 3.

- The main loop refines the partition P_n at every iteration and keeps a queue K containing representatives of the new classes in the partition. It makes use of a function $\text{next}_n(i)$ that returns the state following i in class $\Phi_n[i]$ or the first state in $\Phi_n[i]$ if i is the last state in that class (a fixed, arbitrary order of states is assumed).

Merging all useless states with $\perp$ is supported by the fact that, once inaccessible states are removed, q is coaccessible if and only if $q \not\equiv \perp$. On the other hand, it is clear that after removing useless states, $\text{sig}(p) \neq \text{sig}(q) \Rightarrow p \not\equiv q$ and π can be safely initialized with the classes of states with identical signature.

Algorithm findUseless
Input: A reduced DTA $A = (Q, \Sigma, \Delta, F)$ with $F \neq \emptyset$.
Output: The subset of useless states in A.
Method:

1. For all q in Q create an empty list L_q.
2. For all $\tau_n = (\sigma, i_1, \ldots, i_m, j)$ in Δ add n to L_j (* Store n such that j is the output of τ_n *).
3. $K \leftarrow F$; $U \leftarrow Q - F$
4. While $K \neq \emptyset$ and $U \neq \emptyset$ remove a state q from K and for all n in L_q and for all i_k in $\{i_1, \ldots, i_m\}$ do
   - If $i_k \in U$ then then move i_k from U to K.
5. Return U.

Fig. 3. Algorithm for the identification of useless states in a DTA

The correctness of the main loop requires that all inequivalent pairs are eventually found through the search at step 2. Indeed, according to eq. (6), if $p \not\sim_{n+1} q$ there exist $m > 0$, $k \leq m$ and $(\sigma, r_1, \ldots, r_m, j) \in \Sigma \times Q^{m+1}$ with $r_k = p$ such that

$$\delta_m(\sigma, r_1, \ldots, r_{k-1}, q, r_{k+1}, \ldots, r_m) \not\sim_n j.$$

Let us assume that $j \neq \perp$ (otherwise, one can exchange p and q) and write $p^{[1]} = p$ and, for $s > 0$, $p^{[s+1]} = \text{next}(p^{[s]})$. Then, there is a value of $s > 0$ such that

$$\delta_m(\sigma, r_1, \ldots, r_{k-1}, p^{[s]}, r_{k+1}, \ldots, r_m) \sim_n j$$

and

$$\delta_m(\sigma, r_1, \ldots, r_{k-1}, p^{[s+1]}, r_{k+1}, \ldots, r_m) \not\sim_n j.$$

Therefore, the check performed at step 2 of the minimization algorithm over all $m > 0$, all $k \leq m$ and all transitions in $\Sigma \times Q^m$ can be limited to those

Algorithm minimizeDTA
Input: a DTA $A = (Q, \Sigma, \Delta, F)$ without inaccessible states.
Output: a minimal DTA $A^{\min} = (Q^{\min}, \Sigma, \Delta^{\min}, F^{\min})$.
Method:

1. (* Initialize π and K *)
   - Remove useless states from Q and transitions using them from Δ and set $Q \leftarrow Q \cup \{\bot\}$ and $n \leftarrow 1$.
   - For all $(\sigma, i_1, \ldots, i_m) \in \Delta$ add (σ, m, k) to sig(i_k) for $k = 1, \ldots, m$.
   - For all $q \in F$ add $(\#, 1, 1)$ to sig(q).
   - Create an empty set B_{sig} for every different signature sig and for all $q \in Q$ add q to set $B_{\text{sig}(q)}$.
   - Set $P_0 \leftarrow (Q)$ and $P_1 \leftarrow \{B_s : B_s \neq \emptyset\}$.
   - Enqueue in K the first element from every class in P_1.
2. While K is not empty
   (a) Remove the first state q in K.
   (b) For all $(\sigma, i_1, \ldots, i_m, j) \in \Delta$ such that $j \sim_n q$ and for all $k \leq m$
       i. If $\delta_m(\sigma, i_1, \ldots, \text{next}_n(i_k), \ldots, i_m) \not\sim_n j$ then
           A. Create P_{n+1} from P_n by splitting $\Phi_n[i_k]$ into so many subsets as different classes $\Phi_n[\delta_m(\sigma, i_1, ., i'_k, .., i_m)]$ are found for all $i'_k \in \Phi_n[i_k]$.
           B. Add to K the first element from every subset created at the previous step.
           C. Set $n \leftarrow n + 1$.
3. Output $(Q^{\min}, \Sigma, \Delta^{\min}, F^{\min})$ with
   - $Q^{\min} = \{\Phi_n[q] : q \in Q\}$;
   - $F^{\min} = \{\Phi_n[q] : q \in F\}$;
   - $\Delta^{\min} = \{(\sigma, \Phi_n[i_1], \ldots, \Phi_n[i_m], \Phi_n[j]) : (\sigma, i_1, \ldots, i_m, j) \in \Delta \wedge \Phi_n[j] \neq \Phi_n[\bot]\}$.

Fig. 4. Modified algorithm `minimizeDTA`

transitions in Δ and every $(\sigma, i_1, \ldots, i_m, j) \in \Delta$ needs only to be compared with m transitions of the type $(\sigma, i_1, \ldots, \text{next}(i_k), \ldots, i_m, j')$.

Finally, this minimization algorithm runs in time $\mathcal{O}(|A|^2)$, as can be easily checked if we take into account that, in a DTA without inaccessible states, $|Q| \leq |A|$ and:

- A state may enter K every time a finer class is created in the partition. As the refinement process cannot create more than $2|Q| - 1$ different classes (the number of nodes in a binary tree with $|Q|$ leaves), the main loop, which always removes a state from K, performs at most $2|Q| - 1$ iterations.
- At every iteration, a loop over some transitions in Δ and their arguments is performed: obviously, this internal loop involves at most $|A|$ iterations.
- If $\delta_m(\sigma, i_1, \ldots, \text{next}_n(i_k), \ldots, i_m) \not\sim_n j$ then class $\Phi_n[i_k]$ becomes split and its states are classified according to the transition output using less than $|Q|$

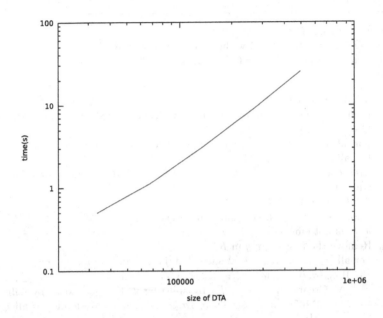

Fig. 5. Time needed to minimize a DTA as a function of the size of the DTA

steps; also updating K adds at most $|Q|$ states. As the maximum number of splits is $|Q| - 1$, the conditional block involves at most $|Q|^2$ steps.

This theoretical bound has been tested by appliyng the algorithm to compress an acyclic DTA accepting parse trees (up to 20 000 trees and 60 labels) obtained from a tree bank [7]. The results, depicted in figure 5, show that the time needed to minimize the DTA grows less than quadratically with the size of the automaton (the best fit for this example is $|A|^{1.47}$).

3   Conclusion

We presented a simple implementation of the standard algorithm for the minimization of deterministic frontier-to-root tree automata which runs in time $\mathcal{O}(|A|^2)$ by showing that the search for inconsistent classes can be efficiently performed and that undefined transitions and the absorption state can be properly handled. As the partition may be initialized with more than two classes and also subsequent refinements beyond binary splitting are possible the convergence is usually reached with fewer iterations. The question if a modification exists with better asymptotic behavior, such as those applicable for sparse string automata [8], remains open. Incremental minimization of DTAs, that is, the construction of a minimal DTA by adding new trees to the language accepted by an existing one, will be addressed elsewhere [9].

Acknowledgments

Work supported by the Spanish CICyT through grant TIN2006-15071-C03-01.

References

1. Brainerd, W.S.: The minimalization of tree automata. Information and Control 13(5), 484–491 (1968)
2. Gécseg, F., Steinby, M.: Tree Automata. Akadémiai Kiadó, Budapest (1984)
3. Comon, H., Dauchet, M., Gilleron, R., Jacquemard, F., Lugiez, D., Tison, S., Tommasi, M.: Tree automata techniques and applications (1997) release (October 1rst, 2002), Available on `http://www.grappa.univ-lille3.fr/tata`
4. Hopcroft, J., Ullman, J.D.: Introduction to Automata Theory, Languages, and Computation. Addison–Wesley, Reading, MA (1979)
5. Blum, N.: An O(n log n) implementation of the standard method for minimizing n-state finite automata. Information Processing Letters 57(2), 65–69 (1996)
6. Watson, B.W.: A taxonomy of finite automata minimization algorithmes. Computing Science Note 93/44, Eindhoven University of Technology, The Netherlands (1993)
7. Marcus, M.P., Santorini, B., Marcinkiewicz, M.: Building a large annotated corpus of english: the penn treebank. Computational Linguistics 19, 313–330 (1993)
8. Paige, R., Tarjan, R.E.: Three partition refinement algorithms. SIAM J. Computing 16(6), 973–989 (1987)
9. Carrasco, R.C., Daciuk, J., Forcada, M.L.: Incremental construction of minimal tree automata (submitted, 2007)

Accelerating Boyer Moore Searches
on Binary Texts

Shmuel T. Klein and Miri Kopel Ben-Nissan

Department of Computer Science, Bar Ilan University, Ramat-Gan 52900, Israel
Tel.: (972–3) 531 8865; Fax: (972–3) 736 0498
{tomi,kopel}@cs.biu.ac.il

Abstract. The Boyer and Moore (BM) pattern matching algorithm is considered as one of the best, but its performance is reduced on binary data. Yet, searching in binary texts has important applications, such as compressed matching. The paper shows how, by means of some pre-computed tables, one may implement the BM algorithm also for the binary case without referring to bits, and processing only entire blocks such as bytes or words, thereby significantly reducing the number of comparisons. Empirical comparisons show that the new variant performs better than regular binary BM and even than BDM.

Keywords: Boyer-Moore, BDM, pattern matching, binary texts, compressed matching.

1 Introduction

One of the important applications of automata theory is to Pattern Matching. Indeed, many matching methods can be reformulated in terms finding an automaton with certain properties, as, e.g., the KMP algorithm [1], and several variations of the Boyer and Moore (BM) method [2]. The Backward DAWG Match (BDM) algorithm uses a suffix automaton and runs in optimal sublinear average time [3]. This papers deals with an extension of the BM algorithm to binary data, which has important applications, for example matching in compressed texts. For the ease of description, we shall stick to the usual pattern matching vocabulary.

BM uses two independent heuristics for shifting the pattern forward, denoted by $delta_1$ and $delta_2$ in their original paper. $delta_1$ shifts the pattern according to the character in the text that caused the mismatch: if the character $T[i]$ does not appear at all in P, the pattern can be shifted by its full length. In the binary case, however, the character $T[i]$ is either 1 or 0, and both will most probably appear in P, even close to its right end, except for a very restricted set of patterns. Thus $delta_1$ will rarely let the pattern to be shifted by more than just a few bits.

The second shift function, $delta_2$, assigns a value for each possible position j of the mismatch in P, noting that if $P[j]$ is the first element from the right that does not match, then the suffix $P[j+1] \cdots P[m]$ does, so one may look

Jan Holub and Jan Žd'árek (Eds.): CIAA 2007, LNCS 4783, pp. 130–143, 2007.

for a reoccurrence of this suffix in the pattern. More precisely, one looks for the reoccurrence of this suffix which is not preceded by $P[j]$, or, if such an occurrence is not found, one looks for the occurrence of the longest suffix of the suffix $P[j + 1] \cdots P[m]$ which is a prefix of P. While $delta_2$ is reported to add only marginally to the performance in the general case, it does in fact all the job on binary data, as $delta_2 \geq delta_1$ in the binary case.

There is, however, an additional problem with using BM on binary input: it forces the programmer to deal at the bit-level, which is more complicated and time consuming. Packing the bits into blocks and processing byte per byte is not a solution, as the location of the pattern in the text is not necessarily byte aligned, in particular when the binary text at hand is the compressed form of some input text. This led to the idea of using 256-ary Huffman codes as compression scheme, especially for very large alphabets for which the loss relative to the optimal binary variant is small [4]. To enable compressed matching, the first bit of each byte serves as tag, which is used to identify the last byte of each codeword, thereby reducing the order of the Huffman tree to 128-ary. These *Tagged Huffman codes* have then been replaced by the better (s, c)-*Dense codes* in [5].

We show in this paper how to apply the BM algorithm even in the binary case by treating only full blocks of k bits at a time, typically, bytes, half-words or words, that is $k = 8$, 16 or 32. This takes advantage of the fact that such k-bit blocks can be processed at the cost of a single operation. The idea is to eliminate any reference to bits and to proceed, by means of some pre-computed tables, block by block, similarly to the fast decoding method of binary Huffman encoded texts, first suggested in [6]. A similar approach has been taken in [7], and the special case of BM compressed matching for LZ encoded texts is treated in [8,9], and for BWT compression in [10]. The details of the algorithm are presented in the next section, an analysis is given in Section 3, and Section 4 brings empirical comparisons.

2   A High-Level Binary BM Variant

Once the block size k is fixed, all references to both text and pattern will only be to entire blocks of k bits. For the ease of description, we shall refer to a k-bit block as a *byte*, though larger values than $k = 8$ could be supported as well.

Let Text$[i]$ and Pat$[i]$ denote, respectively, the i-th byte of the text and of the pattern, starting for $i = 1$ with both text and pattern aligned at the leftmost bit of the first byte. When we need to refer to the individual bits rather than the bytes, we shall use the notation $T[i]$ and $P[i]$. Since the lengths in bits of both text and pattern are not necessarily multiples of k, the last bytes may be only partially defined. In fact, we shall use a sequence of several copies of the pattern: using a shift parameter sh, with $0 \leq sh < k$, denote by Pat$[sh, i]$ the i-th byte of the pattern after an initial shift of sh bits to the right. Figure 1 visualizes these definitions for $k = 8$ and a pattern of length $m = 21$. The bold vertical

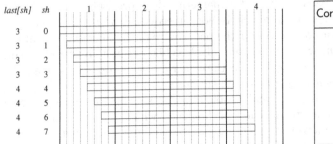

Fig. 1. Schematic representation of shifted copies of the pattern

bars indicate the byte boundaries. Let last[sh] be the index of the last byte of the pattern that has been shifted sh bits, so formally $\text{last}[sh] = \lceil (sh + m)/k \rceil$. In our example in Figure 1, $\text{last}[sh] = 3$ for $0 \leq sh \leq 3$, and $\text{last}[sh] = 4$ for $4 \leq sh \leq 7$. Figure 1 also includes a Table Correct, to be explained below.

The algorithm starts by comparing the last byte of the pattern, of which possibly only a proper prefix belongs really to P, with the corresponding byte of the text. Let sl be the length in bits of the suffix of P in this last byte, that is $sl = 1 + (m - 1) \mod k$, so that $1 \leq sl \leq k$. The variable sl will hold this suffix length throughout the program, but sl may change because of the initial shift sh. When processing the first or last byte of P, the bit positions not belonging to the pattern have to be neutralized by means of pre-computed masks. Define Mask$[sh, j]$ as a binary mask of length k in which a bit is set to 1 if and only if the corresponding bit of Pat$[sh, j]$ belongs to P. For our example of Figure 1, Mask$[0, 3] = 11111000$, Mask$[0, 2] = 11111111$ and Mask$[2, 1] = 00111111$.

In the original BM algorithm, the comparisons are between characters, which either match or not. In this binary variant, more information is available in case of a mismatch, namely, the length of the (possibly empty) suffix of the mismatching byte that still did match. For example, the characters b and j do not match, but their corresponding ASCII encodings, 01100010 and 01101010 are not completely unrelated and share a common suffix of length 3. In fact, they share even more common bits, but we are interested in the longest common suffix, because BM scans from right to left up to the first mismatch, which in this example would be at the 4-th bit from the right.

A way to get the length of the longest matching suffix is to replace comparisons by Xoring. If $C = A$ XOR B, then $C = 0$ if and only if $A = B$, but if $A \neq B$, then the length of the longest common suffix of A and B is the length of the longest run of zeros at the right end of C. In the above example, b XOR j $= 00001000$ and the requested length is 3. Let NRZ$[x]$ be this number of rightmost zeros for a given binary string x of length k. To speedup the computation, we shall keep NRZ as a pre-computed table of size 2^k. This is just 256 for $k = 8$, but for $k = 16$ or even 32, such a table might be too large. Not that requesting enough RAM to store a 2^{16} size table is unreasonable, but with growing k, there will be many cache misses, and they may have a strong impact on the performance. Certainly

2^{32} seems too large, so for larger k, it might pay to compute the function on the fly, still using a table $\mathsf{NRZ}[x]$ for single bytes. For example, for $k = 32$, denoting the four bytes of x by $x_1, \ldots, x_4$ and the rightmost two bytes by x_{34}, the function could be defined by

if $x_{34} = 0$ then   else
   if $x_2 = 0$ then   return $24 + \mathsf{NRZ}[x_1]$ if $x_4 = 0$ then   return $8 + \mathsf{NRZ}[x_3]$
   else   return $16 + \mathsf{NRZ}[x_2]$ else   return $\mathsf{NRZ}[x_4]$

It was mentioned in the introduction that the $delta_1$ heuristic of the original BM algorithm will rarely be useful in the binary case, but it is possible to use an extension of the idea as follows. Refer to Figure 2 for an example of a typical scenario. Suppose the pattern has just been positioned at its current location, being shifted sh bits to the right from a byte boundary and extending sl bits into its rightmost byte, which corresponds to byte i of the text. The first comparison at this position will be between $\mathsf{Text}[i]$ and $\mathsf{Pat}[sh, \mathsf{last}[sh]]$, using the appropriate mask to cancel the rightmost bits of the latter. Suppose we got a mismatch. The original BM $delta_1$ heuristic would ask where the rightmost occurrence of the bit in the text causing the mismatch (which, in the binary case, is the complement of the rightmost bit of P) can be found in P. In the byte oriented version on the other hand, since several bits have been compared already, we know what the first sl bits of $\mathsf{Text}[i]$ are, so one can check whether these bits, corresponding to the shaded area in the Text of the left part of Figure 2, reoccur somewhere in the pattern. This is similar to the idea underlying the original definition of $delta_2$. If yes, we seek the rightmost reoccurrence, which, in our example, is the identically shaded area in P. The pattern can thus be shifted forward so as to align these matching substrings, as can be seen in the bottom line of the example. If the bits do not reoccur, the pattern can be shifted by its full length. The right part of Figure 2 will be referred to below, when dealing with $delta_2$.

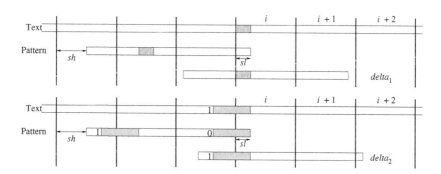

Fig. 2. Typical pattern matching scenarios with binary data: $delta_1$ and $delta_2$

2.1   Definition of $Delta_1$

The amount of shifts for all the possible cases can be computed in advance. We define a sequence of tables $delta_1[sl, B]$, one table for each possible suffix length sl, with $1 \leq sl \leq k$ and $0 \leq B < 2^{sl}$. $delta_1[sl, B] = m - \ell$, where ℓ is the index of the last bit of the rightmost occurrence in P of the sl-bit binary representation of B. For example, if $sl = 4$ and $P = 0010101011101101$, where the rightmost occurrence of $B = 5 = 0101$ is underlined, then $delta_1[4, 5] = 16 - 9 = 7$. In fact, this definition needs a similar amendment as that of $delta_2$ in the original algorithm: if the sl-bit binary representation of B does not occur as a substring of P, but some proper suffix of it appears as a prefix of P, this should still be counted as a plausible reoccurrence. For example, using $sl = 5$ and the same P but letting $B = 17 = 10001$, one sees that B does not occur in P, but its suffix 001 is a prefix of P. The pattern can thus not be shifted by its full length, and $delta_1[5, 17] = 13$ rather than 16. The tables are first initialized with m in each entry; then the prefixes of P are taken care of by:

$$\text{for } r \quad \longleftarrow \quad 1 \quad \text{to} \quad sl - 1$$
$$\text{for all values of } B \text{ such that the prefix } P[1] \cdots P[r] \text{ is a suffix of } B$$
$$delta_1[sl, B] \quad \longleftarrow \quad m - r;$$

finally, the other values are filled in by scanning the pattern left to right:

$$\text{for } t \quad \longleftarrow \quad 1 \quad \text{to} \quad m - sl$$
$$B \quad \longleftarrow \quad P[t] \cdots P[t + sl - 1]$$
$$delta_1[sl, B] \quad \longleftarrow \quad m - t - sl + 1,$$

where the assignment of a bit-string of length sl to B should be understood as considering this string as the binary representation of some number, which is assigned to B.

The formal binary BM algorithm is given in Figure 3 (it contains some details to be explained below). Each iteration of the while loop starting in line 3 corresponds to checking if there is a match at the given position i in the text. The pointer to the pattern is initialized in each iteration to the last byte, and the suffix length is calculated. In the main comparison loop in lines 6–8, the variable *indic* serves as indicator if there has been a match. If not, and the pattern has not yet been found, the else clause starting at line 10 calculates the new position of the pointer i to the text. Lines 11–15 and 16–17 deal, respectively, with Δ_1 and Δ_2, which are based on BM's original $delta_1$ and $delta_2$ functions. In line 18, the new bit position of the text pointer is evaluated by adding the maximum possible shift to *lastbit*, which is throughout the bit-index of the last bit in the text that was aligned with the last bit of the pattern. The new byte oriented values of i and sh are then derived accordingly from the newly calculated bit-position in lines 19–20. Note that contrarily to the original BM algorithm, it is possible that the byte index i is not increased after a mismatch (but then the suffix length sl is), in case the shift is not large enough to cause the crossing of a byte boundary.

If in the first comparison in line 6, between Text[i] and Pat[sh, last[sh]], one gets a match, the preceding bytes of both text and pattern are inspected. This continues either until the pattern is found (line 9), or until a mismatch stops

BLOCKED BOYER-MOORE MATCHING

```
1   i   ⟵   last[0]        sh   ⟵   0
2   lastbit   ⟵   m
3   while i ≤ ⌈n/k⌉    // length of text in bytes
4           j   ⟵   last[sh]
5           sl   ⟵   1 + ((m + sh − 1) mod k)
6           while j > 0 AND (indic ⟵ (Text[i] XOR Pat[sh, j]) AND Mask[sh, j]) = 0
7                   i   ⟵   i − 1
8                   j   ⟵   j − 1
9           if j = 0        print "match at k ∗ i + sh"
10          else
11                  if j = last[sh]
12                          B   ⟵   (Text[i] / 2^{k−sl}) mod 2^K
13                          Δ₁   ⟵   delta₁[min(sl, K), B]
14                  else
15                          Δ₁   ⟵   delta₁[K, Text[i] mod 2^K] − Correct[sh, j]
16                  matchlen   ⟵   sl + NRZ[indic] + (last[sh] − j − 1) ∗ k
17                  Δ₂   ⟵   delta₂[m − matchlen]
18                  lastbit   ⟵   lastbit + max(Δ₁, Δ₂)
19                  i   ⟵   ⌈lastbit / k⌉
20                  sh   ⟵   (lastbit − m) mod k
```

Fig. 3. Formal BM algorithm for binary data

this iteration. In the original BM algorithm, a single $delta_1$ table could be used, regardless of whether the mismatch occurred in the last byte of the pattern or not, because $delta_1$ was in fact the amount by which the current pointer to the text i could be increased, rather than the number of characters the pattern could be shifted. In this binary variant, on the other side, $delta_1$ will only hold the number of bits to shift the pattern, because the increase in i, if there is one at all, has to be calculated. Therefore, if the mismatch is not at the last byte of P, $delta_1$ has to be corrected by subtracting the number of bits i has been moved to the left during the comparison at the current position of the pattern. This correction is constant for a given pair (sh, j), so a table $\mathsf{Correct}[sh, j]$ can be prepared in advance. The table corresponding to the example in Figure 1 is shown at the right side of the figure. It is not defined for $j = \mathsf{last}[sh]$, and for the other values it is given by

$$\mathsf{Correct}[sh, j] = sl + (\mathsf{last}[sh] − 1 − j) \times k.$$

The combined size of all the $delta_1$ tables is $\sum_{sl=1}^{k} 2^{sl} = 2^{k+1} − 2$, which seems reasonable for $k = 8$ or even 16, but not for $k = 32$. One can adapt the algorithm to choose the desired time/space tradeoff by introducing a new parameter $K \leq k$, representing the maximal number of mismatching bits taken into account for deciding by how much to move the pattern. If the mismatch is in the first iteration, that is, between Text$[i]$ and Pat$[sh, \text{last}[sh]]$, and if $sl > K$, then only the K rightmost bits of the sl first bits of Text$[i]$ are taken into account (implemented by the division and the mod function in line 12), for the other iterations, the reference is to the K rightmost bits of the current byte of the text (line 15). This reduces the total sizes of the tables to 2^{K+1} at the cost of sometimes shifting the pattern less than could be done if the full length mismatch had been considered. The possible values of K are not bound to be multiples of 8 and the choice of K is governed solely by the available space.

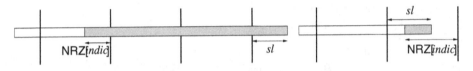

Mismatch at the 4th byte   Mismatch at the last byte

Fig. 4. Examples of mismatch lengths for the definition of $delta_2$

2.2   Definition of $Delta_2$

The $delta_2$ table is a function of the length of the matching suffix. This length, denoted by $matchlen$, consists, in case the mismatch did not occur at the last byte of the pattern, of three parts:

1. the length of the suffix of the pattern in the last byte;
2. the lengths of the full matching bytes;
3. the length of the matching suffix of the byte that finally caused the mismatch.

The first item is sl, the second is a multiple of k and the last is given by NRZ$[indic]$. This general case is represented in the left part of Figure 4, where the matching part of the pattern appears in grey. For the special case in which the mismatch occurred already at the first comparison, depicted in the right part of Figure 4, the length of the match is the length of the matching suffix of the sl-bit prefix of Pat$[sh, \text{last}[sh]]$. This is NRZ$[indic]$, from which the length of the suffix of the byte not belonging to P, $k - sl$, should be subtracted. One can thus describe the length in both cases by the formula

$$\text{NRZ}[indic] + sl + k \times r,$$

where $r = -1$ if the mismatch is at the last byte, $r = 0$ if it is at the second byte from the right, $r = 1$ for the third, etc. In general, one gets that $r = \text{last}[sh] - j - 1$, where j is the index of the current byte of the pattern at which the mismatch occurred.

To be consistent with the original BM algorithm, the parameter of $delta_2$ is not the length of the matching suffix, but the index of the first bit from the right that did not match, which is $m - matchlen$. Figure 5 brings two examples of $delta_2$ tables. The left one corresponds to the example pattern above

j	1	2	3	4	5	6	7	8	9	10	11	12	13	14	15	16
Pat[j]	0	0	1	0	1	0	1	0	1	1	1	0	1	1	0	1
$delta_2[j]$	16	16	16	16	16	16	16	16	16	16	16	3	7	13	2	1

j	1	2	3	4	5	6	7	8	9	10	11	12	13	14	15	16
Pat[j]	1	0	1	0	1	0	1	0	1	1	1	0	1	1	0	1
$delta_2[j]$	13	13	13	13	13	13	13	13	13	13	3	7	15	2	1

Fig. 5. Examples of $delta_2$

$P = 0010101011101101$. The values are filled following the original algorithm, except that as above for $delta_1$, the values stored will be the number of bits the pattern can be shifted to the right, and not the number of bits the text pointer can be moved. For example, position 12 corresponds to a matching suffix 1101 and a mismatch at the 0-bit preceding this suffix. We are thus looking for a reoccurrence of this suffix preceded by the complement of the bit that caused the mismatch.

The situation is schematically represented in the right side of Figure 2, where the greyed suffix of the pattern, preceded by a zero, appears again earlier in the pattern, but preceded there by a 1. The next line in the figure shows how the pattern can be moved so as to align the matching substrings. In the present example, we seek for 11101 in P, which can be found in positions 9–13; the possible shift, which should align the rightmost reoccurrence with the current position of the suffix, in therefore in this case $16 - 13 = 3$. The right side of Figure 5 shows how the $delta_2$ table changes with a slight change in the pattern: the first bit of P has been changed to a 1. Consider, e.g., position 11, corresponding to the suffix 01101; there is no occurrence of 001101 in P, so a priori, the possible shift should be of length 16, but a suffix of the suffix, 101, appears as prefix in P, so the possible shift is only of length 13.

Note that all the operations in the algorithm in Figure 3 refer to entire bytes of either the text or the pattern and there is no processing of individual bits. Moreover, multiplications and divisions, which generally are more time consuming, are all with powers of 2 and can thus be translated to the more economical shifts by the compiler.

Summarizing, the byte oriented search algorithm makes use of the following tables, all of which are prepared in advance as functions of the pattern only: Mask and Correct, both with k lines and $\lceil m/k \rceil$ columns, so using about m bytes each, $delta_2$ with m entries, last with k entries, NRZ with 2^8 entries, even if $k > 8$, and $delta_1$ of size 2^{K+1}, where K is a parameter of our choice, enabling a time/space tradeoff: increasing K by 1 doubles the size of the $delta_1$ tables, but also increases the expected size of the shift after a mismatch, reducing the expected processing time. Summing it up, we need $3m + k + 256 + 2^{K+1}$ entries, and each can be stored in a single byte (assuming the length m of the pattern is less than 256 bits; for longer patterns, more than one byte is needed for each entry). For example for $m = 100$, using $k = 8$, all the tables together need just slightly more than 1K, and even if we use $k = 32$, thereby quadrupling the number of bits processed in a single operation, the overhead is below 9K if we choose $K = 12$.

3 Time Analysis

To compare the number of comparisons of the k-bit block algorithm suggested here with the regular binary BM algorithm, we shall assume the following probabilistic model. The distribution of zeros and ones in the input string is like in a randomly generated one, that is, the probability of occurrence in the text of any binary string of length ℓ is $2^{-\ell}$, and it is independent of the other substrings. This is a reasonable assumption if the binary BM is to be applied on compressed text. For the special case where compression is done using Huffman coding, such "randomness" has been shown to hold in [11], subject to some additional constraints, but in fact any reasonable compression scheme produces output that is quite close to random: if it would not, the remaining redundancy could be removed by applying another compression round on the already compressed text. We moreover assume that this randomness also holds for the input pattern to be searched for.

Let us first concentrate on the binary, unblocked, case, and suppose that the index into the text has just been moved forward to a new location i. The algorithm will now compare $T[i-j]$ with $P[m-j]$ for $j = 0, 1, \ldots$ until a mismatch will allow us to move i forward again. The expected number of comparisons up to and including the mismatch will be

$$1 \cdot \frac{1}{2} + 2 \cdot \frac{1}{4} + 3 \cdot \frac{1}{8} + \cdots = \sum_{j=1}^{m} \frac{j}{2^j} = 2 - 2^{-(m-1)} - m2^{-m} \simeq 2.$$

This follows from the fact that if p denotes the probability of a zero, then the probability of a bit of the text matching a bit of the pattern is $p^2 + (1-p)^2$, and the probability of a mismatch is $2p(1-p)$; in our case, both probabilities are $\frac{1}{2}$, so the probability of having the first mismatch at the jth trial is $\frac{1}{2} \left(\frac{1}{2}\right)^{j-1} = 2^{-j}$.

For the blocked case, denote by NK the random variable giving the number of comparisons between consecutive mismatches. We then have

$$E(NK) = \sum_{i=1}^{\lceil m/k \rceil} P(NK \geq i) = 1 + \sum_{i=1}^{\lceil m/k \rceil} P(\text{match at first } i - 1 \text{ comparisons}).$$

The latter probability depends on the length sl of the suffix in the rightmost k-bit block and is $2^{-sl} + 2^{-(k+sl)} + 2^{-(2k+sl)} + \cdots$. Averaging over the possible values of sl, which all appear with the same probability, we get

$$E(NK) = 1 + \frac{1}{k} \sum_{sl=1}^{k} \sum_{t=1}^{\lceil m/k \rceil} 2^{-(tk+sl)} < 1 + \frac{1}{k} \sum_{sl=1}^{k} 2^{-sl} \sum_{t=1}^{\infty} \left(2^{-k}\right)^t = 1 + \frac{[1 - 2^{-k}]}{k(1 - 2^{-k})} = 1 + \frac{1}{k}.$$

Let M and M' denote, respectively for the unblocked and k-bit blocked variants, the expected number of bits the pattern can be shifted after a mismatch is detected. In fact, if both algorithms would use the same $delta_1$ and $delta_2$ functions, one would have $M = M'$, as they depend only on the length of the longest matching suffix of the pattern at each position, and not on whether this suffix has been detected bit by bit or in blocks. Indeed, both algorithms use the same $delta_2$, but the block variant exploits the fact that several bits have been compared in a single operation to increase, in certain cases, the jump defined by $delta_1$. Our empirical tests show that about 75% of the jumps are due to the revised $delta_1$ in the blocked variant. It therefore follows that $M' \geq M$. If n is the length of the text in bits, the expected number of comparisons for the unblocked case is thus $\frac{2n}{M}$, which is larger than the corresponding number for the blocked case, $\frac{(1+\frac{1}{k})n}{M'}$.

To evaluate M, assume that the first mismatch occurs at the jth trial, $j \geq 1$. The value of $delta_2$ for the rightmost bit of the pattern is usually 1, unless the pattern has ℓ identical characters as suffix, in which case $delta_2$ of the last ℓ positions is ℓ. So if $j = 1$, the expected shift by $delta_2$ is $\sum \frac{\ell}{2^{-\ell}} \simeq 2$. For $j > 1$, the probability of a suffix of length $j-1$ to reoccur with complemented preceding bit is 2^{-j}, thus the expected position of this reoccurrence is 2^j bits to the left, but since the shift is limited, the expected shift caused by $delta_2$ will be $\min(2^j, m)$. Since the probability of having the first mismatch at the jth trial is 2^{-j}, we get as expected size of the shift

$$\frac{1}{2}\,2+\sum_{j=2}^{m}2^{-j}\min(2^j,m)=1+(\log m-1)+m\sum_{j=\log m+1}^{m}2^{-j} = \log m+m2^{-m}-1 \simeq \log m,$$

for large enough m, where the logarithm is with base 2.

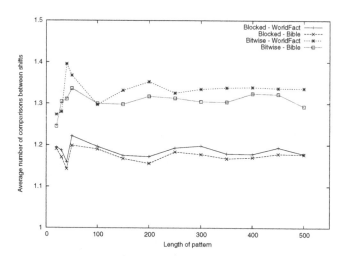

Fig. 6. Average number of comparisons between shifts

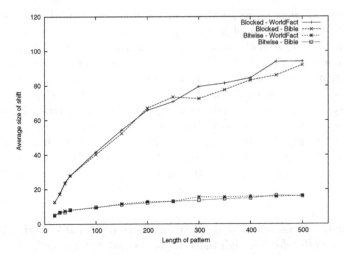

Fig. 7. Expected size of shift after mismatch

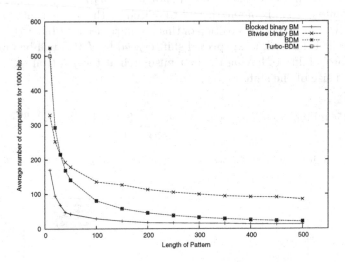

Fig. 8. Expected number of comparisons for 1000 bits

4   Experiments

To get some empirical results, we ran the following tests on the English Bible (2.55 MB, King James Version) and the World Factbook 1992 file of the Gutenberg Project (1.49 MB). Both files were Huffman encoded according to their character distributions. The patterns were chosen as substrings of lengths 10 to 500, starting at 100 randomly chosen positions in the last third of the encoded string, and for each length, the 100 obtained values were averaged. The results are displayed in the plots of Figures 6 to 9, giving the averaged values as function of the length of the pattern m.

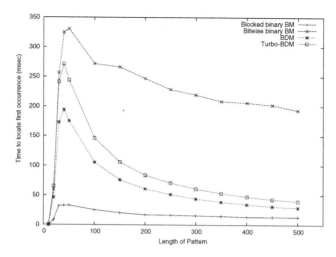

Fig. 9. Time to locate first occurrence of the pattern

Figure 6 gives the average number of comparisons between consecutive shifts. As expected, this number is smaller for the blocked variant than for bit by bit processing, though also for the latter, the obtained values were smaller than 2. The plot in Figure 7 shows the values M and M'. M exhibits indeed logarithmic behavior, and the values of M' can be seen to grow at a faster rate. This may be due to the extended definition of $delta_1$ for the blocked algorithm, which has a dominant influence on the shift size.

The next plots compare the behavior of the blocked and bitwise binary BM variants also with BDM and Turbo-BDM [12,3], the suffix automaton pattern matching techniques, which are among the best alternatives to BM. For lack of space, the displayed results are for the Bible file only; the graphs for the WorldFact file were similar. Figure 8 plots the expected number of comparisons for every 1000 bits passed of the text, showing a significant reduction with the blocked versus the bitwise variant, and improving even on both BDM and Turbo-BDM (which are indistinguishable on these plots). Typical values (for patterns of length 250) were 105.2 comparisons for bitwise BM, 37.9 for both BDM and 16.5 for blocked BM. All graphs show decreasing functions of the pattern length, as expected.

The last graphs, in Figure 9, are timing results measured on an Intel Pentium III processor, 750 MHz, with 256 MB of RAM. The values are the time needed to locate the first occurrence of each pattern, in milliseconds. Here too the blocked BM gives consistently better times than the bitwise variant and also than the two BDM algorithms, with typical values (for patterns of length 250) 228.5 ms for bitwise BM, 70.8 for Turbo-BDM, 51.2 for BDM and 16.6 for blocked BM. Here again the functions are decreasing, except for the lowest values. This can be explained by the fact that we measured the time to locate the *first* occurrence of each of the patterns, and these patterns were chosen from the last third of the file; for the shorter patterns, there were several occurrences and the first one was closer to the beginning of the file, but for the longer patterns, only one occurrence occurred — the one from which the pattern was generated.

5   Conclusion

A variant of the Boyer Moore pattern matching algorithm has been presented, which is suitable in case when both text and pattern are over a binary alphabet, and nevertheless do not use any bit manipulations. Using a set of tables that are prepared in advance and are independent of the text, the algorithm addresses only entire bytes or words. The expected reduction in time and number of comparisons comes at the cost of a space overhead of 1–10K, which can generally be tolerated.

In fact, one could think that the same ideas could also be used to get a similar reduction in the regular ASCII case: instead of comparing the characters one by one, they could be processed by groups of four (i.e., words instead of bytes). But in practice, most of the mismatches occur at the first comparison of each new position (which has led to the Horspool variant [13]), so the overhead of the word-decoding procedure might exceed the expected gain.

References

1. Knuth, D.E., Morris, J.H., Pratt, V.R.: Fast pattern matching in strings. SIAM J. Comput. 6, 323–350 (1977)
2. Boyer, R.S., Moore, J.S.: A fast string searching algorithm. Commun. ACM 20, 762–772 (1977)
3. Crochemore, M., Czumaj, A., Gasieniec, L., Jarominek, S., Lecroq, T., Plandowski, W., Rytter, W.: Speeding up two string-matching algorithms. Algorithmica 12, 247–267 (1994)
4. de Moura, E.S., Navarro, G., Ziviani, N., Baeza-Yates, R.A.: Fast and flexible word searching on compressed text. ACM Transactions on Information Systems 18, 113–139 (2000)
5. Brisaboa, N.R., Farina, A., Navarro, G., Esteller, M.F.: (s,c)-dense coding: An optimized compression code for natural language text databases. In: Nascimento, M.A., de Moura, E.S., Oliveira, A.L. (eds.) SPIRE 2003. LNCS, vol. 2857, pp. 122–136. Springer, Heidelberg (2003)
6. Choueka, Y., Klein, S.T., Perl, Y.: Efficient variants of Huffman codes in high level languages. In: SIGIR 1985. Proceedings of the 8th annual international ACM SIGIR conference on Research and development in information retrieval, pp. 122–130. ACM Press, New York (1985)
7. Fredriksson, K.: Faster string matching with super-alphabets. In: Laender, A.H.F., Oliveira, A.L. (eds.) SPIRE 2002. LNCS, vol. 2476, pp. 44–57. Springer, Heidelberg (2002)
8. Navarro, G., Tarhio, J.: Boyer-Moore string matching over Ziv-Lempel compressed text, pp. 166–180 (2000)
9. Shibata, Y., Matsumoto, T., Takeda, M., Shinohara, A., Arikawa, S.: A Boyer-Moore type algorithm for compressed pattern matching. In: Giancarlo, R., Sankoff, D. (eds.) CPM 2000. LNCS, vol. 1848, pp. 181–194. Springer, Heidelberg (2000)

10. Bell, T., Powell, M., Mukherjee, A., Adjeroh, D.: Searching BWT compressed text with the Boyer-Moore algorithm and binary search. In: DCC 2002. Proceedings of the Data Compression Conference (DCC 2002), pp. 112–121. IEEE Computer Society Press, Washington, DC, USA (2002)
11. Klein, S.T., Bookstein, A., Deerwester, S.: Storing text retrieval systems on CD-ROM: compression and encryption considerations. ACM Trans. Inf. Syst. 7, 230–245 (1989)
12. Crochemore, M., Rytter, W.: Text algorithms. Oxford University Press, Inc., New York (1994)
13. Horspool, R.N.: Practical fast searching in strings. Software Practice and Experience 10, 501–506 (1980)

On the Suffix Automaton with Mismatches*

Maxime Crochemore[1], Chiara Epifanio[2], Alessandra Gabriele[2],
and Filippo Mignosi[3]

[1] Institut Gaspard-Monge, Université de Marne-la-Vallée, France and King's College
London, UK
mac@univ-mlv.fr
[2] Dipartimento di Matematica e Applicazioni, Università di Palermo, Italy
{epifanio,sandra}@math.unipa.it
[3] Dipartimento di Informatica, Università dell'Aquila, Italy
mignosi@di.univaq.it

Abstract. In this paper we focus on the construction of the minimal
deterministic finite automaton S_k that recognizes the set of suffixes of a
word w up to k errors. We present an algorithm that makes use of S_k in
order to accept in an efficient way the language of all suffixes of w up to
k errors in every window of size r, where r is the value of the repetition
index of w. Moreover, we give some experimental results on some well-
known words, like prefixes of Fibonacci and Thue-Morse words, and we
make a conjecture on the size of the suffix automaton with mismatches.

Keywords: combinatorics on words, suffix automata, languages with
mismatches, approximate string matching.

1 Introduction

One of the seminal results in string matching is that the size of the suffix automaton of a word, called also DAWG, is linear [1,2]. In the particular case of
prefixes of the Fibonacci word, a result by Carpi and de Luca [3] implies that
the suffix automaton of any prefix v of the Fibonacci word f has $|v| + 1$ states.

These results are surprising as the maximal number of subwords that may
occur in a word is quadratic according to the length of the word. Suffix trees
are linear too, but they represent strings by pointers to the text, while DAWGs
work without the need of accessing it.

In this work we are interested in an extension of suffix automata, more precisely we consider the DAWG recognizing the set of occurrences of a word w up
to k errors. Literature on data structures recognizing languages with mismatches
involves many results, among the most recent ones [4,5,6,7,8,9,10,11,12]. Several
of these papers deal with approximate string matching. In particular, in [8,9,10]
authors have considered some data structures recognizing words occurring in a
text w up to k errors in each substring of length r of the text. The presence

---

* Partially supported by MIUR National Project PRIN "Automi e Linguaggi Formali:
aspetti matematici e applicativi."

Jan Holub and Jan Žd'árek (Eds.): CIAA 2007, LNCS 4783, pp. 144–156, 2007.
© Springer-Verlag Berlin Heidelberg 2007

of a window in which allowing a fixed number of errors generalizes the classical k-mismatch problem and, at the same time, it allows more errors in all.

In this paper we focus on the minimal deterministic finite automaton that recognizes the set of suffixes of a word w up to k errors, denoted by $S_{w,k}$, or simply by S_k if there are no risks of misunderstanding on w. As first main result we give a characterization of the Nerode's right-invariant congruence relative to S_k. This result generalizes a result described in [1] (see also [13,14]), where it was used in an efficient construction of the suffix automaton with no mismatches, that, up to the set of final states, is also called DAWG (directed acyclic word graph). We think that it is possible to define such an algorithm even when dealing with mismatches. It would be probably more complex than the classical one. It still remains an open problem how to define it. As a second main result, we describe an algorithm that makes use of the automaton S_k in order to accept, in an efficient way, the language of all suffixes of w up to k errors in every windows of size r, for a specific integer r called repetition index.

We have constructed the suffix automaton with mismatches of a great number of words and we have considered overall its structure when the input word is well-known, such as the prefixes of Fibonacci and Thue-Morse words, as well as words of the form bba^n, $a, b \in \Sigma, n \geq 1$ and some random words generated by memoryless sources. We have studied how the number of states grows depending on the length of the input word. By the results of our experiments on these classes of words, we conjecture that the (compact) suffix automaton with k mismatches of any text w has size $O(|w| \cdot \log^k(|w|))$. Given a word v, Gad Landau wondered if a data structure having a size "close" to $|v|$ that allows approximate pattern matching in time proportional to the query plus the number of occurrences exists. This question is still open, even if recent results are getting closer to a positive answer. If our conjecture turns out to be true, it would settle Landau's question as discussed at the end of this paper.

The remainder of this paper is organized as follows. In the second section we give some basic definitions. In the third section we describe a characterization of the Nerode's right invariant congruence relative to S_k. The fourth section is devoted to describe an algorithm that makes use of the automaton S_k in order to accept in an efficient way the language of all suffixes of w up to k errors in every window of size r, where r is the value of the repetition index of w. The fifth section contains our conclusions and some conjectures on the size of the suffix automaton with mismatches based on our experimental results. Finally, appendix contains the proofs of our results.

2   Basic Definitions

Let Σ be a finite set of symbols, usually called *alphabet*. A *word* or *string* w is a finite sequence $w = a_1 a_2 \cdots a_n$ of characters in the alphabet Σ, its length (i.e. the number of characters of the string) is defined to be n and it is denoted by $|w|$. The set of words built on Σ is denoted by Σ^* and the empty word by ε. We denote by Σ^+ the set $\Sigma^* \setminus \{\varepsilon\}$. A word $u \in \Sigma^*$ is a *factor* (resp. a *prefix*, resp. a *suffix*) of a word w if and only if there exist two words $x, y \in \Sigma^*$ such that $w = xuy$ (resp. $w = uy$, resp. $w = xu$). Notice that some authors call *substring* what we have defined as factor. We denote by *Fact(w)* (resp. *Pref(w)*, resp. *Suff(w)*) the set of all factors (resp. prefixes, resp. suffixes) of a word w. We denote an occurrence of a factor in a string $w = a_1 a_2 \cdots a_n$ at position i ending at position j by $w(i,j) = a_i \cdots a_j$, $1 \le i \le j \le n$. The length of a factor $w(i,j)$ is the number of letters that compose it, i.e. $j - i + 1$. We say that u *occurs* in w at position i if $u = w(i,j)$, with $|u| = j - i + 1$.

In order to handle languages with errors, we need a notion of distance between words. In this work we consider the *Hamming distance*, that is defined between two words x and y of the same length as the minimal number of character substitutions that transform x into y. In the field of approximate string matching, typical approaches for finding a string in a text consist in considering a percentage D of errors, or fixing the number k of them. Instead, we use a hybrid approach introduced in [10] that considers a new parameter r and allow at most k errors for any factor of length r of the text.

Definition 1. *Let w be a string over the alphabet Σ, and let k, r be non negative integers such that $k \le r$. A string u occurs in w at position l up to k errors in a window of size r or, simply, k_r-occurs in w at position l, if one of the following two conditions holds:*

- $|u| < r \Rightarrow d(u, w(l, l + |u| - 1)) \le k$;
- $|u| \ge r \Rightarrow \forall i, 1 \le i \le |u| - r + 1, \quad d(u(i, i+r-1), w(l+i-1, l+i+r-2)) \le k$.

A string u satisfying the above property is a k_r-occurrence of w. A string u that k_r-occurs as a suffix of w is a k_r-suffix of w.

We suppose that the text is non-empty, $r \ge 2$ and $0 \le k \le r$, otherwise the above definition would have no meaning. We denote by $L(w, k, r)$ (resp. *Suff*(w, k, r)) the set of words (resp. suffixes) u that k_r-occur in w at position l, for some l, $1 \le l \le |w| - |u| + 1$. Notice that $L(w, k, r)$ is a *factorial language*, i.e. if $u \in L(w, k, r)$ then each factor (or substring) of u belongs to $L(w, k, r)$. Moreover, we denote by *Suff*(w, k) the set of k_r-suffixes of w for $r = |w|$.

Remark 2. The condition $r = |w|$ is equivalent to say that there is not a window in which it is possible to allow errors. Indeed, when the size r of the window is equal to the size of the text w, then the problem of finding all k_r-occurrences of a string u in the text is equivalent to the k-mismatch problem, that consists in finding all occurrences of the string u in w with at most k errors (cf. [15]).

Example 3. Let $w = abaa$ be a string on the alphabet $\Sigma = \{a, b\}$. The set of words that k_r-occur in w, when $k = 1$ and $r = 2$, is $L(w, 1, 2) = \{a, b, aa, ab, ba, bb, aaa, aab, aba, abb, baa, bab, bba, bbb, aaaa, aaab, abaa, abab, abba, bbaa, bbab, bbba\}$.

Notice that words $aab, aaab, bbab, bbba$ occur with one error every $r = 2$ symbols, but with two errors in the whole word. Hence, they belong to $L(w, 1, 2)$, but not to $L(w, 1, 4)$. Moreover, *Suff*$(w, 1, 2) = \{a, b, aa, ab, ba, aaa, aab, baa, bab, bba, aaaa, aaab, abaa, abab, abba, bbaa, bbab, bbba\}$ and *Suff*$(w, 1) = \{a, b, aa, ab, ba, aaa, baa, bab, bba, aaaa, abaa, abab, abba, bbaa\}$.

Now we can recall the definition of the *repetition index*, denoted by $R(w, k, r)$, that plays an important role in the construction of an automaton recognizing the language $L(w, k, r)$ (cf. [10]).

Definition 4. *The* repetition index *of a string w, denoted by $R(w, k, r)$, is the smallest integer h such that all strings of this length k_r-occur at most once in the text w.*

The parameter $R(w, k, r)$ is well defined because the integer $h = |w|$ satisfies the condition. Moreover, it is easy to prove that if $\frac{k}{r} \geq \frac{1}{2}$ then $R(w, k, r) = |w|$ (cf. [8]). In [8] it is proved that $R(w, k, r)$ is a non-increasing function of r and a non-decreasing function of k and that the equation $r = R(w, k, r)$ admits an unique solution. Moreover, it is proved that, under some hypothesis, $R(w, k, r)$ has a logarithmic upper bound in the size of the text w almost surely.

Remark 5. In [10] authors gave an algorithm for building a deterministic finite automaton (DFA) recognizing the language $L(w, k, r)$ of all words that k_r-occur in the string w. They proved that the size of such automaton $\mathcal{A}(w, k, r)$ is bounded by a function that depends on the length $|w|$ of the text w, the repetition index $R(w, k, r)$ and the number k of errors allowed in a window of size $r = R(w, k, r)$, that is $|\mathcal{A}(w, k, r)| = O(|w| \cdot (R(w, k, r))^{k+1})$. In the worst case, when both $R(w, k, r)$ and k are proportional to $|w|$, the size of the automaton $\mathcal{A}(w, k, r)$ is exponential. But, under the hypothesis that w is a sequence generated by a memoryless source with identical symbol probabilities and the number k of errors is fixed for any window of size $r = R(w, k, r)$, the size of this automaton is $O(|w| \cdot \log^{k+1}(|w|))$ almost surely.

Starting from the automaton $\mathcal{A}(w, k, r)$, an automaton recognizing the language $Suff(w, k, r)$ can be simply deduced from a procedure that first builds the automaton $\mathcal{A}(w\$, k, r)$, extending the alphabet Σ by letter \$, then sets as terminal states only those states from which an edge by letter \$ outgoes, and finally removes all edges labeled \$ and the state they reach [13]. In this paper we focus on the minimal automaton recognizing $Suff(w, k)$. It is therefore natural to study the Nerode's congruence corresponding to it.

3   On the Nerode's Congruence

In this section, we introduce a right-invariant congruence relation on Σ^* used to define the suffix automaton of a word up to mismatches and we prove some properties of it. In particular we give a characterization of the Nerode's congruence relative to S_k. This result generalizes a classical result described in [1] (see also [13,14]), where it was used in an efficient construction of the suffix automaton with no mismatches, that is also called DAWG (directed acyclic word graph), up to the set of final states. We think that it is possible to define such an algorithm even when dealing with mismatches. It would be probably more complex than the classical one. In what follows, we do not consider the window,

i. e. we set $r = |w|$. Let us start by introducing the following definition, that is a generalization of the one given in [1].

Definition 6. *Let $w = a_1 \cdots a_n$ be a word in Σ^*. For any nonempty word $y \in \Sigma^*$, the end-set of y in w up to k mismatches, denoted by end-set$_w(y, k)$, is the set of all final positions in which y k-occurs in w, i.e. end-set$_w(y, k) = \{i \mid y$ k-occurs in w with final position $i\}$. Notice that end-set$_w(\varepsilon, k) = \{0, 1, \ldots, n\}$.*

By using Definition 6 we can define a equivalence relation between words on Σ^*.

Definition 7. *Two words x and y in Σ^* are end$_k$-equivalent, or $\equiv_{w,k}$, on w if the following two conditions hold.*

1. *end-set$_w(x, k) = $ end-set$_w(y, k)$;*
2. *for any position $i \in$ end-set$_w(x, k) = $ end-set$_w(y, k)$, the number of errors available in the suffix of w having $i+1$ as first position is the same after the reading of x and of y, i.e. $\min\{|w|-i, k-err_i(x)\} = \min\{|w|-i, k-err_i(y)\}$, where $err_i(u)$ is the number of mismatches of the word u that k_r-occurs in w with final position i.*

We denote by $[x]_{w,k}$ the equivalence class of x with respect to $\equiv_{w,k}$. The degenerate class is the equivalence class of words that are not k-occurrences of w (i.e., words with empty end-set in w up to k mismatches).

In other words, two words x and y in Σ^* are end$_k$-equivalent if, besides having the same end-set in w up to k mismatches as in the exact case [1], the number of errors available in the suffix of w after the reading of x and of y is the same. The definition includes two cases depending on the considered final position $i \in$ end-set$_w(x, k) = $ end-set$_w(y, k)$ of x and y in w:

2.a) if this position is sufficiently "far from" the end of the word, which means that $|w| - i \geq \max\{k - err_i(x), k - err_i(y)\}$, then the number of errors available after this position is the same in both cases, i.e. $k - err_i(x) = k - err_i(y)$, which implies that $err_i(x) = err_i(y)$. In this case
$$\min\{|w|-i, k-err_i(x)\} = k-err_i(x) = k-err_i(y) = \min\{|w|-i, k-err_i(y)\}.$$

2.b) otherwise, if this position is sufficiently "near" the end of the word, which means that $|w| - i \leq \min\{k - err_i(x), k - err_i(y)\}$, then it is possible to have mismatches in any position of the suffix of w having length $|w| - i$. This does not necessarily imply that $err_i(x) = err_i(y)$. Therefore
$$\min\{|w| - i, k - err_i(x)\} = |w| - i = \min\{|w| - i, k - err_i(y)\}.$$

Example 8. Let us consider the prefix of length 10 of the Fibonacci word, $w = abaababaab$, and let us suppose that the number k of errors allowed in any factor is 2.

- If we consider words $x = baba$ and $y = babb$, one has that they have the same end-set, that is end-set$_w(baba, 2) = \{5, 6, 8, 10\} = $ end-set$_w(babb, 2)$, but the two words are not end$_k$-equivalent because it is not true that for any position

$i \in$ end-set$_w(baba, 2) =$ end-set$_w(babb, 2)$, the number of errors available in the suffix of w having $i+1$ as first position is the same after the reading of x and of y. In fact, if we consider $i = 5$, $err_5(baba) = 2$ and $err_5(babb) = 1$ and then $\min\{|w| - 5, 2 - err_5(baba)\} = 0 \neq 1 = \min\{|w| - 5, 2 - err_5(babb)\}$.

- If we consider words $x = abaababa$ and $y = baababa$, one has that they are trivially end_k-equivalent because they have the same end-set, that is end-$set_w(abaababa, 2) = \{8\} = end$-$set_w(baababa, 2)$, and for $i = 8$ the number of errors available in the suffix of w having $i+1$ as first position is the same after the reading of x and of y. In fact, if we consider $i = 8$, $err_8(abaababa) = 0$ and $err_8(baababa) = 0$ and then $\min\{|w| - 8, 2 - err_8(abaababa)\} = 2 = \min\{|w| - 8, 2 - err_8(baababa)\}$.

- If we consider words $x = abaababaa$ and $y = baababab$, one has that they have the same end set, that is end-$set_w(abaababaa, 2) = \{9\} = end$-$set_w(baababab, 2)$, and for $i = 9$ the number of errors available in the suffix of w having $i + 1$ as first position is the same after the reading of x and of y, even if $err_9(abaababaa) = 0$ and $err_9(baababab) = 1$. In fact, one has that $\min\{|w| - 9, 2 - err_9(abaababaa)\} = 1 = \min\{|w| - 9, 2 - err_9(baababab)\}$, and then x and y are end_k-equivalent.

The following lemma and theorem summarize some properties of end_k- equivalence. Before stating them, we recall that an equivalence relation $\equiv$ on Σ^* is *right invariant* if, for any $x, y, z \in \Sigma^*$, $x \equiv y$ implies that $xz \equiv yz$.

Lemma 9. *(i)* $\equiv_{w,k}$ *is a right-invariant equivalence relation on Σ^*.*
(ii) If x and y are end_k-equivalent, then one is a suffix of the other up to $2k$ errors.
(iii) Words xy and y are end_k-equivalent if and only if for any $i \in$ end-set$_w(xy, k)$ $=$ end-set$_w(y, k)$, the k-occurrence of y with final position i is immediately preceded by a t-occurrence of x, where $t = \max\{(k - err_i(y)) - (|w| - i), 0)\}$.

Theorem 10. *Words x and y are end_k-equivalent if and only if they have the same future in w, i.e. for any $z \in \Sigma^*$, xz is a k-suffix of w if and only if yz is a k-suffix of w.*

In what follows we use the term *partial DFA* (with respect to the alphabet Σ) for a deterministic finite automaton in which each state has not necessarily a transition for every letter of Σ. The smallest partial DFA for a given language is the partial DFA that recognizes the language and has the smallest number of states. It is called the minimal DFA recognizing the language. Uniqueness follows from Nerode's Theorem [16] of the right invariant equivalence relation.

By using Nerode's theorem and by Theorem 10 we have the following result.

Corollary 11. *For any $w \in \Sigma^*$, the (partial) deterministic finite automaton having input alphabet Σ, state set $\{[x]_{w,k} \mid x$ is a k occurrence of $w\}$, initial state $[\varepsilon]_{w,k}$, accepting states those equivalence classes that include the k-suffixes of w (i.e., whose end-sets include the position $|w|$) and transitions $\{[x]_{w,k} \xrightarrow{a} [xa]_{w,k} \mid x$ and xa are k-occurrences of $w\}$, is the minimal deterministic finite automaton, denoted by $S_{w,k}$ (or simply by S_k if there are no risks of misunderstanding on w), which recognizes the set $Suff(w, k)$.*

Remark 12. We note that *Suff(w,k)=Suff(w,k,r)* with $r = |w|$ (which is equivalent to saying that there are at most k errors in the entire word without window) and that *Suff(w,k,r)* $\subseteq L(w, k, r)$.

4   Allowing More Mismatches

In this section we present the second main result of the paper. More precisely, we describe an algorithm that makes use of the automaton S_k in order to accept, in an efficient way, the language $Suff(w, k, r)$ of all suffixes of w up to k errors in every window of size $r = R(w, k, r)$. First of all we recall that if $r = R(w, k, r)$ then for any value $x \geq r$ one has that $r = R(w, k, x)$, i.e. the repetition index gets constant. And this is also valid when the parameter x is such that $x = |w|$, which implies that if $r = R(w, k, r)$ then $r = R(w, k, |w|) = R(w, k)$ (cf. [8,9,17]). These two extremal cases are the two cases we are considering. From now on we denote this value simply by r. This fact implies that any word u of length $|u| = r$ has the following property: if u k_r-*occurs* or k-*occurs in* w, then, in both cases, it occurs only once in the text $|w|$.

Before describing our algorithm, we give a preliminary result that is important both for the following and in itself.

Lemma 13. *Given the automaton* S_k, *there exists a linear time algorithm that returns the repetition index* r *such that* $r = R(w, k, r)$.

Remark 14. As a side effect of this algorithm, each state of the automaton S_k is equipped with an integer that represents a distance from this state to the end. For this purpose, it is sufficient to make a linear time visit of the automaton.

Now we can describe the algorithm that accepts the language $Suff(w, k, r)$. We can distinguish two cases.

  i) If a word u has length less than or equal to $r = R(w, k, r)$, then we check if the word u is accepted by the automaton S_k. If u is accepted by this automaton, then it is in the language $Suff(w, k, r)$, otherwise it does not belong to the language.
 ii) If a word u has a length greater than or equal to $r = R(w, k, r)$, then we consider its prefix u' of length $r = R(w, k, r)$. Let q be the state that is reached after reading u' and let i be the integer associated to this state (cf. Remark 14). We have that $|w| - i - r + 1$ is the unique possible initial position of u. Given a position, checking whether a word k_r-occurs at that position in the text w can be done in linear time.

5   Conclusions and Experimental Results

We have constructed the suffix automaton with mismatches of a great number of words and we have considered overall its structure when the input word is well-known, such as the prefixes of Fibonacci and Thue-Morse words, as well as words

of the form bba^n, $a, b \in \Sigma$, $n \geq 1$ and some random words. We have studied how
the number of states grows depending on the length of the input word. In the
case of the prefixes of length n of the Fibonacci word, our experimental results
have led us to the following sequence $\{a_n\}_n$, representing the number of states of
the suffix automaton with one mismatch: $\{a_n\}_n = 2$, 4, 6, 11, 15, 18, 23, 28, 33,
36, 39, 45, 50, 56, 61, 64, 67, 70, 73, 79, 84, 90, 96, 102, 107, 110, 113, 116, 119,
122, 125, 128, 134, 139, 145, 151, 157, 163, 169, 175, 180, 183, 186, 189, 192, 195,
198, 201, 204, 207, 210, 213, 216, 222, 227, 233, 239, 245, 251, 257, 263, 269, ...
This means that the sequence of differences between two consecutive terms is:
$\{a_{n+1} - a_n\}_n = 2$, 2, 5, 4, 3, 5, 5, 5, 3, 3, 6, 5, 6, 5, 3, 3, 3, 3,6, 5, 6, 6, 6, 5, 3, 3,
3, 3, 3, 3, 3, 6, 5, 6, 6, 6, 6, 6, 6, 5, 3, 3, 3, 3, 3, 3, 3, 3, 3, 3, 3, 6, 5, 6, 6, 6, 6, 6,
6, 6, 6, 6, 6, 6, 5, 3, 3, 3, 3, 3, 3, 3, ... We note that after an initial part, there
is one 6, one 5, $(fib_{i-1} - 2)$ consecutive 6s, one 5, $(fib_i - 1)$ consecutive 3s, etc,
where fib_i denotes the i-th Fibonacci number, $i = 4, 5, 6 \ldots$. This leads to the
following recursive formula: $a_{fib_n} = a_{fib_{n-1}} + 3(a_{fib_{n-3}} - 1) + 10 + 6(a_{fib_{n-4}} - 1)$.
From this recursion an explicit formula is easy to find. We did not prove the rule
that describes the growth of the suffix automaton with one mismatch, but we
checked that this rule holds true up to prefixes of length 2000 of the Fibonacci
word f.

Conjecture 15. The size of the suffix automaton with one mismatch of the pre-
fixes of the Fibonacci word grows according to the recursive formula $a_{fib_n} = a_{fib_{n-1}} + 3(a_{fib_{n-3}} - 1) + 10 + 6(a_{fib_{n-4}} - 1)$.

Given a word v, Gad Landau wondered if a data structure having a size "close"
to $|v|$ and that allows approximate pattern matching in time proportional to
the query plus the number of occurrences exists. In the non approximate case,
suffix trees and compact suffix automata do the job (cf. [18,14]). Let us see the
approximate case. In [8,17,10,19,12] it is proved that for a random text w, the
size of its compact suffix automaton with k mismatches is linear times a polylog
of the size of w, i.e. $O(|w| \cdot \log^k |w|)$. By using this data structure, the time
for finding the list $occ(x)$ of all occurrences of any word x in the text w up to
k mismatches is proportional to $|x| + |occ(x)|$. Therefore, for random texts the
open problem of Landau has a positive answer. For prefixes of Fibonacci word
our previous conjecture tells us that suffix automata do the same. In the case
of words of the form bba^n, $a, b \in \Sigma$, $n \geq 1$, our experimental results have led us
to the following formula describing the behaviour of the sequence of differences
between two consecutive terms involving words having n greater than or equal
to 4: $\{a_{n+1} - a_n\} = 19 + 6 * (n - 4)$. We have experimented also on prefixes
of Thue-Morse words and, even if we have not obtained a well-formed formula,
we have tested that the size of the compact suffix automata with 1 mismatch
obtained is less than or equal to $2 \cdot |w| \cdot \log(|w|)$. Moreover, the result is true
even in the case of periodic words. So, we can state the following conjecture.

Conjecture 16. The (compact) suffix automaton with k mismatches of any text
w has size $O(|w| \cdot \log^k(|w|))$.

The minimal deterministic finite automaton S_k can be useful for solving the problem of approximate indexing and some applications of it. Classically, an index (cf. [2]) over a fixed text w is an abstract data type based on the set $Fact(w)$. Such data type is equipped with some operations that allow it to answer to the following queries. 1) Given a word x, say whether it belongs to $Fact(w)$ or not. If not, an index can optionally give the longest prefix of x that belongs to $Fact(w)$. 2) Given $x \in Fact(w)$, find the first (respectively the last) occurrence of x in w. 3) Given $x \in Fact(w)$, find the number of occurrences of x in w. 4) Given $x \in Fact(w)$, find the list of all occurrences of x in w. In the case of exact string matching, there exist classical data structures for indexing such as suffix trees, suffix arrays, DAWGs, factor automata or their compacted versions (cf. [2]). The algorithms that use them run in a time usually independent from the size of the text or at least substantially smaller than it. The last property is required by some authors to be an essential part in the definition of an index (cf. [20]). All the operations defined for an index can easily be extended to the approximate case. But in the case of approximate string matching the problem is somehow different. We refer to [21,22,15,23] and to the references therein for a *panorama* on this subject and on approximate string matching in general. The minimal deterministic finite automaton S_k introduced in this paper can be useful for solving the problem of approximate indexing. More precisely, it is easy to answer queries 1) and 2), but the other questions are more complex and they can be solved by using techniques analogous to those in [10].

Moreover, if the Conjecture 16 is true and constants involved in O-notation are small, our data structure is useful for some classical applications of approximate indexing, such as recovering the original signals after their transmission over noisy channels, finding DNA subsequences after possible mutations, text searching where there are typing or spelling errors, retrieving musical passages, A.I. techniques in feature vector, and so on. It is important even in other applications, like in the field of Web search tools when we deal with *agglutinative languages*, i.e. languages that mainly resort to suffixes and declinations such as many Uralic languages (like Hungarian, Finnish, and Estonian), or in the case of real-time proposal of alternative internet URL in Domain Name Servers, or for deeper analysis of biological sequences.

Finally, we think that it is possible to connect the suffix automaton S_k of the language $Suff(w, k, |w|)$ (without window) to the suffix automaton $S_{k,r}$ of the language $Suff(w, k, r)$ with $r = R(w, k, r)$. More precisely, we conjecture that if S_k and $S_{k,r}$ are the suffix automata of the languages $Suff(w, k)$ (without window) and $Suff(w, k, r)$ with $r = R(w, k, r)$, respectively, then $|S_{k,r}| = O(|S_k|)$.

References

1. Blumer, A., Blumer, J., Haussler, D., Ehrenfeucht, A., Chen, M., Seiferas, J.: The smallest automaton recognizing the subwords of a text. Theoretical Computer Science 40, 31–55 (1985)
2. Crochemore, M., Hancart, C., Lecroq, T.: Algorithmique du texte. Vuibert, pages 347 (2001)

3. Carpi, A., de Luca, A.: Words and special factors. Theoretical Computer Science 259, 145–182 (2001)

4. Amir, A., Keselman, D., Landau, G.M., Lewenstein, M., Lewenstein, N., Rodeh, M.: Indexing and dictionary matching with one error. Journal of Algorithms 37, 309–325 (2000)

5. Buchsbaum, A.L., Goodrich, M.T., Westbrook, J.: Range searching over tree cross products. In: Paterson, M.S. (ed.) ESA 2000. LNCS, vol. 1879, pp. 120–131. Springer, Heidelberg (2000)

6. Chávez, E., Navarro, G.: A metric index for approximate string matching. In: Rajsbaum, S. (ed.) LATIN 2002. LNCS, vol. 2286, pp. 181–195. Springer, Heidelberg (2002)

7. Cole, R., Gottlieb, L., Lewenstein, M.: Dictionary matching and indexing with errors and don't cares. In: STOC 2004. Proceedings of Annual ACM Symposium on Theory of Computing, ACM Press, New York (2004)

8. Epifanio, C., Gabriele, A., Mignosi, F.: Languages with mismatches and an application to approximate indexing. In: De Felice, C., Restivo, A. (eds.) DLT 2005. LNCS, vol. 3572, pp. 224–235. Springer, Heidelberg (2005)

9. Epifanio, C., Gabriele, A., Mignosi, F., Restivo, A., Sciortino, M.: Languages with mismatches (Theoretical Computer Science) (to appear)

10. Gabriele, A., Mignosi, F., Restivo, A., Sciortino, M.: Indexing structure for approximate string matching. In: Petreschi, R., Persiano, G., Silvestri, R. (eds.) CIAC 2003. LNCS, vol. 2653, pp. 140–151. Springer, Heidelberg (2003)

11. Huynh, T.N.D., Hon, W.K., Lam, T.W., Sung, W.K.: Approximate string matching using compressed suffix arrays. In: Sahinalp, S.C., Muthukrishnan, S.M., Dogrusoz, U. (eds.) CPM 2004. LNCS, vol. 3109, pp. 434–444. Springer, Heidelberg (2004)

12. Maass, M.G., Nowak, J.: Text indexing with errors. In: Apostolico, A., Crochemore, M., Park, K. (eds.) CPM 2005. LNCS, vol. 3537, pp. 21–32. Springer, Heidelberg (2005)

13. Crochemore, M., Hancart, C.: Automata for Matching Patterns. In: Rozenberg, G., Salomaa, A. (eds.) Handbook of Formal Languages, Linear Modeling: Background and Application, vol. 2, pp. 399–462. Springer, Heidelberg

14. Inenaga, S., Hoshino, H., Shinohara, A., Takeda, M., Arikawa, S., Mauri, G., Pavesi, G.: On-line construction of compact directed acyclic word graphs. Discrete Applied Mathematics 146(2), 156–179 (2005)

15. Gusfield, D.: Algorithms on Strings, Trees, and Sequences. Cambridge University Press, Cambridge (1997)

16. Lothaire, M.: Combinatorics on Words. Encyclopedia of Mathematics, vol. 17. Cambridge University Press, Cambridge (1983)

17. Gabriele, A.: Combinatorics on words with mismatches, algorithms and data structures for approximate indexing with applications. PhD thesis, University of Palermo (2004)

18. Crochemore, M.: Reducing space for index implementation. Theoretical Computer Science 292, 185–197 (2003)

19. Maass, M.G., Nowak, J.: A new method for approximate indexing and dictionary lookup with one error. Information Processing Letters 96, 185–191 (2005)

20. Amir, A., Keselman, D., Landau, G.M., Lewenstein, M., Lewenstein, N., Rodeh, M.: Indexing and dictionary matching with one error. In: Dehne, F., Gupta, A., Sack, J.-R., Tamassia, R. (eds.) WADS 1999. LNCS, vol. 1663, pp. 181–192. Springer, Heidelberg (1999)

21. Baeza-Yates, R., Navarro, G., Sutinen, E., Tarhio, J.: Indexing methods for approximate string matching. IEEE Data Engineering Bulletin 24, 19–27 (2001) Special issue on Managing Text Natively and in DBMSs. Invited paper.
22. Galil, Z., Giancarlo, R.: Data structures and algorithms for approximate string matching. Journal of Complexity 24, 33–72 (1988)
23. Navarro, G.: A guided tour to approximate string matching. ACM Computing Surveys 33, 31–88 (2001)

Appendix

Proof of Lemma 9

Proof. (i) $\equiv_{w,k}$ is an equivalence relation. Indeed it is obviously reflexive, symmetric and transitive.

Moreover this relation is a right-invariant equivalence. For any $x, y \in \Sigma^*$, if $x \equiv_{w,k} y$, then $end\text{-}set_w(x, k) = end\text{-}set_w(y, k)$ and for any position $i \in end\text{-}set_w(x, k) = end\text{-}set_w(y, k)$, $\min\{|w| - i, k - err_i(x)\} = \min\{|w| - i, k - err_i(y)\}$. Since the number of errors available in the suffix of w having i as first position is the same after the reading of x and of y, then for any $z \in \Sigma^*$ xz is a k-occurrence of w if and only if yz is a k-occurrence of w. Hence, $end\text{-}set_w(xz, k) = end\text{-}set_w(yz, k)$ and for any position $j \in end\text{-}set_w(xz, k) = end\text{-}set_w(yz, k)$ the number of errors available in the suffix of w having j as first position is the same after the reading of xz and of yz.

(ii) By definition x and y are such that $end\text{-}set_w(x, k) = end\text{-}set_w(y, k)$. Therefore, for any $i \in end\text{-}set_w(x, k) = end\text{-}set_w(y, k)$, both x and y k-occur in w with final position i and $d(x, y) \leq d(x, w) + d(w, y) \leq 2k$. Hence x and y are one a $2k$-suffix of the other.

(iii) Let us suppose, by hypothesis, that $xy \equiv_{w,k} y$. Therefore, $end\text{-}set_w(xy, k) = end\text{-}set_w(y, k)$ and for any position $i \in end\text{-}set_w(xy, k) = end\text{-}set_w(y, k)$, $\min\{|w| - i, k - err_i(xy)\} = \min\{|w| - i, k - err_i(y)\}$. Since $err_i(y) \leq err_i(xy)$, then $k - err_i(xy) \leq k - err_i(y)$. For any $i \in end\text{-}set_w(xy, k) = end\text{-}set_w(y, k)$, we can distinguish the following cases.

1. Let $\min\{|w| - i, k - err_i(y)\} = k - err_i(y)$. Since $k - err_i(xy) \leq k - err_i(y) \leq |w| - i$, then $\min\{|w| - i, k - err_i(xy)\} = k - err_i(xy)$. Since $\min\{|w| - i, k - err_i(xy)\} = \min\{|w| - i, k - err_i(y)\}$, then $k - err_i(xy) = k - err_i(y)$ and all the $err_i(xy)$ errors are in y and x occurs exactly in w.

2. Let $\min\{|w| - i, k - err_i(y)\} = |w| - i$. Since $\min\{|w| - i, k - err_i(xy)\} = \min\{|w| - i, k - err_i(y)\}$, one has that the number of errors available in the suffix of w having $i + 1$ as first position is $\min\{|w| - i, k - err_i(xy)\} = |w| - i$. Therefore the maximal allowed number of errors in x is $k - [err_i(y) + (|w| - i)] \geq 0$.

Hence, for any $i \in end\text{-}set_w(xy, k) = end\text{-}set_w(y, k)$, the k-occurrence of y with final position i is immediately preceded by a t-occurrence of x, where $t = \max\{(k - err_i(y) - (|w| - i), 0)\}$.

Let us suppose, now, that for any $i \in end\text{-}set_w(xy, k) = end\text{-}set_w(y, k)$, the k-occurrence of y with final position i is immediately preceded by a t-occurrence of x, where $t = \max\{(k - err_i(y)) - (|w| - i), 0)\}$. By hypothesis, $end\text{-}set_w(xy, k) = end\text{-}set_w(y, k)$. Let us distinguish two cases.

1. Let us consider positions $i \in end\text{-}set_w(xy, k) = end\text{-}set_w(y, k)$ such that $t = 0$. In this case all the $err_i(xy)$ are in y and the number of errors available in the suffix of w having $i + 1$ as first position is the same after the reading of xy and of y.

2. Let us, now, consider positions $i \in end\text{-}set_w(xy, k) = end\text{-}set_w(y, k)$ such that $t = (k - err_i(y)) - (|w| - i)$. In this case $k - err_i(y) \geq |w| - i$ and then $\min\{|w| - i, k - err_i(y)\} = |w| - i$. By hypothesis, this k-occurrence of y is immediately preceded by an occurrence of x up to $t = (k - err_i(y)) - (|w| - i)$ errors. Therefore, $k - err_i(xy) \geq k - [k - (err_i(y) + |w| - i) + err_i(y)] = |w| - i$ and $\min\{|w| - i, k - err_i(xy)\} = |w| - i$. □

Proof of Theorem 10

Proof. By Lemma 9(i), if x and y are end_k-equivalent, then for any $z \in \Sigma^*$ xz and yz are end_k-equivalent and then xz is a k-suffix if and only if yz is a k-suffix.

Let us suppose, now, that for any $z \in \Sigma^*$, xz is a k-suffix if and only if yz is a k-suffix. Therefore $end\text{-}set_w(x, k) = end\text{-}set_w(y, k)$. Moreover, for any z such that xz and yz are suffixes of w, the ending position i of x and y is such that $|w| - i = |z|$. By hypothesis, we can have two cases depending on $|z|$.

- Let $z \in \Sigma^*$ be such that $|z| \leq \min\{k - err_i(x), k - err_i(y)\}$. For such z one has that $\min\{|w| - i, k - err_i(x)\} = |w| - i$ and $\min\{|w| - i, k - err_i(y)\} = |w| - i$ and the thesis is proved.
- Let $z \in \Sigma^*$ be such that $|z| \geq \max\{k - err_i(x), k - err_i(y)\}$. For such z one has that $\min\{|w| - i, k - err_i(x)\} = k - err_i(x)$ and $\min\{|w| - i, k - err_i(y)\} = k - err_i(y)$. By hypothesis, for any position $i \in end\text{-}set_w(x, k) = end\text{-}set_w(y, k)$, any word $z \in \Sigma^*$ having $i + 1$ as first position is such that xz is a k-suffix of w if and only if yz is a k-suffix of w and then $k - err_i(x) = k - err_i(v)$ and the thesis is proved. □

Proof of Corollary 11

Proof. Since the union of the equivalence classes that form the accepting states of $\mathcal{S}_k$ is exactly the set of all k-suffixes of w, by Nerode's Theorem one has that $\mathcal{S}_k$ recognizes the language of all k-suffixes of w, i.e. the set $Suff(w, k)$. The minimality follows by Lemma 9. □

Proof of Lemma 13

Proof. In this proof we consider w to be fixed. Let q_0 be the initial state of $\mathcal{S}_k$ and let δ be its transition function. By abuse of notation, we keep calling δ its extension to words.

If u k-occurs twice in w, then from state $\delta(q_0, u)$ there are two paths having different lengths to a final state. Therefore $r - 1$ will be the greatest length of all words that reach a state from which there are two paths having different lengths to a final state.

We firstly find all such states. Since the graph G underlying S_k is a DAG (its language is finite), the same happens to the inverse $\hat{G}$ of G that is the graph where all arcs are inverted. We can perform a visit of $\hat{G}$ by adding to each node a field distance d and a flag information that can be white, green or red. The flag white means that the node has not yet been met during the visit, the green one means that, up that moment during the visit, the node has been encountered at last once during the visit and that all paths in G to a final state have same length. The flag red means that there are at last two paths in G to a final state having different lengths. In order to simplify the algorithm we add an initial state to $\hat{G}$ that goes with one arc to each final state of S_k. This initial state is set to be green and having distance -1 while all other nodes are set to be white and distance equal to $+\infty$. If a node with white flag is reached starting from a green node, then its flag is set to green and its distance becomes the distance from the initial state, i.e. the distance of previous node plus one. If a node with green flag is reached starting from a green node and if its distance is equal to be the distance of previous node plus one, then the node is not enqueued again, while otherwise it is set to red. Red flags propagate. Details are left to the reader. Nodes with red flags are the ones we were looking for.

At this point we perform a visit on G starting from the initial state (using a topological order) in order to obtain the greatest length of all words that reach a state with a red flag. The repetition index r is the greatest of such values plus one.   □

On String Matching in Chunked Texts

Hannu Peltola and Jorma Tarhio*

Department of Computer Science and Engineering
Helsinki University of Technology
P.O. Box 5400, FI-02015 HUT, Finland
{hpeltola,tarhio}@cs.hut.fi

Abstract. We study exact string matching in special texts, which consist of consecutive fixed-length chunks where each position of a chunk has a character distribution of its own. This kind of setting can also be interpreted so that a chunk represents a character of a larger alphabet. If texts and patterns are of this kind, it may ruin the efficiency of common algorithms. We examine anomalies related to the Horspool and Sunday algorithms in this setting. In addition we present two new algorithms.

Keywords: string matching, experimental comparison, Horspool algorithm.

1 Introduction

String matching algorithms find all positions where a given pattern occurs in a longer string, which is called a text. There are many good practical solutions [8] to string matching. In most algorithms it is assumed that the characters are statistically independent of each other. If the text and the pattern contain similar regularities, well-known string matching algorithms may loose their efficiency. Thierry Lecroq [7] considered string matching in texts with strong regularities. His texts were dumps of memory structures: arrays of numbers. Thus the texts consist of consecutive fixed-length chunks where each position of a chunk has a character distribution of its own. In this paper we will call strings of this kind *chunked*. Though Lecroq's texts were chunked, he did not consider the effects caused by chunks. He was more interested in the effect of the alphabet size. In the following we will present refinements to his work. We use throughout the paper the following notations. We denote a text of length n as $T = t_1 t_2 \cdots t_n$ and a pattern of length m as $P = p_1 p_2 \cdots p_m$. The size of the alphabet is c.

We discovered anomalies in Lecroq's test results. Namely, with the two data sets he used, the Horspool algorithm [4] was considerably slower than Sunday's QS algorithm [10], although these algorithms should behave in a similar way. We analyzed the reasons in detail. We found out that this phenomenon is due to the characteristics of the test data. We were able to construct examples where the Horspool algorithm works in $\mathcal{O}(n/m)$ and QS in $\mathcal{O}(nm)$ and vice versa.

In addition, we introduce two new algorithms suitable for chunked texts and patterns.

---

* Work was supported by the Academy of Finland.

Jan Holub and Jan Žd'árek (Eds.): CIAA 2007, LNCS 4783, pp. 157–167, 2007.
© Springer-Verlag Berlin Heidelberg 2007

2 Lecroq's Experiments

Lecroq tested how well-known exact string matching algorithms behave on dumps of memory structures. He studied the effect of the alphabet size. Besides the traditional byte oriented approach, he considered alphabets where several consecutive bytes represent a character. So a chunk can regarded as one character of a larger alphabet. Lecroq's algorithms and data are available on the Web[1].

We shortly describe Lecroq's two data sets [7] which we use in our tests. *Shorts* or short integers consist of consecutive chunks of two bytes. *Doubles* or double precision numbers consist of consecutive chunks of eight bytes. Each chunk in Lecroq's data sets has been stored such that the high-order byte of the number is at the lowest address (i.e. bytes of the numbers are stored in the big-endian order) and the low-order byte at the highest address. The number of distinct values, counts of the most common values (max. frequency), and counts of zero for each byte is shown in short and double chunks in Table 1, where q denotes the probability that two randomly chosen bytes (in the given position or overall) are the same. In the shorts, the first byte follows a discrete uniform distribution. In the doubles, the proportion of zero bytes is considerable. The overall $1/q$ is moderate, but the different frequencies of zeros among positions of chunks makes searching harder. Lecroq's patterns were consecutive chunks extracted randomly from the texts.

Table 1. Statistics of the bytes of chunks

DOUBLES	1	2	3	4	5	6	7	8	Overall
symbols	5	215	256	256	256	4	1	1	256
max.frequency	100152	6371	863	1344	9667	124889	200000	200000	536705
zeros	3	4	798	1344	9667	124889	200000	200000	536705
$1/q$	2.00	48.07	255.71	254.40	113.98	2.29	1.00	1.00	8.11

SHORTS	1	2	Overall
symbols	256	44	256
max. frequency	1564	12500	14064
zeros	1559	12500	14059
$1/q$	248.25	32.00	86.01

Lecroq's conclusion was that the byte-oriented approach in searching was more efficient than the approach with extended alphabet (excluding the two shortest patterns of doubles). So we consider here only the byte-oriented approach. Lecroq used in his experiments the following algorithms: Boyer–Moore [3], Horspool [4], Sunday's Quick Search [10], and Tuned Boyer–Moore [5]. For them we use abbreviations BM, Hor, QS, and TBM, respectively. Pairwise matching in the Boyer–Moore algorithm works inherently in the reverse order, but the other implementations use C's library routine *memcmp* for matching. Quick Search

---

[1] http://www-igm.univ-mlv.fr/~lecroq/esmms.tar.gz

and Tuned Boyer–Moore use an additional *guard test* [5, pp. 1224–1225] before pairwise comparison (so called Raita's trick [9]). Only the Tuned Boyer–Moore algorithm uses a *ufast3* skip loop [5]. All the other implementations apply a simple skip loop searching for the last character of a pattern. After pairwise matching, it is tested whether the potential occurrence of the pattern is at a correct alignment (phase) and does not extend beyond the end of the text.

Lecroq's data sets are big-endian. If Lecroq's tests were repeated with data corresponding to the same numbers on a little-endian machine, the results would resemble those for texts of natural language. The length of the text is 400 000 bytes with shorts and 1 600 000 bytes with doubles.

3 Why QS Was Faster Than Hor?

Chunked texts and patterns may ruin the efficiency of common algorithms. Moreover, two algorithms may be inefficient in different cases. We illustrate this with the algorithms Hor and QS. These algorithms are closely related, and in practice their performances are similar on data which is not chunked.

In Lecroq's experiments QS used on average 37% less processor time than Hor on the doubles, but he did not give any explanation for this phenomenon. In our experiments this difference was only slightly smaller[2]: 33%. The inspection of shift lengths reveals that something odd has happened: the average shift is over 14 for QS and less than 8 for Hor. From the characteristics of these algorithms we know that if successive bytes do not (statistically) depend on each other, the expected length of shift for QS should be at most one longer than that for Hor.

A similar phenomenon was present in the case of the short integers. QS was considerably faster than Hor for long patterns. Again there is a difference in the average length of shift. We will show that the both differences are due to the characteristics of data.

In addition to Hor, the performance of TBM is poor on Lecroc's data. Because TBM follows closely the behavior pattern of Hor, we decided not to consider it in detail.

3.1 The Speed of QS and Hor Should Be Almost Equal

Theoretically, the speed of QS and Hor should be similar for long patterns in the case of random data. Let t_i be the text character aligned with the last character of the pattern. The main difference of the algorithms is that the shift is based on t_i in Hor and t_{i+1} in QS. If we assume that characters are independent of each other, the expected shift length [1] of Hor is

$$\frac{1-(1-q)^m}{q},$$

---

[2] This difference also depends on the processor: Lecroq used Hyundai SPARC HWS-S310. We used Sun Enterprise 450 and for verification AMD Athlon. The difference was only 13% on the AMD Athlon.

where q is as in section 2. Similarly, it is straightforward to show that the expected shift length of QS is

$$\frac{1 - (1 - q)^{m+1}}{q}$$

When the pattern becomes longer, the expected shift lengths of both algorithms approach $\frac{1}{q}$. This means that the performance of Hor should get closer and closer to the performance of QS, when patterns get longer. Note that pairwise comparisons of these algorithms are equally laborious.

If the characters are from the uniform discrete distribution of c different characters, the average shift approaches c in the case of long patterns. The improvement on expected lengths of shift should be quite clear while the pattern length m grows but still $m < c$ holds.

3.2   Anomaly of Shorts

The data of short integers is not uniformly distributed. The text and patterns consist of chunks of two bytes. The second byte has a skew distribution among 44 values. A hexadecimal dump of the beginning of the text is given in Table 2.

Table 2. The beginning of shorts

```
bf04 5be9 a100 2051 38c4 60a1 3e10 7599
f6a4 edf9 6640 fe81 fea4 71f1 cf90 1909
36c4 ba89 1000 8331 6504 f5c1 9d90 5af9
2f64 b199 ce40 1e61 1be4 dc11 d810 ab69
9084 c329 d100 4011 d344 14e1 af10 7a59
0a24 df39 4840 5841 3b24 9031 5290 37c9
4c44 f5c9 6400 d6f1 0384 3e01 f290 53b9
06e4 f6d9 5440 2c21 dc64 0e51 bf10 3e29
ea04 d269 4900 c7d1 75c4 f121 e810 6719
```

In order to explain the different behavior of QS and Hor, let us consider a simple example. Let $T = (\#a\#b)^{n/4}$ and $P = (\#a\#b)^{m/4}$ be the text and the pattern, where $\#$ represents any character, e.g. $T = xaybcadbsayb$, $P = cadbfaxb$. In this case, a typical shift of Hor is two or four, but the average shift of QS is longer for long patterns. However, for a pattern $P = (a\#b\#)^{m/4}$ aligned differently, a typical shift of QS will be two or four, whereas the average shift of Hor would be longer.

In order to verify that this is the cause of the difference in Lecroq's test results, we ran a test with two possible alignments of patterns. The pattern set of Alignment 1 is the original one (patterns start on even bytes). Another set of 100 patterns, which start on odd bytes, was randomly picked from the text. This set is denoted Alignment 2. The results are shown in Table 3. Hor is clearly faster than QS in the latter case.

Table 3. Running times per pattern in seconds for short integers

	Alignment 1		Alignment 2	
m	Hor	QS	Hor	QS
4	0.286	0.251	0.240	0.243
6	0.200	0.199	0.174	0.193
8	0.197	0.170	0.148	0.164
10	0.151	0.149	0.127	0.140
12	0.144	0.133	0.115	0.126
14	0.130	0.122	0.105	0.118
16	0.131	0.117	0.098	0.111
18	0.109	0.110	0.088	0.101
20	0.107	0.100	0.079	0.091
40	0.078	0.062	0.043	0.055
80	0.065	0.038	0.024	0.039
160	0.056	0.025	0.014	0.032
320	0.054	0.016	0.010	0.031
640	0.053	0.011	0.008	0.030
1280	0.058	0.011	0.010	0.032

The anomaly caused by Lecroq's data is not exceptional. When ASCII characters are represented in UTF-16 (16-bit Unicode Transformation Format) coding, a similar situation appears on little-endian machines: rightmost bytes are zeros.

3.3   Anomaly of Doubles

The double data is far from uniformly distributed. The text and patterns consist of chunks of eight bytes. In a chunk, the two last bytes are zeros and the value of the first byte is either 65 or 193 in practice. Because the last but one character of each pattern is also zero, the shift of Hor on zero is one. Because the frequency of 193 and 65 is high in the first byte, the shift of Hor on 65 or 193 is likely seven and the shift on the other alternatives is $7 + s$, where s is a multiple of eight. These characteristics lead Hor to a repetitive behavior in shifting where Hor has approximately two alignments of the pattern for each alignment of QS.

Moreover, the location of the double zero in the chunks of the pattern is critical. Table 4 shows the results with differently aligned patters. Note that Hor is clearly faster in five cases of eight.

The difference of QS and Hor can be even larger. Let us assume that at each alignment Hor checks the characters under the pattern in the order $p_m, p_1, p_2, ...,$ p_{m-1} and QS in the order $p_1, p_2, ..., p_m$ until a mismatch is found. Moreover QS reads an extra character p_{m+1} at each alignment for shifting. It is known that the worst case complexity of the both algorithms is $\mathcal{O}(nm)$, whereas the best case complexity is $\mathcal{O}(n/m)$. Let us consider two examples:

(1) $P = a^m, T = (a^{m-1}b)^{n/m}$
(2) $P = a^{m-4}ca^3, T = (ba^{m-2}cb)^{n/m}$.

Table 4. Running times per pattern in seconds in Sparc for different alignments of doubles (patterns of 320 bytes)

offset	Hor	QS
0	1.389	1.016
1	0.884	0.257
2	0.181	0.237
3	0.176	0.230
4	0.172	0.237
5	0.178	0.264
6	0.238	2.133
7	2.060	2.016

It is straight-forward to show that in the case (1) Hor works in $\mathcal{O}(n/m)$ and QS in $\mathcal{O}(nm)$, but in the case (2) QS works in $\mathcal{O}(n/m)$ and Hor in $\mathcal{O}(nm)$. These examples were tuned for forward checking in Hor and QS. It is not difficult to modify the examples for backward checking.

4   New Algorithms

Fork. For long patterns it is advantageous to base shifting of pattern on several characters (n-grams) in order to get longer shifts. There are several variations of Boyer–Moore and Horspool algorithms which use 2-grams [1,2,6,11]. 3-grams are not practical, if no transformation is used for reducing the space. According to our experiments consecutive characters yield the longest shift for 2-grams, when the distribution of all bytes is uniform. Lecroq's double data is an example where also 2-grams, which are not consecutive, produce good results. We developed a variation which applies 2-grams which are not consecutive. The left character of the 2-gram is under the last position of the pattern and the right character is at a fixed distance from it to the right in order to make shift longer. This test can be combined with a skip loop. In the case where the character under the end of the pattern yields a shift that does not reach the other character, that shift is the final shift. This algorithm shown as Algorithm 1 is called *Fork*. The parameter h is the offset of the right character of the 2-gram. The value $h = 1$ corresponds to a 2-gram of consecutive characters.

In a way, Fork is an extension the Zhu-Takaoka and Berry-Ravindran algorithms [11,2], which apply 2-grams of consecutive characters. The worst case complexity of Fork is clearly $\mathcal{O}(mn)$. The applying of 2-grams never decreases the average shift length, so the average case complexity is at most the same as for Hor.

Sync. If we know the format of the data beforehand, it is possible to speed up string matching by taking this into consideration. For example, let a text and a pattern consist of consecutive chunks of w bytes. Then the shifts are necessarily multiples of w, if non-aligned matches are not accepted. This was the case in Lecroq's experiments.

Algorithm 1. Fork$(h, P = p_1 p_2 \cdots p_m, T = t_1 t_2 \cdots t_n)$

Require: $m > h > 0$

   /* Preprocessing */

1: **for all** $c \in \Sigma$ **do** $tmpd[c] \leftarrow m$

2: **for** $i \leftarrow 1$ **to** $m - 1$ **do** $tmpd[p_i] \leftarrow m - i$

3: $shift \leftarrow tmpd[p_m]$; $tmpd[p_m] \leftarrow 0$

4: **for all** $c1 \in \Sigma$ **do**

5:      **if** $tmpd[c1] < h$ **then**

6:          **for all** $c2 \in \Sigma$ **do** $d[c1, c2] \leftarrow tmpd[c1]$

7:      **else**

8:          **for all** $c2 \in \Sigma$ **do** $d[c1, c2] \leftarrow m + h$

9:          **for** $i \leftarrow 1$ **to** h **do** $d[c1, p_i] \leftarrow m + h - i$

10: **for** $i \leftarrow 1$ **to** $m - h$ **do**

11:      **if** $tmpd[p_i] \geq h$ **then** $d[p_i, p_{i+h}] \leftarrow m - i$

   /* Searching */

12: $t_{n+1} \cdots t_{n+2*m} \leftarrow P + P$ /* Stopper */

13: $j \leftarrow m$

14: **while** $j \leq n$ **do**

15:      **repeat** $k \leftarrow d[t_j, t_{j+h}]$; $j \leftarrow j + k$ **until** $k = 0$

16:      **if** $j \leq n$ **then**

17:          **if** $t_{j-m+1} \cdots t_{j-1} = p_1 \cdots p_{m-1}$ **and** j is a multiple of w **then**

             Report match

18:          $j \leftarrow j + shift$

Moreover, the shift can be based on any byte of a chunk. So if the bytes of a chunk have different distributions, it is advantageous to base the shift on a byte position with a distribution as uniform as possible over all possible symbols.

Algorithm 2 called *Sync* uses this idea. Sync applies occurrence heuristics and is thus related to the Horspool algorithm [4]. Using the position of the least probable character in the pattern as a test position is also applied in the *Least Cost algorithm* [10], where the whole pairwise matching is made in the increasing order of probability of the characters. The worst case complexity of Sync is clearly $\mathcal{O}(mn)$, and average case complexity is at most the same as for Hor.

Let h be the offset of the examined byte from the end of the pattern. We assume that h is less than w. By making some changes, it would be possible to allow larger values for h, but this extension might be useful only in rare special cases. Actually the while loop starting from line 6 requires one test more: we need to check that we don't report matches beyond the end of the text.

5 Experiments

For performance comparison with Lecroq's implementations the new algorithms were implemented in a similar way in C. All the codes were compiled with gcc version 3.4.4. $Fork_i$ is our 2-gram algorithm, where the subscript i denotes the offset of the right character of the 2-gram. $Sync_i$ is our algorithm that moves

---

Algorithm 2. Sync$(h, P = p_1 p_2 \cdots p_m, T = t_1 t_2 \cdots t_n)$

Require: $w > h \geq 0$ /* Let w be the width of a chunk */
  /* Let h be the distance of the examined byte from the end */
  /* Preprocessing */
1: **for all** $c \in \Sigma$ **do** $d1[c] \leftarrow m$
2: **for** $i \leftarrow w - h$ **step** w **to** $m - h - 1$ **do** $d1[p_i] \leftarrow (m - h) - i$
  /* Searching */
3: $s \leftarrow p_{m-h}$
4: $t_{n+1}..t_{n+m} \leftarrow s^m$ /* Stopper for inner while */
5: $j \leftarrow m$
6: **while** $j \leq n$ **do**
7:     **while** $t_{j-h} \neq s$ **do** $j \leftarrow j + d1[t_{j-h}]$
8:     **if** $t_{j-m+1}..t_j = P$ **then** Report match
9:     $j \leftarrow j + d1[s]$

---

the pattern so that it always remains in the correct alignment with the text. In Sync$_i$ the subscript i denotes the offset of the test character from the end of pattern.

We ran extensive experiments on Lecroq's data of shorts and doubles. Each run includes the processing of 100 patterns extracted randomly from the corresponding text. The tests were run on Sun Enterprise 450 (4 UltraSPARC-II 400MHz processors, 2048 MB main memory with 4 MB Ecache). For verifying purposes the test runs were repeated on a PC with AMD Athlon[TM] Thunderbird 1000 MHz processor and 256 MB main memory (VIA© KT133 chipset) with gcc version 3.3.5. When the test runs were repeated, the variation was at most ± 0.002 seconds.

Table 5 shows the results of our experiments for doubles and Table 6 for shorts. For each algorithm, the mean timing of 50 runs is given and the best value is shown in boldface on each row. Mean timing of preprocessing of 1000 runs is given in parentheses. Each run includes the processing of 100 patterns extracted randomly from the text. The relative performance of algorithms remained quite similar compared to the test runs of Lecroq. The preprocessing times of Hor, QS, TBM, and Sync are small. For Hor, QS, and TBM it is always less than 1% of the corresponding search time. On the other hand BM, Fork, and Sync work so fast with long patterns that preprocessing time becomes relevant with this text. On double precision data with patterns longer than 320 bytes, the preprocessing time of Sync exceeds 1% and grows to nearly 30% (but is less than 0.003 sec.). With shorts the preprocessing time hardly exceeds 0.001 seconds. The preprocessing time of Fork is so large, that the algorithm is practical only with long texts. The preprocessing time of BM grows fastest, and is considerable with patterns longer than 1000 bytes.

On doubles Sync$_4$ outperforms all the other algorithms for all patterns lengths. Fork$_4$ is faster than Hor, QS, and TBM for all patterns lengths. Fork$_4$ is also faster than BM for patterns of at least 320 characters; on the AMD Athlon processor this happened a little earlier.

Table 5. Running times per pattern in seconds for doubles (preprocessing times are in parentheses). Text length is 1 600 000 bytes.

m	BM	Hor	QS	TBM	Fork$_4$	Sync$_4$
16	0.803 (.000)	1.755 (.000)	1.131 (.000)	1.742 (.000)	0.935 (.037)	**0.382** (.000)
24	0.384 (.001)	1.572 (.000)	1.100 (.000)	1.631 (.000)	0.770 (.038)	**0.269** (.000)
32	0.317 (.001)	1.499 (.000)	1.056 (.000)	1.586 (.000)	0.631 (.038)	**0.204** (.000)
40	0.300 (.001)	1.658 (.000)	1.089 (.000)	1.668 (.000)	0.459 (.038)	**0.168** (.000)
48	0.283 (.001)	1.566 (.000)	1.038 (.000)	1.565 (.000)	0.399 (.038)	**0.139** (.000)
56	0.242 (.001)	1.468 (.000)	1.016 (.000)	1.506 (.000)	0.420 (.038)	**0.119** (.000)
64	0.241 (.001)	1.517 (.000)	1.041 (.000)	1.558 (.000)	0.303 (.038)	**0.103** (.000)
72	0.222 (.001)	1.541 (.000)	1.041 (.000)	1.601 (.000)	0.277 (.038)	**0.092** (.000)
80	0.200 (.001)	1.677 (.000)	1.106 (.000)	1.733 (.000)	0.305 (.038)	**0.085** (.000)
160	0.135 (.002)	1.612 (.000)	1.091 (.000)	1.619 (.000)	0.143 (.039)	**0.044** (.000)
320	0.116 (.004)	1.563 (.001)	1.065 (.001)	1.588 (.001)	0.081 (.040)	**0.024** (.000)
640	0.097 (.007)	1.721 (.001)	1.120 (.001)	1.733 (.001)	0.049 (.041)	**0.015** (.000)
1280	0.089 (.015)	1.577 (.002)	1.042 (.003)	1.604 (.002)	0.039 (.048)	**0.011** (.001)
2560	0.094 (.029)	1.633 (.004)	1.120 (.004)	1.686 (.004)	0.032 (.052)	**0.010** (.001)
5120	0.095 (.058)	1.576 (.008)	1.073 (.009)	1.640 (.008)	0.034 (.065)	**0.012** (.003)

On short integers Fork is not competitive. It is obvious that Fork reaches its best performance on data where examined position are enough statistically independent of each other and when $1/q$ is small. TBM is the fastest for short patterns. Sync$_3$ is the fastest for patterns longer than 13 characters. This takeover point depends on the computing platform. On the AMD Athlon processor the takeover point was around 20.

We used a preselected parameter value for Fork and Sync in our tests. One may argue that this is not fair. However, these algorithms were designed for chunked data. If we do not know the structure of the data beforehand, it is not sensible to apply these algorithms. If we know the format, the suitable parameter values can be inferred from the format or they can be achieved by light testing.

Fork is greedy in the sense that if the leftmost test character gives so short shift that we do not reach the rightmost character, then that other character cannot be utilized in computing the shift. On the other hand larger values of h may also produce longer shifts. So the speed of Fork depends on the data more than with the other algorithms and may sometimes be unstable. The behavior of Fork is demonstrated in Table 7. With the offset h longer than 4, at least one of the tested characters hits often a position with a fixed value. With shorter offsets, the performance of Fork is better. On short patterns Fork$_4$ was the fastest while on the longest patterns Fork$_2$ was even slightly faster.

The effect of different values of parameter h to Sync is demonstrated in Table 8. There the double precision patterns that are 320 bytes long are used as the example data. In addition to the search times also average shift lengths, and average visit counts in inner loops are given. Table 8 shows how many times the

Table 6. Running times per pattern in seconds for short integers (preprocessing times are in parentheses). Text length is 400 000 bytes.

m	BM	Hor	QS	TBM	Fork$_3$	Sync$_3$
4	0.267 (.000)	0.290 (.000)	0.256 (.000)	**0.243** (.000)	0.318 (.038)	0.424 (.000)
6	0.190 (.000)	0.200 (.000)	0.201 (.000)	**0.173** (.000)	0.259 (.038)	0.238 (.000)
8	0.177 (.000)	0.195 (.000)	0.171 (.000)	**0.153** (.000)	0.220 (.038)	0.172 (.000)
10	0.144 (.000)	0.154 (.000)	0.151 (.000)	**0.133** (.000)	0.191 (.038)	0.146 (.000)
12	0.133 (.000)	0.145 (.000)	0.134 (.000)	**0.123** (.000)	0.174 (.038)	0.126 (.000)
14	0.120 (.000)	0.131 (.000)	0.121 (.000)	0.114 (.000)	0.162 (.038)	**0.113** (.000)
16	0.115 (.000)	0.133 (.000)	0.118 (.000)	0.117 (.000)	0.156 (.039)	**0.108** (.000)
18	0.101 (.000)	0.108 (.000)	0.109 (.000)	0.096 (.000)	0.136 (.038)	**0.095** (.000)
20	0.098 (.000)	0.107 (.000)	0.102 (.000)	0.090 (.000)	0.123 (.038)	**0.085** (.000)
40	0.054 (.001)	0.080 (.000)	0.062 (.000)	0.065 (.000)	0.072 (.038)	**0.042** (.000)
80	0.031 (.001)	0.064 (.000)	0.038 (.000)	0.051 (.000)	0.045 (.038)	**0.022** (.000)
160	0.022 (.002)	0.056 (.000)	0.025 (.000)	0.041 (.000)	0.032 (.039)	**0.013** (.000)
320	0.018 (.003)	0.057 (.001)	0.016 (.001)	0.038 (.001)	0.023 (.039)	**0.008** (.000)
640	0.020 (.006)	0.054 (.001)	0.013 (.001)	0.038 (.001)	0.027 (.041)	**0.007** (.001)
1280	0.022 (.012)	0.059 (.002)	0.010 (.003)	0.041 (.002)	0.031 (.045)	**0.008** (.001)

Table 7. Comparison of parameter h in Fork with double patterns of 56 bytes

algorithm:	Fork$_1$	Fork$_2$	Fork$_3$	Fork$_4$	Fork$_5$	Fork$_6$	Fork$_7$	Fork$_8$
search time	0.424	0.385	0.488	0.347	1.200	2.031	2.005	1.517
aver. shift	36.12	34.53	29.74	40.75	14.15	8.05	8.16	10.92
$0 <$shift$< h$	–	0.0	31.18	302.94	610.20	265.82	221.46	37361.48
to slow loop	16019.0	18591.9	26488.1	11882.9	64886.0	99660.0	97476.9	71112.9

Table 8. Comparison of parameter h in Sync with double patterns of 320 bytes

algorithm:	Sync$_0$	Sync$_1$	Sync$_2$	Sync$_3$	Sync$_4$	Sync$_5$	Sync$_6$	Sync$_7$
search time	2.375	2.369	0.694	0.028	0.027	0.024	0.033	0.903
average shift	8.00	8.00	24.45	281.13	296.68	296.85	223.10	15.37
in skip loop	0.0	0.0	19954.5	5469.1	5369.1	5367.6	7011.2	52075.8
to slow loop	199961	199961	45479.2	222.5	24.0	22.9	160.8	51994.1

versions of Sync roll inside the skip loop on row 7, and how often they fall to the slow loop after it. The reported numbers are averages per pattern.

The average length of shift is only 7.62 for Hor in the case of Table 8. The search time of Hor according to Table 5 is 1.563. The comparison with Sync$_0$ and Sync$_1$ shows the importance of staying in the skip loop. Hor takes 103967.2 shifts inside the skip loop and falls outside (to the slow loop) 106009.4 times per pattern. The same effect can also be recognized for Sync$_3$ and Sync$_6$.

6   Final Remarks

We considered problems related to chunked data. We introduced two new string matching algorithms for chunked data and showed by experiments that these algorithms work well in practice.

If the text and the pattern are chunked in the same way, common algorithms may loose their efficiency. Lecroq's data contained two repetitive shapes which made Hor considerably slower than QS. We showed that slightly changing the search patterns QS became slower than Hor. The fatal thing is that the least random byte occurs in the test position of an algorithm [1, p. 268].

Everyone knows examples where both Hor and QS are slow, like $P = a^m$, $T = a^n$. However, starting from Lecroq's data we were able to construct two succinct examples where Hor works in $\mathcal{O}(n/m)$ and QS in $\mathcal{O}(nm)$ and vice versa. Though these examples seem to be simple, but they were not easy to discover.

Lecroq used the library routine *memcmp* of C for pairwise matching. On all processors we tested *memcmp* was considerably slower than explicit comparisons. To be able to repeat Lecroq's experiments we did not change the codes. And to make fair comparisons we used *memcmp* also in the implementations of our algorithms.

Pipelining in modern processors may conceal inherent inefficiency of an algorithm. For example when we ran the double test on the AMD Athlon without *memcmp*, Hor and QS were equally fast, though Hor made 63% more comparisons than QS.

References

1. Baeza-Yates, R.: Improved string searching. Software: Practice and Experience 19(3), 257–271 (1989)
2. Berry, T., Ravindran, S.: A fast string matching algorithm and experimental results. In: Proc. of the Prague Stringology Club Workshop 1999, Czech Technical University, Prague, Czech Republic, Collaborative Report DC-99-05, pp. 16–28 (1999)
3. Boyer, R.S., Moore, J.S.: A fast string searching algorithm. Communications of the ACM 20(10), 762–772 (1977)
4. Horspool, R.N.: Practical fast searching in strings. Software: Practice and Experience 10(6), 501–506 (1980)
5. Hume, A., Sunday, D.: Fast string searching. Software: Practice and Experience 21(11), 1221–1248 (1991)
6. Kim, J.Y., Shawe-Taylor, J.: Fast string matching using an n-gram algorithm. Software: Practice and Experience 24(1), 79–88 (1994)
7. Lecroq, T.: Experiments on string matching in memory structures. Software: Practice and Experience 28(5), 561–568 (1998)
8. Navarro, G., Raffinot, M.: Flexible pattern matching in strings. Cambridge University Press, Cambridge (2002)
9. Raita, T.: Tuning the Boyer–Moore–Horspool string searching algorithm. Software: Practice and Experience 22(10), 879–884 (1992)
10. Sunday, D.M.: A very fast substring search algorithm. Communications of the ACM 33(8), 132–142 (1990)
11. Zhu, R.F., Takaoka, T.: On improving the average case of the Boyer–Moore string matching algorithm. Journal of Information Processing 10(3), 173–177 (1987)

Factor Automata of Automata and Applications

Mehryar Mohri[1,2], Pedro Moreno[2], and Eugene Weinstein[1,2]

[1] Courant Institute of Mathematical Sciences
251 Mercer Street, New York, NY 10012
[2] Google Research
76 Ninth Avenue, New York, NY 10011
mohri@cs.nyu.edu, pedro@google.com, eugenew@cs.nyu.edu

Abstract. An efficient data structure for representing the full index of a set of strings is the *factor automaton*, the minimal deterministic automaton representing the set of all factors or substrings of these strings. This paper presents a novel analysis of the size of the *factor automaton of an automaton*, that is the minimal deterministic automaton accepting the set of factors of a finite set of strings, itself represented by a finite automaton. It shows that the factor automaton of a set of strings U has at most $2|Q| - 2$ states, where Q is the number of nodes of a prefix-tree representing the strings in U, a bound that significantly improves over $2\|U\| - 1$, the bound given by Blumer et al. (1987), where $\|U\|$ is the sum of the lengths of all strings in U. It also gives novel and general bounds for the size of the factor automaton of an automaton as a function of the size of the original automaton and the maximal length of a suffix shared by the strings it accepts. Our analysis suggests that the use of factor automata of automata can be practical for large-scale applications, a fact that is further supported by the results of our experiments applying factor automata to a music identification task with more than 15,000 songs.

Keywords: text indexing, inverted files, information retrieval, finite automata, suffix trees, suffix automata, factor automata, music identification.

1   Introduction

Pattern matching in strings is a fundamental problem in computer science and has been extensively studied in the past [1,2]. With the renewed interest in search within the massive amounts of natural language texts, biological sequences, and other widely accessible digitized sequences, this problem has gained further attention and significance.

This paper considers the problem of constructing a full index, or inverted file, for a large set of strings represented by a finite automaton. This problem arises in a number of different contexts, such as those where the set of strings is directly given as an automaton produced by an information extraction or speech recognition system, or when the set of strings is compactly stored as an automaton to reduce storage and increase the efficiency of their use [3,4].

Jan Holub and Jan Žd'árek (Eds.): CIAA 2007, LNCS 4783, pp. 168–179, 2007.
© Springer-Verlag Berlin Heidelberg 2007

An efficient and compact data structure for representing a full index of a set of strings is a *factor automaton*, that is a minimal deterministic automaton representing the set of all factors of a set of strings. Since it is deterministic, the factor automaton can be used to determine if a string x is a factor in time linear in its length $O(|x|)$, which is optimal.

The construction and the size of a factor automaton have been specifically analyzed in the case of a single string [5,6]. These authors demonstrated the remarkable result that the size of the factor automaton of a string x is linear, and that, more precisely, for strings x of length more than three, it has at most $2|x| - 2$ states and $3|x| - 4$ transitions. They also gave on-line linear-time algorithms for constructing a factor automaton from x. Similar results were given for the suffix automata, the minimal deterministic automata accepting exactly the set of suffixes of a string.

The construction and the size of the factor automata has also been previously studied in the case of a finite set of strings $U = \{x_1, \ldots, x_m\}$ [7]. These authors showed that an automaton accepting all factors of U can be constructed that has at most $2\|U\| - 1$ states and $3\|U\| - 3$ transitions, where $\|U\|$ is the sum of the lengths of all strings in U, that is $\|U\| = \sum_{i=1}^{m} |x_i|$.

This paper proves a significantly better bound on the size of the suffix automaton or factor automaton of a set of strings. It shows that the factor automaton of a set of strings U has at most $2|Q| - 2$ states, where Q is the number of nodes of a prefix-tree representation of the strings in U. The number of nodes $|Q|$ can be dramatically smaller than $\|U\|$, the sum of the lengths of all strings. Thus, our space bound clearly improves on previous work [7]. Also, although we are not demonstrating this here, our analysis leads to an algorithm for constructing the factor automaton of U in time $O(|Q|)$. More generally, we give novel bounds for the size of the factor automaton of an acyclic finite automaton as as a function of the size of the original automaton and the maximal length of a suffix shared by the strings accepted by the original automaton.

The original motivation for this work was the design of a large-scale music identification system [4], where we represented the songs found in the database by a compact finite automaton, as we shall briefly describe later in this paper. To facilitate an efficient search of song snippets, we constructed the minimal deterministic factor automaton of the song automaton. Empirically, the size of the factor automaton was not prohibitive. But, to ensure the scalability of our approach to a larger set of songs, e.g., several million songs, we wished to derive a bound on the size of the factor automata of automata. One characteristic of the strings considered in this application as in many others is that the original strings do not share long suffixes. This motivated our analysis of the size of the factor automata with respect to the length of the common suffixes in the original automaton.

The remainder of the paper is organized as follows. Section 2 introduces the string and automata definitions and terminology used throughout the paper. In Section 3, we describe a novel analysis of factor automata and present new bounds on the size of the factor automaton and suffix automaton of an automaton.

Section 4 briefly describes the use of factor automata in music identification and reports several empirical results related to their size.

2   Factors of a Finite Automaton

This section reviews some key properties of factors of a fixed finite automaton, generalizing similar observations made for strings by Blumer et al. (1985).

We denote by Σ a finite alphabet. The length of a string $x \in \Sigma^*$ over that alphabet is denoted by $|x|$. A *factor*, or *substring*, of a string $x \in \Sigma^*$ is a sequence of symbols appearing consecutively in x. Thus, y is a factor of x iff there exist $u, v \in \Sigma^*$ such that $x = uyv$. A *suffix* of a string $x \in \Sigma^*$ is a factor that appears at the end of x. Put otherwise, y is a suffix of x iff there exists $u \in \Sigma^*$ such that $x = uy$. Analogously, y is a *prefix* of x iff there exists $u \in \Sigma^*$ such that $x = yu$. More generally, a factor, suffix, or prefix of a set of strings X or an automaton A, is a factor, suffix, or prefix of a string in X or a string accepted by A, respectively.

In some applications such as music identification the strings considered may be long, e.g., sequences of music sounds, but with relatively short common suffixes. This motivates the following definition.

Definition 1. *Let k be a non-negative integer. We will say that a finite automaton A is* k-suffix unique *if no two strings accepted by A share a suffix of length k. A is said to be* suffix-unique *when it is k-suffix unique with $k = 1$.*

We denote by $F(A)$ the minimal deterministic automaton accepting the set of factors of a finite automaton A, that is the set of factors of the strings accepted by A. Similarly, we denote by $S(A)$ the minimal deterministic automaton accepting the set of suffixes of an automaton A.

The following generalizes to automata some definitions and results given by Blumer et al. (1985) for a single string.

Definition 2. *Let A be a finite automaton. For any string $x \in \Sigma^*$, we define* end-set(x) *as the set of states of A reached by the paths in A labeled with x. We say that two strings x and y in Σ^* are equivalent and denote this by $x \equiv y$, when* end-set$(x) =$ end-set(y). *This defines a right-invariant equivalence relation on Σ^*. We denote by $[x]$ the equivalence class of $x \in \Sigma^*$.*

Lemma 3. *Assume that A is suffix-unique. Then, a non-suffix factor x of the automaton A is the longest member of $[x]$ iff it is either a prefix of A, or both ax and bx are factors of A for distinct $a, b \in \Sigma$.*

Proof. Let x be a non-suffix factor of A. Clearly, if x is not a prefix, then there must be distinct a and b such that ax and bx are factors of A, otherwise $[x]$ would admit a longer member. Conversely, assume that ax and bx are both factors of A with $a \neq b$. Let y be the longest member of $[x]$. Let q be a state in end-set$(x) =$ end-set(y). Since x is not a suffix, q is not a final state, and there exists a non-empty string z labeling a path from q to a final state. Since

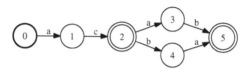

Fig. 1. Finite automaton A accepting the strings $ac, acab, acba$

A is suffix-unique, both xz and yz are suffixes of the same string. Since y is the longest member of $[x]$, x must be a suffix of y. Since ax and bx are both factors of A with $a \neq b$, we must have $y = x$. Finally, if x is a prefix, then clearly it is the longest member of $[x]$. □

Proposition 4. *Assume that A is suffix-unique. Let $S_A = (Q_A, I_A, F_A, E_A)$ be the deterministic automaton whose states are the equivalence classes $Q_A = \{[x] \neq \emptyset : x \in \Sigma^*\}$, its initial state $I_A = \{[\varepsilon]\}$, its final states $F_A = \{[x] : \text{end-set}(x) \cap F \neq \emptyset\}$ where F is the set of final states of A, and its transition set $E = \{([x], a, [xa]) : [x], [xa] \in Q_A\}$. Then, S_A is the minimal deterministic suffix of A: $S_A = S(A)$.*

Proof. By construction, S_A is deterministic and accepts exactly the set of suffixes of A. Let $[x]$ and $[y]$ be two equivalent states of S_A. Then, for all $z \in \Sigma^*$, $[xz] \in F_A$ iff $[yz] \in F_A$, that is z is a suffix of A iff yz is a suffix of A. Since A is suffix-unique, this implies that either x is a suffix of y or vice-versa, and thus that $[x] = [y]$. Thus, S_A is minimal. □

In much of what follows, we will be interested in the case where the automaton A is acyclic. We denote by $|A|_Q$ the number of states of A, by $|A|_E$ the number of transitions of A, and by $|A|$ the *size of A* defined as the sum of the number of states and transitions of A.

3 Space Bounds for Factor Automata

The objective of this section is to derive new bounds on the size of $S(A)$ and $F(A)$ in the case of interest for our applications where A is an acyclic automaton, typically deterministic and minimal, representing a set of strings.

When A represents a single string, there are standard algorithms for constructing $S(A)$ and $F(A)$ from A in linear time [5,6]. In the general case, $S(A)$ can be constructed from A as follows: add an ε-transition from the initial state of A to each state of A, then apply an ε-removal algorithm, followed by determinization and minimization to obtain $S(A)$. $F(A)$ can be obtained similarly by further making all states final before applying ε-removal, determinization, and minimization. It can also be obtained from $S(A)$ by making all states of $S(A)$ final and applying minimization. Figure 1 shows a simple automaton A accepting three strings and Figure 2 its suffix automaton $S(A)$.

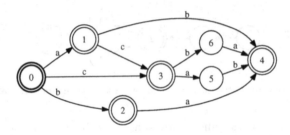

Fig. 2. Suffix automaton $S(A)$ of the automaton A of Figure 1

When A represents a single string x, the size of the automata $S(A)$ and $F(A)$ can be proved to be linear in $|x|$. More precisely, the following bounds hold for $|S(A)|$ and $|F(A)|$ [6,5]:

$$|S(A)|_Q \le 2|x| - 1 \quad |S(A)|_E \le 3|x| - 4$$
$$|F(A)|_Q \le 2|x| - 2 \quad |F(A)|_E \le 3|x| - 4. \tag{1}$$

These bounds are tight for strings of length more than three. [7] gave similar results for the case of a set of strings U by showing that the size of the factor automaton $F(U)$ representing this set is bounded as follows

$$|F(U)|_Q \le 2\|U\| - 1 \quad |F(U)|_E \le 3\|U\|_E - 3, \tag{2}$$

where $\|U\|$ denotes the sum of the lengths of all strings in U.

In general, the size of an acyclic automaton A representing a finite set of strings U can be substantially smaller than $\|U\|$. In fact, $|A|$ can be exponentially smaller than $\|U\|$. Thus, we are interested in bounding the size of $S(A)$ or $F(A)$ in terms of the size of A, rather than the sum of the lengths of all strings accepted by A.

For any state q of $S(A)$, we denote by $\mathrm{suff}(q)$ the set of strings labeling the paths from q to a final state. We also denote by $N(q)$ the set of states in A from which a non-empty string in $\mathrm{suff}(q)$ can be read to reach a final state.

Lemma 5. *Let A be a suffix-unique automaton and let q and q' be two states of $S(A)$ such that $N(q) \cap N(q') \ne \emptyset$, then*

$$\big(\mathrm{suff}(q) \subseteq \mathrm{suff}(q') \text{ and } N(q) \subseteq N(q')\big) \text{ or } \big(\mathrm{suff}(q') \subseteq \mathrm{suff}(q) \text{ and } N(q') \subseteq N(q)\big). \tag{3}$$

Proof. Since $S(A)$ is a minimal automaton, its states are accessible from the initial state. Let u be the label of a path from the initial I of $S(A)$ to q and similarly u' the label of a path from I to q'.

By assumption, there exists $p \in N(q) \cap N(q')$. Thus, there exist non-empty strings $v \in \mathrm{suff}(q)$ and $v' \in \mathrm{suff}(q')$ such that both v and v' label paths from p to a final state.

By definition of u and u', both uv and $u'v'$ are suffixes of A. Since A is suffix-unique and v is non-empty, there exists a unique string accepted by A and ending with v. There exists also a unique string accepted by A and ending with uv. Thus, these two strings must coincide.

Fig. 3. Illustration of the situation described in Lemma 5. uv and $u'v$ are suffixes of the same string x. Thus, u and u' are also suffixes of the same string. Thus, u is a suffix of u' or vice-versa.

This implies that any string accepted by A and admitting v as suffix also admits uv as suffix. In particular, the label of any path from an initial state to p must admit u as suffix. Reasoning in the same way for v' let us conclude that the label of any path from an initial state to p must also admit u' as suffix. Thus, u and u' are suffixes of the same string. Thus, u is a suffix of u' or vice-versa. Figure 3 illustrates this situation.

Assume without loss of generality that u is a suffix of u'. Then, for any string w, if $u'w$ is a suffix of A so is uw. Thus, $\mathrm{suff}(q') \subseteq \mathrm{suff}(q)$, which implies $N(q') \subseteq N(q)$. When u' is a suffix of u, we obtain similarly the other case of the statement of the lemma. $\qquad\square$

Note that Lemma 5 holds even when A is a non-deterministic automaton.

Lemma 6. *Let A be a suffix-unique deterministic automaton and let q and q' be two distinct states of $S(A)$ such that $N(q) = N(q')$, then either q is a final state and q' is not, or q' is a final state and q is not.*

Proof. Assume that $N(q) = N(q')$. By Lemma 5, this implies $\mathrm{suff}(q) = \mathrm{suff}(q')$. Thus, the same non-empty strings label the paths from q to a final state or the paths from q' to a final state. Since $S(A)$ is a minimal automaton, the distinct states q and q' are not equivalent. Thus, one must admit an empty path to a final state and not the other. $\qquad\square$

The following proposition extends the results of [5] which hold for a set of strings, to the case where A is an automaton.

Proposition 7. *Let A be a suffix-unique deterministic and minimal automaton accepting strings of length more than three. Then, the number of states of the suffix automaton of A is bounded as follows*

$$|S(A)|_Q \leq 2|A|_Q - 3. \tag{4}$$

Proof. If the strings accepted by A are all of the form a^n, $S(A)$ can be derived from A simply by making all its states final and the bound is trivially achieved. In the remaining of the proof, we can thus assume that not all strings accepted by A are of this form.

Let F be the unique final state of $S(A)$ with no outgoing transitions. Lemmas 5-6 help define a tree T associated to all states of $S(A)$ other than F by using the ordering:

$$N(q) \sqsubseteq N(q') \text{ iff } \begin{cases} N(q) \subset N(q') \text{ or} \\ N(q) = N(q') \text{ and } q' \text{ final}, q \text{ non-final}. \end{cases} \tag{5}$$

We will identify each node of T with its corresponding state in $S(A)$. By Proposition 4, each state q of $S(A)$ can also be identified with an equivalence class $[x]$. Let q be a state of $S(A)$ distinct from F, and let $[x]$ be its corresponding equivalence class. Observe that since A is suffix-unique, $end\text{-}set(x)$ coincides with $N(q)$.

We will show that the number of nodes of T is at most $2|A|_Q - 4$, which will yield the desired bound on the number of states of $S(A)$. To do so, we bound separately the number of non-branching and branching nodes of T.

Let q be a node of T and let $[x]$ be the corresponding equivalence class, with x its longest member. The children of q are the nodes corresponding to the equivalence classes $[ax]$ where $a \in \Sigma$ and ax is a factor of A.

By Lemma 3, if x is a non-suffix and non-prefix factor, then there exist factors ax and bx with $a \neq b$. Thus, q admits at least two children corresponding to $[ax]$ and $[bx]$ and is thus a branching node. Thus non-branching nodes can only be either nodes q where x is a prefix, or those where x is a suffix, that is when q is a final state of $S(A)$.

Since the strings accepted by A are not all of the form a^n for some $a \in \Sigma$, the empty prefix ε occurs at least in two distinct left contexts a and b with $a \neq b$. Thus, the prefix ε, which corresponds to the root of T, is necessarily branching. Also, let f be the unique final state of A with no outgoing transitions. The equivalence class of the longest factor ending in f, that is the longest string accepted by A corresponds to the state F in $S(A)$ which is not included in the tree T. Thus, there are at most $|A|_Q - 2$ non-branching prefixes.

There can be at most one non-branching node for each string accepted by A. Let N_{str} denote the number of strings accepted by A, then, the number of non-branching nodes N_{nb} of T is at most $N_{nb} \leq |A|_Q - 2 + N_{str}$.

To bound the number of branching nodes N_b of T, observe that since A is suffix-unique, each string accepted by A must end with a distinct symbol a_i, $i = 1, \ldots, N_{str}$. Each a_i represents a distinct left context for the empty factor ε, thus the root node $[\varepsilon]$ admits all $[a_i]$s, $i = 1, \ldots, N_{str}$, as children. Let T_{a_i} represent the sub-tree rooted at $[a_i]$ and let n_{a_i} represent the number of leaves of T_{a_i}. Let a_j, $j = N_{str} + 1, \ldots, N_{str} + k$ denote the other children of the root and let T_{a_j} denote each of the corresponding sub-tree. A tree with n_{a_i} leaves has less than n_{a_i} branching nodes. Thus, the number of branching nodes of T_{a_i} is at most $n_{a_i} - 1$. The total number of leaves of T is at most the number of disjoint subsets of Q excluding the initial state and f.

Note however that when the root node $[\varepsilon]$ admits only $[a_i]$s, $i = 1, \ldots, N_{str}$, as children, that is when $k = 0$, then there is at least one a_i, say a_1, that is also a prefix of A since any other symbol would have been the root node's child. The node a_1 will then have also a child since it corresponds to a suffix or final state of $S(A)$. Thus, a_1 cannot be a leaf in that case. Thus, there are at most as many as $\sum_{i=1}^{N_{str}+k} n_{a_i} \leq |A|_Q - 2 - 1_{k=0}$ leaves and the total number of branching nodes of T, including the root is at most $N_b \leq \sum_{i=1}^{N_{str}+k} (n_{a_i} - 1) + 1 \leq |A|_Q - 2 - 1_{k=0} - (N_{str} + k) + 1 \leq |A|_Q - 2 - N_{str}$. The total number of nodes of the tree T is thus at most $N_{nb} + N_b \leq 2|A|_Q - 4$. $\square$

In the specific case where A represents a single string x, the bound of Proposition 7 matches that of [6] or [5] since $|A|_Q = |x| + 1$. The bound of Proposition 7 is tight for strings of length more than three and thus is also tight for automata accepting strings of length more than three. Note that the automaton of Figure 1 is suffix-unique, deterministic, and minimal and has $|A|_Q = 6$ states. The number of states of the minimal suffix automaton of A is $|S(A)|_Q = 7 < 2|A|_Q - 3$.

Corollary 8. *Let A be a suffix-unique deterministic and minimal automaton accepting strings of length more than three. Then, the number of states of the factor automaton of A is bounded as follows*

$$|F(A)|_Q \leq 2|A|_Q - 3. \tag{6}$$

Proof. As mentioned earlier, a factor automaton $F(A)$ can be obtained from a suffix automaton $S(A)$ by making all states final and applying minimization. Thus, $|F(A)| \leq |S(A)|$. The result follows Proposition 7. □

Blumer et al. (1987) showed that an automaton accepting all factors of a set of strings U has at most $2\|U\| - 1$ states, where $\|U\|$ is the sum of the lengths of all strings in U. The following gives a significantly better bound on the size of the factor automaton of a set of strings U as a function of the number of nodes of a prefix-tree representing U, which is typically substantially smaller than $\|U\|$.

Corollary 9. *Let $U = \{x_1, \ldots, x_m\}$ be a set of strings of length more than three and let A be a prefix-tree representing U. Then, the number of states of the factor automaton $F(U)$ and that of the suffix tree $S(U)$ of the strings of U are bounded as follows*

$$|F(U)|_Q \leq 2|A|_Q - 2 \quad |S(U)|_Q \leq 2|A|_Q - 2. \tag{7}$$

Proof. Let B be a prefix-tree representing the set $U' = \{x_1\$_1, \ldots, x_m\$_m\}$, obtained by appending to each string of U a new symbol $\$_i$, $i = 1, \ldots, m$, to make their suffixes distinct and let B' be the automaton obtained by minimization of B. By construction, B has m more states than A, but since all final states of B are equivalent and merged after minimization, B' has at most one more state than A.

By construction, B' is a suffix-unique automaton and by Proposition 7, $|S(B')|_Q \leq 2|B'|_Q - 3$. Removing from $S(B')$ the transitions labeled with the extra symbols $\$_i$ and connecting the resulting automaton yields the minimal suffix automaton $S(U)$. In $S(B')$, there must be a final state reachable by the transitions labeled with $\$_i$ and only such transitions, which becomes non-accessible after removal of the extra symbols. Thus, $S(U)$ has at least one state less than $S(B')$, which gives:

$$|S(U)|_Q \leq |S(B')|_Q - 1 \leq 2|B'|_Q - 4 = 2|A|_Q - 2. \tag{8}$$

A similar bound holds for the factor automaton $F(U)$ following the argument given in the proof of Corollary 8. □

When A is k-suffix-unique with a relatively small k as in our applications of interest, the following proposition provides a convenient bound on the size of the suffix automaton.

Proposition 10. *Let A be a k-suffix-unique deterministic automaton accepting strings of length more than three and let n be the number of strings accepted by A. Then, the following bound holds for the number of states of the suffix automaton of A:*

$$|S(A)|_Q \le 2|A_k|_Q + 2kn - 3, \tag{9}$$

where A_k is the part of the automaton of A obtained by removing the states and transitions of all suffixes of length k.

Proof. Let A be a k-suffix-unique deterministic automaton accepting strings of length more than three and let the alphabet Σ be augmented with n temporary symbols $\$_1, \ldots, \$_n$. By marking each string accepted by A with a distinct symbol $\$_i$, we can turn A into a suffix-unique deterministic automaton A'.

To do that, we first unfold all k-length suffixes of A. In the worst case, all these (distinct) suffixes were sharing the same $(k-1)$-length suffix. Unfolding can thus increase the number of states of A by as many as $kn - n$ states in the worst case. Marking the end of each suffix with a distinct $\$$-sign further increases the size by n. The resulting automaton A' is deterministic and $|A'|_Q \le |A_k|_Q + kn$. By Proposition 7, the size of the suffix automaton of A' is bounded as follows: $|S(A')| \le 2|A'| - 3$. Since transitions labeled with a $\$$-sign can only appear at the end of successful paths in $S(A')$, we can remove these transitions and make their origin state final, and minimize the resulting automaton to derive a deterministic automaton A'' accepting the set of suffixes of A. The statement of the proposition follows the fact that $|A''| \le |S(A')|$.   □

Since the size of $F(A)$ is always less than or equal to that of $S(A)$, we obtain directly the following result.

Corollary 11. *Let A be a k-suffix-unique automaton accepting strings of length more than three. Then, the following bound holds for the factor automaton of A:*

$$|F(A)|_Q \le 2|A_k|_Q + 2kn - 3. \tag{10}$$

The bound given by the corollary is not tight for relatively small values of k in the sense that in practice, the size of the factor automaton does not depend on kn, the sum of the lengths of suffixes of length k, but rather on the number of states of A used for their representation, which for a minimal automaton can be substantially less. However, for large k, e.g., when all strings are of the same length and k is as long as the length of the strings accepted by A, our bound coincides with that of [7].

Similar results can be obtained for the number of transitions of the suffix automaton or factor automaton of a suffix-unique automaton ($|S(A)|_E \le 3|A|_E - 4$) and k-suffix-unique automaton ($|S(A)|_E \le 3|A_k|_E + 3kn - 3k - 1$), as in the string case.

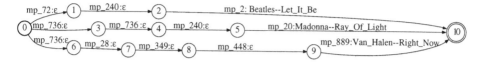

Fig. 4. Finite-state transducer T_0 mapping each song to its identifier

4   Factor Automata for Music Identification

We have verified the above insights into factor automata in the context of a music identification system [4]. Music identification is the task of matching an audio stream to a particular song. In our system, we learn an inventory of music phone units similar to phonemes in speech and a unique sequence of music phones characterizing each song. We view the music phone set as our alphabet and the music phone sequences as a set of strings, transforming the task into a factor recognition problem. Our approach is to construct a compact transducer mapping music phone sequences to corresponding song identifiers.

4.1   Factor Transducer Construction

Let Σ denote the set of music phones and let the set of music phone sequences describing m songs be $U = \{x_1, \ldots, x_m\}, x_i \in \Sigma^*$ for $i \in \{1, \ldots, m\}$. In our experiments, $m = 15{,}455$, $|\Sigma| = 1{,}024$ and the average length of a transcription x_i is more than 1,700. Thus, in the worst case, there can be as many as $15{,}455 \times 1{,}700^2 \approx 45 \times 10^9$ factors. The size of a naive prefix-tree-based representation would thus be prohibitive, and hence we endeavor to represent the set of factors with a much more compact factor automaton. We construct a deterministic and minimal automaton representing the sequences in U and subsequently a deterministic and minimal finite-state transducer mapping each song to its identifier using transducer determinization and minimization algorithms [8,9].

Let T_0 be the transducer mapping phone sequences to song identifiers before determinization and minimization. Figure 4 shows T_0 when U is reduced to three short songs. Let A be the acceptor obtained by omitting the output labels of T_0. The factor automaton $F(A)$ is constructed as described in Section 3: by creating ε-transitions from the initial state of A to all other states, making all states final, and applying epsilon-removal, determinization, and minimization. This leads to a compact automaton representing the factors of U (see Figure 5(a)), but it does not allow us to output the song identifier associated with each factor.

To accomplish this, we create a compact weighted acceptor over the tropical semiring accepting the factors of U that associates the total weight s_x to each factor x. A crucial advantage of this representation is the use of weighted determinization and minimization [8] during which the song identifier is treated as a weight that can be distributed along a path. The property that the sum of the weights along the path labeled with x is s_x is preserved by these operations. Let $F_w(A)$ be the automaton constructed analogously to $F(A)$, but where each ε-transition added is weighted with the song identifier corresponding to that

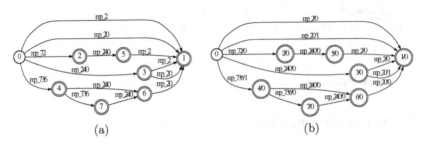

(a)   (b)

Fig. 5. (a) Deterministic and minimal unweighted factor acceptor $F(A)$ for two songs. (b) Deterministic and minimal weighted factor acceptor $F_w(A)$ for two songs.

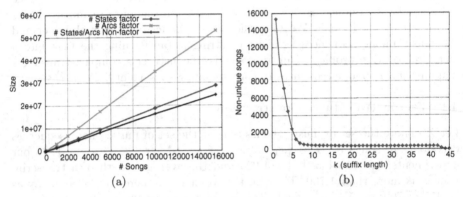

(a)   (b)

Fig. 6. (a) Comparison of automaton sizes for different numbers of songs. "#States/Arcs Non-factor" is the size of the automaton A accepting the entire song transcriptions. "# States factor" and "# Arcs factor" is the number of states and transitions in the weighted factor acceptor $F_w(A)$, respectively. (b) Number of strings in U for which the suffix of length k is also a suffix of another string in U.

transition. The weighted acceptor $F_w(A)$, obtained after determinization and minimization over the tropical semiring, is transformed into a song recognition transducer T by treating each output weight integer as a regular output symbol. Given a music phone sequence as input, the associated song identifier is obtained by summing the outputs yielded by T.

4.2   Automata Size

Figure 5(b) shows the weighted automaton $F_w(A)$ corresponding to the unweighted automaton $F(A)$ of Figure 5(a). Note that $F_w(A)$ is no larger than $F(A)$. Remarkably, even in the case of 15,455 songs, the total number of transitions of $F_w(A)$ was 53.0 M, only about 0.004% more than $F(A)$. We also have $|F(A)|_E \approx 2.1|A|_E$. As is illustrated in Figure 6(a), this multiplicative relationship is maintained as the song set size is varied between 1 and 15,455. Furthermore, for the case of 15,455 songs, U is 45-suffix-unique. Figure 6(b) demonstrates that the number of suffix "collisions" drops rapidly as the suffix size is increased. We also have

$|F_w(A)|_Q \approx 28.8\,\mathrm{M} \approx 1.2|A|_Q$, meaning the bound of Corollary 11 is verified in this empirical context.

5   Conclusion

We presented a novel analysis of the size of the factor automaton of an automaton in terms of the size of the original automaton and described the use of factor automata in a large-scale application. Our analysis shows that factor automata can be practical for a large number of strings. Our application to a large-scale music identification task further demonstrates this fact. Factor automata of automata are likely to form a useful and compact index for very large-scale tasks.

Acknowledgments

We thank Cyril Allauzen for several discussions about the material presented. The research of Mehryar Mohri and Eugene Weinstein was partially supported by the New York State Office of Science Technology and Academic Research (NYSTAR). This project was also sponsored in part by the Department of the Army Award Number W81XWH-04-1-0307. The U.S. Army Medical Research Acquisition Activity, 820 Chandler Street, Fort Detrick MD 21702-5014 is the awarding and administering acquisition office. The content of this material does not necessarily reflect the position or the policy of the Government and no official endorsement should be inferred.

References

1. Gusfield, D.: Algorithms on Strings, Trees, and Sequences. Cambridge University Press, Cambridge, UK (1997)
2. Crochemore, M., Rytter, W.: Jewels of Stringology. World Scientific, Singapore (2002)
3. Allauzen, C., Mohri, M., Saraclar, M.: General Indexation of Weighted Automata – Application to Spoken Utterance Retrieval. In: Proceedings of the Workshop on Interdisciplinary Approaches to Speech Indexing and Retrieval (HLT/NAACL 2004), Boston, Massachusetts, pp. 33–40 (2004)
4. Weinstein, E., Moreno, P.: Music Identification with Weighted Finite-State Transducers. In: Proceedings of ICASSP 2007, Honolulu, Hawaii (2007)
5. Blumer, A., Blumer, J., Haussler, D., Ehrenfeucht, A., Chen, M., Seiferas, J.: The smallest automaton recognizing the subwords of a text. Theoretical Computer Science 40, 31–55 (1985)
6. Crochemore, M.: Transducers and repetitions. Theoretical Computer Science 45, 63–86 (1986)
7. Blumer, A., Blumer, J., Ehrenfeucht, A., Haussler, D., McConnell, R.: Complete inverted files for efficient text retrieval and analysis. Journal of the ACM 34, 578–589 (1987)
8. Mohri, M.: Finite-state transducers in language and speech processing. Computational Linguistics 23, 269–311 (1997)
9. Mohri, M.: Statistical Natural Language Processing. In: Lothaire, M. (ed.) Applied Combinatorics on Words, Cambridge University Press, Cambridge (2005)

Subset Seed Automaton

Gregory Kucherov[1], Laurent Noé[1], and Mikhail Roytberg[2]

[1] LIFL/CNRS/INRIA, Bât. M3 Cité Scientifique, 59655, Villeneuve d'Ascq cedex,
France
{Gregory.Kucherov,Laurent.Noe}@lifl.fr
[2] Institute of Mathematical Problems in Biology, Pushchino, Moscow Region,
142290, Russia
mroytberg@mail.ru

Abstract. We study the pattern matching automaton introduced in [1] for the purpose of seed-based similarity search. We show that our definition provides a compact automaton, much smaller than the one obtained by applying the Aho-Corasick construction. We study properties of this automaton and present an efficient implementation of the automaton construction. We also present some experimental results and show that this automaton can be successfully applied to more general situations.

Keywords: spaced seed, subset seed, automaton, seed sensitivity.

1 Introduction

The technique of *spaced seeds* for similarity search in strings (sequences) was introduced about five years ago [2,3] and constituted an important algorithmic development [4,5]. Its main applications have been approximate string matching [2] and local alignment of DNA sequences [3,6,7] but the underlying idea applies also to other algorithmic problems on strings [8,9].

Since the invention of spaced seeds, different generalizations have been proposed, such as seeds with match errors [10,11], *daughter seeds* [12], *indel seeds* [13], or *vector seeds* [14]. In [1], we proposed the notion of *subset seeds* and demonstrated its advantages and its usefulness for DNA sequence alignment. In the formalism of subset seeds, an alignment is viewed as a text over some alphabet $\mathcal{A}$, and a seed as a pattern over a subset alphabet $\mathcal{B} \subseteq 2^{\mathcal{A}}$. The only requirements made is that $\mathcal{A}$ contains a special letter 1, $\mathcal{B}$ contains a letter $\# = \{1\}$, and every letter of $\mathcal{B}$ contains 1 in its set. The matching relation is naturally defined: a seed letter $b \in \mathcal{B}$ matches a letter $a \in \mathcal{A}$ iff a belongs to the set b.

For any seed-based similarity search method, including all above-mentioned types of seeds, an important issue is an accurate estimation of the sensitivity of a seed with respect to a given probabilistic model of alignments. For different probabilistic models, this problem has been studied in [15,16,17]. In [1] we proposed a general framework for this problem that allows one to compute the seed sensitivity for different definitions of seed and different alignment models. This approach is based on a finite automata representation of the set of target alignments and the set of alignments matched by a seed, as well as on a representation of the probabilistic model of alignments as a finite-state transducer.

Jan Holub and Jan Žd'árek (Eds.): CIAA 2007, LNCS 4783, pp. 180–191, 2007.

A key ingredient of the approach of [1] is a finite automaton that recognizes the set of alignments matched (or *hit*) by a given subset seed. We call this automaton a *subset seed automaton*. The size (number of states) of the subset seed automaton is crucial for the efficiency of the whole algorithm of [1]. Note that the algorithm of [16] is also based on an automaton construction, namely on the Aho-Corasick automaton implied by the well-known string matching algorithm.

Besides its application to the seeding technique for similarity search and string matching, constructing an efficient subset seed automaton is an interesting problem in its own, as it provides a solution to a variant of the *subset matching problem* studied in literature [18,19,20].

In this paper, we study properties of the subset seed automaton and present an efficient implementation of its construction. More specifically, we obtain the following results:

- we present a construction of subset seed automaton that has $\mathcal{O}(w2^{s-w})$ states, compared to $\mathcal{O}(w|\mathcal{A}|^{s-w})$ implied by the Aho-Corasick construction, where s and w are respectively the *span* and the *weight* of the seed defined in the next Section,
- we further motivate our construction by showing that for some seeds, our construction gives the minimal automaton,
- we prove that our automaton is *always* smaller than the one obtained by the Aho-Corasick construction; we provide experimental data that confirm that for $|\mathcal{A}| = 2$, our automaton is on average about 1.3 times bigger than the minimal one, while the Aho-Corasick automaton is about 2.5 times bigger. For $|\mathcal{A}| = 3$ the difference is much more substantial: while our automaton is still about 1.3 times bigger than the minimal one, the Aho-Corasick automaton turns out to be about 17 times bigger,
- we provide an efficient algorithm that implements the construction of the automaton such that each transition is computed in constant time,
- we show that our construction can be applied to the case of multiple seeds and to the general subset matching problem.

The presented automaton construction is implemented in full generality in HEDERA software package (http://bioinfo.lifl.fr/yass/hedera.php) and has been applied to the design of efficient seeds for the comparison of genomic sequences.

2 Subset Seed Matching

The goal of seeds is to specify short string patterns that, if shared by two strings, have best chances to belong to a larger similarity region common to the two strings. To formalize this, a similarity region is modeled by an alignment between two strings. Usually one considers *gapless alignments* that, in the simplest case, are viewed as sequences of matches and mismatches and are easily specified by binary strings $\{0,1\}^*$, where 1 is interpreted as "match" and 0 as "mismatch". A *spaced seed* is a string over binary alphabet $\{\#, \_\}$. The length of π is called its *span* and the number of # is called its *weight*. A spaced seed $\pi \in \{\#, \_\}^s$ *matches* (or *hits*) an alignment $A \in \{0, 1\}^*$ at a position p if for all $i \in [1..s]$, $\pi[i] = \#$ implies $A[p + i - 1] = 1$.

In [1], we proposed a generalization of this basic framework, based on the idea to distinguish between different types of mismatches in the alignments. This leads to representing both alignments and seeds as words over larger alphabets. In the general case, consider an alignment alphabet $\mathcal{A}$ of arbitrary size. We always assume that $\mathcal{A}$ contains a symbol 1, interpreted as "match". A *subset seed* is defined as a word over a *seed alphabet* $\mathcal{B}$, such that

- each letter $b \in \mathcal{B}$ denotes a subset of $\mathcal{A}$ that contains 1 ($b \in 2^{\mathcal{A}} \setminus 2^{\mathcal{A} \setminus \{1\}}$),
- $\mathcal{B}$ contains a letter # that denotes subset $\{1\}$.

As before, s is called the *span* of π, and the *#-weight* of π is the number of # in π. A subset seed $\pi \in \mathcal{B}^s$ *matches* an alignment $A \in \mathcal{A}^*$ at a position p iff for all $i \in [1..s]$, $A[p + i - 1] \in \pi[i]$.

Example 1. For DNA sequences over the alphabet $\{A, C, G, T\}$, in [21] we considered the alignment alphabet $\mathcal{A} = \{1, h, 0\}$ representing respectively a match, a transition mismatch ($A \leftrightarrow G$, $C \leftrightarrow T$), or a transversion mismatch (other mismatch). In this case, the appropriate seed alphabet is $\mathcal{B} = \{\#, @, \_\}$ corresponding respectively to subsets $\{1\}$, $\{1, h\}$, and $\{1, h, 0\}$. Thus, seed $\pi = \#@\_\#$ matches alignment $A = 10h1h1101$ at positions 4 and 6. The span of π is 4, and the #-weight of π is 2.

One can view the problem of finding seed occurrences in an alignment as a special string matching problem. In particular, it can be considered as a special case of *subset matching* [18] where the text is composed of individual characters. It is also an instance of the problem of matching in indeterminate (degenerate) strings [19,20]. Therefore, an efficient automaton construction that we present in the following sections applies directly to these instances of string matching. One can also freely use the string matching terminology by replacing words "seed" and "alignment" by "pattern" and "text" respectively.

3   Subset Seed Automaton

Let us fix an alignment alphabet $\mathcal{A}$, a seed alphabet $\mathcal{B}$, and a seed $\pi = \pi_1 \cdots \pi_s \in \mathcal{B}^*$ of span s and #-weight w. Denote $r = s - w$ and let R_π, $|R_\pi| = r$, be the set of all non-# positions in π. Throughout the paper, we identify each position $z \in R_\pi$ with the corresponding prefix $\pi_{1..z} = \pi_1 \cdots \pi_z$ of π, and we interchangeably regard elements of R_π as positions or as prefixes of π.

We now define an automaton $S_\pi = \langle Q, q_0, Q_F, \mathcal{A}, \psi : Q \times \mathcal{A} \to Q \rangle$, $q_0 \in Q$, $Q_F \subseteq Q$, that recognizes the set of all alignments matched by π. The states Q are defined as pairs $\langle X, t \rangle$ such that $X = \{x_1, \ldots, x_k\} \subseteq R_\pi$, $t \in [0, \ldots, s]$, $\max\{X\} + t \leq s$. The automaton maintains the following invariant condition. Suppose that S_π has read a prefix $a_1 \cdots a_p$ of an alignment A and has come to a state $\langle X, t \rangle$. Then t is the length of the longest suffix of $a_1 \cdots a_p$ of the form

(a) $\pi = \text{\#@\#\_\#\#\_\#\#\#}$

(b) $A = \text{111h1011h11}$

(c)
$$\overset{a_9 \quad t}{\text{111h1011h}\overline{\text{11}}}$$
$$\pi_{1..7} = \text{\#@\#\_\#\#\_}$$
$$\pi_{1..4} = \text{\#@\#\_}$$
$$\pi_{1..2} = \text{\#@}$$

Fig. 1. Illustration to Example 2

1^i, $i \leq s$, and X contains all positions $x_i \in R_\pi$ such that prefix $\pi_{1..x_i}$ matches a suffix of $a_1 \cdots a_{p-t}$.

Example 2. In the framework of Example 1, consider a seed π and an alignment prefix $A = a_1 \cdots a_p$ of length $p = 11$ given in Figure 1(a) and (b) respectively. The length t of the last run of 1's of A is 2. The last non-1 letter of A is $a_9 = \text{h}$. The set R_π of non-# positions of π is $\{2, 4, 7\}$ and π has 3 prefixes belonging to R_π (Figure 1(c)). Prefixes $\pi_{1..2}$ and $\pi_{1..7}$ do match suffixes of $a_1 a_2 \cdots a_9$, but prefix $\pi_{1..4}$ does not. Thus, the state of the automaton after reading $a_1 a_2 \cdots a_{11}$ is $\langle \{2, 7\}, 2 \rangle$.

The initial state q_0 of S_π is the state $\langle \emptyset, 0 \rangle$. Final states Q_F of S_π are all states $q = \langle X, t \rangle$, where $\max\{X\} + t = s$. All final states are merged into one state $\langle \rangle$.

The transition function $\psi(q, a)$ is defined as follows. If q is a final state, then $\forall a \in \mathcal{A}$, $\psi(q, a) = q$. If $q = \langle X, t \rangle$ is a non-final state, then

- if $a = 1$ then $\psi(q, a) = \langle X, t+1 \rangle$,
- otherwise $\psi(q, a) = \langle X_U \cup X_V, 0 \rangle$ with
  - $X_U = \{x \mid x \leq t+1 \text{ and } a \in \pi_x\}$
  - $X_V = \{x + t + 1 \mid x \in X \text{ and } a \in \pi_{x+t+1}\}$

Example 3. Still in the framework of Example 1, consider seed $\pi = \text{\#\_@\#}$. Then the set R_π is $\{2, 3\}$. Possible non-final states $\langle X, t \rangle$ of S_π are states $\langle \emptyset, 0 \rangle$, $\langle \emptyset, 1 \rangle$, $\langle \emptyset, 2 \rangle$, $\langle \emptyset, 3 \rangle$, $\langle \{2\}, 0 \rangle$, $\langle \{2\}, 1 \rangle$, $\langle \{3\}, 0 \rangle$, $\langle \{2, 3\}, 0 \rangle$. All these states are reachable in S_π. Figure 2 shows the resulting automaton.

We now study main properties of automaton S_π.

Lemma 4. *The automaton S_π accepts all alignments $A \in \mathcal{A}^*$ matched by π.*

Proof. It can be verified by induction that the invariant condition on the states $\langle X, t \rangle \in Q$ is preserved by the transition function ψ. The final state verifies $\max\{X\} + t = s$ which implies that at the first time S_π gets into the final state, π matches a suffix of $a_1 \cdots a_p$.   □

Lemma 5. *The number of states of the automaton S_π is no more than $(w+1)2^r$, where w is the #-weight of π.*

Proof. Assume that $R_\pi = \{z_1, z_2, \ldots, z_r\}$ and $z_1 < z_2 \cdots < z_r$. Let Q_i be the set of non-final states $\langle X, t \rangle$ with $\max\{X\} = z_i$. For states $q = \langle X, t \rangle \in Q_i$ there are 2^{i-1} possible values of X and $s - z_i$ possible values of t between 0 and $s - z_i - 1$, as $\max\{X\} + t \leq s - 1$.

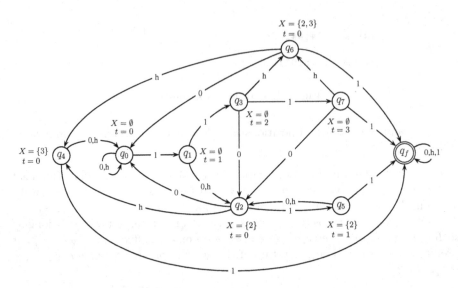

Fig. 2. Illustration to Example 3

Thus,

$$|Q_i| \leq 2^{i-1}(s - z_i) \leq 2^{i-1}(s - i), \text{ and} \tag{1}$$

$$\sum_{i=1}^{r} |Q_i| \leq \sum_{i=1}^{r} 2^{i-1}(s - i) = (s - r + 1)2^r - s - 1. \tag{2}$$

Besides states Q_i, Q contains s states $\langle \emptyset, t \rangle$ ($t \in [0..s - 1]$) and one final state. Thus, $|Q| \leq (s - r + 1)2^r = (w + 1)2^r$. □

Note that if π starts with #, which is always the case for spaced seeds, then $X_i \geq i + 1$, $i \in [1..r]$, and the bound of (1) rewrites to $2^{i-1}(s - i - 1)$. This results in the same $w2^r$ bound on number of states as the one for the Aho-Corasick automaton proposed in [16] for spaced seeds (see also Lemma 7 below).

The next Lemma shows that the construction of automaton S_π is optimal in the sense that no two states can be merged in general.

Lemma 6. *Let* $\mathcal{A} = \{0, 1\}$ *and* $\mathcal{B} = \{#, \_\}$, *where* $# = \{1\}$ *and* $\_ = \{0, 1\}$. *Consider a seed* $\pi = #\_\cdots\_#$ *with* r *letters* '$\_$' *between two #'s. Then the automaton* S_π *is reduced, that is*

(i) each of its states q is reachable, and
(ii) any two non-final states q', q'' *are not equivalent.*

Proof. (i) Let $q = \langle X, t \rangle$ be a non-final state of the automaton S_π, and let $X = \{x_1, \ldots, x_k\}$ with $x_1 < \cdots < x_k$. Let $A = a_1 \cdots a_{x_k} \in \{0, 1\}^*$ be an alignment of length x_k defined as follows: $a_p = 1$ if, for some $i \in [1..k]$, $p = x_k - x_i + 1$, and $a_p = 0$ otherwise. Note that $1 \notin X$ and thus $a_{x_k} = 0$. Thus $\psi(\langle \emptyset, 0 \rangle, A) = \langle X, 0 \rangle$ and finally $\psi(\langle \emptyset, 0 \rangle, A \cdot 1^t) = q$.

(ii) For a set $X = \{x_1, \ldots, x_k\}$ and an integer t, denote $X \oplus t = \{x_1 + t, \ldots, x_k + t\}$. Let $q' = \langle X', t' \rangle$ and $q'' = \langle X'', t'' \rangle$ be non-final states of S_π. If $\max\{X'\} + t' > \max\{X''\} + t''$, then let $d = (r+2) - (\max\{X'\} + t')$. Obviously, $\psi(q', 1^d)$ is a final state, and $\psi(q'', 1^d)$ is not.

Now assume that $\max\{X'\} + t' = \max\{X''\} + t''$. Let $g = \max\{v | (v \in X' \oplus t'$ and $v \notin X'' \oplus t'')$ or $(v \in X'' \oplus t''$ and $v \notin X' \oplus t')\}$. By symmetry, assume that the maximum is reached on the first condition, i.e. $g = x_i' + t'$ for some $x_i' \in X'$. Let $d = (r+1) - g$ and consider word $0^d 1$. It is easy to see that $\psi(q', 0^d 1)$ is a final state. We claim that $\psi(q'', 0^d 1)$ is not. To see this, observe that none of the seed prefixes corresponding to $x \in X''$ with $x + t'' > x_i' + t'$ can lead to the final state on $0^d 1$, due to the last $\#$ symbol of π. The details are left to the reader.   □

Another interesting property of S_π is the existence of a surjective mapping from the states of the Aho-Corasick automaton onto reachable states of S_π. This mapping proves that even if S_π is not always minimized, it has *always* a smaller number of states than the Aho-Corasick automaton. Here, by the Aho-Corasick (AC) automaton, we mean the automaton with the states corresponding to nodes of the trie built according to the classical Aho-Corasick construction [22] from the set of all instances of the seed π. More precisely, given a seed π of span s, the set of states of the AC-automaton is $Q_{AC} = \{A \in \mathcal{A}^* \mid |A| \leq s$ and A is matched by prefix $\pi_{1..|A|}\}$. The transition $\psi(A, a)$ for $A \in Q_{AC}$, $a \in \mathcal{A}$ yields the *longest* $A' \in Q_{AC}$ which is a suffix of Aa. We assume that all final states are merged into a single sink state.

Lemma 7. *Consider an alignment alphabet $\mathcal{A}$, a seed alphabet $\mathcal{B}$ and a seed $\pi \in \mathcal{B}^s$ of span s. There exists a surjective mapping $f : Q_{AC} \rightarrow Q$ from the set of states of the Aho-Corasick automaton to the set of reachable states of the subset seed automaton S_π.*

Proof. We first define the mapping f. Consider a state $A \in Q_{AC}$, $|A| = p < s$, where A is matched by $\pi_{1..p}$. Decompose $A = A' 1^t$, where the last letter of A' is not 1. If A' is empty, define $f(A) = \langle \emptyset, t \rangle$. Otherwise, $\pi_{1..p-t}$ matches A' and $\pi[p - t] \neq \#$. Let X be a set of positions that contains $p - t$ together with all positions $i < p - t$ such that $\pi_{1..i}$ matches a suffix of A'. Define $f(A) = \langle X, t \rangle$. It is easy to see that $\langle X, t \rangle \in Q$, that $\langle X, t \rangle$ exists in S_π and is reachable by string A.

Now show that for every reachable state $\langle X, t \rangle \in Q$ of S_π there exists $A \in Q_{AC}$ such that $f(A) = \langle X, t \rangle$. Consider a string $C \in \mathcal{A}^*$ that gets S_π to the state $\langle X, t \rangle$. Then $C = C' 1^t$ and the last letter of C' is not 1. If X is empty then define $A = 1^t$. If X is not empty, then consider the suffix A' of C' of length $x = \max\{X\}$ and define $A = A' 1^t$. Since $\pi_{1..x}$ matches A', and $x + t \leq s$, then $\pi_{1..x+t}$ matches A and therefore $A \in Q_{AC}$. It is easy to see that $f(A) = \langle X, t \rangle$.   □

Observe that the mapping of Lemma 7 is actually a morphism from the Aho-Corasick automaton to S_π.

Table 1 shows experimentally estimated average sizes of the Aho-Corasick automaton, subset seed automaton, and minimal automaton. The two tables

Table 1. Average number of states of Aho-Corasick, S_π and minimal automaton

$\|\mathcal{A}\|=2$ w	Aho-Corasick avg.	ratio	S_π avg.	ratio	Minimized avg.	$\|\mathcal{A}\|=3$ w	Aho-Corasick avg.	ratio	S_π avg.	ratio	Minimized avg.
9	130.98	2.46	67.03	1.260	53.18	9	1103.5	16.46	86.71	1.293	67.05
10	140.28	2.51	70.27	1.255	55.98	10	1187.7	16.91	90.67	1.291	70.25
11	150.16	2.55	73.99	1.254	58.99	11	1265.3	17.18	95.05	1.291	73.65
12	159.26	2.57	77.39	1.248	62.00	12	1346.1	17.50	98.99	1.287	76.90
13	168.19	2.59	80.92	1.246	64.92	13	1419.3	17.67	103.10	1.284	80.31

correspond respectively to the binary alphabet (spaced seeds) and ternary alphabet (see Example 1). For Aho-Corasick and subset seed automata, the ratio to the average size of the minimal automaton is shown. Each line corresponds to a seed weight (#-weight for $|\mathcal{A}| = 3$). In each case, 10 000 random seeds of different span have been generated to estimate the average.

4   Subset Seed Automaton Implementation

As in section 3, consider a subset seed π of #-weight w and span s, and let $r = s - w$ be the number of non-# positions. A straightforward generation of the transition table of the automaton S_π can be performed in time $\mathcal{O}(r \cdot w \cdot 2^r \cdot |\mathcal{A}|)$. In this section, we show that S_π can be constructed in time proportional to its size, which is bounded by $(w+1)2^r$, according to Lemma 5. In practice, however, the number of states is usually much smaller.

The algorithm generates the states of the automaton incrementally by traversing them in the breadth-first manner. Transitions $\psi(\langle X, t\rangle, a)$ are computed using previously computed transitions $\psi(\langle X', t\rangle, a)$. A tricky part of the algorithm corresponds to the case where state $\psi(\langle X, t\rangle, a)$ has already been created before and should be retrieved.

The whole construction of the automaton is given in Algorithm 1. We now describe it in more details.

Let $R_\pi = \{z_1, \ldots, z_r\}$ and $z_1 < z_2 \cdots < z_r$. Consider $X \subseteq R_\pi$. To retrieve the maximal element of X, the algorithm maintains a function $k(X)$ defined by

$$k(X) = \max\{i | z_i \in X\},\ k(\emptyset) = 0.$$

Let $q = \langle X, t\rangle$ be a non-final and reachable state of S_π, $X = \{x_1, \ldots, x_i\} \subseteq R_\pi$ and $x_1 < x_2 \cdots < x_i$. We define $X' = X \setminus \{z_{k(X)}\} = \{x_1, \ldots, x_{i-1}\}$ and $q' = \langle X', t\rangle$. The following lemma holds.

Lemma 8. If $q = \langle X, t\rangle$ is reachable, then $q' = \langle X', t\rangle$ is reachable and has been processed before in a breadth-first computation of S_π.

Proof. First prove that $\langle X', t\rangle$ is reachable. If $\langle X, t\rangle$ is reachable, then $\langle X, 0\rangle$ is reachable due to the definition of transition function for $t > 0$. Thus, there is a word A of length $x_i = z_{k(X)}$ such that $\forall j \in [1..r]$, $z_j \in X$ iff the seed suffix $\pi_{1..z_j}$ matches the word suffix $A_{x_i - z_j + 1} \cdots A_{x_i}$. Define A' to be the suffix of A of length $x_{i-1} = z_{k(X')}$ and observe that reading A' gets the automaton to the state $\langle X', 0 \rangle$, and then reading $A' \cdot 1^t$ leads to the state $\langle X', t \rangle$. Finally, as $|A' \cdot 1^t| < |A \cdot 1^t|$, then the breadth-first traversal of states of A_π always processes state $\langle X', t \rangle$ before $\langle X, t \rangle$. □

To retrieve X' from X, the algorithm maintains a function $\text{FAIL}(q)$, similar to the *failure* function of the Aho-Corasick automaton, such that $\text{FAIL}(\langle X, t \rangle) = \langle X', t \rangle$ for $X \neq \emptyset$, and $\text{FAIL}(\langle \emptyset, t \rangle) = \langle \emptyset, max\{t - 1, 0\} \rangle$.

We now explain how values $\psi(q, a)$ are computed by Algorithm 1. Note first that if $a = 1$, state $\psi(q, a) = \langle X, t + 1 \rangle$ can be computed in constant time (part a. of Algorithm 1). Moreover, since this is the only way to reach state $\langle X, t + 1 \rangle$, it is created and added once to the set of states.

Assume now that $a \neq 1$. To compute $\psi(q, a) = \langle Y, 0 \rangle$, we retrieve state $q' = \text{FAIL}(q) = \langle X', t \rangle$ and then retrieve $\psi(q', a) = \langle Y', 0 \rangle$. Note that this is well-defined as by Lemma 8, q' has been processed before q.

Observe now that since X' and X differ by only one seed prefix $\pi_{1..z_k(X)}$ the only possible difference between Y and Y' can be the prefix $\pi_{1..z_k(X)+t+1}$ depending on whether $\pi_{z_k(X)+t+1}$ matches a or not. As $a \neq 1$, this is equivalent to testing whether $(z_k(X) + t + 1) \in R_\pi$ and $\pi_{z_k(X)+t+1}$ matches a. This information can be precomputed for different values $k(X)$ and t.

For every $a \neq 1$, we define

$$V(k, t, a) = \begin{cases} \{z_k + t + 1\} & \text{if } z_k + t + 1 \in R_\pi \text{ and } \pi_{z_k+t+1} \text{ matches } a, \\ \emptyset & \text{otherwise.} \end{cases}$$

Thus, $Y = Y' \cup V(k(X), t, a)$ (part c. of Algorithm 1). Function $V(k, t, a)$ can be precomputed in time and space $\mathcal{O}(|\mathcal{A}| \cdot r \cdot s)$.

Note that if $V(k, t, a)$ is empty, then $\langle Y, 0 \rangle$ is equal to an already created state $\langle Y', 0 \rangle$ and no new state needs to be created in this case (part e. of Algorithm 1).

If $V(k, t, a)$ is not empty, we need to find out if $\langle Y, 0 \rangle$ has already been created or not and if it has, we need to retrieve it. To do that, we need an additional construction. For each state $q' = \langle X', t \rangle$, we maintain another function $\text{REVMAXFAIL}(q')$, that gives the *last created* state $q = \langle X, t \rangle$ such that $X \backslash z_{k(X)} = X'$ (part d. of Algorithm 1). Since the state generation is breadth-first, new states $\langle X, t \rangle$ are created in a non-decreasing order of the quantity $(z_{k(X)} + t)$. Therefore, among all states $\langle X, t \rangle$ such that $\text{FAIL}(\langle X, t \rangle) = \langle X', t \rangle$, $\text{REVMAXFAIL}(\langle X', t \rangle)$ returns the one with the largest $z_{k(X)}$.

Now, observe that if $V(k, t, a)$ is not empty, i.e. $Y = Y' \cup \{z_{k(X)} + t + 1\}$, then $\text{FAIL}(\langle Y, 0 \rangle) = \langle Y', 0 \rangle$. Since state $\langle Y, 0 \rangle$ has the maximal possible current value $z_{k(Y)} + 0 = z_{k(X)} + t + 1$, by the above remark, we conclude that if $\langle Y, 0 \rangle$ has already been created, then $\text{REVMAXFAIL}(\langle Y', 0 \rangle) = \langle Y, 0 \rangle$. This allows us to check if this is indeed the case and to retrieve the state $\langle Y, 0 \rangle$ if it exists (part d. of Algorithm 1).

The generation of states $\langle X, t \rangle$ with $X = \emptyset$ represents a special case (part b. of Algorithm 1). Here another precomputed function is used:

$$U(t, a) = \cup \{x | x \leq t + 1 \text{ and } a \text{ matches } \pi_x\}$$

Algorithm 1. computation of S_π

Data: a seed $\pi = \pi_1\pi_2\ldots\pi_s$
Result: an automaton $S_\pi = \langle Q, q_0, q_F, \mathcal{A}, \psi \rangle$
$q_F \leftarrow createstate(\langle\rangle)$; $q_0 \leftarrow createstate(\langle\emptyset, 0\rangle)$;
/* process the first level of states to set FAIL and REVMAXFAIL */
for $a \in \mathcal{A}$ **do**

    if $a \in \pi_1$ **then**

        if $a = 1$ **then**

            | $\langle Y, t_y \rangle \leftarrow \langle \emptyset, 1 \rangle$;

        else

            $\lfloor$ $\langle Y, t_y \rangle \leftarrow \langle \{1\}, 0 \rangle$;

        if $z_{k(Y)} + t_y \geq s$ **then**

            | $q_y \leftarrow q_F$;

        else

            $q_y \leftarrow createstate(\langle Y, t_y \rangle)$;

            FAIL$(q_y) \leftarrow q_0$; REVMAXFAIL$(q_0) \leftarrow q_y$;

            $\lfloor$ push$(Queue, q_y)$;

    else

        $\lfloor$ $q_y \leftarrow q_0$;

    $\psi(q_0, a) \leftarrow q_y$;

/* breadth-first processing */
while $Queue \neq \emptyset$ **do**

    $q : \langle X, t_X \rangle \leftarrow pop(Queue)$;

    $q' \leftarrow$ FAIL(q);

    for $a \in \mathcal{A}$ **do**

        /* compute $\psi(\langle X, t_X \rangle, a) = \langle Y, t_y \rangle$ */

        $q'_y : \langle Y', t'_y \rangle \leftarrow \psi(q', a)$;

        if $a = 1$ **then**

            $Y \leftarrow X$;

a $t_y \leftarrow t_X + 1$;

        else

            if $X = \emptyset$ **then**

b | $Y \leftarrow U(t_X, a)$;

            else

c $\lfloor$ $Y \leftarrow Y' \cup V(k(X), t_X, a)$;

            $t_y \leftarrow 0$;

        /* create a new state unless it already exists or it is final */

        $q_{rev} : \langle Y_{rev}, t_{rev} \rangle \leftarrow$ REVMAXFAIL(q'_y);

        if $defined(q_{rev})$ **and** $t_y = t_{rev}$ **and** $Y = Y_{rev}$ **then**

d | $q_y \leftarrow q_{rev}$;

        else if $t_y = t'_y$ **and** $Y = Y'$ **then**

e | $q_y \leftarrow q'_y$;

        else

            if $z_{k(Y)} + t_y \geq s$ **then**

               | $q_y \leftarrow q_F$;

            else

               $q_y \leftarrow createstate(\langle Y, t_y \rangle)$;

               FAIL$(q_y) \leftarrow q'_y$; REVMAXFAIL$(q'_y) \leftarrow q_y$;

               $\lfloor$ push$(Queue, q_y)$;

        $\psi(q, a) \leftarrow q_y$;

$U(t, a)$ gives the set of seed prefixes that match the word $1^t \cdot a$. In this case, checking if resulting states have been already added is done in a similar way to $V(k, t, a)$. Details are left out.

We summarize the results of this section with the following Lemma.

Lemma 9. *After a preprocessing of seed π within time $\mathcal{O}(|\mathcal{A}|\cdot s^2)$, the automaton S_π can be constructed by incrementally generating all reachable states so that every transition $\psi(q, a)$ is computed in constant time.*

5   Possible Extensions

An important remark is that the automaton defined in this paper can be easily generalized to the case of multiple seeds. For seeds $\pi^1, \ldots, \pi^k$, a state of the automaton recognizing the alignments matched by one of the seeds would be a tuple $\langle X_1, \ldots, X_k, t \rangle$, where $X_1, \ldots, X_k$ contain the set of respective prefixes, similarly to the construction of the paper. Interestingly, Lemma 7 still holds for the case of multiple seeds. This means that although the size of the union of individual seed automata could potentially grow as the product of sizes, it actually does not, as it is bounded by the size of the Aho-Corasick automaton which grows additively with respect to subsets of underlying words. In practice, our automaton is still substantially smaller than the Aho-Corasick automaton, as illustrated by Table 2. Similar to Table 1, 10 000 random seed pairs have been generated here in each case to estimate the average size.

Table 2. *Average number of states of Aho-Corasick, S_π and minimized automata for the case of two seeds*

| $|\mathcal{A}| = 2$ | Aho-Corasick | | S_π | | Minimized | $|\mathcal{A}| = 3$ | Aho-Corasick | | S_π | | Minimized |
w	avg.	ratio	avg.	ratio	avg.	w	avg.	ratio	avg.	ratio	avg.
9	224.49	2.01	122.82	1.10	111.43	9	2130.6	12.09	201.69	1.15	176.27
10	243.32	2.07	129.68	1.10	117.71	10	2297.8	12.53	209.75	1.14	183.40
11	264.04	2.11	137.78	1.10	125.02	11	2456.5	12.86	218.27	1.14	191.04
12	282.51	2.15	144.97	1.10	131.68	12	2600.6	13.14	226.14	1.14	198.00
13	300.59	2.18	151.59	1.10	137.74	13	2778.0	13.39	236.62	1.14	207.51

Another interesting observation is that the construction of a matching automaton where each state is associated with a set of "compatible" prefixes of the pattern is a general one and can be applied to the general problem of subset matching [18,23,19,20]. Recall that in subset matching, a pattern is composed of subsets of alphabet letters. This is the case, for example, with IUPAC genomic motifs, such as motif ANDGR representing the subset motif $A[ACGT][AGT]G[AG]$. Note that the text can also be composed of subset letters, with two possible matching interpretations [20]: a seed letter b matches a text letter a either if $a \subseteq b$ or if $a \cap b \neq \emptyset$.

Interestingly, the automaton construction of this paper still applies to these cases with minor modifications due to the absence of text letter 1 matched by any seed letter. With this modification, the automaton construction algorithm of Section 4 still applies. As a test case, we applied it to subset motif $[GA][GA]GGGNNNNAN[CT]ATGNN[AT]\ NNNNN[CTG]$ mentioned in [20] as a motif describing the translation initiation site in the *E.coli* genome. For a regular 4-letters genomic text, the automaton obtained with our approach has only 138 states, while the minimal automaton has 126 states. For a text composed of 15 subsets of 4 letters and the inclusion matching relation, our automaton contains 139 states, compared to 127 states of the minimal automaton. However, in the case of intersection matching relation, the automaton size increases drastically: it contains 87 617 states compared to the 10 482 states of the minimal automaton.

References

1. Kucherov, G., Noé, L., Roytberg, M.: A unifying framework for seed sensitivity and its application to subset seeds. JBCB 4, 553–569 (2006)
2. Burkhardt, S., Kärkkäinen, J.: Better filtering with gapped *q*-grams. Fundamenta Informaticae 56, 51–70 (2003)
3. Ma, B., Tromp, J., Li, M.: PatternHunter: Faster and more sensitive homology search. Bioinformatics 18, 440–445 (2002)
4. Brown, D., Li, M., Ma, B.: A tutorial of recent developments in the seeding of local alignment. JBCB 2, 819–842 (2004)
5. Brown, D.: A survey of seeding for sequence alignments. In: Bioinformatics Algorithms: Techniques and Applications (to appear, 2007)
6. Li, M., Ma, B., Kisman, D., Tromp, J.: PatternHunter II: Highly sensitive and fast homology search. Journal of Bioinformatics and Computational Biology 2, 417–439 (2004)
7. Noé, L., Kucherov, G.: YASS: enhancing the sensitivity of DNA similarity search. Nucleic Acids Research 33(web-server issue), W540–W543 (2005)
8. Califano, A., Rigoutsos, I.: Flash: A fast look-up algorithm for string homology. In: Proceedings of the 1st International Conference on Intelligent Systems for Molecular Biology (ISMB), pp. 56–64 (1993)
9. Tsur, D.: Optimal probing patterns for sequencing by hybridization. In: Bücher, P., Moret, B.M.E. (eds.) WABI 2006. LNCS (LNBI), vol. 4175, pp. 366–375. Springer, Heidelberg (2006)
10. Schwartz, S., Kent, J., Smit, A., Zhang, Z., Baertsch, R., Hardison, R., Haussler, D., Miller, W.: Human–mouse alignments with BLASTZ. Genome Research 13, 103–107 (2003)
11. Sun, Y., Buhler, J.: Choosing the best heuristic for seeded alignment of DNA sequences. BMC Bioinformatics 7 (2006)
12. Csűrös, M., Ma, B.: Rapid homology search with two-stage extension and daughter seeds. In: Wang, L. (ed.) COCOON 2005. LNCS, vol. 3595, pp. 104–114. Springer, Heidelberg (2005)
13. Mak, D., Gelfand, Y., Benson, G.: Indel seeds for homology search. Bioinformatics 22, e341–e349 (2006)
14. Brejová, B., Brown, D., Vinar, T.: Vector seeds: An extension to spaced seeds. Journal of Computer and System Sciences 70, 364–380 (2005)
15. Keich, U., Li, M., Ma, B., Tromp, J.: On spaced seeds for similarity search. Discrete Applied Mathematics 138, 253–263 (2004) preliminary version in 2002.
16. Buhler, J., Keich, U., Sun, Y.: Designing seeds for similarity search in genomic DNA. In: Proceedings of the 7th Annual International Conference on Computational Molecular Biology (RECOMB), pp. 67–75 (2003)

17. Brejová, B., Brown, D., Vinar, T.: Optimal spaced seeds for homologous coding regions. Journal of Bioinformatics and Computational Biology 1, 595–610 (2004)
18. Cole, R., Hariharan, R., Indyk, P.: Tree pattern matching and subset matching in deterministic $O(n \log^3 n)$-time. In: Proceedings of 10th Symposium on Discrete Algorithms (SODA), pp. 245–254 (1999)
19. Holub, J., Smyth, W.F., Wang, S.: Fast pattern-matching on indeterminate strings. Journal of Discrete Algorithms (2006)
20. Rahman, S., Iliopoulos, C., Mouchard, L.: Pattern matching in degenerate DNA/RNA sequences. In: Proceedings of the Workshop on Algorithms and Computation (WALCOM), pp. 109–120 (2007)
21. Noé, L., Kucherov, G.: Improved hit criteria for DNA local alignment. BMC Bioinformatics 5 (2004)
22. Aho, A.V., Corasick, M.J.: Efficient string matching: An aid to bibliographic search. Communications of the ACM 18, 333–340 (1975)
23. Amir, A., Porat, E., Lewenstein, M.: Approximate subset matching with don't cares. In: Proceedings of 12th Symposium on Discrete Algorithms (SODA), pp. 305–306 (2001)

A Measure for the Degree of Nondeterminism of Context-Free Languages

František Mráz[1,*], Martin Plátek[1], and Friedrich Otto[2]

[1] Charles University, Faculty of Mathematics and Physics
Department of Computer Science, Malostranské nám. 25
118 00 Praha 1, Czech Republic
mraz@ksvi.ms.mff.cuni.cz, Martin.Platek@mff.cuni.cz
[2] Fachbereich Elektrotechnik/Informatik, Universität Kassel
34109 Kassel, Germany
otto@theory.informatik.uni-kassel.de

Abstract. Restarting automata can be seen as analytical variants of classical automata as well as of regulated rewriting systems. We study some measures for the degree of nondeterminism of (context-free) languages in terms of lexicalized deterministic restarting automata. These measures are based on the number of auxiliary symbols (categories) used for recognizing a language as the projection of its characteristic language onto its input alphabet. This type of recognition is typical for analysis by reduction, a method used in linguistics for the creation and verification of formal descriptions of natural languages. Our main results establish a two-dimensional hierarchy of classes of (context-free) languages based on the expansion factor of a language and on the number of different auxiliary symbols available in the underlying characteristic language.

Keywords: measure of nondeterminism, restarting automaton, analysis by reduction.

1 Introduction

Automata with a restart operation were originally introduced in order to describe a method of grammar-checking for the Czech language (see, e.g., [1]). These automata, which work in a fashion similar to the automata used in this paper, started the investigation of restarting automata as a suitable tool for modeling the so-called *analysis by reduction*. Analysis by reduction facilitates the development and testing of categories for syntactic and semantic disambiguation of sentences of natural languages. It is often used (implicitly) for developing grammars for natural languages based on the notion of *dependency* [2]. In particular, the Functional Generative Description (FGD) for the Czech language developed in Prague (see, e.g., [3]) is based on this method.

* F. Mráz and M. Plátek were partially supported by the program 'Information Society' under project 1ET100300517. F. Mráz was also partially supported by the Grant Agency of Charles University in Prague under Grant-No. 358/2006/A-INF/MFF.

Jan Holub and Jan Žd'árek (Eds.): CIAA 2007, LNCS 4783, pp. 192–202, 2007.
© Springer-Verlag Berlin Heidelberg 2007

Analysis by reduction consists in stepwise simplifications (reductions) of a given extended sentence (enriched by syntactic and semantic categories) until a correct simple sentence is obtained. Each simplification replaces a small part of the sentence by an even shorter phrase. Here we formalize analysis by reduction by using lexicalized deterministic restarting automata for characteristic languages, that is, these automata work on languages that include auxiliary symbols (categories) in addition to the input symbols. By requiring that the automata considered are *lexicalized* we restrict the lengths of the blocks of auxiliary symbols that are allowed on the tape by a constant. This restriction is quite natural from a linguistic point of view, as these blocks of auxiliary symbols model the meta-language categories from all linguistic layers with which an input string is being enriched when its disambiguated form is being produced (see, e.g., [3]). We use deterministic restarting automata in order to ensure the *correctness preserving property* for the analysis.

While it is well-known that monotone deterministic restarting automata without auxiliary symbols recognize exactly the deterministic context-free languages [4], we will see that exactly the context-free languages are recognized as proper languages of lexicalized deterministic restarting automata that are monotone. Then we define the *word-expansion factor* of a restarting automaton M. This is the maximal number of auxiliary symbols that M uses simultaneously on its tape when processing a word from the characteristic language $L_C(M)$. If L is a (context-free) language, then the minimal word-expansion factor for any lexicalized deterministic restarting automaton M with proper language L can be seen as a measure for the degree of nondeterminism of L. This is quite natural from a language-theoretic point of view, as the auxiliary symbols inserted in an input sentence can be interpreted as information that is used to single out a particular computation of an otherwise nondeterministic restarting automaton. Corresponding notions have been investigated before for finite-state automata, and for some other devices [5,6,7]. An overview about degrees of non-determinism for pushdown automata can be found in [8].

Here we establish a two-dimensional hierarchy of language classes that is based on the word-expansion factor and on the number of auxiliary symbols in the working alphabet of the restarting automaton considered. Actually, we obtain four such hierarchies, two for (strongly) lexicalized deterministic restarting automata that are monotone, and two for the non-monotone case. Observe that due to our result above the hierarchies for the monotone cases are hierarchies of context-free languages above the level of deterministic context-free languages.

The paper is structured as follows. In Section 2 we define the model of restarting automata we will use and restate some basic results on these automata. Then in Section 3 we introduce our measure of nondeterminism and derive the announced results. In the concluding section (Section 4) we summarize our results and present some open problems for future work.

2 Definitions and Notation

Here we describe in short the type of restarting automaton we will be dealing with. More details on restarting automata in general can be found in [9]. In what follows, λ denotes the empty word, and $\mathbb{N}_+$ and $\mathbb{N}$ denote the set of positive and the set of nonnegative integers, respectively.

A *one-way deterministic restarting automaton*, det-RRWW-automaton for short, is a deterministic machine $M = (Q, \Sigma, \Gamma, \mathcal{c}, \$, q_0, k, \delta)$ with a finite set of (internal) states Q, a flexible tape, and a read/write window of a fixed size $k \geq 1$. The work space is bounded by the left sentinel $\mathcal{c}$ and the right sentinel $\$$, which cannot be removed from the tape. The tape alphabet Γ of M contains the input alphabet Σ, but it may also contain a finite number of so-called *auxiliary symbols*. The behaviour of M is described by a transition relation δ that associates a transition step to each pair (q, u) consisting of a state q and a possible content u of the read/write window. There are four types of transition steps: *move-right steps*, *rewrite steps*, *restart steps*, and *accept steps*. A *rewrite step* replaces the content of the read/write window by a shorter word, in this way shortening the tape. A *restart step* causes M to place its read/write window over the left end of the tape, so that the first symbol it sees is the left sentinel $\mathcal{c}$, and to reenter the initial state q_0. However, it is more convenient to describe M by a finite set of so-called *meta-instructions* (see below).

A *configuration* of M is described by a string $\alpha q \beta$, where $q \in Q$, and either $\alpha = \lambda$ and $\beta \in \{\mathcal{c}\} \cdot \Gamma^* \cdot \{\$\}$ or $\alpha \in \{\mathcal{c}\} \cdot \Gamma^*$ and $\beta \in \Gamma^* \cdot \{\$\}$; here q represents the current state, $\alpha\beta$ is the current content of the tape, and it is understood that the head scans the first k symbols of β or all of β when $|\beta| \leq k$. A *restarting configuration* is of the form $q_0 \mathcal{c} w \$$, where $w \in \Gamma^*$.

A *rewriting meta-instruction* for M has the form $(E_1, u \rightarrow v, E_2)$, where E_1 and E_2 are regular languages (often given in terms of regular expressions), and $u, v \in \Gamma^*$ are words satisfying $|u| > |v|$. On trying to execute this meta-instruction M will get stuck (and so it rejects) starting from the restarting configuration $q_0 \mathcal{c} w \$$, if w does not admit a factorization of the form $w = w_1 u w_2$ such that $\mathcal{c} w_1 \in E_1$ and $w_2 \$ \in E_2$. On the other hand, if w does have factorizations of this form, then the leftmost of these factorizations is chosen, and $q_0 \mathcal{c} w \$$ is transformed into $q_0 \mathcal{c} w_1 v w_2 \$$. This computation is called a *cycle* of M. It is expressed as $w \vdash_M^c w_1 v w_2$. In order to describe the tails of accepting computations we use *accepting meta-instructions* of the form (E_1, Accept), where the strings from the regular language E_1 are accepted by M after scanning them from left to right.

A word $w \in \Gamma^*$ is *accepted* by M, if there is a computation which, starting from the restarting configuration $q_0 \mathcal{c} w \$$, consists of a finite sequence of cycles that is followed by an application of an accepting meta-instruction. By $L_C(M)$ we denote the language consisting of all words accepted by M. It is the *characteristic language* of M.

By Pr^Σ we denote the projection from Γ^* onto Σ^*, that is, Pr^Σ is the morphism defined by $a \mapsto a$ $(a \in \Sigma)$ and $A \mapsto \lambda$ $(A \in \Gamma \smallsetminus \Sigma)$. If $v := \mathsf{Pr}^\Sigma(w)$, then v is the *Σ-projection* of w, and w is an *expanded version* of v. For a language $L \subseteq \Gamma^*$, $\mathsf{Pr}^\Sigma(L) := \{\, \mathsf{Pr}^\Sigma(w) \mid w \in L \,\}$.

In recent papers (see, e.g., [9]) restarting automata are mainly used as acceptors. The *(input) language* accepted by a restarting automaton M is the set $L(M) := L_C(M) \cap \Sigma^*$, that is, it is the set of input words $w \in \Sigma^*$ for which there exists an accepting computation starting from the configuration $q_0 \text{\textcent} w \$$. Here, motivated by linguistic considerations to model the processing of sentences that are enriched by syntactic and semantic categories, we are rather interested in the so-called *proper language of* M, which is the set of words $L_P(M) := \Pr^\Sigma(L_C(M))$. Hence, a word $v \in \Sigma^*$ belongs to $L_P(M)$ if and only if there exists an expanded version u of v such that $u \in L_C(M)$.

We are also interested in some restrictions on rewrite-instructions (expressed by the second part of the class name): -WW denotes no restriction, -W means that no auxiliary symbols are available (that is, $\Gamma = \Sigma$), -λ means that no auxiliary symbols are available and that each rewrite step is simply a deletion (that is, if $u \to v$ is a rewrite instruction of M, then v is obtained from u by deleting some symbols).

The following property is of central importance (see, e.g., [4]).

Definition 1. (Correctness Preserving Property.) *An* RRWW-*automaton M is* correctness preserving *if $u \in L_C(M)$ and $u \vdash_M^{c*} v$ imply that $v \in L_C(M)$.*

Each deterministic RRWW-automaton is correctness preserving. In proofs we will repeatedly use the following simple generalization of a fact given in [9].

Proposition 2. *For any* RRWW-*automaton M there exists a constant p such that the following holds. Assume that $uvw \vdash_M^c uv'w$, where $u = u_1 u_2 \cdots u_n$ for some non-empty words $u_1, \ldots, u_n$ and a constant $n > p$. Then there exist $r, s \in \mathbb{N}_+$, $1 \le r < s \le n$, such that*
$$u_1 \cdots u_{r-1}(u_r \cdots u_{s-1})^i u_s \cdots u_n vw \vdash_M^c u_1 \cdots u_{r-1}(u_r \cdots u_{s-1})^i u_s \cdots u_n v'w$$
holds for all $i \ge 0$, that is, $u_r \cdots u_{s-1}$ is a 'pumping factor' in the above cycle. Similarly, such a pumping factor can be found in any factorization of length greater than p of w. Such a pumping factor can also be found in any factorization of length greater than p of a word accepted in a tail computation.

As deterministic restarting automata only accept Church-Rosser languages (see, e.g., [9]), we have the following complexity result.

Proposition 3. *If M is a deterministic* RRWW-*automaton, then the membership problem for the language $L_C(M)$ is solvable in linear time.*

3   Lexicalized Deterministic RRWW-Automata

A deterministic RRWW-automaton $M = (Q, \Sigma, \Gamma, \text{\textcent}, \$, q_0, k, \delta)$ is called *lexicalized* if there exists a constant $j \in \mathbb{N}_+$ such that, whenever $v \in (\Gamma \smallsetminus \Sigma)^*$ is a factor of a word $w \in \Gamma^*$ which is not immediately rejected by M (that is, in a tail computation), then $|v| \le j$. M is called *strongly lexicalized* if it is lexicalized, and if each of its rewrite operations only deletes symbols. Strong lexicalization is a technique that is used in dependency (or categorially) based formal descriptions of natural languages [3]. All the results presented here for lexicalized RRWW-automata are valid for strongly lexicalized RRWW-automata as well.

If M is a lexicalized RRWW-automaton, and if w is an extended version of an input word $v = \mathsf{Pr}^\Sigma(w)$ such that w is not immediately rejected by M, then $|w| \leq (j+1) \cdot |v| + j$ for some constant $j > 0$. Accordingly we have the following result.

Corollary 4. *If M is a lexicalized* RRWW-*automaton, then the proper language $L_P(M)$ is context-sensitive.*

In what follows we are only interested in lexicalized RRWW-automata and their proper languages. By lex-RRWW we denote the class of these automata. Recall from the definition that lexicalized RRWW-automata are deterministic. Further, we are interested in RRWW-automata that are *monotone*.

Each computation of an RRWW-automaton M can be described by a sequence of cycles $C_1, C_2 \ldots, C_n$, where C_n is the last cycle, which is followed by the tail of the computation. Each cycle C_i of this computation contains a unique configuration of the form $\mathfrak{c}xquy\$$ in which a rewrite step is executed. By $D_r(C_i)$ we denote the *right distance* $|y\$|$ of this cycle. The sequence of cycles $C_1, C_2, \ldots, C_n$ is called *monotone* if $D_r(C_1) \geq D_r(C_2) \geq \cdots \geq D_r(C_n)$ holds. A computation of M is called *monotone* if the corresponding sequence of cycles is monotone. Observe that the tail of the computation is not taken into account here. Finally, an RRWW-automaton is called *monotone* if each of its computations is monotone.

Theorem 5. *The class* CFL *of context-free languages coincides with the class of proper languages of monotone lexicalized* RRWW-*automata, that is,* CFL $= \mathcal{L}_P(\text{mon-lex-RRWW})$.

Proof. If M is a monotone RRWW-automaton, then its characteristic language $L_C(M)$ is context-free [4]. As $L_P(M) = \mathsf{Pr}^\Sigma(L_C(M))$, and as CFL is closed under morphisms, it follows that $L_P(M)$ is context-free.

Conversely, assume that $L \subseteq \Sigma^*$ is a context-free language. Without loss of generality we may assume that L does not contain the empty word. Thus, there exists a context-free grammar $G = (N, \Sigma, S, P)$ for L that is in *Greibach normal form*, that is, each rule of P has the form $A \to \alpha$ for some string $\alpha \in \Sigma \cdot N^*$ (see, e.g., [10]). For the following construction we assume that the rules of G are numbered from 1 to m.

From G we construct a new grammar $G' := (N, \Sigma \cup B, S, P')$, where $B := \{ \nabla_i \mid 1 \leq i \leq m \}$ is a set of new terminal symbols that are in one-to-one correspondence to the rules of G, and

$$P' := \{ A \to \nabla_i \alpha \mid (A \to \alpha) \text{ is the } i\text{-th rule of } G, 1 \leq i \leq m \}.$$

Obviously, a word $\omega \in (\Sigma \cup B)^*$ belongs to $L(G')$ if and only if ω has the form $\omega = \nabla_{i_1} a_1 \nabla_{i_2} a_2 \cdots \nabla_{i_n} a_n$ for some integer $n > 0$, where $a_1, \ldots, a_n \in \Sigma$, $i_1, \ldots, i_n \in \{1, \ldots, m\}$, and these indices describe a (left-most) derivation of

$w := a_1 a_2 \cdots a_n$ from S in G. Thus, $\mathsf{Pr}^{\Sigma}(L(G')) = L(G) = L$. From ω this derivation can be reconstructed deterministically. In fact, the language $L(G')$ is deterministic context-free. Hence, there exists a monotone deterministic RR-automaton M for this language [4]. By interpreting the symbols of B as auxiliary symbols, we obtain a monotone deterministic RRWW-automaton M' such that $\mathsf{Pr}^{\Sigma}(L_C(M')) = \mathsf{Pr}^{\Sigma}(L(M)) = \mathsf{Pr}^{\Sigma}(L(G')) = L$.

It remains to verify that M' is lexicalized. From the observation above we see that within each word $\omega \in L(G')$, symbols from B and terminal symbols from Σ occur alternatingly. As the RR-automaton M is correctness preserving, each restarting configuration of M within an accepting computation is of the form $q_0 \mathfrak{c} \gamma \$$ for some $\gamma \in L(G')$. Thus, it only contains factors from B^+ of length one. It follows that M' is lexicalized with constant 1. $\qquad \square$

In the following we will only consider RRWW-automata that are lexicalized (and therewith deterministic).

Definition 6. *Let* $M = (Q, \Sigma, \Gamma, \mathfrak{c}, \$, q_0, k, \delta)$ *be an* RRWW-*automaton, and let* $m \in \mathbb{N}$. *We say that* M *has* word-expansion m, *denoted by* $\mathsf{W}(M) = m$, *if each word from* $L_C(M)$ *contains at most* m *occurrences of auxiliary symbols, that is, for each word* $w \in L_C(M)$, *we have* $|\mathsf{Pr}^{\Gamma \smallsetminus \Sigma}(w)| \leq m$.

In addition, M *is said to have* word-alphabet-expansion (m, j), *denoted by* $\mathsf{WA}(M) = (m, j)$, *if* $\mathsf{W}(M) = m$, *and if* Γ *contains at most* j *different auxiliary symbols, that is,* $|\Gamma \smallsetminus \Sigma| \leq j$.

Notation. By $\mathsf{W}(m)$-RRWW we denote the class of lexicalized RRWW-automata with word-expansion of degree m, and by $\mathsf{WA}(m, j)$-RRWW we denote the class of lexicalized RRWW-automata that simultaneously have word-expansion of degree m and alphabet-expansion of degree j. The corresponding classes of characteristic languages are denoted by $\mathcal{L}_C(\mathsf{W}(m)$-RRWW$)$ and $\mathcal{L}_C(\mathsf{WA}(m, j)$-RRWW$)$, respectively, and the corresponding classes of proper languages are denoted by $\mathcal{L}_P(\mathsf{W}(m)$-RRWW$)$ and $\mathcal{L}_P(\mathsf{WA}(m, j)$-RRWW$)$, respectively. The monotone variants of these classes will be distinguished by the additional prefix mon-.

Theorem 7. *If* M *is a* $\mathsf{W}(m)$-RRWW-*automaton for some constant* $m \geq 0$, *then the membership problem for the language* $L_P(M)$ *is solvable in deterministic polynomial time.*

Proof. Assume that $M = (Q, \Sigma, \Gamma, \mathfrak{c}, \$, q_0, k, \delta)$ is a lexicalized RRWW-automaton with word-expansion of degree $m \geq 0$. Then a word $w \in \Sigma^*$ belongs to the language $L_P(M)$ if and only if there exists an expansion $u \in \Gamma^*$ of w such that $u \in L_C(M)$. Thus, u is obtained from w by inserting at most m auxiliary letters. There are $j := |\Gamma \smallsetminus \Sigma|$ many such symbols available to M, and there are $\binom{|w|+m}{m}$ options to place m symbols within the expanded version of w of length $|w| + m$. Hence, there are at most $\binom{|w|+m}{m} \cdot j^{m+1}$ many words of the form required for u. Accordingly, these words can be enumerated in a systematic way, and for each of them it can be checked in linear time whether or not it belongs to $L_C(M)$ (Proposition 3). This gives the announced result. Actually, the resulting time bound is $O(j^{m+1} \cdot (n + m)^{m+1}) = O(n^{m+1})$. $\qquad \square$

Here we are particularly interested in the classes $\mathcal{L}_P(W(m)(\text{-mon})\text{-RRWW})$ and $\mathcal{L}_P(WA(m,j)(\text{-mon})\text{-RRWW})$. As monotone deterministic RR-automata accept the deterministic context-free languages [4], we have the following result.

Proposition 8. $DCFL = \mathcal{L}_P(W(0)\text{-mon-RRWW}) = \mathcal{L}_C(W(0)\text{-mon-RRWW})$.

Thus, the proper languages of lexicalized RRWW-automata with word-expansion of degree 0 are exactly the deterministic context-free languages, while the proper languages of lexicalized RRWW-automata with unbounded word-expansion cover all context-free languages (Theorem 5). Accordingly, the degree of word-expansion of lexicalized RRWW-automata can be interpreted as a measure for the degree of nondeterminism of context-free languages. It remains to be shown that the resulting classes of proper languages form an infinite hierarchy. For doing so we consider a number of example languages.

We begin with $L_3 := \bigcup_{1 \leq k \leq 3}\{\, a^n(b^k)^n \mid n \geq 0 \,\}$ over $\Sigma_0 := \{a, b\}$.

Proposition 9. $L_3 \in \mathcal{L}_P(WA(1,1)\text{-mon-RRWW}) \smallsetminus \mathcal{L}_P(W(0)\text{-RRWW})$.

Proof. Here, as well as in the proofs that follow, we use upper case letters to denote auxiliary symbols.

Let M_3 be the RRWW-automaton that is given through the following meta-instructions:

(1) $(\mathfrak{c} \cdot a^*, ab \to \lambda, b^* \cdot \$)$,   (3) $(\mathfrak{c} \cdot aCa^*, abbb \to \lambda, b^+ \cdot \$)$,
(2) $(\mathfrak{c} \cdot Ca^*, abb \to \lambda, b^* \cdot \$)$,   (4) $(\mathfrak{c} \cdot (C + aCbbb + \lambda) \cdot \$, \text{Accept})$.

M_3 is deterministic as to each word over $\Sigma_0 \cup \{C\}$ at most one of its meta-instructions is applicable and the place of rewriting is unambiguous. Also M_3 is monotone, and it is easily seen that $WA(M_3) = (1, 1)$ and that $L_P(M_3) = \Pr^{\Sigma_0}(L_C(M_3)) = L_3$.

In order to show that $L_3 \notin \mathcal{L}_P(W(0)\text{-RRWW})$ it suffices to prove that L_3 is not accepted by any deterministic RRW-automaton. Assume that M' is a deterministic RRW-automaton on $\Gamma = \Sigma = \Sigma_0$ such that $L(M') = L_3$. For $l \geq 0$ and $r \in \{1, 2, 3\}$, we define $v_l^{(r)} := a^l b^{r \cdot l}$. As $v_l^{(r)} \in L_3$, M' accepts on input $v_l^{(r)}$. For sufficiently large values of l, M' cannot accept $v_l^{(3)}$ in a tail computation. Thus, the accepting computation of M' on input $v_l^{(3)}$ begins with a cycle of the form $v_l^{(3)} \vdash_{M'}^c w_1$ for some $w_1 \in \Sigma_0^*$. As M' satisfies the correctness preserving property, it follows that $w_1 = a^{l-s}b^{3l-3s}$ for some integer s satisfying $0 < s < k$, where k denotes the size of the read/write window of M'. Now consider the word $v_l^{(1)} \in L_3$. As M' is deterministic, it will execute the same rewrite operation at the same place as in the cycle $v_l^{(3)} \vdash_{M'}^c w_1$. Continuing with this cycle, M' cannot reject as $v_l^{(1)} \in L_3$, and so M' will restart with the word $a^{l-s}b^{l-3s}$. This, however, contradicts the correctness preserving property, as $a^{l-s}b^{l-3s} \notin L_3$. Thus, $L_3 \neq L(M')$. $\square$

This proof nicely illustrates the proof technique for establishing lower bound results. The next result will be used below.

Proposition 10. *The language of palindromes* $L_{pal} := \{ w \in \Sigma_0^* \mid w = w^R \}$ *belongs to the class* $\mathcal{L}_P(WA(1,1)$-mon-RRWW$)$, *but it is not contained in the class* $\mathcal{L}_P(W(0)$-RRWW$)$, *either.*

Proof. Consider the RRWW-automaton M_{pal} that is given through the following meta-instructions, where $x, y, z, t \in \Sigma_0$ and $x \neq y$:

(1) $(\mathbb{c} \cdot \Sigma_0^*, zxCxxt \to zCxt, \Sigma_0^* \cdot \$)$,
(2) $(\mathbb{c} \cdot \Sigma_0^*, zyxCxyz \to yxCxy, \Sigma_0^* \cdot \$)$,
(3) $(\mathbb{c} \cdot \Sigma_0^*, zyCxyz \to yCxy, \Sigma_0^* \cdot \$)$,
(4) $(\mathbb{c}, \omega \to C, \$)$ for all $\omega \in \{Cx, xCx, xCzx, xzCzx\}$,
(5) $(\mathbb{c} \cdot C \cdot \$, \mathsf{Accept})$.

Let $L_e = \{ wCw^R \mid w \in \Sigma_0^* \}$, that is, L_e contains the palindromes of even length with C inserted in the middle, and let $L_o = \{ wCxw^R \mid w \in \Sigma_0^*, x \in \Sigma_0 \}$, that is, L_o contains the palindromes of odd length with C inserted just to the left of the middle. Let $\alpha \vdash^c_{M_{pal}} \beta$, and assume that one of the meta-instructions (1) to (3) is used in this cycle. If (1) is used, then α and β belong both to L_e, or α and β belong both to L_o, or α and β are both outside of L_{pal}. If (2) is used, then α and β belong both to L_e, or α and β are both outside of L_{pal}. If (3) is used, then α and β belong both to L_o, or α and β are both outside of L_{pal}. It follows by induction that $L_C(M_{pal}) = L_e \cup L_o$, which implies that $L_P(M_{pal}) = L_{pal}$. M_{pal} is deterministic, as to each word over the alphabet $\Sigma_0 \cup \{C\}$ at most one of its meta-instructions applies, and the place of rewriting is unambiguous. Further, M_{pal} is monotone, and $WA(M_{pal}) = (1,1)$.

The proof that $L_{pal} \notin \mathcal{L}_P(W(0)$-RRWW$)$ is similar to the corresponding part in the proof of the previous proposition. $\square$

For $j \in \mathbb{N}_+$, let $L_j := \bigcup_{1 \leq i \leq j} \{ a^n (b^i)^n \mid n \geq 0 \}$, and

$$L_p(1,j) := \{ ucvcw \mid uw \in L_{pal}, |u| \geq |w| \geq 0, \text{ and } v \in L_j \}.$$

Based on the construction of M_{pal} we can construct a monotone RRWW-automaton $M_{1,j}^p$ that has word-alphabet-expansion $(1,j)$ and that satisfies $L_P(M_{1,j}^p) = L_p(1,j)$. In fact, the following result can be proved.

Proposition 11. *For all* $j \in \mathbb{N}_+$, $L_p(1,j) \in \mathcal{L}_P(WA(1,j)$-mon-RRWW$)$, *while for* $j > 1$, $L_p(1,j) \notin \mathcal{L}_P(WA(1,j-1)$-RRWW$)$.

Now, for all $m, j \in \mathbb{N}_+$, let $L_p(m,j) := L_p(1,j) \cdot (\{d\} \cdot L_{pal})^{m-1}$.

Proposition 12. (a) *For all* $m, j \geq 1$, $L_p(m,j) \in \mathcal{L}_P(WA(m,j)$-mon-RRWW$)$.
(b) *For all* $m, j \geq 1$, $L_p(m,j) \notin \mathcal{L}_P(W(m-1)$-RRWW$)$.
(c) *For all* $m \geq 1$ *and* $j \geq 2$, $L_p(m,j) \notin \mathcal{L}_P(WA(m,j-1)$-RRWW$)$.

Proof. A monotone RRWW-automaton $M^p_{m,j}$ with word-alphabet-expansion (m, j) such that $L_P(M^p_{m,j}) = L_p(m, j)$ can be constructed by combining the automaton $M^p_{1,j}$ with an automaton accepting L_{pal}.

Each element of $L_p(m, j)$ is a concatenation of m palindromes, where these palindromes are separated from each other by an occurrence of the symbol d. In addition, the first palindrome contains an insertion of the form $c \cdot a^n \cdot b^{i \cdot n} \cdot c$, where $n \geq 0$ and $i \in \{1, \ldots, j\}$. As a lexicalized RRWW-automaton M' satisfying $L_P(M') = L_p(m, j)$ is deterministic, the middle of each of these palindromes must be marked by an auxiliary symbol. Hence, M' has word-expansion of degree at least m. This proves part (b).

Finally, in processing a word from $L_p(m, j)$, a lexicalized RRWW-automaton M' must be able to distinguish between the j possible values for the parameter i in the factor $c \cdot a^n \cdot b^{i \cdot n} \cdot c$ inserted within the first of the above palindromes. As it scans its tape strictly from left to right, it only has the first of the above-mentioned auxiliary symbols to encode the correct value. It follows that j different auxiliary symbols must be available to M'. This proves part (c). □

From this proposition we obtain the following proper hierarchy results.

Theorem 13. *For all* $X \in \{$RRWW, mon-RRWW$\}$*, we have the following proper inclusions:*

(a) $\mathcal{L}_P(W(m)\text{-}X) \subset \mathcal{L}_P(W(m+1)\text{-}X)$ *for all* $m \geq 0$.

(b) $\mathcal{L}_P(WA(m, j)\text{-}X) \subset \mathcal{L}_P(WA(m+1, j)\text{-}X)$ *for all* $m \geq 0$ *and all* $j \geq 1$.

(b) $\mathcal{L}_P(WA(m, j)\text{-}X) \subset \mathcal{L}_P(WA(m, j+1)\text{-}X)$ *for all* $m, j \geq 1$.

Let M be a lexicalized RRWW-automaton with word-expansion of degree m. Then M necessarily has word-alphabet-expansion (m, j) for some $j \geq 0$. Here j is simply the number of auxiliary symbols of M. Hence, it follows that

$$\bigcup_{j \geq 0} \mathcal{L}_P(WA(m, j)\text{-}(\text{mon-})RRWW) = \mathcal{L}_P(W(m)\text{-}(\text{mon-})RRWW)$$

holds for all $m \geq 0$. Finally, let $L_{pal+} := \bigcup_{i \geq 1}(\{d\} \cdot L_{pal,e})^i$, where $L_{pal,e}$ denotes the language of palindromes of even length.

Proposition 14. $L_{pal+} \notin \mathcal{L}_P(W(m)\text{-}RRWW)$ *for any* $m \geq 0$.

Proof. Let M' be a lexicalized RRWW-automaton with word-expansion of degree m, and let $w := dw_1 dw_2 d \cdots dw_{m+1}$, where $w_1, \ldots, w_{m+1}$ are palindromes of sufficient length over Σ_0^2. In order to enable M' to accept the word w, auxiliary symbols are needed to mark the middle of each of these palindromes just as in the proofs above. However, as M' only has word-expansion of degree m, the middle of at most m of these palindromes can be marked by an auxiliary symbol. It follows that $L_P(M') \neq L_{pal+}$. □

On the other hand, it is easily seen that L_{pal+} is the proper language of the lexicalized RRWW-automaton M_{pal+} on $\Gamma := \{a, b, d, C\}$ that is given through the following meta-instructions, where $f \in \Sigma_0$:

(1) $(\math00 \cdot (dC)^* \cdot d \cdot \Sigma_0^*, fCf \rightarrow C, \Sigma_0^* \cdot (d \cdot \Sigma_0^* \cdot C \cdot \Sigma_0^*)^* \cdot \$)$,

(2) $(\math00 \cdot (dC)^+ \cdot \$, \text{Accept})$.

Obviously, M_{pal+} is monotone, but it has unbounded word expansion. Thus, we obtain the following proper inclusion.

Corollary 15. $\bigcup_{m \geq 0} \mathcal{L}_P(\mathsf{W}(m)\text{-(mon-)RRWW}) \subset \mathcal{L}_P(\mathsf{lex}\text{-(mon-)RRWW})$.

4 Conclusion

We have introduced new measures for the degree of nondeterminism for proper languages of restarting automata: the degree of word-expansion and the word-alphabet-expansion. Based on these measures we have obtained infinite hierarchies of language classes for monotone and for non-monotone RRWW-automata that are (strongly) lexicalized. In the monotone case these classes form an infinite hierarchy between DCFL and CFL. In addition, we have seen that for each finite degree m of word-expansion, the number of available different auxiliary symbols yields an infinite hierarchy within $\mathcal{L}_P(\mathsf{W}(m)(\text{-mon-})\mathsf{RRWW})$.

Any lexicalized RRWW-automaton has word-expansion that is bounded from above by a linear function. It remains to study those languages that are obtained as proper languages of lexicalized RRWW-automata for which the word-expansion is non-constant, but bounded from above by a slowly growing function.

References

1. Kuboň, V., Plátek, M.: A grammar based approach to a grammar checking of free word order languages. In: COLING 1994. 15th International Conference on Computational Linguistics, Kyoto, Japan, vol. II, pp. 906–910 (1994)
2. Lopatková, M., Plátek, M., Kuboň, V.: Modeling syntax of free word-order languages: Dependency analysis by reduction. In: Matoušek, V., Mautner, P., Pavelka, T. (eds.) TSD 2005. LNCS (LNAI), vol. 3658, pp. 140–147. Springer, Heidelberg (2005)
3. Lopatková, M., Plátek, M., Sgall, P.: Functional generative description, restarting automata and analysis by reduction. In: Abstracts of Formal Description of Slavic Languages Conference 6.5 (2006)
4. Jančar, P., Mráz, F., Plátek, M., Vogel, J.: On monotonic automata with a restart operation. Journal of Automata, Languages and Combinatorics 4, 287–311 (1999)
5. Bordihn, H., Dassow, J.: A note on the degree of nondeterminism. In: Developments in Language Theory, pp. 70–80 (1993)
6. Goldstine, J., Kintala, C.M.R., Wotschke, D.: On measuring nondeterminism in regular languages. Information and Computation 86, 179–194 (1990)

7. Goldstine, J., Leung, H., Wotschke, D.: Measuring nondeterminism in pushdown automata. Journal of Computer and System Sciences 71, 440–466 (2005). An extended abstract appeared In: Reischuk, R., Morvan, M. (eds.) STACS 97. LNCS, vol. 1200, pp. 295–306. Springer, Heidelberg (1997)
8. Salomaa, K., Yu, S.: Nondeterminism degrees for context-free languages. In: Dassow, J., Rosenberg, G., Salomaa, A. (eds.) Developments in Language Theory II, Proc., pp. 154–165. World Scientific, Singapore (1996)
9. Otto, F.: Restarting automata. In: Ésik, Z., Martin-Vide, C., Mitrana, V. (eds.) Recent Advances in Formal Languages and Applications. Studies in Computational Intelligence, vol. 25, pp. 269–303. Springer, Berlin (2006)
10. Hopcroft, J., Ullman, J.: Introduction to Automata Theory, Languages, and Computation. Addison-Wesley, Reading, MA (1980)

Efficient Computation of Throughput
Values of Context-Free Languages

Didier Caucal[1], Jurek Czyzowicz[2], Wojciech Fraczak[2], and Wojciech Rytter[3]

[1] IGM-CNRS, Marne-la-Vallée, France
[2] Dépt d'informatique, Université du Québec en Outaouais, Gatineau PQ, Canada
[3] Inst. of Informatics, Warsaw University, Warsaw, Poland
fraczak@gmail.com

Abstract. We give the first deterministic polynomial time algorithm that computes the *throughput* value of a given context-free language L. The language is given by a grammar G of size n, together with a weight function assigning a positive weight to each symbol. The *weight* of a word $w \in L$ is defined as the sum of weights of its symbols (with multiplicities), and the *mean weight* is the weight of w divided by length of w. The *throughput* of L, denoted by *throughput(L)*, is the smallest real number t, such that the mean value of each word of L is not smaller than t. Our approach, to compute *throughput(L)*, consists of two phases. In the first one we convert the input grammar G to a grammar G', generating a finite language L', such that *throughput(L) = throughput(L')*. In the next phase we find a word of the smallest mean weight in a finite language L'. The size of G' is polynomially related to the size of G.

The problem is of practical importance in system-performance analysis, especially in the domain of network packet processing, where one of the important parameters is the *"guaranteed throughput"* of a system for on-line network packet processing.

Keywords: context-free grammar, push-down automaton, throughput, minimal mean weight.

1 Introduction

In this paper we propose the first polynomial time algorithm computing the throughput of context-free languages. An algorithm computing the approximation of the value of throughput of a context-free grammar was proposed in [1]. The algorithms are applicable in the context of system-performance analysis, particularly in the context of network packet processing. As described in [7], the essential criterion for the evaluation of a system is the measure of its worst case speed of processing data, i.e., its *throughput*. More precisely, this criterion is the lower bound (the infimum) of the greatest ratio of the length of processed input packet to its processing time, taken over all possible input packets. In some cases, a simple system allows a representation by a regular language (a finite automaton) with each alphabet symbol representing a constant time *task* consuming a constant amount of packet data. As noted in [2], in such a case

Jan Holub and Jan Žd'árek (Eds.): CIAA 2007, LNCS 4783, pp. 203–213, 2007.

any standard algorithm for minimum mean cycle calculation, e.g., [5], would do. In practice, however, especially when more complex systems are analyzed and a better accuracy is required, context-free grammars have to be used to adequately describe the behavior of the systems. As a consequence, the practical worst case throughput computation of a system is equivalent to the context-free grammar throughput computation, which is the subject of this paper.

2   Notation

Let Σ be a finite alphabet with a weight function $\rho : \Sigma \mapsto \mathbb{N}$, where $\mathbb{N}$ is the set of positive integers. A word over Σ is any finite sequence of letters. The set of all words is denoted by Σ^*, and the set of all non-empty words by Σ^+. The length of a word w is denoted by $|w|$ and the empty word is denoted by ε.

The weight function defined over Σ extends onto non-empty words in the following way:

$$\rho(a_1 a_2 \cdots a_n) \overset{\text{def}}{=} \rho(a_1) + \rho(a_2) + \cdots \rho(a_n).$$

The *mean weight* of a non-empty word w is defined as

$$\overline{\rho}(w) \overset{\text{def}}{=} \frac{\rho(w)}{|w|}.$$

Given a non-empty language $L \subseteq \Sigma^+$, we define *throughput* of L as the infimum of the mean weight of all words of L:

$$throughput(L) \overset{\text{def}}{=} \inf \{\overline{\rho}(w) \mid w \in L\}.$$

In other words, *throughput* of L is a real value $t \in \mathbb{R}$ such that:

1. $\forall w \in L, \ \overline{\rho}(w) \geq t$, and
2. $\forall \epsilon > 0, \exists w \in L, \ \overline{\rho}(w) < t + \epsilon$.

Note that the mean weight of a word w is independent of the order of symbols used in w. Hence, the alphabet commutativity may be used in our approach. Parikh [6] showed that the commutative image of every context-free language is the commutative image of some regular language. Consequently, for every context-free language L we can find a regular language R such that $throughput(L) = throughput(R)$. However, a direct transformation of a language given by a context-free grammar G to a commutatively equivalent regular expression (or a finite automaton) may yield the result of an exponential size with respect to the size of G. Also, it is worth noting that the Hopkins-Kozen acceleration methods from [4,3], which are built around the Parikh's theorem, do not apply in the context of throughput calculation.

A context-free grammar $G = (\Sigma, N, P, S)$ is composed of a finite set Σ of *terminals*, a finite set N of *nonterminals* disjoint from Σ, a finite set $P \subseteq N \times (N \cup \Sigma)^*$ of *production rules*, and an axiom $S \in N$. The *size of the grammar* is defined as the sum of the number of terminals, nonterminals, and the lengths of right hand sides of production rules.

A context-free grammar $G = (\Sigma, N, P, S)$ defines the set of *syntax trees*, i.e., ordered rooted trees with inner nodes labeled by nonterminals and leaves labeled by $\Sigma \cup \{\varepsilon\}$. For every inner node v labeled by $X \in N$, with k children $v_1, \ldots, v_k$ there exists a production $X \to A_1, \ldots, A_k \in P$, with $A_i \in \Sigma \cup N$, such that v_i is labeled by A_i, for $i \in [1, k]$; otherwise $k = 1$, $X \to \varepsilon \in P$, and v_1 is a leaf labeled by ε.

Every syntax tree T defines a word $w(T)$ over Σ; it is the concatenation of its leaf labels (read from left to right). The set of all words over Σ generated by all syntax trees of a grammar $G = (\Sigma, N, P, S)$ with root labeled by $A \in N \cup \Sigma$, is denoted by $L_G(A)$. E.g., if $A = a \in \Sigma$, $L_G(a) = \{a\}$. The language of G is defined as $L_G(S)$ and denoted by $L(G)$.

Every grammar G of size n may be converted in $O(n)$ time to a *2-reduced* grammar G' of size $O(n)$, such that $L(G) = L(G')$. A grammar is *2-reduced* if it is trimmed (there are no useless nonterminals), and each of its production rules has zero, one or two symbols on the right-hand side. Assume that the grammar does not generate the empty word. Nevertheless, it can still use the empty production rules (i.e., rules with ε on the right-hand side). However, the empty rules can be removed from the grammar without affecting the generated language and increasing the size of the grammar linearly. We omit the proof. Therefore, without loss of generality, we assume, until the end of the paper, that the language L does not contain the empty word and that the context-free grammars under consideration are 2-reduced grammars without empty rules.

3   Throughput of a Finite Language

In the case of an infinite language it is possible that its throughput is not equal to the mean weight of any of its words, e.g., as it is the case for the regular language ab^*, when $\rho(a) > \rho(b)$.

However, in the case of a finite language L there always exists a word in L, whose mean weight equals the throughput of L.

In this section we give an algorithm which, given a grammar generating a finite language L, finds a word w such that $\overline{\rho}(w) = throughput(L)$.

Let $L \subset \Sigma^+$ be a finite non-empty language with weight function $\rho : \Sigma \mapsto \mathbb{N}$. Given a positive real value t, we define *throughput balance* of L with respect to t, denoted by $tb(L, t)$, as the following real value:

$$tb(L, t) \overset{\text{def}}{=} \min \{(\rho(w) - |w|t) \mid w \in L\}$$

Intuitively, $tb(L, t)$ can be seen as a measurement of the "surplus/deficit" of L with respect to a given throughput t; If $tb(L, t) > 0$ (resp., $tb(L, t) < 0$) then language L has a "surplus" (resp., "deficit") in achieving throughput t.

Note 1. The real value $tb(L,t)$, which may be negative, corresponds to the minimal weight of a word in L with respect to the modified weight function $\rho_t : \Sigma \mapsto \mathbb{R}$ defined as $\rho_t(a) \stackrel{\text{def}}{=} \rho(a) - t$.

Lemma 2. *Let L be a finite language over a weighted alphabet and t be a positive real value. We have:*

$$tb(L,t) \geq 0 \iff throughput(L) \geq t$$

Proof. L is finite, hence $throughput(L) = \min_{w \in L} \overline{\rho}(w)$.

$$\min_{w \in L} \frac{\rho(w)}{|w|} \geq t \iff \min_{w \in L} \left(\frac{\rho(w)}{|w|} - t \right) \geq 0 \iff \min_{w \in L} \frac{\rho(w) - |w|t}{|w|} \geq 0$$

consequently we have that for all $w \in L$, $|w| > 0$:

$$\min_{w \in L} \frac{\rho(w) - |w|t}{|w|} \geq 0 \iff tb(L,t) \geq 0.$$

$\square$

Lemma 3. *Let $G = (\Sigma, N, P, S)$ be a grammar of size n generating a non-empty finite language $L \subset \Sigma^+$ with weight function $\rho : \Sigma \to \mathbb{N}$. Given a positive real value t, we can decide in $O(n)$ time whether $throughput(L) \geq t$.*

Proof. By Note 1 and Lemma 2, deciding whether $throughput(L) \geq t$ can be done by finding the minimal weight of a word in L with respect to the modified weight function ρ_t.

For all $a \in \Sigma$, we have $tb(L_G(a),t) = \rho_t(a) = \rho(a) - t$.

L is finite, consequently there exists a partial ordering of the nonterminals of G, such that for any $X, Y \in N$ we have $X < Y$ if there exists a syntax tree of some word of L in which X is a descendant of Y. We topologically sort, in $O(n)$ time, the nonterminals of G, which gives such an ordering.

Then, for every $X \in N$, in the increasing order, we compute $tb(L_G(X),t)$.

More precisely, $tb(L_G(X),t)$ is computed as the minimum, over all rules with X on the left side, of the sums of the throughput balances of the right-hand side symbols. The value $tb(L_G(X),t)$ is stored in an array requiring $O(|N|)$ memory space.

Each production rule is taken into consideration once only, consequently the overall cost is linear in the size of the input grammar. $\square$

The following lemma shows that we can bound the density of the set of mean weights of words of a finite language.

Lemma 4. *Let $L \subset \Sigma^+$ be a finite language, $\rho : \Sigma \mapsto \mathbb{N}$ a weight function, and m the maximum length of a word of L, i.e., $m = \max\{|w| \mid w \in L\}$. The minimum difference between mean weight of two words of L is not smaller than $\frac{1}{m^2}$. I.e., for every $w_1, w_2 \in L$:*

$$\overline{\rho}(w_1) > \overline{\rho}(w_2) \implies \overline{\rho}(w_1) - \overline{\rho}(w_2) \geq \frac{1}{m^2}.$$

Proof. We have:

$$\Delta = \frac{\rho(w_1)}{|w_1|} - \frac{\rho(w_2)}{|w_2|} > 0, \quad |w_1||w_2|\Delta = |w_2|\rho(w_1) - |w_1|\rho(w_2) > 0.$$

Since $|w_2|\rho(w_1) - |w_1|\rho(w_2)$ is an integer, $|w_1||w_2|\Delta \geq 1$. i.e., $\Delta \geq \frac{1}{m^2}$. □

Theorem 5. *Let G be a grammar of size n defining a finite language L with weight function ρ over alphabet Σ such that $\max_{a \in \Sigma} \rho(a) - \min_{a \in \Sigma} \rho(a) = d$. There exists an $O(n \log md)$ time algorithm that computes throughput(L), where m is the maximum length of a word of L.*

Proof. The throughput of L belongs to the interval $[\min_{a \in \Sigma} \rho(a), \max_{a \in \Sigma} \rho(a)]$. Using Lemma 3, we can perform a binary search in this interval to determine the sub-interval $[r - \frac{1}{m^2}, r]$, for some real value r, which must contain the throughput of L, i.e., $r - \frac{1}{m^2} \leq$ throughput$(L) \leq r$ or equivalently, by Lemma 2,

$$tb(L, r - \frac{1}{m^2}) \geq 0 \geq tb(L, r).$$

Let w_r be that word from L for which $\rho_r(w_r) = tb(L, r)$. One can show that $\overline{\rho}(w_r)$ and throughput(L) are both in the interval. Consequently, by Lemma 4, throughput$(L) = \overline{\rho}(w_r)$.

The binary search reducing an interval of size d to a size not bigger than $\frac{1}{m^2}$ takes $O(\log md)$ iterations and, by Lemma 3, each iteration works in $O(n)$ time. Finding word w_r and then computing its mean weight $\overline{\rho}(w_r)$ can be done in $O(n)$ time. For that, during the last iteration the procedure described in the proof of Lemma 3 has to be slightly extended; for every $X \in N$, we need to store a production rule correponding to the throughput balance $tb(L_G(X), r)$, i.e., for which the sum of the throughput balance of the right-hand side symbols equals $tb(L_G(X), r)$. The set of the stored production rules defines a one-word grammar corresponding to w_r, from which $\overline{\rho}(w_r)$ can be easily calculated in $O(|N|)$ time. Thus, the overall time complexity of finding throughput(L) is $O(n \log md)$. □

4   Throughput Invariant Grammar Transformation

In this section we show how to convert any context-free grammar $G = (\Sigma, N, P, S)$ into another grammar $G' = (\Sigma, N', P', S')$ that generates a finite language, such that throughput$(L(G)) =$ throughput$(L(G'))$. The main idea behind the transformation is the observation that the throughput of $L(G)$ is either equal to the mean weight of some word $w \in L(G)$, whose syntax tree is at most of depth $|N|$, or it is equal to the mean weight of some word $w_1 w_2 \in \Sigma^+$, not necessarily in $L(G)$, such that there exists in G a syntax tree T_X of type as shown in Figure 1, for some $X \in N$.

Let $G = (\Sigma, N, P, S)$ be a 2-reduced grammar of size n. We define the following grammar $Fin(G) \stackrel{\text{def}}{=} G' = (\Sigma, N', P', S')$ generating a finite language as follows:

Fig. 1. Syntax tree T_X: nodes v_0 and v_1 are labeled by the same nonterminal X

- The set of nonterminals N' is defined as the union $N' = N'_f \cup N'_r \cup \{S'\}$, where:
  - S' is the new axiom symbol,
  - For every $X \in N$ and $k \in \{1, \ldots, |N|\}$ there is a nonterminal X_k in N'_f. Intuitively, for every nonterminal $X \in N$, we create $|N|$ nonterminals $X_1, \ldots, X_{|N|}$ in N'_f; $L_{G'}(X_k)$ will correspond to the finite subset of $L_G(X)$ with syntax trees not higher than k. In particular, if $L_G(X)$ is finite then $L_G(X) = L_{G'}(X_{|N|})$.
  - For every $X, Y \in N$ and $k \in \{1, \ldots, |N|\}$, there is X_k^Y in N'_r.
    We say that $X \in N$ is *recursive* if there is a syntax tree in G with two nodes both labeled by X and such that one node is a proper ancestor of the other. For every recursive nonterminal $X \in N$ and a nonterminal $Y \in N$, we create $|N|$ nonterminals $X_1^Y, \ldots, X_{|N|}^Y$ in N'_r. For every syntax tree in G' with its root labeled by $X_{|N|}^X$ there will exist an infinite number of syntax trees in G as depicted in Figure 2.

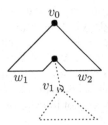

Fig. 2. Every syntax tree in G' (solid lines) corresponds to an initial part of many syntax trees in G (solid and dashed lines). The root v_0 is labeled by $X_{|N|}^X$ in G' and by X in G. Every inner node on the path from v_0 to v_1 is labeled by Y_k^X in G', for some $Y \in N$ and $k \in \{1, \ldots, |N|\}$, and by Y in G. All other inner nodes of solid-line tree are labeled by Y_k in G', for some $Y \in N$ and $k \in \{1, \ldots, |N|\}$, and by Y in G. The subtree rooted in v_1 (dashed lines) is any syntax tree in G with v_1 labeled by X.

- The set of production rules is the union $P' = P_f \cup P_r \cup P_i$.

  In order to define those production rules we will introduce the following partial mappings:

$\psi : \mathbb{N} \times (N \cup \Sigma) \mapsto (N'_f \cup \Sigma)^*$ — is defined as

$$\psi(k, A) \stackrel{\text{def}}{=} \begin{cases} A & \text{if } A \in \Sigma \\ A_{k-1} & \text{if } A \in N, k > 1 \\ \texttt{undefined} & \text{otherwise} \end{cases}$$

$\phi : \mathbb{N} \times N \times (N \cup \Sigma) \mapsto (N'_r \cup \Sigma)^*$ — is defined as

$$\phi(k, X, A) \stackrel{\text{def}}{=} \begin{cases} \varepsilon & \text{if } A = X \\ A^X_{k-1} & \text{if } A \in N, A \neq X, k > 1 \\ \texttt{undefined} & \text{otherwise} \end{cases}$$

- For every $X \to A_1 \cdots A_j \in P$ and $k \in \{1, \ldots, |N|\}$ such that $\psi(k, A_i)$ is defined for all $i \in \{1, \ldots, j\}$, there is a rule

$$X_k \to \psi(k, A_1) \cdots \psi(k, A_j)$$

in P_f.
- For every $X \to A_1 \cdots A_j \in P$, $Y \in N$, $k \in \{1, \ldots, |N|\}$, and $l \in \{1, \ldots, j\}$, such that $\phi(k, Y, A_l)$ and $\psi(k, A_i)$ are defined for all $i \in \{1, \ldots, l-1, l+1, \ldots, j\}$, there is a rule

$$X^Y_k \to \psi(k, A_1) \cdots \psi(k, A_{l-1}) \phi(k, Y, A_i) \psi(k, A_{l+1}) \cdots \psi(k, A_j)$$

in P_r.
- $P_i = \{S' \to X^X_{|N|} \mid X \in N\} \cup \{S' \to S_{|N|}\}$

The new grammar G' generates a finite number of syntax trees not higher than $|N| + 1$. G' is of size $O(n^3)$, where n is the size of G.

Example 6. Consider the following context-free grammar $G = (\Sigma, N, P, S)$ where

- $\Sigma = \{a, b, c\}$,
- $N = \{X, Y\}$,
- $P = \{X \to b, \ X \to aY, \ Y \to Xc\}$,
- $S = X$.

The corresponding finite language grammar $Fin(G) = G' = (\Sigma, N', P', S')$ is:

- $N' = N'_f \cup N'_r \cup \{S'\}$, where:
  $N'_f = \{X_1, X_2, Y_1, Y_2\}$
  $N'_r = \{X^X_1, X^X_2, Y^X_1, Y^X_2, X^Y_1, X^Y_2, Y^Y_1, Y^Y_2\}$
- $P' = P_f \cup P_r \cup P_i$ where:
  $P_f = \{X_2 \to b, \ X_1 \to b, \ X_2 \to aY_1, \ Y_2 \to X_1 c\}$
  $P_r = \{X^X_2 \to aY^X_1, \ Y^X_2 \to c, \ Y^X_1 \to c, \ X^Y_2 \to a, \ X^Y_1 \to a, \ Y^Y_2 \to X^Y_1 c\}$
  $P_i = \{S' \to X_2, \ S' \to X^X_2, \ S' \to Y^Y_2\}$

After trimming, the grammar has the following set of productions:

$$X_2 \rightarrow b, \ X_2^X \rightarrow aY_1^X, \ Y_1^X \rightarrow c, \ X_1^Y \rightarrow a, \ Y_2^Y \rightarrow X_1^Y c,$$
$$S' \rightarrow X_2, \ S' \rightarrow X_2^X, \ S' \rightarrow Y_2^Y.$$

with axiom S'. The language of the grammar is $\{b, ac\}$.

In order to prove that $throughput(L(G)) = throughput(L(G'))$ we need some auxiliary results (the proof is omitted).

Lemma 7. *For all $w, u \in \Sigma^+$ we have:*

$$\overline{p}(w) \leq \overline{p}(u) \ \Rightarrow \ \overline{p}(w) \leq \overline{p}(wu) = \overline{p}(uw) \leq \overline{p}(u).$$

Let T be a syntax tree of G. By $\langle T \rangle$ we denote the number of different pairs of nodes (v_1, v_2) of T such that v_1 and v_2 both carry the same label, and v_1 is a proper ancestor of v_2.

Lemma 8. *Let $G = (\Sigma, N, P, S)$ and $G' = (\Sigma, N', P', S')$ be context-free grammars such that $G' = Fin(G)$. For every syntax tree T of G either:*

1. *there exists a word $w' \in L(G')$ such that $\overline{p}(w') \leq \overline{p}(w(T))$; or*
2. *there exists a syntax tree T_0 of G such that $\langle T_0 \rangle < \langle T \rangle$ and $\overline{p}(w(T_0)) \leq \overline{p}(w(T))$.*

Proof. If $\langle T \rangle = 0$ then by construction of G', $w(T) \in L_{G'}(S_{|N|}) \subseteq L(G')$ and the first statement of the lemma holds.

Otherwise, consider Figure 3, where $w(T) = u_1 u_2 u_3 u_4 u_5$. Let (v_1, v_2) denote a pair of occurrences of the same nonterminal $X \in N$ in the syntax tree T, such that the level of v_1 is minimal, i.e., there is no pair of nodes (p_1, p_2) in the syntax tree T and that p_1 is a proper descendant of v_1 and p_1, p_2 have the same labels. Therefore, in the syntax tree T the distance between v_1 and v_2, and between v_1 and all the leaves of v_1 which are not leaves of v_2 (i.e., u_2, u_4) is at most $|N|$.

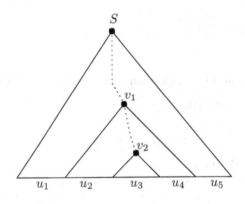

Fig. 3. A syntax tree T with $\langle T \rangle > 0$. Nodes v_1 and v_2 are labeled by the same nonterminal

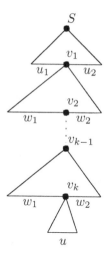

Fig. 4. A syntax tree T_k of $G = (\Sigma, N, P, S)$ generating word $u_1 w_1^k u w_2^k u_2$. Nodes $v_1, \ldots, v_k$ are all labeled by the same $X \in N$.

Thus, $u_2 u_4$ is a word in $L_{G'}(X_{|N|}^X)$, i.e., in $L_{G'}(S')$, and the tree T_0 obtained from T by replacing sub-tree v_1 by v_2, is the syntax tree of G such that $\langle T_0 \rangle < \langle T \rangle$ and $w(T_0) = u_1 u_3 u_5$. By Lemma 7, either $\bar{\rho}(u_2 u_4) \leq \bar{\rho}(w(T))$ or $\bar{\rho}(u_1 u_3 u_5) \leq \bar{\rho}(w(T))$. $\qquad \square$

Lemma 9. *For each word* $w \in L(G)$, *there exists a word* $w' \in L(G')$, *such that* $\bar{\rho}(w') \leq \bar{\rho}(w)$.

Proof. By induction on $\langle T \rangle$ for a syntax tree for w in G using Lemma 8. $\qquad \square$

Lemma 10. *For any* $\epsilon > 0$ *there exists a word* $w \in L(G)$, *such that*

$$\bar{\rho}(w) < throughput(L(G')) + \epsilon \ .$$

Proof. G' generates a finite language, consequently there exists a non-empty word $w_0 \in L(G')$, such that $\bar{\rho}(w_0) = throughput(L(G'))$.

If w_0 is generated by a syntax tree with its root labeled by a nonterminal $X_{|N|} \in N_f'$, by construction of G', we have $w_0 \in L(G)$, and the statement of the lemma is obviously true.

Otherwise, w_0 is generated by a syntax tree T' of G' with its root labeled by $X_{|N|}^X \in N_r'$, as depicted in Figure 2 (solid lines), with $w_0 = w_1 w_2$.

For every $k > 0$ there exists a syntax tree T_k of G, as depicted in Figure 4, which generates $u_1 w_1^k u w_2^k u_2$ for some $u_1, u_2, u \in \Sigma^*$.

For any $\epsilon > 0$ and any $y \in \Sigma^*$, there exists a sufficiently large k such that

$$\bar{\rho}(w_0^k y) < \bar{\rho}(w_0) + \epsilon$$

In particular, for $y = u_1uu_2$, we have

$$\overline{\rho}(w(T_k)) = \overline{\rho}(u_1w_1^kuw_2^ku_2) = \overline{\rho}(w_0^ku_1uu_2) < \overline{\rho}(w_0) + \epsilon,$$

which proves the statement of the lemma.   □

Lemmas 9 and 10 imply directly that our transformation of a context-free grammar does not change the throughput of the language. This can be formulated formally as follows:

Lemma 11. *For every context-free grammar G, we have:*

$$throughput(L(G)) = throughput(L(Fin(G))) .$$

5   Polynomial-Time Algorithm for Throughput Computation of a Context-Free Language

Results from two previous sections, namely Theorem 5 and Lemma 11 lead us to the following procedure calculating throughput of a language given by a context-free grammar G.

Algorithm Throughput-Calculation;

Phase 1: Compute grammar $G' = Fin(G)$ as described in Section 4;
Phase 2: Find the throughput of $L(G')$ and report it as the throughput of $L(G)$.

Theorem 12. *Let $G = (\Sigma, N, P, S)$ be a context-free grammar of size n, and $\rho : \Sigma \mapsto \mathbb{N}$ a weigh function such that $\max_{a \in \Sigma} \rho(a) - \min_{a \in \Sigma} \rho(a) = d$. There exists an $O(n^4 + n^3 \log d)$ time algorithm finding throughput$(L(G))$.*

Proof. We have already proved that the two step procedure for calculating throughput of $L(G)$ gives the correct result.

By construction, transformation $Fin(G)$ yields a context free grammar G' of size $O(n^3)$ with all syntactic trees no higher than n. Thus, the maximum length m of a word from $L(G')$ is in $O(2^n)$.

Finally, by Theorem 5, finding the throughput of $L(G')$ takes $O((n^3) \log md)$ time, i.e., $O(n^4 + n^3 \log d)$ since m is in $O(2^n)$.   □

6   Conclusions

We presented the first polynomial-time algorithm computing the throughput of context-free languages. The only previously known solution to this problem was an approximate approach presented in [1]. Our solution may be viewed as a generalization of the technique of Karp [5], working for finite digraphs, to the case of the class of graphs generated by context-free grammars. However, the approach presented here is different from that given by Karp.

Unfortunately the complexity of our approach is substantially higher. An open problem is then to improve the proposed time complexity, possibly by using a completely different approach. In particular, one can try to exploit explicitly the commutative property of the given grammar, i.e., the fact that permuting the symbols of a word or permuting the symbols on the right-hand side of production rules does not affect the throughput of the generated language. We implicitly used (to some extent) the commutation property in our paper while we constructed the transformation *Fin* of a given grammar to one generating a finite language. The resulting language, though finite, could be of doubly exponential size. Fortunately it was possible to overcome the doubly exponential barrier.

More explicit, direct application of the commutation property may lead to better algorithmic bounds.

Our interest in this problem was directly fuelled by its application in system-performance analysis and, more precisely, in the performance measurement of network packet processing engines. We believe that other applications, in particular in string processing or some optimization problems are also possible.

References

1. Czyzowicz, J., Fraczak, W., Yazdani, M.: Throughput of high-performance concatenation state machines. In: AWOCA 2005. Proceedings of the sixteenth Australasian Workshop on Combinatorial Algorithms, pp. 85–94 (2005)
2. Dasdan, A., Gupta, R.: Faster maximum and minimum mean cycle algorithms for system-performance analysis. IEEE Transactions on Computer-Aided Design of Integrated Circuits and Systems 17(10), 889–899 (1998)
3. Esparza, J., Kiefer, S., Luttenberger, M.: On fixed point equations over commutative semirings. In: Thomas, W., Weil, P. (eds.) STACS 2007. LNCS, vol. 4393, pp. 296–307. Springer, Heidelberg (2007)
4. Hopkins, M.W., Kozen, D.: Parikh's theorem in commutative Kleene algebra. In: Logic in Computer Science, pp. 394–401 (1999)
5. Karp, R.M.: A characterization of the minimum cycle mean in a digraph. Discrete Mathematics 23, 309–311 (1978)
6. Parikh, R.J.: On context-free languages. J. ACM 13(4), 570–581 (1966)
7. Yazdani, M., Fraczak, W., Welfeld, F., Lambadaris, I.: A criterion for speed evaluation of content inspection engines. In: ICN/ICONS/MCL 2006. Fifth International Conference on Networking and the International Conference on Systems, pp. 19–24. IEEE Computer Society, Los Alamitos (2006)

Analyzing Ambiguity of Context-Free Grammars

Claus Brabrand[1], Robert Giegerich[2], and Anders Møller[1]

[1] Department of Computer Science, University of Aarhus, Denmark
{brabrand,amoeller}@brics.dk
[2] Practical Computer Science, Faculty of Technology, Bielefeld University, Germany
robert@techfak.uni-bielefeld.de

Abstract. It has been known since 1962 that the ambiguity problem for context-free grammars is undecidable. Ambiguity in context-free grammars is a recurring problem in language design and parser generation, as well as in applications where grammars are used as models of real-world physical structures.

We observe that there is a simple linguistic characterization of the grammar ambiguity problem, and we show how to exploit this to conservatively approximate the problem based on local regular approximations and grammar unfoldings. As an application, we consider grammars that occur in RNA analysis in bioinformatics, and we demonstrate that our static analysis of context-free grammars is sufficiently precise and efficient to be practically useful.

Keywords: CFG ambiguity, regular approximation, RNA analysis.

1 Introduction

When using context-free grammars to describe formal languages, one has to be aware of potential ambiguity in the grammars, that is, the situation where a string may be parsed in multiple ways, leading to different parse trees. We propose a technique for detecting ambiguities in a given grammar. As the problem is in general undecidable [1] we resort to conservative approximation. This is much like, for example, building an $LR(k)$ parse table for the given grammar and checking for conflicts. The analysis we propose has two significant advantages:

1. The $LR(k)$ condition has since its discovery by Knuth in 1965 been known as a powerful test for unambiguity [2]. An example of an even larger class of unambiguous grammars is LR-Regular [3]. However, not even LR-Regular is sufficient for a considerable class of grammars involving palindromic structures, which our technique can handle. Additionally, unlike $LR(k)$, our approach works well without separating lexical descriptions from the grammars.
2. The ambiguity warnings that our approach can produce if a potential ambiguity is detected are more human readable than those typically produced by, for example, Bison [4]. (Any user of Bison or a similar tool will recognize the difficulty in finding the true cause of a conflict being reported.) Our technique is in many cases able to produce shortest possible examples of strings that

Jan Holub and Jan Žd'árek (Eds.): CIAA 2007, LNCS 4783, pp. 214–225, 2007.

may be parsed in multiple ways and precisely identify the relevant location in the grammar, thereby pinpointing the cause of the ambiguity.

An increasing number of parser generators, for example, Bison [4], SDF [5], and Elkhound [6], support general context-free grammars rather than unambiguous subclasses, such as LL(k), LR(k), or LALR(k). Such tools usually handle ambiguities by dynamically (that is, during parsing) disambiguating or merging the resulting parse trees [7,8]. In contrast, our approach is to *statically* analyze the grammars for potential ambiguities. Also, we aim for a *conservative* algorithm, unlike many existing ambiguity detection techniques (e.g. [9,10]). The recent approach by Schmitz is conservative; for a comparison with our approach see the paper [11]. Another conservative approach, expressed in terms of pushdown acceptors, is described in an article by Kuich [12].

In bioinformatics, context-free grammars in various guises have important applications, for example in sequence comparison, motif search, and RNA secondary structure analysis [13,14]. Recently, ambiguity has gained attention in this field, as several important algorithms (such as the Viterbi algorithm on stochastic CFGs) have been shown to deliver incorrect results in the presence of ambiguity [15,16]. The ambiguity problem arises in biosequence analysis from the necessity to check a static property of the dynamic programming algorithms employed – the question whether or not an element of the search space may be evaluated more than once. If so, probabilistic scoring schemes yield incorrect results, and enumeration of near-optimal solutions drowns in redundancy. It may seem surprising that the static analysis of this program property can be approached as a question of language ambiguity on the formal language level. We will explain this situation in some detail in Section 5.

Before we start presenting our method, we state two requirements on a practical ambiguity checker that result from the biosequence analysis domain and must be kept in mind in the sequel: First, the grammars to be checked are actually abstractions from richer programming concepts. They may look strange from a formal language design point of view – for example, they may contain "redundant" nonterminal symbols generating the same language. However, different nonterminals model different physical structures with different semantics that are essential for subsequent algorithmic processing. Hence, the grammar must be checked as is, and cannot be transformed or simplified by, for instance, coalescing such nonterminal symbols. Second, the domain experts are typically molecular biologists with little programming expertise and no training in formal language theory. Hence, when ambiguity is discovered, it must be reported in a way that is meaningful to this category of users.

Besides the applications to biosequence analysis, our motivation behind the work we present here has been analyzing reversibility of transformations between XML and non-XML data [17]. This involves scannerless parsing, that is, lexical descriptions are not separated from the grammars, so LR(k) is not applicable.

Contributions. Despite decades of work on parsing techniques, which in many cases involve the problem of grammar ambiguity, we have been unable to find tools that are applicable to grammars in the areas mentioned above. This paper contributes with the following results:

- We observe that there is a simple linguistic characterization of grammar ambiguity. This allows us to shift from reasoning about grammar derivations to reasoning about purely linguistic properties, such as, language inclusion.
- We show how Mohri and Nederhof's regular approximation technique for context-free grammars [18] can be adapted in a local manner to detect many common sources of ambiguity, including ones that involve palindromic structures. Also, a simple grammar unfolding trick can be used to improve the precision of the analysis.
- We demonstrate that our method can handle "real-world" grammars of varying complexity taken from the bioinformatics literature on RNA analysis, acquitting the unambiguous grammars and pinpointing the sources of ambiguity (with shortest possible examples as witnesses) in two grammars that are in fact ambiguous.

We here work with plain, context-free grammars. Generalizing our approach to work with parsing techniques that involve interoperability with a lexical analyzer, precedence/associativity declarations, or other disambiguation mechanisms is left to future work.

Overview. We begin in Section 2 by giving a characterization of grammar ambiguity that allows us to reason about the *language* of the nonterminals in the grammar rather than the *structure* of the grammar. In particular, we reformulate the ambiguity problem in terms of language intersection and overlap operations. Based on this characterization, we then in Section 3 formulate a general framework for conservatively approximating the ambiguity problem. In Section 4 we show how regular approximations can be used to obtain a particular decidable approximation. Section 5 discusses applications in the area of biosequence analysis where context-free grammars are used to describe RNA structures. It also summarizes a number of experiments that test the precision and performance of the analysis. In the technical report [19] we show how the precision can be improved by selectively unfolding parts of the given grammar, and we provide proofs of the propositions.

2   A Characterization of Grammar Ambiguity

We begin by briefly recapitulating the basic terminology about context-free grammars.

Definition 1 (Context-free grammar and ambiguity). *A context-free grammar (CFG) G is defined by $G = (\mathcal{N}, \Sigma, s, \pi)$ where $\mathcal{N}$ is a finite set of nonterminals, Σ is a finite set of alphabet symbols (or terminals), $s \in \mathcal{N}$ is the start nonterminal, and $\pi : \mathcal{N} \to \mathcal{P}(E^*)$ is the production function where $E = \Sigma \cup \mathcal{N}$. We write $\alpha n \omega \Rightarrow \alpha \theta \omega$ when $\theta \in \pi(n)$ and $\alpha, \omega \in E^*$, and $\Rightarrow^*$ is the reflexive* *transitive closure of* $\Rightarrow$. *We assume that every nonterminal* $n \in \mathcal{N}$ *is reachable from* s *and derives some string, that is,* $\exists \alpha, \phi, \omega \in \Sigma^* : s \Rightarrow^* \alpha n \omega \Rightarrow^* \alpha \phi \omega$. *The language of a sentential form* $\alpha \in E^*$ *is* $\mathcal{L}_G(\alpha) = \{x \in \Sigma^* \mid \alpha \Rightarrow^* x\}$, *and the language of* G *is* $\mathcal{L}(G) = \mathcal{L}_G(s)$.

Assume that $x \in \mathcal{L}(G)$, *that is,* $s = \phi_0 \Rightarrow \phi_1 \Rightarrow \ldots \Rightarrow \phi_n = x$. *Such a derivation sequence gives rise to a* derivation tree *where each node is labeled with a symbol from* E, *the root is labeled* s, *leaves are labeled from* Σ, *and the labels of children of a node with label* e *are in* $\pi(e)$. G *is* ambiguous *if there exists a string* x *in* $\mathcal{L}(G)$ *with multiple derivation trees, and we then say that* x *is* ambiguous relative to G.

We now introduce the properties *vertical* and *horizontal unambiguity* and show that they together characterize grammar unambiguity.

Definition 2 (Vertical and horizontal unambiguity). *A grammar* G *is* vertically unambiguous *iff* $\forall n \in \mathcal{N}, \alpha, \alpha' \in \pi(n), \alpha \neq \alpha' : \mathcal{L}_G(\alpha) \cap \mathcal{L}_G(\alpha') = \emptyset$. *A grammar* G *is* horizontally unambiguous *iff*
$$\forall n \in \mathcal{N}, \alpha \in \pi(n), i \in \{1, \ldots, |\alpha|-1\} : \mathcal{L}_G(\alpha_0 \cdots \alpha_{i-1}) \ \text{\M} \ \mathcal{L}_G(\alpha_i \cdots \alpha_{|\alpha|-1}) = \emptyset$$
where $\text{\M}$ *is the* language overlap *operator defined by*

$$X \ \text{\M} \ Y = \{ xay \mid x, y \in \Sigma^* \wedge a \in \Sigma^+ \wedge x, xa \in X \wedge y, ay \in Y \}.$$

Intuitively, vertical unambiguity means that, during parsing of a string, there is never a choice between two different productions of a nonterminal. The overlap $X \ \text{\M} \ Y$ is the set of strings in XY that can be split non-uniquely in an X part and a Y part. For example, if $X = \{\text{x}, \text{xa}\}$ and $Y = \{\text{a}, \text{ay}\}$ then $X \ \text{\M} \ Y = \{\text{xay}\}$. Horizontal unambiguity then means that, when parsing a string according to a production, there is never any choice of how to split the string into substrings corresponding to the entities in the production.

Proposition 3 (Characterization of Ambiguity).
    G is vertically and horizontally unambiguous $\Leftrightarrow$ *G is unambiguous*

Proof. Intuitively, any ambiguity must result from a choice between two productions of some nonterminal or from a choice of how to split a string according to a single production. A detailed proof is given in [19]. $\square$

This proposition essentially means that we have transformed the problem of context-free grammar ambiguity from a *grammatical* property to a *linguistic* property dealing solely with the languages of the nonterminals in the grammar rather than with derivation trees. As we shall see in the next section, this characterization can be exploited to obtain a good conservative approximation for the problem without violating the two requirements described in Section 1.

Note that this linguistic characterization of grammar ambiguity should not be confused with the notion of *inherently ambiguous languages* [1]. (A language is inherently ambiguous if all its grammars are ambiguous.)

We now give examples of vertical and horizontal ambiguities.

Example 4 (a vertically ambiguous grammar).

Z   : $\boxed{\texttt{A 'y'}}$

| $\boxed{\texttt{'x' B}}$;

A   :   `'x' 'a'`   ;

B   :   `'a' 'y'`   ;

The string **xay** can be parsed in two ways by choosing either the first or the second production of Z. The name *vertical* ambiguity comes from the fact that productions are often written on separate lines as in this example.

Example 5 (a horizontally ambiguous grammar).

Z   : $\boxed{\texttt{'x' A}}\leftrightarrow\boxed{\texttt{B}}$;

A   :   `'a'`

| ε ;

B   :   `'a' 'y'`

| `'y'`   ;

Also here, the string **xay** can be parsed in two ways, by parsing the **a** either in $\boxed{\texttt{'x' A}}$ (using the first production of A and the second of B) or in $\boxed{\texttt{B}}$ (using the second production of A and the first of B). Here, the ambiguity is at a split-point between entities on the right-hand side of a particular production, hence the name *horizontal* ambiguity.

3   A Framework for Conservative Approximation

The characterization of ambiguity presented above can be used as a foundation for a framework for obtaining decidable, conservative approximations of the ambiguity problem. When the analysis says "unambiguous grammar!", we know that this is indeed the case. The key to this technique is that the linguistic characterization allows us to reason about languages of nonterminals rather than derivation trees.

Definition 6 (Grammar over-approximation). *A grammar over-approximation relative to a CFG G is a function* $\mathcal{A}_G : E^* \to \mathcal{P}(\Sigma^*)$ *where* $\mathcal{L}_G(\alpha) \subseteq \mathcal{A}_G(\alpha)$ *for every* $\alpha \in E^*$. *An* approximation strategy $\mathcal{A}$ *is a function that returns a grammar over-approximation* $\mathcal{A}_G$ *given a CFG G.*

Definition 7 (Approximated vertical and horizontal unambiguity). *A grammar G is* vertically unambiguous relative to a grammar over-approximation $\mathcal{A}_G$ *iff*

$$\forall n \in \mathcal{N}, \alpha, \alpha' \in \pi(n), \alpha \neq \alpha' : \mathcal{A}_G(\alpha) \cap \mathcal{A}_G(\alpha') = \emptyset.$$

Similarly, G is horizontally unambiguous relative to $\mathcal{A}_G$ *iff*

$$\forall n \in \mathcal{N}, \alpha \in \pi(n), i \in \{1, \ldots, |\alpha|-1\} : \mathcal{A}_G(\alpha_0 \cdots \alpha_{i-1}) \between \mathcal{A}_G(\alpha_i \cdots \alpha_{|\alpha|-1}) = \emptyset.$$

Finally, we say that an approximation strategy $\mathcal{A}$ *is* decidable *if the following problem is decidable: "Given a grammar G, is G vertically and horizontally unambiguous relative to* $\mathcal{A}_G$*?"*

Proposition 8 (Approximation soundness). *If G is vertically and horizontally unambiguous relative to $\mathcal{A}_G$ then G is unambiguous.*

Proof. The result follows straightforwardly from Definitions 2, 6, and 7 and Proposition 3. For details, see [19].   □

As an example of a decidable but not very useful approximation strategy, the one which returns the constant Σ^* approximation corresponds to the trivial analysis that reports that every grammar may be (vertically and horizontally) ambiguous at all possible locations. In the other end of the spectrum, the approximation strategy which for every grammar G returns $\mathcal{L}_G(\alpha)$ for each α has full precision but is undecidable (since it involves checking language disjointness for context-free grammars).

Also note that two different approximations, $\mathcal{A}_G$ and $\mathcal{A}'_G$, may be combined: the function $\mathcal{A}''_G$ defined by $\mathcal{A}''_G(\alpha) = \mathcal{A}_G(\alpha) \cap \mathcal{A}'_G(\alpha)$ is a grammar over-approximation that subsumes both $\mathcal{A}_G$ and $\mathcal{A}'_G$. Such a pointwise combination is generally better than running the two analyses independently as one of the approximations might be good in one part of the grammar, and the other in a different part.

4   Regular Approximation

One approach for obtaining decidability is to consider *regular* approximations, that is, ones where $\mathcal{A}_G(\alpha)$ is a regular language for each α: the family of regular languages is closed under both intersection and overlap, and emptiness on regular languages is decidable (for an implementation, see [20]). Also, shortest examples can easily be extracted from non-empty regular languages. As a concrete approximation strategy we propose using Mohri and Nederhof's algorithm for constructing regular approximations of context-free grammars [18].

We will not repeat their algorithm in detail, but some important properties are worth mentioning. Given a CFG G, the approximation results in another CFG G' which is right linear (and hence its language is regular), $\mathcal{L}(G) \subseteq \mathcal{L}(G')$, and G' is at most twice the size of G. Whenever $n \Rightarrow^* \alpha n \omega$ and $n \Rightarrow^* \theta$ in G for some $\alpha, \omega, \theta \in E$ and $n \in \mathcal{N}$, the grammar G' has the property that $n \Rightarrow^* \alpha^m \theta \omega^k$ for any m, k. Intuitively, G' keeps track of the order that alphabet symbols may appear in, but it loses track of the fact that α and ω must appear in balance.

Definition 9 (Mohri-Nederhof approximation strategy). *Let MN be the approximation strategy that given a CFG $G = (\mathcal{N}, \Sigma, s, \pi)$ returns the grammar over-approximation MN_G defined by $MN_G(\alpha) = \mathcal{L}(G_\alpha)$ where G_α is the Mohri-Nederhof approximation of the grammar $(\mathcal{N} \cup \{s_\alpha\}, \Sigma, s_\alpha, \pi[s_\alpha \mapsto \{\alpha\}])$ for some $s_\alpha \notin \mathcal{N}$.*

In other words, whenever we need to compute $\mathcal{A}_G(\alpha)$ for some $\alpha \in E^*$, we apply Mohri and Nederhof's approximation algorithm to the grammar G modified to derive α as the first step.

Example 10 (palindromes). A classical example of an unambiguous grammar that is not LR(k) (nor LR-Regular) is the following whose language consists of all palindromes over the alphabet $\{a, b\}$:

```
P  :  'a' P 'a'  |  'b' P 'b'  |  'a'  |  'b'  |  ε  ;
```

Running our analysis on this grammar immediately gives the result "unambiguous grammar!". It computes MN_G for each of the five right-hand sides of productions and all their prefixes and suffixes and then performs the checks described in Definition 7. As an example, $MN_G(\text{'a' P 'a'})$ is the regular language $a(a+b)^*a$, and $MN_G(\text{'b' P 'b'})$ is $b(a+b)^*b$. Since these two languages are disjoint, there is no vertical ambiguity between the first two productions.

A variant of the grammar above is the following language, AntiPalindromes, which our analysis also verifies to be unambiguous:

```
R  :  'a' R 'b'  |  'b' R 'a'  |  'a'  |  'b'  |  ε  ;
```

As we shall see in Section 5, this grammar is closely related to grammars occurring naturally in biosequence analysis.

Example 11 (ambiguous expressions). To demonstrate the capabilities of producing useful warning messages, let us run the analysis on the following tiny ambiguous grammar representing simple arithmetical expressions:

```
Exp[plus]    :    Exp '+' Exp
   [mult]    |    Exp '*' Exp
   [var]     |    'x'          ;
```

(Notice that we allow productions to be labeled.) The analysis output is

```
*** vertical ambiguity: E[plus] <--> E[mult]
    ambiguous string: "x*x+x"
*** horizontal ambiguity at E[plus]: Exp <--> '+' Exp
    ambiguous string: "x+x+x"
*** horizontal ambiguity at E[plus]: Exp '+' <--> Exp
    ambiguous string: "x+x+x"
*** horizontal ambiguity at E[mult]: Exp <--> '*' Exp
    ambiguous string: "x*x*x"
*** horizontal ambiguity at E[mult]: Exp '*' <--> Exp
    ambiguous string: "x*x*x"
```

Each source of ambiguity is clearly identified, even with example strings that have been verified to be non-spurious (of course, it is easy to check with a CFG parser whether a concrete string is ambiguous or not). Obviously, these messages are more useful to a non-expert than, for example, the shift/reduce conflicts and reduce/reduce conflicts being reported by Bison.

5   Application to Biosequence Analysis

The languages of biosequences are trivial from the formal language point of view. The alphabet of DNA is $\Sigma_{\text{DNA}} = \{A, C, G, T\}$, of RNA it is $\Sigma_{\text{RNA}} = \{A, C, G, U\}$, and for proteins it is a 20 letter amino acid code. In each case, the language of biosequences is Σ^*. Biosequence analysis relates two sequences to each other (sequence alignment, similarity search) or one sequence to itself (folding). The latter is our application domain – RNA structure analysis.

RNA is a chain molecule, built from the four *bases* adenine (A), cytosine (C), guanine (G), and uracil (U), connected via a *backbone* of sugar and phosphate. Mathematically, it is a string over Σ_{RNA} of moderate length (compared to genomic DNA), ranging from 20 to 10,000 bases.

RNA forms structure by folding back on itself. Certain bases, located at different positions in the backbone, may form hydrogen bonds. Such bonded *base pairs* arise between *complementary* bases $G - C$, $A - U$, and $G - U$. By forming these bonds, the two pairing bases are arranged in a plain, and this in turn enables them to stack very densely onto adjacent bases also forming pairs. Helical structures arise, which are energetically stable and mechanically rather stiff. They enable RNA to perform its wide variety of functions.

Because of the backbone turning back on itself, RNA structures can be viewed as palindromic languages. Starting from palindromes in the traditional sense (as described in Example 10) we can characterize palindromic languages for RNA structure via five generalizations: (1) a letter does not match to itself but to a complementary base (cf. Example 12); (2) the two arms of a palindrome may be separated by a non-palindromic string (of length at least 3) called a *loop*; (3) the two arms of the palindrome may hold non-pairing bases called *bulges*; (4) a string may hold several adjacent palindromes separated by unpaired bases; and (5) palindromes can be recursively nested, that is, a loop or a bulge may contain further palindromes.

Example 12 (RNA "palindromes" – base pairs only).

```
R   :   'C' R 'G'   |   'G' R 'C'
    |   'A' R 'U'   |   'U' R 'A'
    |   'G' R 'U'   |   'U' R 'G'   |   ε   ;
```

Context-free grammars are used to describe the structures that can be formed by a given RNA sequence. (The grammars G1 through G8, which we describe later, are different ways to achieve this.) All grammars generate the full language Σ^*_{RNA}, the different derivations of a given RNA string corresponding to its possible physical structures in different ways.

Figure 1 shows an RNA sequence and two of its possible structures, presented in the graphical form commonly used in biology, and as a so-called Vienna (or "dot-bracket") string, where base pairs are represented as matching parentheses and unpaired bases as dots.

The number of possible structures under the rules of base pairing is exponentially related to the length of the molecule. In formal language terms, each string has an exponential number of parse trees. This has been termed the "good" ambiguity in a grammar describing RNA structure. The set of all structures is the search space from which we want to extract the "true" structure. This is achieved by evaluating structures under a variety of scoring schemes.

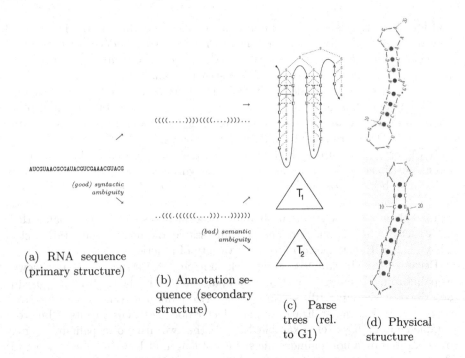

$(((((.....)))))(((((....)))))...$

$\nearrow$

AUCGUAACGCGAUACGUCGAAACGUACG

(good) syntactic
ambiguity

$\searrow$

$...(((.(((((((....)))...))))))$

(bad) semantic
ambiguity

$\searrow$

(a) RNA sequence
(primary structure)

(b) Annotation se-
quence (secondary
structure)

(c) Parse
trees (rel.
to G1)

(d) Physical
structure

Fig. 1. Good and bad ambiguity in RNA folding

A CYK-style parser [21] constructs the search space and applies dynamic programming along the way.

The problem at hand arises when different parse trees correspond to the same physical structure. In Figure 1, parse trees T_1 and T_2 denote different parse trees for the same physical structure, shown to their right. In this case, the scoring schemes are misled. The number of structures is wrongly counted, and the most likely parse does not find the most likely structure. We say that the algorithm exhibits the "bad" kind of ambiguity. It makes no sense to check the grammar for ambiguity *as is*, since (using a phrase from [22]) the bad ambiguity hides within the good.

Fortunately, the grammar can be transformed such that the good ambiguity is eliminated, while the bad persists and can now be checked by formal language techniques such as ours. The grammar remains structurally unchanged in the transformation, but is rewritten to no longer generate RNA sequences, but Vienna strings. They represent structures uniquely, and if one of them has two different parse trees, then the original grammar has the bad type of ambiguity.

We applied our ambiguity checker to several grammars that were obtained by the above transformation from stochastic grammars used in the bioinformatics literature [16,22,23]. Grammars G1 and G2 were studied as ambiguous grammars in [16], and our algorithm nicely points out the sources of ambiguity by indicating shortest ambiguous words. In [16], G2 was introduced as a refinement of G1, to bring it closer to grammars used in practice. Our ambiguity checker detects an extra vertical ambiguity in G2 (see Table 1) and clearly reports it by producing the ambiguous word "()" for the productions P[aPa] and P[S]. Grammars G3 through G8 are unambiguous grammars, taken from the same source. Our approach demonstrates their unambiguity.

Grammars used for thermodynamic RNA folding are rather large in order to accommodate the elaborate free energy model where the energy contribution of a single base or base pair strongly depends on its context. Grammars with bad ambiguity can still be used to find the minimum free energy structure, but not for the enumeration of near-optimal structures, and not for Boltzmann statistics scoring.

The grammar *Voss* from [23] has 28 nonterminals and 65 productions. This grammar clearly asks for automatic support (even for experts in formal grammars). We demonstrate this application in two steps. First, we study a grammar, *Voss-Light*, which demonstrates an essential aspect of the *Voss* grammar: unpaired bases in bulges and loops (the dots in the transformed grammar) must be treated differently, and they hence are derived from different nonterminal symbols even though they recognize the same language. This takes the grammar *Voss-Light* (and consequently also *Voss*) beyond the capacities of, for example, LR(k) parsing, whereas our technique succeeds in verifying unambiguity.

Example 13 (Voss-Light).

```
P  :  '(' P ')'  |  '(' O ')'  ;           // P: closed structure
O  :  L P  |  P R  |  S P S  |  H ;         // O: open structure
L  :  '.' L  |  '.'  ;                       // L: left bulge
R  :  '.' R  |  '.'  ;                       // R: right bulge
S  :  '.' S  |  '.'  ;                       // S: singlestrand
H  :  '.' H  |  '.' '.' '.'  ;               // H: hairpin 3+ loop
```

As the second step, we took the full grammar, which required four simple unfolding transformations (see [19]) due to spurious ambiguities related to multiloops. Our method succeeded to show unambiguity, which implies that the Boltzmann statistics computed according to [23] are indeed correct.

5.1   Summary of Biosequence Analysis Experiments

Table 1 summarizes the results of running our ambiguity analysis and that of LR(k) on the example grammars from biosequence analysis presented in this paper. The first column lists the name of the grammar along with a source reference. The second column quantifies the size of a grammar (in bytes). The third column elaborates this size measure where n is the total number of nonterminals, v is the maximum number of productions for a nonterminal, and h is the maximum number of entities on the right-hand-side of a production. The fourth column shows the results of running automatic LR(k) and LALR(1) analyses: if the grammar is ambiguous, we list the number of shift/reduce and reduce/reduce conflicts as reported by LR(k) for increasing k, starting at $k = 1$. We have manually inspected that the ones marked as non-LR(k) are in fact non-LR-Regular. The last column shows the verdict from our analysis, reporting no false positives.

All example grammars, except *Voss*, take less than a second to analyze (including two levels of unfolding, as explained in [19], in the case of G7 and G8).

Table 1. Benchmark results

Grammar	Bytes	(n, v, h)	LR(k)	Our
Palindromes (Ex. 10)	125	(1,5,3)	**non-LR(k)**	*unamb.*
AntiPalindromes (Ex. 10)	125	(1,5,3)	**non-LR(k)**	*unamb.*
Base pairs (Ex. 12)	144	(1,7,3)	**non-LR(k)**	*unamb.*
G1 [16]	91	(1,5,3)	24/12, 70/36, 195/99, ...	5V + 1H
G2 [16]	126	(2,5,3)	25/13, 59/37, 165/98, ...	6V + 1H
G3 [16]	154	(3,4,3)	**non-LR(k)**	*unamb.*
G4 [16]	115	(2,3,4)	LALR(1)	*unamb.*
G5 [16]	59	(1,3,4)	LALR(1)	*unamb.*
G6 [16]	116	(3,2,3)	LALR(1)	*unamb.*
G7 [16]	261	(5,4,3)	**non-LR(k)**	*unamb.*
G8 [16]	227	(4,3,4)	LALR(1)	*unamb.*
Voss-Light (Ex. 13)	243	(6,4,3)	**non-LR(k)**	*unamb.*
Voss [23]	2,601	(28,9,7)	**non-LR(k)**	*unamb.*

The larger *Voss* grammar takes about a minute on a standard PC. Note that in 7 cases, our technique verifies unambiguity where LR(k) fails.

With the recent *Locomotif* system [24], users draw graphical representation of physical structures (cf. Figure 1(d)), from which in a first step CFGs augmented with scoring functions are generated, which are subsequently compiled into dynamic programming algorithms coded in C. With this system, biologists may generate specialized RNA folding algorithms for many RNA families. Today more than 500 are known, with a different grammar implied by each – and all have to be checked for unambiguity.

6   Conclusion

We have presented a technique for statically analyzing ambiguity of context-free grammars. Based on a linguistic characterization, the technique allows the use of grammar transformations, in particular regular approximation and unfolding, without sacrificing soundness. Moreover, the analysis is often able to pinpoint sources of ambiguity through concrete examples being automatically generated. The analysis may be used when LR(k) and related techniques are inadequate, for example in biosequence analysis, as our examples show. Our experiments indicate that the precision, the speed, and the quality of warning messages are sufficient to be practically useful.

References

1. Hopcroft, J.E., Ullman, J.D.: Introduction to Automata Theory, Languages and Computation. Addison-Wesley, Reading (1979)
2. Knuth, D.E.: On the translation of languages from left to right. Information and Control 8, 607–639 (1965)

3. Culik II, K., Cohen, R.S.: LR-regular grammars - an extension of LR(k) grammars. Journal of Computer and System Sciences 7(1), 66–96 (1973)
4. Scott, E., Johnstone, A., Hussein, S.S.: Tomita style generalised parsers. Technical Report CSD-TR-00-A, Royal Holloway, University of London (2000)
5. Visser, E.: Syntax Definition for Language Prototyping. PhD thesis, University of Amsterdam (1997)
6. McPeak, S., Necula, G.C.: Elkhound: A fast, practical GLR parser generator. In: Duesterwald, E. (ed.) CC 2004. LNCS, vol. 2985, Springer, Heidelberg (2004)
7. van den Brand, M., Scheerder, J., Vinju, J.J., Visser, E.: Disambiguation filters for scannerless generalized LR parsers. In: Horspool, R.N. (ed.) CC 2002 and ETAPS 2002. LNCS, vol. 2304, Springer, Heidelberg (2002)
8. Brabrand, C., Schwartzbach, M.I., Vanggaard, M.: The metafront system: Extensible parsing and transformation. In: LDTA 2003. Proc. 3rd ACM SIGPLAN Workshop on Language Descriptions, Tools and Applications, ACM Press, New York (2003)
9. Gorn, S.: Detection of generative ambiguities in context-free mechanical languages. Journal of the ACM 10(2), 196–208 (1963)
10. Cheung, B.S.N., Uzgalis, R.C.: Ambiguity in context-free grammars. In: SAC 1995. Proc. ACM Symposium on Applied Computing, ACM Press, New York (1995)
11. Schmitz, S.: Conservative ambiguity detection in context-free grammars. In: ICALP 2007. Proc. 34th International Colloquium on Automata, Languages and Programming (2007)
12. Kuich, W.: Systems of pushdown acceptors and context-free grammars. Elektronische Informationsverarbeitung und Kybernetik 6(2), 95–114 (1970)
13. Durbin, R., Eddy, S.R., Krogh, A., Mitchison, G.: Biological Sequence Analysis. Cambridge University Press, Cambridge (1998)
14. Giegerich, R., Meyer, C., Steffen, P.: A discipline of dynamic programming over sequence data. Science of Computer Programming 51(3), 215–263 (2004)
15. Giegerich, R.: Explaining and controlling ambiguity in dynamic programming. In: Giancarlo, R., Sankoff, D. (eds.) CPM 2000. LNCS, vol. 1848, pp. 46–59. Springer, Heidelberg (2000)
16. Dowell, R.D., Eddy, S.R.: Evaluation of several lightweight stochastic context-free grammars for RNA secondary structure prediction. BMC Bioinformatics 5(71) (2004)
17. Brabrand, C., Møller, A., Schwartzbach, M.I.: Dual syntax for XML languages. In: Bierman, G., Koch, C. (eds.) DBPL 2005. LNCS, vol. 3774, Springer, Heidelberg (2005)
18. Mohri, M., Nederhof, M.J.: 9: Regular Approximation of Context-Free Grammars through Transformation. In: Robustness in Language and Speech Technology, Kluwer Academic Publishers, Dordrecht (2001)
19. Brabrand, C., Giegerich, R., Møller, A.: Analyzing ambiguity of context-free grammars. Technical Report RS-07-10, BRICS (2007)
20. Møller, A.: dk.brics.automaton – finite-state automata and regular expressions for Java (2007), http://www.brics.dk/automaton/
21. Aho, A.V., Ullman, J.D.: The Theory of Parsing, Translation and Compiling, vol. 1: Parsing. Prentice-Hall, Englewood Cliffs (1972)
22. Reeder, J., Steffen, P., Giegerich, R.: Effective ambiguity checking in biosequence analysis. BMC Bioinformatics 6(153) (2005)
23. Voss, B., Giegerich, R., Rehmsmeier, M.: Complete probabilistic analysis of RNA shapes. BMC Biology 4(5) (2006)
24. Reeder, J., Giegerich, R.: A graphical programming system for molecular motif search. In: GPCE 2006. Proc. 5th International Conference on Generative Programming and Component Engineering, pp. 131–140. ACM Press, New York (2006)

Efficient Enumeration of Regular Languages

Margareta Ackerman and Jeffrey Shallit

University of Waterloo, Waterloo ON, Canada
mackerma@uwaterloo.ca, shallit@graceland.uwaterloo.ca

Abstract. The cross-section enumeration problem is to list all words
of length n in a regular language L in lexicographical order. The enumeration problem is to list the first m words in L according to radix
order. We present an algorithm for the cross-section enumeration problem that is linear in n. We provide a detailed analysis of the asymptotic
running time of our algorithm and that of known algorithms for both
enumeration problems. We discuss some shortcomings of the enumeration algorithm found in the Grail computation package. In the practical
domain, we modify Mäkinen's enumeration algorithm to get an algorithm
that is usually the most efficient in practice. We performed an extensive
performance analysis of the new and previously known enumeration and
cross-section enumeration algorithms and found when each algorithm is
preferable.

Keywords: enumeration, regular language, nondeterministic finite automaton, lexicographical order, radix order.

1 Introduction

Given an NFA N, we wish to enumerate the words accepted by N. By "enumerate" we mean list the words, as opposed to only counting them. Given words
$u = u_1 u_2 \cdots u_n$ and $v = v_1 v_2 \cdots v_m$, $u < v$ according to *radix order* if $n < m$ or
if $n = m$, $u \neq v$, and $u_i < v_i$ for the minimal i where $u_i \neq v_i$. Sorting a set S of
words according to radix order is equivalent to sorting words in S of equal length
according to lexicographic order and then sorting S by length. Given an NFA
accepting a language L, the *enumeration problem* is to enumerate the first m
words in L according to their radix order. Let the nth *cross-section* of a language
$L \subseteq \Sigma^*$ be $L \cap \Sigma^n$. Given an NFA accepting language L, the *cross-section enumeration problem* is to enumerate the nth cross-section of L in lexicographical
order.

Enumeration algorithms enable correctness testing of NFAs and regular expressions. (If a regular language is represented via a regular expression, we first
convert it to an NFA.) While such a technique provides evidence that the correct
NFA or regular expression has been found, the technique can also be used to
fully verify correctness once sufficiently many words have been enumerated [1,
p. 11].

In addition, regular language enumeration leads to an alternative solution
to the next k-subset of an n-set problem. The problem is, given a set $T =$

Jan Holub and Jan Žd'árek (Eds.): CIAA 2007, LNCS 4783, pp. 226–242, 2007.

$\{e_1, e_2, \ldots, e_n\}$, we wish to enumerate all k-subsets of T in alphabetical order. Nijenhuis and Wilf provide a solution to this problem [5, p. 27]. A cross-section enumeration algorithm yields an alternative solution, as follows. Construct an NFA N over the alphabet $\{0, 1\}$ that accepts all words with exactly k 1s. The nth cross-section of N is in bijection with the set of k subsets of T via the function that takes a word $w = a_1 a_2 \cdots a_n$ in the nth cross-section of N to the k-subset $\{e_i \mid a_i = 1\}$. Therefore, we enumerate the nth cross-section of $L(N)$, which is in bijection with the set of k-subsets of T.

Our contributions are two-fold. On the complexity theoretic side, we give a cross-section enumeration algorithm, crossSectionLM, with running time linear in n, the length of words in the cross-section. The best previously known algorithm is quadratic in n. This cross-section enumeration algorithm has a corresponding enumeration algorithm, enumLM. To refer to both algorithms together, we call them the *lookahead-matrix* algorithms. In addition, we perform a theoretical analysis of the previously known algorithms and our algorithms. We analyze the algorithms in terms of their output size, the parameters of the NFA, and the length of words in the cross-section for the cross-section enumeration algorithms. The output size, t, is the total number of characters over all words enumerated by the algorithm. An NFA is a five-tuple $N = (Q, \Sigma, \delta, q_0, F)$ where Q is the set of states, Σ is the alphabet, δ is the transition function, q_0 is the start state, and F is the set of final states. In our analysis we consider $s = |Q|$ and $\sigma = |\Sigma|$.

In the practical domain, we give enumeration algorithms, crossSectionMäkinenII and enumMäkinenII, both of which usually perform better than the other discussed algorithms for their respective problems. The algorithms crossSectionMäkinenII and enumMäkinenII are a combination of Mäkinen's algorithm [4] and the lookahead-matrix enumeration algorithms. We perform extensive performance analysis of both previous enumeration algorithms and the algorithms presented here, and find when each algorithm performs well. For example, one of our findings is a set of regular languages on which crossSectionLM outperforms crossSectionMäkinenII.

Here is an outline of the paper. We first introduce the general framework for the enumeration algorithms, after which we describe enumeration algorithms based on Mäkinen's regular language enumeration algorithm [4]. Then we introduce the lookahead-matrix algorithms. Next, we discuss an enumeration algorithm found in the symbolic computation environment, Grail+ 3.0 [3], list a few bugs, and provide a theoretical analysis of the algorithm. We conclude with an analysis and comparison of how these algorithms perform in practice.

2   Enumeration Algorithms

2.1   Enumerating the nth Cross-Section

We introduce a general framework for enumerating the nth cross-section of a language accepted by an NFA, N. First, we find the minimal word $w = a_1 a_2 \cdots a_n$ in the cross-section with respect to radix order, or determine that the cross-section is empty. We say that state q is *i-complete* if starting from q in N there is a path of length i ending at a final state. Let $S_0 = \{q_0\}$ and $S_i = \cup_{q \in S_{i-1}} \delta(q, a_i) \cap \{q \mid q$ is $(n-i)$-complete$\}$, for $1 \le i < n$. That is, S_i is the set of $(n-i)$-complete states reachable from the states in S_{i-1} on a_i. We find w while storing the sets of states $S_0, S_1, S_2, \ldots, S_{n-1}$ on the *state stack*, S, which we assume is global. We present two methods for finding the minimal word in the following two sections. For now we assume that there is some implementation of the method $\texttt{minWord}(n, N)$, which returns the minimal word w of length n accepted by NFA N starting from one of the states on top of the state stack, or returns NULL if no such word exists. To find the next word, we scan the minimal word $a_1 a_2 \cdots a_n$ from right to left, looking for the shortest suffix that can be replaced such that the new word is in $L(N)$. It follows that the suffix $a_i \cdots a_n$ can be replaced if the set of $(n-i)$-complete states reachable from S_{i-1} on any symbol greater than a_i is not empty. As we search for the next word of length n, we update the state stack. Therefore, each consecutive word can be found using the described procedure. The algorithm is outlined in detail in $\texttt{nextWord}$. Note that the algorithms use indentation to denote the scope of loops and if-statements.

Algorithm 1. nextWord(w, N)

```
INPUT: A word w = a₁a₂···aₙ and an NFA N.
OUTPUT: Returns the next word in the nᵗʰ cross-section of L(N) according
        to radix order, if it exists. Otherwise, return NULL. Updates S
        for a potential subsequent call to nextWord or minWord.
```

INPUT: A word $w = a_1 a_2 \cdots a_n$ and an NFA N.

OUTPUT: Returns the next word in the nth cross-section of $L(N)$ according to radix order, if it exists. Otherwise, return NULL. Updates S for a potential subsequent call to nextWord or minWord.

$\texttt{FOR } i \leftarrow n, \ldots, 1$
  $S_{i-1} = \texttt{top}(S)$
  $R = \{v \in \cup_{q \in S_{i-1}, a \in \Sigma} \delta(q, a) \mid v \text{ is } (n-i)\text{-complete}\}$
  $A = \{a \in \Sigma \mid \cup_{q \in S_{i-1}} \delta(q, a) \cap R \ne \emptyset\}$
  $\texttt{IF for all } a \in A, a \le a_i$
    $\texttt{pop}(S)$
  $\texttt{ELSE}$
    $b_i = \min\{a \in A \mid a > a_i\}$
    $S_i = \{v \in \cup_{q \in S_{i-1}} \delta(q, b_i) \mid v \text{ is } (n-i)\text{-complete}\}$
    $\texttt{IF } i \ne n$
      $\texttt{push}(S, S_i)$
    $w' = w[1 \cdots i - 1] \cdot b_i \cdot \texttt{minWord}(n - i, N)$
    $\texttt{RETURN } w'$
$\texttt{RETURN NULL}$

Algorithm 2. enumCrossSection(n, N)

INPUT: A nonnegative integer n and an NFA N.

OUTPUT: Enumerates the nth cross-section of $L(N)$.

$S = \texttt{empty stack}$
$\texttt{push}(S, \{q_0\})$
$w = \texttt{minWord}(n, N)$
$\texttt{WHILE } w \ne \texttt{NULL}$

```
visit w
w = nextWord(w, N)
```

The algorithms `nextWord` and `enumCrossSection` can be used in conjunction with any algorithms for `minWord` and for determining if a state is i-complete. We will use `nextWord` and `enumCrossSection` to form enumeration algorithms based on Mäkinen's algorithm. We will also use these algorithms to form the basis for the lookahead-matrix enumeration algorithms.

2.2   Enumerating the First m Words

We provide a structure for an algorithm that enumerates the first m words accepted by an NFA. The algorithm `enum` finds the minimal word in each cross-section and calls `nextWord` to get the rest of the words in the cross-section, until the required number of words is found.

Algorithm 3. enum(m, N)

```
INPUT: A nonnegative integer m and an NFA N.
OUTPUT: Enumerates the first m words accepted by N according to radix
        order, if there are at least m words. Otherwise, enumerates all
        words accepted by N.
```

```
i = 0
numCEC = 0
len = 0
WHILE i < m AND numCEC < s DO
    S = empty stack
    push(S, {q₀})
    w = minWord(len, N)
    IF w = NULL
        numCEC = numCEC+1
    ELSE
        numCEC = 0
        WHILE w ≠ NULL AND i < m
            visit w
            w = nextWord(w, N)
            i = i + 1
    len = len+1
```

The variable $numCEC$ counts the number of consecutive empty cross-sections. If the count ever hits s, the number of states in N, then all the words accepted by N have been visited. This bound is tight, as it is reached in the NFA consisting of a cycle of states, with the start state final. The proof for the following lemma appears in the appendix.

Lemma 1. *Let N be an NFA with s states accepting an infinite language L. The maximum number of consecutive empty cross-sections in L is $s - 1$.*

We will use `enum` as a base for creating a number of enumeration algorithms.

3   Mäkinen's Algorithm

Mäkinen [4] presented a cross-section enumeration algorithm. His algorithm assumes that the language is represented by a regular grammar. A regular grammar is equivalent to an NFA and these representations have the same space complexity. For consistency, we present and analyze Mäkinen's algorithm on NFAs. The algorithm is separated into two parts: finding the first word of length n and finding the remaining words of length n. The original algorithm for finding the remaining words applies only to DFAs, and so the NFA has to be converted to a DFA before the algorithm can be applied. By using enumCrossSection, we demonstrate an enumeration algorithm that uses parts of Mäkinen's algorithm and works directly on NFAs, without incurring the exponential size blow-up of subset construction.

To find the minimal word of length n, first find the lexicographically minimal words of length 1 through $n-1$ starting at each state, via dynamic programming. Theorem 3.2 in [4] states that the minimal and maximal words of length n can be found in $O(n)$ time and space. Mäkinen analyzes the algorithm in the unit-cost model, treating the size of the grammar as a constant. In the unit-cost model all operations, regardless of the size of the operands, have a cost of 1. Since Mäkinen's algorithm uses operands of length n, this model does not fully capture the complexity of the problem. We analyze the algorithm in the bit-complexity model and also take into account the number of states in the NFA.

Algorithm 4. minWordMäkinen(n, N)

INPUT: A positive integer n and an NFA N.
OUTPUT: Table $A^{min}[1 \cdots n]$ for each state $A \in Q$ where $A^{min}[i]$ is the minimal
      word of length i starting at state A.

FOR each $A \in Q$
    IF for all $a \in \Sigma$, $\delta(A,a) \cap F = \emptyset$
        $A^{min}[1] =$ NULL
    ELSE
        $A^{min}[1] = \min\{a \in \Sigma \mid \delta(A,a) \cap F \neq \emptyset\}$
FOR $i \leftarrow 2, \ldots, n$
    FOR each $A \in Q$
        $min =$ NULL
        FOR each $B \in Q$ and minimal $a \in \Sigma$ such that $B \in \delta(A,a)$
            IF $B^{min}[i-1] \neq$ NULL
                IF $aB^{min}[i-1] < min$ OR $min =$ NULL
                    $min \leftarrow aB^{min}[i-1]$
        $A^{min}[i] = min$
RETURN $\{A^{min} \mid A \in Q\}$

We assume that the complexity of comparison of two words of length n is in the order of the position of the first index where the words differ. We can store the NFA as an adjacency list, keeping track of the edge with the minimal character between any pair of states, which adds constant time and linear space to the implementation of the NFA. Therefore, the running time of `minWordMäkinen` is independent of the alphabet size. The following theorem is proved in the appendix.

Theorem 2. *The algorithm* `minWordMäkinen` *uses* $\Theta(sn)$ *space and* $\Theta(s^2n^2)$ *operations in the worst case.*

The algorithm `minWordMäkinen` finds the minimal word of length n in linear time on DFAs, since the determinism causes all words compared by the algorithm to differ on the leftmost character.

In all variations of Mäkinen's algorithm, to determine if a state is i-complete we check if $A^{min}[i]$ is not NULL. To use `minWordMäkinen` with `enumCrossSection` and `enum`, store the sets of states $S_0, S_1, \ldots, S_{n-1}$ on the state stack and then invoke `nextWord`. We know that a cross-section has been fully enumerated when the state stack is emptied, that is, when `nextWord` returns NULL. We call this the `enumCrossSection` *cross-section termination method*. Mäkinen introduces an alternative method for determining when a cross-section has been fully enumerated. In addition to finding the minimal word, his algorithm finds the maximal word in the cross-section in a method similar to finding the minimal word. When the maximum word in the cross-section is found we know that the cross-section has been fully enumerated. We call this method *Mäkinen's cross-section termination method*.

When `enumCrossSection` is used with `minWord` replaced by `minWordMäkinen` and Mäkinen's cross-section termination method, we get the algorithm `cross SectionMäkinenI`. When instead of Mäkinen's cross-section termination method the `enumCrossSection` cross-section termination method is used, we get the algorithm `crossSectionMäkinenII`. Similarly, `enumMäkinenI` is `enum` with `minWord` replaced by `minWordMäkinen` and Mäkinen's cross-section termination method. The function `enumMäkinenII` is the same as `enumMäkinenI`, except that it uses the `enumCrossSection` cross-section termination method.

Consider Mäkinen's cross-section termination method. Finding the maximal words adds an overhead of $\Theta(s^2n^2)$ in the worst case and $\Theta(sn)$ in the best case. The `enumCrossSection` cross-section termination method recognizes that a cross-section has been enumerated when the first character of the last word found cannot be replaced. This takes $\Theta(s^2n)$ time in the worst case and constant time in the best case. Recall that the output size, t, is the total number of characters over all words enumerated by an algorithm. With either termination method, once the first word in the cross-section is found, the rest of the work is $O(\sigma s^2 t)$. Therefore, `crossSectionMäkinenI` and `crossSectionMäkinenII` use $O(s^2n^2 + \sigma s^2 t)$ operations. The difference in the best and worst case performance between these two versions is significant for practical purposes, as will be discussed in Section 6.2.

Theorem 3. *The algorithms* `crossSectionMäkinenI` *and* `crossSectionMäkinenII` *use* $O(s^2n^2 + \sigma s^2 t)$ *operations.*

In the algorithms `enumMäkinenI` and `enumMäkinenII`, after enumerating the nth cross-section we have a table $A^{min}[1 \cdots n]$ for each state A. To improve the performance of these algorithms, when `minWord` is called for $n+1$, we reuse these tables, extending the tables by index $n + 1$. Therefore, each call to `minWord`(i, S) costs $O(s^2i)$. Finding the rest of the words in the cross-section costs $O(\sigma s^2 t)$. For each empty cross-section, the algorithm does $O(s^2)$ operations. Therefore, `enumMäkinenI` and `enumMäkinenII` have $O(\sigma s^2 t + s^2 e)$ operations, where e is the number of empty cross-sections found throughout the enumeration.

Theorem 4. *The algorithms* `enumMäkinenI` *and* `enumMäkinenII` *are* $O(\sigma s^2 t + s^2 e)$, *where* e *is the number of empty cross-sections encountered throughout the enumeration.*

4   Lookahead-Matrix Algorithm

To find the minimal words of length n, Mäkinen's algorithms find the minimal words of length 1 through $n-1$. An alternative approach for finding the minimal word of length n is to generate the characters of the word one at a time, while avoiding going down paths that would not lead to a final state within the required number of transitions. To do so, we need a method of quickly determining whether a word of length i can be completed to a word of length n in $n - i$ steps.

Given an NFA, we precompute M, the adjacency matrix of the NFA; $M_{p,q} = 1$ if there is a transition from state p to state q, and $M_{p,q} = 0$ otherwise. Then compute $M^2, M^3, \ldots, M^{n-1}$ using boolean matrix multiplication. Observe that $M^i_{p,q} = 1$ if and only if there is a path from state p to state q of length exactly i. Note that M^0 is the identity matrix.

To find the minimal word of length n, find the set of $(n-1)$-complete states, S_1, reachable from the start state on the minimal possible symbol a_1. Then find the set of $(n-2)$-complete states, S_2, reachable from any state in S_1 on the minimal symbol. Continue this process for a total of n iterations. Then $a_1 a_2 \cdots a_n$ is the minimal word of length n. The algorithm `minWordLM`(n,N) finds the minimal word of length n starting from a state in the set of states on top of the state stack S and ending at a final state, or determines that no such word exists. To find the minimal word of length n accepted by N, place $S_0 = \{q_0\}$ on the state stack S and call `minWordLM`.

Algorithm 5. `minWordLM`(n, N)

```
INPUT: A nonnegative integer n and an NFA N.
OUTPUT: The minimal word of length n accepted by N. Updates state stack
        S for a potential subsequent call to minWord or nextWord.
```

Compute $M, M^2, \ldots, M^n$, if they have not been precomputed
$S_0 = \text{top}(S)$
IF $M^n_{q,f} = 0$ for all $f \in F, q \in S_0$
    return NULL
w = empty word
FOR $i \leftarrow 0, \ldots, n - 1$
    $a_{i+1} = \min(a \in \Sigma \mid \exists u \in S_i, f \in F \text{ where } M^{n-1-i}_{v,f} = 1 \text{ for some } v \in \delta(u, a))$

$w = wa_{i+1}$
$S_{i+1} = \{v \in \cup_{u \in S_i} \delta(u, a_{i+1}) \mid M_{v,f}^{n-1-i} = 1 \text{ for some } f \in F\}$
IF $i \neq n - 1$
    push(S, S_{i+1})
return w

Since the matrices require $O(s^2 n)$ space, minWordLM uses $O(s^2 n)$ space. Finding each character of the minimal word can be implemented in a way that uses $O(s^2)$ operations. The standard matrix multiplication algorithm is $O(s^3)$. Strassen's matrix multiplication algorithm has $O(s^{2.81})$ operations [6]. The best bound on the matrix multiplication problem is $O(s^{2.376})$ [2]. All other operations in the algorithm cost $O(s^2 n)$. Therefore, minWordLM can be made to run in $O(s^{2.376} n)$ operations. However, the matrices have to be unreasonably large before the differences in these multiplication methods become apparent in practice.

Theorem 5. *The algorithm* minWordLM *finds the minimal word of length n in* $O(s^{2.376} n)$ *time and* $O(s^2 n)$ *space.*

Note that minWordLM can be easily modified to find the maximal word of length n. In the bit-complexity model, minWordMäkinen is quadratic in n. The algorithm minWordLM is linear in n in the bit-complexity model. Theorem 3.2 of [4] states that the minimal and maximal words of length n in a regular language can be found in linear time in n in the unit-cost model. The algorithm minWordLM proves that this is also true in the bit-complexity model.

Replace minWord by minWordLM in nextWord and use the matrices to determine i-completeness to get the method nextWordLM. Then using nextWordLM instead of nextWord, we get modified versions of enumCrossSection and enum, which we call crossSectionLM and enumLM, respectively. See appendix for details. Looking for the minimal word costs $O(s^{2.376} n)$ and finding all consecutive words costs $O(\sigma s^2 t)$. Therefore crossSectionLM costs $O(s^{2.376} n + \sigma s^2 t)$.

Theorem 6. *The algorithm* crossSectionLM *uses* $O(s^{2.376} n + \sigma s^2 t)$ *operations.*

If an empty cross-section is encountered in enumLM, the algorithm performs $O(s^{2.376})$ operations to determine that. Therefore, enumLM uses $O(s^{2.376}(m+e) + \sigma s^2 t)$ operations, where e is the number of empty cross-sections encountered during the enumeration. Note that if the total number of cross-sections encountered by the algorithm is c, then the running time of enumLM is $O(s^{2.376} c + \sigma s^2 t)$.

Theorem 7. *The algorithm* enumLM *uses* $O(s^{2.376}(m + e) + \sigma s^2 t)$ *operations, where e is the number of empty cross-sections encountered throughout the enumeration.*

5   Grail Enumeration Algorithm

The symbolic computation environment Grail+ 3.0 has an fmenum function that finds the m lexicographically first words accepted by an NFA. Consider the potentially infinite tree of paths that can be traversed on an NFA. The function fmenum performs breadth first search (BFS) on that tree until the required number of words is found. More precisely, it looks for all words of length n by searching all paths of length n starting at the start state, distinguishing paths that terminate at a final state. It searches for words of length $n+1$ by completing the paths of length n. Based on the Grail algorithm, we present a cross-section enumeration algorithm crossSectionBFS.

Let the nth *NFA-cross-section* be the set of all words appearing on paths of length n of an NFA that start at the start state. Given all words in the $(n-1)^{st}$ NFA-cross-section and the ends states of the corresponding paths, nextCrossSection finds all words in the nth NFA-cross-section as well as the end states of the corresponding paths. To find all words of length n accepted by an NFA, fmenum finds the words in the nth NFA-cross-section and selects all words for which there is a path that ends at a final state.

Algorithm 6. nextNFACrossSection(N, prevSec, prevSecStates)

INPUT: NFA N. The set, prevSec, of all words of some length $l \geq 0$ that
       occur on paths in N starting at s_0. An array, prevSecStates, where
       prevSecStates$[w] = \delta(q_0, w)$ for all $w \in$ prevSec.
OUTPUT: Returns the pair (nextSec, nextSecStates), where nextSec is the
       set of all words in $L(N)$ of length $l + 1$ and nextSecStates$[w] =$
       $\delta(q_0, w)$ for all $w \in$ nextSec.

```
nextSec = ∅
FOR i ← 1,...,size(prevSec)
  currWord = prevSec[i]
  currNodes = prevSecStates[currWord]
  FOR each currNode in currNodes
    FOR each edge adjacent to currNode
      newWord = currWord + value(edge)
      IF newWord ∉ nextSec
        nextSec = nextSec ∪ newWord
        nextSecStates[newWord] = ∅
      nextSecStates[newWord] = nextSecStates[newWord] ∪ destination(edge)
RETURN (nextSec, nextSecStates)
```

Algorithm 7. crossSectionBFS(n, N)

INPUT: A nonnegative integer n and an NFA N.
OUTPUT: Visits all words of length n accepted by N in lexicographical
order. FOR each state in N
         sort outgoing edges

```
words = ∅
emptyWord = ""
crossSec = {emptyWord}
crossSecStates[emptyWord] = {q0}
IF n = 0
  IF q0 ∈ F
```

```
        visit emptyWord
ELSE
    FOR i ← 1,...,n
        (crossSec, crossSecStates) = nextNFACrossSection(N, crossSec,
                                        crossSecStates)
    sort(crossSec)
    FOR each word in crossSec
        IF crossSectionStates[word]∩F ≠ ∅
            visit word
```

The BFS enumeration algorithm, enumBFS, calls crossSectionBFS until the required number of words is found. When we refer to our implementation of the BFS enumeration algorithm we call it enumBFS and when we refer to the original Grail implementation, we call it fmenum.

We found a number of bugs in fmenum. The function does not always display words in the cross-sections in radix order (equivalently, lexicographic order). When asked to enumerate the first two words accepted by the NFA in Figure 1(a), the following input to fmenum results in an output of 1 followed by a 0.

(START) |− 0

0 1 1
0 0 2
1 −| (FINAL)
2 −| (FINAL)

In addition, fmenum does not always display all words it should. When fmenum is called with $n = 1000$ and a DFA that accepts words over $(0 + 1)^*$ such that the number of 1s is congruent to 0 mod 3 (see Figure 1(b)), fmenum is missing 11000000000001.

Without explicit sorting of the words, words found by BFS algorithms will likely not be visited in radix order. Sorting the edges based on their alphabet symbol reduces the frequency of the problem, but does not eliminate it. If we call enumBFS on the NFA in Figure 1(c), then while enumerating words of length 2 we attempt to complete the string "0", which was found while enumerating the previous cross-section. Since both states B and C are reached on the symbol 0, state B may be chosen to complete the word. Thus, the algorithm finds "01" before it finds "00". To solve this problem, we sort the words after they are found.

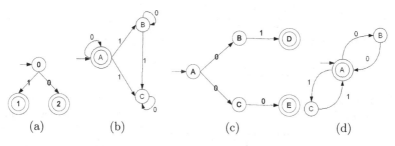

(a)   (b)   (c)   (d)

Fig. 1.

The algorithm `crossSectionBFS` may do exponential work in n for empty output. Consider the NFA in Figure 1(d). If we enumerate the nth cross-section of this NFA for $n = 2j+1, j \geq 0$, the algorithm performs over $(2j) \cdot 2^j \in \Theta(n2^{n/2})$ operations and has empty output. Note that the NFA in Figure 1(d) is minimal. On non-minimal NFAs, the running time could be worse. The running time of the BFS enumeration algorithms depends on the structure of the NFA. The ith NFA-cross-section contains at most σ^i words and the algorithm does $O(\sigma s^2)$ operations per word in the ith NFA-cross-section when enumerating the $(i+1)^{st}$ NFA-cross-section. Therefore, the algorithm performs $O(\sigma^i s^2)$ operations for the ith NFA-cross-section. Therefore, `crossSectionBFS` is $O(s^2 \sigma^n)$. The algorithm `enumBFS`(m, N) is bounded by $O(s^2 \sigma^k)$, where k is the length of the last cross-section examined. Further, $k \leq ms$ as for every word enumerated by `enumBFS` there are at most s empty cross-sections examined.

Theorem 8. *The algorithm* `crossSectionBFS`(n, N) *has* $O(s^2 \sigma^n)$ *operations. The algorithm* `enumBFS`(m, N) *has* $O(s^2 \sigma^k)$ *operations, where* $k \leq ms$ *is the length of the last cross-section examined.*

6   Experimental Results

6.1   Implementation

We discussed the following algorithms: `enumMäkinenI`, `crossSectionMäkinenI`, `enumMäkinenII`, `crossSectionMäkinenII`, `enumLM`, `crossSectionLM`, `enumBFS`, and `crossSectionBFS`. We also introduce the naive algorithm, `enumNaive`, which generates words over Σ^* in radix order and checks which are accepted by the NFA, until the required number of words is found or it is determined by the `enumCrossSection` cross-section termination method that the language is finite. The algorithm `enumNaive` has a corresponding cross-section enumeration algorithm, `crossSectionNaive`, that generates all words over Σ^n in radix order and checks which are accepted by the NFA. The running time of `crossSectionNaive` is $O(s^2 \sigma^n)$, since the algorithm may have to do up to s^2 operations for every character in a word in Σ^n. The algorithm `enumNaive`(m, N) costs $O(s^2 \sigma^k)$, where k is the length of the last word examined by the algorithm. As in `enumBFS`, $k \leq ms$. We implemented these algorithms and compared their performance. We represent NFAs as adjacency-lists. To improve performance, edges adjacent to each vertex are sorted based their associated Σ symbols.

6.2   Performance Comparison

A large body of tests was randomly generated. Most tests follow the following format: 100 NFAs were randomly generated with a bound on the number of vertices and alphabet size. The probability of placing an edge between any two states was randomly generated. The probability of any state being final or the number of final states was randomly generated within a specified range. The algorithms were tested on NFAs with differing number of states, varying edge densities, various alphabet sizes, and different proportions of final states. Each algorithm was run between 1 and 10 times on each NFA, and the average running time was recorded.

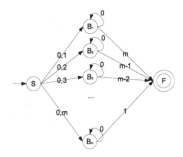

Fig. 2. NFA L_m

In addition to randomly generated tests, the algorithms were tested on the DFA that accepts the language 1^*, the DFA that accepts the language $(0 + 1)^*$, and some NFAs from the set $L = \{L_m \mid m \geq 2\}$, found in Figure 2. The NFAs in L are important because they take quadratic time on crossSectionMäkinen.

The naive algorithms perform reasonably well on small NFAs when the alphabet is of size less than 3, but even in these cases they tend to be slower than the other algorithms. With an alphabet size greater than 3, the naive algorithms are unreasonably slow. For large values of s, the naive algorithms are very slow, even on NFAs over the binary alphabet. The only case found in which the naive algorithms outperform the other algorithms is on NFAs with a unary alphabet where all states are final.

The BFS algorithms tend to perform well on small NFAs for small values of n. The algorithms enumBFS and crossSectionBFS outperform the other enumeration algorithms on 1^*, and crossSectionBFS outperforms the other algorithms for L_2 and L_9 (see Figure 2). In addition, the BFS algorithms are faster than the naive algorithms. However, enumBFS and crossSectionBFS are significantly slower than both Mäkinen and lookahead-matrix on most test cases.

Mäkinen and lookahead-matrix were slower than BFS on the language 1^*, for which Mäkinen and lookahead-matrix are particularly poorly suited. After each minimal word is found, the Mäkinen and lookahead-matrix algorithms go through the state stack searching for a character that can be replaced, finding none. Both algorithms end up performing a lot of redundant work on this particular language.

The efficiency of Mäkinen and lookahead-matrix on any NFA N can be estimated by the average length of the common prefix between two consecutive words in the same cross-section of $L(N)$. Therefore, Mäkinen and lookahead-matrix are particularly well suited for dense languages. This is confirmed in practice, as the performance of the Mäkinen and lookahead-matrix algorithms improves as the alphabet size increases. Performance improves further when, in addition to a larger alphabet, the number of edges or final states increases.

The top competing algorithms on almost all randomly generated tests are MäkinenII and lookahead-matrix. As the alphabet size increases, the difference between the efficiency of the algorithms decreases. On average, MäkinenII performs best. The performance of lookahead-matrix is consistently close to that of MäkinenII. Lookahead-matrix overtakes MäkinenII on some test cases where there is only a single final state.

As expected, MäkinenII is significantly more efficient than MäkinenI on NFAs with unary alphabets, due to the overhead in MäkinenI of searching for the maximal word in each cross-section where all cross-sections have a unique element. MäkinenII is also much more efficient on NFAs corresponding to sparse graphs. While on a few other test cases there is a significant disparity in the performance of the algorithms, their performance is similar on average, with MäkinenII performing a little better on most tests.

The algorithm `minWordMäkinen` is $O(s^2 n^2)$ in the worst case and $O(sn)$ in the best case. We implemented the lookahead-matrix algorithms with the standard $O(s^3)$ matrix multiplication algorithm. Therefore, our implementation of `minWordLM` is $O(s^3 n)$. Finding the rest of the words is $O(s^2 t)$ for both algorithms. All other operations in the algorithms are identical. The performance difference in the average case can be explained by the additional factor of s in lookahead-matrix when searching for the minimal word of length n and the hypothesis that the worst case of $O(s^2 n^2)$ for `minWordMäkinen` is not usually reached on random NFAs. This provides a theoretical basis for the proposition that the slightly faster average performance of `crossSectionMäkinenII` and `enumMäkinenII` over that of the lookahead-matrix algorithms is not symptomatic of a larger problem with the lookahead-matrix algorithms.

On NFAs where Mäkinen's cross-section enumeration algorithms are quadratic in n, `crossSectionLM` performs significantly better than Mäkinen's cross-section algorithms. On L_9, `crossSectionLM` runs over 50 times faster than `crossSectionMäkinenI` and `crossSectionMäkinenII`. Note also that it is sufficient for an NFA to have an NFA in L as a subgraph in order for the Mäkinen algorithms to have a quadratic running time in n.

From these results, we find that on typical data, Mäkinen algorithms with the `enumCrossSection` cross-section termination method tend to perform slightly faster than all other algorithms. However, in applications where a bounded worst case running time is essential, the lookahead-matrix algorithms are preferable.

The tests were run on Microsoft Windows XP Professional Version 2002 Service Pack 2, AMD Sempron(tm) 1.89 GHz, 1.00 GB of RAM.

Acknowledgements

We would like to thank David Loker for proofreading this paper and for his helpful suggestions.

References

1. Conway, J.H.: Regular Algebra and Finite Machines. Chapman and Hall, London (1971)
2. Coppersmith, D., Winograd, S.: Matrix multiplication via arithmetic progressions. J. Symb. Comput. 9, 251–280 (1990)
3. Department of Computer Science, University of Western Ontario, Canada, http://www.csd.uwo.ca/Research/grail/index.html
4. Mäkinen, E.: On lexicographic enumeration of regular and context-free languages. Acta Cybern. 13, 55–61 (1997)
5. Nijenhuis, A., Wilf, H.S.: Combinatorial Algorithms: For Computers and Calculators. Academic Press, Inc, NY, USA (1978)
6. Strassen, V.: Gaussian elimination is not optimal. Journal Numerische Mathematik 13, 354–356 (1969)

Appendix

Lemma 9. *Let N be an NFA with s states accepting an infinite language L. The maximum number of consecutive empty cross-sections in L is $s - 1$.*

Proof. Suppose L is infinite but contains s consecutive empty cross-sections, say of length $m, m + 1, \ldots, m + s - 1$. Let $w = a_1 a_2 \cdots a_r$ be a shortest word in L of length $\geq m + s$. Such a word exists because L is infinite. Consider the accepting configuration $q_0, q_1, \ldots, q_r$ of w in N. Now look at the sequence of states $q_m, q_{m+1}, \ldots, q_{m+s-1}$. None of these s states are accepting, since otherwise there would be a word in the associated cross-section. But there is at least one accepting state in N. So there are at most $s - 1$ distinct states in the sequence. Therefore some state is repeated. If we cut out the loop, we get either a shorter word in L of length $\geq m + s$ or a word of length between m and $m + s - 1$. $\square$

Theorem 10. *The algorithm* minWordMäkinen *uses $\Theta(sn)$ space and $\Theta(s^2 n^2)$ operations in the worst case.*

Proof. The two expensive operations are concatenation and comparison of words. Concatenation of words can be performed in constant time by changing the mode of storage: Instead of storing a word w of length i in $A^{min}[i]$, store the pair (a, B) such that $w = aB^{min}[i-1]$. With this modification, minWordMäkinen uses $\Theta(sn)$ space.

The time complexity of comparing two words of length n is $O(n)$. The number of symbols compared throughout the algorithm is $O(n^2)$. Since the states of an NFA can form a complete graph, the worst case running time is $O(s^2 n^2)$. This bound is reached on the NFA in Figure 3.

To fill in $A_j^{min}[i]$, which represents the minimal word of length i starting at state A_j, the minimal words of length $i - 1$ starting at states $B_1, B_2, \ldots, B_{\frac{s-2}{2}}$ are compared. The minimal word of length $i - 1$ starting at state B_l is $0^{i-2}l$. Therefore, comparing each pair of minimal words requires $i - 1$ steps, and there is a total of $\frac{s-2}{2} - 1$ comparisons. So filling all the tables A_i^{min} takes $\Theta(s^2 n^2)$ operations. $\square$

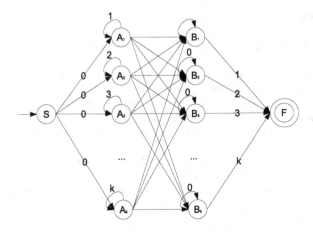

Fig. 3. $\delta(A_i, a_i) = \{B_1, B_2, \ldots, B_k\}$ for all distinct a_i

Algorithm 8. crossSectionLM(n, N)

INPUT: A nonnegative integer n and an NFA N.
OUTPUT: Enumerates the nth cross-section of $L(N)$.

```
Find M, M², ..., Mⁿ
S = empty stack
push(S, {q₀})
w = minWordLM(n,N)
WHILE w ≠ NULL
    visit w
    w = nextWordLM(w,N)
```

Algorithm 9. enumLM(m, N)

INPUT: A nonnegative integer m and an NFA N.
OUTPUT: Enumerates the first m words accepted by N according to radix
        order, if there are at least m words. Otherwise, enumerates all
        words accepted by N.

```
i = 0
len = 0
numCEC = 0
WHILE i < m AND numCEC < s DO
    IF len > 1
        find Mⁱ
    S = empty stack
    push(S, {q₀})
    w = minWordLM(len,S)
    IF w = NULL
        numCEC = numCEC+1
    ELSE
```

```
    numCEC = 0
    WHILE w ≠ NULL AND i < m
        visit w
        w = nextWordLM(w, N)
        i = i+1
len = len+1
```

The following tables list some of the running times of the algorithms. The first table lists the results of the described enumeration algorithms and the second lists the results of the cross-section enumeration algorithms. When an "x" appears, the test case has not been run to completion due to an unreasonably high running time.

Table 1 (cross-section timings).

NFA type	num NFAs	num runs	n	crossSectionBFS	crossSectionMäkinenI	crossSectionMäkinenII	crossSectionLM	naive
1* dfa	1	5	10000	0.2	0.24	0.43	0.26	0.33
1* dfa	1	5	50000	8.48	9.11	21.27	8.95	18.47
(0+1)* dfa	1	10	15	0.71	0.18	5.17	0.16	0.42
(0+1)* dfa	1	10	20	x	0.05	5.11	5.43	16.86
L_2	1	5	1000	0.05	0.05	0.19	0.02	x
L_2	1	5	10000	3.2	21.75	21.91	0.53	x
L_9	1	5	1000	0.32	1.48	1.46	0.1	x
L_9	1	1	10000	6.3	52.69	54.45	1.02	x
Alp. size 2, ∨|∨| 10 nodes	100	5	4	1.99	0.23	0.24	0.24	0.27
Alp. size 2, 10 nodes	100	5	5	35.69	2.72	2.79	3.03	3.26
Alp. size 5, ≤ 10 nodes	100	5	4	x	7.48	7.51	7.49	x
Alp. size 20, ≤ 10 nodes	100	1	x	x	01:04.27	01:03.78	01:08.28	x
Alp. size 20, ≤ 10 nodes, all final	100	3	x		15.98	15.97	17.13	x

Table 2 (enumeration timings).

NFA type	num NFAs	num runs	m	enumBFS	enumMäkinenII	enumMäkinenI	enumLM	naive
1* dfa	1	1	1000	0.01	1.78	2.91	1.93	1.4
1* dfa	1	3	2000	0.02	10.91	16.69	12.15	9.82
(0+1)* dfa	1	10	1000	0.01	0.01	0	0	0.01
(0+1)* dfa	1	10	2000	0.02	0.01	0	0.01	0.02
(0+1)* dfa	1	5	100000	1.79	0.53	0.48	0.5	1.25
(0+1)* dfa	1	5	1000000	18.48	4.73	4.75	5.35	14.68
L_2	1	5	1000	0.02	0.33	0.41	0.41	x
L_2	1	5	5000	0.25	15.84	20.39	18.91	x
L_2	1	5	10000	0.59	01:31.84	01:58.11	01:57.20	x
L_9	1	5	1000	0.01	0.05	0.05	0.16	16.6
L_9	1	5	5000	0.05	1.31	1.36	1.7	x
L_9	1	5	10000	0.18	6.17	6.48	8.33	x
Alp. Size 1, ≤ 10 nodes, 1 final	100	1	7	03:30.41	00:21.03	00:46.28	00:30.20	01:02.72
Alp. Size 1, ≤ 10 nodes, all final	100	1	8	43.33	14.17	29.13	17.06	12.34
Alp. Size 1, ∨|∨| 10 nodes	100	10	8	55.23	15.98	34.25	19.75	17.05
Alp. size 2, 10 nodes	100	10	10	0.2	0.08	0.08	0.08	4.6
Alp. size 2, 10 nodes	100	3	50	35.36	1.74	1.94	2.13	x
Alp. size 5, 10 nodes	100	10	100	x	38.77	40.09	44.33	x
Alp. size 5, 10 nodes	100	5	100	4.63	0.31	0.33	0.32	x
Alp. size 10, 10 nodes	100	5	1000	1.14	43.94	50.61	47.66	16.6
Alp. size 10, 10 nodes	100	1	100	24.84	0.17	0.16	0.16	x
Alp. size 10, 10 nodes	100	5	500	40.42	1.03	1.17	1.03	x
Alp. size 10, 10 nodes	100	1	5000	06:02.81	3.15	4.19	3.32	x
Alp. 2, ∨|∨| 10 n, 1 final state	19	1	5000	x	02:02.22	03:12.94	02:23.81	x
Alp. 5, ∨|∨| 10 n, 1 final state	100	20	100	x	0.18	0.26	0.17	x
Alp. 10, ∨|∨| 10 n, 1 final state	100	5	1000	x	0.27	28.5	0.25	x
Alp. 10, ∨|∨| 10 n, 1 final state	100	20	100	x	0.17	0.16	0.16	x
Alp. 10, ∨|∨| 10 n, 1 final state	100	5	1000	x	1.43	1.44	1.52	x
Alp. size 2, 10 nodes, dense grph	100	5	5000	x	29.64	29.75	32.72	x
Alp. size 10, 10 nodes, dense grph	100	5	5000	x	22.46	24.19	26.33	x
Alp. size 10, 10 nodes, dense grph	100	5	100	x	0.19	0.19	0.18	x
Alp. size 10, 10 nodes, dense grph	100	5	1000	x	1.79	1.81	1.86	x
Alp. size 2, 10 nodes, sparse grph	100	5	5000	x	37.71	37.79	40.18	x
Alp. size 10, 10 nodes, sparse grph	100	5	1000	x	0.28	0.33	0.32	x
Alp. size 10, ∨|∨| 10 nodes, sparse grph	100	10	1000	2.35	26.99	40.18	31.08	x
Alp. size 5, ≤ 10 nodes, all final	100	5	100	01:36.57	0.13	0.15	0.14	x
Alp. size 5, 10 nodes, all final	100	5	500	0.26	7.58	12.28	8.58	x
Alp. size 2, 10 nodes, all final	100	5	500	2.53	0.25	0.27	0.26	x
Alp. size 5, 3n, all final	100	5	30	31.32	4.11	4.68	4.29	x
Alp. size 5, 3n, all final	100	5	100	31.95	3.12	6.31	5.79	x
Alp. size 5, 3n, all final	100	5	500	30.4	0.18	0.21	0.2	x
Alp. size 5, 20n, all final	100	5	1000	x	3.26	4.9	3.63	x
Alp. size 5, 20n, all final	100	5	100	3.29	17.01	29.07	20.18	x
Alp. size 20, ∨|∨| 10 nodes, all final	100	5	150	x	1.97	2.07	2.06	0.49
Alp. size 20, 10 nodes, all final	100	5	1000	x	1.97	2.01	2.07	x

Multi-grain Relations

François Barthélemy[1,2]

[1] CNAM (Cédric), 292 rue Saint-Martin
75003 Paris, France
[2] INRIA (Atoll), domaine de Voluceau
78153 Le Chesnay cedex, France
barthe@cnam.fr

Abstract. In this paper, a subclass of rational relations is defined for which there is not only a global correspondence between strings of a given tuple, but also a structured correspondence between substrings. This structure is denoted in strings using postfixed inner-node markers. These relations are closed under rational operations. Some additional conditions are defined to obtain also a closure under intersection. This approach is interesting for applications where several level of analysis are relevant. An example in Natural Language Processing is given.

Keywords: rational relation, tree transduction, two-level morphology.

1 Introduction

Rational relations are a class of relations which are implemented by finite-state machines. They are closed under rational operations and composition but not under intersection.

Some subclasses of relations are closed under intersection. It is the case of recognizable relations which are the finite union of Cartesian products of independent rational languages. It is also the case of length preserving relations where all the strings of a given tuple in the relation have the same length. Such a tuple of strings may also be described as a sequence of tuples of symbols, so the length-preserving relations are sometimes used to formalize a symbol-to-symbol correspondence between strings of two domains.

For instance, the two-level morphology by Kimmo Koskenniemi [1], in the field of Natural Language Processing, relate an abstract and a concrete description of words using a length preserving relation described, roughly speaking, by regular expressions over symbol pairs. A special symbol 0 is inserted when a symbol of one side has no actual counterpart on the other side.

In this paper, we define a class of relations which generalize the idea of term-to-term correspondence between members of tuples in such a way that substrings of arbitrary length may be paired. The strings of a given tuple have not the same number of symbols, but they are split into the same number of substrings. There are two different levels in such a description: the level of symbols and the level of substrings. Different operations may be used at one level or the other.

Jan Holub and Jan Žd'árek (Eds.): CIAA 2007, LNCS 4783, pp. 243–252, 2007.
© Springer-Verlag Berlin Heidelberg 2007

The relations described using this model are called *two-grain relations*. They are not closed under intersection, but some subclasses are.

The first application of two-grain relations is the morphological analysis of Natural Language [2]. Typically, a morpheme is a substring of words which has some properties. We use the two grains of symbols and morphemes to describe different properties of words.

The next section defines two-grains relations. Section 3 is devoted to three subclasses closed under intersection. Then we generalize the concept to n-ary relations with possibly more than two level of analysis.

2   Two-Grain Relations

The definition of two-grain relation relies on the definitions of rational languages and relations. A rational language (resp. relation) over an alphabet A (resp. two alphabets A and B) is a subset of the free monoid A^* (resp. the non-free monoid $A^* \times B^*$) closed under disjunction, product and star. The notation $\text{Rat}_1(A^*)$ (resp. $\text{Rat}_2(A^* \times B^*)$) is used to denote the set of all rational languages (resp. relations).

Definition 1. *Two-Grain Sets*
A two-grain set is characterized by a rational language $L \in \text{Rat}_1(\Sigma^*)$ and a function $\mu : \Sigma \to \text{Rat}(A^* \times B^*)$. It is a set of strings of pairs from $A^* \times B^*$ defined by:
$$TGS(L, \mu) = \{(v_1, w_1) \cdots (v_n, w_n) \in (A^* \times B^*)^* \mid$$
$$\exists a_1 \cdots a_n \in L, (v_1, w_1) \in \mu(a_1), \ldots, (v_n, w_n) \in \mu(a_n)\}.$$

The members of Σ and their images by μ are called the coarse grains of the set and the members of A and B are called the fine grains. The distinction between the two scales is mostly visible when considering the product (concatenation): the product of two coarse grains is not equal to the product of their components. For instance, $(v_1, w_1)(v_2, w_2)$ is different from $(v_1 v_2, w_1 w_2)$. Therefore, the two levels are really separated and a string $a_1 \cdots a_n$ in L contains more information than the product $\mu(a_1) \cdots \mu(a_n)$. It contains also the number of coarse grains and the position of the frontiers between them.

Note that the symbols in Σ do not appear in the members of a two-grain set, but only the symbols in A and B. The symbols of Σ are therefore not very important. Renaming these symbols does not change the members of the set.

Property 2. Two-grain sets are closed under product, union and star.

These operations involve only coarse grains. The only problem is that the same symbol may map on two different rational expressions in the two operands. In this case, a renaming is to be performed before applying the relevant operation on the regular language.

Property 3. Two-grain sets are not closed under intersection and complementation.

This comes from the fact that relations in the image of μ are not closed under these operations either.

Property 4. Let $S_1 = TGS(L_1, \mu_1)$ and $S_2 = TGS(L_2, \mu_2)$ be two two-grain sets. If all the relations in the image of μ_1 and μ_2 belong to the same subclass of relations closed under intersection, then $S_1 \cap S_2$ is a two-grain set.

If $\Sigma_1 \cap \Sigma_2 = \emptyset$, then let $\Sigma_3 = \Sigma_1 \times \Sigma_2$ and $\forall (a, b) \in \Sigma_3, \mu_3((a, b)) = \mu_1(a) \cap \mu_2(b)$. L_3 is the language defined by $L_3 = \{(a_1, b_1) \cdots (a_n, b_n) \in \Sigma_3^* \mid a_1 \cdots a_n \in L_1 \wedge b_1 \cdots b_n \in L_2\}$. L_3 is rational. $S_3 = TGS(L_3, \mu_3)$ is a two-grain set equal to $S_1 \cap S_2$.

Two-grain sets are useful to introduce the concept and make the two scales clear, but they have two drawbacks. The first one is that there is a multiplicity of characterization for a given set. The symbols in Σ are not significant and may be freely renamed. Furthermore, different regular languages may be used to describe the same relation, like in the example (we note relations using regular expressions where the semicolon denotes the Cartesian product):

$$L1 = a|b, L_2 = c, \mu_1 = \{(a, x : y), (b, x : z)\}, \mu_2 = \{(c, x : (y|z))\},$$
$$TGS(L_1, \mu_1) = TGS(L_2, \mu_2) = \{(x, y), (x, z)\}$$

Unlike product, the union is distributive with respect to grains. The equivalence of two-grain sets is therefore not easily described.

The second drawback is that deriving an operational device from the definition is not straightforward. In order to avoid the two problems, we now define an intermediate form which is a subclass of rational relations, more convenient and which is equivalent to two-grain sets. The idea is to represent the frontiers between coarse grains using a special symbol read on both sides of the relation. This allows to concatenate the relations of fine grains.

Definition 5. *Two-grain relation*
A two-grain relation over two alphabets A, B and a terminator ω is a rational subset of $(A^* \omega \times B^* \omega)^*$.

The set of all two-grain relations using a given terminator ω is written TGR_ω. The strings in a pair belonging to a two-grain relation have the same number of occurrences of ω and both are ending with an ω.

Definition 6. *Canonical homomorphism*
Let $(u_1, v_1) \cdots (u_n, v_n)$ be a string of pairs from $A^* \times B^*$ and ω a symbol neither in A nor B. $\Phi_\omega((u_1, v_1) \cdots (u_n, v_n)) = (u_1 \omega \cdots u_n \omega, v_1 \omega \cdots v_n \omega)$.
Let TGS be a two-grain set. Then $\Phi_\omega(TGS) = \{u | \exists e \in TGS \text{ and } \Phi_\omega(e) = u\}$.

Property 7. The image of a two-grain set by Φ_ω is a two-grain Relation and the image of a two-grain Relation by Φ_ω^{-1} is a two-grain set.

3   Three Classes Closed Under Intersection

The property 4 states that two-grain sets where all the rational relations belong to a given class closed under intersection are closed under intersection. In this section, we will consider successively three classes of rational relations closed under intersection and set difference, namely *recognizable, same-length* and *left-synchronized relations*. The set of two-grain sets where the image of μ is included in a class of relations C will be written $TGS(C)$, and the corresponding set of two-grain Relations $TGR(C)$.

Recognizable relations were defined by [3]. The definition given in [4] is the following: a recognizable relation of $A^* \times B^*$ is the finite union of Cartesian products of the form $S \times T$ where S is a rational subset of A^* and T a rational subset of B^*. The notation $Rec(A^* \times B^*)$ stands for the set of all the recognizable relations of $A^* \times B^*$.

$TGR(Rec(A^* \times B^*))$ is not included in $Rec((A \cup \{\omega\})^* \times (B \cup \{\omega\})^*)$. The numbers of occurrences of ω in both strings of a tuple are equal and this number is not bounded whenever there is a star over a coarse grain. It is typically the kind of things which cannot be expressed using a finite union of Cartesian products.

Length Preserving Relations (also called *same-length relations*) were also defined by [3]. A Length-Preserving (Rational) Relation is a Rational Relation such that for all member (u, v) of the relation, the length of u is equal to the length of v. The notation $LP(A^* \times B^*)$ denotes the set of all the Length Preserving Relations of $A^* \times B^*$.

$TGR(LP(A^* \times B^*))$ is obviously included in $LP((A \cup \{\omega\})^* \times (B \cup \{\omega\})^*)$.

Left-Synchronized Relations were defined (under another name) by [3] and described in [4]. Let $\text{Diff}_{Rat} = \{(S \times 1) \cup (1 \times T) | S \in Rat(A^*), T \in Rat(B^*)\}$. A rational Relation is Left-Synchronized if and only if it is the finite union of products of Length Preserving Relations by elements of Diff_{Rat}. The set of left-synchronized relations of $A^* \times B^*$ is written $Sync(A^* \times B^*)$.

$Sync(A^* \times B^*)$ is closed under intersection and difference, but not under product and star. The resynchronization is not possible when the Diff_{Rat} part of the first operand has not a bounded length, like for instance $(a, a)^*(a, 1)^*$.

$TGR(Sync)$ is not included in $Sync$. For instance, $(a, x)^*(b, 1)^* \in Sync$, $(a, x)^*(b, 1)^*(\omega, \omega)^* \in TGR(Sync)$ but $(a, x)^*(b, 1)^*(\omega, \omega)^*$ is not left-synchronized.

$TGR(Sync)$ is not formally a superset of $Sync$, because all the strings in members of a two-grain relation end with an ω, which is not the case of arbitrary synchronous relations.

If we change the definition in such a way that ω is a separator between coarse grains instead of a terminator at the end of such grains, there is no more ω at the end of the last coarse grain. The number of ω of a string is the number of coarse grains minus one, so now, synchronized relations are two-grain relations. TGS is then a strict superset of left-synchronized relations which is closed under intersection and difference. It is also a superset of Rec_2 and LP_2 which are themselves included in $Sync_2$. We know no bigger class of relations fulfilling these closure properties.

On the other hand, the final ω is useful to obtain closure of two-grain relations under product and star, so we let the definition 5 unchanged. $TGR(Sync)$ has all the most useful closure properties and is a wide class.

4   Multi-grain Relations

The aim of this section is to generalize the approach to cases where there are more than two kinds of grains.

There is an immediate way of achieving this goal. A *TGS* is characterized by a pair (Σ, μ) where μ may maps symbols from Σ to elements of a two-grain relation. In this case, there are two grains with respect to the TGS and two grains with respect to the image of μ. They are such that the fine grain of the former is the coarse grain of the later. Such a TGS belongs to $TGS(TGR_\omega(Rat(A^* \times B^*)))$. It does not belong to the domain of Φ_ω, which is not defined because ω belongs to the alphabet of the inner relations. A new symbol ω' must be chosen to denote the end of the coarser grains.

$TGR_{\omega'}(TGR_\omega(R))$ is closed under intersection if R is closed under intersection.

The multiplicity of grains leads to a tree structure where each level in the tree corresponds to a given grain. Let us take an example. There are two representations of English words, one is the usual written form, the other is a phonetic representation using a phonetic alphabet. There is a term-to-term correspondence between substrings of both representations, but sometimes a unique phoneme is written using 2 or 3 letters, like for example **sh**, and conversely, a unique letter corresponds to several signs of the phonetic alphabet. There is another level of analysis, which is the notion of morpheme. Morphemes are the smallest linguistic units having a semantic meaning. For instance, the form **shyly** is composed of two morphemes, the nominal root **shy** and the derivational suffix **ly** which makes an adverb out of a noun.

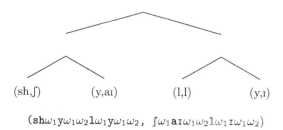

$(\mathbf{sh}\omega_1\mathbf{y}\omega_1\omega_2\mathbf{l}\omega_1\mathbf{y}\omega_1\omega_2\,, \;\int\omega_1\mathbf{a\textsc{i}}\omega_1\omega_2\mathbf{l}\omega_1\textsc{i}\omega_1\omega_2)$

Fig. 1. The tree structure for the form *shyly* ans its linearization using two terminators ω_1 and ω_2

The strings are a postfix notation of the tree where these two symbols label the inner nodes. Different symbols are needed for different levels in the trees because there may be empty grains, so two consecutive terminators denote either a node and its father or a node and its empty sibling.

This approach generalizes two-grain relations to relations with several embedded levels of grains. The next generalization concerns the arity of the relations. When there are more than two members in a relation, the number of grains is

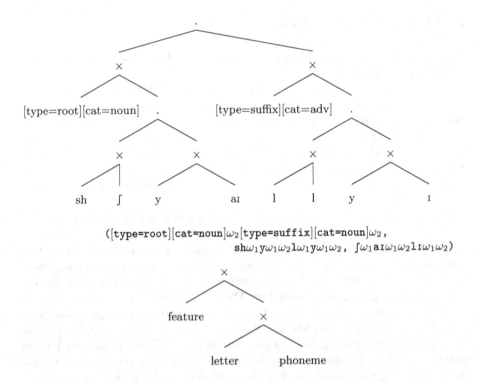

$$([\text{type=root}][\text{cat=noun}]\omega_2[\text{type=suffix}][\text{cat=noun}]\omega_2,$$
$$\text{sh}\omega_1\text{y}\omega_1\omega_2\text{l}\omega_1\text{y}\omega_1\omega_2, \int\omega_1\text{aı}\omega_1\omega_2\text{lı}\omega_1\omega_2)$$

Fig. 2. the word *shyly*: tree, linearization and domain tree

not necessarily the same for all the components. So far, all the leaves of trees labeled by symbols of $A^* \times B^*$ are at the same depth of the tree. Now, we would like to allow the different components of a n-ary relation to be at different depth in the tree structure. To achieve this goal, the formalism is extended by allowing rational relations at other places than leaves, namely at any level of the tree.

For instance, we would like to enrich our example by adding some information about the morphemes, such as the syntactic category (verb, noun, etc), the type (root, prefix, suffix, inflection) and so on. This information is related to morphemes, i.e. the coarsest grains of the description. We will write [name=value] a single symbol encoding a piece of information (feature).

Definition 8. ω-*subtree relation*
Let A be a finite alphabet, Ω a finite set of terminators, t a tree, and TERM, a bijection between nodes of t and Ω.

- let ν be a leaf of t. Then, a rational language of $Rat(A)$ is a TERM(ν)-subtree relation.
- let ν_0 be a node with n children. $\{(\omega, \ldots, \omega)\}$ is a TERM(ν_0)-subtree relation.
- let ν_0 be a node in t, with n subtrees $\nu_1, \ldots, \nu_n$ and $\omega = $ TERM(ν_0). Let $r_1, \ldots, r_n$ be respectively a TERM(ν_1)-subtree relation,..., a TERM(ν_n)-subtree relation. $(r_1 \times \cdots \times r_n)\{(\omega, \ldots, \omega)\}$ is an ω-subtree relation.

– let r_1 and r_2 be two ω-subtree relations. Then $r_1 r_2$, $r_1 \cup r_2$ and r_1^* are ω-subtree relations.

Definition 9. *Multi-grain relation*
Let A be a finite alphabet, Ω a finite set of terminators, t a tree, and TERM, *a bijection between nodes of t and Ω. A* TERM($\text{ROOT}(t)$)-*subtree relation is called a multi-grain relation.* $(A, \Omega, t, \text{TERM})$ *is called the domain of the relation and t the domain tree of the relation.*

A multi-grain relation is a rational relation because its definition uses only rational operators and the Cartesian product which preserves the rationality. The rationality mentioned here and in the remainder of the paper is rationality of the relation, not of the underlying trees.

Property 10. Multi-grain relations defined over the same domain are closed under union, product and star.

This comes directly from the definition of ω-subtree relations.

The tree t is somehow a type of structure which is used in members of multi-grain relations. Each node in t is a description of a class of nodes in the members of relations, more precisely the Cartesian product nodes. Each leaf in t corresponds to a component of the relation. All the actual symbols of this component in all the trees of members of the relation are accessible through a path having the same number and type of Cartesian product as the path of this leaf in t. In addition, there are some product nodes which appear in the trees of members of the relation and not in t (cf. Fig.2).

In this definition, the terminators are used to denote unambiguously the structure in flat strings. Let $(w_1, \ldots, w_n)$ be a member of a multi-grain relation. If $\omega \in \Omega$ appears in both w_i and w_j, then there is the same number of occurrences of ω in w_i and w_j.

Definition 11. *Multi-level characterization*
Let A be a finite alphabet of terminal symbols, Σ a finite alphabet of non-terminal symbols, $i \in A$ called the initial symbol, t a tree and REL, *a function which associates to each node ν in t a function μ_ν from Σ to $Rat(B_1^* \times \cdots \times B_n^*)$ where n is the arity of ν, $B_i = A$ if the ith child of ν is a leaf and $B_i = \Sigma$ the if i^{th} child is an inner node.* $(A, \Sigma, i, t, \text{REL})$ *is called a Multi-level characterization.*

A Multi-level characterization $(A, \Sigma, i, t, \text{REL})$ defines a multi-grain relation using a function NGR defined by:

– Let ν_0 be a node in t, with $\nu_1, \ldots, \nu_n$ as children. Let $r = \mu_{\nu_0}(a)$. $\text{NGR}(\nu_0, a) = \text{NGR}(\nu_1, \ldots, \nu_n, r)\{(\omega_{\nu_0}, \ldots, \omega_{\nu_0})\}$.
– $\text{NGR}(\nu_0, a) = a$ if $a \in A$.
– $\text{NGR}(\nu_0, 1) = 1$
– $\text{NGR}(\nu_1, \ldots, \nu_n, r_1 \times \cdots \times r_n) = \text{NGR}(\nu_1, r_1) \times \cdots \times \text{NGR}(\nu_n, r_n)$
– $\text{NGR}(\nu_1, \ldots, \nu_n, r^*) = \text{NGR}(\nu_1, \ldots, \nu_n, r)^*$
– $\text{NGR}(\nu_1, \ldots, \nu_n, r_1 r_2) = \text{NGR}(\nu_1, \ldots, \nu_n, r_1)\text{NGR}(\nu_1, \ldots, \nu_n, r_2)$

NGR(ROOT(t), i) is the multi-grain relation defined by the multi-level characterization.

The fact that the image of NGR is a multi-grain relation is proved by induction on the depth of the subtree of its first argument.

Conversely, it is possible to build a multi-level characterization from a multi-grain relation as follows. Let $R = MGR(A, \Omega, t, \text{TERM})$ be a multi-grain relation. Let $\Sigma = \{\sigma_1, \ldots, \sigma_n\}$ be a finite set of symbols disjoint from A. For each leaf ν in t, there are only a finite number of ν-subtree relations used in the definition of R. Replace each of these by a distinct symbol from Σ, remove the trailing ω and add a couple between this symbol and the subtree-relation to a function μ. Remove the leaves in t. Iterate until t is empty.

Property 12. Let R_1 and R_2 be two multi-grain relations having multi-level characterization defined over the same alphabet A and the same tree t. Let REL$_1$, REL$_2$ be their respective functions from nodes to relations. If for all node ν in t, the images of REL$_1$(ν) and REL$_2$(ν) belong to the same subclass of relations closed under intersection, then $R_1 \cap R_2$ is a multi-grain relation.

The proof works by induction, bottom-up in the tree. An interesting detail of this property is that the subclass of relations need not be the same for all the functions in the image of REL, but a different subclass may be used for different nodes. For instance, in our example, the relation between phonemes and letter will be typically recognizable whereas the relation between morpheme information and morphemes will be length preserving.

Multi-grain relations are based on trees. They are tree transductions [5] with some special properties. They are n-ary relations with no input/output notion. Two trees from a tuple of the relation share a common structure in their upper part (context) and differs possibly in the lower parts (subtrees). The trees considered have a very restricted form, with Cartesian products and products. The Cartesian products are organized by the domain tree whereas products use only linear subtrees (cf. Fig.2).

Multi-grain relations closed under intersection give a sufficient support for morphological applications. All the morphemes may be described in specialized lexica: for instance, one lexicon for each kind of root (verb, noun, etc), one lexicon for prefixes, one for derivation suffixes, one for inflection suffixes. Union applied on root lexica merge them into a multi-grain relation. Then, product allows to add prefixes and suffixes to roots. Some constraints on valid affix concatenation may be expressed as contextual rules which may be compiled into multi-grain relations using the algorithms from [6] and [7]. These algorithms use intersection and set difference. The constraints are then intersected with the result of product to filter valid forms. This gives a multi-grain relation representing all the words. Another operation is necessary to use this representation to analyze actual form, which is a composition, an operation not considered here.

The implementation of multi-grain relations uses multi-tape transducers. The number of tapes is equal to the number of leaves in the domain tree. The tapes are partially synchronized on terminator symbols. Other symbols are synchronized or not, depending on the underlying rational relations. We have made a prototype implementation of multi-grain relations based on the FSM toolkit from AT&T [8]. We have written a number of sample grammars describing portions of natural language morphology. The greatest example so far is a 16-tape transducer with a domain tree of depth 3. The system uses a standardization of transducers where the transitions read a single symbol on one tape and nothing on the other tapes.

5 Conclusion

In this paper, we define classes of n-ary relations where there is more than a correspondence between complete strings: there is also a structured correspondence between substrings. They are not a theoretically powerful formalism; the goal of this work is not to extend the formal power but to keep the closure properties of finite-state automata.

For morphological applications, the product and union operations are the way to achieve modular descriptions. Intersection and set difference are very important to compile contextual rules such as the surface coercion and context restriction rules defined in [1] or the generalized restriction rules from [7].

Multi-grain relations, under some conditions (cf. property 12), are closed under these operations. They offer different levels of analysis which is interesting whenever these levels correspond to concepts of the user's universe.

In the future, we would like to define operations which change the structure of the relations. For instance a projection which forgets some parts of the tree and a join which merge two trees identifying some of their nodes but possibly not all of them. Another issue concerns operations distributed on the inner grains. At the moment, union and product act on the coarsest grains, on the first level of the tree structure. Union and product could be performed smaller grain by smaller grain, on inner nodes of trees.

Acknowledgements

The author is grateful to Jacques Sakarovitch for a valuable discussion.

References

1. Koskenniemi, K.: Two-level morphology: a general computational model for word-form recognition and production. Technical Report 11, Department of General Linguistics, University of Helsinki (1983)
2. Sproat, R.: Morphology and Computation. The MIT Press, Cambridge, Massachusetts (1992)
3. Elgot, C.C., Mezei, J.E.: On relations defined by generalized finite automata. IBM journal of Research and Development 9, 47–68 (1965)
4. Frougny, C., Sakarovitch, J.: Synchronized rational relations of finite and infinite words. Theoretical Computer Science 108, 45–82 (1993)
5. Comon, H., Dauchet, M., Gilleron, R., Jacquemard, F., Lugiez, D., Tison, S., Tommasi, M.: Tree automata techniques and applications (1997) release (September 6, 2005) Available on http://www.grappa.univ-lille3.fr/tata

6. Kaplan, R.M., Kay, M.: Regular models of phonological rule systems. Computational Linguistics 20(3), 331–378 (1994)
7. Yli-Jyrä, A.M., Koskenniemi, K.: Compiling contextual restrictions on strings into finite-state automata. In: Proceedings of the Eindhoven FASTAR Days 2004, Eindhoven, The Netherlands (September 3–4, 2004)
8. Mohri, M., Pereira, F.C.N., Riley, M.: Weighted finite-state transducers in speech recognition. Computer Speech and Language 16, 69–88 (2002)
9. Sakarovitch, J.: Éléments de theorie des automates. Éditions Vuibert (Paris, France) (2003)

Memory Reduction for Strategies in Infinite Games

Michael Holtmann and Christof Löding

RWTH Aachen, Lehrstuhl für Informatik 7, 52056 Aachen, Germany
{holtmann,loeding}@i7.informatik.rwth-aachen.de

Abstract. We deal with the problem of reducing the memory necessary for implementing winning strategies in infinite games. We present an algorithm that is based on the notion of game reduction. The key idea of a game reduction is to reduce the problem of computing a solution for a given game to the problem of computing a solution for a new game which has an extended game graph but a simpler winning condition. The new game graph contains the memory to solve the original game. Our algorithm computes an equivalence relation on the vertices of the extended game graph and from that deduces equivalent memory contents. We apply our algorithm to Request-Response and Staiger-Wagner games where in both cases we obtain a running time polynomial in the size of the extended game graph. We compare our method to the technique of minimising strategy automata and present an example for which our approach yields a substantially better result.

Keywords: memory reduction, infinite games, request-response game, Staiger-Wagner game, strategy, attractor, automaton, reduction, Büchi, DWA, GASt.

1 Introduction

Infinite games constitute a powerful tool for synthesis and verification of reactive systems such as protocols and controllers (cf. [1]). We consider the case of two players, Player 0 corresponds to the system and Player 1 to the environment. The system is represented by a finite directed graph $G = (Q, E)$ with each vertex belonging to either player. The players move in alternation building up a play ρ. After infinitely many steps Player 0 is declared the winner if ρ satisfies the winning condition φ (modelling the requirements demanded from the system). A solution to an infinite game is indicated by the sets of vertices from where the players can win, and corresponding winning strategies. Accordingly, solving an infinite game amounts to constructing controller programmes that realise certain specifications.

A Muller winning condition is given by a family $\mathcal{F} = \{F_1, \ldots, F_k\}$ with $F_i \subseteq Q$ (cf. [2]). A play is won by Player 0 if the set of vertices visited infinitely often is one of the F_i. Büchi and Landweber showed that the problem of finding a solution to a Muller game is decidable (cf. [3]). Gurevich and Harrington showed

Jan Holub and Jan Žd'árek (Eds.): CIAA 2007, LNCS 4783, pp. 253–264, 2007.

that in Muller games there exist winning strategies for both players that need only finite memory (cf. [4]). The amount of memory needed to realise a specific strategy corresponds to the size of the respective controller programme, e.g. a finite automaton with output. Hence, the problem of memory reduction has been intensely investigated. Whereas some winning conditions can be solved by positional strategies, others require an exponential memory (cf. [5],[6]). In [7] it is shown that there exist Muller games requiring a memory of size at least $n!$ if $\mathcal{O}(n)$ is the size of the game graph. A similar result is shown for Streett games in [8]. There, the lower bound on the size of the needed memory is $k!$ where k is the number of Streett pairs.

Even if worst case lower bounds exist for specific games the average case requires less memory. One approach to memory reduction is to compute a strategy and then minimise the corresponding automaton. This procedure may yield a result of arbitrary size depending on the computed strategy. As a remedy, we present an algorithm which is applied before computing a strategy. It is based on the concept of game reduction, i.e. simulation of a winning condition by a simpler one at the expense of the size of the game graph. The idea is to reduce the size of the extended game graph before computing a winning strategy. Basically, this leads to simplifying the winning strategies in the original game. For reducing the game graph we proceed via a transformation to ω-automata and introduce a notion of equivalent memory contents.

Generally, our algorithm is applicable to all common winning conditions but we have implemented it only for Request-Response and Staiger-Wagner games. In a Request-Response game we are given a set $\mathcal{F} = \{(P_1, R_1), \ldots, (P_k, R_k)\}$ with $P_i, R_i \subseteq Q$. Player 0 wins if each visit to the set P_i is eventually followed by a visit to the set R_i. This type of game can be reduced to a Büchi game using a memory of size $2^k \cdot k$ which can be shown to be asymptotically optimal (cf. [9]). In a Staiger-Wagner game we are given a set $\mathcal{F} = \{F_1, \ldots, F_k\}$ with $F_i \subseteq Q$, and Player 0 wins if the vertices visited at least once form one of the sets F_i. Staiger-Wagner games can be solved by a reduction to weak parity games and require a memory exponential in the size of the game graph (cf. [10]).

In the next section we introduce the basic notions on infinite games and the term game reduction. After that we present the two approaches to memory reduction and compare them to each other: We present a family of games where the game reduction algorithm produces a memory of exponential size which is then reduced to constant size by our new algorithm. The minimisation algorithm for finite automata with output fails to do so because the algorithm for solving the game yields a too complicated strategy whose minimal automaton is of exponential size. We conclude by giving some remarks on the implementation of our algorithm.

This article is based on [10], and any further details can be found there.

2   Preliminaries

We assume that the reader is familiar with the basic theory of ω-automata, as e.g. described in [11], and restrict this introduction to infinite games. An *infinite game* $\Gamma = (G, \varphi)$ is played by two players on a finite directed graph $G = (Q, E)$ with no dead ends. The set $Q = Q_0 \,\dot{\cup}\, Q_1$ is a disjoint union of Player 0 and Player 1 vertices. A *play* is a sequence $\rho = q_0 q_1 q_2 \cdots \in Q^\omega$ such that $(q_i, q_{i+1}) \in E$ for every $i \in \mathbb{N}$. The *winning condition* $\varphi \subseteq Q^\omega$ denotes the set of plays winning for Player 0.

A *strategy* for Player 0 is a partial function $f : Q^* Q_0 \dashrightarrow Q$ that assigns to any play prefix $q_0 \cdots q_i$ with $q_i \in Q_0$ a state q_{i+1} such that $(q_i, q_{i+1}) \in E$. The function f is called a *winning strategy for Player 0 from q* if any play ρ starting in vertex q that is played according to f is won by Player 0. The *winning region* W_0 of Player 0 is the set of all vertices from where Player 0 has a winning strategy. A *strategy automaton* for Player 0 is a Mealy automaton $\mathcal{A} = (S, Q, s_0, \sigma, \tau)$ with a memory update function $\sigma : S \times Q \rightarrow S$ and a transition choice function $\tau : S \times Q_0 \rightarrow Q$. The strategy $f_{\mathcal{A}}$ implemented by $\mathcal{A}$ is defined as $f_{\mathcal{A}}(q_0 \cdots q_i) := \tau(\sigma^*(s_0, q_0 \cdots q_{i-1}), q_i)$ for $q_i \in Q_0$. A strategy f is called *positional* if it can be implemented by a strategy automaton with one state. The *size* of a strategy is the minimal number of states among all automata implementing this strategy. By a *solution* to an infinite game we mean the winning regions of the two players and corresponding winning strategies.

We now briefly introduce the winning conditions that are relevant for us. In a Büchi game we are given a designated set $F \subseteq Q$ and Player 0 wins if and only if the set of vertices visited infinitely often contains a state from F. Büchi games can be solved by positional strategies. In a weak parity game we are given a colouring $c : Q \rightarrow \{0, \ldots, k\}$ with $k \in \mathbb{N}$. Player 0 wins ρ if and only if the maximal colour occurring in ρ is even. Weak parity games can be solved by a conventional algorithm where we obtain positional winning strategies for both players (cf. [12]). We perform a backward breadth-first search through the game graph and compute for each even (resp. odd) colour the sets of vertices from where Player 0 (resp. Player 1) can win by reaching a vertex of this colour. Since each vertex can be removed after it has been visited the overall running time of the algorithm is in $\mathcal{O}(|E|)$.

There are more complex winning conditions which are not solvable by positional strategies. In a Request-Response game we are given a family of pairs $\mathcal{F} = \{(P_1, R_1), \ldots, (P_k, R_k)\}$ and Player 0 wins if and only if for all $i = 1, \ldots, k$ any visit to the set P_i is eventually followed by a visit to the set R_i. In a Staiger-Wagner game we are given a family $\mathcal{F} = \{F_1, \ldots, F_k\}$ and Player 0 wins if and only if the set of visited vertices is one of the sets in $\mathcal{F}$ (cf. weak Muller games in [13]). To solve these games we introduce the notion of game reduction: From the given game graph we construct a new game graph extended by a memory component, such that on this new game graph a simpler winning condition suffices to simulate the original game. The new edge relation comprises the memory update. Usually, the extended game graph gets exponentially large in the size of the original game graph.

Definition 1. *Let $\Gamma = (G, \varphi)$ and $\Gamma' = (G', \varphi')$ be infinite games with game graphs $G = (Q, E)$ and $G' = (Q', E')$ and φ, φ' the winning conditions. We say that Γ is reducible to Γ' (short: $\Gamma \leq \Gamma'$) if and only if the following hold:*

1. $Q' = S \times Q$ *for a finite memory set* S *(and* $q \in Q_i \iff (s, q) \in Q'_i$*)*
2. *Every play* ρ *of* Γ *is transformed into a unique play* ρ' *of* Γ' *by*
   (a) $\exists s_0 \in S, \forall q \in Q : \rho(0) = q \implies \rho'(0) = (s_0, q)$
   (b) *Let* $(s, q) \in Q'$:
      i. $(q, q') \in E \implies \exists s' \in S : ((s, q), (s', q')) \in E'$
      ii. $((s, q), (s_1, q_1)) \in E', ((s, q), (s_2, q_2)) \in E' \implies s_1 = s_2$
   (c) $((s, q), (s', q')) \in E' \implies (q, q') \in E$
3. ρ *is winning for Player 0 in* $\Gamma \iff \rho'$ *is winning for Player 0 in* Γ'

From a positional winning strategy for Player 0 in Γ' we can directly construct a strategy automaton $\mathcal{A}$ implementing a winning strategy for Player 0 in Γ in the following way: The transition structure of G' yields the memory update function σ, and any positional winning strategy for Player 0 in Γ' yields a feasible output function τ for the automaton $\mathcal{A}$.

We now give a game reduction algorithm from Staiger-Wagner to weak parity games. As memory S we use the powerset of Q, i.e. $S = 2^Q$. The idea is to start with the empty set ($s_0 := \emptyset$) and accumulate the visited states in the memory. Note that in our definition of game reduction the memory update only depends on the source vertex of a transition (cf. item 2.(b).ii). This means for any $s \in S$ and any transition (q, q') in G we get a transition $((s, q), (s \cup \{q\}, q'))$ in G' (and no other transitions). The colouring c for the weak parity condition is defined as follows:

$$c((R, q)) := \begin{cases} 2 \cdot |R \cup \{q\}| - 1 & , \text{ if } R \cup \{q\} \notin \mathcal{F} \\ 2 \cdot |R \cup \{q\}| & , \text{ if } R \cup \{q\} \in \mathcal{F} \end{cases}$$

With these definitions of S, E' and c one can easily verify that the properties from Def. 1 are satisfied. For a game reduction from Request-Response to Büchi games we refer to [9].

3   Reduction of Strategy Automata

3.1   Minimisation of DFA with Output

Our aim is to present an algorithm for reducing the needed memory. One approach could be to compute a strategy and then minimise the corresponding automaton, i.e. a DFA with output (cf. [14]). Two states are considered equivalent if taking either of them as initial state the same output functions are computed. This technique has a certain drawback because it depends on the implemented strategy. Consider the Staiger-Wagner game in the left part of Fig. 1 with $\mathcal{F} = \{\{0, 1\}, \{0, 2\}, \{0, 1, 2, 3\}\}$. (Player 0 vertices are drawn as circles.)

Player 0 has the winning region $W_0 = \{0, 1\}$ but does not have any positional winning strategy. If vertex 1 is visited then Player 0 has to move from vertex 2 to vertex 3. Otherwise, he has to stay at vertex 2 forever. To implement this winning strategy we need a memory of size two. Consider the strategy automaton $\mathcal{A}_n$ from the right part of Fig. 1 which, of course, is not the automaton obtained by a standard algorithm but only used to illustrate the problem. $\mathcal{A}_n$ implements the following strategy f_n: If vertex 1 is visited then stay in vertex 2 for exactly

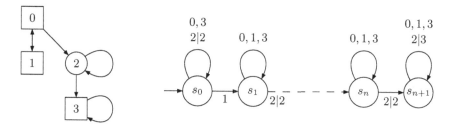

Fig. 1. Simple Staiger-Wagner game

n times, then move on to vertex 3. If vertex 1 is not visited then stay in vertex 2. Obviously, for any $n \in \mathbb{N}$ this strategy is winning for Player 0 from W_0. Note that $\mathcal{A}_n$ is minimal w.r.t. the implemented strategy because we need the states $s_1, \ldots, s_n$ to count the number of revisits to vertex 2. If we assume a large value for n then this is very unsatisfying. In Sect. 3.3 we provide a family of games for which a standard algorithm computes a complicated winning strategy although a simple one exists.

A second argument against the above minimisation technique is the fact that numerous transitions in a strategy automaton can be irrelevant for the definition of the implemented strategy. The general reason for this is that a strategy is a partial function. For a further discussion on problems arising in the minimisation of partially specified Mealy automata see [15].

3.2 Reduction of Game Graphs

We present an algorithm which is independent of the winning strategies a player has in a specific game. The idea is to modify the output of the game reduction before constructing the strategy automaton. More precisely, we reduce the size of G' by computing an equivalence relation on S. We view Γ' as an ω-automaton accepting the winning plays for Player 0 in Γ and compute an equivalence relation $\approx$ on $S \times Q$. From $\approx$ we derive the equivalence relation $\approx_S$ on S. As the new memory we obtain the set $S' := S/_{\approx_S}$. Our algorithm is illustrated in Fig. 2.

Definition 2. *Let* $\Gamma = (G, \varphi)$ *and* $\Gamma' = (G', \varphi')$ *be two infinite games and* $\Gamma \leq \Gamma'$. *We define the (deterministic) game automaton* $\mathcal{A} = ((S \times Q) \,\dot\cup\, \{q_0, q_{sink}\}, Q_0, Q, q_0, \delta, \psi)$ *where* $Q_0 \subseteq Q$ *is used to keep the information on the partition of the vertices. Basically,* δ *is adopted from* E' *and a transition is labelled by the Q-component of its target state. For* $q' \in Q$ *we set* $\delta(q_0, q') := (s_0, q')$ *and* $\delta(q_{sink}, q') := q_{sink}$. *For* $s \in S, q, q' \in Q$ *with* $(q, q') \notin E$ *we set* $\delta((s, q), q') := q_{sink}$. *The acceptance condition* ψ *is defined on an abstract level: A run* $q_0\rho'$ *of* $\mathcal{A}$ *is defined to be accepting if and only if* ρ' *is a winning play for Player 0 in* Γ'. *Constructing an infinite game from a given game automaton works the other way round. (For that we need* Q_0.) *We call this an automaton game.*

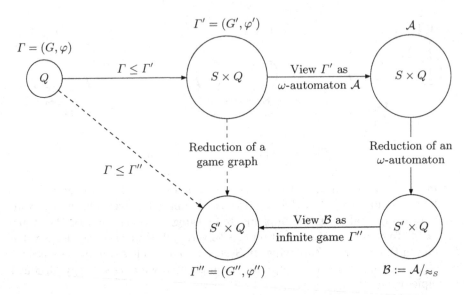

Fig. 2. Algorithm for Memory Reduction

Our idea is to reduce the game automaton in such a way that the properties of a game reduction are preserved. This primarily requires two things. First, to retain item 1. from Def. 1 we are only allowed to modify the set S even if we proceed via an equivalence relation on the set $S \times Q$. Second, to achieve item 3. we have to preserve the recognised language. To be able to define the quotient automaton in a natural way we require the following structural properties for $\approx$.

Definition 3. *Let $\mathcal{A}$ be a game automaton and let $\approx$ be an equivalence relation on $S \times Q$. We say that $\approx$ is compatible with $\mathcal{A}$ if and only if the following hold:*

1. *For all $s_1, s_2 \in S, q, q' \in Q$:*
   $(s_1, q) \approx (s_2, q) \implies \delta((s_1, q), q') \approx \delta((s_2, q), q')$
2. *Let ρ and ρ' be two runs in $\mathcal{A}$ starting at arbitrary states such that $\rho(i) \approx \rho'(i)$ for all $i \geq 0$. Then ρ is accepting if and only if ρ' is accepting.*

The quotient automaton of $\mathcal{A}$ w.r.t. $\approx_S$ is defined on the basis of the following observation. If $(s_1, q) \approx (s_2, q)$ holds then from these two states exactly the same inputs are accepted. (Note that $\mathcal{A}$ gets as inputs the plays of the game Γ.) If this is true for all $q \in Q$ then s_1 and s_2 can be considered equivalent.

Definition 4. *Let $\mathcal{A}$ be a game automaton and let $\approx$ be a compatible equivalence relation on $S \times Q$. The equivalence relation $\approx_S$ on S is defined as follows:*

$$s_1 \approx_S s_2 :\Longleftrightarrow \forall q \in Q : (s_1, q) \approx (s_2, q)$$

For $s \in S$, $[s]$ denotes the equivalence class of s w.r.t. $\approx_S$. Given $s_1 \approx_S s_2$ and $(q, q') \in E$, let $(s'_i, q') := \delta((s_i, q), q')$ for $i = 1, 2$. According to Def. 3 we know that $(s'_1, q') \approx (s'_2, q')$ holds. However, $s'_1 \approx_S s'_2$ does not hold necessarily. To get the q'-successor of $([s_1], q)$ well-defined we use some fixed total order $\prec_S$ on S.

Definition 5. *Let $\approx$ be compatible and $\approx_S$ be derived from it as above. We define the quotient automaton $\mathcal{A}/\approx_S = ((S/\approx_S \times Q) \,\dot\cup\, \{q_0, q_{sink}\}, Q_0, Q, q_0, \delta/\approx_S, \psi/\approx_S)$. Given $([s], q) \in S/\approx_S \times Q$ and $(q, q') \in E$ we define*

$$\delta/\approx_S (([s], q), q') := ([s_{min}], q')$$

where

$$s_{min} := \min\{\hat{s}' \mid \exists \hat{s} : \hat{s} \approx_S s \text{ and } \delta((\hat{s}, q), q') = (\hat{s}', q')\}.$$

The rest of $\delta/\approx_S$ is defined analogously. Let $\rho = q_0([s_1], q_1)([s_2], q_2) \cdots$ be a run of $\mathcal{A}/\approx_S$. We define ρ to be accepting if and only if the run $\rho' = q_0(s_1', q_1)(s_2', q_2) \cdots$ of $\mathcal{A}$ (which is uniquely determined by ρ) is accepting.

The run ρ' is uniquely determined by ρ because both $\mathcal{A}$ and $\mathcal{A}/\approx_S$ are deterministic. The acceptance condition for $\mathcal{A}/\approx_S$ immediately implies $L(\mathcal{A}) = L(\mathcal{A}/\approx_S)$. For reducing Büchi and weak parity game automata there exist equivalence relations which are computable efficiently (cf. Sect. 4). Moreover, in [10] we show that each of these relations satisfies Def. 3 and that the respective quotient according to Def. 5 can be defined with the same type of acceptance condition. The claim of the following theorem is that the automaton game Γ'' of $\mathcal{A}/\approx_S$ has the same structural properties as Γ', i.e. Γ is reducible to Γ'' (indicated by the left dashed arrow in Fig. 2).

Theorem 6. *Let $\Gamma = (G, \varphi)$ and $\Gamma' = (G', \varphi')$ be infinite games and Γ be reducible to Γ'. Let $\mathcal{A}$ be the game automaton of Γ' and $\approx$ a compatible equivalence relation on $S \times Q$. Then Γ is reducible to the unique automaton game Γ'' of $\mathcal{A}/\approx_S$.*

Proof. We do not give the full proof here but refer to [10] for the details. From Def. 5 it follows that $\mathcal{A}/\approx_S$ has the state set $(S' \times Q) \,\dot\cup\, \{q_0, q_{sink}\}$ for some finite set S'. Hence, $\mathcal{A}/\approx_S$ is a game automaton and we can transform it into a unique automaton game $\Gamma'' = (G'', \varphi'')$.

To prove that Γ is reducible to Γ'' we verify items 1. to 3. from Def. 1. Item 1. is immediately satisfied by our remarks above. As the initial memory content from item 2.(a) we choose the equivalence class $[s_0]$ of s_0 and obtain as initial game positions the set $\{([s_0], q) \mid q \in Q\}$. To show that the edge relation E transfers to E'' as required in items 2.(b).i and 2.(c) we argue by simple implications using Defs. 2 and 5 and the fact that Γ is reducible to Γ'. Since edge relation E', hence also δ, has the required properties and each transition in $\mathcal{A}/\approx_S$ corresponds to a unique set of transitions in $\mathcal{A}$ we get that E'' also has the required properties. For item 2.(b).ii we show that the uniqueness of the memory update in G'' follows from the uniqueness of the memory update in G'. The proof is accomplished by contraposition.

What remains to be shown is that Player 0 wins a play ρ of Γ if and only if he wins the corresponding play ρ'' of Γ'' (item 3.). This is a simple consequence of the fact that automata $\mathcal{A}$ and $\mathcal{A}/\approx_S$ are equivalent. $\qquad\square$

Since $S' = S/\approx_S$ we get that $|S'| \leq |S|$. Of course, we want that $|S'| < |S|$. In the latter case the strategy automaton extracted from the game reduction $\Gamma \leq \Gamma''$

has less states than the one extracted from the game reduction $\Gamma \leq \Gamma'$. We now present the full memory reduction algorithm from Fig. 2 on page 258.

Algorithm 7. (MEMORY REDUCTION)
Input: Infinite game $\Gamma = (G, \varphi)$
Output: Strategy automaton $\mathcal{A}_f$ for Player 0 from W_0

1. Establish a game reduction from Γ to a new game Γ' in which Player 0 has a positional winning strategy from W_0' (cf. Def. 1).
2. View Γ' as ω-automaton $\mathcal{A}$ (cf. Def. 2).
3. Reduce ω-automaton $\mathcal{A}$: Use a compatible equivalence relation $\approx$ on $S \times Q$ to compute $\approx_S$ on S and construct the corresponding quotient game automaton $\mathcal{B} := \mathcal{A}/\approx_S$ (cf. Defs. 3,5).
4. Transform $\mathcal{B}$ into the unique automaton game $\Gamma'' = (G'', \varphi'')$ (cf. Def. 2).
5. Compute a positional winning strategy for Player 0 in Γ'' and from it construct the strategy automaton $\mathcal{A}_f$.

Note that Alg. 7 does not depend on the actual winning condition φ but that we only need a suitable relation $\approx$ to execute step 3. Moreover, Thm. 6 is even valid if Γ' does not admit positional winning strategies.

3.3   Comparison of the Two Approaches

In this section we present a family of games where our new approach yields a substantial reduction of the used memory. Consider the Staiger-Wagner game $\Gamma_n = (G_n, \varphi_n)$ with game graph G_n from Fig. 3 and φ_n determined by the set

$$\mathcal{F}_n = \{U \mid U \subseteq \{v, u_1, \ldots, u_n\}, v \in U\} \cup \{R \mid R \supseteq \{x, y\}\}.$$

Accordingly, Player 0 wins if the play remains within $\{v, u_1, \ldots, u_n\}$ or reaches both x and y. Reducing Γ_n to the weak parity game $\Gamma_n' = (G_n', \varphi_n')$ we obtain exponentially many reachable memory contents in G_n'. A memory content s is reachable if there exist $q, q' \in Q$ such that (s, q') is reachable from (s_0, q). If we solve Γ_n' with the algorithm from [12] then this yields an exponential winning strategy for Player 0 in Γ_n. If, however, we use our new algorithm to reduce G_n' before solving the game then we obtain a winning strategy of constant size.

Lemma 8. *Let $\Gamma_n = (G_n, \varphi_n)$ be defined as above and let $\Gamma_n' = (G_n', \varphi_n')$ be the weak parity game to which Γ_n is reduced to (as described on page 256). Then Player 0 wins Γ_n from vertex v such that the following hold:*

1. *The positional winning strategy f_n' for Player 0 in Γ_n' from $(\emptyset, v)$ computed by the algorithm from [12] yields a winning strategy f_n of exponential size for Player 0 in Γ_n from v.*
2. *The reduced game graph G_n'' computed by Alg. 7 has constantly many memory contents.*

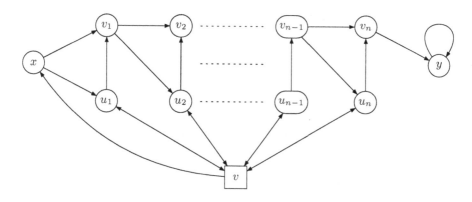

Fig. 3. Staiger-Wagner game graph G_n

Proof. We assume a play starting in vertex v and Player 1 eventually moving to vertex x. Thus, a play is of the form $\rho = v\rho_1 x\rho_2$. For abbreviation we set $U_v := \{U \mid U \subseteq \{v, u_1, \ldots, u_n\}, v \in U\}$. If we apply the game reduction algorithm from page 256 to Γ_n then we obtain a weak parity game Γ_n' where the game graph G_n' contains as memory the set of vertices visited in ρ. The algorithm for solving Γ_n' computes sets A_i from where a player can force a win by reaching the set $C_i := c^{-1}(i)$ (cf. [12]). It starts with the highest colour which is $k := 2 \cdot (2 \cdot n + 3)$ in our case. The first observation is that the algorithm will direct Player 0 to reach C_k. This is only possible if the play in ρ_2 visits each of the vertices u_i not visited in ρ_1. Secondly, Player 0 will be directed in ρ_2 to skip all vertices u_i already visited in ρ_1. This is because the computed attractor strategy chooses the shortest way into C_k. The set of u_i-vertices visited in ρ_1 uniquely determines the strategy for Player 0 after the visit to x. For example, if Player 1 moves from v directly to x without visiting any u_i then Player 0 will play the strategy that visits each vertex u_i to reach C_k. This means we get the play $\rho = vxu_1v_1 \cdots u_nv_ny^\omega$. If Player 1 visits each u_i before moving to x then we get e.g. $\rho = vu_1v \cdots u_nvxv_1 \cdots v_ny^\omega$ because in this case the shortest way into C_k is to skip all vertices u_i. Altogether, for each i the vertex u_i is visited between x and y if and only if it has not been visited between v and x. Any of the 2^n subsets in U_v yields a different strategy each requiring its own state in the strategy automaton. Hence, this automaton will be of exponential size.

To see item 2. of the lemma we have to determine the classes of $\approx_S$. First we reduce the problem of computing $\approx$ for the game automaton $\mathcal{A}$ of Γ_n' to the problem of computing the standard equivalence relation $\approx_{\mathcal{A}'}$ for a DFA $\mathcal{A}'$ uniquely determined by $\mathcal{A}$ (cf. Sect. 4 and [16]). This yields for two given states that $(s_1, q) \approx (s_2, q) \iff L(\mathcal{A}_{(s_1,q)}) = L(\mathcal{A}_{(s_2,q)})$ which allows us to identify equivalence of states with winning the same plays from the corresponding vertices in the game. The automaton $\mathcal{A}_{(s_1,q)}$ is the same as $\mathcal{A}$ except for the initial state set to (s_1, q). From $\approx$ we compute $\approx_S$ and obtain that the set $S/_{\approx_S}$ has five elements and that all sets in U_v are equivalent. Table 1 gives a review of the five equivalence classes where the sets from U_v are all in class three. $\qquad\square$

Table 1. Equivalence classes of $\approx_S$

Class	Description		Representative
	Winning Plays	Losing Plays	
1	y^ω	None	Q
2	Reach y	otherwise	$\{x\}$
3	Stay in U_v or reach both x and y	otherwise	$\{v, u_1\}$
4	Reach both x and y	otherwise	$\{v, u_1, v_1, u_2\}$
5	None	y^ω	$\{y\}$

The above lemma shows that there exist infinite games where our algorithm yields a substantial reduction of the needed memory. In [10] we also present a family of games where the situation is converse: After applying our algorithm the set of memory contents is still exponentially large. Nevertheless, we obtain a positional winning strategy for Player 0 in the original game by minimising the strategy automaton.

Generally speaking, when solving an infinite game via game reduction it is possible to use Alg. 7 for reducing the memory. The only requirement is the existence of a compatible, language-preserving equivalence relation to reduce the game automaton of Γ'. Additionally, the classical approach of minimising the strategy automaton can be executed after solving the simplified game.

4   Implementation

GASt is a tool for synthesis problems in infinite games (cf. [17]). We have integrated our memory reduction algorithm for two types of winning conditions, Request-Response and Staiger-Wagner. Request-Response games are reducible to Büchi games. For the reduction of Büchi game automata we use the notion of delayed simulation presented in [18]. It can be computed in time $\mathcal{O}(m \cdot \log(n))$.[1] This reveals a technique for memory reduction for any type of game which is reducible to a Büchi game, e.g. generalised Büchi or upwards-closed Muller. Staiger-Wagner games can be reduced to weak parity games. The corresponding weak parity game automaton is equivalent to a deterministic weak Büchi automaton (DWA). The minimisation problem for DWA can be solved in time $\mathcal{O}(n \cdot \log(n))$ by a reduction to the minimisation problem for standard DFA (cf. [16]). Both algorithms and any further details on how to compute the used equivalence relations can be found in [10]. Whereas GASt provides algorithms based on both the enumerative and symbolic representation of the state space we have considered only the enumerative case. Due to the state space explosion the running time of our algorithm grows very rapidly. Sometimes considering only the reachable vertices of G' already yields a substantial reduction of the needed memory. In this case we have to restrict the definition of $\approx_S$ further. More on this can be found in Sect. 6.1 in [10]. The following table summarises

---

[1] Let n denote the number of states and m the number of transitions.

Table 2. Computation results

n	Q_n	Γ'_n				Memory Reduction		Γ''_n		
		Create	S_n	Q'_n	Solve	$\approx_S$	Quotient	S'_n	Q''_n	Solve
2	7	40 ms	69	699	68 ms	1.8 s	0.3 s	5	23	$\leq$ 5 ms each
3	9	39 ms	203	2906	0.31 s	31.5 s	3.7 s	5	29	
4	11	0.26 s	609	11291	3.15 s	684 s	56 s	5	35	

some computation results for the game from La. 8 for the values $n = 2, 3, 4$ with and without the memory reduction algorithm.

5   Conclusion

We have presented an algorithm that reduces the memory for implementing winning strategies in infinite games. It is based on the notion of game reduction. The idea is to compute an equivalence relation on the set S of memory contents where two memory contents are considered equivalent if, from them, Player 0 wins exactly the same plays. The actual reduction is carried out via a transformation to ω-automata. Our algorithm has as parameters a game reduction and a compatible equivalence relation which mainly determine the running time. In La. 8 we have given a family of Staiger-Wagner games for which Alg. 7 reduces the needed memory to constant size whereas (without this reduction) the minimisation algorithm for strategy automata returns a memory of exponential size. This is because the algorithm from [12] computes a very complicated winning strategy for this family of examples. Our algorithm can also be applied to Muller and Streett games which can both be reduced to (strong) parity games. For the reduction of parity game automata we use the right-hand delayed simulation for alternating parity automata introduced in [19], whose computation, in our case, amounts to solving a Büchi game of size $\mathcal{O}(n^2 \cdot k)$ where n is the number of states of the game automaton and k the number of colours.

References

1. Walukiewicz, I.: A landscape with games in the background. In: Proceedings of the 19th LICS, pp. 356–366. IEEE Computer Society Press, Los Alamitos (2004)
2. Muller, D.E.: Infinite sequences and finite machines. In: Proceedings of the Fourth Annual Symposium on Switching Circuit Theory and Logical Design, Chicago, Illinois, pp. 3–16. IEEE Computer Society Press, Los Alamitos (1963)
3. Büchi, J.R., Landweber, L.H.: Solving sequential conditions by finite-state strategies. Transactions of the AMS 138, 295–311 (1969)
4. Gurevich, Y., Harrington, L.: Trees, automata and games. In: Proceedings of the 14th STOC, San Francisco, CA, pp. 60–65 (1982)
5. Thomas, W.: On the synthesis of strategies in infinite games. In: Mayr, E.W., Puech, C. (eds.) STACS 95. LNCS, vol. 900, pp. 1–13. Springer, Heidelberg (1995)
6. Zielonka, W.: Infinite games on finitely coloured graphs with applications to automata on infinite trees. Theoretical Computer Science 200, 135–183 (1998)

7. Dziembowski, S., Jurdziński, M., Walukiewicz, I.: How much memory is needed to win infinite games? In: Proceedings of the 12th LICS, Washington - Brussels - Tokyo, pp. 99–110. IEEE Computer Society Press, Los Alamitos (1997)
8. Horn, F.: Streett games on finite graphs. GDV (2005)
9. Wallmeier, N., Hütten, P., Thomas, W.: Symbolic synthesis of finite-state controllers for request-response specifications. In: Ibarra, O.H., Dang, Z. (eds.) CIAA 2003. LNCS, vol. 2759, pp. 11–22. Springer, Heidelberg (2003)
10. Holtmann, M.: Memory reduction for strategies in infinite games. Diploma Thesis (revised version), RWTH Aachen (2007), http://www-i7.informatik.rwth-aachen.de/~holtmann/
11. Thomas, W.: Languages, automata, and logic. Technical report, Christian-Albrechts-Universität Kiel, Institut für Informatik und Praktische Mathematik (1996)
12. Chatterjee, K.: Linear time algorithm for weak parity games. Technical report, EECS Department, University of California, Berkeley (2006)
13. Thomas, W.: Infinite games and verification. In: Brinksma, E., Larsen, K.G. (eds.) CAV 2002. LNCS, vol. 2404, pp. 58–64. Springer, Heidelberg (2002)
14. Hopcroft, J.E.: An nlogn-algorithm for minimizing states in a finite automaton. Technical report, Stanford University, Department of Computer Science (1971)
15. Kohavi, Z.: Switching and Finite Automata Theory. McGraw-Hill, New York (1970)
16. Löding, C.: Efficient minimization of deterministic weak ω-automata. IPL 79, 105–109 (2001)
17. Wallmeier, N.: Symbolische Synthese zustandsbasierter reaktiver Programme. Diplomarbeit, RWTH Aachen (2003)
18. Etessami, K., Wilke, T., Schuller, R.A.: Fair simulation relations, parity games, and state space reduction for Büchi automata. SIAM Journal on Computing 34, 1159–1175 (2005)
19. Fritz, C., Wilke, T.: Simulation relations for alternating parity automata and parity games. In: Ibarra, O.H., Dang, Z. (eds.) DLT 2006. LNCS, vol. 4036, pp. 59–70. Springer, Heidelberg (2006)

Syntax-Directed Translations and Quasi-alphabetic Tree Bimorphisms

Magnus Steinby[1] and Cătălin Ionuţ Tîrnăucă[2]

[1] Department of Mathematics, University of Turku
FIN-20014 Turku, Finland
[2] Research Group on Mathematical Linguistics, Rovira i Virgili University
Pl. Imperial Tàrraco 1, Tarragona 43005, Spain
steinby@utu.fi, catalinionut.tirnauca@estudiants.urv.es

Abstract. We introduce a class of tree bimorphisms that define exactly the translations performed by syntax-directed translation schemata. We also show that these "quasi-alphabetic" tree bimorphisms preserve recognizability, and that their class is closed under composition and inverses.

Keywords: syntax-directed translations, regular tree languages, tree bimorphisms, natural language processing.

1 Introduction

There is an increasing demand for various forms of automatic processing of natural languages, and this has stimulated the development of appropriate mathematical models and tools. In many applications finite-state recognizers and transducers, usually with some probability or weight features, have been used with considerable success (cf. [1,2,3], for example). Finite-state machines have many attractive properties and a well-developed theory. However, finite transducers cannot perform some of the syntax-sensitive transformations and reorderings of parts of sentences frequently encountered in translations from one natural language to another, and therefore more powerful translation defining devices are called for.

The syntax-directed translation schema (SDTS) to be considered in this paper was originally introduced as a simple model of a compiler [4,5]. An SDTS consists of two context-free (CF) grammars working in parallel: an input grammar that generates the strings of the source language, and an output grammar that generates the translations of these strings. The generation of an input-output pair by an SDTS may also be viewed as a procedure in which parse trees for the input string and the output string are implicitly produced in parallel. As proposed in [6,7], for example, the quality of machine translations may be expected to improve if one utilizes the syntactic structures of the input and output sentences. This suggests the use of tree transducers (cf. [8,9] for surveys and further references) to explicitly transform input trees to output trees.

In natural language processing, closure under composition and the preservation of recognizability are important features of translations [6]. Unfortunately,

Jan Holub and Jan Žd'árek (Eds.): CIAA 2007, LNCS 4783, pp. 265–276, 2007.

the tree transformations defined by many common types of tree transducers are neither closed under composition nor do they preserve the recognizability of tree languages [10,11,8,9,7].

A tree bimorphism $B = (\varphi, R, \psi)$ consists of a (regular) tree language R and two tree homomorphisms φ and ψ, and the tree transformation defined by B is the set of all the pairs $(r\varphi, r\psi)$, where $r \in R$. Extensively studied especially in the 1970s and 1980s (cf. [12,13,14], for example), tree bimorphisms offer an elegant algebraic formalism for defining tree transformations. Moreover, by imposing suitable restrictions on the tree language or the tree homomorphisms, one can get classes of tree bimorphisms with special properties that may also be useful for applications in linguistics. By taking the yields of input and output trees, a tree bimorphism is turned into a device defining a string-to-string translation. In [15] a class of tree bimorphisms that define exactly the rational translations is given, and Shieber [16] shows that the translations defined by synchronized tree-substitution grammars are also defined by a well-known class of tree bimorphisms studied already by Arnold and Dauchet [12].

In this paper, we show that syntax-directed translation schemata are effectively equivalent to tree bimorphisms in which the tree language is local and the two homomorphisms are "quasi-alphabetic". With linguistic applications in mind, we also prove that the class of tree transformations defined by these tree bimorphisms is closed under composition and inverses, and that the transformations preserve the recognizability of tree languages. Moreover, it is shown that the same class of translations is obtained even if we either restrict the tree languages appearing in the bimorphisms to local tree languages accepted by deterministic top-down tree recognizers, or if we allow any regular tree languages.

2   Preliminaries

For any positive integer n, we denote by $[n]$ the set $\{i \mid 1 \leq i \leq n\}$. Let A, B be sets, and consider a relation $\rho \subseteq A \times B$. The fact that $(a, b) \in \rho$ for some elements $a \in A$ and $b \in B$, can also be expressed by writing $a\rho b$. For any $a \in A$, let $a\rho = \{b \mid a\rho b\}$. More generally, for any $A' \subseteq A$, $A'\rho$ is the set of all $b \in B$ such that $(a, b) \in \rho$ for some $a \in A'$. The *inverse* of ρ is the relation $\rho^{-1} = \{(b, a) \mid (a, b) \in \rho\}$ $(\subseteq B \times A)$. The *domain* and the *range* of ρ are the sets $B\rho^{-1}$, and $A\rho$, respectively. The *composition* of two relations $\rho \subseteq A \times B$ and $\rho' \subseteq B \times C$ is the relation $\rho \circ \rho' = \{(a, c) \mid a \in A, c \in C, (\exists b \in B)(a, b) \in \rho, (b, c) \in \rho'\}$. The *diagonal relation* $\{(a, a) \mid a \in A\}$ of a set A is denoted δ_A. A mapping $\varphi : A \to B$ may also be viewed as a relation $(\subseteq A \times B)$, and $a\varphi$ $(a \in A)$ denotes either the image $\varphi(a)$ of a or the set formed by it.

A *ranked alphabet* Σ is a finite set of symbols each of which has a given nonnegative integer arity. For any $m \geq 0$, the set of m-ary symbols in Σ is denoted by Σ_m. In addition to ranked alphabets, we use ordinary finite alphabets, that we call *leaf alphabets*, disjoint from the ranked alphabets.

For any ranked alphabet Σ and leaf alphabet X, the set $T_\Sigma(X)$ of Σ-*terms with variables in* X is the smallest set M such that $X \cup \Sigma_0 \subseteq M$, and $f(t_1, \ldots, t_m)$

$\in M$ whenever $m > 0$, $f \in \Sigma_m$ and $t_1, \ldots, t_m \in M$. Such terms are regarded as representations of labeled trees, and we call them ΣX-*trees*. The label of the root of a tree t is denoted by $\text{root}(t)$. Subsets of $T_\Sigma(X)$ are called ΣX-*tree languages*. We may also speak about *trees* and *tree languages* without specifying the alphabets.

The *yield* $\text{yd}(t)$, the *height* $\text{hg}(t)$ and the set $\text{fork}(t)$ of *forks* of a ΣX-tree t are defined as usual (see [8,9]):

(1) $\text{yd}(x) = x$, $\text{hg}(x) = 0$ and $\text{fork}(x) = \emptyset$ for $x \in X$;
(2) $\text{yd}(c) = \lambda$, $\text{hg}(c) = 0$ and $\text{fork}(c) = \emptyset$ for $c \in \Sigma_0$;
(3) $\text{yd}(t) = \text{yd}(t_1) \cdots \text{yd}(t_m)$, $\text{hg}(t) = \max\{\text{hg}(t_1), \ldots, \text{hg}(t_m)\} + 1$ and $\text{fork}(t) = \text{fork}(t_1) \cup \ldots \cup \text{fork}(t_m) \cup \{f(\text{root}(t_1), \ldots, \text{root}(t_m))\}$ for $t = f(t_1, \ldots, t_m)$ $(m > 0)$.

The (finite) set of all possible forks of ΣX-trees is denoted by $\text{fork}(\Sigma, X)$.

In what follows Σ, Ω and Γ are ranked alphabets, and X, Y and Z leaf alphabets. Furthermore, $\Xi = \{\xi_1, \xi_2, \ldots\}$ is a set of *variables* disjoint from all the other alphabets. For any $m \geq 0$, let $\Xi_m = \{\xi_1, \ldots, \xi_m\}$.

A *nondeterministic top-down* (ndT) ΣX-*recognizer* is a triple $\mathbf{A} = (Q, P, I)$, where $Q = Q_1$ is a unary ranked alphabet of *states* such that $Q \cap (\Sigma \cup X) = \emptyset$, $I \subseteq Q$ is the set of *initial states*, and P is a finite set of *transition rules*, each one of one of the following two types:

(1) $q(d) \to d$, where $d \in X \cup \Sigma_0$ and $q \in Q$;
(2) $q(f(\xi_1, \ldots, \xi_m)) \to f(q_1(\xi_1), \ldots, q_m(\xi_m))$, where $m > 0$, $f \in \Sigma_m$ and q, $q_1, \ldots, q_m \in Q$.

For any $s, t \in T_{Q \cup \Sigma}(X)$, $s \Rightarrow_\mathbf{A} t$ means that t is obtained by replacing an occurrence of

(i) a subtree $q(d)$ of s by d, where $q(d) \to d$ is a rule of type (1) in P, or
(ii) a subtree $q(f(t_1, \ldots, t_m))$ of s by the tree $f(q_1(t_1), \ldots, q_m(t_m))$ by using a type (2) rule $q(f(\xi_1, \ldots, \xi_m)) \to f(q_1(\xi_1), \ldots, q_m(\xi_m))$ appearing in P.

The reflexive and transitive closure of $\Rightarrow_\mathbf{A}$ is denoted by $\Rightarrow_\mathbf{A}^*$. The set $T(\mathbf{A}) = \{t \in T_\Sigma(X) \mid q(t) \Rightarrow_\mathbf{A}^* t \text{ for some } q \in I\}$ is the tree language *recognized* by $\mathbf{A}$. A ΣX-tree language R is said to be *recognizable*, or *regular*, if $R = T(\mathbf{A})$ for some ndT ΣX-recognizer $\mathbf{A}$. Let $\text{Rec}_\Sigma(X)$ be the set of recognizable ΣX-tree languages, and let Rec denote the family of all recognizable tree languages.

A *deterministic top-down* (dT) ΣX-*recognizer* is an ndT ΣX-recognizer $\mathbf{A} = (Q, P, I)$ with exactly one initial state, at most one rule of type (1) for each $d \in X \cup \Sigma_0$ and $q \in Q$, and exactly one transition of type (2) for any $f \in \Sigma_m, m > 0$ and $q \in Q$. A ΣX-tree language is *deterministic recognizable*, *dT-recognizable* for short, if it is recognized by a dT ΣX-recognizer. The family of dT-recognizable tree languages is denoted by DRec, and $\text{DRec}_\Sigma(X)$ denotes the set of all dT-recognizable ΣX-tree languages. It is well known that $\text{DRec} \subset \text{Rec}$ (see [8] or [9]).

For any $D \subseteq \Sigma \cup X$ and $E \subseteq \text{fork}(\Sigma, X)$, let $L(D, E)$ denote the set

$$\{t \in T_\Sigma(X) \mid \text{root}(t) \in D, \text{fork}(t) \subseteq E\}.$$

A ΣX-tree language R is *local (in the strict sense)*, if $R = L(D, E)$ for some D and E. Let $\text{Loc}_\Sigma(X)$ be the set of all local ΣX-tree languages, and Loc the family of local tree languages. We recall that every local tree language is regular [8].

3   Quasi-alphabetic Tree Bimorphisms

First, recall that a *tree homomorphism* (cf. [8,9,17]) $\varphi : T_\Sigma(X) \to T_\Omega(Y)$ is determined by a mapping $\varphi_X : X \to T_\Omega(Y)$ and mappings $\varphi_m : \Sigma_m \to T_\Omega(Y \cup \Xi_m)$, for all $m \geq 0$ such that $\Sigma_m \neq \emptyset$, as follows:

(1) $x\varphi = \varphi_X(x)$ for any $x \in X$,
(2) $c\varphi = \varphi_0(c)$ for any $c \in \Sigma_0$, and
(3) $t\varphi = \varphi_m(f)(\xi_1 \leftarrow t_1\varphi, \ldots, \xi_m \leftarrow t_m\varphi)$ for $t = f(t_1, \ldots, t_m)$ $(m > 0)$.

Such a tree homomorphism φ is said to be

- *linear*, if for all $m > 0$ and $f \in \Sigma_m$, no ξ_i $(i \in [m])$ appears more than once in $\varphi_m(f)$, and otherwise it is *nonlinear*;
- *non-deleting*, or *complete*, if for all $m > 0$ and $f \in \Sigma_m$, every ξ_i $(i \in [m])$ appears at least once in $\varphi_m(f)$, and otherwise it is *deleting*;
- *symbol-to-symbol*, if $\varphi_X(x) \in Y$ for every $x \in X$, $\varphi_0(c) \in \Omega_0$ for every $c \in \Sigma_0$, and for all $m > 0$ and $f \in \Sigma_m$, $\varphi_m(f)$ is of the form $g(\xi_{i_1}, \ldots, \xi_{i_k})$, where $k > 0$, $g \in \Omega_k$ and $1 \leq i_1, \ldots, i_k \leq m$;
- *alphabetic*, if $\varphi_X(x) \in Y$ for every $x \in X$, $\varphi_0(c) \in \Omega_0$ for every $c \in \Sigma_0$, and for all $m > 0$ and $f \in \Sigma_m$, $\varphi_m(f) = g(\xi_1, \ldots, \xi_m)$ for some $g \in \Omega_m$.

We denote by lH, nH, ssH, and aH the classes of all linear, non-deleting, symbol-to-symbol, and alphabetic tree homomorphisms, respectively. Further subclasses of tree homomorphisms can be obtained by combining any of these restrictions. For example, lnH is the class of all linear non-deleting tree homomorphisms.

We call a tree homomorphism $\varphi : T_\Sigma(X) \to T_\Omega(Y)$ *quasi-alphabetic*, if

(1) $\varphi_X(x) \in Y$ for every $x \in X$, and
(2) for all $m \geq 0$ and $f \in \Sigma_m$, $\varphi_m(f)$ is of the form

$$g(y_1^1, \ldots, y_1^{k_1}, \xi_{\sigma(1)}, y_2^1, \ldots, y_m^{k_m}, \xi_{\sigma(m)}, y_{m+1}^1, \ldots, y_{m+1}^{k_{m+1}}),$$

where σ is a permutation of $[m]$, for each $i \in [m+1]$, $k_i \geq 0$ and $y_i^1, \ldots, y_i^{k_i} \in Y$, and $g \in \Omega_{m'}$ for $m' = m + k_1 + \cdots + k_{m+1}$. For any φ and f as above, let $\sigma(f, \varphi)$ denote the permutation σ of the variables in $\varphi_m(f)$.

Let qH denote the class of all quasi-alphabetic tree homomorphisms.

Clearly, any quasi-alphabetic tree homomorphism is linear and non-deleting. Moreover, it is a symbol-to-symbol tree homomorphism with a special feature: a constant symbol is always mapped to a tree of height 0 or 1. We also note the following facts to be used later.

Remark 1. If $\varphi \in$ lnssH, $\psi \in$ qH and $\eta \in$ aH, then $\varphi \circ \psi, \eta \circ \psi \in$ qH.

Recall now that a *tree bimorphism* (cf. [12,8,9], for example) is a triple $B = (\varphi, R, \psi)$, where $R \subseteq T_\Gamma(Z)$ is a regular tree language, and $\varphi : T_\Gamma(Z) \to T_\Sigma(X)$ and $\psi : T_\Gamma(Z) \to T_\Omega(Y)$ are tree homomorphisms. The *tree transformation defined by* B is

$$\tau_B = \varphi^{-1} \circ \delta_R \circ \psi = \{(r\varphi, r\psi) \mid r \in R\} \ (\subseteq T_\Sigma(X) \times T_\Omega(Y)),$$

and the *translation* performed by B is the relation

$$\mathrm{yd}(\tau_B) = \{(\mathrm{yd}(r\varphi), \mathrm{yd}(r\psi)) \mid r \in R\} \ (\subseteq X^* \times Y^*).$$

For any classes H_1 and H_2 of tree homomorphisms and any class $\mathcal{R}$ of regular tree languages, we denote by $\mathbf{B}(H_1, \mathcal{R}, H_2)$ the class of all tree bimorphisms $B = (\varphi, R, \psi)$ with $\varphi \in H_1$, $R \in \mathcal{R}$ and $\psi \in H_2$, and by $\mathcal{B}(H_1, \mathcal{R}, H_2)$ the corresponding class of tree transformations. In particular, $\mathbf{B}(\mathrm{qH}, \mathrm{Loc}, \mathrm{qH})$ is the class of *quasi-alphabetic tree bimorphisms* in which the two tree homomorphisms are quasi-alphabetic and the tree language is local, and $\mathcal{B}(\mathrm{qH}, \mathrm{Loc}, \mathrm{qH})$ is the class of all the tree transformations defined by quasi-alphabetic tree bimorphisms.

4 Syntax-Directed Translation Schemata

Let us recall that a syntax-directed translation schema (cf. [4,5]) is a CF grammar with translation elements attached to each production. Whenever a production is used in the derivation of an input sentence, the associated translation element generates a part of the output sentence.

Formally, a *syntax-directed translation schema*, a SDTS, for short, is a device $T = (N, X, Y, P, S)$, where N is a finite set of *nonterminal symbols*, X is a finite *input alphabet*, Y is a finite *output alphabet*, P is a finite set of *productions* of the form $A \to \alpha; \beta$, where $\alpha \in (N \cup X)^*$, $\beta \in (N \cup Y)^*$ and the nonterminals in β are a permutation of the nonterminals in α, and $S \in N$ is the *start symbol*.

Let p be any production $A \to \alpha; \beta$ in P. The *head* A of p is denoted $\mathrm{head}(p)$. Furthermore, let σ be the permutation that shows how the nonterminals in β are related to those in α, i.e., $\sigma(i) = j$ means that the ith nonterminal in β corresponds to the jth nonterminal in α. Then, the rule p is of the form

$$A \to u_1 A_1 u_2 \cdots u_m A_m u_{m+1}; v_1 A_{\sigma(1)} v_2 \cdots v_m A_{\sigma(m)} v_{m+1}, \qquad (*)$$

where $m \geq 0$, $A, A_1, \ldots, A_m \in N$, σ is a permutation of $[m]$, and for every $i \in [m+1]$, $u_i = x_i^1 \cdots x_i^{k_i} \in X^*$ $(k_i \geq 0)$ and $v_i = y_i^1 \cdots y_i^{l_i} \in Y^*$ $(l_i \geq 0)$.

The *translation forms* of T are defined inductively as follows:

(1) (S, S) is a translation form, and the two Ss are said to be *associated*.
(2) If $(\gamma A\delta, \gamma' A\delta')$ is a translation form in which the two explicit instances of A are associated, and $A \to \alpha; \beta$ is a production in P, then $(\gamma\alpha\delta, \gamma'\beta\delta')$ is a translation form. The nonterminals of α and β are associated in the translation form exactly as they are associated in the rule. The nonterminals of γ and δ are associated with those of γ' and δ' in the new translation form exactly as in the original one.

If $(\gamma A\delta, \gamma' A\delta')$ and $(\gamma\alpha\delta, \gamma'\beta\delta')$ are as above, we write $(\gamma A\delta, \gamma' A\delta') \Rightarrow_T (\gamma\alpha\delta, \gamma'\beta\delta')$. Furthermore, for any translation forms (γ, δ) and (γ', δ'), $(\gamma, \delta) \Rightarrow_T^* (\gamma', \delta')$ means that, for some $n \geq 0$, there exists a *derivation*

$$(\gamma, \delta) \Rightarrow_T (\gamma_1, \delta_1) \Rightarrow_T \cdots \Rightarrow_T (\gamma_{n-1}, \delta_{n-1}) \Rightarrow_T (\gamma', \delta')$$

of (γ', δ') from (γ, δ) in T. The *translation defined* by T is the relation

$$\tau_T = \{(u, v) \in X^* \times Y^* \mid (S, S) \Rightarrow_T^* (u, v)\}.$$

The translations defined by SDTSs will be called simply *syntax-directed translations*.

Finally, the *input grammar* of an SDTS $T = (N, X, Y, P, S)$ is the CF grammar $G^{\text{in}} = (N, X, P^{\text{in}}, S)$, where $P^{\text{in}} = \{A \to \alpha \mid A \to \alpha; \beta \text{ in } P\}$. Similarly, the grammar $G^{\text{out}} = (N, Y, P^{\text{out}}, S)$, where $P^{\text{out}} = \{A \to \beta \mid A \to \alpha; \beta \text{ in } P\}$, is called the *output grammar* of T.

5   The Connection Between SDTSs and B(qH, Loc, qH)

In this section we exhibit the connection between SDTSs and quasi-alphabetic tree bimorphisms. Not only do they define the same translations but the derivations in an SDTS can be retrieved from the tree structures of their bimorphism counterpart.

First we show how to construct for a given SDTS $T = (N, X, Y, P, S)$ a quasi-alphabetic tree bimorphism that defines the same translation. Let Σ^P be the ranked alphabet in which, for each $m \geq 0$, the symbols in Σ_m^P are the productions in P with m pairs of nonterminals. We also consider two more ranked alphabets Σ^{in} and Σ^{out} that correspond to input grammar G^{in} and output grammar G^{out}, respectively. For any $m \geq 0$, let

$$\Sigma_m^{\text{in}} = \{[A \to \alpha] \mid A \to \alpha \in P^{\text{in}}, |\alpha| = m\}.$$

In an analogous way, Σ^{out} is defined.

The set of *derivation trees* $\text{Deriv}_T \subseteq T_{\Sigma^P}$ of T is defined inductively:

(1) $\Sigma_0^P \subseteq \text{Deriv}_T$;
(2) $p(t_1, \ldots, t_m) \in \text{Deriv}_T$ for any $m > 0$, $p \in \Sigma_m^P$ of the form (*) and $t_1, \ldots, t_m \in \text{Deriv}_T$ such that $\text{head}(\text{root}(t_i)) = A_i$ for all $i \in [m]$.

Let $E \subseteq \text{fork}(\Sigma^P, \emptyset)$ be the set of forks $p(p_1, \ldots, p_m)$, where $m > 0$, $p \in \Sigma_m^P$ is of the form (*) and $\text{head}(p_i) = A_i$ for all $i \in [m]$.

The following lemma is easily verified by tree induction on t.

Lemma 2. *For any $t \in T_{\Sigma^P}$, $t \in \text{Deriv}_T$ if and only if $\text{fork}(t) \subseteq E$.*

If we set $R_T = \{t \in \text{Deriv}_T \mid \text{head}(\text{root}(t)) = S\}$ and $D = \{p \in \Sigma^P \mid \text{head}(p) = S\}$, then $R_T = L(D, E)$ by Lemma 2. Hence, we get

Proposition 3. *For any SDTS T, the tree language R_T is local.*

Let us define two quasi-alphabetic tree homomorphisms $\varphi : T_{\Sigma^P} \to T_{\Sigma^{\text{in}}}(X)$ and $\psi : T_{\Sigma^P} \to T_{\Sigma^{\text{out}}}(Y)$ as follows. If $p = A \to u_1; v_1 \in \Sigma_0^P$, where $u_1 = x_1^1 x_1^2 \cdots x_1^{k_1}$ $(k_1 \geq 0)$ and $v_1 = y_1^1 y_1^2 \cdots y_1^{l_1}$ $(l_1 \geq 0)$, we set $\varphi_0(p) = [A \to u_1](x_1^1, x_1^2, \ldots, x_1^{k_1})$ and $\psi_0(p) = [A \to v_1](y_1^1, y_1^2, \ldots, y_1^{l_1})$.

If $t = p(t_1, \ldots, t_m)$ for some $m > 0$, and $p = A \to \alpha; \beta \in \Sigma_m^P$ is of the form (*), then let

$$\varphi_m(p) = [A \to \alpha](x_1^1, \ldots, x_1^{k_1}, \xi_1, x_2^1, \ldots, x_m^{k_m}, \xi_m, x_{m+1}^1, \ldots, x_{m+1}^{k_{m+1}}),$$

and

$$\psi_m(p) = [A \to \beta](y_1^1, \ldots, y_1^{l_1}, \xi_{\sigma(1)}, y_2^1, \ldots, y_m^{l_m}, \xi_{\sigma(m)}, y_{m+1}^1, \ldots, y_{m+1}^{l_{m+1}}).$$

Also the following lemma can be verified by tree induction.

Lemma 4. *If $t \in \text{Deriv}_T$ and $A = \text{head}(\text{root}(t\varphi))$, $(A, A) \Rightarrow_T^* (\text{yd}(t\varphi), \text{yd}(t\psi))$.*

The following converse of Lemma 4 can be proved by induction on the length of the derivation.

Lemma 5. *If $(A, A) \Rightarrow_T^* (u, v)$ with $u \in X^*$ and $v \in Y^*$, there exists t in Deriv_T such that $\text{head}(\text{root}(t\varphi)) = A$ and $(u, v) = (\text{yd}(t\varphi), \text{yd}(t\psi))$.*

Now, we get the following first part of the main theorem.

Proposition 6. *For every SDTS T, one can define a tree bimorphism B in $\mathbf{B}(\text{qH}, \text{Loc}, \text{qH})$ such that $\tau_T = \text{yd}(\tau_B)$.*

Proof. Let $T = (N, X, Y, P, S)$ be an SDTS, and let us consider the tree bimorphism $B = (\varphi, R_T, \psi)$ with φ, ψ and R_T constructed as above. Clearly, $B \in \mathbf{B}(\text{qH}, \text{Loc}, \text{qH})$. It suffices to show that $\tau_T = \text{yd}(\tau_B)$.

If $(u, v) \in \tau_T$, there exists a derivation $(S, S) \Rightarrow_T^* (u, v)$, and hence by Lemma 5, there is a t in Deriv_T such that $\text{root}(t\varphi) = S$ and $(u, v) = (\text{yd}(t\varphi), \text{yd}(t\psi))$. But then $t \in R_T$, and hence $(u, v) \in \text{yd}(\tau_B)$.

If $t \in R_T$, then $t \in \text{Deriv}_T$ and $\text{head}(\text{root}(t)) = S$, and hence $\text{root}(t\varphi) = S$. Using Lemma 4, we get $(\text{yd}(t\varphi), \text{yd}(t\psi)) \in \tau_T$. $\square$

Next, we consider the converse construction.

Proposition 7. *For each quasi-alphabetic tree bimorphism B, one can define a syntax-directed translation schema T such that $\mathrm{yd}(\tau_B) = \tau_T$.*

Proof. Let $B = (\varphi, R, \psi)$ be a tree bimorphism such that $\varphi : T_\Gamma \to T_\Sigma(X)$ and $\psi : T_\Gamma \to T_\Omega(Y)$ are quasi-alphabetic tree homomorphisms, and $R = L(D, E) \in \mathrm{Loc}_\Gamma$. We construct an SDTS $T = (N, X, Y, P, S)$ as follows. For each $f \in \Gamma$, we introduce a nonterminal $\hat{f}$, and let $N = \{S\} \cup \{\hat{f} \mid f \in \Gamma\}$, where S is a new nonterminal. Let P consist of the following rules.

(1) If $f \in D$, then $S \to \hat{f}; \hat{f}$ is in P.
(2) If $c \in \Gamma_0$, then $\hat{c} \to \mathrm{yd}(\varphi_0(c)); \mathrm{yd}(\psi_0(c))$ is in P.
(3) Consider any element $f(f_1, \ldots, f_m)$ of E. If

$$\varphi_m(f) = g(x_1^1, \ldots, x_1^{k_1}, \xi_{\sigma(1)}, x_2^1, \ldots, x_m^{k_m}, \xi_{\sigma(m)}, x_{m+1}^1, \ldots, x_{m+1}^{k_{m+1}})$$

and

$$\psi_m(f) = h(y_1^1, \ldots, y_1^{l_1}, \xi_{\theta(1)}, y_2^1, \ldots, y_m^{l_m}, \xi_{\theta(m)}, y_{m+1}^1, \ldots, y_{m+1}^{l_{m+1}}),$$

with $g \in \Sigma$, $h \in \Omega$, σ and θ permutations of $[m]$, and $k_i \geq 0$, $l_i \geq 0$, $x_i^j \in X$ $(j \in [k_i])$ and $y_i^l \in Y$ $(l \in [l_i])$ for each $i \in [m + 1]$, then P includes the rule

$$\hat{f} \to u_1 \hat{f}_{\sigma(1)} u_2 \cdots u_m \hat{f}_{\sigma(m)} u_{m+1}; v_1 \hat{f}_{\theta(1)} v_2 \cdots v_m \hat{f}_{\theta(m)} v_{m+1},$$

where for every $i \in [m + 1]$, $u_i = x_i^1 x_i^2 \cdots x_i^{k_i}$ and $v_i = y_i^1 y_i^2 \cdots y_i^{l_i}$.

To obtain the inclusion $\mathrm{yd}(\tau_B) \subseteq \tau_T$, it suffices to show by tree induction on $t \in T_\Gamma$ that if $\mathrm{root}(t) = f$ and $\mathrm{fork}(t) \subseteq E$, then $(\hat{f}, \hat{f}) \Rightarrow_T^* (\mathrm{yd}(t\varphi), \mathrm{yd}(t\psi))$. Indeed, if $t \in R$, then $\mathrm{root}(t) = f$ belongs to D and $\mathrm{fork}(t) \subseteq E$. Hence, $S \to \hat{f}; \hat{f} \in P$ and $(\hat{f}, \hat{f}) \Rightarrow_T^* (\mathrm{yd}(t\varphi), \mathrm{yd}(t\psi))$, so $(\mathrm{yd}(t\varphi), \mathrm{yd}(t\psi)) \in \tau_T$.

To show $\tau_T \subseteq \mathrm{yd}(\tau_B)$, one first proves by induction on the number of derivation steps that if $(\hat{f}, \hat{f}) \Rightarrow_T^* (u, v)$ for some $f \in \Gamma$, $u \in X^*$ and $v \in Y^*$, then there exists a tree t in T_Γ such that $\mathrm{root}(t) = f$, $\mathrm{fork}(t) \subseteq E$, and $(u, v) = (\mathrm{yd}(t\varphi), \mathrm{yd}(t\psi))$. Assuming that this has be done, we can argue as follows: if $(u, v) \in \tau_T$, then $(S, S) \Rightarrow_T^* (u, v)$, and hence there exists a nonterminal $\hat{f} \in N$ such that $S \to \hat{f}; \hat{f}$ is in P and $(\hat{f}, \hat{f}) \Rightarrow_T^* (u, v)$. But $\mathrm{root}(t) = f \in D$, $\mathrm{fork}(t) \subseteq E$ and $(u, v) = (\mathrm{yd}(t\varphi), \mathrm{yd}(t\psi))$, and hence $(u, v) \in \mathrm{yd}(\tau_B)$. $\square$

Propositions 6 and 7 can be summed up as follows:

Theorem 8. *The class of syntax-directed translations is effectively equal to the class of translations defined by quasi-alphabetic tree bimorphisms.*

We may now use tree language theory for proving properties of syntax-directed translations. The following fact may then be useful.

Lemma 9. *Quasi-alphabetic tree bimorphisms preserve recognizability, i.e., if $B \in \mathbf{B}(\mathrm{qH}, \mathrm{Loc}, \mathrm{qH})$ and R' is a regular tree language, then so is $R'\tau_B$.*

Proof. If $B = (\varphi, R, \psi)$ is in $\mathbf{B}(\mathrm{qH}, \mathrm{Loc}, \mathrm{qH})$ and R' is any recognizable tree language, then $R'\tau_B = (R'\varphi^{-1} \cap R)\psi$ is also recognizable because regular tree languages are closed under linear tree homomorphisms, inverse tree homomorphisms and intersection (see [8,9], for example). ☐

It is even easier to show, for example, that the domain and range of any syntax-directed translation are context-free languages. Indeed, let $B = (\varphi, R, \psi)$ be a quasi-alphabetic tree bimorphism such that $\tau_T = \mathrm{yd}(\tau_B)$ for a given SDTS T. Then $\mathrm{dom}(\tau_T)$ is a context-free language as the yield of the regular tree language $\mathrm{dom}(\tau_B) = (T_\Omega(Y)\psi^{-1} \cap R)\varphi = R\varphi$. Similarly, $\mathrm{range}(\tau_T) = \mathrm{yd}(R\psi)$ is seen to be context-free.

6   Classes Equivalent to B(qH, Loc, qH)

In this section we show that the essential feature of the bimorphisms in the class $\mathbf{B}(\mathrm{qH}, \mathrm{Loc}, \mathrm{qH})$ is that the tree homomorphisms are quasi-alphabetic; we may either limit or extend the class of tree languages allowed.

The construction required by the following proposition is possible because the symbols in Σ^P contain also the full information about the righthand sides of the rules in P.

Proposition 10. *For any SDTS T, the language R_T is recognizable by a deterministic top-down recognizer.*

If we add Proposition 10 to Proposition 3, the proof of Theorem 8 turns into a proof of the following fact.

Theorem 11. *The class of all syntax-directed translations is effectively equal to the class of translations defined by the tree bimorphisms belonging to the class $\mathbf{B}(\mathrm{qH}, \mathrm{Loc} \cap \mathrm{DRec}, \mathrm{qH})$.*

Next, we note that we may allow any regular language in a quasi-alphabetic tree bimorphism.

Theorem 12. *The class of all syntax-directed translations is effectively equal to the class of translations defined by the tree bimorphisms belonging to the class $\mathbf{B}(\mathrm{qH}, \mathrm{Rec}, \mathrm{qH})$.*

Proof. Let $B = (\varphi, R, \psi)$ be a tree bimorphism, where $\varphi : T_\Gamma \to T_\Sigma(X)$ and $\psi : T_\Gamma \to T_\Omega(Y)$ are quasi-alphabetic, and $R \in \mathrm{Rec}_\Gamma$. It is well known (cf. [8]) that there exist a ranked alphabet Δ, a local tree language $R' \subseteq T_\Delta$ and an alphabetic tree homomorphism $\eta : T_\Delta \to T_\Gamma$ such that $R = R'\eta$. It is easy to see that $\tau_B = \tau_{B'}$ for $B' = (\eta \circ \varphi, R', \eta \circ \psi)$. On the other hand, by Remark 1, the tree bimorphism B' is in $\mathbf{B}(\mathrm{qH}, \mathrm{Loc}, \mathrm{qH})$, and hence also $\mathrm{yd}(\tau_{B'})$ is syntax-directed by Theorem 8. ☐

7   Closure Properties of B(qH, Loc, qH)

For any tree bimorphism $B = (\varphi, R, \psi)$, the tree bimorphism (ψ, R, φ) defines the inverse of τ_B. Hence, the following fact is obvious.

Theorem 13. *The class* $\mathcal{B}(\mathrm{qH}, \mathrm{Loc}, \mathrm{qH})$ *is closed under inverses.*

Next, we shall prove that $\mathcal{B}(\mathrm{qH}, \mathrm{Loc}, \mathrm{qH})$ is closed under composition. The following useful observation is an immediate consequence of the definition of quasi-alphabetic tree homomorphisms.

Remark 14. If $\psi : T_\Gamma \to T_\Omega(Y)$ and $\varphi : T_\Lambda \to T_\Omega(Y)$ are two quasi-alphabetic tree homomorphisms, and $t\psi = t'\varphi$ for some $t = f(t_1, \ldots, t_m)$ in T_Γ and $t' = g(t'_1, \ldots, t'_{m'})$ in T_Λ, then $m = m'$, and for all $i \in [m]$, $t_{\sigma(i)}\psi = t'_{\varsigma(i)}\varphi$, where $\sigma = \sigma(f, \psi)$ and $\varsigma = \sigma(g, \varphi)$. Moreover, the $\Omega(Y \cup \Xi_m)$-trees $\psi_m(f)$ and $\varphi_m(g)$ are equal modulo a permutation of the variables $\xi_1, \ldots, \xi_m$, and we express this fact by writing $\psi_m(f) \approx \varphi_m(g)$.

The proof of Theorem 16 is based on the following lemma.

Lemma 15. *Let* $\psi : T_\Gamma \to T_\Omega(Y)$ *and* $\varphi : T_\Lambda \to T_\Omega(Y)$ *be two quasi-alphabetic tree homomorphisms, and* $R \subseteq T_\Gamma$ *and* $R' \subseteq T_\Lambda$ *two local tree languages. Then, there exist a ranked alphabet* Θ, *a local tree language* $R'' \subseteq T_\Theta$ *and two linear, non-deleting, symbol-to-symbol tree homomorphisms* $\mu : T_\Theta \to T_\Gamma$ *and* $\eta : T_\Theta \to T_\Lambda$ *such that* $\mu^{-1} \circ \delta_{R''} \circ \eta = \delta_R \circ \psi \circ \varphi^{-1} \circ \delta_{R'}$.

Proof. Let Θ be the ranked alphabet such that for every $m \geq 0$,

$$\Theta_m = \{\langle f, g \rangle \mid f \in \Gamma_m, g \in \Lambda_m, \psi_m(f) \approx \varphi_m(g)\},$$

and define the tree homomorphisms $\mu : T_\Theta \to T_\Gamma$ and $\eta : T_\Theta \to T_\Lambda$ by the following mappings $\mu_m : \Theta_m \to T_\Gamma(\Xi_m)$ and $\eta_m : \Theta_m \to T_\Lambda(\Xi_m)$, $m \geq 0$:

- $\mu_0(\langle a, b \rangle) = a$ and $\eta_0(\langle a, b \rangle) = b$;
- $\mu_m(\langle f, g \rangle) = f(\xi_{\sigma^{-1}(1)}, \ldots, \xi_{\sigma^{-1}(m)})$ and $\eta_m(\langle f, g \rangle) = g(\xi_{\varsigma^{-1}(1)}, \ldots, \xi_{\varsigma^{-1}(m)})$, where $m > 0$, $\sigma = \sigma(f, \psi)$ and $\varsigma = \sigma(g, \varphi)$.

Clearly, μ and η are linear, non-deleting, symbol-to-symbol tree homomorphisms.

Because R and R' are local, there exist $D_R \subseteq \Gamma$, $D_{R'} \subseteq \Lambda$, $E_R \subseteq \mathrm{fork}(\Gamma, \emptyset)$ and $E_{R'} \subseteq \mathrm{fork}(\Lambda, \emptyset)$ such that $R = L(D_R, E_R)$ and $R' = L(D_{R'}, E_{R'})$. The local tree language $R'' = L(D, E)$ ($\subseteq T_\Theta$) is defined as follows. In D we include all the symbols $\langle f, g \rangle \in \Theta_m$ ($m \geq 0$) such that $f \in D_R$ and $g \in D_{R'}$. The set $E \subseteq \mathrm{fork}(\Theta, \emptyset)$ contains all the forks

$$\langle f, g \rangle(\langle f_{\sigma(1)}, g_{\varsigma(1)} \rangle, \ldots, \langle f_{\sigma(m)}, g_{\varsigma(m)} \rangle),$$

where $m > 0$, $f(f_1, \ldots, f_m) \in E_R$, $g(g_1, \ldots, g_m) \in E_{R'}$, $\sigma = \sigma(f, \psi)$ and $\varsigma = \sigma(g, \varphi)$.

Let us show that $\delta_R \circ \psi \circ \varphi^{-1} \circ \delta_{R'} \subseteq \mu^{-1} \circ \delta_{R''} \circ \eta$. First we prove by tree induction on t that if $t \in T_\Gamma$ and $t' \in T_\Lambda$ are such that $\mathrm{fork}(t) \subseteq E_R$, $\mathrm{fork}(t') \subseteq E_{R'}$, $\mathrm{root}(t) = f$, $\mathrm{root}(t') = g$ and $t\psi = t'\varphi$, then there exists a tree r in T_Θ such that $\mathrm{fork}(r) \subseteq E$, $\mathrm{root}(r) = \langle f, g \rangle$, $r\mu = t$ and $r\eta = t'$.

(1) If $t = f \in \Gamma_0$, then $t' = g \in \Lambda_0$, and one can take $r = \langle f, g \rangle$.

(2) If $t = f(t_1, \ldots, t_m)$ for some $m > 0$, then $t' = g(t'_1, \ldots, t'_m)$ for some $t'_1, \ldots, t'_m \in T_\Gamma$. Let $\sigma = \sigma(f, \psi)$, $\varsigma = \sigma(g, \varphi)$, and for all $i \in [m]$, assume that $\mathrm{root}(t_i) = f_i \in \Gamma_{k_i}$ and $\mathrm{root}(t'_i) = g_i \in \Lambda_{k_i}$. Because $\mathrm{fork}(t) \subseteq E_R$ and $\mathrm{fork}(t') \subseteq E_{R'}$, we have $f(f_1, \ldots, f_m) \in E_R$, $g(g_1, \ldots, g_m) \in E_{R'}$, and for all $i \in [m]$, $\mathrm{fork}(t_i) \subseteq E_R$ and $\mathrm{fork}(t'_i) \subseteq E_{R'}$. Moreover, by Remark 2, $\psi_m(f) \approx \varphi_m(g)$ and $t_{\sigma(i)}\psi = t'_{\varsigma(i)}\varphi$ for every $i \in [m]$, and hence by the induction assumption, there exist $r_1, \ldots, r_m \in T_\Theta$ such that for each $i \in [m]$, $\mathrm{fork}(r_i) \subseteq E$, $\mathrm{root}(r_i) = \langle f_{\sigma(i)}, g_{\varsigma(i)} \rangle$, $r_i\mu = t_{\sigma(i)}$ and $r_i\eta = t'_{\varsigma(i)}$. Let $r = \langle f, g \rangle(r_1, \ldots, r_m)$. Because $t_{\sigma(i)}\psi = t'_{\varsigma(i)}\varphi$, we have $\psi_{k_i}(f_{\sigma(i)}) \approx \varphi_{k_i}(g_{\varsigma(i)})$ for every $i \in [m]$, and hence

$$\langle f, g \rangle(\langle f_{\sigma(1)}, g_{\varsigma(1)} \rangle, \ldots, \langle f_{\sigma(m)}, g_{\varsigma(m)} \rangle) \in E.$$

Thus, $\mathrm{fork}(r) \subseteq E$. But the fact that $r_i\mu = t_{\sigma(i)}$ and $r_i\eta = t'_{\varsigma(i)}$ for all $i \in [m]$, implies that $r_{\sigma^{-1}(j)}\mu = t_j$ and $r_{\varsigma^{-1}(j)}\eta = t'_j$ for all $j \in [m]$. Finally, we obtain $t = f(r_{\sigma^{-1}(1)}\mu, \ldots, r_{\sigma^{-1}(m)}\mu) = r\mu$, and $t' = g(r_{\varsigma^{-1}(1)}\eta, \ldots, r_{\varsigma^{-1}(m)}\eta) = r\eta$.

If in addition, $t \in R$ and $t' \in R'$, i.e., if $(t, t') \in \delta_R \circ \psi \circ \varphi^{-1} \circ \delta_{R'}$, then we also have $f \in D_R$ and $g \in D_{R'}$, implying that $\mathrm{root}(r) \in D$. Therefore $r \in R''$, and hence $(t, t') \in \mu^{-1} \circ \delta_{R''} \circ \eta$.

To prove the converse inclusion $\mu^{-1} \circ \delta_{R''} \circ \eta \subseteq \delta_R \circ \psi \circ \varphi^{-1} \circ \delta_{R'}$, we first show by tree induction that if $r \in T_\Theta$ is such that $\mathrm{fork}(r) \subseteq E$, then $\mathrm{fork}(r\mu) \subseteq E_R$, $\mathrm{fork}(r\eta) \subseteq E_{R'}$ and $r\mu\psi = r\eta\varphi$.

(1) If $r = \langle f, g \rangle \in \Theta_0$, then $\psi_0(f) = \varphi_0(g)$, $\mathrm{fork}(r\mu) = \emptyset \subseteq E_R$ and $\mathrm{fork}(r\eta) = \emptyset \subseteq E_{R'}$.

(2) If $r = \langle f, g \rangle(r_1, \ldots, r_m)$ for some $m > 0$, then $\mathrm{fork}(r_i) \subseteq E$ for every $i \in [m]$, and hence by the induction assumption, $\mathrm{fork}(r_i\mu) \subseteq E_R$, $\mathrm{fork}(r_i\eta) \subseteq E_{R'}$ and $r_i\mu\psi = r_i\eta\varphi$. Also, $\langle f, g \rangle(\mathrm{root}(r_1), \ldots, \mathrm{root}(r_m))$ is in E which implies that for all $i \in [m]$, $\mathrm{root}(r_i) = \langle f_{\sigma(i)}, g_{\varsigma(i)} \rangle$, $\psi_{k_i}(f_{\sigma(i)}) \approx \varphi_{k_i}(g_{\varsigma(i)})$, $f(f_1, \ldots, f_m) \in E_R$, $g(g_1, \ldots, g_m) \in E_{R'}$, where $\sigma = \sigma(f, \psi)$ and $\varsigma = \sigma(g, \varphi)$. Because $r\mu = f(r_{\sigma^{-1}(1)}\mu, \ldots, r_{\sigma^{-1}(m)}\mu)$ and $\mathrm{root}(r_{\sigma^{-1}(i)}\mu) = f_i$ for all $i \in [m]$, we have $\mathrm{fork}(r\mu) \subseteq E_R$. By a similar argument, $\mathrm{fork}(r\eta) \subseteq E_{R'}$. Because $\psi_m(f) \approx \varphi_m(g)$ and $r_i\mu\psi = r_i\eta\varphi$ for all $i \in [m]$, $\psi_m(f)(r_1\mu\psi, \ldots, r_m\mu\psi) = \varphi_m(g)(r_1\eta\varphi, \ldots, r_m\eta\varphi)$, and hence $r\mu\psi = r\eta\varphi$.

Now, if $r \in R''$, then $\mathrm{fork}(r) \subseteq E$ and $\mathrm{root}(r) \in D$, and hence $\mathrm{fork}(r\mu) \subseteq E_R$, $\mathrm{fork}(r\eta) \subseteq E_{R'}$, $r\mu\psi = r\eta\varphi$, and $\mathrm{root}(r) = \langle f, g \rangle$ with $f \in D_R$ and $g \in D_{R'}$. So, $r\mu \in R$ and $r\eta \in R'$ which concludes the proof of our lemma. $\qquad \square$

Now we can state and prove the following theorem.

Theorem 16. *The class* $\mathcal{B}(\mathrm{qH}, \mathrm{Loc}, \mathrm{qH})$ *is closed under composition.*

Proof. Let $B_1 = (\varphi_1, R_1, \psi_1)$ and $B_2 = (\varphi_2, R_2, \psi_2)$ be two tree bimorphisms in $\mathbf{B}(\mathrm{qH}, \mathrm{Loc}, \mathrm{qH})$, where $\varphi_1 : T_\Gamma \to T_\Sigma(X)$, $\psi_1 : T_\Gamma \to T_\Omega(Y)$, $\varphi_2 : T_\Lambda \to T_\Omega(Y)$, $\psi_2 : T_\Lambda \to T_\Delta(Z)$, $R_1 \in \mathrm{Rec}_\Gamma$ and $R_2 \in \mathrm{Rec}_\Lambda$.

By virtue of Lemma 15, there exist a ranked alphabet Θ, a local tree language $R \subseteq T_\Theta$ and two linear, non-deleting, symbol-to-symbol tree homomorphisms $\mu : T_\Theta \to T_\Gamma$ and $\eta : T_\Theta \to T_\Lambda$ such that $\mu^{-1} \circ \delta_R \circ \eta = \delta_{R_1} \circ \psi_2 \circ \varphi_2^{-1} \circ \delta_{R_2}$.

If we set $B = (\mu \circ \varphi_1, R, \eta \circ \psi_2)$, then $B \in \mathbf{B}(\mathrm{qH}, \mathrm{Loc}, \mathrm{qH})$ by Remark 1. Moreover, $\tau_{B_1} \circ \tau_{B_2} = \varphi_1^{-1} \circ \delta_{R_1} \circ \psi_1 \circ \varphi_2^{-1} \circ \delta_{R_2} \circ \psi_2 = \varphi_1^{-1} \circ \mu^{-1} \circ \delta_R \circ \eta \circ \psi_2 = (\mu \circ \varphi_1)^{-1} \circ \delta_R \circ (\eta \circ \psi_2) = \tau_B$.   □

References

1. Mohri, M.: Finite-state transducers in language and speech processing. Computational Linguistics 23(2), 269–311 (1997)
2. Brown, P.F., Della Pietra, S.A., Della Pietra, V.J., Mercer, R.L.: The mathematics of statistical machine translation: Parameter estimation. Computational Linguistics 19(2), 263–312 (1993)
3. Knight, K., Al-Onaizan, Y.: Translation with finite-state devices. In: Farwell, D., Gerber, L., Hovy, E. (eds.) Proc. of the AMTA 1998, pp. 421–437. Springer, London, UK (1998)
4. Irons, E.T.: A syntax directed compiler for ALGOL 60. Communications of the ACM 4(1), 51–55 (1961)
5. Aho, A.V., Ullman, J.D.: The Theory of Parsing, Translation, and Compiling, vol. 1: Parsing. Prentice Hall Professional Technical Reference, New Jersey (1972)
6. Knight, K., Graehl, J.: An overview of probabilistic tree transducers for natural language processing. In: Gelbukh, A. (ed.) CICLing 2005. LNCS, vol. 3406, pp. 1–24. Springer, Heidelberg (2005)
7. Graehl, J., Hopkins, M., Knight, K.: Extended top-down tree transducers. submitted to HLT-NAACL 2006, New York, USA (2006)
8. Gécseg, F., Steinby, M.: Tree Automata. Akadémiai Kiadó, Budapest (1984)
9. Gécseg, F., Steinby, M.: Tree languages. In: Salomaa, A., Rozenberg, G. (eds.) Handbook of Formal Languages, vol. 3. Beyond Words, pp. 1–68. Springer, Heidelberg (1997)
10. Engelfriet, J.: Bottom-up and top-down tree transformations - a comparison. Mathematical Systems Theory 9(3), 198–231 (1975)
11. Baker, B.S.: Composition of top-down and bottom-up tree transductions. Information and Control 41(2), 186–213 (1979)
12. Arnold, A., Dauchet, M.: Morphismes et bimorphismes d'arbres. Theoretical Computer Science 20, 33–93 (1982)
13. Takahashi, M.: Rational relations of binary trees. In: Salomaa, A., Steinby, M. (eds.) ICALP 1977. LNCS, vol. 72, pp. 524–538. Springer, Heidelberg (1977)
14. Bozapalidis, S.: Alphabetic tree relations. Theoretical Computer Science 99(2), 177–211 (1992)
15. Steinby, M.: On certain algebraically defined tree transformations. In: Demetrovics, J., Budach, L., Salomaa, A. (eds.) Algebra, Combinatorics and Logic in Computer Science, vol. I, II (Györ 1983). Colloquia Mathematica Societatis János Bolyai, North-Holland, vol. 42, pp. 745–764 (1986)
16. Shieber, S.M.: Synchronous grammars as tree transducers. In: Proc. of the TAG+ 7, Vancouver, Canada (2004)
17. Comon, H., Dauchet, M., Gilleron, R., Jacquemard, F., Lugiez, D., Tison, S., Tommasi, M.: Tree automata techniques and applications (1997), Available online http://www.grappa.univ-lille3.fr/tata

Finite State Automata Representing
Two-Dimensional Subshifts

Nataša Jonoska[1,*] and Joni B. Pirnot[2]

[1] University of South Florida, Department of Mathematics, Tampa, FL 33620
[2] Manatee Community College, Department of Mathematics, Bradenton, FL 34207
jonoska@math.usf.edu, pirnotj@mccfl.edu

Abstract. We employ a two-dimensional automaton defined in [5] to recognize a class of two-dimensional shifts of finite type having the property that every admissable block found within the related local picture language can be extended to a point of the subshift. Here, we show that the automaton accurately represents the image of the represented two-dimensional shift of finite type under a block code. We further show that such automata can be used to check for a certain type of two-dimensional transitivity in the factor language of the corresponding shift space and how this relates to periodicity in the two-dimensional case. The paper closes with a notion of "follower sets" used to reduce the size of the automata representing two-dimensional sofic shifts.

Keywords: two-dimensional subshift, transitivity, periodicity.

1 Introduction

To each two-dimensional subshift, one may associate a factor language based on blocks appearing in points of the subshift. For two-dimensional shifts of finite type, there is also a notion of the language of the subshift being contained within a local picture language defined by a finite set of 2×2 blocks. Unlike one-dimensional subshifts, two-dimensional subshifts need not contain a periodic point [1,6] which leads to the undecidabilty of the emptiness problem. Specifically, it is undecidable whether blocks appearing in the local language of a two-dimensional shift of finite type also appear in the factor language of the subshift. This makes properties of languages related to two-dimensional shift spaces difficult to analyze; many properties that are straightforward in one dimension are undecidable in higher dimensions [3,7,8].

Every recognizable picture language can be obtained as the projection of a so-called hv-local picture language [9], where the 2×2 blocks defining the language are replaced by horizontal and vertical dominoes - 1×2 and 2×1 blocks, respectively. This permits separate horizontal and vertical scanning of the pictures, which suggests representation of two-dimensional languages through the use of two separate graphs/matrices [4,11]. In symbolic dynamics however,

* Supported in part by NSF Grants CCF #0523928 and #0432009.

Jan Holub and Jan Žd'árek (Eds.): CIAA 2007, LNCS 4783, pp. 277–289, 2007.
© Springer-Verlag Berlin Heidelberg 2007

one disadvantage to separate graphs for horizontal and vertical movement is that when a block map is applied to graphs representing two-dimensional shifts of finite type, the newly-labeled graphs often fail to correspond to the sofic subshift that is the image of the map [2]. We note that in the case when the language defined by the shift of finite type X is precisely the local language determined by the set of defining blocks, the factor language of the sofic shift obtained as an image of X is a recognizable language (as defined in [3], but without the boundary symbol #) that contains all its factors.

A single graph representing certain two-dimensional subshifts was introduced in [5]. Here, Proposition 7 shows how the underlying graph of this automaton can be used to accurately represent the sofic shift space that results from application of a block code to the represented shift of finite type. Theorem 9 then provides an algorithm to determine whether the factor language of the represented shift space exhibits a type of two-dimensional transitivity referred to as uniform horizontal transitivity, and Theorem 10 relates uniform horizontal transitivity to periodicity in the two-dimensional case. We show that a notion similar to that of follower sets (right context) in one-dimensional languages can be associated to the two-dimensional automaton. This provides state reduction possibility of the automaton similar to that obtained as a result of the Myhill-Nerode Theorem.

2   Notation and Terminology

A discussion of one-dimensional symbolic dynamical systems can be found in [10]; here we supply additional notation and terminology required for the two-dimensional case. Let Σ be a finite alphabet and define the *two-dimensional full Σ-shift* to be $\Sigma^{\mathbb{Z}^2}$. A *point* $x \in \Sigma^{\mathbb{Z}^2}$ is a function $x : \mathbb{Z}^2 \to \Sigma$. For $x \in \Sigma^{\mathbb{Z}^2}$ and $w \in \mathbb{Z}^2$, we may denote $x(w)$ as x_w; for $x \in \Sigma^{\mathbb{Z}^2}$ and $R \subseteq \mathbb{Z}^2$, x_R denotes the restriction of x to R. We call R a region, and we call a finite region $S \subset \mathbb{Z}^2$ a *shape*. In particular, $[-j,j]^2$ is the square shape centered at the origin. The set $\Sigma^{\mathbb{Z}^2}$ is a compact metric space with metric $\rho(x,y) = 2^{-j}$, where for $x, y \in \Sigma^{\mathbb{Z}^2}$, j is the largest integer such that $x_{[-j,j]^2} = y_{[-j,j]^2}$. (When $x = y$, define $\rho(x,y) = 0$.) For $v \in \mathbb{Z}^2$, define the *two-dimensional translation in direction v* as σ^v where σ^v is defined by $(\sigma^v(x))_w = x_{w+v}$. A subset $X \subseteq \Sigma^{\mathbb{Z}^2}$ is said to be translation invariant if for all $v \in \mathbb{Z}^2$, $\sigma^v(X) \subseteq X$. If $X \subseteq \Sigma^{\mathbb{Z}^2}$ is translation invariant and closed with respect to the metric ρ, we say that X is a *two-dimensional shift space* (or a *subshift* of the full shift). Define a *design* γ on a shape S to be a function $\gamma : S \to \Sigma$, where S has been *normalized* so that $\min\{i : (i,j) \in S\} = 0$ and $\min\{j : (i,j) \in S\} = 0$. If Γ is a set of designs on a fixed shape S, then a *two-dimensional shift of finite type* is the set

$$X := \{x \in \Sigma^{\mathbb{Z}^2} : \forall v \in \mathbb{Z}^2, (\sigma^v(x))_S \in \Gamma\}. \tag{1}$$

For a design γ on a rectangular shape $T \subset \mathbb{Z}^2$ having m rows and n columns, we call γ an $m \times n$ *block* and denote such designs by $B_{m,n}$. (We may drop the subscripts when the number of rows and columns is irrelevant.) We say that an

$m \times n$ block has *height* m, *length* n, and *thickness* $k = \max\{m, n\}$. For a design $B : T \to \Sigma$, a *subblock* B' of B is the restriction of the design to a rectangular subset $T' \subseteq T \subset \mathbb{Z}^2$. In such cases, we say that B *encloses* B' and denote this by $B' \sqsubseteq B$. For fixed r and c, the set of all $r \times c$ subblocks of B is denoted as $F_{r,c}(B)$, and the set of all rectangular subblocks of B is denoted with $F(B)$. The set of all blocks of any size over Σ is denoted by Σ^{**}, with a *picture language* over the alphabet Σ being any subset of Σ^{**}. The blocks of a shift space form a picture language: say block $B : T \to \Sigma$ *occurs* in $X \subseteq \Sigma^{\mathbb{Z}^2}$ if there exists an $x \in X$ such that $x_T = B$. Then the *factor language* of a shift space X is the picture language of all blocks that occur in points of X. That is,

$$F(X) := \{F_{m,n}(x) : m, n \geq 0, x \in X\}. \tag{2}$$

The factor language of a shift space uniquely determines the shift space; that is, for shift spaces X and Y, $X = Y$ if and only if $F(X) = F(Y)$ [10].

A *local picture language* L is one such that $B \in L$ if and only if $F_{k,k}(B) \subseteq Q$, where Q is a finite set of allowed $k \times k$ blocks. For a two-dimensional shift of finite type X defined by a set of designs Γ on shape S, let T be the $r \times c$ rectangular shape of minimal dimension that contains S. For thickness $k = \max\{r, c\}$, set $Q = F_{k,k}(X)$ and let ψ be a normalized $k \times k$ square shape. There is no loss of generality in assuming that X is defined by Q rather than by Γ. The *allowed blocks* of a shift of finite type X is the local picture language

$$A(X) := \{B \in \Sigma^{**} : F_{k,k}(B) \subseteq Q\}. \tag{3}$$

(For $B = B_{m,n}$ with $m < k$ or $n < k$, we say $B_{m,n}$ is in $A(X)$ if there exists $B'_{m',n'}$ with $m', n' \geq k$ such that $B'_{m',n'}$ is in $A(X)$ and $B_{m,n} \sqsubset B'_{m',n'}$.) We point out that for $B \in \Sigma^{**}$, $F_{k,k}(B) \subseteq Q$ is necessary for $B \in F(X)$ but is not sufficient. That is, for a two-dimensional shift of finite type, a block in $A(X)$ need not appear as a block in $F(X)$ since the emptiness problem raises the question of whether all blocks allowed by the structure of the local picture language may appear as subblocks of some point in the shift space.

For a two-dimensional shift of finite type X, we can transform $x \in X$ into a new point $y \in Y \subseteq \Delta^{\mathbb{Z}^2}$ over some new alphabet Δ. For a $k \times k$ square shape T, a function $\Phi : F_{k,k}(X) \to \Delta$ that maps $k \times k$ blocks in $F(X)$ to symbols in Δ by $\Phi(x_{T+w}) = y_w$ is called a $k \times k$-*block map*. The map $\phi : X \to \Delta^{\mathbb{Z}^2}$ defined by $y = \phi(x)$ with y_w induced by Φ is called a $k \times k$-*block code*, and its image $Y = \phi(X)$ is called a *two-dimensional sofic shift*. When the block code ϕ is invertible, it is said that ϕ is a *conjugacy* and that the spaces X and Y are *conjugate*. If ϕ is not one-to-one, then $\phi(X) = Y$ need no longer be a shift of finite type, in which case we say that Y is a *strictly sofic shift*.

3   Automata Representing Two-Dimensional Sofic Shifts

A two-dimensional automaton can be viewed as a finite directed graph with two disjoint sets of directed edges representing horizontal and vertical transitions. For subshifts whose languages contain all their factors, we take every state (vertex) to be initial and terminal. The graph construction defined in [5] is based on interlacing horizontal and vertical movement in the graph's transitions, which allows the input data to consist of $m \times n$ blocks that can be scanned locally (and intermittently) by both horizontal and vertical transitions. The general idea is that given an input block, sequences of symbols appearing in a window of fixed size are read as the block is scanned from the lower-left corner to the upper-right corner by traveling in two directions (up and/or to the right) within the constraints of the block's dimensions. If the automaton accepts all such sequences of symbols appearing as a result of these moves, and the set of all such sequences overlaps progressively, then the block is accepted by the automaton.

Proposition 1. *[5] Let X be a two-dimensional shift of finite type having the property $F(X) = A(X)$. Then there exists a finite state two-dimensional automaton $\mathcal{M}_{F(X)}$ such that the language recognized by $\mathcal{M}_{F(X)}$ is $F(X)$.*

Example 2. Define $X \subseteq \{a, b\}^{\mathbb{Z}^2}$ to be a two-dimensional shift of finite type such that for every point $x \in X$, any appearance of b is surrounded by a's. This subshift has the property that $A(X) = F(X)$ since for any block $B \in A(X)$, one can simply surround B with a configuration of the plane populated entirely with a's. The language of the shift space X is defined through the set of allowed 2×2 blocks $Q = F_{2,2}(X)$ depicted as states in Figure 1. By applying a 2×2 invertible block code, X is seen to be conjugate to $X' \subseteq \{p, q_1, q_2, q_3, q_4\}^{\mathbb{Z}^2}$. Using solid lines to represent horizontal transitions and dashed lines to represent vertical transitions, the graph depicted in Figure 1 accurately represents both X and X'.

In one dimension, the set of labels of bi-infinite paths of an automaton are precisely the points of the represented shift space. An analogous representation

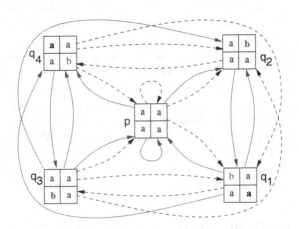

Fig. 1. Shift of finite type X where any b is surrounded entirely by a's. A representation of the sofic shift X' is achieved by using $Q' = \{p, q_1, q_2, q_3, q_4\}$.

of bi-infinite paths in two dimensions will require the following definition. In Definition 3, square brackets are used to avoid the confusion of the symbol $q_{(i,j)} = a \in \Sigma$ with the state associated to the ordered pair $(i,j) \in \mathbb{Z}^2$.

Definition 3. *A* grid-infinite path *Π in $\mathcal{M}_{F(X)} = (Q, E, s, t, \lambda)$ is defined by a pair of maps, $\Pi_h : \mathbb{Z}^2 \to Q$ and $\Pi_v : \mathbb{Z}^2 \to Q$, and is denoted as a collection of states $\{q_{[i,j]}\}$ and the transitions that accompany these states.*

$$
\begin{array}{ccccccc}
& \vdots & & \vdots & & \vdots & \\
& \uparrow & & \uparrow & & \uparrow & \\
\cdots & q_{[-1,1]} & \to & q_{[0,1]} & \to & q_{[1,1]} & \to \cdots \\
& \uparrow & & \uparrow & & \uparrow & \\
\cdots & q_{[-1,0]} & \to & q_{[0,0]} & \to & q_{[1,0]} & \to \cdots \\
& \uparrow & & \uparrow & & \uparrow & \\
\cdots & q_{[-1,1]} & \to & q_{[0,-1]} & \to & q_{[1,-1]} & \to \cdots \\
& \vdots & & \vdots & & \vdots &
\end{array}
$$

This collection is such that $\forall (i,j) \in \mathbb{Z}^2$, the following hold:
i) $q_{[i,j]} \in Q$,
ii) $q_{[i,j]} \to q_{[i+1,j]} = e_h \in E$ *is a horizontal transition, and*
iii) $q_{[i,j]} \uparrow q_{[i,j+1]} = e_v \in E$ *is a vertical transition.*

A grid-infinite path commutes in the sense that any block described by a subset of a grid-infinite path is independent of the order in which the edges are traversed. Proposition 4 uses this fact to establish a $1-1$ correspondence between blocks in the local language and subsets of grid-infinite paths.

Proposition 4. *Let $\mathcal{M}_{F(X)} = (Q, E, s, t, \lambda)$ be the graph representation of the shift of finite type X. For a grid-infinite path Π of $\mathcal{M}_{F(X)}$, let β be a 2×2 subset of Π comprised of four adjacent states $q_{[i,j]}, q_{[i+1,j]}, q_{[i,j+1]}, q_{[i+1,j+1]}$ and the transitions that connect them. Then β represents a unique $(k+1) \times (k+1)$ block that is recognized by $\mathcal{M}_{F(X)}$.*

Corollary 5. *If X is a two-dimensional shift of finite type represented by $\mathcal{M}_{F(X)}$, then there exists a $1-1$ correspondence between points in X and grid-infinite paths in $\mathcal{M}_{F(X)}$.*

In the sequel, we sometimes refer to an $m \times n$ subset β of a grid-infinite path Π as a *block path*. Note that an $m \times n$ block path is comprised of (not necessarily distinct) mn states and describes a block $B \in F(X)$ of size $(m+k-1) \times (n+k-1)$. The labeling of a block path is denoted with $\lambda(\beta) = B$ and the states are denoted by $\beta(i,j)$ for $0 \le i \le n-1, 0 \le j \le m-1$. For example, when $\mathcal{M}_{F(X)}$ is defined via 2×2 states, a 3×7 block of symbols would be represented by a 2×6 block path. It is important that the language of the automaton $L(\mathcal{M}_{F(X)})$ be based on blocks rather than on k-phrases alone. That is, all "strings" found within an accepted block must be represented by paths in $\mathcal{M}_{F(X)}$ that originate in a single state representing the lower-left corner of the block and that terminate in a single state representing the upper-right corner of the block. For a two-dimensional shift of finite type then, points in the shift space X are precisely the labels of the grid-infinite paths found in the graph $\mathcal{M}_{F(X)}$. That is, we have the following.

Definition 6. Block $B_{m,n}$ is accepted by the automaton $\mathcal{M}_{F(X)}$ if and only if there exists a block path β in $\mathcal{M}_{F(X)}$ having $\lambda(\beta) = B_{m,n}$.

If X is a two-dimensional shift of finite type over Σ having the property that $A(X) = F(X)$, then the image of the block code $\phi : X \to \Delta^{\mathbb{Z}^2}$ induced by the $d \times d$ block map $\Phi : B_{d,d}(X) \to \Delta$ can be represented by the underlying graph of $\mathcal{M}_{F(X)}$ with states and labels adjusted accordingly. In the one-dimensional case, a graph is *deterministic* if given a label and a vertex, there is at most one path starting at the given vertex with the specified label. The graph $\mathcal{M}_{F(X)}$ is a deterministic graph in this sense, since given a state and a $k \times (k+1)$ label, at most one horizontal transition is specified. (Analogously, given a state and a $(k+1) \times k$ label, at most one vertical transition is specified.) Once a block code is applied to the states of $\mathcal{M}_{F(X)}$, the states need no longer have distinct labels and the new graph need not be deterministic. However, while there may no longer exist a $1 - 1$ correspondence between grid-infinite paths and their labels, it is still the case that points in the represented two-dimensional shift space Y are precisely the labels of the grid-infinite paths found in the graph.

Proposition 7. Let X be a two-dimensional shift of finite type represented by $\mathcal{M}_{F(X)} = (Q, E, s, t, \lambda)$, and let $Y = \phi(X)$ be the shift space that is the image of X under the block code ϕ induced by a block map Φ. If $\mathcal{M}^{\Phi}_{F(X)}$ is the finite automaton having underlying graph $\mathcal{M}_{F(X)}$ with state set Q' relabeled according to $Q' = \phi(Q)$ and edge set E' relabeled according to $\phi(\lambda(e))$, then $L(\mathcal{M}^{\Phi}_{F(X)}) = F(Y)$.

Proof. Suppose $B' \in F(Y)$ is given. Since $F(Y) = \phi(F(X)) = \phi(L(\mathcal{M}_{F(X)}))$, there exists some $B \in F(X)$ such that $\phi(B) = B'$. So for the graph $\mathcal{M}_{F(X)}$, $B \in L(\mathcal{M}_{F(X)}) = F(X)$. However, $\mathcal{M}_{F(X)}$ and $\mathcal{M}^{\Phi}_{F(X)}$ have the same underlying edge set so that $B \in L(\mathcal{M}_{F(X)}) \Rightarrow B' \in L(\mathcal{M}^{\Phi}_{F(X)})$. Therefore $F(Y) \subseteq L(\mathcal{M}^{\Phi}_{F(X)})$.

For the reverse inclusion, say $B' \in L(\mathcal{M}^{\Phi}_{F(X)})$ is given. In this case, there must exist some block path β' in $\mathcal{M}^{\Phi}_{F(X)}$ such that $\lambda(\beta') = B'$. Using the underlying portion of the graph representing β', we can find a block path β with labels from $\mathcal{M}_{F(X)}$ such that $\lambda(\beta) = B \in L(\mathcal{M}_{F(X)}) = F(X)$. In other words, $\phi(B) = B' \in F(Y)$. Therefore $L(\mathcal{M}^{\Phi}_{F(X)}) \subseteq F(Y)$.   □

We comment that although the block paths β and β' found in the proof of Proposition 7 are of the same size, the blocks B and B' that they represent need not be. That is, the image $\phi(q) = q'$ of each state $q \in Q$ has thickness $k' = 1 + k - d$. (We may assume that $k \geq d$ since whenever $F_{k,k}(X)$ defines X, then $F_{K,K}(X)$ also defines X for all $K \geq k$.)

Example 8. For the shift space X' of Example 2, apply a non-invertible 1×1 block code to create a strictly sofic shift space Y by defining ϕ such that $\phi(p) = p$ and $\phi(q_i) = q$ for $i = 1, ..., 4$. By inspection, any occurrence of q_1 in a point $x \in X'$ must be preceded horizontally by q_2 and followed vertically by q_3, whereas q_3 must be preceded horizontally by q_4. So for any point $y \in Y$, the q symbol always appears in 2×2 blocks, so that one can picture the shift space Y to be the collection of all points that result from concatenations of 1×1 blocks labeled p and 2×2 blocks labeled with q's. This subshift was introduced in [2] as an illustration of the difficulty in presenting two-dimensional sofic shifts with two graphs. However, if we use the $\mathcal{M}_{F(X)}$ construction to represent the X' as defined in Example 2, then the sofic system Y that is the image of the 1×1 block code ϕ is accurately represented by the underlying graph of Figure 1.

4   Uniform Horizontal Transitivity and Periodicity

For two-dimensional languages, it is of interest whether a given pair of blocks can coexist within a single point of the shift space. In one dimension, such a question is one of transitivity in the associated factor language. Unlike the one-dimensional case, however, there are several types of transitivity that appear in two-dimensional languages. (See [5] for a discussion of the various types of two-dimensional transitivity.) Here, we focus on uniform directional transitivity, which most closely resembles the notion of one-dimensional transitivity, since one can examine a bi-infinite sequence of "blocks" in the specified direction. Informally, we say that a two-dimensional language L is *horizontally transitive* if for every pair of blocks $B', B'' \in L$ there exists a block $B \in L$ that encloses B' and B'' in such a way that the bottom row of B intersects the bottom rows of both B' and B''. (See the first diagram in Figure 2.) In this situation, the *distance* at which B' meets B'' is taken to be the number of columns in B that separate the two blocks. *Uniform horizontal transitivity* in a picture language guarantees there is a $k > 0$ such that any two blocks from the language can be horizontally enclosed by a third block in the language at a distance less than k. For example, it is clear that the shift space X of Example 2 has factor language $F(X)$ that is uniformly horizontally transitive at distance 1. (*Uniform*) *vertical transitivity* can be defined in a similar manner.

The existence of uniform horizontal transitivity in the factor language of a shift space is not always so easily determined, since the distance at which the two blocks meet may depend on the height of the blocks. However, if X is a shift of finite type having property $A(X) = F(X)$, then given $K \geq 0$ it is decidable whether $F(X)$ exhibits uniform horizontal (vertical) transitivity at distance K. We outline how the $\mathcal{M}_{F(X)}$ construction facilitates the proof.

Suppose we are given blocks $B'_{m',n'}, B''_{m'',n''} \in F(X)$. To show uniform horizontal transitivity, it suffices to find a block $B \in F(X)$ that encloses B' and B'' in such a way that the bottom left corners of B' and B'' appear on a horizontal vector at $(0,0)$ and $(n' + k, 0)$, respectively, for some $k \leq K$. The assumption that $A(X) = F(X)$ implies that blocks can always be extended upward to have the same height m. Let $\mathcal{M}_{F(X)}$ be a representation of $F(X)$, using 2×2 blocks as states. (One may extend the alphabet if needed.) Then for every $m \times n$ block $B \in F(X)$, there must exist some $(m-1) \times (n-1)$ block path in $\mathcal{M}_{F(X)}$ that recognizes B. So suppose that B' is recognized by an $(m-1) \times (n'-1)$ block path β' and that B'' is recognized by an $(m-1) \times (n''-1)$ block path β'', assuming without loss of generality that $n', n'' \geq 2$. Horizontal transitivity can be illustrated by finding a block path β in $\mathcal{M}_{F(X)}$ such that the states in the initial (left) column of β agree with the states in the final (right) column of β' and such that the states in the final column of β agree with the the states in the initial column of β''. Note that a block path of length $k+3$ is needed to represent a block of length $k+4$ that overlaps the final two columns of symbols (comprising one v-path in β) and initial two columns of symbols in blocks B' and B'', respectively. For example, if a block path of length 3 overlaps the given blocks in the desired way, then the distance at which the two blocks meet would be zero, since this implies that the original two blocks touch.

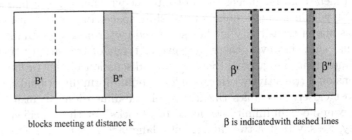

blocks meeting at distance k   β is indicatedwith dashed lines

Fig. 2. Over 2×2 states, we seek $\lambda(\beta)$ with length $k+4$

Theorem 9. *If X is a two-dimensional subshift representd by $\mathcal{M}_{F(X)}^{\Phi}$, then given a distance K, there is an algorithm which decides whether $F(X)$ has uniform horizontal transitivity at distance K.*

The proof will be comprised of four steps. To begin, the uniformity condition is used to place the question into the framework of one-dimensional languages so that several well-known results concerning one-dimensional recognizable languages may be applied. We first use the fact that if two one-dimensional languages are recognizable, then both their union and their product are known to be recognizable. (The product $L_1 L_2$ of two one-dimensional languages L_1 and L_2 is given by $L_1 L_2 := \{x_1 x_2 : x_1 \in L_1, x_2 \in L_2\}$.) We then use the well-known result that it is decidable whether two one-dimensional languages are equal or not.

Proof. (sketch) Step 1: Let $\mathcal{G} = \mathcal{M}_{F(X)}^{\Phi} = (Q, E, s, t, \lambda)$ be a graph representation of $F(X)$. For $i \in \{1, 2, \ldots, k+2\}$, form the set $\mathcal{H}_i$ of all h-paths of length i found in $\mathcal{G}$. For each $\mathcal{H}_i$, form the one-dimensional finite automaton $\mathcal{G}_i$ in the following way.

- Define the states of $\mathcal{G}_i$ to be the set $\mathcal{H}_i$.
- Define a transition from state $h = q_0 \rightharpoonup q_1 \rightharpoonup \cdots \rightharpoonup q_{i-1}$ to state $h' = q'_0 \rightharpoonup q'_1 \rightharpoonup \cdots \rightharpoonup q'_{i-1}$ if and only if $\forall j \in \{0, 1, \ldots, i-1\} \exists e_v \in E$ such that $s(e_v) = q_j$ and $t(e_v) = q'_j$ $(q_j \uparrow q'_j)$.
- An edge from h to h' is given the label h.

Note that each $\mathcal{G}_i$ is essentially a one-dimensional vertex shift representing the set of all block paths of length $i+1$ that represent blocks in $F(X)$.

Step 2: For each finite automaton $\mathcal{G}_i$, form the language $\mathcal{L}_i$ by taking products of the sequences of states found in the lower portions of the first and last columns of the represented block paths in the following way. First distinguish between states in the left and right columns of a block by forming two different alphabets Q and Q'. Then let $\mathcal{L}_i := \{\alpha_j \omega_j\}$, where if $\beta = h_0 h_1 \cdots h_m \in L(\mathcal{G}_i)$ is a path of "height" m, then for all $j \in \{0, 1, \ldots, m-1\}$, $\alpha_j = \beta(0,0)\beta(0,1)\cdots\beta(0,j) = q_0^0 q_0^1 \cdots q_0^j$ is a sequence of states found in the bottom part of the first column of β; that is, q_0^s is the source of the h-path h_s for $s \in \{0, 1, \ldots, j\}$. In a similar fashion, $\omega_j = [\beta(i-1,0)]'[\beta(i-1,1)]'\cdots[\beta(i-1,j')]' = q_i'^0 q_i'^1 \cdots q_i'^j$ is a sequence of states found in the bottom part of the last column of the same block path β; that is, $q_i'^s$ is the target of the h-path h_s for $s \in \{0, 1, \ldots, j\}$. Now define the recognizable language $\mathcal{L}$ to be $\mathcal{L}_1 \cup \mathcal{L}_2 \cup \cdots \cup \mathcal{L}_{k+2}$. Thus defined, $\mathcal{L}$ represents the set of all blocks that can meet on a horizontal vector at distance $k \leq K$ in $F(X)$. (The language $\mathcal{L}$ is formed from the labels of bi-infinite sequences of the vertex shifts $\mathcal{G}_i$ and is not necessarily finite.)

Step 3: Consider $\mathcal{G}^v = (Q, E_v, s, t, \lambda)$, the restriction of the graph representation of $F(X)$ to vertical transitions only. Relabel $\mathcal{G}^v$ to be a vertex shift where the transition $q \uparrow r$ is labeled with q. (We are interested in columnar block paths rather than the symbols from the alphabet Σ.) Denote by L the language recognized by this relabeled finite automaton, and create a second language L' from L by attaching a prime to each state's symbol. So if the alphabet for L is $Q = \{q_1, q_2, \ldots, q_f\}$, then the alphabet for L' is $Q' = \{q'_1, q'_2, \ldots, q'_f\}$. Now define the recognizable language LL' to be the product of L and L'. This language LL' represents the possibility of any two blocks in $F(X)$ meeting on a horizontal vector.

Step 4: It is decidable whether $LL' = \mathcal{L}$. $\qquad\qquad\qquad\square$

Theorem 9 can be reworded in terms of uniform vertical transitivity at distance K. Transitivity in the horizontal and/or vertical direction is of particular interest, since in the literature, the definition of periodicity in the two-dimensional case is based on horizontal and vertical movement. Specifically, given the two-dimensional shift space X, $x \in X$ is said to be *periodic* of period $(a, b) \in \mathbb{Z}^2 \setminus \{(0, 0)\}$ iff $x_{(i,j)} = x_{(i+a,j+b)}$ for every $(i, j) \in \mathbb{Z}^2$. The existence of uniform horizontal transitivity (or uniform vertical transitivity) for $L(\mathcal{M}_{F(X)}) = F(X)$ guarantees that the shift space X has a periodic point.

Theorem 10. *Let X be a two-dimensional shift of finite type representd by $\mathcal{M}^\phi_{F(X)}$. If $F(X)$ exhibits uniform horizontal transitivity at some distance K, then X has a periodic point of period (a, b) for some $a \leq K + 2$.*

Proof. (sketch) Using 2×2 states, let $\mathcal{G} = \mathcal{M}_{F(X)}$ represent $F(X)$ and consider some v-cycle contained in $\mathcal{G}^v$, say $\theta = q_0 \mathbin{1} q_1 \mathbin{1} \cdots \mathbin{1} q_p = q_0$. (Such a v-cycle must exist since $\mathcal{G}^v$ represents a one-dimensional sofic shift space, which must contain a periodic point.) Denote by B the $(p+2) \times 2$ block described by $\lambda(\theta)$, and for $i \geq 1$ consider the set $\{B_i\}$ of $(ip+2) \times 2$ blocks that result from repeatedly traveling the v-cycle θ. Since $F(X)$ exhibits uniform horizontal transitivity, B_i meets B_i at a distance $k \leq K$. As the set $\{B_i\}$ is infinite, there must exist $m \leq K$ such that blocks from a (countably) infinite subset $S \subseteq \{B_i\}$ all meet themselves at distance m. For each $B_i^j \in S$, let $C_i^1, C_i^2, \ldots, C_i^j, \ldots$ be the blocks that connect B_i^j with B_i^j. Since $\{C_i^j\}$ is also infinite and since each block C_i^j has length m, there must exist a block C_I^J with the property that the h-path connecting q_0 to q_0 whose label describes the bottom row of C_I^J equals the h-path connecting q_0 to q_0 whose label describes the top row of C_I^J. (There exist only a finite number of h-paths connecting q_0 to q_0 since the graph $\mathcal{G}$ is finite.) Finally, define the block $B_{Ip+1,m+2}$ as follows.

$$B_{Ip+1,m+2}(i,j) = \begin{cases} B_I(i,j) & \text{for } 0 \leq i \leq 1, 0 \leq j \leq Ip \\ C_I^J(i-2,j) & \text{for } 2 \leq i \leq m+2, 0 \leq j \leq Ip \end{cases} \tag{4}$$

Then $B_{Ip+1,m+2}$ contains all but the top row of symbols in blocks B_I and C_I^J so that $B_{Ip+1,m+2}(i,j) = B_{Ip+1,m+2}(i+a, j+b)$ with $a = m+2, b = Ip+2$ is a block describing a periodic point of period (a,b). $\square$

5   State Merging

Similarly to the notion of "right context" or "follower sets" of states in the Myhill-Nerode Theorem for one-dimensional recognizable languages, we can define follower sets for the states in $\mathcal{M}_{F(X)}^{\Phi}$.

Definition 11. *The* <u>follower set</u> *of state* $q \in \mathcal{G} = \mathcal{M}_{F(X)}^{\Phi}$ *is the set of labels of block paths starting at* q:

$$\mathcal{F}_{\mathcal{G}}(q) = \{B_{m,n} : \exists \text{ block path } \beta \text{ in } \mathcal{G} \text{ with } \lambda(\beta) = B_{m,n}, \beta(0,0) = q\}.$$

We say that graph $\mathcal{G}$ is *follower separated* if each state has a distinct follower set. When the states of $\mathcal{G}$ have distinct labels, $\mathcal{G}$ is naturally follower separated: in this case, $q' \in \mathcal{F}_{\mathcal{G}}(q)$ if and only if $q = q'$. However when the labels on the states are not distinct, it may be the case that two states have the same follower set. For one-dimensional automatons, such states can be merged to create a smaller graph representing the same language. Similarly, states in $\mathcal{M}_{F(X)}^{\Phi}$ can be merged without affecting the recognized language, i.e., the represented shift space.

Proposition 12. *For a graph* $\mathcal{G} = \mathcal{M}_{F(X)}^{\Phi} = \{Q, E, s, t, \lambda\}$ *with the equivalence relation* $q \sim q'$ *iff* $\mathcal{F}_{\mathcal{G}}(q) = \mathcal{F}_{\mathcal{G}}(q')$, *partition the set of states* Q *into disjoint equivalence classes* $Q_1, Q_2, \ldots, Q_v$. *Define graph* $\mathcal{G}'$ *with states* $Q' = \{Q_1, Q_2, \ldots, Q_v\}$ *and for* $i, j \in \{1, 2, \ldots, v\}$ *define an edge from* Q_i *to* Q_j *iff there are vertices* $q \in Q_i$ *and* $q' \in Q_j$ *having an edge in* $\mathcal{G}$ *from* q *to* q'. *Then* $L(\mathcal{G}) = L(\mathcal{G}')$.

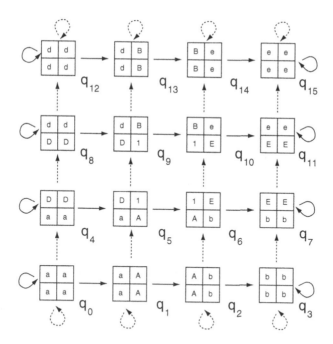

Fig. 3. $\mathcal{M}_{F(X)}$ follower separated; $\mathcal{M}_{F(X)}^{\Phi}$ not follower separated

There is a similar notion of the predecessor set of state $q \in \mathcal{G} = \mathcal{M}_{F(X)}^{\Phi}$ defined as the set of labels of block paths terminating in q:

$$\mathcal{P}_{\mathcal{G}}(q) = \{B_{m,n} : \exists \text{ block path } \beta \text{ in } \mathcal{G} \text{ with } \lambda(\beta) = B_{m,n}, \beta(n-2, m-2) = q\}.$$

Example 13. For the shift of finite type X represented by the graph $\mathcal{M}_{F(X)}$ of Figure 3, define the 1×1 block map Φ such that $\Phi(z) = 1$ if $z = 1$, but $\Phi(z) = 0$ otherwise. Then the strictly sofic shift space $Y = \phi(X)$ is the set of all configurations of the plane containing at most one 1.

The graph $\mathcal{M}_{F(X)}^{\Phi} = \mathcal{G}$ is not follower separated. To see this, let y_0 be the configuration of the plane populated entirely with 0's and let $F(y_0)$ denote all factors of this point, i.e., the set of all blocks populated entirely with 0's. Then for $i \in \{3, 7, 11, 12, 13, 14, 15\}$, $\mathcal{F}_{\mathcal{G}}(q_i) = F(y_0)$. We can merge these states in graph $\mathcal{G}$ to create a smaller graph $\mathcal{G}'$ representing the same shift space Y.

Notice that for $i \in \{0, 1, 2, 3, 4, 8, 12\}$, $\mathcal{P}_{\mathcal{G}}(q_i) = F(y_0)$. Alternatively then, we could have merged these states in graph $\mathcal{G}$ to create a smaller graph representing Y. However, if we now merge these states in graph $\mathcal{G}'$, the new graph will no longer represent the subshift Y as points will be accepted that contain more than a single 1. Note that in $\mathcal{M}_{F(X)}$, only states q_3 and q_{12} have both predecessor and follower set equal to $F(y_0)$. So if we merge states q_i for $i \in \{0, 1, 2, 4, 8\}$ to create graph $\mathcal{G}''$ from graph $\mathcal{G}'$, we will have reduced the size of the graph while still maintaining distinct initial and terminal states for blocks in the language $F(Y)$

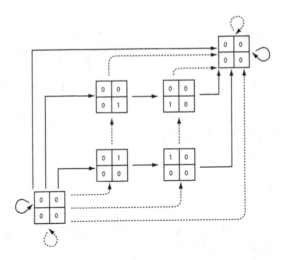

Fig. 4. Graph of reduced size recognizing Y

that contain a single 1. In other words, the graph $\mathcal{G}''$ also represents Y. See Figure 4 for the merged graph $\mathcal{G}''$ with states labeled according to ϕ.

6   Concluding Remarks

The automata defined with this paper represent shifts of finite type as well as their strictly sofic images when the condition $F(X) = A(X)$ is required for the shift of finite type. As the emptiness problem in two-dimensional subshifts is undecidable, we feel that this is the best single graph representation that we can obtain. When they exist, periodic points of a given period (a, b) can be located for two-dimensional subshifts through use of the $\mathcal{M}_{F(X)}$ graph representation regardless of whether $L(\mathcal{M}_{F(X)})$ exhibits uniform horizontal transitivity or not. An algorithm for finding periodic points with the $\mathcal{M}_{F(X)}$ construction can be found in [12] along with other results on periodicity. It remains to be seen what further properties of subshifts can and cannot be observed from the graph presentation used herein. Moreover, it would be advantageous to identify classes of graphs with two types of transitions (horizontal and vertical) that will always represent a non-empty two-dimensional sofic shift.

References

1. Berger, R.: The undecidability of the domino problem. Memoirs AMS 66 (1966)
2. Coven, E.M., Johnson, A., Jonoska, N., Madden, K.: The symbolic dynamics of multidimensional tiling systems. Ergodic Theory Dynam. Systems 23(2), 447–460 (2003)
3. Giammarresi, D., Restivo, A.: Two-dimensional languages. Handbook of formal languages 3, 215–267 (1997)

4. Johnson, A.S., Madden, K.: The decomposition theorem for two-dimensional shifts of finite type. Proc. Amer. Math. Soc. 127(5), 1533–1543 (1999)
5. Jonoska, N., Pirnot, J.B.: Transitivity in two-dimensional local languages defined by dot systems. International Journal of Foundations of Computer Science 17(2), 435–464 (2006)
6. Kari, J.: A small aperiodic set of wang tiles. Discrete Mathematics 160, 259–264 (1996)
7. Kitchens, B., Schmidt, K.: Automorphisms of compact groups. Ergod. Th. & Dynam. Sys. 9, 691–735 (1989)
8. Kitchens, B., Schmidt, K.: Markov subgroups of $(\mathbb{Z}/2\mathbb{Z})^{\mathbb{Z}^2}$. Symbolic Dynamics and its Applications, Contemporary Mathematics 135, 265–283 (1992)
9. Latteux, M., Simplot, D.: Recognizable picture languages and domino tiling. Theoretical Computer Science 178, 275–283 (1997)
10. Lind, D., Marcus, B.: An introduction to symbolic dynamics and coding. Cambridge University Press, Cambridge (1995)
11. Markley, N., Paul, M.: Matrix subshifts for $\mathbb{Z}^{\nu}$ symbolic dynamics. Proc. London Math. Soc. 43, 251–272 (1981)
12. Pirnot, J.B.: Graph representation of periodic points in two-dimensional subshifts (in preparation)

Tiling Automaton: A Computational Model for Recognizable Two-Dimensional Languages*

Marcella Anselmo[1], Dora Giammarresi[2], and Maria Madonia[3]

[1] Dipartimento di Informatica ed Applicazioni, Università di Salerno I-84084
Fisciano (SA) Italy
anselmo@dia.unisa.it
[2] Dipartimento di Matematica. Università di Roma "Tor Vergata",
via della Ricerca Scientifica, 00133 Roma, Italy
giammarr@mat.uniroma2.it
[3] Dip. Matematica e Informatica, Università di Catania, viale Andrea Doria 6/a,
95125 Catania, Italy
madonia@dmi.unict.it

Abstract. Two-dimensional languages can be recognized by tiling systems. A tiling system becomes an effective device for recognition when a *scanning strategy* on pictures is fixed. We define a *Tiling Automaton* as a tiling system together with a scanning strategy and a suitable data structure. In this framework it is possible to define determinism, non-determinism and unambiguity. The class of languages accepted by tiling automata coincides with REC family. Tiling automata are able to simulate on-line tessellation automata. Then (deterministic) tiling automata are compared with the other known (deterministic) automata models for recognition of two-dimensional languages.

Keywords: automata, two-dimensional languages, determinism.

1 Introduction

Two-dimensional languages appeared in the theory of formal languages in 1967 when M. Blum and C. Hewitt [4] defined them as sets of finite rectangular arrays of symbols from a finite alphabet. Main goal was to define a class of (finite state) recognizable two-dimensional languages that generalizes the class of regular string languages together with all its properties. With this aim they defined an automaton model for two-dimensional languages called *four-way automaton (4FA)* that generalizes the two-way automaton for strings by allowing the input head to move up and down besides right and left. Many automaton-like devices were introduced so far [3,11,12,13]. Furthermore, many other approaches appeared in the literature following other classical ways to define regular languages, namely grammars, logics and regular expressions [7]. In 1991, an unifying point of view was presented by A. Restivo and D. Giammarresi who defined the

---

* Work partially supported by PRIN project *Linguaggi Formali e Automi: aspetti matematici e applicativi.*

Jan Holub and Jan Žd'árek (Eds.): CIAA 2007, LNCS 4783, pp. 290–302, 2007.

family REC of *recognizable picture languages* (see [6] and [7]). A two-dimensional language is *tiling system recognizable* if it can be obtained as a projection of a local picture language. REC is the family of all recognizable two-dimensional languages. REC family inherits several properties from the class of regular string languages and it has several characterizations.

The starting motivation of this paper is the major observation that despite a tiling system generalizes to two dimensions a particular characterization of string finite automaton (local set plus a projection are effectively a description of the state-graph of an automaton), it does not correspond to an effective procedure of recognition. To verify that a picture p belongs to a language, we have to look for a counter-image p' in the local alphabet that matches the set of tiles: no scanning procedure of the picture p is proposed. To get an automaton in a common sense we need also a procedure to process the input and to define the steps of computations (where it starts, where/when it accepts the input).

In the case of conventional finite automata for strings, it is defined (implicitly!) an *a priori* scanning procedure, and then separately a transition function that takes a pair (state, symbol) and gives the new state. All the inputs will be read by this automaton with the same scanning procedure, namely starting from the leftmost position and going right at each step. In the case of two-way finite automata, instead, we have a unique function for the transition and for the next-position function: it takes a pair (state, symbol) and gives the new state and the new position. Then, a given automaton may read two different inputs by two completely different sequences of positions! No need to recall that the two models of automata correspond to the same class of string languages.

The idea is that to make tiling systems becoming "real automata" we have to provide them with an input scanning procedure: we have to fix the starting position and the sequence of all positions of each picture we read. Moreover to apply the transition function described as set of tiles, it is necessary a data structure that maintains the necessary information. We remark that the languages accepted by tiling automata will not depend on the scanning strategy associated to the automata (namely the REC class) despite it is necessary to consider all possible scanning strategies when defining *deterministic tiling automata*.

The paper recalls first some basic definitions and notations. Then we propose motivations and intuitions for the definition of tiling automata to prepare the reader to the more formal definitions given later. We conclude by comparing the tiling automaton with the other finite devices for recognizing two-dimensional languages. We discuss both model simulations and accepted languages.

2   Preliminaries

We introduce some definitions about two-dimensional languages. The notations used and more details can be mainly found in [7].

A *two-dimensional string* (or a *picture*) over a finite alphabet Σ is a two-dimensional rectangular array of elements of Σ. The set of all pictures over Σ is denoted by Σ^{**} and a *two-dimensional language* over Σ is a subset of Σ^{**}. Given a picture $p \in \Sigma^{**}$, we let $p_{(i,j)}$ denote the symbol in p with coordinates (i,j) where position $(1,1)$ corresponds to top-left corner. Moreover if p has m rows and n columns we refer to the pair (m,n) as the *size* of the picture p. For any picture p of size (m,n), we consider the *bordered picture* $\hat{p}$ of size $(m+2, n+2)$ obtained by surrounding p with a special *boundary symbol* $\# \notin \Sigma$.

A *tile* is a picture of size $(2,2)$ and $B_{2,2}(p)$ is the set of all blocks of size $(2,2)$ of a picture p. Given an alphabet Γ, a two-dimensional language $L \subseteq \Gamma^{**}$ is *local* if there exists a finite set Θ of tiles over $\Gamma \cup \{\#\}$ (the set of *allowed blocks*) such that $L = \{p \in \Gamma^{**} | B_{2,2}(\hat{p}) \subseteq \Theta\}$ and we will write $L = L(\Theta)$. A *tiling system* is a quadruple $(\Sigma, \Gamma, \Theta, \pi)$ where Σ and Γ are finite alphabets, Θ is a finite set of tiles over $\Gamma \cup \{\#\}$ and $\pi : \Gamma \rightarrow \Sigma$ is a projection. A two-dimensional language $L \subseteq \Sigma^{**}$ is *tiling recognizable* if there exists a tiling system $(\Sigma, \Gamma, \Theta, \pi)$ such that $L = \pi(L(\Theta))$ (extending π in the usual way).

We denote by REC the family of all *tiling recognizable* picture languages. REC family is closed under union, intersection, rotation and under some concatenation operations. The main important difference with the one dimensional case is that REC family is *not* closed under complement (see [7]); moreover, it was proved that the problem of parsing in REC is NP-complete [13]. As a consequence it was crucial to have a definition for a deterministic version of REC. Very recently *DREC* and *UREC* classes have been introduced (see [1,6]) as deterministic and unambiguous subfamilies of REC, respectively. In [1] it is shown that DREC $\subset$ UREC $\subset$ REC with all strict inclusions.

Example 1. Let $L_{lastr=lastc}$ be the language of squares over $\Sigma = \{a, b\}$ with last row equal to the last column. We show that $L_{lastr=lastc} \in$ REC by describing a tiling system $(\Sigma, \Gamma, \Theta, \pi)$ recognizing it. The tiling system is such that, for any picture p, the information on each letter of the last row is brought up till the diagonal and then right towards the last column. More precisely, we use a local alphabet $\Gamma = \{0_x^y, 1_x^y, 2_x^y\}$ with $x, y \in \{a, b\}$ and let symbols 0 occur only below the diagonal, symbols 1 occur only in the diagonal and symbols 2 only above the diagonal. Moreover the superscript symbols correspond to the "real value" of the symbol (i.e. $\pi(0_x^y) = \pi(1_x^y) = \pi(2_x^y) = y$) while the subscript symbols correspond to information we are bringing from the last row to the last column (making a turn at the diagonal). Here below it is given a picture $p \in L_{lastr=lastc}$ together with the corresponding local picture p' (i.e. $\pi(p') = p$).

$$p = \begin{array}{|c|c|c|c|c|}
\hline
b & a & a & a & a \\
\hline
a & a & a & b & b \\
\hline
b & a & a & b & b \\
\hline
a & b & b & b & a \\
\hline
a & b & b & a & a \\
\hline
\end{array}
\qquad
p' = \begin{array}{|c|c|c|c|c|}
\hline
1_a^b & 2_a^a & 2_a^a & 2_a^a & 2_a^a \\
\hline
0_a^a & 1_b^a & 2_b^a & 2_b^b & 2_b^b \\
\hline
0_a^b & 0_a^a & 1_b^a & 2_b^b & 2_b^b \\
\hline
0_a^a & 0_b^b & 0_b^b & 1_a^b & 2_a^a \\
\hline
0_a^a & 0_b^b & 0_b^b & 0_a^a & 1_a^a \\
\hline
\end{array}$$

An interesting model of automaton to recognize picture languages is the *on-line tessellation automaton* (OTA) introduced in [9]. In a sense the OTA is an infinite array of identical finite-state automata in a two dimensional space. The computation goes by anti-diagonals starting from top-left towards bottom-right corner of the picture. A run of an OTA on a picture consists in associating a state to each position of the picture. The state for some position (i, j) is given by the transition function and depends on symbol in that position and on the states already associated to positions $(i, j-1)$, $(i-1, j-1)$ and $(i-1, j)$. A deterministic version of this model is referred to as DOTA. The family of languages recognized by the two versions of the model $(\mathcal{L}(OTA), \mathcal{L}(DOTA))$ are different. Although this kind of automaton is quite difficult to manage, this is actually the machine counterpart of a tiling system: in [10], it is proved that REC = $\mathcal{L}(OTA)$.

Another model of two-dimensional automaton is the *4-way automaton* (4NFA or 4DFA for the deterministic version): it is defined as an extension of the two-way automaton for strings (cf. [4]) by allowing it to move in four directions: *Left, Right, Up, Down*. It is proved that also for 4-way automata, the deterministic version of the model defines a class of languages $(\mathcal{L}(4DFA))$ smaller than the corresponding one defined by non-deterministic version $(\mathcal{L}(4NFA))$ (see [7,4]).

3   Tiling Automata

We concentrate on tiling systems and define a model of *Tiling Automaton* as an effective computational device whose transitions are given by a tiling system.

We try first to understand precisely the situation in one-dimensional case to make an accurate generalization to two dimensions. Consider the proof in [5] that shows that a (string) language is accepted by a finite automaton if and only if it is the projection of a local language of words. The local language of words is given by a set of allowed blocks of length 2 that in fact correspond to the edges of the state-graph of the automaton. Then, in a sense what we call tiling system, in one dimension, represents the transition function of the automaton. Remark that such edges that describe the transition function are actually *non-oriented* edges (since are given just as words of length 2). The whole automaton is recovered by assuming the conventional way of reading the string (starting from leftmost symbol and proceeding from left to right) and therefore by choosing a direction for such edges. Moreover at each step, to apply the transition function, we maintain the current local symbol that corresponds somehow to the current state of the automaton. Remark that we could also assume to read the string starting from rightmost symbol and going left (probably more natural for Arabs!): from the same tiling system we would get another automaton that accepts the same language but processes strings from right to left.

Hence a tiling system is part of an automaton, i.e. a computation device, if it is equipped with a scanning strategy that "gives the instructions" on how to use it for the computation. We extend these reasonings to two dimensions. For a scanning strategy on a picture we have much more possibilities: we are going from writing in a single tape to writing in a whole sheet. To fix the ideas we choose the scanning strategy that seems "the most natural one": for any picture, it goes, row by row, from left to right and from top to bottom (probably oriental people would find more natural going column by column!).

Let us see in details how this could be accomplished. First of all we need a function that, at any step of the computation, gives the next position to be scanned. Observe that, to handle the borders, this position depends not only from the current position but also from the size (m, n) of the picture: if the current position (i, j) is the last one in the h-th row, then the next position is the first one in the $(h + 1)$-th row, otherwise the next position is $(i, j + 1)$. More formally, we consider a *next-step function* $f(i, j, m, n)$ equal to $(i, j+1)$ if $j \leq n - 1$ and equal to $(i+1, 1)$ if $j = n$ and $i < m$. First position of the scanning will be the top-left corner: applying iteratively such next-step function to current position, we obtain a complete scanning sequence for the input picture. Note also that, when we have reached position (i, j), we have already visited its top-left contiguous positions (i.e. positions $(i - 1, j - 1)$, $(i - 1, j)$, $(i, j - 1)$) and so we have already "chosen" the local symbols for those positions. Now, at this step of the computation, it is possible to choose a suitable tile for the four positions (i, j), $(i - 1, j - 1)$, $(i - 1, j)$ and $(i, j - 1)$ and compute the local symbol for (i, j). Remark that for the computation, it is necessary to remember some of the local symbols associated to the positions of p already scanned. In particular when we have reached position (i, j), we need to remember the local symbols in the positions of the $(i - 1)$-th row, from the $(j - 1)$-th column to the last one, and the local symbols in the positions of the i-th row, from the first column to the $(j - 1)$-th one. We do this with a suitable data structure. For example, we can use a list of $n + 2$ symbols. After applying the transition function (i.e. using a tile to get the next local symbol) the data structure is updated consequently.

The following figure shows the step of the computation when reading the symbol $p_{(i,j)}$. All the positions already scanned have been assigned some γ symbol from the local alphabet Γ. The data structure that supports the computation at that step contains $\gamma_{i-1,j-1}, \gamma_{i-1,j}, \ldots, \gamma_{i-1,n}, \#, \gamma_{i,1}, \ldots, \gamma_{i,j-1}$, while one step later it will contain $\gamma_{i-1,j}, \ldots, \gamma_{i-1,n}, \#, \gamma_{i,1}, \ldots, \gamma_{i,j-1}, \gamma_{i,j}$.

To sum up briefly, our computational device is defined by a tiling system plus a scanning strategy (that uses a next-step function) plus a data structure (equipped with some operations).

We remark that we can adopt other scanning strategies: we will get a different tiling automaton but the class of recognized languages will be the same, namely REC. The main difference will arise in the case of a definition of deterministic automaton. In particular (see proof of Proposition 15 and Example 11) it can be proved that, depending on the chosen scanning strategy, deterministic tiling automata define different classes of languages. Observe that also in the one-dimensional case, determinism is an oriented notion: if the automaton that reads strings form right to left is deterministic, we use the term of *co-deterministic automaton*. All these considerations give the evidence that a tiling automaton should be defined without fixing a particular (natural) scanning strategy for the pictures but indeed in a much more general setting.

We are ready for the definition of tiling automaton. We start with some terminology. A *position* in a picture of size (m, n) is any pair in $P(m, n) = \{0, 1, \ldots, m+1\} \times \{0, 1, \ldots, n+1\}$. *External positions* are pairs (i, j) with $i = 0$, $i = m+1, j = 0$ or $j = n+1$, while *internal positions* are the non-external ones. *Corner positions* are the ones in the set $\{(0,0), (0, n+1), (m+1, 0), (m+1, n+1)\}$. Given a position (i, j) with $i = 1, \ldots, m+1$ and $j = 1, \ldots, n+1$ its *top-left- (tl- for short) contiguous positions* are the positions: $(i, j-1)$, $(i-1, j-1)$, and $(i-1, j)$. In a similar way for tr, bl, and br. Here t, b, l, and r are used for *top, bottom, left* and *right* respectively. For any internal position, its *contiguous positions* are all the tl-, tr-, br-, and bl-ones.

Definition 2. *A next-position function for pictures is a computable partial function $f : \mathbb{N}^4 \to \mathbb{N}^2$ associating to a quadruple (i, j, m, n), with $(i, j) \in P(m, n)$, a position $(i', j') \in P(m, n)$.*

The sequence of visited positions by f at step k, starting from position (i_0, j_0), is the sequence $V_{f,k}(m, n) = (v_1(m, n), v_2(m, n), \ldots, v_{k-1}(m, n))$ where $v_1(m, n) = (i_0, j_0)$ and for any $h = 2, \ldots, k-1$, $v_h(m, n) = f(i, j, m, n)$ with $(i, j) = v_{h-1}(m, n)$.

Definition 3. *A scanning strategy is a next-position function S such that for any $m, n \in \mathbb{N}$ the sequence of visited positions by S at step $(m+2)(n+2)+1$ starting from a corner, say $V(m, n) = (v_1(m, n), v_2(m, n), \ldots, v_{(m+2)(n+2)}(m, n))$, satisfies:*

1. *$V(m, n)$ is a permutation of $P(m, n)$*
2. *for any $k = 2, \ldots, (m+2)(n+2)$, the tl- (or tr-, or bl-, or br- resp.) contiguous positions of $v_k(m, n)$ (when defined) are all in $V_{S,k}(m, n)$.*

   Furthermore, a scanning strategy is said continuous when it satisfies condition 3 below; it is said normalized when it satisfies condition 4.
3. *for any $k = 2, \ldots, (m+2)(n+2)$, $v_k(m, n)$ is a contiguous position of $v_{k-1}(m, n)$ unless eventually when $v_{k-1}(m, n)$ is an external position and, in this case, $v_k(m, n)$ is an external position too.*
4. *$v_{(m+2)(n+2)}(m, n)$ is a corner.*

Note that when a next-position function is given, there is one starting corner at most, verifying conditions 1 and 2. Property 3 forbids "taking the pen off" the picture unless on external positions; in this case we may jump only to some other external position. This condition avoids that two non-contiguous regions of a picture are both scanned during a scanning process. Note that some spiral-like scanning strategy (as in Example 4) is continuous, while allowing the presence of 'holes' in the scanned region. Properties 3 and 4 together forbid the existence of 'holes' in the picture during the scanning process, because once a hole is filled we could not jump to a final corner. The following examples show the richness and extent of possibilities that arise when going from one to two dimensions.

Example 4. We list some possible scanning strategies for pictures.
1. The strategy of scanning pictures row by row from left to right and from top to bottom (as at the beginning of this section) can be formalized as follows. The next-position function S_{row} is defined on (i, j, m, n) such that $(i, j) \in P(m, n)$ and $(i, j) \neq (m + 1, n + 1)$ by: $S_{row}(i, j, m, n) = \begin{cases} (i, j + 1) & \text{if } j \leq n \\ (i + 1, 1) & \text{if } j = n + 1, \ i \leq m \end{cases}$

and for any $m, n \in \mathbb{N}$, $v_1(m, n) = (0, 0)$. S_{row} is continuous and normalized.

In a similar way one can also depict a scanning strategy S_{col} that starts in the bottom-right corner and proceeds, column by column, from bottom to top and from right to left.

2. The scanning strategy S_{diag} starts in the top-left corner and proceeds following the counter-diagonal direction from top-right to bottom-left. The next-position function S_{diag} is defined on (i, j, m, n) such that $(i, j) \in P(m, n)$ and $(i, j) \neq (m + 1, n + 1)$ by:

$$S_{diag}(i, j, m, n) = \begin{cases} (i + 1, j - 1) & \text{if } j \neq 0 \text{ and } i \neq m + 1 \\ (0, i + j + 1) & \text{if } j = 0 \text{ or } i = m + 1 \text{ and } i + j \leq n \\ (i + j - n, n + 1) & \text{otherwise} \end{cases}$$

and for any $m, n \in \mathbb{N}$, $v_1(m, n) = (0, 0)$. S_{diag} is continuous and normalized.

3. Let S_{snake} be the scanning strategy that starts in position $(0, 0)$ and proceeds snake-like. The next-position function S_{snake} is defined on (i, j, m, n) such that $(i, j) \in P(m, n)$ and $(i, j) \neq (m + 1, n + 1)$ if m is odd, $(i, j) \neq (m + 1, 0)$ if m is even, as follows:

$$S_{snake}(i, j, m, n) = \begin{cases} (i, j + 1) & \text{if } i \text{ is even and } j \leq n \\ (i + 1, n + 1) & \text{if } i \text{ is even and } j = n + 1 \\ (i, j - 1) & \text{if } i \text{ is odd and } j \geq 1 \\ (i + 1, 0) & \text{if } i \text{ is odd and } j = 0 \end{cases}$$

S_{snake} satisfies conditions 1-4. Note that, contrarily to previous cases, for positions of i-th rows with even i, the tl-contiguous positions are already visited, while for odd i, the tr-contiguous positions are in the sequence of visited positions.

More informally, one could also consider a next-position function defined as S_{snake} on the left half part of the picture, and whatever on the remaining right half-part. This is not a scanning strategy since, after scanning position $(0, \lfloor n/2 \rfloor)$ the next position $(1, \lfloor n/2 \rfloor)$ has not 3 contiguous positions (against property 2).

Further a spiral-like way of proceeding is an example of a continuous but not normalized scanning strategy, since it does not stop in a corner. While an example of a scanning strategy that is neither continuous nor normalized is the one proceeding row by row from top to bottom scanning each row from left to right till the "middle" position is reached, and then from right to left.

Let us now introduce tiling automata as a pair of a tiling system plus a scanning strategy. To make this definition more effective we will consider only scanning strategies of a restricted type, that more naturally generalize the ones in string automata. This is not a restriction in what concerns the class of accepted picture languages (namely REC). Remark that in one-dimensional case, there are only two possible directions (from the left and from the right): once a direction is fixed there is only one scanning strategy compatible with that direction. In two-dimensional case, even if a direction is fixed, there is an huge number of scanning strategies along that direction. This is the reason to consider those scanning strategies that follow a main direction from a corner to the opposite one. In the sequel *tl2br* will be the short form for *from top-left corner to bottom-right corner*; similarly for the other corner-to-corner directions *tr2bl*, *bl2tr*, *br2tl*.

Definition 5. *A scanning strategy S is* tl2br-directed *if for any $(m, n) \in I\!N \times I\!N$ and $k = 1, \ldots, (m + 2)(n + 2)$ the tl-contiguous positions of $v_k(m, n)$ (when defined) are in the set of visited positions at step k. In a similar way define d-directed scanning strategies for any corner-to-corner direction d. A scanning strategy is said* corner-to-corner directed (c2c-directed) *if it is d-directed for some corner-to-corner direction.*

Example 6. Referring to Example 4, the scanning strategies S_{row} and S_{diag} are *tl2br*-directed, S_{col} is *br2tl*-directed, while S_{snake} is not *c2c*-directed.

According to a scanning strategy, a tiling system becomes a device able to effectively process a picture and decide whether it has to be accepted or not, whenever we can (easily) keep track of all information needed for the next steps of the computation. In other words for any scanning strategy, we need a proper data structure that supports operations of retrieval of the three states defined in the three contiguous positions and the update of structure itself. (In the simple example at the beginning of the section such data structure was a list.)

Definition 7. *A Tiling Automaton of type tl2br is a quadruple $\mathcal{A} = (T, S, D_0, \delta)$ where $T = (\Sigma, \Gamma, \Theta, \pi)$ is a tiling system, S is a tl2br-directed scanning strategy, D_0 is the initial content of a data structure that supports operations* state$_1$(D), state$_2$(D), state$_3$(D), update(D,γ), *for $\gamma \in \Gamma \cup \{\#\}$, and $\delta : (\Gamma \cup \{\#\})^3 \times (\Sigma \cup \{\#\}) \to 2^{\Gamma \cup \{\#\}}$ is a partial function such that $\gamma_4 \in \delta(\gamma_1, \gamma_2, \gamma_3, \sigma)$ if the tile* $\begin{array}{|c|c|} \hline \gamma_1 & \gamma_2 \\ \hline \gamma_3 & \gamma_4 \\ \hline \end{array} \in \Theta$ *and $\pi(\gamma_4) = \sigma$ if $\sigma \in \Sigma$, $\gamma_4 = \#$, otherwise.*

Similarly, we define a tiling automaton of type d for any corner-to-corner direction d. TA is the short form for tiling automaton.

Definition 8. *A tiling automaton $\mathcal{A} = (T, S_f, D_0, \delta)$ is deterministic if for any $\gamma_1, \gamma_2, \gamma_3 \in \Gamma \cup \{\#\}$ and $\sigma \in \Sigma \cup \{\#\}$ there exists at most one symbol γ_4 such that $\gamma_4 \in \delta(\gamma_1, \gamma_2, \gamma_3, \sigma)$.*

Let us define how the computation of a tiling automaton goes on a picture and when it accepts. An *instantaneous configuration* of $\mathcal{A} = (T, S, D_0, \delta)$ is a quadruple (p, i, j, D) where p is a picture, $(i, j) \in \mathbb{N} \times \mathbb{N}$, and D is the content of the data structure. The initial instantaneous configuration for a picture p of size (m, n) is (p, i, j, D_0) with $(i, j) = v_1(m, n)$; D_0 plays the role of an "initial state". The next instantaneous configuration is given by the relation $(p, i, j, D) \vdash (p, i', j', D')$ defined as follows. When $f(i, j, m, n)$ and $\delta(\texttt{state}_1(D), \texttt{state}_2(D), \texttt{state}_3(D), p_{(i,j)})$ are both defined, $(p, i, j, D) \vdash (p, i', j', D')$ if $(i', j') = f(i, j, m, n)$ and D' is the content of the data structure after calling $\texttt{update}(D, \gamma_4)$, with $\gamma_4 \in \delta(\texttt{state}_1(D), \texttt{state}_2(D), \texttt{state}_3(D), p_{(i,j)})$. When $f(i, j, m, n)$ is defined and $\delta(\texttt{state}_1(D), \texttt{state}_2(D), \texttt{state}_3(D), p_{(i,j)})$ is not defined, $\mathcal{A}$ stops without accepting. When $f(i, j, m, n)$ is not defined, the next instantaneous configuration is not defined, $\mathcal{A}$ stops and accepts p. Note that a particular attention should be payed when dealing with external positions.

$\mathcal{L}(\mathcal{A})$ denotes the language (of all pictures) accepted by $\mathcal{A}$.

Example 9. Let $\mathcal{T} = (\Sigma, \Gamma, \Theta, \pi)$ be a tiling system for a language L. We construct a tiling automaton $\mathcal{A}_{col} = (\mathcal{T}, \mathcal{S}_{col}, D_{col_0}, \delta_{col})$, for L, based on $\mathcal{T}$ and on the scanning strategy $\mathcal{S}_{col}$, as in Example 4. We need to define the data structure associated to $\mathcal{S}_{col}$ and how it can (efficiently) support the operations $\texttt{state}_1(D)$, $\texttt{state}_2(D)$, $\texttt{state}_3(D)$, $\texttt{update}(D, \gamma)$, as in Definition 7.

As in the beginning of this section, we can use a list of size $m + 2$ for a picture p of size (m, n), with pointers to the first, second and last elements. At the beginning D_{col_0} is empty and reading the last column (column of index $n + 1$) $m + 2$ symbols $\#$ are inserted. Then, when position (i, j) of p is considered, the list D stores (in order) the symbols associated to the visited positions $(i+1, j+1)$, $(i, j + 1), \ldots, (0, j + 1), (m, j), \ldots, (i + 1, j)$. The call to $\texttt{state}_1(D)$, $\texttt{state}_2(D)$, $\texttt{state}_3(D)$, will return (in $O(1)$ time) the first, second and last symbols in the list that are the ones in positions $(i + 1, j + 1)$, $(i, j + 1)$ and $(i + 1, j)$, say γ_1, γ_2 and γ_3, respectively. Value $\gamma_4 \in \delta_{col}(\gamma_1, \gamma_2, \gamma_3, p_{(i,j)})$ is such that $\begin{array}{|c|c|} \hline \gamma_4 & \gamma_2 \\ \hline \gamma_3 & \gamma_1 \\ \hline \end{array} \in \Theta$ and $\pi(\gamma_4) = p_{(i,j)}$ if $p_{(i,j)} \in \Sigma$, $\gamma_4 = \#$, otherwise. A call to $\texttt{update}(D, \gamma_4)$ deletes the first symbol in the list (γ_1) and inserts γ_4 as last element (in $O(1)$ time).

Example 10. Let $\mathcal{T} = (\Sigma, \Gamma, \Theta, \pi)$ be a tiling system for a language L. We sketch a tiling automaton $\mathcal{A}_{diag} = (\mathcal{T}, \mathcal{S}_{diag}, D_{diag_0}, \delta_{diag})$ recognizing L, based on $\mathcal{T}$ and on the scanning strategy $\mathcal{S}_{diag}$ as in Example 4. As data structure we use a list of size $\min\{m, n\} + 2$ at most for a picture p of size (m, n), with pointers to the first, second and last elements. At the beginning, D_{diag_0} is empty. Suppose position (i, j) of p is considered and $\gamma_{h,k}$ is the symbol associated to the visited position (h, k). At each time we have to keep track of the symbols already associated to some positions in the two counter-diagonals up position (i, j). So we store in the list D, in a proper order, all the computed tiles with bottom-right element in some positions on the previous two counter-diagonals. This way we know whether the list increases, decreases or is constant in length, following we have just inserted a corner tile or not. Increment and decrement are handled on external positions. For all internal positions the call to $\texttt{state}_1(D)$, $\texttt{state}_2(D)$, $\texttt{state}_3(D)$, will return (in $O(1)$ time) the symbols $\gamma_{i-1,j-1}$ and

$\gamma_{i-1,j}$ from the first tile in the list, and $\gamma_{i,j-1}$ from the second tile in the list. A value $\gamma_4 \in \delta_{diag}(\gamma_{i-1,j-1}, \gamma_{i-1,j}, \gamma_{i,j-1}, p_{(i,j)})$ of the transition function is a symbol such that the tile $\begin{array}{|c|c|} \hline \gamma_{i-1,j-1} & \gamma_{i-1,j} \\ \hline \gamma_{i,j-1} & \gamma_4 \\ \hline \end{array} \in \Theta$ and $\pi(\gamma_4) = p_{(i,j)}$.

Example 11. Let $L_{lastr=lastc}$ be the language of squares over a two-letters alphabet $\Sigma = \{a, b\}$ with last row equal to the last column. Consider the tiling system as in Example 1, and the tiling automata $\mathcal{A}_{col}$ and $\mathcal{A}_{diag}$ based on $\mathcal{T}$, as in Examples 9 and 10. We have that $\mathcal{A}_{col}$ is a deterministic tiling automaton, whereas $\mathcal{A}_{diag}$ is not. In fact there exist $\gamma_1 = 1_a^b$, $\gamma_2 = 2_a^a$, $\gamma_3 = 0_a^a$, $\gamma_4 = 1_b^a$, $\gamma_4' = 1_a^a \in \Gamma$, $\sigma = a \in \Sigma$ such that $\gamma_4 \neq \gamma_4'$ and $\gamma_4, \gamma_4' \in \delta_{diag}(\gamma_1, \gamma_2, \gamma_3, \sigma)$.

Let us now briefly discuss some complexity issues. In the examples shown, the next-position functions are all computable in $O(1)$ time; whereas the data structure used for the computation of a picture of size (m, n) occupies $O(m + n)$ space and the operations for retrieving information and updating it are achieved in time $O(1)$ each. When such conditions hold, the parsing of a picture of size (m, n) by a deterministic tiling automaton will require $O(mn)$ time (i.e. linear in the size) with $O(m + n)$ extra space. This is stated in the following proposition.

Proposition 12. *Let $\mathcal{A}$ be a deterministic tiling automaton where the next-position function is computable in $O(1)$ time, the data structure used for the computation of a picture of size (m, n) occupies $O(m + n)$ space and the operations* state$_1$(D), state$_2$(D), state$_3$(D), update(D,γ), *require $O(1)$ time each. Then the parsing of a picture of size (m, n) by $\mathcal{A}$ requires $O(mn)$ time with $O(m + n)$ extra space.*

4   Languages of Tiling Automata

We now establish some relations among the languages accepted by tiling automata and other classes of two-dimensional languages defined by finite devices. In particular we will consider recognizability by tiling systems, on-line tessellation automata and 4-way automata and their deterministic counterparts.

Let $\mathcal{L}(TA)$ denote the class of languages accepted by tiling automata. Then denote $\mathcal{L}(DTA)$ ($\mathcal{L}(UTA)$, resp.) the class of languages accepted by deterministic (unambiguous, resp.) tiling automata (a tiling automaton is unambiguous when for any picture there exists at most one accepting computation). We show that the recognition power of a tiling system is independent from the scanning strategy we choose: $\mathcal{L}(TA)$ coincides with REC family. Furthermore, we have that $\mathcal{L}(DTA) = $ DREC and $\mathcal{L}(UTA) = $ UREC, where DREC (UREC, resp.) is the class of all deterministic (unambiguous, resp.) recognizable languages (see Section 2).

In fact deterministic tiling automata are the computational model capturing the notion of determinism as introduced for DREC family. The same remark holds for UREC. Hence $\mathcal{L}(DTA)$, $\mathcal{L}(UTA)$ inherit several properties of the classes DREC and UREC (see [1,2]).

Proposition 13. *The following properties hold.*
(i) $\mathcal{L}(\text{TA}) = \text{REC}$
(ii) $\mathcal{L}(\text{DTA}) \subset \mathcal{L}(\text{UTA}) \subset \mathcal{L}(\text{TA})$, *where the inclusions are strict*
(iii) $\mathcal{L}(\text{DTA})$ *is closed under complementation*
(iv) *It is decidable whether a tiling automaton is deterministic.*

Proof. We only prove the statement (i): the other ones can be proved using some results in [1,2]. $\mathcal{L}(\text{TA}) \subseteq \text{REC}$: let $L = \mathcal{L}(\mathcal{A})$ where $\mathcal{A} = (\mathcal{T}, \mathcal{S}, D_0, \delta)$ is a tiling automaton. Then L is recognized by the tiling system $\mathcal{T}$. $\text{REC} \subseteq \mathcal{L}(\text{TA})$: let $L \in \text{REC}$ and $\mathcal{T}$ a tiling system recognizing L. Then the tiling automaton obtained from $\mathcal{T}$ equipped with any scanning strategy realizable by a data structure (as in Examples 9, 10) accepts L.   □

Tiling automata can be viewed as a more general model than OTA, since the computation done by a OTA can be simulated by a tiling automaton of a certain type. Nevertheless OTA and tiling automata have the same recognition power, that is they recognize the same class of languages (namely REC). On the contrary when restricted to their deterministic counterparts, DOTA are less powerful than deterministic tiling automata.

Proposition 14. *Any OTA can be simulated by a tiling automaton of type tl2br.*

Proof. The run of an OTA is usually defined as going in parallel following the counter-diagonals (see Example 10), but indeed the transitions of an OTA could be used by any TA of type *tl2br*.   □

Proposition 15. *The following properties hold.*
(i) $\mathcal{L}(\text{OTA}) = \mathcal{L}(\text{TA})$
(ii) $\mathcal{L}(\text{DOTA}) \subset \mathcal{L}(\text{DTA})$, *where the inclusion is strict*
(iii) $\mathcal{L}(\text{DTA})$ *is equal to the closure by rotation of* $\mathcal{L}(\text{DOTA})$

Proof. (i) Use Proposition 13 and the equivalence $\mathcal{L}(\text{OTA}) = \text{REC}$.
(ii) Applying Proposition 14, one can show that $\mathcal{L}(\text{DOTA})$ coincides with the class of languages accepted by DTA of type *tl2br*. Language $L_{lastr=lastc}$ (see Example 11) is an example of the strict inclusion. In fact it belongs to DREC $= \mathcal{L}(\text{DTA})$ [1], but it cannot be accepted by a DOTA [9].
(iii) $\mathcal{L}(\text{DTA}) = \text{DREC}$ and it is the closure by rotation of $\mathcal{L}(\text{DOTA})$ [1].   □

Consider now 4-way automata. The tiling automaton is a model conceptually different from 4FA. While the next move of a 4FA is determined from the pair (state, symbol), in a TA the direction of the computation is fixed in advance. Furthermore 4FA can visit the same position many times, while this is forbidden for tiling automata. And in fact $\mathcal{L}(\text{4NFA})$ is strictly contained in $\mathcal{L}(\text{TA}) = \text{REC}$. When restricting to determinism, the two models diverge: Propositions 16 and 17 show that $\mathcal{L}(\text{DTA})$ is incomparable with $\mathcal{L}(\text{4DFA})$, still remaining inside $\mathcal{L}(\text{UTA})$.

Proposition 16. *The class $\mathcal{L}(DTA)$ is incomparable with $\mathcal{L}(4DFA)$.*

Proof. We exhibit a language in $\mathcal{L}(4DFA)$ but not in $\mathcal{L}(DTA)$ and a language in $\mathcal{L}(DTA)$ but not in $\mathcal{L}(4DFA)$. For this, consider language L_{frames} equal to the language of all square pictures over a two-letters alphabet $\Sigma = \{0, 1\}$ with the last row equal to the last column, the second row equal to the reverse of the second-last column, the first row equal to the first column and the second-last row equal to the reverse of the second column. In [1] it is shown that $L_{frames} \notin$ DREC, and DREC $= \mathcal{L}(DTA)$ (see Proposition 13). On the other hand, it is easy to construct a 4DFA for L_{frames} so that $L_{frames} \in \mathcal{L}(4DFA)$. In fact it is known (cf. [9]) that $L_{lastr=lastc} \in \mathcal{L}(4DFA)$ and $\mathcal{L}(4DFA)$ is closed by rotation and intersection (cf. [7]). Moreover, in [9], an example of language in $\mathcal{L}(DOTA)$ (and then in $\mathcal{L}(DTA)$) but not in $\mathcal{L}(4DFA)$ is given and this concludes the proof.
$\square$

Proposition 17. $\mathcal{L}(DTA) \cup \mathcal{L}(4DFA) \subset \mathcal{L}(UTA)$, *where the inclusion is strict.*

Proof. The inclusion $\mathcal{L}(DTA) \subseteq \mathcal{L}(UTA)$ easily follows: the uniqueness of the next local symbol implies the uniqueness of the counter-image of any picture.

Let us show that $\mathcal{L}(4DFA) \subseteq \mathcal{L}(UTA)$. For this, we refer to the proof in [9] (Lemma 4.1), that $\mathcal{L}(4NFA) \subseteq \mathcal{L}(OTA)$. Informally, the authors associate to any picture accepted by a given 4NFA, a set of pictures over an expanded alphabet, called "satisfactory description tapes", which describes the possible accepting computations of the 4NFA on the original picture. Such set can be recognized by a properly constructed OTA. The resulting OTA is not in general deterministic, even if the starting 4FA is: it cannot keep true the local property of determinism along the different ways of visiting the pictures. Nevertheless, the one-to-one correspondence ensures the uniqueness of the satisfactory description tape associated to a picture recognized by a 4FA, in the case such automaton is deterministic (and hence unambiguous). So $\mathcal{L}(4DFA) \subseteq \mathcal{L}(UOTA)$. The equivalence $\mathcal{L}(UOTA) = UREC$ (see [2] and [14]) gives the inclusion.

An example of the strict inclusion is the language L of pictures of size (m, n) whose first column is equal to the i-th column and the last column is equal to the j-th one, for some $1 \leq i, j \leq n$, $i \neq 1$, $j \neq n$. In [1] it is shown that $L \in UREC \setminus DREC$, that is $L \in \mathcal{L}(UTA) \setminus \mathcal{L}(DTA)$. On the other hand L cannot be recognized by a 4DFA (by similar arguments used in [9]).
$\square$

References

1. Anselmo, M., Giammarresi, D., Madonia, M.: From determinism to non-determinism in recognizable two-dimensional languages. In: Procs. DLT 2007. LNCS, vol. 4588, pp. 36–47. Springer, Heidelberg (2007)
2. Anselmo, M., Giammarresi, D., Madonia, M., Restivo, A.: Unambiguous recognizable two-dimensional languages. RAIRO - Inf. Theor. Appl. 40, 277–293 (2006)
3. Anselmo, M., Madonia, M.: Simulating two-dimensional recognizability by pushdown and queue automata. In: Farré, J., Litovsky, I., Schmitz, S. (eds.) CIAA 2005. LNCS, vol. 3845, pp. 43–53. Springer, Heidelberg (2006)

4. Blum, M., Hewitt, C.: Automata on a two-dimensional tape. In: IEEE Symposium on Switching and Automata Theory, pp. 155–160. IEEE Computer Society Press, Los Alamitos (1967)
5. Eilenberg, S.: Automata, Languages and Machines, vol. A. Academic Press, London (1974)
6. Giammarresi, D., Restivo, A.: Recognizable picture languages. Int. Journal Pattern Recognition and Artificial Intelligence 6(2&3), 241–256 (1992)
7. Giammarresi, D., Restivo, A.: Two-dimensional languages. In: Rozenberg, G. (ed.) Handbook of Formal Languages, vol. III, pp. 215–268. Springer, Heidelberg (1997)
8. Giammarresi, D., Restivo, A., Seibert, S., Thomas, W.: Monadic second order logic over pictures and recognizability by tiling systems. Information and Computation 125(1), 32–45 (1996)
9. Inoue, K., Nakamura, A.: Some properties of two-dimensional on-line tessellation acceptors. Information Sciences 13, 95–121 (1977)
10. Inoue, K., Takanami, I.: A characterization of recognizable picture languages. In: Nakamura, A., Saoudi, A., Inoue, K., Wang, P.S.P., Nivat, M. (eds.) ICPIA 1992. LNCS, vol. 654, Springer, Heidelberg (1992)
11. Inoue, K., Takanami, I., Taniguchi, H.: Two-dimensional alternating Turing machines. Theor. Comp. Sc. 27, 61–83 (1983)
12. Kinber, E.B.: Three-way automata on rectangular tapes over a one-letter alphabet. Information Sciences 35, 61–77 (1985)
13. Lindgren, K., Moore, C., Nordahl, M.: Complexity of two-dimensional patterns. Journal of Statistical Physics 91(5-6), 909–951 (1998)
14. Mäurer, I.: Weighted picture automata and weighted logics. In: Torra, V., Narukawa, Y., Valls, A., Domingo-Ferrer, J. (eds.) MDAI 2006. LNCS (LNAI), vol. 3885, pp. 313–324. Springer, Heidelberg (2006)

REGAL: A Library to Randomly and Exhaustively Generate Automata

Frédérique Bassino, Julien David, and Cyril Nicaud

Institut Gaspard Monge, UMR CNRS 8049
Université de Marne-la-Vallée, 77454 Marne-la-Vallée Cedex 2, France
{bassino,jdavid01,nicaud}@univ-mlv.fr

Keywords: finite automata, random generation, C++ library.

Description of the Library REGAL

The C++ library REGAL [1] is devoted to the random and exhaustive generation of finite deterministic automata. The random generation of automata can be used for example to test properties of automata, to experimentally study average complexities of algorithms dealing with automata or to compare different implementations of the same algorithm. The exhaustive generation allows one to check conjectures on small automata.

The algorithms implanted are due to Bassino and Nicaud, the reader can refer to [1] for the description and the proofs of the algorithms used. The uniform generation, based on Boltzmann samplers, of deterministic and accessible automata runs in average time $\mathcal{O}(n^{3/2})$ where n is the number of states of the generated automata.

REGAL works with generics automata. To interface it with another software platform, the user has to define some basic methods (adding a state or a transition for example). REGAL also defines an implementation of automata that can be used directly.

To generate automata, either randomly or exhaustively, a generator object has to be instancied with the following parameters: the type of the states, the type of the alphabet, the class of the output automaton, the number of states of the output automaton and the alphabet.

The exhaustive generator provides methods to compute the first automaton, to go to the next automaton, and to test whether the last automaton is reached.

To randomly and equally likely generate automata of a given size, one has to initialize a random generator and then use the method random() as shown in the example below.

Experimental Results

Using the exhaustive generator, we computed the exact number of minimal automata on a two-letters alphabet, for small values of n.

---

[1] available at: http://igm.univ-mlv.fr/~jdavid01/regal.php

Jan Holub and Jan Žd'árek (Eds.): CIAA 2007, LNCS 4783, pp. 303–305, 2007.

```
DFAAutomaton<int,char> * result; //Result DFA
Alphabet<char> alpha; //Create an alphabet
alpha.insert ('a');   alpha.insert ('b');
RandomDFAGenerator<int,char,DFAAutomaton<int,char>> rg(50 ,alpha);
for(int counter=0; counter<10000; counter++) a=rg->random();
```

Fig. 1. Random generation of 10 000 DFA with 50 states on $A = \{a, b\}$

Number of states	2	3	4	5	6	7
Minimal automata	24	1 028	56 014	3 705 306	286 717 796	25 493 886 852

Using the random generator, the proportion of minimal automata amongst deterministic and accessible ones can be estimated. The tests in the following array are made with 20 000 automata of each size.

Size	50	100	500	1 000	2 000	3 000	5 000
Minimal automata	84.77 %	85.06 %	85.32 %	85.09 %	85.42 %	85.64 %	85.32 %

On a two-letters alphabet we tested how the size of a random automaton is reduced by minimization. The following array summarizes the results obtained on 4 000 automata of size 10 000:

Reduction of the size	0	1	2	3
Proportion of automata	85.26 %	13.83 %	0.89 %	0.02 %

In Fig. 2 the mean time of execution of Moore's and Hopcroft's algorithms has been measured on an Intel 2.8 GHz. We used 10 000 automata of each size

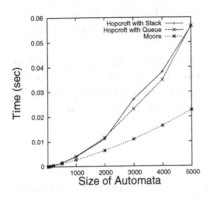

Fig. 2. Time complexities of Moore's and Hopcroft's algorithms

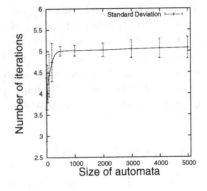

Fig. 3. Number of iterations in the main loop of Moore's algorithm

to compute the mean value. Two different implementations have been tested for Hopcroft's algorithm: either with a stack or with a queue.

In Fig. 3 the mean number of partitions refinements in Moore's algorithm is analysed. Its very slow growth could explain why this algorithm seems efficient in the average (its worst case complexity of $\mathcal{O}(n^2)$ is reached for n refinements).

Reference

1. Bassino, F., Nicaud, C.: Enumeration and random generation of accessible automata. Theoret. Comput. Sci. (to appear) Available at
   http://www-igm.univ-mlv.fr/~bassino/publi.html

A Finite-State Super-Chunker

Olivier Blanc, Matthieu Constant, and Patrick Watrin

Université de Marne-la-Vallée, Institut Gaspard Monge, France
patrick.watrin@univ-mlv.fr

Abstract. Language is full of multiword unit expressions that form basic semantic units. The identification of these structures limits the combinatorial complexity induced by lexical ambiguity. In this paper, we detail an experiment that largely integrates these notions in a finite-state procedure of segmentation into super-chunks, preliminary to a parser. We show that the chunker, developped for French, reaches 92.9% precision and 98.7% recall.

Keywords: local grammar, lexical resources, natural language processing, multiword units, super-chunking.

1 Introduction

Language is full of multiword units (MWUs) that form basic semantic units. The identification of these structures limits the combinatorial complexity induced by lexical ambiguity. To study this phenomenon, we implemented an incremental finite-state *chunker* based on the notion of *super-chunk* and on the programs of the Outilex plateform [1]. Super-chunks are standard chunks [2] where adjectival and prepositional lexical attachment is integrated. For instance, *marge d'exploitation* (trading margin) is considered as a standard noun. Our system is composed of three successive stages : (1) lexical segmentation into simple and MWUs ; (2) identification and tagging of super-chunks ; (3) disambiguation process.

2 Lexical Segmentation

The lexical segmentation is entirely based on lexical resources either developed by linguists or automatically learnt from raw texts. These resources include a large-coverage morpho-syntactic dictionary of inflected French forms [3] that is composed of 746,198 inflected simple forms and 249,929 inflected compounds. They also include a library of 190 lexicalized local grammars [4] representing MWUs. The lexical analyzer also uses a set of 1,493 nominal collocations that have been automatically extracted from corpora [5]. This module takes as an input a text segmented in sentences and in tokens. First, the dictionary lookup

Jan Holub and Jan Žd'árek (Eds.): CIAA 2007, LNCS 4783, pp. 306–308, 2007.

associates each token with all its possible linguistic tags and recognizes compounds. The output of the process is a Text FSA (TFSA). Then, local grammars are directly applied to the TFSA, which is then augmented with the analyses of the matching MWUs.

3   Chunk Segmentation

Chunk segmentation is based on a cascade of FSTs applied on the TFSA, which is then augmented each time a new chunk is found. It is composed of height stages and uses a network of 18 graphs. The identified chunks inherit morpho-syntactic properties from their components.

4   Incremental Disambiguation

The chunk segmentation produces a set of possible analyses in chunks. In order to remove ambiguity, the chunker includes an incremental disambiguation module composed of three stages. First, the Shortest Path Heuristic (SPH) that only keeps the shortest paths of the TFSA can be applied. It is based on the idea of preferring multiword expression analyses to sequences of simple analyses. Then, a module of disambiguation with 26 manually constructed rules can also be applied. Each rule consists of three parts: two contextual parts (left and right) that are represented by local grammars; a central ambiguous part that is a list of possible analyses. If the ambiguity is found in the TFSA with the defined left and right contexts, then an analysis is selected. The others are then removed. Finally, we can apply stochastic rules consisting in keeping the analysis that is the most frequent in a learning tagged corpus.

5   Evaluation

Our evaluation process has been carried out on a corpus composed of broadcast news. This 13,492-word corpus includes 6,901 super-chunks. The 3-stage process described above was applied to the corpus. Precision and recall were evaluated manually by two persons. The super-chunker reaches 92.9% precision and 98.7% recall. From a general point of view, we observed that most of errors are due to incomplete lexical and syntactic resources. These results led us to a double conclusion. First, our disambiguation procedure reaches excellent recall and precision rates without the use of any tagger. Then, a significant amount (36.6%) of attachments within noun and prepositional phrases are actually resolved by the use of a large-coverage set of MWUs, and therefore do not have to be computed at the syntactic level.

Future work will focus on the improvement of the chunker by improving the lexical and syntactic resources and by integrating a more sophisticated statistical disambiguation module (*e.g.* HMM). We wish to extend it in order to process less stable textual data such as spoken texts or emails. Moreover, we would like to evaluate the impact of the chunker when it is integrated in a parser.

References

1. Blanc, O., Constant, M.: Outilex, a linguistic platform for text processing. In: Proc. of the COLING/ACL 2006 Interactive Presentation Sessions, pp. 73–76 (2006)
2. Abney, S.: Partial parsing via finite-state cascades. Natural Language Engineering 2, 337–344 (1996)
3. Courtois, B.: Un système de dictionnaires électroniques pour les mots simples du français. Langue Française 87, 11–22 (1990)
4. Gross, M.: The construction of local grammars. In: Roche, E., Schabes, Y. (eds.) Finite State Language Processing, pp. 329–352. The MIT Press, Cambridge, Mass. (1997)
5. Watrin, P.: Une approche hybride de l'extraction d'information: sous-langages et lexique-grammaire. PhD thesis, Thèse de Doctorat de l'Université Catholique de Louvain-la-Neuve (2006)

The Constrained Longest Common Subsequence Problem for Degenerate Strings*

Costas Iliopoulos[1,3], M. Sohel Rahman[1,3],
Michal Voráček[2,4], and Ladislav Vagner[2,4]

[1] Algorithm Design Group
Department of Computer Science, King's College London, UK
http://www.dcs.kcl.ac.uk/adg
[2] Department of Computer Science and Engineering
Czech Technical University, Czech Republic
[3] {csi,sohel}@dcs.kcl.ac.uk
[4] {voracem,xvagner}@fel.cvut.cz

In this paper, we present a finite automata based algorithm for solving the *constrained longest common subsequence* problem for *degenerate strings*. A *string* is a sequence of symbols from a given alphabet Σ. A *subsequence* u of a string x is obtained by deleting some characters from u (not necessarily contiguous). Given two strings x and y, u is a *common subsequence* of x and y, if u is a subsequence of both x and y. And, u is a *longest common subsequence* (LCS) of x and y, if it is the longest among all such subsequences. Given two strings x and y, the LCS problem aims to compute a longest common subsequence of them. We study a newer variant of the classic LCS problem, namely the Constrained LCS problem (CLCS). In CLCS, the computed longest common subsequence must also be a supersequence of a third given string, say z [3,2,1].

The CLCS problem was introduced, quite recently, by Tsai in [3], where an algorithm was presented solving the problem in $\mathcal{O}(n^2m^2r)$ time complexity. Here $n = |x|, m = |y|$ and $r = |z|$. Later, Chin et al. [1] and independently, Arslan and Eğecioğ [2] presented improved algorithm with $\mathcal{O}(nmr)$ time and space complexity. We consider the CLCS problem for degenerate strings, i.e. strings that may have a set of letters in each position. In our case, all the three input strings are degenerate. Our algorithm is based on the following lemma:

Lemma 1. *Let $\tilde{x}$, $\tilde{y}$ and $\tilde{z}$ be degenerate strings over an alphabet Σ, then the following holds:*

$$CLCSub(\tilde{x}, \tilde{y}, \tilde{z}) = MaxLen(Sub(\tilde{x}) \cap Sub(\tilde{y}) \cap Super(\tilde{z})).$$

Here, $CLCSub(\tilde{x}, \tilde{y}, \tilde{z})$ denotes the set of constrained longest common subsequences of $\tilde{x}, \tilde{y}$ and $\tilde{z}$, $Sub(\tilde{x})$ (resp. $Super(\tilde{x})$) denotes the set of all subsequences

* Partially supported by the Ministry of Education under research program MSM 6840770014 and the Czech Science Foundation as project No. 201/06/1039.

Jan Holub and Jan Žďárek (Eds.): CIAA 2007, LNCS 4783, pp. 309–311, 2007.

(resp. supersequences) of $\tilde{x}$ and $MaxLen$ is a function that, given a set of strings, returns the (sub)set of strings with maximum length. All the sets considered in Lemma 1, form regular languages. This implies that we can represent each of them by a finite automaton. Given an automaton M, we use $\mathcal{L}(M)$ to denote the language represented by M. The steps of our algorithm are as follows:

1. Given degenerate string $\tilde{x}$ (resp. $\tilde{y}$) construct automaton M_1 (resp. M_2) such that $\mathcal{L}(M_1) = Sub(\tilde{x})$ (resp. $\mathcal{L}(M_2) = Sub(\tilde{y})$).

2. Construct automaton M_3 such that $\mathcal{L}(M_3) = \mathcal{L}(M_1) \cap \mathcal{L}(M_2)$.

3. Given degenerate string $\tilde{z}$ construct automaton M_4 such that $\mathcal{L}(M_4) = Super(\tilde{z})$.

4. Construct automaton M_5 such that $\mathcal{L}(M_5) = \mathcal{L}(M_3) \cap \mathcal{L}(M_4)$.

5. Construct automaton M such that $\mathcal{L}(M) = MaxLen(\mathcal{L}(M_5))$.

Our approach utilizes two novel types of finite automata, namely *subsequence automaton for degenerate strings* and *supersequence automaton for degenerate strings*. Given a degenerate string $\tilde{x}$, the automaton accepting the set $Sub(\tilde{x})$ (*subsequence automaton*) can be constructed online in $\mathcal{O}(n|\Sigma|)$ time and space, where $n = |\tilde{x}|$, and it is deterministic acyclic, minimal and has exactly $n + 1$ states and $\mathcal{O}(|\Sigma|n)$ transitions. Similarly, given degenerate string $\tilde{x}$, the automaton accepting the set $Super(\tilde{x})$ (*supersequence automaton*) can be constructed online in $\mathcal{O}(n|\Sigma|)$ time and space and it is deterministic, minimal and has exactly $n + 1$ states and $|\Sigma|(n + 1)$ transitions. For the construction of an automaton for the intersection of languages we use a variant of standard algorithm that creates only accessible states. This algorithm builds the resulting automaton by simultaneous traversal of the input automata and works in $\mathcal{O}(|\Sigma|nm)$ time, where n and m are the number of states of the two input automata. The algorithm realizing the function $MaxLen$ is a modification of the longest-path algorithm for directed acyclic graphs (DAGs) based on the topological ordering of nodes (states). This algorithms works $\mathcal{O}(n)$ time, where n is the number of transitions of the input automaton. The resulting automaton has at most as many states and at most as many transitions as the original automaton. The result of the above discussion is summarized in the following lemma.

Lemma 2. *Given degenerate strings $\tilde{x}$, $\tilde{y}$ and $\tilde{z}$ of length n, m and r, respectively, we can construct the finite automaton M accepting langauge $\mathcal{L}(M) = CLCSub(\tilde{x}, \tilde{y}, \tilde{z})$ in $\mathcal{O}(|\Sigma|nmr)$ time.*

Based on Lemma 1 and 2, we get the following theorem which is the main result of this paper.

Theorem 3. *CLCS problem for degenerate strings can be solved in $\mathcal{O}(|\Sigma|nmr)$ time.*

References

1. Chin, F.Y.L., De Santis, A., Ferrara, A.L., Ho, N.L., Kim, S.K.: A simple algorithm for the constrained sequence problems. Inf. Process. Lett. 90(4), 175–179 (2004)
2. Arslan, A.N., Egecioglu, Ö.: Algorithms for the constrained longest common subsequence problems. Int. J. Found. Comput. Sci. 16(6), 1099–1109 (2005)
3. Tsai, Y.T.: The constrained common subsequence problem. Inf. Process. Lett. 88, 173–176 (2003)

Finite Automata Accepting Star-Connected Languages

Barbara Klunder

Faculty of Mathematics and Computer Science, Nicolaus Copernicus University
Toruń, Poland
klunder@mat.uni.torun.pl

Abstract. In this paper we characterize star-connected languages using finite automata: any language is star-connected if and only if it is accepted by a finite automaton with cycles which are proper composition of connected cycles. Star-connected (flat) languages play an important role in the theory of recognizable languages of monoids with partial commutations. In addition we introduce a flat counterpart of the concurrent star operation used in this theory.

Keywords: finite automaton, trace monoid, star-connected language.

The theory of traces (i.e. monoids with partial commutations) has two independent origins: combinatorial problems and the theory of concurrent systems. Since the fundamental Mazurkiewicz's paper, trace languages are regarded as a powerful means for description of behaviours of concurrent systems.

Let $I \subseteq A \times A$ be a symmetric and irreflexive relation on A. Such a relation is named the *independency relation*; it expresses possibilities of concurrent executions of atomic actions of systems. The complement $D = A \times A \setminus I$ of I is named the *dependency relation*.

The couple (A, I) or (A, D) is said to be a *concurrent alphabet*. Given a concurrent alphabet (A, I), the *trace monoid* $A^\star/I$ is the quotient of the free monoid $A^\star$ by the least congruence on $A^\star$ containing the relation $\{ab = ba | aIb\}$. Members of $A^\star/I$ are called *traces*, and sets of traces (i.e. subsets of $A^\star/I$) are called *trace languages*. Any word $w \in A^\star$ induces a trace $[w] \in A^\star/I$ - the congruence class of w. Any flat language $L \subseteq A^\star$ induces a trace language $[L] = \{[w] | w \in L\}$ - the set of all traces induced by members of L.

A *word* $w \in A^\star$ (*trace* $[w]$) is *connected* (w.r.t. D) iff the graph $D|_{Alph(w)}$ induced by the set of all letters occurring in w is connected; A *flat language* $L \subseteq A^\star$ (*trace language* $T \subseteq A^\star/I$) is *connected* iff all its members are connected; Connected trace languages play important role in trace theory. We know that star may destroy recognizability. It is not the case, if the iterated language is connected. The following result is due to E. Ochmański [1]:

If $T \subseteq A^\star/I$ is recognizable and connected, then $T^\star$ is recognizable.

We say that, for a given concurrent alphabet (A, D), a regular expression r is *star-connected* if every sub-expression $s^\star$ of r defines connected language. Then r

---

[1] E. Ochmański: *Regular Behaviour of Concurrent Systems*. Bulletin of EATCS 27, pp. 56-67, 1985.

Jan Holub and Jan Žd'árek (Eds.): CIAA 2007, LNCS 4783, pp. 312–313, 2007.
© Springer-Verlag Berlin Heidelberg 2007

defines *star-connected* language. Star-connected flat languages induce the whole class of recognizable trace languages. In fact $T \subseteq A^\star / I$ is recognizable iff $T = [L]$ for some star-connected language $L \subseteq A^\star$ [1].

Definition 1 (Composition of cycles). *Let* $\mathbf{A} = \langle A, Q, \delta, q, F \rangle$ *be an automaton. A cycle of* $\mathbf{A}$ *is a path* $s_0 a_1 s_1 a_2 s_2 \cdots a_n s_n$ *such that* $n > 0$ *and* $s_0 = s_n$; *a cycle is simple if* $s_i \neq s_j$ *whenever* $i \neq j$ *(for* $i, j = 0, \ldots, n-1$*). A cycle is connected if its label* w *is a connected word. If for some* $k \geq 0$ *and* $i_0 = 0 < i_1 < \cdots < i_k < i_{k+1} = n$ *equations* $s_{i_j} = s_0$ *hold the cycle is a composition in* s_0 *of cycles* $s_{i_j} a_{i_j + 1} \cdots s_{i_{j+1}}$ *for* $0 \leq j \leq k$. *If the sequence* $i_0 = 0 < i_1 < \cdots < i_k < i_{k+1} = n$ *contains all occurrences of* s_0 *then the composition is proper. For every* $0 < i < n$ *the cycle* $s_i a_{i+1} \cdots a_n s_n a_1 s_1 \cdots a_i s_i$ *is isomorphic to* $s_0 a_1 s_1 a_2 s_2 \cdots a_n s_n$.

It is easy to see that for any $L \subseteq A^\star$, L is star-connected iff $L \setminus \{\varepsilon\}$ is star-connected. We consider finite automata without ε-transitions.

Lemma 2. *For every star-connected language* L *such that* $L \setminus \{\varepsilon\} = L$ *there exists an automaton* $\mathbf{A} = \langle A, Q, \delta, q, F \rangle$ *accepting* L *(i.e.* $L = L(\mathbf{A})$*) such that*

1. *every simple cycle of* $\mathbf{A}$ *is connected;*
2. *for every cycle* $s_0 a_1 s_1 a_2 s_2 \cdots a_n s_0$ *there exist* $0 \leq i \leq n$ *such that the isomorphic cycle* $s_i a_{i+1} \cdots a_n s_0 a_1 s_1 \cdots a_i s_i$ *is a proper composition in* s_i *of connected cycles.*

In this way we obtain stronger version of the previous result [2]. This result implies very interesting pumping lemmas for every star-connected flat language L. Firstly, we can require that the pumping element is connected, in the classical version of the lemma. Secondly, there exist $m > 0$ such that for all $z \in L$ if $|z| \geq m$ then for some $u, v_1, v_2, v_3, w \in A^\star$: $z = u v_1 v_2 v_3 w$, words $v_2, v_3 v_1$ are nonempty and connected, $u v_1 (v_2 \cup v_3 v_1)^\star v_3 w \subseteq L$.

Using this property it is easy to prove that the language $L = (a \cup b a^\star b)^\star$ is not star-connected. For $n > 0$ the word $(ab)^{2n}$ does not satisfy this condition.

Let X be any subset of A. We put $\pi_X(a) = a$ if $a \in X$ and $\pi_X(a) = \varepsilon$ otherwise.

The unique extension of π_X to $A^\star$ we call the projection (on X) and denote in the same way.

Proposition 3. *Let* (A, I) *be any concurrent alphabet. Let* $X \subset A$ *be such that* X *and* $A \setminus X$ *are independent:* $X \times (A \setminus X) \subset I$. *Let* $\mathbf{A} = \langle A, Q, \delta, q, F \rangle$ *be any automaton satisfying conditions 1 and 2 of Lemma 2. Then the language* $\pi_X(L(\mathbf{A}))$ *is star-connected.*

Thus we obtain a characterization of star-connected languages via automata accepting them. Proposition 3. let us to define the concurrent star operation on star-connected languages previously used in the theory of trace languages.

---

[1] ibid.

[2] B. Klunder: *Star-Connected Flat Languages and Automata*, Fundamenta Informaticae 72 (1-3), pp. 235-243, 2006.

Efficiently Matching with Local Grammars Using Prefix Overlay Transducers

Clemens Marschner[1,2]

[1] Centrum für Informations- und Sprachverarbeitung,
Ludwig-Maximilians-Universität München, 80538 München, Germany
[2] Fast Search and Transfer Deutschland GmbH, Rablstr. 26, 81667 München
marschner@cis.uni-muenchen.de

Abstract. Prefix Overlay Transducers (POTs) are effective filters on
the search space of Local Grammars (LG, [1]) which are used for searching on large corpora that are annotated with linguistic features, such as
part-of-speech tags or other syntactic or semantic annotations.

LGs are a way to describe language constructs by means of nested syntax dia-
grams that may also contain output symbols. In each "box" of these grammars,
the formalism allows for query patterns (often called "labels") like "here be a
token having the lemma 'live' and part of speech 'N'". Large grammars tend
to become highly non-deterministic for various reasons: e.g. sub graph calls and
overlapping result sets, among others. Hence, the search space quickly becomes
prohibitely large.

LGs are transformed into Recursive Transition Networks (RTNs)[4]. An RTN
consists of a set of (named) graphs G with name $N(g), g \in G$ with a specific top
graph $g_0 \in G$. Each graph g consists of the tuple $\langle Q, \Sigma, \Gamma, q_0, F, \delta, \rangle$, where Q is
the set of states, Σ is the input alphabet, Γ is the output alphabet, $q_0 \in Q$ is
a special initial state, $F \subseteq Q$ is the set of final states, and $\delta \subset Q \times \{\Sigma \cup \epsilon \cup
N(G)\} \times \Gamma \times Q$ is the transition function. The input symbols of RTNs consist
of search patterns which are composed from expressions of the kind "$feature =
value$" and are closed under conjunction (&) and negation (!). Examples would
be "$pos = N$" and "$lemma = live \quad \& \quad pos = N$". Both would be assigned to
different transitions in the RTN.

The default matching algorithm therefore needs to use backtracking while
evaluating the intersection between the input and the grammar, for which a
partial ordering is introduced for transitions leaving each state. Leaving the
question of non-deterministic input aside, the control state of the matcher is
therefore determined by a position in the text and a path through the RTN,
represented through a series of numbers (The path $\langle 1, 2 \rangle$ would signify that,
from the start state, first transition 1 was followed, then from its target state,
transition 2). Determining which transitions to follow may require hundreds or
even thousands of comparisons, whereas the number of matching sequences is
usually small.

The idea of this paper is to use a *lexical transducer* as an overlay to the initial state of the RTN, taking advantage of their favorable scalability. Lexical

Jan Holub and Jan Žd'árek (Eds.): CIAA 2007, LNCS 4783, pp. 314–316, 2007.

transducers are acyclic, deterministic, minimal transducers containing single characters as input alphabet and output only at final states. They are used for representing large dictionaries. Since their alphabet is known and small, outgoing transitions at a state can be represented through an array whose indices represent the symbols. This means, for a given input character, the matching outgoing transitions can be found in $O(1)$, regardless of the size of the automaton[2].

The overlay maps string representations of finite RTN paths, consisting of a sequence of concatenated *keys* being computed from the patterns, to their numerical representations (a single string representation can map to more than one path). Since not all types of patterns may be representable as keys in a way that it can serve for matching purposes, by default they are represented using the key "+", which means that the transition at the end of the path needs to be evaluated "by hand"[1]. For ϵ-transitions (which includes sub graph calls and -returns) the key is empty. Patterns of the form "feature=value" can be represented by appending a delimiter symbol "$", e.g. "*pos = N$*", or even shorter using single-character feature identifiers such as "*pN$*" when the set of features is known and small. Other patterns such as ones containing ! may not be representable (unless the alphabet is known).

The overlay automaton is built breadth-first, and limits such as: maximum number of non-empty keys per string ("depth"), maximum number of cycles unfolded, and maximum automaton size need to be given. Encounting a "+" key is also a limit. After determinization, by virtue of the delimiter symbol $, the automaton will consist of two alternating parts: states whose outgoing transitions contain feature names and/or "+" need to be evaluated linearly. Deterministic sub-automata that represent sets of feature values followed by delimiter symbols can be traversed in constant time for each input character.

Theoretical comparisons between the naive approach and our extension are hard to give, as performance is dependent on the complexity of the search patterns, which may depend on soft factors such as the author's style. In our experiments, the implementation was for example able to process a text using a grammar recognizing time adverbials (65 graphs containing 1277 states and 4209 transitions) at a speed of about 280 KB/second using this technique alone, a 19-fold improvement to naive backtracking, using a modest overlay automaton of depth 2.

Acknowledgements. The author wishes to thank Klaus U. Schulz, Franz Guenthner, Petra Maier-Meyer, Tomasz Mikolajewski and other anonymous reviewers for their support while preparing this paper.

References

1. Gross, M.: Lexicon-Grammar And The Syntactic Analysis Of French. In: Proc. COLING 1984, pp. 275–282 (1984)
2. Liang, F.M.: Word Hyphenation by Computer. Ph.D. thesis, Stanford (1983)

---

[1] This includes that the overlay does not introduce a restriction on the formalism of the local grammar.

3. Paumier, S.: Weak Greibach Normal of Recursive Transition Networks. In: Proc. Journées Montoises d'Informatique Théorique (2004)
4. Woods, W.A.: Transition network grammars for natural language analysis. Comm. ACM 13(10), 591–606 (1970)

Significant Subpatterns Matching*

Jan Šupol

Department of Computer Science and Engineering, Faculty of Electrical Engineering,
Czech Technical University in Prague, Karlovo nám. 13, 121 35 Prague 2
jan.supol@gmail.com

Abstract. We present an algorithm for matching significant subpatterns of a given pattern in a text. The significant subpattern is any subpattern of the pattern which is at least of some specified length. We use bit-parallel simulation of an automaton for matching all subpatterns. The bit-parallel approach enables us to count the length of longest subpatterns.

Notions. Let A be a *finite alphabet*. A set of strings over A is denoted A^*, A^l is a set of strings of length $l \geq 0$. Let $T = t_1 t_2 \cdots t_n$ be a text and let $P = p_1 p_2 \cdots p_m$ be a pattern in text T, $m \leq n$. Set $Subp(X) = \{Y : X = UYV, U, V, X, Y \in A^*\}$ is a set of all subpatterns of string X. A finite nondeterministic automaton (NFA) is a quintuple (Q, A, δ, I, F) where Q is a finite set of states, A is a finite input alphabet, $F \subseteq Q$ is a set of final states, δ is a mapping $Q \times A \mapsto P(Q)$, and $I \subseteq Q$ is a set of initial states.

Preliminaries. For the subpattern matching, we use a well-known simulation technique of pattern matching using NFA called "shift-or" bit-parallel algorithm [1] which uses matrix R of size $m \times (n+1)$, and matrix D of size $m \times |A|$. Each element $r_{j,i} \in R, 0 < j \leq m, 0 \leq i \leq n$, corresponds to one state of the NFA, and it contains 0, if $p_1 p_2 \cdots p_j = t_{i-j+1} t_{i-j+2} \cdots t_i$, or 1, otherwise. Each element $d_{j,x}, 0 < j \leq m, x \in A$, contains 0, if $p_j = x$, or 1, otherwise. The bit-vectors $R_i, 0 \leq i \leq n$, are computed as follows:

$$\begin{aligned} r_{j,0} &= 1, & 0 < j \leq m \\ R_i &= \mathbf{shl}(R_{i-1}) \text{ or } D[t_i], 0 < i \leq n \end{aligned} \quad (1)$$

Operation **shl** is the standard shift-left bitwise operation and operation **or** is the standard bitwise OR operation. In what follows, we also use the standard bitwise AND operation denoted **and**, and the operation **shl** performed i times on bit-vector x denoted $\mathbf{shl}^i(x)$. Term $\mathbf{shl}(R_{i-1})$ or $D[t_i]$ represents matching–position i in text T is increased, the position in pattern P is increased by operation $\mathbf{shl}()$, and the active states of NFA are selected by term **or** $D[t_i]$.

---

* This research has been partially supported by the Ministry of Education, Youth, and Sport of the Czech Republic under research program MSM6840770014, and by the Czech Science Foundation as project No. 201/06/1039.

Jan Holub and Jan Žd'árek (Eds.): CIAA 2007, LNCS 4783, pp. 317–319, 2007.

Algorithm Outline. We need to store the lengths of accepted subpatterns. To handle this, we use a technique explained in [2], where a cell of λ bits $[C_j]_\lambda$ corresponds to state j. Therefore each bit-vector R_i, $0 \leq i \leq n$ has the following structure:

$$0[C_m]_\lambda 0[C_{m-1}]_\lambda \cdots 0[C_1]_\lambda$$

One extra bit extension before each cell is for computational purposes.

Note that m cells (integers) in a bit-vector are computed at a time. The integers in cells contain values from 0 to m for active states and one more value for inactive states, thus we set $\lambda = \log(m+2)$. From now on, we represent inactive state j as $[C_j]_\lambda = 1^\lambda$. Here, we need to redefine the matrix D of size $m(\lambda + 1) \times |A|$. Each cell$[C_j]_\lambda$ of element $d_{j,x}$, $0 < j \leq m$, $x \in A$, contains 0^λ, if $p_j = x$, or 1^λ, otherwise. Note that matrix R is of size $m(\lambda + 1) \times n$.

We need to compute the length of subpattern found. After each iteration of the algorithm, we add 1 to the value of each cell $[C_j]_\lambda$ corresponding to the active state. To handle this, Algorithm *AddOne* is used.

AddOne(X)
1 $T \leftarrow (10^\lambda)^m$; $U \leftarrow (0^\lambda 1)^m$
2 $Z \leftarrow ((X \text{ or } T) - \text{not } T) \text{ and } T$
3 $Z \leftarrow Z - \text{shr}^\lambda(Z)$
4 **Return** $(X \text{ and } Z) \text{ or } ((X + U) \text{ and not } (Z \text{ or } T))$

The meaning is as follows. The bit-vector Z contains either 00^λ for active states, or 10^λ for inactive states at line 2. Then, the bit-vector Z contains 01^λ for inactive states at line 3. At line 4, either inactive state, or the active state with value incremented by one is returned.

The subpattern, however, may start at any position ℓ in text T, $i-j+1 \leq \ell \leq i$. Therefore, we set any nonactive state ℓ as active with the cell value of 0 in the beginning of every iteration according to Algorithm *ResetInactive*.

ResetInactive(X)	**MainIteration(i)**
1 $T \leftarrow (10^\lambda)^m$	1 $R_i \leftarrow$ **ResetInactive**(R_{i-1})
2 $Z \leftarrow ((X \text{ or } T) - \text{not } T) \text{ and } T$	2 $R_i \leftarrow \text{shl}^{\lambda+1}(R_i) \text{ or } D[t_i]$
3 $Z \leftarrow Z - \text{shr}^\lambda(Z)$	3 $R_i \leftarrow$ **AddOne**(R_i)
4 **Return** $(X \text{ and not } Z)$	4 **Return** (R_i)

Finally, we define the subpattern matching formula as follows:

$$\begin{aligned} R_0 &= (01^\lambda)^m \\ R_i &= \textbf{MainIteration}(i), \quad 0 < i \leq n \end{aligned} \tag{2}$$

In order to check the subpatterns of significant length, each cell is compared to some threshold value. If the threshold is less than the value, the significant subpattern is found. This comparison takes the same time complexity as the computation of matrix R itself.

Conclusion. Since each bit-vector has $(\lambda+1)m = (\log(m+2)+1)m$ bits, the time complexity of our subpatterns matching algorithm is $\mathcal{O}(\frac{(\log(m+2)+1)mn}{w})$, where w is the length of a computer word. Note that for a significant approximate subpattern matching, the time complexity is k times higher, where k is the number of allowed edit operations.

References

1. Baeza-Yates, R.A., Gonnet, G.H.: A new approach to text searching. Commun. ACM 35, 74–82 (1992)
2. Navarro, G.: Approximate regular expression searching with arbitrary integer weights. Nordic J. of Computing 11, 356–373 (2004)

A New Method for Compiling Parallel Replacement Rules

Anssi Yli-Jyrä and Kimmo Koskenniemi

[1] Language Research Service, CSC Scientific Computing Ltd., Finland
[2] Department of General Linguistics, University of Helsinki, Finland
anssi.yli-jyra@csc.fi

Keywords: regular relations, conditional replacement, two-level rules, finite-state compilation.

Kempe and Karttunen [1] have presented a method that compiles a set of parallel conditional replacement (rewriting) rules into a finite-state transducer. Other, simpler methods exist for single rules or for rules of a restricted type, but they can be used only in restricted situations.

We introduce a new compilation method that is simpler, general, and more optimizable and extensible than the previous solutions. We have already implemented it in our subversion of the Stuttgart FS tool, and in addition, tested even the directed and scattered variants of the method with XFST. The method allows expressing rules that were not previously possible. The method uses parameters that allow for obtaining directional, gradient, scattered, or disjunctively ordered replace or markup rules as its extensions and optimizations in several special cases. The full technical report, further articles on the parameters and pointers to implementations are collected at http://www.ling.helsinki.fi/~aylijyra/replace/.

Most prior methods for simple and parallel replacement rely heavily on the use of brackets that indicate the (non)occurrences of substrings in strings, and a separated concatenation closure that make changes in bracketed replace regions. In contrast, our method is considerably simpler since it packs the set of rules and their context conditions into a single language representing all the rules. The packing eliminates the need for computing Kaplan and Kay's if-then idioms [2] or Mohri and Sproat's [3] marking transducers. As a byproduct, the set of possible rules is closed under the Boolean operations, which enables expressing disjunctive ordering and negative default rules.

The orientation of contexts is expressed in traditional methods by ordering the algorithm-encapsulated transducers differently under the composition operation. In our method, the contexts are languages over the symbol-pair alphabet, and their unknown tapes can be left under-specified by the user or the rule compiler to account for left-, right-, down- or up-ward contexts [4].

In most previous methods, the user specifies possible replacement centers as pairs of input and output languages. In contrast, our method assumes, along with van Noord and Gerdemann [5], that changes in replacement centers are specifiable with a transducer.

Jan Holub and Jan Žd'árek (Eds.): CIAA 2007, LNCS 4783, pp. 320–321, 2007.
© Springer-Verlag Berlin Heidelberg 2007

The prior methods unanimously exclude, along with Kaplan and Kay (KK) [2], the part of string already rewritten from further rewriting. This assumption makes rules $xax \rightarrow xbx$ and $a \rightarrow b/x\_x$ nonequivalent, although they have been traditionally considered as notational variants of each other. In contrast, Generalized Two-Level Grammars [6] provides a relaxed interpretation for optional replacement that actually treats both forms of rules equivalently. Our current work extends these grammars with a correct interpretation for obligatory rules.

The double arrow rules of two-level grammars would lead to a too strict, local interpretation of obligatoriness. For example in the case of input ABC and a rule pair: A:aB:p<=>_ and B:bC:c<=>_, there is no output. For this reason, we define obligatory rules by first applying the rules as optional and then ordering the obtained mappings according to the matching [7] replace regions. This is implemented in following steps:

1. interpretation of the oriented contexts as two-level contexts;
2. insertion of a pair of brackets to the alphabet and freely to the oriented contexts; embracing the centers with such brackets;
3. insertion of a context restriction rule that bans all occurences of non-identity pairs and brackets by default; insertion of context restriction rules obtained from the bracketed centers and two-level contexts
4. extraction of the 0-free domain [2] from the generalized two-level grammar [6]; its worsening by manipulation [7] of brackets;
5. constraining the domain of the previous regular relation with the complement of the worsened language; removal of the brackets and 0's in both domain and range sides.

References

1. Kempe, A., Karttunen, L.: Parallel replacement in finite state calculus. In: 16th COLING 1996, Proc. Conference, Copenhagen, Denmark, vol. 2, pp. 622–627 (1996)
2. Kaplan, R.M., Kay, M.: Regular models of phonological rule systems. Computational Linguistics 20, 331–378 (1994)
3. Mohri, M., Sproat, R.: An efficient compiler for weighted rewrite rules. In: 34th ACL 1996, Proc. Conference, Santa Cruz, CA, USA, pp. 231–238 (1996)
4. Karttunen, L.: The replace operator. In: 33th ACL 1995, Proceedings of the Conference, Cambridge, MA, USA, pp. 16–23 (1995)
5. Gerdemann, D., van Noord, G.: Transducers from rewrite rules with backreferences. In: 9th EACL 1999, Proceedings of the Conference, pp. 126–133 (1999)
6. Yli-Jyrä, A., Koskenniemi, K.: Compiling generalized two-level rules and grammars. In: Salakoski, T., Ginter, F., Pyysalo, S., Pahikkala, T. (eds.) FinTAL 2006. LNCS (LNAI), vol. 4139, Springer, Heidelberg (2006)
7. Gerdemann, D., van Noord, G.: Approximation and exactness in Finite-State Optimality Theory. In: Eisner, J., Karttunen, L., Thériault, A. (eds.) SIGPHON 2000, Finite State Phonology (2000)

Author Index

Lecture Notes in Computer Science

Sublibrary 1: Theoretical Computer Science and General Issues

For information about Vols. 1– 4490
please contact your bookseller or Springer